TWENTY ONE-ACT PLAYS
AN ANTHOLOGY
FOR AMATEUR PERFORMING GROUPS

Books and Plays by Stanley Richards

BOOKS:

The Tony Winners
America on Stage: Ten Great Plays of American History
Best Plays of the Sixties
Great Musicals of the American Theatre: Volume One
Great Musicals of the American Theatre: Volume Two
Best Mystery and Suspense Plays of the Modern Theatre
10 Classic Mystery and Suspense Plays of the Modern Theatre
Modern Short Comedies from Broadway and London
Best Short Plays of the World Theatre: 1968–1973
Best Short Plays of the World Theatre: 1958–1967
The Best Short Plays 1978
The Best Short Plays 1977
The Best Short Plays 1976
The Best Short Plays 1975
The Best Short Plays 1974
The Best Short Plays 1973
The Best Short Plays 1972
The Best Short Plays 1971
The Best Short Plays 1970
The Best Short Plays 1969
The Best Short Plays 1968
Canada on Stage

PLAYS:

Through a Glass, Darkly
August Heat
Sun Deck
Tunnel of Love
Journey to Bahia
O Distant Land
Mood Piece
Mr. Bell's Creation

The Proud Age
Once to Every Boy
Half-Hour, Please
Know Your Neighbor
Gin and Bitterness
The Hills of Bataan
District of Columbia

TWENTY
ONE-ACT PLAYS

An Anthology for Amateur Performing Groups
Edited with
Prefaces and an Introductory Note by

STANLEY RICHARDS

Dolphin Books
DOUBLEDAY & COMPANY, INC.
GARDEN CITY, NEW YORK

DESIGN BY RAYMOND DAVIDSON

Library of Congress Cataloging in Publication Data

Main entry under title:
Twenty one-act plays.

1. One-act plays. 2. Amateur theatricals.
I. Richards, Stanley, 1918–
PN6120.05T85   808.82′41
ISBN: 0-385-12865-7
Library of Congress Catalog Card Number 77–12873

for
PAUL MYERS

CONTENTS

AN INTRODUCTORY NOTE

This volume has a dual purpose: to entertain the reader and to provide exceptional source material for producing groups.

The short play always has been an attractive commodity in little theatres and, within the past couple of decades, in the professional theatre as well. Of the twenty plays represented in this collection, seventeen were produced commercially, most with conspicuous success. Their taut construction, economy of dialogue, and their immediate establishment of characters rivet audience attention within moments after the curtain has risen. They are, for amateur groups, splendid material with which they can hone their skills while simultaneously entertaining their audiences.

Without a doubt, the major, most striking influence on the modern short play was Eugene O'Neill, whose initial work to be staged, *Bound East for Cardiff*, was presented by the Provincetown Players in 1916. Always an experimentalist and innovator, O'Neill brought the craft to a high point of development with his short plays of the sea, and also succeeded in attracting unprecedented critical attention to the form. Unquestionably, he elevated its stature to new artistic levels and serious consideration.

The contemporary dramatist, who now chooses to employ this form of expression (and these include some of our most prominent authors), is free to portray consequential themes, on his own terms, untenanted by fusty restrictions. As the veteran New York drama critic Richard Watts, Jr., pointed out: "It is a form which tends to set free the imagination and the spirit of the playwright and to send it bounding through time and space, ignoring the customary fetters of convention and length. Almost any playwright can say what he wants to say in less time than the full-length play requires, and the short work is joyously free of the usual padding. It is a sprightly form and a splendidly easygoing one."

No theme is too strong or too ample for the modern short drama. If a theme is worthy of dramatic exploration, it is worth the telling in any form conceived by the writer. One cannot stretch a rubber band beyond its determined length. The same theory is applicable to drama: If an author has something important to say, and it fits into the dimensions of the short play, then that is its rightful place.

It is a form unto itself: It must be concise, stringent, and have an instantaneous impact upon the viewer. After all, a short bell ring can be as effective as a protracted bell ring: Its hearer is alerted in either case. The short play therefore can—and *must*—alert and stimulate audiences just as the long play purportedly does.

For noncommercial groups short plays are ideal to stage. Simpler and less intricate to produce, they also are less costly, scenically and otherwise, to mount. Royalties for the plays in this volume are comparatively modest. While costs have risen drastically in other areas of present-day living, somehow the fees for permission to present these plays have remained more or less constant, generally ranging from ten to twenty-five dollars a performance. All one has to do, if interested in staging one or more plays in this collection, is to contact the rights holder mentioned in the caution notice that precedes the text of each play. Licenses are then issued after the applicant provides basic information about the prospective production and pays the requisite royalty fee which should not strain even the most economically minded amateur group's budget.

If a group chooses to fill an entire evening with, say, two or three plays selected from this anthology, there is a wide choice ranging from comedy and farce to serious and thought-provoking drama that would make for a diversified and compelling theatrical experience. Their audience appeal has been proven and the pleasure to perform in them has been duly manifested in their initial and subsequent productions. In their own short way they provide a world of notable and artistically profitable entertainment.

STANLEY RICHARDS

TWENTY ONE-ACT PLAYS
AN ANTHOLOGY
FOR AMATEUR PERFORMING GROUPS

THE PATIENT

Agatha Christie

Agatha Christie

More than half a century after she revolutionized detective fiction with her first published novel, *The Mysterious Affair at Styles*—which introduced her immortal character, Hercule Poirot, to the world—Agatha Christie (1890–1976) remains, even after her death, supreme in her realm. Her eighty-five or so books, translated into many languages, have enjoyed world-wide sales of close to 400 million copies. Yet, with all due consideration to her prodigious reputation as a mystery novelist, it must be acknowledged that she was a formidable figure in the theatre as well. Since 1928, when *Alibi*, the Michael Morton dramatization of her classic *The Murder of Roger Ackroyd* ran for 250 performances at the Prince of Wales Theatre in London, Agatha Christie has been represented on stage by approximately twenty plays that either she herself wrote or that were adapted by others from her stories. During one period, 1953–54, she became England's first distaff playwright to have three offerings running concurrently in the West End: *The Mousetrap; Spider's Webb;* and *Witness for the Prosecution.*

That, however, was merely Agatha Christie's foothold on theatrical records. In due time, *The Mousetrap*, which opened in London on November 25, 1952, went on to become the longest-running play in theatre history. As of this writing, it is entering its twenty-fifth consecutive year and has played well over 10,000 performances. Before its legendary opening, the author regarded it as "a well-constructed little play that might well run for six months or so." Her producer, Peter Saunders, was somewhat more optimistic: He prophesied an engagement of about fourteen months. Thereafter, both managed to evade any further predictions about its final count, for the end still is not even remotely in sight.

Agatha Christie's other plays include: *Witness for the Prosecution* (winner of the 1954–55 New York Drama Critics' Circle Award as the year's best foreign play—the only mystery and suspense drama ever accorded this accolade); *Ten Little Indians; Verdict; Hidden Horizon; Towards Zero; The Hollow; The Unexpected Guest; Appointment with Death; Black Coffee; Go Back for Murder; Fiddlers Five;* and *Love from a Stranger,* which she dramatized with Frank Vosper.

Her theatre pieces, and some twenty motion pictures culled from her works, amply justified the recent observation of a leading British critic, Ivor Brown, who wrote: "Nowadays we live, not only as readers, but as play and filmgoers, in a whirl of Christie criminology."

As Agatha Mary Clarissa Miller, she was born in Torquay, Devonshire, the English countryside that served as the setting for many of her stories. In her youth she studied piano and voice in Paris, and with the encouragement of her mother and the novelist-dramatist Eden Phillpotts, a Devon neighbor, began to write what she described as "stories of unrelieved gloom, where most of the characters died" (a somewhat prophetic preamble to an extraordinary career!). In 1914 she married Archibald Christie, and although the marriage was dissolved fourteen years later, she retained the Christie name professionally. Her second husband was the noted archaeologist Sir Max Mallowan, whom she married in 1930. She often served as his assistant on expeditions in the Middle East.

In 1971 Agatha Christie was created a Dame of the Order of the British Empire by Queen Elizabeth II. Her autobiography, which she began to write at the age of sixty and continued to work on for many years, was published in 1977.

The Patient (published for the first time in the United States in this collection) originally was produced at the Duchess Theatre, London, on December 20, 1962. It was the final play in a triptych of three short Christie plays; its companion pieces were *The Rats* and *Afternoon at the Seaside.*

Characters:

Lansen
Nurse
Dr. Ginsberg
Inspector Cray
Bryan Wingfield
Emmeline Ross
William Ross
Brenda Jackson
The Patient

SCENE: *A private room in a nursing home. An autumn afternoon.*

The room is square, plain and hygienic-looking. In the right wall are two sets of double doors. Across the back is a large window covered by Venetian blinds which are at present down but not "closed". Up left, and extending across half the window is a curtained alcove, the curtains drawn back. Inside the alcove is a cabinet. An electrical apparatus, with dials, red light, etc., is down left center. A hospital trolley is up right center in the window, and a wall telephone down right. Down right center is a small table, with an elbow chair to right of it and four small chairs in a rough semicircle to left of it. These have the appearance of having been brought into the room for a purpose and not really belonging to it. On the trolley is a sterilizer with boiling water.

When the curtain rises, the lights fade up from a blackout. LANSEN, *a tall gangling young man with spectacles, wearing a long white hospital overall, is fiddling with an electrical apparatus on castors. The* NURSE, *a tall, good-looking woman, competent and correct, slightly inhuman and completely submissive to everything the doctor says, is at the trolley. She lifts the lid of the sterilizer, removes a needle with a forceps, places it in a tray, crosses to the cabinet, takes out a towel, and crosses back to put it on the trolley. A buzzer sounds.*

DR. GINSBERG *enters and goes to the telephone. He is a dark, clever-looking man in his middle forties.*

GINSBERG: All right, Nurse, I'll answer it. [*At the telephone*] Yes? . . . Oh, Inspector Cray, good. Ask him to come up to Room Fourteen, will you? [*He crosses to the electrical apparatus*] How are you doing, Lansen? Got it fixed up?

LANSEN: Yes, everything's in order. I'll plug in here, Dr. Ginsberg.

GINSBERG: You're quite sure about this, now? We can't afford to have a slip up.

LANSEN: Quite sure, Doctor. It'll work a treat.

GINSBERG: Good. [*He turns and looks at the chairs*] Oh, a little less formal, I think, Nurse. Let's move these chairs a bit. [*He moves one*] Er—that one over there against the wall.

[GINSBERG *exits*]

NURSE: Yes, Doctor. [*She comes down and lifts the chair*]

LANSEN: Careful! [*He takes it and places it against the wall*]

NURSE: [*Indicating the apparatus, with slight curiosity*] What is this thing?

LANSEN: [*Grinning*] New electrical gadget.

NURSE: [*Bored*] Oh, one of those. [*She moves up to the trolley*]

LANSEN: Trouble with you people is you've no respect for science.

[INSPECTOR CRAY *enters. He is a middle-aged man of delusively mild appearance.* GINSBERG *enters with him*]

INSPECTOR: Good afternoon.

GINSBERG: Everything's ready.

INSPECTOR: [*Indicating the electrical apparatus*] Is this the contraption?

LANSEN: Good afternoon, Inspector.

GINSBERG: Yes. It's been well tested, Inspector.

LANSEN: It works perfectly. The least touch will make a connection. I guarantee there will be no hitch.

GINSBERG: All right, Lansen. We'll call you when we need you. [LANSEN *exits. To* NURSE] Has Nurse Cartwright got the patient ready?

NURSE: Yes, Doctor. Quite ready.

GINSBERG: [*To the* INSPECTOR] Nurse Bond here is going to stay and assist me during the experiment.

INSPECTOR: Oh, good. That's very kind of you.

NURSE: Not at all, Inspector. I'll do anything I can to help. I'd never have gone off duty, if I'd thought that Mrs. Wingfield was unduly depressed.

GINSBERG: Nobody's blaming you, Nurse. [*The* NURSE *moves to the trolley*] You say the others have arrived?

INSPECTOR: Yes, they're downstairs.

GINSBERG: All four of them?

INSPECTOR: All four of them. Bryan Wingfield, Emmeline Ross, William Ross and Brenda Jackson. They can't leave. I've posted my men.

GINSBERG: [*Formally*] You must understand, Inspector, that the well-being of my patient comes before anything else. At the first sign of collapse or undue excitement—any indication that the experiment is having an adverse effect—I shall stop the proceedings. [*To* NURSE] You understand that, Nurse?

NURSE: Yes, Doctor.

INSPECTOR: Quite so, quite so—I shouldn't expect anything else. [*Uneasily*] You don't think it's *too* risky?

GINSBERG: [*Sitting in the elbow chair; coldly*] If I thought it was too risky I should not permit the experiment. Mrs. Wingfield's condition is mainly psychological—the result of severe shock. Her temperature, heart and pulse are now normal. [*To the* NURSE] Nurse, you are already acquainted with the family. Go down to the waiting room and bring them up here. If they ask you any questions, please be strictly non-committal in your answers.

NURSE: Yes, Doctor.

[*The* NURSE *exits*]

INSPECTOR: Well, here we go.

GINSBERG: Yes.

INSPECTOR: Let's hope we have luck. Have any of them been allowed to see her?

GINSBERG: Her husband, naturally. And also her brother and sister for a few minutes. The nurse assigned to look after her here, Nurse Cartwright, was present all the time. [*He pauses*] Miss Jackson has not visited Mrs. Wingfield, nor asked to do so.

INSPECTOR: Quite so. You'll give them a little preliminary talk, will you? Put them in the picture.

GINSBERG: Certainly, if you wish. [*The* INSPECTOR *strolls up to the window*] I see that Mrs. Wingfield fell from the second-story balcony.

INSPECTOR: Yes. Yes, she did.

GINSBERG: [*Rising*] Remarkable, really, that she wasn't killed. Head contusions, dislocated shoulder and fracture of the left leg.

[*The* NURSE *opens the door.* BRYAN WINGFIELD, WILLIAM ROSS *and* EMMELINE ROSS *enter.* WINGFIELD *is a short, stocky man of about thirty-five, attractive, with a quiet manner normally and rather a poker-face.* ROSS *is a man of the same age, also short, but dark-haired, rather mercurial in temperament.* EMMELINE, *his sister, is a tall, grim-faced woman of forty. They are all in a state of emotional disturbance. The* NURSE *exits*]

GINSBERG: [*Shaking hands with* EMMELINE] Good afternoon, Miss Ross, will you sit down? [*He shakes hands with* ROSS] Mr. Ross! Good afternoon, Mr. Wingfield. [*He shakes hands with* WING-FIELD]

WINGFIELD: You sent for us—it's not—my wife? There's not bad news?

GINSBERG: No, Mr. Wingfield. No bad news.

WINGFIELD: Thank God. When you sent for us I thought there might be a change for the worse.

GINSBERG: There is no change of any kind—neither for the worse, nor —alas—for the better.

EMMELINE: Is my sister *still* unconscious?

GINSBERG: She is still completely paralysed. She cannot move or speak.

EMMELINE: [*Sitting*] It's terrible! Simply terrible!

INSPECTOR: Was Miss Jackson with you?

WINGFIELD: She was following us. [BRENDA JACKSON *enters. She is a tall, extremely pretty young woman of twenty-five*] Dr. Ginsberg, my secretary, Miss Jackson.

GINSBERG: Good afternoon.

[*She turns and looks at the electrical apparatus*]

ROSS: Poor Jenny, what an awful thing to happen to anyone. Sometimes I feel it would have been better if she'd been killed outright by the fall.

WINGFIELD: No. Anything but that.

ROSS: I know what you feel, Bryan. But this—I mean, it's a living death, isn't it, Doctor?

GINSBERG: There's still some hope for your sister, Mr. Ross.

BRENDA: But she won't stay like this? I mean—she'll get better, won't she?

GINSBERG: In cases of this kind—it is very difficult to forecast the progress of a patient. Her injuries will heal, yes. The bones will knit, the dislocation has already been reduced, the wounds in the head are nearly healed.

WINGFIELD: Then why shouldn't she get well? Why shouldn't she be herself again in every way?

GINSBERG: You are touching there on a field in which we are still ignorant. Mrs. Wingfield's state of paralysis is due to shock.

EMMELINE: The result of her accident?

GINSBERG: Her accident was the ostensible cause.

ROSS: Just what do you mean by ostensible?

GINSBERG: Mrs. Wingfield must have suffered unusual fears as she fell from the balcony. It is not so much her *physical* injuries but something in her *mind* that has produced this state of complete paralysis.

[BRENDA *sits*]

WINGFIELD: You're not trying to say——[GINSBERG *sits behind the table*]—you're not thinking what I'm sure the Inspector has been more or less suggesting—that my wife tried to commit suicide? That I don't believe for a moment.

INSPECTOR: I haven't *said* I thought it was suicide, Mr. Wingfield.

WINGFIELD: [*Sitting*] You must think something of the kind or you and your people wouldn't keep hanging round like vultures.

INSPECTOR: We have to be quite clear as to the cause of this—accident.

ROSS: My God, isn't it simple enough? She's been ill for months. She'd been feeling weak, up for the first time, or practically the first time. Goes over to the window, out on to the balcony—leans over, is suddenly taken giddy and falls to the ground. That balcony's very low.

EMMELINE: Don't get so excited, William, don't shout.

ROSS: [*Turning to* EMMELINE] It's all very well, Bunny, but it makes me mad, all this business. [*To* GINSBERG] Do you think it's pleasant for us having the police mixing themselves up in our family affairs?

WINGFIELD: Now, Bill, if anyone should complain it's myself, and I don't.

[ROSS *moves to the window*]

BRENDA: What have we been asked to come here for?

INSPECTOR: One moment, Miss Jackson. [*To* EMMELINE] Miss Ross, I wish you could tell me a little more about your sister. Was she at all subject to fits of melancholy—depression?

EMMELINE: She was always highly strung, nervous.

ROSS: Oh, I wouldn't say that at all.

EMMELINE: Men don't realize these things. I know what I'm talking about. I think it is quite possible, Inspector, that her illness had left her particularly low and depressed, and that with other things she had to worry and distress her . . .

[BRENDA *rises and moves towards the door. The* INSPECTOR *moves towards her.* GINSBERG *and* WINGFIELD *rise*]

INSPECTOR: Where are you going, Miss Jackson?

BRENDA: I'm leaving. I'm not one of the family, I'm only Mr. Wingfield's secretary. I don't see the point of all this. I was asked to come with the others, but if all you're going to do is to go over and over again about the accident—whether it was accident or attempted suicide—well, I don't see why I should stay.

INSPECTOR: But it's not going to be the same thing over and over again, Miss Jackson. We are about to make an experiment.

BRENDA: An experiment? What kind of experiment?

INSPECTOR: Dr. Ginsberg will explain. Sit down, Miss Jackson. [BRENDA *moves back to her chair and sits.* WINGFIELD *and* GINSBERG *sit*] Dr. Ginsberg!

GINSBERG: I had better perhaps recapitulate what I know or have been told. Mrs. Wingfield has been suffering in the last two months from an illness somewhat mysterious in nature which was puzzling the doctor in attendance on her, Dr. Horsefield. This I have on the authority of Dr. Horsefield himself. She was, however, showing decided signs of improvement and was convalescent, though there was still a nurse in the house. On the day in question, exactly ten days ago, Mrs. Wingfield got up from bed after lunch and was settled by Nurse Bond in an easy chair near the open window, it being a fine, mild afternoon. She had books beside her, and a small radio. After seeing her patient had all she needed, nurse went out for her afternoon walk as usual. What happened during the course of the afternoon is a matter of conjecture.

[*The* INSPECTOR *moves to above* WINGFIELD]

But at half past three a cry was heard. Miss Ross, who was sitting in the room below, saw a falling body cross the window. It was the body of Mrs. Wingfield, who had fallen from the balcony of her room. There was no one with her at the time when she fell, but there were *four* people in the house, the four people who are assembled here now.

INSPECTOR: Perhaps, Mr. Wingfield, you would like to tell us in your own words just what happened then?

WINGFIELD: I should have thought I'd told it often enough already. I was correcting proofs in my study. I heard a scream, a noise from outside. I rushed to the side door, went out on the terrace and found—and found poor Jenny. [*He rises*] Emmeline joined me a moment later, and then William and Miss Jackson. We telephoned for the doctor and . . . [*His voice breaks*]

GINSBERG: I—I . . .

INSPECTOR: Yes, yes, Mr. Wingfield, there's no need to go into any more. [*He turns to* BRENDA] Miss Jackson, will you tell us again your side of the story?

BRENDA: I had been asked to look up a reference in the encyclopaedia for Mr. Wingfield. I was in the library when I heard a commotion and people running. I dropped the book and came out and joined them on the terrace.

INSPECTOR: [*Turning to* ROSS] Mr. Ross?

ROSS: What? Oh—I'd been playing golf all the morning—always play golf on a Saturday. I'd come in, eaten a hearty lunch and was feeling whacked. I lay down on my bed upstairs. It was Jenny's scream that woke me up. I thought for a moment I must have been dreaming. Then I heard the row down below and I looked out of my window. There she was on the terrace with the others gathered round. [*Fiercely, facing the* INSPECTOR] Oh, God, have we got to go over this again and again?

INSPECTOR: I only wanted to stress the point that nobody who was in the house can tell us exactly what happened that afternoon. [*He pauses*] Nobody, that is, except Mrs. Wingfield herself.

ROSS: It's all perfectly simple, as I've said all along. Poor Jenny thought she was stronger than she was. She went out on the balcony, leant over, and that's that. [*He sits on the chair, takes off his spectacles and wipes them*] Perfectly simple accident—might have happened to anybody.

WINGFIELD: Somebody ought to have been with her. [*He moves up to the window*] I blame myself for leaving her alone.

EMMELINE: But she was supposed to rest in the afternoon, Bryan, that was part of the doctor's orders. We were all going to join her at half past four for tea, but she was supposed to rest every afternoon from three o'clock until then.

INSPECTOR: Miss Ross—the accident seems a little difficult to explain. The railings of the balcony did not give way.

ROSS: No, no. She got giddy and overbalanced. I leant over myself to test it afterwards and it could easily happen.

INSPECTOR: Mrs. Wingfield is a very small woman. It wouldn't be so easy for her to overbalance even if she was taken giddy.

EMMELINE: I hate to say it, but I think you're right in what you suspect. I think poor Jenny was worried and troubled in her mind. I think a fit of depression came over her . . .

WINGFIELD: [*Moving to* EMMELINE] You keep saying she tried to commit suicide. I don't believe it. I won't believe it!

EMMELINE: [*With meaning*] She had plenty to make her depressed.

WINGFIELD: What do you mean by that?

EMMELINE: [*Rising*] I think you know quite well what I mean. I'm not blind, Bryan.

WINGFIELD: Jenny wasn't depressed. She'd nothing to be depressed about. You've got an evil mind, Emmeline, and you just imagine things.

ROSS: Leave my sister alone.

BRENDA: [*Rising and facing* EMMELINE] It was an accident. Of course it was an accident. Miss Ross is just trying to—trying to . . .

EMMELINE: [*Facing* BRENDA] Yes, what am I trying to do?

BRENDA: It's women like you that write anonymous letters—poison pen letters. Just because no man has ever looked at you . . .

EMMELINE: How dare you!

ROSS: [*Rising*] Oh, my God! Women! Cut it out, both of you.

WINGFIELD: I think we're all rather overexcited, you know. We're talking about things that are quite beside the point. What we really want to get at is, what was Jenny's state of mind on the day she fell? Well, I'm her husband, I know her pretty well, and I don't think for a moment she meant to commit suicide.

EMMELINE: Because you don't want to think so—you don't want to feel responsible!

WINGFIELD: Responsible? What do you mean by responsible?

EMMELINE: Driving her to do what she did!

ROSS: ⎫ ⎧ What do you mean by that?
WINGFIELD: ⎬ [*Together*] ⎨ How dare you!
BRENDA: ⎭ ⎩ It's not true!

GINSBERG: [*Rising*] Please—please! When I asked you to come here, it was not my object to provoke recriminations.

ROSS: [*Angrily*] Wasn't it? I'm not so sure. [*He wheels round and looks suspiciously at the* INSPECTOR]

GINSBERG: No, what I had in mind was to conduct an experiment.

BRENDA: We've already been told that, but you still haven't told us what kind of experiment.

GINSBERG: As Inspector Cray said just now—only one person knows what happened that afternoon—Mrs. Wingfield herself.

WINGFIELD: [*Sighing*] And she can't tell us. It's too bad.

EMMELINE: She will when she's better.

GINSBERG: I don't think you quite appreciate the medical position, Miss Ross. [*He crosses to the electrical apparatus.* BRENDA *sits*] It may be months—it may even be years before Mrs. Wingfield comes out of this state.

WINGFIELD: Surely not!

GINSBERG: Yes, Mr. Wingfield. I won't go into a lot of medical details, but there are people who have gone blind as a result of shock and have not recovered their sight for fifteen or twenty years. There have been those paralysed and unable to walk for the same periods of time. Sometimes another shock precipitates recovery. But there's no fixed rule. [*To the* INSPECTOR] Ring the bell, please.

[*The* INSPECTOR *crosses and rings the bell below the doors*]

WINGFIELD: I don't quite understand what you are driving at, Doctor. [*He looks from* GINSBERG *to the* INSPECTOR]

INSPECTOR: You're about to find out, Mr. Wingfield.

GINSBERG: Miss Jackson . . .

[BRENDA *rises.* GINSBERG *moves the chair left of the table close to it, lifting* EMMELINE's *handbag, which he hands to her*]

EMMELINE: Thank you.

[GINSBERG *crosses to the window and closes up the Venetian blinds. The lights dim.* GINSBERG *switches on the upstage lights*]

GINSBERG: Inspector, do you mind?

[*The* INSPECTOR *switches on the downstage lights.*
LANSEN *opens the doors up right and pulls on the* PATIENT *on the trolley, the* NURSE *following. They place the trolley down-*

stage, parallel to the footlights, with the PATIENT's *head to right. The* PATIENT's *head is heavily bandaged so that nothing of the features show but the eyes and nose. She is quite motionless. Her eyes are open but she does not move.*

The NURSE *stands about two feet from the* PATIENT's *head.* LANSEN *moves the electrical apparatus round and nearer to the* PATIENT. GINSBERG *moves above the trolley*]

WINGFIELD: Jenny, darling!

[EMMELINE *advances but does not speak*]

BRENDA: What's going on? What are you trying to do?

GINSBERG: Mrs. Wingfield, as I have told you, is completely paralysed. She cannot move or speak. But we are all agreed that she knows what happened to her on that day.

BRENDA: She's unconscious. She may be unconscious—oh—for years, you said.

GINSBERG: I did not say *unconscious*. Mrs. Wingfield cannot move and cannot speak, but she *can* see and hear; and I think it highly probable that her mind is as keen as ever it was. She knows what happened. She would like to communicate it to us, but unfortunately she can't do so.

WINGFIELD: You think she can hear us? You think she does know what we are saying to her, what we're feeling?

GINSBERG: I think she knows.

WINGFIELD: [*Moving to the head of the* PATIENT] Jenny! Jenny, darling! Can you hear me? It's been terrible for you, I know, but everything's going to be all right.

GINSBERG: Lansen!

LANSEN: [*Adjusting the electrical apparatus*] I'm ready, sir, when you are.

GINSBERG: I said Mrs. Wingfield could not communicate with us, but it is possible that a way has been found. Doctor Zalzbergen, who has been attending her, and who is a specialist on this form of paralysis, became aware of a very slight power of movement in the fingers of the right hand. It is very slight—hardly noticeable. She could not raise her arm or lift anything, but she can very slightly move the two fingers and thumb on her right hand. Mr. Lansen here has fixed up a certain apparatus of an electrical nature. You see, there is a small rubber bulb. When that bulb is pressed, a red light appears on the top of the apparatus. The slightest pressure will operate it. If you please, Lansen! [LANSEN *presses the bulb twice. The red light on the apparatus goes up twice*] Nurse, uncover the patient's right arm. [*The* NURSE *lays the* PATIENT's *arm on the coverlet*] Lansen, between the thumb and two fingers. Gently. [LANSEN *places the bulb in the* PATIENT's *right hand and crosses to the electrical apparatus*] Now I'm going to ask Mrs. Wingfield some questions.

ROSS: Ask her questions? What do you mean? Questions about what?

GINSBERG: Questions about what happened on that Saturday afternoon.

ROSS: [*Moving to face the* INSPECTOR] This is *your* doing!

GINSBERG: The experiment was suggested by Mr. Lansen and myself.

WINGFIELD: But you can't possibly put any reliance on what might be purely muscular spasms.

GINSBERG: I think we can soon find out whether Mrs. Wingfield can answer questions or not.

WINGFIELD: I won't have it! It's dangerous for her. It'll set her recovery back. I won't allow this! I won't agree to it.

BRENDA: [*Warningly*] Bryan! [*She turns to face* WINGFIELD, *then senses the* INSPECTOR *watching her, crosses to a chair and sits*]

GINSBERG: Mrs. Wingfield's health will be fully safeguarded, I assure you. Nurse! [WINGFIELD *moves away. The* NURSE *moves over and takes up her position by the* PATIENT *with her fingers on the* PATIENT's *wrist. To the* NURSE] At the least sign of collapse, you know what to do.

NURSE: Yes, Doctor. [*She takes the* PATIENT's *pulse*]

[*The* INSPECTOR *moves in to right of the* NURSE]

BRENDA: [*Almost under her breath*] I don't like this—I don't like it.

EMMELINE: I'm sure you don't like it.

BRENDA: Do you?

EMMELINE: I think it might be interesting. [*She goes and sits on chair*]

ROSS: ⎫ [*Together*] ⎧ I don't believe for a . . .
WINGFIELD: ⎭　　　　　 ⎩ Inspector, I hope . . .

INSPECTOR: Quiet, please! We must have absolute quiet. The doctor is about to begin.

[WINGFIELD *sits.* ROSS *moves down right. There is a pause*]

GINSBERG: Mrs. Wingfield, you have had a very narrow escape from death and are now on the way to recovery. Your physical injuries are healing. We know that you are paralysed and that you cannot speak or move. What I want is this——

[WINGFIELD *rises*]

—if you understand what I am saying to you, try and move your fingers so that you press the bulb. Will you do so?

[*There is a pause, then the* PATIENT's *fingers move slightly and the red light comes on. There is a gasp from all the four people. The* INSPECTOR *is now closely watching, not the* PATIENT *but the four visitors.* GINSBERG, *on the other hand, is intent on the* PATIENT. LANSEN *is intent on his apparatus, and beams with pleasure every time the light goes on*]

You have heard and understood what we have been saying, Mrs. Wingfield?

[*One red light*]

Thank you. Now what I propose is this: when the answer to a question is "yes" you press the bulb once; if the answer is "no" you will press it twice. Do you understand?

[*One red light*]

Now, Mrs. Wingfield, what is the signal for "no"?

[*Two red lights in rapid succession*]

I think, then, it must be clear to all of you that Mrs. Wingfield can understand what I'm saying and can reply to my questions. I'm going back to the afternoon of Saturday the fourteenth. Have you a clear recollection of what happened that afternoon?

[*One red light*]

As far as possible, I will ask you questions that will save you too much fatigue. I am assuming, therefore, that you had lunch, got up, and that Nurse here settled you in a chair by the window. You were alone in your room with the window open and were supposed to rest until four-thirty. Am I correct?

[*One red light*]

Did you, in fact, sleep a little?

[*One red light*]

And then you woke up . . .

[*One red light*]

Went out on to the balcony?

[*One red light*]

You leant over?

[*One red light*]

You lost your balance and fell?

[*There is a pause.* LANSEN *bends over to adjust the electrical apparatus*]

Just a minute, Lansen! You fell?

[*One red light*]

But you did not lose your balance.

[*Two red lights. A gasp from everyone*]

You were giddy—felt faint?

[*Two red lights*]

WINGFIELD: Inspector, I . . .
INSPECTOR: Sssh!

[WINGFIELD *turns away*]

GINSBERG: Mrs. Wingfield, we have come to the point where you
have to tell us what happened. I am going to say over the letters
of the alphabet. When I come to the letter of the word you want,
will you press the bulb. I'll begin. A, B, C, D, E, F, G, H, I, J, K,
L, M, N, O, P.

[*One red light*]

You have given me the letter "P". I'm going to hazard a guess—I
want you to tell me if I am right. Is the word in your mind
"pushed"?

[*One red light. There is a general sensation.* BRENDA *shrinks
away, her face in her hands.* ROSS *swears.* EMMELINE *is still*]

BRENDA: No, it can't be true!
ROSS: What the hell!
WINGFIELD: This is iniquitous!
GINSBERG: Quiet, please. I cannot have the patient agitated. Mrs.
Wingfield, you obviously have more to tell us. I'm going to spell
again. A, B, C, D, E, F, G, H, I, J, K, L, M.

[*One red light*]

M? The letter "M" is probably followed by a vowel. Which vowel,
Mrs. Wingfield? A, E, I, O, U.

[*One red light. The* INSPECTOR *moves to left of* LANSEN *above the electrical apparatus*]

M-U?

[*One red light*]

Is the next letter "R"?

[*One red light. The* INSPECTOR *and* GINSBERG *exchange a look*]

M-U-R- . . . Mrs. Wingfield, are you trying to tell us that what happened that afternoon was not an accident; are you trying to tell us that it was attempted murder?

[*One red light. There is an immediate reaction*]

BRYAN:		It's incredible! Absolutely incredible. It's impossible, I tell you, impossible!
BRENDA:		It's not true. She doesn't know what she's saying.
EMMELINE:	[*Together*]	[*Rising*] This is nonsense! Poor Jenny doesn't know what she's doing.
ROSS:		Murder! Murder! It can't be murder! D'you mean someone got in?

GINSBERG: Please. Quiet, please!

EMMELINE: She doesn't know what she's saying.

INSPECTOR: I think she does.

GINSBERG: Mrs. Wingfield, did some unknown person come in from outside and attack you?

[*Two red lights sharply*]

Was it someone in the house who pushed you?

[*A pause, then one red light*]

WINGFIELD: My God!

[*The red light flashes several times*]

NURSE: Doctor, her pulse is quickening.

INSPECTOR: [*Crossing close to* GINSBERG] Not much further. We must have the name.

GINSBERG: Mrs. Wingfield, do you know who pushed you?

[*One red light*]

I'm going to spell out the name. Do you understand?

[*One red light*]

Good. A, B.

[*One red light*]

B. Is that right?

[*Several red lights*]

NURSE: Doctor! She's collapsed.

GINSBERG: It's no good. I daren't go on, Nurse! [*The* NURSE *moves to the trolley upstage for the hypodermic and comes down to the* PA- TIENT, *handing the syringe to* GINSBERG. BRENDA *sits*] Thank you, Lansen. [*He breaks the ampule head, fills the syringe and injects it in the* PATIENT's *arm*]

[LANSEN *switches off the electrical apparatus, removes the bulb from the* PATIENT *and the plug from the wall. He wheels the electrical apparatus into the curtained recess, and exits. The* NURSE *returns the syringe to the trolley upstage. The* INSPECTOR *moves below the* PATIENT]

GINSBERG: Nurse, would you unplug the sterilizer?

NURSE: Yes, Doctor.

[*The* NURSE *unplugs the sterilizer.* GINSBERG *moves to the small trolley, and with the* NURSE *wheels it to the left wall*]

WINGFIELD: Is she all right?

GINSBERG: The strain and excitement have been too much for her. She'll be all right. She must rest for a while. We should be able to resume in about half an hour.

WINGFIELD: I forbid you to go on with it! It's dangerous.

GINSBERG: I think you must allow me to be the best judge of that. We'll move Mrs. Wingfield up nearer the window. She'll be all right there.

[GINSBERG *and the* NURSE *move the* PATIENT *upstage, with her head near the doors up right, the* NURSE *at the head*]

EMMELINE: There's not much doubt is there, who she meant? "B." [*She looks at* WINGFIELD] Not much doubt about that, is there, Bryan?

WINGFIELD: You always hated me, Emmeline. You always had it in for me. I tell you here and now, I didn't try to kill my wife.

EMMELINE: Do you deny that you were having an affair with that woman there? [*She points at* BRENDA]

BRENDA: [*Rising*] It's not true.

EMMELINE: Don't tell me that. You were head over ears in love with him.

BRENDA: [*Facing the others*] All right, then. I *was* in love with him. But that was all over ages ago. He didn't really care for me. It's all over, I tell you. All *over!*

EMMELINE: In that case it seems odd you stayed on as his secretary.

BRENDA: I didn't want to go. I—oh, all right, then! [*Passionately*] I still wanted to be near him. [*She sits*]

EMMELINE: And perhaps you thought that if Jenny were out of the way, you'd console him very nicely, and be Mrs. Wingfield Number Two . . .

WINGFIELD: Emmeline, for heaven's sake!

EMMELINE: Perhaps it's "B" for Brenda.

BRENDA: You horrible woman! I hate you. It's not true.

ROSS: [*Rising*] Bryan—and Brenda. It seems to narrow it down to one of you two all right.

WINGFIELD: I wouldn't say that. It could be "B" for brother, couldn't it? Or Bill?

ROSS: She always called me William.

WINGFIELD: After all, who stands to gain by poor Jenny's death? Not me. It's you. You and Emmeline. It's you two who get her money.

GINSBERG: Please—please! I can't have all this argument. Nurse, will you take them down to the waiting room.

NURSE: Yes, Doctor.

ROSS: [*Turning to* GINSBERG] We can't stay cooped up in a little room with all of us slanging each other.

INSPECTOR: You can go where you please on the hospital premises, but none of you is actually to leave the place. [*Sharply*] Is that understood?

WINGFIELD: All right.

ROSS: Yes.

EMMELINE: I have no wish to leave. My conscience is clear.

BRENDA: [*Going up to her*] I think—*you* did it.

EMMELINE: [*Sharply*] What do you mean?

BRENDA: You hate her—you've always hated her. And you get the money—you and your brother.

EMMELINE: My name does *not* begin with a "B," I'm thankful to say.

BRENDA: [*Excitedly*] No—but it needn't. [*She turns to the* INSPECTOR] Supposing that, after all, Mrs. Wingfield *didn't* see who it was who pushed her off the balcony.

EMMELINE: She has told us that she did.

BRENDA: But supposing that she didn't. [*Crosses to the* INSPECTOR] Don't you see what a temptation it might be to her? She was jealous of me and Bryan—oh, yes, she knew about us—and she was jealous. And when that machine there—[*She gestures towards the electrical apparatus*] gave her a chance to get back at us—at me—don't you see how tempting it was to say "Brenda pushed me . . ." It could have been like that, it could!

INSPECTOR: A little far-fetched.

BRENDA: No, it isn't! Not to a jealous woman. You don't know what women are like when they're jealous. And she'd been cooped up there in her room—thinking—suspecting—wondering if Bryan and I were still carrying on together. It isn't far-fetched, I tell you. It could easily be true. [*She looks at* WINGFIELD]

WINGFIELD: [*Thoughtfully*] It is quite possible, you know, Inspector.

BRENDA: [*To* EMMELINE] And you *do* hate her.

EMMELINE: Me? My own sister?

BRENDA: I've seen you looking at her often. You were in love with Bryan—he was half engaged to you—and then Jenny came home from abroad and cut you out. [*Facing* EMMELINE] Oh, she told me the whole story one day. You've never forgiven her. I think you've hated her ever since. I think that you came into her room that day, and you saw her leaning over the balcony, and it was too good a chance to be missed—you came up behind her and—[*With a gesture*] pushed her over . . .

EMMELINE: Inspector! Can't you stop this kind of thing?

INSPECTOR: I don't know that I want to, Miss Ross. I find it all very informative.

GINSBERG: I'm afraid I must insist on your leaving now. The patient must rest. We should be able to resume in twenty minutes. [*He moves to the upstage light switch and turns off part of the lights*] Nurse will take you downstairs.

NURSE: Yes, Doctor. [*She opens the door*]

[ROSS, EMMELINE, WINGFIELD *and* BRENDA *move to exit*]

INSPECTOR: Miss Ross, would you mind waiting a moment?

[*They pause, then* BRENDA *exits, followed by* ROSS, *the* NURSE *and* WINGFIELD]

EMMELINE: Well, what is it?

[*The* INSPECTOR *eases the chair left of the table a little farther.* EMMELINE *sits on it. The* INSPECTOR *moves to behind the table*]

INSPECTOR: There are one or two questions I should like to put to you. I didn't want to embarrass your brother . . .

EMMELINE: [*Interrupting sharply*] Embarrass William? You don't know him. He has no self-respect at all. Never ashamed to admit that he doesn't know where to turn for the next penny!

INSPECTOR: [*Politely*] That's very interesting—but it was your brother-in-law that I thought might be embarrassed by the questions I am about to ask you.

EMMELINE: [*A little taken aback*] Oh, Bryan. What do you want to know?

INSPECTOR: Miss Ross, you know the family very well. A person of your—intelligence—would not be deceived as to what went on in it. You know the lives of your sister and your brother-in-law, and what the relations were between them. It is reasonable that, up to now, you would say as little as you could. But now that you know what our suspicions are—and the way they have been confirmed only a minute or two ago—well, that alters matters, doesn't it?

EMMELINE: Yes, I suppose it does. [*She puts her bag on the floor*] What do you want me to tell you?

INSPECTOR: This affair between Mr. Wingfield and Miss Jackson, was it serious?

EMMELINE: Not on his part. His affairs never are.

INSPECTOR: There actually *was* an affair.

EMMELINE: Of course. You heard her. She as good as admitted it.

INSPECTOR: You know it of your own knowledge?

EMMELINE: I could tell you various details to prove it, but I do not propose to do so. You will have to accept my word for it.

INSPECTOR: It started—when?

EMMELINE: Nearly a year ago.

INSPECTOR: And Mrs. Wingfield found out about it?

EMMELINE: Yes.

INSPECTOR: And what was her attitude?

EMMELINE: She taxed Bryan with it.

INSPECTOR: And he?

EMMELINE: He denied it, of course. Told her she was imagining things. You know what men are! Lie their way out of anything! [*The* INSPECTOR *and* GINSBERG *exchange a look*] She wanted him to send the girl away, but he wouldn't—said she was far too good a secretary to lose.

INSPECTOR: But Mrs. Wingfield was very unhappy about it?

EMMELINE: Very.

INSPECTOR: Unhappy enough to want to take her own life?

EMMELINE: Not if she'd been well and strong. But her illness got her down. And she got all kinds of fancies.

GINSBERG: [*Showing interest*] What kinds of fancies, Miss Ross?

EMMELINE: Just fancies.

INSPECTOR: Why was Mrs. Wingfield left alone that afternoon?

EMMELINE: She preferred it. One of us always offered to sit with her, but she had her books and her radio. For some reason she preferred to be alone.

INSPECTOR: Whose idea was it to send the nurse off duty?

GINSBERG: In private nursing that's standard practice. She would have two hours off every afternoon.

INSPECTOR: Miss Jackson has told us that "it was all over ages ago," referring to her affair with Mr. Wingfield. Do you say that that was *not* so.

EMMELINE: I think they broke with each other for a while. Or possibly they were very careful. But at the time of the accident, it was on again all right. Oh, yes!

INSPECTOR: You seem very sure of that.

EMMELINE: I lived in the house, didn't I? [*She pauses*] And I'll show you something. [*She reaches for her bag, takes out a piece of notepaper and hands it to the* INSPECTOR] I found it in the big Ming vase on the hall table. They used it as a postbox, it seems.

INSPECTOR: [*Reading*] "Darling, we must be careful. I think she suspects. B." [*He looks at Ginsberg*]

EMMELINE: It's Bryan's writing all right. So, you see!

GINSBERG: Do you mind if I ask a question or two?

INSPECTOR: No, Doctor, please do.

GINSBERG: I'm interested in those "fancies" you mentioned, Miss Ross. You had some particular fancy in mind, I think.

EMMELINE: Just a sick woman's imaginings. She was ill, you see, and she felt she wasn't making the progress she should have done.

GINSBERG: And she thought there was a reason for that?

EMMELINE: She was—just upset.

INSPECTOR: [*Leaning on the table and stressing his words*] She thought there was a reason for it.

EMMELINE: [*Uneasily*] Well—yes.

GINSBERG: [*Quietly*] She thought those two were poisoning her? That's it, isn't it?

[*There is a pause. The* INSPECTOR *sits on the table*]

EMMELINE: [*Reluctantly*] Yes.

GINSBERG: She said so to you?

EMMELINE: Yes.

GINSBERG: And what did you say?

EMMELINE: I told her it was all nonsense of course.

GINSBERG: Did you take any steps yourself?

EMMELINE: I don't know what you mean.

GINSBERG: Did you discuss it with the doctor attending her? Take any samples of food?

EMMELINE: [*Shocked*] Of course not. It was just a sick woman's fancy.

GINSBERG: Well, it happens, you know. Far more often than is known. The symptoms of arsenic poisoning, it's almost always arsenic, are practically indistinguishable from gastric disorders.

EMMELINE: Bryan couldn't—he just couldn't.

GINSBERG: It might have been the girl.

EMMELINE: Yes! Yes, I suppose so. [*She sighs*] Well, we shall never know now.

GINSBERG: You're quite wrong there, Miss Ross. There are ways of telling. Traces of arsenic can be found in the hair, you know, and in the fingernails . . .

EMMELINE: [*Rising*] I can't believe it! I can't believe it of Bryan! [*Turning to the* INSPECTOR *agitatedly*] Do you want me any longer, Inspector?

INSPECTOR: No, Miss Ross. [EMMELINE *moves towards the table to take the paper, but the* INSPECTOR *rises and picks it up first*] I'll keep this. It's evidence.

EMMELINE: Yes, of course.

[EMMELINE *exits*]

GINSBERG: [*Rubbing his hands*] Well, we got something.

INSPECTOR: [*Sitting in the elbow chair*] Yes. [*He looks at the piece of paper*] From the Ming vase in the hall. Interesting.

GINSBERG: It's his writing?

INSPECTOR: Oh, yes, it's Bryan Wingfield's writing all right. You know, he was quite a one for the ladies. Bowled them over like ninepins. Unfortunately they always took him seriously.

GINSBERG: Doesn't strike me as the Casanova type. Writes all those historical novels. Very erudite.

INSPECTOR: There's quite a lot of dirt in history. Oh . . . [*He notices he is in* GINSBERG's *chair; rises*]

GINSBERG: Thank you. [*He sits in the elbow chair*] So it wasn't all over!

INSPECTOR: Get four people all het up and accusing each other, get an embittered and malicious woman on her own and invite her to spill the beans—it gives one some material to work on, doesn't it?

GINSBERG: In addition to what you had already. What did you have?

INSPECTOR: [*Smiling*] Just some good solid facts. [*He sits*] I went into the financial angle. Bryan Wingfield's a poor man, his wife's a rich woman. Her life's insured in favour of him—not for a very large sum, but it would enable him to marry again, if he wanted to. Her money came to her in trust. If she dies childless, it's divided between her brother and sister. The brother's a wastrel, always trying to get money out of his rich sister. According to Bryan, she told her brother she wasn't going to pay for him any more. [*Thought-fully*] But I dare say she would have done—in the end.

GINSBERG: So which is it? B for Bryan? B for Brenda? B for Brother Bill? Or Emmeline without a B?

INSPECTOR: [*Rising*] Emmeline without the—Emmeline? Wait a min-ute—something I heard this afternoon, while they were all here . . . No, it's gone.

GINSBERG: Could it be B for burglar?

INSPECTOR: No, that's definitely out. We've got conclusive evidence on that point. The road was up in front of the house and there was a constable on duty there. Both the side and the front gate were directly under his eye. Nobody entered or left the house, that afternoon.

GINSBERG: You know, you asked me to co-operate, but you were very careful not to put all your cards on the table. Come on! What *do* you think?

INSPECTOR: It's not a question of thinking. I know.

GINSBERG: What?

INSPECTOR: I may be wrong, but I don't think so. You think it over. [GINSBERG *enumerates on his fingers*] You've got seven minutes.

GINSBERG: Huh! Oh, yes. [*He rises and moves to the* PATIENT. *The* IN-SPECTOR *joins him*] Mrs. Wingfield. Thank you for your help, Mrs. Wingfield. We come now to the crucial moment in the ex-periment.

INSPECTOR: Mrs. Wingfield, we are about to leave you here, ap-parently unguarded. None of the suspects knows that you regained your powers of speech yesterday. They don't know that you did not in fact see who pushed you off that balcony. You realize what that means?

PATIENT: One of them will—will try to . . .

INSPECTOR: Someone will almost certainly enter this room.

GINSBERG: Are you sure you want to go through with this, Mrs. Wingfield?

PATIENT: Yes, yes. I must know—I must know who . . .

INSPECTOR: Don't be afraid. We shall be close at hand. If anyone approaches you or touches you . . .

PATIENT: I know what to do.

INSPECTOR: Thank you, Mrs. Wingfield, you're a wonderful woman. Just be brave for a few moments longer and we shall trap our killer. Trust me. Trust both of us, eh?

GINSBERG: Ready?

[*They move the trolley downstage*]

INSPECTOR: Right.

GINSBERG: Why don't you come into my office? [*Holding the door open*] In view of this poisoning suggestion, you might like to look over the files.

INSPECTOR: Yes, I'd like another look at those X-ray plates too, if I may. [*He switches off the downstage lights*]

[GINSBERG *and the* INSPECTOR *exit. When off, they switch off the light in the passage.*

In the blackout, the NURSE *enters upstage, with a small syringe, and crosses left to behind the curtain*]

PATIENT: Help! Help!!

[*The* INSPECTOR *enters*]

INSPECTOR: All right, Mrs. Wingfield, we're here!

[GINSBERG *enters and switches on the lights by the upstage switch. He rushes straight to the* PATIENT]

PATIENT: Help! Murder! [*Pointing to the curtains*] There!

[*The* INSPECTOR *crosses to the* PATIENT]

INSPECTOR: Is she all right?

GINSBERG: She's all right. You've been very brave, Mrs. Wingfield.

INSPECTOR: Thank you, Mrs. Wingfield. The killer has played right into our hands. [*He faces* GINSBERG] That note in the Ming vase was all I needed. Bryan Wingfield would hardly need to write secret notes to a secretary he sees every day. He wrote that note to someone else. And that constable on duty. He swears that nobody entered or left the house that afternoon. [*He faces the curtain*] So it seems you didn't take your off-duty walk that day. [*He moves towards the curtain*] You may come out from behind that curtain now, Nurse Bond.

[NURSE BOND *comes out from behind the curtain and takes a pace downstage. The lights black out and—*]

THE CURTAIN FALLS

FUMED OAK

Noël Coward

Noël Coward

Described by its author as "an unpleasant comedy in two scenes," *Fumed Oak* was one of nine short plays presented on three separate evenings under the omnibus title *Tonight at 8:30*. An enormous success in England in 1936, it was produced later in the same year at the National Theatre, New York, with its two glittering costars, Noël Coward and Gertrude Lawrence.

In his introduction to the original publication of the play, Coward wrote: "*Fumed Oak* is a comedy based on the good old 'Worm will turn' theme. I loved Henry Gow from the moment I started writing him, and I loved playing him more, I think, than anything else in the repertoire."

Through four decades, the comedy's popularity has remained undiminished. It has enjoyed frequent revivals with some of the theatre's top luminaries, and in 1952 it served as the centerpiece for the film *Meet Me Tonight*, with Stanley Holloway as Henry Gow.

One of the giants of the modern theatre, Noël Coward (who was knighted by Queen Elizabeth II in 1970) was born in Teddington, England, on December 16, 1899. He made his acting debut at the age of twelve as Prince Mussel in a children's play, *The Goldfish*, and when he was twenty-one, his first produced play, *I'll Leave It to You*, opened in the West End. As he personally described the event: "The first night was a roaring success, and I made a boyish speech. The critics were mostly enthusiastic, and said a lot about it having been a great night, and that a new playwright had been discovered, etc., but unfortunately their praise was not potent enough to lure audiences to the New Theatre for more than five weeks; so the run ended miserably. . . ."

It was in 1924 that Sir Noël sprang to international prominence with *The Vortex*, and ever since that eventful year he symbolized glistening sophistication, trenchant wit, and impeccable style in the theatre. His originality and superb craftsmanship and the fact that he was one of the few playwrights to have created a world of his own and made one enter into it on his own terms made him a legendary figure. Few indeed could match his prolificacy as dramatist, composer, lyricist, director, and performer.

In the five decades that followed *The Vortex*, the unique theatrical wizardry of Noël Coward lured hundreds of thousands into theatres throughout the world. Among his forty plays, musicals, and revues are such landmarks of their respective eras as *Hay Fever*; *Easy Virtue*; *This Year of Grace*; *Bitter Sweet*; *Private Lives*; *Design for Living*; *Cavalcade*; *Words and Music*; *Conversation Piece*; *Tonight at 8:30*; *Set to Music*; *Present Laughter*; *This Happy Breed*; *Blithe Spirit*; *Sigh No More*; *Peace in Our Time*; and *Relative Values*.

A Renaissance man of the theatre, Sir Noël also made some notable contributions to films (*In Which We Serve*; *Brief Encounter*; *This Happy Breed*) and added substantially to international library shelves with four volumes of memoirs, five collections of short stories, three of revue sketches and lyrics, a popular novel, *Pomp and Circumstance*, and of course his forty or so published plays.

In spite of the fact that he occasionally came under critical fire from some disciples of the "new wave" for persistently clinging to traditional—and ignoring exploratory—forms in the theatre, Sir Noël maintained his undeniable status as the grand *padrone* of modern stage comedy. This was reaffirmed unequivocally in 1964 when Britain's celebrated National Theatre, under the leadership of Lord (Laurence) Olivier, triumphantly revived his indestructible comedy, *Hay Fever*, with Dame Edith Evans, Maggie Smith, and Lynn Redgrave heading the cast. Its success with press and public sparked an extraordinary resurgence of interest in the author and his works and summoned forth a spate of revivals of his most prominent plays. Additionally, two revues culled from his songs and writings *Cowardy Custard* and *Oh, Coward* played to capacity houses in, respectively, London and New York. ("People have constantly written me off and are surprised that I've come back," Coward wryly observed at the time. "Now, I wish they would tell me where I am supposed to have been.")

In April 1966, Sir Noël once again brightened the West End as author and costar (with Lilli Palmer and Irene Worth) of *Suite in Three Keys*. Lauded by the London *Daily Express* as "Coward at his zenith," it was his last major work and his final official appearance on stage.

Coward was frequently likened to an earlier master of "artificial comedy," Oscar Wilde, for he, too, was a supreme precisionist at entertainingly tearing away at social pretensions. Beneath the surface of his characteristically witty, cutting, and pointed dialogue, there was invariably a flow of pertinent commentary on contemporary society and its values.

Would his plays—particularly the early plays—have been different if he had started writing them later? Shortly before his death, in March 1973, at his home in Jamaica, Sir Noël Coward reflected: "I would continue to write what I wanted to write and about people who are interesting . . . and both peers and charwomen are interesting to me."

Characters:

Henry Gow
Doris, *his wife*
Elsie, *his daughter*
Mrs. Rockett, *his mother-in-law*

SCENE ONE

The Gows' sitting room is indistinguishable from several thousand other suburban sitting rooms. The dominant note is refinement. There are French windows at the back opening on to a narrow lane of garden. These are veiled discreetly by lace curtains set off by a pelmet and side pieces of rather faded blue casement cloth. There is a tiled fireplace on the right; an upright piano between it and the window; a fumed oak sideboard on the left and, below it, a door leading to the hall, the stairs of the front door. There is a fumed oak dining room suite consisting of a table, and six chairs; a sofa; an armchair in front of the fire; a radio, and a plentiful sprinkling over the entire room of ornaments and framed photographs.

When the curtain rises it is about eight-thirty on a spring morning. Rain is trickling down the windows and breakfast is laid on the table.

MRS. ROCKETT *is seated in the armchair by the fire; on a small table next to her is a cup of tea, and a work basket. She is a fattish, grey-looking woman dressed in a blouse and skirt and a pepper and salt jumper of artificial silk. Her pince-nez snap in and out of a little clip on her bosom and her feet are bad which necessitates the wearing of large quilted slippers in the house.*

DORIS, *aged about thirty-five, is seated at the table reading a newspaper propped up against the cruet. She is thin and anæmic and whatever traces of past prettiness she might have had are obscured by the pursed-up, rather sour gentility of her expression. She wears a nondescript coat-frock, a slave bangle and necklace of amber glass beads.* ELSIE, *her daughter aged about fourteen, is sitting opposite to her, cutting her toast into strips in order to dip them into her boiled egg. She is a straight-haired ordinary-looking girl dressed in a navy blue school dress with a glacé red leather waist belt.*

There is a complete silence broken only by the occasional rat-

tle of a spoon in a cup or a sniffle from ELSIE *who has a slight head cold.*

    HENRY GOW *comes into the room. He is tall and spare, neatly dressed in a blue serge suit. He wears rimless glasses and his hair is going grey at the sides and thin on the top. He sits down at the table without a word.* DORIS *automatically rises and goes out, returning in a moment with a plate of haddock which she places in front of him and resumes her place.* HENRY *pours himself out some tea.* DORIS, *without looking at him, being immersed in the paper, passes him the milk and sugar.*

    The silence continues until ELSIE *breaks it.*

ELSIE: Mum?

DORIS: What?

ELSIE: When can I put my hair up?

DORIS: [*Snappily*] When you're old enough.

ELSIE: Gladys Pierce is the same age as me and she's got hers up.

DORIS: Never you mind about Gladys Pierce, get on with your breakfast.

ELSIE: I don't see why I can't have it cut. That would be better than nothing. [*This remark is ignored*] Maisie Blake had hers cut last week and it looks lovely.

DORIS: Never you mind about Maisie Blake neither. She's common.

ELSIE: Miss Pritchard doesn't think so. Miss Pritchard likes Maisie Blake a lot, she said it looked ever so nice.

DORIS: [*Irritably*] What?

ELSIE: Her hair.

DORIS: Get on with your breakfast. You'll be late.

ELSIE: [*Petulantly*] Oh, Mum——

DORIS: And stop sniffling. Sniffle sniffle sniffle! Haven't you got a handkerchief?

ELSIE: Yes, but it's a clean one.

DORIS: Never mind, use it.

MRS. ROCKETT: The child can't help having a cold.

DORIS: She can blow her nose, can't she, even if she has got a cold?

ELSIE: [*Conversationally*] Dodie Watson's got a terrible cold, she's had it for weeks. It went to her chest and then it went back to her head again.

MRS. ROCKETT: That's the worst of schools, you're always catching something.

ELSIE: Miss Pritchard's awful mean to Dodie Watson, she said she'd had enough of it.

DORIS: Enough of what?

ELSIE: Her cold.

[*There is silence again which is presently shattered by the wailing of a baby in the house next door*]

MRS. ROCKETT: There's that child again. It kept me awake all night.

DORIS: I'm very sorry, I'm sure.

MRS. ROCKETT: [*Fiddling in her work-basket*] I wasn't blaming you.

DORIS: The night before last it was the hot-water pipes.

MRS. ROCKETT: You ought to have them seen to.

DORIS: You know as well as I do you can't stop them making that noise every now and then.

MRS. ROCKET: [*Threading a needle*] I'm sure I don't know why you don't get a plumber in.

DORIS: [*Grandly*] Because I do not consider it necessary.

MRS. ROCKETT: You would if you slept in my room—gurgle gurgle gurgle all night long—it's all very fine for you, you're at the end of the passage.

DORIS: [*With meaning*] You don't have to sleep there.

MRS. ROCKETT: What do you mean by that?

DORIS: You know perfectly well what I mean.

MRS. ROCKETT: [*With spirit*] Listen to me, Doris Gow. I've got a perfect right to complain if I want to and well you know it. It isn't as if I was staying here for nothing.

DORIS: I really don't know what's the matter with you lately, Mother, you do nothing but grumble.

MRS. ROCKETT: Me, grumble! I like that, I'm sure. That's rich, that is.

DORIS: Well, you do. It gives me a headache.

MRS. ROCKETT: You ought to do something about those headaches of yours. They seem to pop on and off at the least thing.

DORIS: And I wish you wouldn't keep passing remarks about not staying here for nothing.

MRS. ROCKETT: Well, it's true, I don't.

DORIS: Anyone would think we was taking advantage of you.

MRS. ROCKETT: Well, they wouldn't be far wrong.

DORIS: Mother, how can you! You're not paying a penny more than you can afford.

MRS. ROCKETT: I never said I was. It isn't the money, it's the lack of consideration.

DORIS: Pity you don't go and live with Nora for a change.

MRS. ROCKETT: Nora hasn't got a spare room.

DORIS: Phyllis has, a lovely one, looking out over the railway. I'm sure her hot-water pipes wouldn't annoy you, there isn't hot water in them.

MRS. ROCKETT: Of course, if I'm not wanted here, I can always go to a boardinghouse or a private hotel.

DORIS: Catch you!

MRS. ROCKETT: I'm not the sort to outstay my welcome anywhere——

DORIS: Oh, for heaven's sake don't start that again——

MRS. ROCKETT: [*Addressing the air*] It seems as though some of us had got out of bed the wrong side this morning.

ELSIE: Mum, can I have some more toast?

DORIS: No.

ELSIE: I could make it myself over the kitchen fire.

DORIS: No, I tell you. Can't you understand plain English? You've had quite enough and you'll be late for school.

MRS. ROCKETT: Never mind, Elsie, here's twopence, you can buy yourself a sponge cake at Barret's.

ELSIE: [*Taking the twopence*] Thanks, Grandma.

DORIS: You'll do no such thing, Elsie. I'm not going to have a child of mine stuffing herself with cake in the middle of the High Street.

MRS. ROCKETT: [*Sweetly*] Eat it in the shop, dear.

DORIS: Go on, you'll be late.

ELSIE: Oh, Mum, it's only ten to.

DORIS: Do as I tell you.

ELSIE: Oh, all right.

[*She goes sullenly out of the room and can be heard scampering noisily up the stairs*]

MRS. ROCKETT: [*Irritatingly*] Poor little soul.

DORIS: I'll trouble you not to spoil Elsie, Mother.

MRS. ROCKETT: Spoil her! I like that. Better than half starving her.

DORIS: [*Hotly*] Are you insinuating——

MRS. ROCKETT: I'm not insinuating anything. Elsie's getting a big girl, she only had one bit of toast for her breakfast and she used that for her egg, I saw her.

DORIS: It's none of your business and in future I'd be much obliged if you'd keep your twopences to yourself.

MRS. ROCKETT: [*Hurt*] Very well, of course if I'm to be abused every time I try to bring a little happiness into the child's life——

DORIS: Anyone would think I ill-treated her the way you talk.

MRS. ROCKETT: You certainly nag her enough.

DORIS: I don't do any such thing and I wish you'd be quiet.

[*She flounces up from the table and goes over to the window, where she stands drumming her fingers on the pane.* HENRY *quietly appropriates the newspaper she has flung down*]

MRS. ROCKETT: [*Unctuously*] There's no need to lose your temper.

DORIS: I am not losing my temper.

MRS. ROCKETT: If I'd known when you were Elsie's age what you were going to turn out like I'd have given you what for, I can tell you.

DORIS: Pity you didn't, I'm sure.

MRS. ROCKETT: One thing, I never stinted any of my children.

DORIS: I wish you'd leave me bring up my own child in my own way.

MRS. ROCKETT: That cold's been hanging over her for weeks and a fat lot you care——

DORIS: I've dosed her for it, haven't I? The whole house stinks of Vapex. What more can I do?

MRS. ROCKETT: She ought to have had Doctor Bristow last Saturday when it was so bad. He'd have cleared it up in no time.

DORIS: You and your Doctor Bristow.

MRS. ROCKETT: Nice thing if it turned to bronchitis. Mrs. Henderson's Muriel got bronchitis, all through neglecting a cold; the poor child couldn't breathe, they had to have two kettles going night and day——

DORIS: I suppose your precious Doctor Bristow told you that.

MRS. ROCKETT: Yes, he did, and what's more he saved the girl's life, you ask Mrs. Henderson.

DORIS: Catch me ask Mrs. Henderson anything, not likely, stuck up thing——

MRS. ROCKETT: Mrs. Henderson's a very nice lady-like woman, just because she's quiet and a bit reserved you say she's stuck up——

DORIS: Who does she think she is anyway, Lady Mountbatten?

MRS. ROCKETT: Really, Doris, you make me tired sometimes, you do really.

DORIS: If you're so fond of Mrs. Henderson it's a pity you don't see more of her. I notice you don't go there often.

MRS. ROCKETT: [With dignity] I go when I am invited.

DORIS: [Triumphantly] Exactly.

MRS. ROCKETT: She's not the kind of woman that likes people dropping in and out all the time. We can't all be Amy Fawcetts.

DORIS: What's the matter with Amy Fawcett?

[ELSIE comes into the room wearing a mackintosh and a tam-o'-shanter. She stamps over to the piano and begins to search untidily through the pile of music on it]

MRS. ROCKETT: Well, she's common for one thing, she dyes her hair for another, and she's a bit too free and easy all round for my taste.

DORIS: She doesn't put on airs, anyway.

MRS. ROCKETT: I should think not, after the sort of life she's led.

DORIS: How do you know what sort of a life she's led?

MRS. ROCKETT: Everybody knows, you only have to look at her; I'm a woman of the world, I am, you can't pull the wool over my eyes——

DORIS: Don't untidy everything like that, what are you looking for?

ELSIE: "The Pixie's Parade," I had it last night.

DORIS: If it's the one with the blue cover it's at the bottom.

ELSIE: It isn't—oh dear, Miss Pritchard will be mad at me if I can't find it.

MRS. ROCKETT: Perhaps you put it in your satchel, dear, here, let me look——[*She opens* ELSIE's *satchel, which is hanging over the back of a chair and fumbles in it*] Is this it?

ELSIE: Oh yes, thanks, Grandma.

DORIS: Go along now, for heaven's sake, you'll be late.

ELSIE: Oh, all right, Mum. Good-bye, Mum, good-bye, Grandma, good-bye, Dad.

HENRY: Good-bye.

MRS. ROCKETT: Good-bye, dear, give Grandma a kiss. [ELSIE *does so*]

DORIS: Don't dawdle on the way home.

ELSIE: Oh, all right, Mum.

[*She goes out. The slam of the front door shakes the house*]

DORIS: [*Irritably*] There now.

MRS. ROCKETT: [*With studied politeness*] If you are going down to the shops this morning, would it be troubling you too much to get me a reel of white cotton?

DORIS: I thought you were coming with me.

MRS. ROCKETT: I really don't feel up to it.

DORIS: I'll put it on my list.

[*She takes a piece of paper out of the sideboard drawer and scribbles on it*]

MRS. ROCKETT: If it's out of your way, please don't trouble, it'll do another time.

DORIS: Henry, it's past nine.

HENRY: [*Without looking up*] I know.

DORIS: You'll be late.

HENRY: Never mind.

DORIS: That's a nice way to talk, I must say.

MRS. ROCKETT: I'm sure if my Robert had ever lazed about like that in the mornings, I'd have thought the world had come to an end.

DORIS: Henry'll do it once too often, mark my words.

MRS. ROCKETT: [*Biting off her thread*] Well, that corner's finished.

DORIS: [*To* HENRY] You'll have to move now, I've got to clear.

HENRY: [*Rising—absently*] All right.

MRS. ROCKETT: Where's Ethel?

DORIS: Doing the bedroom.

[*She takes a tray which is leaning against the wall by the sideboard and proceeds to stack the breakfast things on to it.* HENRY *quietly goes out of the room*]

DORIS: Look at that wicked waste. [*Throws more scraps in fire*]

MRS. ROCKETT: What's the matter with him?

DORIS: Don't ask me, I'm sure I couldn't tell you.

MRS. ROCKETT: He came in very late last night, I heard him go into the bathroom. [*There is a pause*] That cistern makes a terrible noise.

DORIS: Does it indeed!

MRS. ROCKETT: Yes, it does.

DORIS: [*Slamming the teapot on to the tray*] Very sorry, I'm sure.

MRS. ROCKETT: Where'd he been?

DORIS: How do I know?

MRS. ROCKETT: Didn't you ask him?

DORIS: I wouldn't demean myself.

MRS. ROCKETT: Been drinking?

DORIS: No.

MRS. ROCKETT: Sounded very like it to me, all that banging about.

DORIS: You know Henry never touches a drop.

MRS. ROCKETT: I know he says he doesn't.

DORIS: Oh, do shut up, Mother, we're not all like father.

MRS. ROCKETT: You watch your tongue, Doris Gow, don't let me hear you saying anything against the memory of your poor father.

DORIS: I wasn't.

MRS. ROCKETT: [*Belligerently*] Oh yes, you were, you were insinuating again.

DORIS: [*Hoisting up the tray*] Father drank and you know it—everybody knew it.

MRS. ROCKETT: You're a wicked woman.

DORIS: It's true.

MRS. ROCKETT: Your father was a gentleman, which is more than your husband will ever be, with all his night-classes and his book reading—night-classes indeed!

DORIS: Who's insinuating now?

MRS. ROCKETT: [*Angrily*] I am, and I'm not afraid to say so.

DORIS: What of it?

MRS. ROCKETT: [*With heavy sarcasm*] I suppose he was at a night-class last night?

[HENRY *comes in wearing his mackintosh and a bowler hat*]

HENRY: What's up?

DORIS: Where were you last night?

HENRY: Why?

DORIS: Mother wants to know and so do I.

HENRY: I was kept late at the shop and I had a bit of dinner in town.

DORIS: Who with?

HENRY: Charlie Henderson.

[*He picks up the paper off the table and goes out. After a moment the front door slams. The baby next door bursts into fresh wails*]

MRS. ROCKETT: There goes that child again. It's my belief it's hungry.

DORIS: Wonder you don't go and give it twopence to buy sponge cake.

[*She pulls the door open with her foot and goes out with the tray as the lights fade on the scene*]

SCENE TWO

It is about seven-thirty in the evening. ELSIE *is sitting at the piano practising with the loud pedal firmly down all the time.*

MRS. ROCKETT *is sitting in her chair by the fire, but she is dressed in her street things and wearing a black hat with a veil.*

DORIS, *also in street clothes, is clearing some paper patterns and pieces of material from the table.*

There is a cloth across the end of the table on which is set a loaf, a plate of cold ham, a saucer with two tomatoes in it, a bottle of A.1 sauce and a teapot, teacup, sugar basin, and milk jug.

HENRY *comes in, taking off his mackintosh. He gives one look round the room and goes out into the hall again to hang up his things.* ELSIE *stops playing and comes over to* DORIS.

ELSIE: Can we go now?

DORIS: In a minute.

ELSIE: We'll miss the Mickey.

DORIS: Put on your hat and don't worry.

ELSIE: [*Grabbing her hat from the sideboard*] Oh, all right.

[HENRY *re-enters*]

DORIS: Your supper's all ready, the kettle's on the gas stove when you want it. We've had ours.

HENRY: Oh!

DORIS: And you needn't look injured either.

HENRY: Very well.

DORIS: If you managed to get home a bit earlier it'd save a lot of trouble all round.

HENRY: [*Amiably*] Sorry, dear.

DORIS: It's all very fine to be sorry, you've been getting later and later these last few weeks, they can't keep you overtime every night.

HENRY: All right, dear, I'll tell them.

DORIS: Here, Elsie, put these away in the cupboard.

[*She hands her a pile of material and pieces of paper. ELSIE obediently takes them and puts them in the left-hand cupboard of the sideboard*]

HENRY: [*Sitting at the table*] Cold ham, what a surprise!

DORIS: [*Looking at him sharply*] What's the matter with it?

HENRY: I don't know, yet.

DORIS: It's perfectly fresh, if that's what you mean?

HENRY: Why are you all so dressed up?

ELSIE: We're going to the pictures.

HENRY: Oh, I see.

DORIS: You can put everything on the tray when you've finished and leave it in the kitchen for Ethel.

HENRY: Good old Ethel.

DORIS: [*Surprised*] What?

HENRY: I said good old Ethel.

DORIS: Well, it sounded very silly, I'm sure.

MRS. ROCKETT: [*Scrutinising him*] What's the matter with you?

HENRY: Nothing, why?

MRS. ROCKETT: You look funny.

HENRY: I feel funny.

MRS. ROCKETT: Have you been drinking?

HENRY: Yes.

DORIS: Henry!

MRS. ROCKETT: I knew it.

HENRY: I had a whisky and soda in town and another one at the Plough.

DORIS: [*Astounded*] What for?

HENRY: Because I felt like it.

DORIS: You ought to be ashamed of yourself.

HENRY: I'm going to have another one too, a bit later on.

DORIS: You'll do no such thing.

HENRY: That hat looks awful.

DORIS: [*Furiously*] Don't you speak to me like that.

HENRY: Why not?

DORIS: [*Slightly nonplussed*] Because I won't have it, so there.

HENRY: It's a common little hat and it looks awful.

DORIS: [*With an admirable effort at control*] Now listen to me, Henry Gow, the next time I catch you drinking and coming home here and insulting me, I'll——

HENRY: [*Interrupting her gently*] What will you do, Dorrie?

DORIS: [*Hotly*] I'll give you a piece of my mind, that's what I'll do!

HENRY: It'll have to be a very little piece, Dorrie, you can't afford much! [*He laughs delighted at his own joke*]

DORIS: I'd be very much obliged if you'd kindly tell me what this means?

HENRY: I'm celebrating.

DORIS: What do you mean, celebrating? What are you talking about?

HENRY: Tonight's our anniversary.

DORIS: Don't talk so soft, our anniversary's not until November.

HENRY: I don't mean that one. Tonight's the anniversary of the first time I had an affair with you and you got in the family way.

DORIS: [*Shrieking*] Henry!

HENRY: [*Delighted with his carefully calculated effect*] Hurray!

DORIS: [*Beside herself*] How dare you say such a dreadful thing, in front of the child, too.

HENRY: [*In romantic tones*] Three years and a bit after that wonderful night our child was born! [*Lapsing into his normal voice*] Considering all the time you took forming yourself, Elsie, I'm surprised you're not a nicer little girl than you are.

DORIS: Go upstairs, Elsie.

HENRY: Stay here, Elsie.

DORIS: Do as I tell you.

ELSIE: But, Mum——

DORIS: Mother, take her for God's sake! There's going to be a row.

HENRY: [*Firmly*] Leave her alone and sit down. [MRS. ROCKETT *hesitates*] Sit down, I tell you.

MRS. ROCKETT: [*Subsiding into a chair*] Well, I never, I——

HENRY: [*Happily*] See? It works like a charm.

DORIS: A fine exhibition you're making of yourself, I must say.

HENRY: Not bad, is it? As a matter of fact I'm rather pleased with it myself.

DORIS: Go to bed!

HENRY: Stop ordering me about. What right have you got to nag at me and boss me? No right at all. I'm the one that pays the rent and works for you and keeps you. What do you give me in return, I'd like to know! Nothing! I sit through breakfast while you and mother wrangle. You're too busy being snappy and bad-tempered even to say good morning. I come home tired after working all day and ten to one there isn't even a hot dinner for me; here see this ham? This is what I think of it! [*He throws it at her feet*] And the tomatoes and the A.1 bloody sauce! [*He throws them, too*]

DORIS: [*Screaming*] Henry! All over the carpet.

HENRY: [*Throwing the butter-dish face downwards on the floor*] And that's what I think of the carpet, now then!

DORIS: That I should live to see this! That I should live to see the man I married make such a beast of himself!

HENRY: Stop working yourself up into a state, you'll need all your control when you've heard what I'm going to say to you.

DORIS: Look here——

HENRY: Sit down. We'll all sit down, I'm afraid you'll have to miss the pictures for once.

DORIS: Elsie, you come with me.

MRS. ROCKETT: Yes, go on, Ducks.

[*She makes a movement towards the door, but* HENRY *is too quick for her. He locks the door and slips the key into his pocket*]

HENRY: I've been dreaming of this moment for many years, and believe me it's not going to be spoilt for me by you running away.

DORIS: [*On the verge of tears*] Let me out of this room.

HENRY: You'll stay where you are until I've had my say.

DORIS: [*Bursting into tears and sinking down at the table*] Oh! Oh! Oh!——

ELSIE: [*Starting to cry, too*] Mum—oh, Mum——

HENRY: Here you, shut up, go and get the port out of the sideboard and give some to your mother—go on, do as I tell you. [ELSIE, *terrified and hypnotised into submission, goes to the sideboard cupboard and brings out a bottle of invalid port and some glasses, snivelling as she does so.* DORIS *continues to sob.*] That's right.

MRS. ROCKETT: [*Quietly*] You drunken brute, you!

HENRY: [*Cheerfully*] Worse than that, Mother, far worse. Just you wait and see.

MRS. ROCKETT: [*Ignoring him*] Take some port, Dorrie, it'll do you good.

DORIS: I don't want any—it'd choke me——

HENRY: [*Pouring some out*] Come on—here——

DORIS: Keep away from me.

HENRY: Drink it and stop snivelling.

DORIS: I'll never forgive you for this, never, never, never as long as I live! [*She gulps down some port*]

HENRY: [*Noting her gesture*] That's better.

MRS. ROCKETT: Pay no attention, Dorrie, he's drunk.

HENRY: I'm not drunk. I've only had two whiskies and sodas, just to give me enough guts to take the first plunge. You'd never believe how scared I was, thinking it over in cold blood. I'm not scared any more though, it's much easier than I thought it was going to be. My only regret is that I didn't come to the boil a long time ago, and tell you to your face, Dorrie, what I think of you, what I've been thinking of you for years, and this horrid little kid, and that old bitch of a mother of yours.

MRS. ROCKETT: [*Shrilly*] Henry Gow!

HENRY: You heard me, old bitch was what I said, and old bitch was what I meant.

MRS. ROCKETT: Let me out of this room, I'm not going to stay here and be insulted—I'm not——

HENRY: You're going to stay here just as long as I want you to.

MRS. ROCKETT: Oh, am I? We'll see about that——

[*With astonishing quickness she darts over to the window and manages to drag one open.* HENRY *grabs her by the arm*]

HENRY: No, you don't.

MRS. ROCKETT: Let go of me.

DORIS: Oh, Mother, don't let the neighbours know all your business.

HENRY: Not on your life!

MRS. ROCKETT: [*Suddenly screaming powerfully*] Help! Help! Police! Help! Mrs. Harrison—help!——

[HENRY *drags her away from the window, turns her round and gives her a light slap on the face, she staggers against the piano, meanwhile he shuts the window again, locks it and pockets the key*]

DORIS: [*Looking at him in horror*] Oh, God! Oh, my God!

ELSIE: [*Bursting into tears again*] Oh, Mum, Mum, he hit Grandma! Oh, Mum——

[*She runs to* DORIS *who puts her arm around her protectively*]

MRS. ROCKETT: [*Gasping*] Oh—my heart! I think I'm going to faint —oh—my—heart——

HENRY: Don't worry, I'll bring you round if you faint——

MRS. ROCKETT: Oh—oh—oh, dear——

[MRS. ROCKETT *slides on to the floor, perceptibly breaking her fall by clinging on to the piano stool.* DORIS *jumps up from the table*]

DORIS: Mother!

HENRY: Stay where you are.

[HENRY *goes to the sideboard and pours out a glass of water.* DORIS, *disobeying him, runs over to her mother.* ELSIE *wails*]

HENRY: Stand out of the way, Doris, we don't all want to get wet.

[He *approaches with the glass of water.* MRS. ROCKETT *sits up weakly*]

MRS. ROCKETT: [*In a far-away voice*] Where am I?

HENRY: Number Seventeen Cranworth Road, Clapham.

MRS. ROCKETT: Oh—oh, dear!

HENRY: Look here, Mother, I don't want there to be any misunderstanding about this. I liked slapping you just now, see? It was lovely, and if you don't behave yourself and keep quiet I shall slap you again. Go and sit in your chair and remember if you feel faint the water's all ready for you. [He *helps her up and escorts her to her chair by the fire. She collapses into it and looks at him balefully*] Now then. Sit down, Dorrie, you look silly standing about.

DORIS: [*With a great effort at control*] Henry——

HENRY: [*Slowly, but very firmly*] Sit down! And keep Elsie quiet or I'll fetch her one, too.

DORIS: [*With dignity*] Come here, Elsie. Shut up, will you!

[*She sits at the table, with* ELSIE]

HENRY: That's right. [He *walks round the room slowly and in silence, looking at them with an expression of the greatest satisfaction on his face. Finally he goes over to the fireplace;* MRS. ROCKETT *jumps slightly as he approaches her, but he smiles at her reassuringly and lights a cigarette. Meanwhile* DORIS, *recovering from her fear, is beginning to simmer with rage, she remains still, however, watching]* Now then. I'm going to start quietly, explaining a few things to you.

DORIS: Enjoying yourself, aren't you?

HENRY: You've said it.

DORIS: [*Gaining courage*] You'll grin on the other side of your face before I've done with you.

HENRY: [*Politely*] Very likely, Dorrie, very likely indeed!

DORIS: And don't you Dorrie me, either! Coming home here drunk, hitting poor mother and frightening Elsie out of her wits.

HENRY: Maybe it'll do her good, do 'em both good, a little excitement in the home. God knows, it's dull enough as a rule.

DORIS: [*With biting sarcasm*] Very clever, oh, very clever, I'm sure.

HENRY: Fifteen, no sixteen years ago to-night, Dorrie, you and me had a little rough and tumble in your Aunt Daisy's house in Stansfield Road, do you remember?

DORIS: Henry——

HENRY: [*Ignoring her*] We had the house to ourselves, it being a Sunday, your Aunt had popped over to the Golden Calf with Mr. Simmonds, the lodger, which, as the writers say, was her wont——

MRS. ROCKETT: This is disgusting, I won't listen to another word.

HENRY: [*Rounding on her*] You will! Shut up!

DORIS: Pay no attention, Mother, he's gone mad.

HENRY: Let me see now, where was I? Oh yes, Stansfield Road. You had been after me for a long while, Dorrie, I didn't know it then, but I realised it soon after. You had to have a husband, what with Nora married and Phyllis engaged, both of them younger than you, you had to have a husband, and quick, so you fixed me. You were pretty enough and I fell for it hook, line and sinker; then, a couple of months later you'd told me you'd clicked, you cried a hell of a lot, I remember, said the disgrace would kill your mother if she ever found out. I didn't know then that it'd take a sight more than that to kill that leathery old mare——

MRS. ROCKETT: [*Bursting into tears*] I won't stand it, I won't! I won't!

HENRY: [*Rising above her sobs*] I expect you were in on the whole business, in a refined way of course, you knew what was going on all right, you knew that Dorrie was no more in the family way than I was, but we got married; you both saw to that, and I chucked up all the plans I had for getting on, perhaps being a steward in a ship and seeing a bit of the world. Oh yes, all that had to go and we settled down in rooms and I went into Ferguson's Hosiery.

DORIS: I've given you the best years of my life and don't you forget it.

HENRY: You've never given me the best of anything, not even yourself. You didn't even have Elsie willingly.

DORIS: [*Wildly*] It's not true—stop up your ears, Elsie, don't listen to him, he's wicked—he's wicked——

HENRY: [*Grimly*] It's true all right, and you know it as well as I do.

DORIS: [*Shrilly*] It was only right that you married me. It was only fair! You took advantage of me, didn't you? You took away my innocence. It was only right that you paid for it.

HENRY: Come off it, Dorrie, don't talk so silly. I was the innocent one, not you. I found out you'd cheated me a long, long time ago, and when I found out, realized it for certain, I started cheating you. Prepare yourself, Dorrie, my girl, you're going to be really upset this time. I've been saving! Every week for over ten years I've been earning a little bit more than you thought I was. I've managed, by hook and by crook, to put by five hundred and seventy-two pounds—d'you hear me?—five hundred and seventy-two pounds!

MRS. ROCKETT: [*Jumping to her feet*] Henry! You never have—it's not true——

DORIS: [*Also jumping up*] You couldn't have—you'd have given it away—I should have found out——

HENRY: I thought that'd rouse you, but don't get excited, don't get worked up. I haven't got it on me, it's in the bank. And it's not for you, it's for me—all but fifty pounds of it, that much is for you, just fifty pounds, the last you'll ever get from me——

DORIS: Henry! You couldn't be so cruel! You couldn't be so mean!

HENRY: I've done what I think's fair and what I think's fair is damn sight more than you deserve. I've transferred the freehold of this

house into your name, so you'll always have a roof over your head—
you can take in lodgers at a pinch, though God help the poor
bastards if you do!

DORIS: Five hundred and seventy-two pounds! You've got all that and
you're going to leave me to starve!

HENRY: Cut out the drama, Dorrie, and have a look at your mother's
savings bank book—I bet you'll find she's got enough to keep you
in comfort till the day you die. She soaked her old man plenty,
I'm sure—before he took to soaking himself!

MRS. ROCKETT: It's a lie!

HENRY: Now listen to me, Mother Machree—You've 'ad one sock in
the jaw this evening and you're not just asking for another, you're
sitting up and begging for it.

MRS. ROCKETT: I'll have you up for assault. I'll have the police on you,
my fine fellow!

HENRY: They'll have to be pretty nippy—my boat sails first thing in
the morning.

DORIS: [Horrified] Boat!

HENRY: I'm going away. I've got my ticket here in my pocket, and
my passport. My passport photo's a fair scream, I wish I could
show it to you, but I don't want you to see the nice new name I've
got.

DORIS: You can't do it, I can have you stopped by law. It's desertion.

HENRY: That's right, Dorrie, you've said it. Desertion's just exactly
what it is.

DORIS: [Breathlessly] Where are you going, you've got to tell me.
Where are you going?

HENRY: Wouldn't you like to know? Maybe Africa, maybe China,
maybe Australia. There are lots of places in the world you know
nothing about, Dorrie. You've often laughed at me for reading
books, but I've found out a hell of a lot from books. There are
islands in the South Seas for instance with cocoa palms and turtles
and sunshine all the year round—you can live there for practically
nothing, then there's Australia or New Zealand, with a little bit of
capital I might start in a small way sheep-farming. Think of it;
miles and miles of open country stretching as far as the eye can see
—good food and fresh air—that might be very nice, that might

suit me beautifully. Then there's South America. There are coffee
plantations, there, and sugar plantations, and banana plantations.
If I go to South America I'll send you a whole crate. 'Ave a banana,
Dorrie! 'Ave a banana!

DORIS: Henry, listen to me, you can't do this dreadful thing, you
can't! If you don't love me any more, think of Elsie.

HENRY: [*Still in his dream*] Then there's the sea, not the sea we know
at Worthing with the tide going in and out regular and the band
playing on the pier. The real sea's what I mean. The sea that
Joseph Conrad wrote about, and Rudyard Kipling and lots of other
people, too, a sea with whacking great waves and water spouts and
typhoons and flying-fish and phosphorus making the foam look as
if it was lit up. Those people knew a thing or two I can tell you.
They knew what life could be like if you give it a chance. They
knew there was a bit more to it than refinement and fumed oak
and lace curtains and getting old and miserable with nothing to
show for it. I'm a middle-aged man, but my health's not too bad
taken all round. There's still time for me to see a little bit of real
life before I conk out. I'm still fit enough to do a job of work—
real work, mind you—not bowing and scraping and wearing myself
out showing fussy old cows the way to the lace and the chinaware
and the bargain basement.

DORIS: [*Hysterically*] God will punish you, you just see if He doesn't,
you just see——

HENRY: God's been punishing me for fifteen years, it's high time He
laid off me now. He's been punishing me good and proper for
being damn fool enough to let you get your claws into me in the
first place——

DORIS: [*Changing tactics*] Henry, have pity, please don't be so cruel,
please—please——

HENRY: And don't start weeping and wailing either, that won't cut
any ice with me, I know what you're like, I know you through and
through. You're frightened now, scared out of your wits, but give
you half a chance and you'd be worse than ever you were. You're
a bad lot, Dorrie, not what the world would call a bad lot, but
what I call a bad lot. Mean and cold and respectable. Good-bye,
Dorrie——

DORIS: [*Flinging her arms round him and bursting into tears*] Listen
to me, Henry, you've got to listen—you must. You can't leave us

to starve, you can't throw us on to the streets—if I've been a bad wife to you, I'm sorry—I'll try to be better, really I will, I swear to God I will—— You can't do this, if you won't forgive me, think of Elsie, think of poor little Elsie——

HENRY: Poor little Elsie, my eye! I think Elsie's awful. I always have ever since she was little. She's never done anything but whine and snivel and try to get something for nothing——

ELSIE: [*Wailing*] Oh, Mum, did you hear what he said? Oh, Dad, oh dear——

MRS. ROCKETT: [*Comforting her*] There, there, dear, don't listen to him——

HENRY: Elsie can go to work in a year or so, in the meantime, Dorrie, you can go to work yourself, you're quite a young woman still and strong as an ox.— Here's your fifty pounds——

[*He takes an envelope out of his pocket and throws it on to the table. Then he goes towards the door.* DORIS *rushes after him and hangs on to his arm*]

DORIS: Henry, Henry, you shan't go, you shan't——

HENRY: [*Struggling with her*] Leave hold of me!

DORIS: Mother, mother—help—help me, don't let him go——

[HENRY *frees himself from her and, taking her by the shoulders, forces her back into a chair, then he unlocks the door and opens it*]

HENRY: I'm taking my last look at you, Dorrie. I shall never see you again as long as I live——

DORIS: Mother! Oh God!—oh, my God!——

[*She buries her head in her arms and starts to sob loudly.* ELSIE *runs and joins her, yelling.* MRS. ROCKETT *sits transfixed, staring at him murderously*]

HENRY: [*Quietly*] Three generations. Grandmother, Mother and Kid. Made of the same bones and sinews and muscles and glands, millions of you, millions just like you. You're past it now, Mother, you're past the thick of the fray, you're nothing but a music hall joke, a mother-in-law with a bit of money put by. Dorrie, the next few years will show whether you've got guts or not. Maybe what I'm doing to you will save your immortal soul in the long run, that'd be a bit of all right, wouldn't it? I doubt it, though, your immortal soul's too measly. You're a natural bully and a cheat, and I'm sick of the sight of you; I should also like to take this opportunity of saying that I hate that bloody awful slave bangle and I always have. As for you, Elsie, you've got a chance, it's a slim one, I grant you, but still it's a chance. If you learn to work and be independent and, when the time comes, give what you have to give freely and without demanding life-long payment for it, there's just a bit of hope that you'll turn into a decent human being. At all events, if you'll take one parting piece of advice from your cruel, ungrateful father, you'll spend the first money you ever earn on having your adenoids out. Good-bye, one and all. Nice to have known you!

[*The wails of* DORIS *and* ELSIE *rise in volume as he goes jauntily out, slamming the door behind him*].

CURTAIN

PORTRAIT OF A MADONNA

Tennessee Williams

Tennessee Williams

The life and career of Tennessee Williams (born Thomas Lanier Williams in Columbus, Mississippi, on March 26, 1911) have been so thoroughly documented in countless periodicals and books, as well as in critical and biographical studies, that there seems little need for reiteration in the pages of this collection. Merely to list Mr. Williams' plays is sufficient for the evocation of many memorable moments in the theatre, for he has peopled the world's stages with characters so durably vibrant that their presences still stalk the corridors of a playgoer's memory.

Named by *Time* magazine as "the greatest living playwright in the Western World," Tennessee Williams, recipient of two Pulitzer Prizes and four New York Drama Critics' Circle Awards, remains, indisputably, a consummate master of theatre. His plays pulsate with the heart's blood of the drama: passion. When one re-examines Mr. Williams' predominant works, one cannot but be awed by the dazzling skill of a remarkable dramatist whose major plays no longer tend to be merely plays but, somehow, through the process of creative genius, have transcended into haunting realities.

As he often has stated, his special compassion is for "the people who are not meant to win—the lost, the odd, the strange, the difficult people—fragile people who lack talons for the jungle," and the tragic heroine of *Portrait of a Madonna* most certainly comes within this concept.

The author first won general recognition with the 1945 production of *The Glass Menagerie*, starring Laurette Taylor. Thereafter, he attained world-wide repute with a succession of impressive plays, notably: *A Streetcar Named Desire* (1947); *Summer and Smoke* (1948); *The Rose Tattoo* (1951); *Cat on a Hot Tin Roof* (1955); and *The Night of the Iguana* (1961). Among his other plays in nonchronological order: *Sweet Bird of Youth; Camino Real; Orpheus Descending; Period of Adjustment; The Milk Train Doesn't Stop Here Anymore; Kingdom of Earth* (known in its Broadway manifestation as *The Seven Descents of Myrtle*); *In the Bar of a Tokyo Hotel; Out Cry; Small Craft Warnings; This Is (An Entertainment); The Red Devil Battery Sign;* and *Vieux Carré.*

In addition to *Portrait of a Madonna,* Mr. Williams has written a number of other short plays, including: 27 *Wagons Full of Cotton; This Property Is Condemned; I Rise in Flame, Cried the Phoenix; The Lady of Larkspur Lotion; The Last of My Solid Gold Watches; Moony's Kid Don't Cry; Suddenly Last Summer; Slapstick Tragedy (The Mutilated* and *The Gnädiges Fräulein); I Can't Imagine Tomorrow; The Frosted Glass Coffin;* and *A Perfect Analysis Given by a Parrot.*

He also has published several volumes of short stories, a book of poetry, and a novella, *The Roman Spring of Mrs. Stone.* In 1975 he published his *Memoirs,* which remained on the best-seller list for a number of months.

A firm disciplinarian where his work is concerned, the dramatist dedicates four hours of each day—"year in, year out"—to writing and about every two years completes a new full-length work. Before settling down to the actual task of writing, however, he "marinates impressions, characters, experiences."

In 1969 Tennessee Williams received a Gold Medal for Drama from the prestigious National Institute of Arts and Letters and, more recently, he was given the National Theatre Conference Annual Award honoring his "countless contributions to the American theatre spanning the past three decades."

Characters:

Miss Lucretia Collins
The Porter
The Elevator Boy
The Doctor
The Nurse
Mr. Abrams

SCENE: *The living room of a moderate-priced city apartment. The furnishings are old-fashioned and everything is in a state of neglect and disorder. There is a door in the back wall to a bedroom, and on the right to the outside hall.*

MISS COLLINS: Richard! [*The door bursts open and* MISS COLLINS *rushes out, distractedly. She is a middle-aged spinster, very slight and hunched of figure with a desiccated face that is flushed with excitement. Her hair is arranged in curls that would become a young girl and she wears a frilly negligee which might have come from an old hope chest of a period considerably earlier*] No, no, no, no! I don't care if the whole church hears about it! [*She frenziedly snatches up the phone*] Manager, I've got to speak to the manager! Hurry, oh, please hurry, there's a *man—*! [*Wildly aside as if to an invisible figure*] Lost all respect, absolutely no respect! . . . Mr. Abrams? [*In a tense hushed voice*] I don't want any reporters to hear about this but something awful has been going on upstairs. Yes, this is Miss Collins' apartment on the top floor. I've refrained from making any complaint because of my connections with the church. I used to be assistant to the Sunday School superintendent and I once had the primary class. I helped them put on the Christmas pageant. I made the dress for the Virgin and Mother, made robes for the Wise Men. Yes, and now this has happened, I'm not responsible for it, but night after night after night this man has been coming into my apartment and—indulging his senses! Do you understand? Not once but repeatedly, Mr. Abrams! I don't know whether he comes in the door or the window or up the fire escape or whether there's some secret entrance they know about at the church, but he's here now, in my bedroom, and I can't force him to leave, I'll have to have some assistance! No, he isn't a thief, Mr. Abrams, he comes of a very fine family in Webb, Mississippi, but this woman has ruined his character, she's destroyed his respect for ladies! Mr. Abrams? Mr. Abrams! Oh, goodness! [*She slams up the receiver and looks dis-*

tractedly about for a moment; then rushes back into the bedroom]
Richard!

[*The door slams shut. After a few moments an old* PORTER
*enters in drab gray cover-alls. He looks about with a sorrowfully
humorous curiosity, then timidly calls*]

PORTER: Miss Collins?

[*The elevator door slams open in hall and the* ELEVATOR BOY,
wearing a uniform, comes in]

ELEVATOR BOY: Where is she?

PORTER: Gone in 'er bedroom.

ELEVATOR BOY: [*Grinning*] She got him in there with her?

PORTER: Sounds like it.

[MISS COLLINS' *voice can be heard faintly protesting with the
mysterious intruder*]

ELEVATOR BOY: What'd Abrams tell yuh to do?

PORTER: Stay here an' keep a watch on 'er till they git here.

ELEVATOR BOY: Jesus!

PORTER: Close 'at door.

ELEVATOR BOY: I gotta leave it open a little so I can hear the buzzer.
Ain't this place a holy sight though?

PORTER: Don't look like it's had a good cleaning in fifteen or twenty
years. I bet it ain't either. Abrams'll bust a blood-vessel when he
takes a lookit them walls.

ELEVATOR BOY: How comes it's in this condition?

PORTER: She wouldn't let no one in.

ELEVATOR BOY: Not even the paperhangers?

PORTER: Naw. Not even the plumbers. The plaster washed down in
the bathroom underneath hers an' she admitted her plumbin' had
been stopped up. Mr. Abrams had to let the plumber in with this
here pass-key when she went out for a while.

ELEVATOR BOY: Holy Jeez! I wunner if she's got money stashed around here. A lotta freaks do stick away big sums of money in ole mattresses an' things.

PORTER: She ain't. She got a monthly pension check or something she always turned over to Mr. Abrams to dole it out to 'er. She tole him that Southern ladies was never brought up to manage finanshul affairs. Lately the checks quit comin'.

ELEVATOR BOY: Yeah?

PORTER: The pension give out or somethin'. Abrams says he got a contribution from the church to keep 'er on here without 'er knowin' about it. She's proud as a peacock's tail in spite of 'er awful appearance.

ELEVATOR BOY: Lissen to 'er in there!

PORTER: What's she sayin'?

ELEVATOR BOY: Apologizin' to him! For callin' the *police!*

PORTER: She thinks police 're comin'?

MISS COLLINS: [*From bedroom*] Stop it, it's got to stop!

ELEVATOR BOY: Fightin' to protect her honor again! What a commotion, no wunner folks are complainin'!

PORTER: [*Lighting his pipe*] This here'll be the last time.

ELEVATOR BOY: She's goin' out, huh?

PORTER: [*Blowing out the match*] Tonight.

ELEVATOR BOY: Where'll she go?

PORTER: [*Slowly moving to the old gramophone*] She'll go to the state asylum.

ELEVATOR BOY: Holy G!

PORTER: Remember this ole number? [*He puts on a record of "I'm Forever Blowing Bubbles"*]

ELEVATOR BOY: Naw. When did that come out?

PORTER: Before your time, sonny boy. Machine needs oilin'.

[*He takes out small oil-can and applies oil about the crank and other parts of gramophone*]

ELEVATOR BOY: How long is the old girl been here?

PORTER: Abrams says she's been livin' here twenty-five, thirty years, since before he got to be manager even.

ELEVATOR BOY: Livin' alone all that time?

PORTER: She had an old mother died of an operation about fifteen years ago. Since then she ain't gone out of the place excep' on Sundays to church or Friday nights to some kind of religious meeting.

ELEVATOR BOY: Got an awful lot of ol' magazines piled aroun' here.

PORTER: She used to collect 'em. She'd go out in back and fish 'em out of the incinerator.

ELEVATOR BOY: What'n hell for?

PORTER: Mr. Abrams says she used to cut out the Campbell soup kids. Them red-tomato-headed kewpie dolls that go with the soup advertisements. You seen 'em, ain'tcha?

ELEVATOR BOY: Uh-huh.

PORTER: She made a collection of 'em. Filled a big lot of scrapbooks with them paper kiddies an' took 'em down to the Children's Hospitals on Xmas Eve an' Easter Sunday, exactly twicet a year. Sounds better, don't it? [*Referring to gramophone, which resumes its faint, wheedling music*] Eliminated some a that crankin' noise . . .

ELEVATOR BOY: I didn't know that she'd been nuts *that* long.

PORTER: Who's nuts an' who ain't? If you ask me the world is populated with people that's just as peculiar as she is.

ELEVATOR BOY: Hell! She don't have brain *one*.

PORTER: There's important people in Europe got less'n she's got. Tonight they're takin' her off 'n' lockin' her up. They'd do a lot better to leave 'er go an' lock up some a them maniacs over there. She's harmless; they ain't. They kill millions of people an' go scot free!

ELEVATOR BOY: An ole woman like her is disgusting, though, imaginin' somebody's raped her.

PORTER: Pitiful, not disgusting. Watch out for them cigarette ashes.

ELEVATOR BOY: What's uh diff'rence? So much dust you can't see it. All a this here goes out in the morning, don't it?

PORTER: Uh-huh.

ELEVATOR BOY: I think I'll take a couple a those ole records as curiosities for my girl friend. She's got a portable in 'er bedroom, she says it's better with music!

PORTER: Leave 'em alone. She's still got 'er property rights.

ELEVATOR BOY: Aw, she's got all she wants with them dream-lovers of hers!

PORTER: *Hush up!* [*He makes a warning gesture as* MISS COLLINS *enters from bedroom. Her appearance is that of a ravaged woman. She leans exhaustedly in the doorway, hands clasped over her flat, virginal bosom*]

MISS COLLINS: [*Breathlessly*] Oh, Richard—Richard . . .

PORTER: [*Coughing*] Miss—Collins.

ELEVATOR BOY: Hello, Miss Collins.

MISS COLLINS: [*Just noticing the men*] Goodness! You've arrived already! Mother didn't tell me you were here! [*Self-consciously she touches her ridiculous corkscrew curls with the faded pink ribbon tied through them. Her manner becomes that of a slightly coquettish but prim little Southern belle*] I must ask you gentlemen to excuse the terrible disorder.

PORTER: That's all right, Miss Collins.

MISS COLLINS: It's the maid's day off. Your No'thern girls receive such excellent domestic training, but in the South it was never considered essential for a girl to have anything but prettiness and charm! [*She laughs girlishly*] Please do sit down. Is it too close? Would you like a window open?

PORTER: No, Miss Collins.

MISS COLLINS: [*Advancing with delicate grace to the sofa*] Mother will bring in something cool after while . . . Oh, my! [*She touches her forehead*]

PORTER: [*Kindly*] Is anything wrong, Miss Collins?

MISS COLLINS: Oh, no, no, thank you, nothing! My head is a little bit heavy. I'm always a little bit—malarial—this time of year! [*She sways dizzily as she starts to sink down on the sofa*]

PORTER: [*Helping her*] Careful there, Miss Collins.

MISS COLLINS: [*Vaguely*] Yes, it is, I hadn't noticed before. [*She peers at them near-sightedly with a hesitant smile*] You gentlemen have come from the church?

PORTER: No, ma'am. I'm Nick, the porter, Miss Collins, and this boy here is Frank that runs the elevator.

MISS COLLINS: [*Stiffening a little*] Oh? . . . I don't understand.

PORTER: [*Gently*] Mr. Abrams just asked me to drop in here an' see if you was getting along all right.

MISS COLLINS: Oh! Then he must have informed you of what's been going on in here!

PORTER: He mentioned some kind of—disturbance.

MISS COLLINS: Yes! Isn't it outrageous? But it mustn't go any further, you understand. I mean you mustn't repeat it to other people.

PORTER: No, I wouldn't say nothing.

MISS COLLINS: Not a word of it, please!

ELEVATOR BOY: Is the man still here, Miss Collins?

MISS COLLINS: Oh, no. No, he's gone now.

ELEVATOR BOY: How did he go, out the bedroom window, Miss Collins?

MISS COLLINS: [*Vaguely*] Yes . . .

ELEVATOR BOY: I seen a guy that could do that once. He crawled straight up the side of the building. They called him The Human Fly! Gosh, that's a wonderful publicity angle, Miss Collins— "Beautiful Young Society Lady Raped by The Human Fly!"

PORTER: [*Nudging him sharply*] Git back in your cracker box!

MISS COLLINS: Publicity? No! It would be so humiliating! Mr. Abrams surely hasn't reported it to the papers!

PORTER: No, ma'am. Don't listen to this smarty pants.

MISS COLLINS: [*Touching her curls*] Will pictures be taken, you think? There's one of him on the mantel.

ELEVATOR BOY: [*Going to the mantel*] This one here, Miss Collins?

MISS COLLINS: Yes. Of the Sunday School faculty picnic. I had the little kindergardeners that year and he had the older boys. We rode in the cab of a railroad locomotive from Webb to Crystal Springs. [*She covers her ears with a girlish grimace and toss of her curls*] Oh, how the steam-whistle blew! Blew! [*Giggling*] Blewwwww! It frightened me so, he put his arm round my shoulders! But she was there, too, though she had no business being. She grabbed his hat and stuck it on the back of her head and they—they *rassled* for it, they actually *rassled* together! Everyone said it was *shameless*! Don't you think that it was?

PORTER: Yes, Miss Collins.

MISS COLLINS: That's the picture, the one in the silver frame up there on the mantel. We cooled the watermelon in the springs and afterwards played games. She hid somewhere and he took ages to find her. It got to be dark and he hadn't found her yet and everyone whispered and giggled about it and finally they came back together—her hangin' on to his arm like a common little strumpet —and Daisy Belle Huston shrieked out, "Look, everybody, the seat of Evelyn's skirt!" It was—covered with—grass-stains! Did you ever hear of anything as outrageous? It didn't faze her, though, she laughed like it was something very, very amusing! Rather *triumphant* she was!

ELEVATOR BOY: Which one is him, Miss Collins?

MISS COLLINS: The tall one in the blue shirt holding onto one of my curls. He loved to play with them.

ELEVATOR BOY: Quite a Romeo—1910 model, huh?

MISS COLLINS: [*Vaguely*] Do you? It's nothing, really, but I like the lace on the collar. I said to Mother, "Even if I don't wear it, Mother, it will be *so* nice for my hope chest!"

ELEVATOR BOY: How was he dressed tonight when he climbed into your balcony, Miss Collins?

MISS COLLINS: Pardon?

ELEVATOR BOY: Did he still wear that nifty little stick-candy-striped blue shirt with the celluloid collar?

MISS COLLINS: He hasn't changed.

ELEVATOR BOY: Oughta be easy to pick him up in that. What color pants did he wear?

MISS COLLINS: [*Vaguely*] I don't remember.

ELEVATOR BOY: Maybe he didn't wear any. Shimmied out of 'em on the way up the wall! You could get him on grounds of indecent exposure, Miss Collins!

PORTER: [*Grasping his arm*] Cut that or git back in your cage! Understand?

ELEVATOR BOY: [*Snickering*] Take it easy. She don't hear a thing.

PORTER: Well, you keep a decent tongue or get to hell out! Miss Collins here is a lady. You understand that?

ELEVATOR BOY: Okay. She's Shoiley Temple.

PORTER: She's a *lady!*

ELEVATOR BOY: Yeah! [*He returns to the gramophone and looks through the records*]

MISS COLLINS: I really shouldn't have created this disturbance. When the officers come I'll have to explain that to them. But you can understand my feelings, can't you?

PORTER: Sure, Miss Collins.

MISS COLLINS: When men take advantage of common white-trash women who smoke in public there is probably some excuse for it, but when it occurs to a lady who is single and always com-*pletely* above reproach in her moral behavior, there's really nothing to do but call for police protection! Unless of course the girl is fortunate enough to have a father and brothers who can take care of the matter privately without any scandal.

PORTER: Sure. That's right, Miss Collins.

MISS COLLINS: Of course it's bound to cause a great deal of very disagreeable talk. Especially 'round the *church!* Are you gentlemen Episcopalian?

PORTER: No, ma'am. Catholic, Miss Collins.

MISS COLLINS: Oh. Well, I suppose you know in England we're known as the English Catholic church. We have direct Apostolic succession through St. Paul who christened the Early Angles— which is what the original English people were called—and established the English branch of the Catholic church over there. So when you hear ignorant people claim that our church was founded by—by Henry the *Eighth*—that horrible, *lech*erous old man who had so many wives—as many as *Blue*-beard they say!—you can see how ridiculous it *is* and how thoroughly ob*nox*-ious to anybody who really *knows* and under*stands* Church *His*tory!

PORTER: [*Comfortingly*] Sure, Miss Collins. Everybody knows that.

MISS COLLINS: I wish they *did*, but they need to be in*struct*ed! Before he died, my father was Rector at the Church of St. Michael and St. George at Glorious Hill, Mississippi . . . I've literally grown up right in the very *shadow* of the Episcopal church. At Pass Christian and Natchez, Biloxi, Gulfport, Port Gibson, Columbus and Glorious Hill! [*With gentle, bewildered sadness*] But you know I sometimes suspect that there has been some kind of spiritual schism in the modern church. These northern dioceses have completely departed from the good old church traditions. For instance our Rector at the Church of the Holy Communion has never darkened my door. It's a fashionable church and he's terribly busy, but even so you'd think he might have time to make a stranger in the congregation feel at home. But he doesn't though! Nobody seems to have the time any more . . . [*She grows more excited as her mind sinks back into illusion*] I ought not to mention this, but do you know they actually take a malicious de-*light* over there at the Holy Communion—where I've recently transferred my letter —in what's been going on here at night in this apartment? Y*es!!* [*She laughs wildly and throws up her hands*] They take a malicious de*LIGHT* in it!! [*She catches her breath and gropes vaguely about her wrapper*]

PORTER: You lookin' for somethin', Miss Collins?

MISS COLLINS: My—handkerchief . . . [*She is blinking her eyes against tears*]

PORTER: [*Removing a rag from his pocket*] Here. Use this, Miss Collins. It's just a rag but it's clean, except along that edge where I wiped off the phonograph handle.

MISS COLLINS: Thanks. You gentlemen are very kind. Mother will bring in something cool after while . . .

ELEVATOR BOY: [*Placing a record on machine*] This one is got some kind of foreign title. [*The record begins to play Tschaikowsky's "None But the Lonely Heart"*]

MISS COLLINS: [*Stuffing the rag daintily in her bosom*] Excuse me, please. Is the weather nice outside?

PORTER: [*Huskily*] Yes, it's nice, Miss Collins.

MISS COLLINS: [*Dreamily*] So wa'm for this time of year. I wore my little astrakhan cape to service but had to *carry* it *home*, as the weight of it actually seemed *oppres*sive to me. [*Her eyes fall shut*] The sidewalks seem so dreadfully long in summer . . .

ELEVATOR BOY: This ain't summer, Miss Collins.

MISS COLLINS: [*Dreamily*] I used to think I'd never get to the end of that last block. And that's the block where all the trees went down in the big tornado. The walk is simple *glit*-tering with sunlight.

[*Pressing her eyelids*] Impossible to shade your face and I *do* perspire so freely! [*She touches her forehead daintily with the rag*] Not a branch, not a leaf to give you a little protection! You simply *have* to en-*dure* it. Turn your hideous red face away from all the front-porches and walk as fast as you decently *can* till you get *by* them! Oh, dear, dear Savior, sometimes you're not so lucky and you *meet* people and have to *smile!* You can't *avoid* them unless you cut *across* and that's so *ob*-vious, you know . . . People would say you're pe*cu*liar . . . His house is right in the middle of that awful leafless block, *their* house, his and *hers*, and they have an automobile and always get home early and sit on the porch and *watch* me walking by—Oh, Father in Heaven—with a ma*li*cious de*light!* [*She averts her face in remembered torture*] She has such *penetrating* eyes, they look straight through me. She sees that terrible choking thing in my throat and the pain I have in *here*— [*Touching her chest*]—and she points it out and laughs and whispers to him, "There she goes with her shiny big red nose, the poor old maid—that *loves* you!" [*She chokes and hides her face in the rag*]

PORTER: Maybe you better forget all that, Miss Collins.

MISS COLLINS: Never, never forget it! Never, never! I left my parasol once—the one with long white fringe that belonged to Mother—I left it behind in the cloakroom at the church so I didn't have anything to cover my face with when I walked by, and I couldn't turn back either, with all those people behind me—giggling back of me, poking fun at my clothes! Oh, dear, dear! I had to walk straight forward—past the last elm tree and into that *merciless* sunlight. Oh! It beat down on me, *scorching* me! Whips! . . . Oh, Jesus! . . . Over my face and my body! . . . I tried to walk on fast but was dizzy and they kept closer behind me—! I stumbled, I nearly fell, and all of them burst out laughing! My face turned so *horribly* red, it got so red and wet, I knew how ugly it was in all that merciless glare—not a single shadow to hide in! And then—[*Her face contorts with fear*]—their automobile drove up in front of their house, right where I had to pass by it, and *she* stepped out, in white, so fresh and easy, her stomach round with a baby, the first of the *six*. Oh, God! . . . And he stood smiling behind her, white and easy and cool, and they stood there waiting for me. *Waiting!* I had to keep on. What else could I do? I couldn't turn *back*, could I? *No!* I said dear *God*, strike me *dead!* He didn't, though. I put my head way down like I couldn't see them! You know what she did? She stretched out her hand to *stop* me! And *he*—he stepped up straight in front of me, *smiling*, blocking the walk with his terrible big white body! "*Lucretia*," he said, "Lucretia *Collins!*" I—I tried to speak but I couldn't, the breath went out of my body! I covered my face and—ran! . . . Ran! . . . *Ran!* [*Beating the arm of the sofa*] Till I reached the end of the block—and the elm trees—*started* again . . . Oh, Merciful Christ in Heaven, how *kind* they were! [*She leans back exhaustedly, her hand relaxed on sofa. She pauses and the music ends*] I said to Mother, "Mother, we've got to leave town!" We *did* after that. And now after all these years he's finally remembered and come *back!* Moved away from that house and the woman and come *here*—I saw him in the back of the church one day. I wasn't sure —but it *was*. The night after that was the night that he first broke in—and indulged his senses with me . . . He doesn't realize that I've changed, that I can't feel again the way that I used to feel, now that he's got six children by that Cincinnati girl—three in high-school already! Six! Think of that? Six children! I don't know what he'll say when he knows another one's coming! He'll probably blame *me* for it because a man always *does!* In spite of the fact that he *forced* me!

ELEVATOR BOY: [*Grinning*] Did you say—*a baby*, Miss Collins?

MISS COLLINS: [*Lowering her eyes but speaking with tenderness and pride*] Yes—I'm expecting a *child*.

ELEVATOR BOY: *Jeez!* [*He claps his hand over his mouth and turns away quickly*]

MISS COLLINS: Even if it's not legitimate, I think it has a perfect right to its father's name—don't you?

PORTER: Yes. Sure, Miss Collins.

MISS COLLINS: A child is innocent and pure. No matter how it's conceived. And it must *not* be made to suffer! So I intend to dispose of the little property Cousin Ethel left me and give the child a private education where it won't come under the evil influence of the Christian church! I want to make sure that it doesn't grow up in the shadow of the cross and then have to walk along blocks that scorch you with terrible sunlight!

[*The elevator buzzer sounds from the hall*]

PORTER: Frank! Somebody wants to come up. [*The* ELEVATOR BOY *goes out. The elevator door bangs shut. The* PORTER *clears his throat*] Yes, it'd be better—to go off some place else.

MISS COLLINS: If only I had the courage—but I don't. I've grown so used to it here, and people outside—it's always so *hard* to *face* them!

PORTER: Maybe you won't—have to face nobody, Miss Collins.

[*The elevator door clangs open*]

MISS COLLINS: [*Rising fearfully*] Is someone coming—here?

PORTER: You just take it easy, Miss Collins.

MISS COLLINS: If that's the officers coming for Richard, tell them to go away. I've decided not to prosecute Mr. Martin.

[MR. ABRAMS *enters with the* DOCTOR *and the* NURSE. *The* ELEVATOR BOY *gawks from the doorway. The* DOCTOR *is the weary, professional type, the* NURSE *hard and efficient.* MR. ABRAMS *is a small, kindly person, sincerely troubled by the situation*]

MISS COLLINS: [*Shrinking back, her voice faltering*] I've decided not to prosecute Mr. Martin . . .

DOCTOR: Miss Collins?

MR. ABRAMS: [*With attempted heartiness*] Yes, this is the lady you wanted to meet, Dr. White.

DOCTOR: Hmmm. [*Briskly to the* NURSE] Go in her bedroom and get a few things together.

NURSE: Yes, sir. [*She goes quickly across to the bedroom*]

MISS COLLINS: [*Fearfully shrinking*] Things?

DOCTOR: Yes, Miss Tyler will help you pack up an overnight bag. [*Smiling mechanically*] A strange place always seems more homelike the first few days when we have a few of our little personal articles around us.

MISS COLLINS: A strange—place?

DOCTOR: [*Carelessly, making a memorandum*] Don't be disturbed, Miss Collins.

MISS COLLINS: I know! [*Excitedly*] You've come from the Holy Communion to place me under arrest! On moral charges!

MR. ABRAMS: Oh, no, Miss Collins, you got the wrong idea. This is a doctor who—

DOCTOR: [*Impatiently*] Now, now, you're just going away for a while till things get straightened out. [*He glances at his watch*] Two-twenty-five! Miss Tyler?

NURSE: Coming!

MISS COLLINS: [*With slow and sad comprehension*] Oh . . . I'm going away . . .

MR. ABRAMS: She was always a lady, Doctor, such a perfect lady.

DOCTOR: Yes. No doubt.

MR. ABRAMS: It seems too bad!

MISS COLLINS: Let me—write him a note. A pencil? Please?

MR. ABRAMS: Here, Miss Collins. [*She takes the pencil and crouches over the table. The* NURSE *comes out with a hard, forced smile, carrying a suitcase*]

DOCTOR: Ready, Miss Tyler?

NURSE: All ready, Dr. White. [*She goes up to* MISS COLLINS] Come along, dear, we can tend to that later!

MR. ABRAMS: [*Sharply*] Let her finish the note!

MISS COLLINS: [*Straightening with a frightened smile*] It's—finished.

NURSE: All right, dear, come along. [*She propels her firmly toward the door*]

MISS COLLINS: [*Turning suddenly back*] Oh, Mr. Abrams!

MR. ABRAMS: Yes, Miss Collins?

MISS COLLINS: If he should come again—and find me gone—I'd rather you didn't tell him—about the baby . . . I think its better for *me* to tell him *that*. [*Gently smiling*] You know how men *are*, don't you?

MR. ABRAMS: Yes, Miss Collins.

PORTER: Goodbye, Miss Collins.

[*The* NURSE *pulls firmly at her arm. She smiles over her shoulder with a slight apologetic gesture*]

MISS COLLINS: Mother will bring in—something cool—after while . . . [*She disappears down the hall with the* NURSE. *The elevator door clangs shut with the metallic sound of a locked cage. The wires hum*]

MR. ABRAMS: She wrote him a note.

PORTER: What did she write, Mr. Abrams?

MR. ABRAMS: "Dear—Richard. I'm going away for a while. But don't worry, I'll be back. I have a secret to tell you. Love—Lucretia." [*He coughs*] We got to clear out this stuff an' pile it down in the basement till I find out where it goes.

PORTER: [*Dully*] Tonight, Mr. Abrams?

MR. ABRAMS: [*Roughly to hide his feeling*] No, no, not tonight, you old fool. Enough has happened tonight! [*Then gently*] We can do it tomorrow. Turn out that bedroom light—and close the window. [*Music playing softly becomes audible as the men go out slowly, closing the door, and the light fades out*]

CURTAIN

VISITOR FROM FOREST HILLS

Neil Simon

Neil Simon

Ever since 1961, Neil Simon has reigned supreme as America's foremost writer of contemporary comedies. His gilt-edged chain of successes began with his initial Broadway play, *Come Blow Your Horn*, which ran for 677 performances. This was followed by the book for the musical *Little Me* (1962); *Barefoot in the Park* (1963); *The Odd Couple* (1965); the musical *Sweet Charity* (1966); and *The Star-Spangled Girl* (1966).

When *Plaza Suite* opened on February 14, 1968, it was immediately apparent that Mr. Simon once again had mined theatrical gold. The play was hailed as "a triple-barreled explosion of comedy" that provided "a wonderfully happy and gratifying evening of sheer entertainment." The production, which originally costarred Maureen Stapleton and George C. Scott, was directed by Mike Nichols and it had an engagement of 1,097 performances. It is the final play of this trio of short comedies (each transpires, at different times, in the identical suite at the Plaza Hotel, New York) that appears in this anthology.

In December of that same year, Mr. Simon unveiled another success, the musical *Promises, Promises* (with music by Burt Bacharach and lyrics by Hal David). In 1969 his Broadway entry was *Last of the Red Hot Lovers*; followed in almost annual succession by *The Gingerbread Lady* (1970); *The Prisoner of Second Avenue* (1971); *The Sunshine Boys* (1972); *The Good Doctor*—adapted from short stories of Chekhov (1973); *God's Favorite* (1974); *California Suite* (1976); and *Chapter Two* (1977).

The author was born in the Bronx, New York, on July 4, 1927. He attended New York University and the University of Denver. His first theatrical affiliation came as a sketch writer (in collaboration with his brother Danny) for resort revues at Camp Tamiment,

Pennsylvania. From there he moved on to television, supplying comedy material for such personalities as Phil Silvers, Jackie Gleason, Red Buttons, Tallulah Bankhead, and, notably, for Sid Caesar and Imogene Coca in *Your Show of Shows*. An accomplished hand at comedy, he later contributed sketches to two Broadway revues, *Catch a Star* (1955) and *New Faces of 1956*.

In 1965 the dramatist won an Antoinette Perry (Tony) Award as the year's best author for *The Odd Couple*, and in 1968 he was the recipient of the Sam S. Shubert Award in recognition of his outstanding contribution to the American theatre. A similar honor was bestowed upon him in 1975 by the presentation of a Special Tony Award for his over-all work in the theatre.

While Neil Simon's plays may be regarded by some as merely lighthearted entertainments, there is, if one digs deeply enough beyond the surface of laughter, an underlying element of human truths, particularly in his more recent efforts. As London's respected drama critic Herbert Kretzmer wrote in the *Daily Express*: "Mr. Simon's genius has been not only to write some of the funniest one-line gags now being spoken on the English-speaking stage, but to suggest also something of the pain, aspiration and panic behind all those flip phrases."

His wit and comedic expertise also have brightened many films. Besides preparing the movie versions of his own plays, he has enlivened the screen with his scenarios for, among others, *The Out-of-Towners; The Heartbreak Kid;* and *Murder by Death*.

Characters:

Norma Hubley
Roy Hubley
Borden Eisler
Mimsey Hubley

SCENE: *A suite at the Plaza Hotel on the seventh floor, overlooking Central Park. The set is divided into two rooms. The room at stage right is the living room. It is a well-appointed room, tastefully furnished, with an entrance door at the extreme right and windows that look out over the park. A door leads into the bedroom, which has a large double bed, etc., and a door that leads to the bathroom. The room also contains a large closet.*

It is three o'clock on a warm Saturday afternoon in spring.

The living room is bedecked with vases and baskets of flowers. In the bedroom one opened valise containing a young woman's street clothes rests on the floor. A very large box, which had held a wedding dress, rests on the luggage rack, and a man's suit lies on the bed. A fur wrap and gloves are thrown over the back of the sofa. Telegrams of congratulation and newspapers are strewn about. The suite today is being used more or less as a dressing room, since a wedding is about to occur downstairs in one of the reception rooms.

As the lights come up, NORMA HUBLEY *is at the phone in the bedroom, impatiently tapping the receiver. She is dressed in a formal cocktail dress and a large hat, looking her very best, as any woman would want to on her daughter's wedding day. But she is extremely nervous and harassed, and with good cause—as we'll soon find out.*

NORMA: [*On the phone*] Hello? . . . Hello, operator? . . . Can I have the Blue Room, please . . . The Blue Room . . . Is there a Pink Room? . . . I want the Hubley-Eisler wedding . . . The Green Room, that's it. Thank you . . . Could you please hurry, operator, it's an emergency . . . [*She looks over at the bathroom nervously. She paces back and forth*] Hello? . . . Who's this? . . . Mr. Eisler . . . It's Norma Hubley . . . No, everything's fine . . . Yes, we're coming right down . . . [*She is smiling and trying to act as pleasant and as calm as possible*] Yes, you're right, it certainly *is* the big day . . . Mr. Eisler, is my husband there? . . . Would you, please? . . . Oh! Well, I'd like to wish you the very best of luck, too . . . Borden's a wonderful boy . . . Well, they're *both* wonderful kids . . . No, no. She's as calm as a cucumber . . . That's the younger generation, I guess . . . Yes, everything seems to be going along beautifully . . . Absolutely beautifully . . . Oh, thank you. [*Her husband has obviously just come on the other end, because the expression on her face changes violently and she screams a rasping whisper filled with doom. Sitting on the bed*] Roy? You'd better get up here right away, we're in big trouble . . . Don't ask questions, just get up here . . . I hope you're not drunk because I can't handle this alone . . . Don't say anything. Just smile and walk leisurely out the door . . . and then get the hell up here as fast as you can. [*She hangs up, putting the phone back on the night table. She crosses to the bathroom and then puts her head up against the door. Aloud through the bathroom door*] All right, Mimsey, your father's on his way up. Now, I want you to come out of that bathroom and get married. [*There is no answer*] Do you hear me? . . . I've had enough of this nonsense . . . Unlock that door! [*That's about the end of her authority. She wilts and almost pleads*] Mimsey, darling, please come downstairs and get married, you know your father's temper . . . I know what you're going through now, sweetheart, you're just nervous . . . Everyone goes through that on their wedding day . . . It's going to be all right, darling. You love Borden and he loves you. You're both going to have a wonderful future. So please come out of the bathroom! [*She listens; there is no answer*] Mimsey, if you don't care about your life, think about mine. Your father'll kill me. [*The front doorbell rings.* NORMA *looks off nervously and moves to the other side of the bed*] Oh, God, he's here! . . . Mimsey! Mimsey, please, spare me this . . . If you want, I'll have it annulled next week, but please come out and get married! [*There is no answer from the bathroom but the front doorbell rings impatiently*] All right, I'm letting your father in. And heaven help the three of us!

[*She crosses through the bedroom into the living room. She crosses to the door and opens it as* ROY HUBLEY *bursts into the room.* ROY *is dressed in striped trousers, black tail coat, the works. He looks elegant but he's not too happy in this attire. He is a volatile, explosive man equipped to handle the rigors of the competitive business world, but a nervous, frightened man when it comes to the business of marrying off his only daughter*]

ROY: Why are you standing here? There are sixty-eight people down there drinking my liquor. If there's gonna be a wedding, let's have a wedding. Come on! [*He starts back out the door but sees that* NORMA *is not going anywhere. She sits on the sofa. He comes back in*] . . . Didn't you hear what I said? There's another couple waiting to use the Green Room. Come on, let's go!

[*He makes a start out again*]

NORMA: [*Very calm*] Roy, could you sit down a minute? I want to talk to you about something.

ROY: [*She must be mad*] You want to talk *now*? You had twenty-one years to talk while she was growing up. I'll talk to you when they're in Bermuda. Can we please have a wedding?

NORMA: We can't have a wedding until you and I have a talk.

ROY: Are you crazy? While you and I are talking here, there are four musicians playing downstairs for seventy dollars an hour. I'll talk to you later when we're dancing. Come on, get Mimsey and let's go.

[*He starts out again*]

NORMA: That's what I want to talk to you about.

ROY: [*Comes back*] Mimsey?

NORMA: Sit down. You're not going to like this.

ROY: Is she sick?

NORMA: She's not sick . . . exactly.

ROY: What do you mean, she's not sick exactly? Either she's sick or she's not sick. Is she sick?

NORMA: She's not sick.

ROY: Then let's have a wedding! [*He crosses into the bedroom*] Mimsey, there's two hundred dollars' worth of cocktail frankfurters getting cold downstairs . . . [*He looks around the empty room*] Mimsey? [*He crosses back to the living room to the side of the sofa. He looks at* NORMA] . . . Where's Mimsey?

NORMA: Promise you're not going to blame me.

ROY: Blame you for what? What did you do?

NORMA: I didn't do anything. But I don't want to get blamed for it.

ROY: What's going on here? Are you going to tell me where Mimsey is?

NORMA: Are you going to take an oath you're not going to blame me?

ROY: *I take it! It take it!* NOW WHERE THE HELL IS SHE?

NORMA: . . . She's locked herself in the bathroom. She's not coming out and she's not getting married.

[ROY *looks at* NORMA *incredulously. Then, because it must be an insane joke, he smiles at her. There is even the faint glint of a chuckle*]

ROY: [*Softly*] . . . No kidding, where is she?

NORMA: [*Turns away*] He doesn't believe me. I'll kill myself.

[ROY *turns and storms into the bedroom. He crosses to the bathroom and knocks on the door. Then he tries it. It's locked He tries again. He bangs on the door with his fist*]

ROY: Mimsey? . . . Mimsey? . . . MIMSEY? [*There is no reply. Girding himself, he crosses back through the bedroom into the living room to the sofa. He glares at* NORMA] . . . All right, what did you say to her?

NORMA: [*Jumping up and moving away*] I knew it! I knew you'd blame me. You took an oath. God'll punish you.

ROY: I'm not blaming you. I just want to know what *stupid* thing you said to her that made her do this.

NORMA: I didn't say a word. I was putting on my lipstick, she was in the bathroom, I heard the door go click, it was locked, my whole life was over, what do you want from me?

ROY: And you didn't say a word?

NORMA: Nothing.

ROY: [*Ominously moving toward her as* NORMA *backs away*] I see. In other words, you're trying to tell me that a normal, healthy, intelligent twenty-one-year-old college graduate, who has driven me crazy the last eighteen months with wedding lists, floral arrangements and choices of assorted hors d'oeuvres, has suddenly decided to spend this, the most important day of her life, locked in the Plaza Hotel john?

NORMA: [*Making her stand at the mantel*] Yes! Yes! Yes! Yes! Yes!

ROY: [*Vicious*] YOU MUSTA SAID SOMETHING!

[*He storms into the bedroom,* NORMA *goes after him*]

NORMA: Roy . . . Roy . . . What are you going to do?

ROY: [*Stopping below the bed*] First I'm getting the college graduate out of the bathroom! Then we're gonna have a wedding and then you and I are gonna have a big talk! [*He crosses to the bathroom door and pounds on it*] Mimsey! This is your father. I want you and your four-hundred-dollar wedding dress out of there in five seconds!

NORMA: [*Standing at the side of the bed*] Don't threaten her. She'll never come out if you threaten her.

ROY: [*To* NORMA] I got sixty-eight guests, nine waiters, four musicians and a boy with a wedding license waiting downstairs. This is no time to be diplomatic. [*Bangs on the door*] Mimsey! . . . Are you coming out or do we have the wedding in the bathroom?

NORMA: Will you lower your voice! Everyone will hear us.

ROY: [*To* NORMA] How long you think we can keep this a secret? As soon as that boy says "I do" and there's no one standing next to him, they're going to suspect something. [*He bangs on the door*] You can't stay in there forever, Mimsey. We only have the room until six o'clock . . . *You hear me?*

[*There is still no reply from the bathroom*]

NORMA: Roy, will you please try to control yourself.

ROY: [*With great display of patience, moves to the foot of the bed and sits*] All right, I'll stay here and control myself. You go downstairs and marry the short, skinny kid. [*Exploding*] What's the matter with you? Don't you realize what's happening?

NORMA: [*Moving to him*] Yes. I realize what's happening. Our daughter is nervous, frightened and scared to death.

ROY: Of what? OF WHAT? She's been screaming for two years if he doesn't ask her to marry him, she'll throw herself off the Guggenheim Museum . . . What is she scared of?

NORMA: I don't know. Maybe she's had second thoughts about the whole thing.

ROY: [Getting up and moving to the bathroom door] Second thoughts? This is no time to be having second thoughts. It's costing me eight thousand dollars for the first thoughts. [He bangs on the door] Mimsey, open this door.

NORMA: Is that all you care about? What it's costing you? Aren't you concerned about your daughter's happiness?

ROY: [Moving back to her below the bed] Yes! Yes, I'm concerned about my daughter's happiness. I'm also concerned about that boy waiting downstairs. A decent, respectable, intelligent young man . . . who I hope one day is going to teach that daughter of mine to grow up.

NORMA: You haven't the faintest idea of what's going through her mind right now.

ROY: Do you?

NORMA: It could be anything. I don't know, maybe she thinks she's not good enough for him.

ROY: [Looks at her incredulously] . . . Why? What is he? Some kind of Greek god? He's a plain kid, nothing . . . That's ridiculous. [Moves back to the door and bangs on it] Mimsey! Mimsey, open this door. [He turns to NORMA] Maybe she's not in there.

NORMA: She's in there. [Clutches her chest and sits on the side of the bed] Oh, God, I think I'm having a heart attack.

ROY: [Listening at the door] I don't hear a peep out of her. Is there a window in there? Maybe she tried something crazy.

NORMA: [Turning to him] That's right. Tell a woman who's having a heart attack that her daughter jumped out the window.

ROY: Take a look through the keyhole. I want to make sure she's in there.

NORMA: She's in there, I tell you. Look at this, my hand keeps bouncing off my chest.

[It does]

ROY: Are you gonna look in there and see if she's all right or am I gonna call the house detective?

NORMA: [*Getting up and moving below the bed*] Why don't *you* look?

ROY: Maybe she's taking a bath.

NORMA: Two minutes before her own wedding?

ROY: [*Crossing to her*] What wedding? She just called it off.

NORMA: Wouldn't I have heard the water running?

ROY: [*Making a swipe at her hat*] With that hat you couldn't hear Niagara Falls! . . . Are you going to look to see what your daughter's doing in the bathroom or do I ask a stranger?

NORMA: [*Crossing to the door*] I'll look! I'll look! I'll look! [*Reluctantly she gets down on one knee and looks through the keyhole with one eye*] Oh, my God!

ROY: What's the matter?

NORMA: [*To him*] I ripped my stockings.

[*Getting up and examining her stockings*]

ROY: Is she in there?

NORMA: She's in there! She's in there! [*Hobbling to the far side of the bed and sitting down on the edge*] Where am I going to get another pair of stockings now? How am I going to go to the wedding with torn stockings?

ROY: [*Crossing to the bathroom*] If *she* doesn't show up, who's going to look at *you*? [*He kneels at the door and looks through the keyhole*] There she is. Sitting there and crying.

NORMA: I *told* you she was in there . . . The only one in my family to have a daughter married in the Plaza and I have torn stockings.

ROY: [*He is on his knees, his eye to the keyhole*] Mimsey, I can see you . . . Do you hear me? . . . Don't turn away from me when I'm talking to you.

NORMA: Maybe I could run across to Bergdorf's. They have nice stockings.

[*Crosses to her purse on the bureau in the bedroom and looks through it*]

ROY: [*Still through the keyhole*] Do you want me to break down the door, Mimsey, is that what you want? Because that's what I'm doing if you're not out of there in five seconds . . . Stop crying on your dress. Use the towel!

NORMA: [*Crossing to* ROY *at the door*] I don't have any money. Give me four dollars, I'll be back in ten minutes.

ROY: [*Gets up and moves below the bed*] In ten minutes she'll be a married woman, because I've had enough of this nonsense. [*Yells in*] All right, Mimsey, stand in the shower because I'm breaking down the door.

NORMA: [*Getting in front of the door*] Roy, don't get crazy.

ROY: [*Preparing himself for a run at the door*] Get out of my way.

NORMA: Roy, she'll come out. Just talk nicely to her.

ROY: [*Waving her away*] We already had nice talking. Now we're gonna have door breaking. [*Through the door*] All right, Mimsey, I'm coming in!

NORMA: No, Roy, don't! Don't!

[*She gets out of the way as* ROY *hurls his body, led by his shoulder, with full force against the door. It doesn't budge. He stays against the door silently a second; he doesn't react. Then he says calmly and softly*]

ROY: Get a doctor.

NORMA: [*Standing below the door*] I knew it. I knew it.

ROY: [*Drawing back from the door*] Don't tell me I knew it, just get a doctor [*Through the door*] I'm not coming in, Mimsey, because my arm is broken.

NORMA: Let me see it. Can you move your fingers?

[*Moves to him and examines his fingers*]

ROY: [*Through the door*] Are you happy now? Your mother has torn stockings and your father has a broken arm. How much longer is this gonna go on?

NORMA: [*Moving* ROY's *fingers*] It's not broken, you can move your fingers. Give me four dollars with your other hand, I have to get stockings.

[*She starts to go into his pockets. He slaps her hands away*]

ROY: Are you crazy moving a broken arm?

NORMA: Two dollars, I'll get a cheap pair.

ROY: [*As though she were a lunatic*] I'm not carrying any cash today. Rented, everything is rented.

NORMA: I can't rent stockings. Don't you even have a charge-plate?

[*Starts to go through his pockets again*]

ROY: [*Slaps her hands away. Then pointing dramatically*] Wait in the Green Room! You're no use to me here, go wait in the Green Room!

NORMA: With torn stockings?

ROY: Stand behind the rented potted plant. [*Takes her by the arm and leads her below the bed. Confidentially*] They're going to call from downstairs any second asking where the bride is. And *I'm* the one who's going to have to speak to them. *Me! Me! Me!* [*The phone rings. Pushing her toward the phone*] That's them. *You* speak to them!

NORMA: What happened to *me me me*?

[*The phone rings again*]

ROY: [*Moving to the bathroom door*] Answer it. Answer it.

[*The phone rings again*]

NORMA: [*Moving to the phone*] What am I going to say to them?

ROY: I don't know. Maybe something'll come to you as you're talking.

NORMA: [*Picks the phone up*] Hello? . . . Oh, Mr. Eisler . . . Yes, it certainly is the big moment.

[*She forces a merry laugh*]

ROY: Stall 'em. Stall 'em. Just keep stalling him. Whatever you do, stall 'em!

[Turns to the door]

NORMA: [On the phone] Yes, we'll be down in two minutes.

[Hangs up]

ROY: [Turns back to her] Are you crazy? What did you say that for? I told you to stall him.

NORMA: I stalled him. You got two minutes. What do you want from me?

ROY: [Shakes his arm at her] You always panic. The minute there's a little crisis, you always go to pieces and panic.

NORMA: [Shaking her arm back at him] Don't wave your broken arm at me. Why don't you use it to get your daughter out of the bathroom?

ROY: [Very angry, kneeling to her on the bed] I could say something to you now.

NORMA: [Confronting him, kneels in turn on the bed] Then why don't you say it?

ROY: Because it would lead to a fight. And I don't want to spoil this day for you. [He gets up and crosses back to the bathroom door] Mimsey, this is your father speaking . . . I think you know I'm not a violent man. I can be stern and strict, but I have never once been violent. Except when I'm angry. And I am really angry now, Mimsey. You can ask your mother.

[Moves away so NORMA can get to the door]

NORMA: [Crossing to the bathroom door] Mimsey, this is your mother speaking. It's true, darling, your father is very angry.

ROY: [Moving back to the door] This is your father again, Mimsey. If you have a problem you want to discuss, unlock the door and we'll discuss it. I'm not going to ask you this again, Mimsey. I've reached the end of my patience. I'm gonna count to three . . . and by God, I'm warning you, young lady, by the time I've reached three . . . *this door better be open!* [*Moving away to below the bed*] All right—One! . . . Two! . . . THREE! [*There is no reply or movement from behind the door.* ROY *helplessly sinks down on the foot of the bed*] . . . Where did we fail her?

NORMA: [*Crosses to the far side of the bed, consoling him as she goes, and sits on the edge*] We didn't fail her.

ROY: They're playing "Here Comes the Bride" downstairs and she's barricaded in a toilet—we must have failed her.

NORMA: [*Sighs*] All right, if it makes you any happier, we failed her.

ROY: You work and you dream and you hope and you save your whole life for this day, and in one click of a door, suddenly every-thing crumbles. Why? What's the answer?

NORMA: It's not your fault, Roy. Stop blaming yourself.

ROY: I'm not blaming myself. I know *I've* done my best.

NORMA: [*Turns and looks at him*] What does that mean?

ROY: It means we're not perfect. We make mistakes, we're only hu-man. I've done my best and we failed her.

NORMA: Meaning *I* didn't do my best?

ROY: [*Turning to her*] I didn't say that. I don't know what your best is. Only *you* know what your best is. Did you do your best?

NORMA: Yes, I did my best.

ROY: And I did my best.

NORMA: Then we *both* did our best.

ROY: So it's not our fault.

NORMA: That's what I said before.

[*They turn away from each other. Then:*]

ROY: [*Softly*] Unless one of us didn't do our best.

NORMA: [*Jumping up and moving away*] I don't want to discuss it any more.

ROY: All right, then what are we going to do?

NORMA: I'm having a heart attack, *you* come up with something.

ROY: How? All right, I'll go down and tell them.

[*Gets up and moves to the bedroom door*]

NORMA: [*Moving to the door in front of him*] Tell them? Tell them what?

[*As they move into the living room, she stops him above the sofa*]

ROY: I don't know. Those people down there deserve some kind of an explanation. They got all dressed up, didn't they?

NORMA: What are you going to say? You're going to tell them that my daughter is not going to marry their son and that she's locked herself in the bathroom?

ROY: What do you want me to do, start off with two good jokes? They're going to find out *some* time, aren't they?

NORMA: [*With great determination*] I'll tell you what you're going to do. If she's not out of there in five minutes, we're going to go out the back door and move to Seattle, Washington! . . . You don't think I'll be able to show my face in this city again, do you? [ROY *ponders this for a moment, then reassures her with a pat on the arm. Slowly he turns and moves into the bedroom. Suddenly, he loses control and lets his anger get the best of him. He grabs up the chair from the dresser, and brandishing it above his head, he dashes for the bathroom door, not even detouring around the bed but rather crossing right over it.* NORMA *screams and chases after him*] ROY!

[*At the bathroom door,* ROY *manages to stop himself in time from smashing the chair against the door, trembling with frustration and anger. Finally, exhausted, he puts the chair down below the door and straddles it, sitting leaning on the back.* NORMA *sinks into the bedroom armchair*]

ROY: . . . Would you believe it, last night I cried. Oh, yes. I turned my head into the pillow and lay there in the dark, crying, because today I was losing my little girl. Some stranger was coming and taking my little Mimsey away from me . . . so I turned my back to you—and cried . . . Wait'll you hear what goes on *tonight!*

NORMA: [*Lost in her own misery*] I should have invited your cousin Lillie. [*Gestures to the heavens*] She wished this on me, I know it. [*Suddenly* ROY *begins to chuckle.* NORMA *looks at him. He chuckles louder, although there is clearly no joy in his laughter*] Do you find something funny about this?

ROY: Yes, I find something funny about this. I find it funny that I hired a photographer for three hundred dollars. I find it hysterical that the wedding pictures are going to be you and me in front of a locked bathroom! [*Gets up and puts the chair aside*] All right, I'm through sitting around waiting for that door to open.

[*He crosses to the bedroom window and tries to open it*]

NORMA: [*Following after him*] What are you doing?

ROY: What do you think I'm doing?

[*Finding it impossible to open it, he crosses to the living room and opens a window there. The curtains begin to blow in the breeze*]

NORMA: [*Crosses after him*] If you're jumping, I'm going with you. You're not leaving *me* here alone.

ROY: [*Looking out the window*] I'm gonna crawl out along that ledge and get in through the bathroom window.

[*He starts to climb out the window*]

NORMA: Are you crazy? It's seven stories up. You'll kill yourself.

[*She grabs hold of him*]

ROY: It's four steps, that's all. It's no problem, I'm telling you. Now will you let go of me?

NORMA: [*Struggling to keep him from getting out the window*] Roy, no! Don't do this. We'll leave her in the bathroom. Let the hotel worry about her. Don't go out on the ledge.

[*In desperation, she grabs hold of one of the tails of his coat*]

ROY: [*Half out the window, trying to get out as she holds onto his coat*] You're gonna rip my coat. Let go or you're gonna rip my coat. [*As he tries to pull away from her, his coat rips completely up the back, right up to the collar. He stops and slowly comes back into the room.* NORMA *has frozen in misery by the bedroom door after letting go of the coat.* ROY *draws himself up with great dignity and control. He slowly turns and moves into the bedroom, stopping by the bed. With great patience, he calls toward the bathroom*] Hey, you in there . . . Are you happy now? Your mother's got torn stockings and your father's got a rented ripped coat. Some wedding it's gonna be. [*Exploding, he crosses back to the open window in the living room*] Get out of my way!

NORMA: [*Puts hand to her head*] I'm getting dizzy. I think I'm going to pass out.

ROY: [*Getting her out of the way*] . . . You can pass out *after* the wedding . . . [*He goes out the window and onto the ledge*] Call room service. I want a double Scotch the minute I get back.

[*And he disappears from view as he moves across the ledge.* NORMA *runs into the bedroom and catches a glimpse of him as he passes the bedroom window, but then he disappears once more*]

NORMA: [*Bemoaning her fate*] . . . He'll kill himself. He'll fall and kill himself, that's the way my luck's been going all day. [*She staggers away from the window and leans on the bureau*] I'm not going to look. I'll just wait until I hear a scream [*The telephone rings and* NORMA *screams in fright*] Aggghhh! . . . I thought it was him . . . [*She crosses to the phone by the bed. The telephone rings again*] Oh, God, what am I going to say? [*She picks it up*] Hello? . . . Oh, Mr. Eisler. Yes, we're coming . . . My husband's getting Mimsey now . . . We'll be right down. Have some more hors d'oeuvres . . . Oh, thank you. It certainly *is* the happiest day of my life. [*She hangs up*] No, I'm going to tell him I've got a husband dangling over Fifty-ninth Street. [*As she crosses back to the opened window, a sudden torrent of rain begins to fall. As she gets to the window and sees it*] I knew it! I knew it! It had to happen . . . [*She gets closer to the window and tries to look out*] Are you all right, Roy? . . . Roy? [*There's no answer*] He's not all right, he

fell. [*She staggers into the bedroom*] He fell, he fell, he fell, he fell
. . . He's dead, I know it. [*She collapses onto the armchair*] He's
laying there in a puddle in front of Trader Vic's . . . I'm passing
out. This time I'm really passing out! [*And she passes out on the
chair, legs and arms spread-eagled. The doorbell rings; she jumps
right up*] I'm coming! I'm coming! Help me, whoever you are,
help me! [*She rushes through the bedroom into the living room
and to the front door*] Oh, please, somebody, help me, please!

[*She opens the front door and* ROY *stands there dripping wet,
fuming, exhausted and with clothes disheveled and his hair
mussed*]

ROY: [*Staggering into the room and weakly leaning on the mantelpiece. It takes a moment for him to catch his breath.* NORMA, *concerned, follows him*] She locked the window, too. I had to climb
in through a strange bedroom. There may be a lawsuit.

[*He weakly charges back into the bedroom, followed by* NORMA,
*who grabs his coattails in an effort to stop him. The rain outside
stops*]

NORMA: [*Stopping him below the bed*] Don't yell at her. Don't get
her more upset.

ROY: [*Turning back to her*] Don't get her *upset*? I'm hanging seven
stories from a gargoyle in a pouring rain and you want me to worry
about *her*? . . . You know what she's doing in there? She playing with her false eyelashes. [*Moves to the bathroom door*] I'm
out there fighting for my life with pigeons and she's playing with
eyelashes . . . [*Crossing back to* NORMA] . . . I already made up
my mind. The minute I get my hands on her, I'm gonna kill her.
[*Moves back to the door*] Once I show them the wedding bills, no
jury on earth would convict me . . . And if by some miracle she
survives, let there be no talk of weddings . . . She can go into a
convent. [*Slowly moving back to* NORMA *below the bed*] . . . Let
her become a librarian with thick glasses and a pencil in her hair,
I'm not paying for any more canceled weddings . . . [*Working
himself up into a frenzy, he rushes to the table by the armchair
and grabs up some newspapers*] Now get her out of there or I start
to burn these newspapers and smoke her out.

[NORMA *stops him, soothes him, and manages to get him calmed down. She gently seats him on the foot of the bed*]

NORMA: [*Really frightened*] I'll get her out! I'll get her out! [*She crosses to the door and knocks*] Mimsey! Mimsey, please! [*She knocks harder and harder*] Mimsey, you want to destroy a family? You want a scandal? You want a story in the *Daily News*? . . . Is that what you want? Is it? . . . Open this door! *Open it!* [*She bangs very hard, then stops and turns to* ROY] . . . Promise you won't get hysterical.

ROY: What did you do?

[*Turns wearily to her*]

NORMA: I broke my diamond ring.

ROY: [*Letting the papers fall from his hand*] Your good diamond ring?

NORMA: How many do I have?

ROY: [*Yells through the door*] Hey, you with the false eyelashes! [*Getting up and moving to the door*] . . . You want to see a broken diamond ring? You want to see eighteen hundred dollars' worth of crushed baguettes? . . . [*He grabs* NORMA's *hand and holds it to the keyhole*] Here! Here! This is a worthless family heirloom [*Kicks the door*]—and this is a diamond bathroom door! [*Controlling himself. To* NORMA] Do you know what I'm going to do now? Do you have any idea? [NORMA *puts her hand to her mouth, afraid to hear.* ROY *moves away from the door to the far side of the bed*] I'm going to wash my hands of the entire Eisler-Hubley wedding. You can take all the Eislers and all the hors d'oeuvres and go to Central Park and have an eight-thousand-dollar picnic . . . [*Stops and turns back to* NORMA] I'm going down to the Oak Room with my broken arm, with my drenched rented ripped suit—and I'm gonna get blind! . . . I don't mean drunk, I mean totally blind . . . [*Erupting with great vehemence*] because I don't want to see you or your crazy daughter again, if I live to be a thousand.

[*He turns and rushes from the bedroom, through the living room to the front door. As he tries to open it,* NORMA *catches up to him, grabs his tail coat and pulls him back into the room*]

NORMA: That's right. Run out on me. Run out on your daughter. Run out on everybody just when they need you.

ROY: You don't need me. You need a rhinoceros with a blowtorch—because no one else can get into that bathroom.

NORMA: [*With rising emotion*] I'll tell you who can get into that bathroom. Someone with love and understanding. Someone who cares about that poor kid who's going through some terrible decision now and needs help. Help that only *you* can give her and that *I* can give her. *That's* who can get into that bathroom now.

[ROY *looks at her solemnly . . . Then he crosses past her, hesitates and looks back at her, and then goes into the bedroom and to the bathroom door.* NORMA *follows him back in. He turns and looks at* NORMA *again. Then he knocks gently on the door and speaks softly and with some tenderness*]

ROY: Mimsey! . . . This is Daddy . . . Is something wrong, dear? . . . [*He looks back at* NORMA, *who nods encouragement, happy about his new turn in character. Then he turns back to the door*] . . . I want to help you, darling. Mother and I both do. But how can we help you if you won't talk to us? Mimsey can you hear me?

[*There is no answer. He looks back at* NORMA]

NORMA: [*At the far side of the bed*] Maybe she's too choked up to talk.

ROY: [*Through the door*] Mimsey, if you can hear me, knock twice for yes, once for no. [*There are two knocks on the door. They look at each other encouragingly*] Good. Good . . . Now, Mimsey, we want to ask you a very, very important question. Do you want to marry Borden or don't you?

[*They wait anxiously for the answer. We hear one knock, a pause, then another knock*]

NORMA: [*Happily*] She said yes.

ROY: [*Despondently*] She said no.

[*Moves away from the door to the front of the bed*]

NORMA: It was two knocks. Two knocks is yes. She wants to marry him.

ROY: It wasn't a double knock "yes." It was two single "no" knocks. She doesn't want to marry him.

NORMA: Don't tell me she doesn't want to marry him. I heard her distinctly knock "yes." She went [*Knocks twice on the foot of the bed*] "Yes, I want to marry him."

ROY: It wasn't [*Knocks twice on the foot of the bed*] . . . It was [*Knocks once on the foot of the bed*] . . . and then another [*Knocks once more on the foot of the bed*] . . . That's "no," twice, she's not marrying him.

[*Sinks down on the side of the bed*

NORMA: [*Crossing to the door*] Ask her again. [*Into the door*] Mimsey, what did you say? Yes or no? [*They listen. We hear two distinct loud knocks.* NORMA *turns to* Roy] . . . All right? There it is in plain English . . . You never *could* talk to your own daughter.

[*Moves away from the door*]

ROY: [*Getting up wearily and moving to the door*] Mimsey, this is not a good way to have a conversation. You're gonna hurt your knuckles . . . Won't you come out and talk to us? . . . Mimsey?

NORMA: [*Leads* ROY *gently to the foot of the bed*] Don't you understand, it's probably something she can't discuss with her father. There are times a daughter wants to be alone with her mother. [*Sits* ROY *down on the foot of the bed, and crosses back to the door*] Mimsey, do you want me to come in there and talk to you, just the two of us, sweetheart? Tell me, darling, is that what you want? [*There is no reply. A strip of toilet paper appears from under the bathroom door.* ROY *notices it, pushes* NORMA *aside, bends down, picks it up and reads it*] What? What does it say? [ROY *solemnly hands it to her.* NORMA *reads it aloud*] "I would rather talk to Daddy."

[NORMA *is crushed. He looks at her sympathetically. We hear the bathroom door unlock.* ROY *doesn't quite know what to say to* NORMA. *He gives her a quick hug*]

ROY: I—I'll try not to be too long.

[He opens the door and goes in, closing it behind him, quietly.
NORMA, *still with the strip of paper in her hand, walks slowly
and sadly to the foot of the bed and sits. She looks glumly down
at the paper]*

NORMA: *[Aloud]* . . . "I would rather talk to Daddy" . . . Did she
have to write it on this kind of paper? *[She wads up the paper]*
. . . Well—maybe I didn't do my best . . . I thought we had such
a good relationship . . . Friends. Everyone thought we were
friends, not mother and daughter . . . I tried to do everything
right . . . I tried to teach her that there could be more than just
love between a mother and daughter . . . There can be trust and
respect and friendship and understanding . . . *[Getting angry, she
turns and yells toward the closed door]* Just because *I* don't speak
to my mother doesn't mean *we* can't be different!

*[She wipes her eyes with the paper. The bathroom door opens.
A solemn ROY steps out, and the door closes and locks behind
him. He deliberately buttons his coat and crosses to the bedroom phone, wordlessly.* NORMA *has not taken her eyes off him.
The pause seems interminable]*

ROY: *[Into the phone]* The Green Room, please . . . Mr. Borden
Eisler. Thank you.

[He waits]

NORMA: *[Getting up from the bed]* . . . I'm gonna have to guess, is
that it? . . . It's so bad you can't even tell me . . . Words can't
form in your mouth, it's so horrible, right? . . . Come on, I'm a
strong person, Roy. Tell me quickly, I'll get over it . . .

ROY: *[Into the phone]* Borden? Mr. Hubley . . . Can you come up to
719? . . . Yes, now . . . *[He hangs up and gestures for* NORMA *to
follow him. He crosses into the living room and down to the ot-
toman where he sits.* NORMA *follows and stands waiting behind
him. Finally]* She wanted to talk to me because she couldn't bear
to say it to both of us at the same time . . . The reason she's
locked herself in the bathroom . . . is she's afraid.

NORMA: Afraid? What is she afraid of? That Borden doesn't love her?

ROY: Not that Borden doesn't love her.

NORMA: That she doesn't love Borden?

ROY: Not that she doesn't love Borden.

NORMA: Then what is she afraid of?

ROY: . . . She's afraid of what they're going to become.

NORMA: I don't understand.

ROY: Think about it.

NORMA: [*Crossing above the sofa*] What's there to think about? What are they going to become? They love each other, they'll get married, they'll have children, they'll grow older, they'll become like us [*Comes the dawn. Stops by the side of the sofa and turns back to* ROY]—I never thought about that.

ROY: Makes you stop and think, doesn't it?

NORMA: I don't think we're so bad, do you? . . . All right, so we yell and scream a little. So we fight and curse and aggravate each other. So you blame me for being a lousy mother and I accuse you of being a rotten husband. It doesn't mean we're not happy . . . does it? . . . [*Her voice rising*] Well? . . . Does it? . . .

ROY: [*Looks at her*] . . . She wants something better. [*The doorbell rings. He crosses to open the door.* NORMA *follows*] Hello, Borden.

BORDEN: [*Stepping into the room*] Hi.

NORMA: Hello, darling.

ROY: [*Gravely*] Borden, you're an intelligent young man, I'm not going to beat around the bush. We have a serious problem on our hands.

BORDEN: How so?

ROY: Mimsey—is worried. Worried about your future together. About the whole institution of marriage. We've tried to allay her fears, but obviously we haven't been a very good example. It seems you're the only one who can communicate with her. She's locked herself in the bathroom and is not coming out . . . It's up to you now.

[*Without a word,* BORDEN *crosses below the sofa and up to the bedroom, through the bedroom below the bed and right up to the bathroom door. He knocks*]

BORDEN: Mimsey? . . . This is Borden . . . Cool it! [*Then he turns and crosses back to the living room. Crossing above the sofa, he passes the Hubleys, and without looking at them, says*] See you downstairs!

[*He exits without showing any more emotion. The Hubleys stare after him as he closes the door. But then the bathroom door opens and* NORMA *and* ROY *slowly turn to it as* MIMSEY, *a beautiful bride, in a formal wedding gown, with veil, comes out*]

MIMSEY: I'm ready now!

[NORMA *turns and moves into the bedroom toward her.* ROY *follows slowly, shaking his head in amazement*]

ROY: Now you're ready? Now you come out?

NORMA: [*Admiring* MIMSEY] Roy, please . . .

ROY: [*Getting angry, leans toward her over the bed*] I break every bone in my body and you come out for "Cool it"?

NORMA: [*Pushing* MIMSEY *toward* ROY] You're beautiful, darling. Walk with your father, I want to look at both of you.

ROY: [*Fuming. As she takes his arm, to* NORMA] That's how he communicates? That's the brilliant understanding between two people? "Cool it"?

NORMA: [*Gathering up* MIMSEY's *train as they move toward the living room*] Roy, don't start in.

ROY: What kind of a person is that to let your daughter marry?

[*They stop above the sofa.* MIMSEY *takes her bridal bouquet from the table behind the sofa, while* NORMA *puts on her wrap and takes her gloves from the back of the sofa*]

NORMA: Roy, don't aggravate me. I'm warning you, don't spoil this day for me.

ROY: Kids today don't care. Not like they did in my day.

NORMA: Walk. Will you walk? In five minutes he'll marry one of the flower girls. Will you walk—

[MIMSEY *takes* ROY *by the arm and they move to the door, as* NORMA *follows*]

ROY: [*Turning back to* NORMA] Crazy. I must be out of my mind, a boy like that. [*Opens the door*] She was better off in the bathroom. You hear me? Better off in the bathroom . . . [*They are out the door . . .*]

CURTAIN

TABLE NUMBER SEVEN

Terence Rattigan

Terence Rattigan

When Terence Rattingan's *Separate Tables* opened in London on September 22, 1954, *Theatre World Annual* reported that the author's second attempt at a double bill—the first was *Playbill* in 1948 —proved brilliantly successful. "In a way he set himself a harder task by giving the two plays in *Separate Tables* the same setting and largely the same characters. Nor does the mood differ essentially from play to play—the psychological stresses of *Table by the Window* giving place to the even more harrowing human problems of *Table Number Seven*," which appears in this volume.

The account continues: "The year certainly provided no more enthralling entertainment than these shrewdly observed studies of the guests in a South Coast private hotel. Mr. Rattigan's understanding of humanity was never deeper. . . ."

The production ran in the West End for 726 performances, and in 1956 came to New York with Margaret Leighton and Eric Portman in their original roles. It met with equal acclaim here: Richard Watts, Jr., of the New York *Post* described it as "a triumph," while Brooks Atkinson declared in the New York *Times* that it was "the finest thing Rattigan has written."

A film version of the combined plays was released in 1958 with Deborah Kerr as Sibyl Railton-Bell and David Niven as the beleagured Major Pollock. Others in the cast included Burt Lancaster, Rita Hayworth, Wendy Hiller, and Gladys Cooper.

A pre-eminent British playwright, Sir Terence Rattigan—already a Commander of the Order of the British Empire, he was raised to knighthood by Queen Elizabeth II in 1971—was born in London on June 10, 1911. Educated at Harrow and Trinity College, Oxford, he sprang to prominence in 1936 with his comedy *French Without Tears*, which ran for over a thousand performances. Seven years later, he was to duplicate this theatrical feat with *While the Sun Shines*, a West End landmark for 1,154 performances.

Among Sir Terence's other noted plays are *Flare Path; Love in Idleness* (retitled *O Mistress Mine* for Broadway, where it was performed by Alfred Lunt and Lynn Fontanne for almost two years); *The Winslow Boy* (recipient of the Ellen Terry Award for the best play produced on the London stage during 1946, it won the 1947–48 New York Drama Critics' Circle Award as the season's best foreign play); *The Browning Version* (the Ellen Terry Award play for 1948); *Adventure Story; Who Is Sylvia?; The Deep Blue Sea; The Sleeping Prince; Man and Boy; Separate Tables; Ross; A Bequest to the Nation;* and *In Praise of Love.*

In addition to his works for the stage, he wrote more than fifteen major films and a number of original television plays.

At one of the countless galas in 1971 to celebrate his sixtieth birthday, Sir Terence was lauded for his "mastery of craft, high entertainment values, compassion, care for clarity, and concern for human beings as individuals." A staunch defender of craftsmanship, he has expressed his thoughts on the subject in a preface to the collected edition of his works: "The school of thought that condemns firm dramatic shape derives, I suppose, originally from Chekhov, an author who, in my impertinent view, is not usually properly understood either by his worshippers or his active imitators. I believe that his plays are as firmly shaped as Ibsen's. The stream that seems to meander its casual length along does so between strong artificial banks, most carefully and cunningly contrived by a master craftsman. To admire the stream and ignore the artifice that gave it its course seems to me a grave oversight, and may well have led over the years to the present critical misapprehension by which laziness of construction is thought a virtue and the shapelessness of a play is taken as evidence of artistic integrity."

As of this writing, the author is represented on the London stage with *Cause Celebre*, a courtroom drama based on a celebrated English murder case that took place in the 1930s.

Sir Terence died at his home in Hamilton, Bermuda, on November 30, 1977.

Characters:

Jean Stratton
Charles Stratton
Major Pollock
Mr. Fowler
Miss Cooper
Mrs. Railton-Bell
Miss Railton-Bell
Lady Matheson
Miss Meacham
Mabel
Doreen·

SCENE 1: *Lounge. After Tea.*
SCENE 2: *Dining room. Dinner.*

SCENE ONE

The lounge of the Beauregard Private Hotel, Bournemouth, a seaside town on the south coast of England. The dining room door is upstage right, and the other door leading to the hall is at back. French windows are at the left, and there is a fireplace downstage right. There is a re-arrangement of chairs to accord with the summer season, and a set of new covers on those chairs.

CHARLES STRATTON, in flannels and sports-shirt, lies on the sofa, reading some large medical treatise. Through the french windows, which are open, JEAN STRATTON appears pulling a pram.

JEAN: [*To the unseen baby*] Tum along now. Tum along. Tum and see Daddy—Daddy will give you a little tiss and then beddy-byes——

[*CHARLES's face shows his annoyance at the interruption to his studies*]

CHARLES: Bed time, already?

JEAN: After six. How are you getting along?

CHARLES: Miles behind. Endless interruptions. It was idiotic to come back to this place. I should have remembered what it was like from the last time. We could have borrowed David's cottage——

JEAN: Nasty air in the Thames Valley. Not good for baby. Bournemouth air much better, [*To baby*] isn't it, my little lammykins? He says, Yes Mummy, lovely air, lovely sun, makes baby teep like an ickle top—

CHARLES: He doesn't say anything of the sort. All he ever appears to say is "goo." I'm getting a bit worried.

JEAN: Don't be silly, darling. What do you expect him to do at five months? Quote T. S. Eliot?

CHARLES: I think all this "tum along" stuff you smother him in is bad for him. It's very dangerous, too, you know. It can lead to arrested development later on—

JEAN: [*Complacently*] What nonsense you do talk. [*She has now sat on the sofa beside him and kisses him fondly. He turns from the caress a trifle brusquely*] Give me a proper kiss.

CHARLES: [*Murmuring*] A kiss, but not a tiss.

[*He kisses her with a little more warmth, then breaks off*]

JEAN: Go on.

CHARLES: No.

JEAN: Why not?

CHARLES: It's too early.

JEAN: You're so horribly coarse-grained sometimes that I wonder why I love you so much. But I do, you know, that's the awful thing. I've been thinking all the afternoon how much I loved you. Funny how it seems sort of to have crept up on me like this—Did it creep up on you too, or did you lie in your teeth before we got married?

CHARLES: I lied in my teeth. Now take baby up to beddy-byes, dear, and leave Daddy to his worky-perky—or Daddy won't ever become a docky-wocky.

[*There is the sound of a loud jovial voice in the garden*]

MAJOR POLLOCK: [*Off*] Hullo, 'ullo, Miss Meacham. Working out the form, eh? Got any tips for tomorrow?

MISS MEACHAM: [*Off*] Let me see.

CHARLES: Oh, God! Here's the Major. Go on, darling, for heaven's sake. If he sees the baby we're lost. He'll talk for hours about infant welfare in Polynesia or something.

JEAN: All right. [*To baby*] Tum along then—[*She meets* CHARLES's *eyes. Firmly:*] Come along, then, Vincent Michael Charles. It is time for your bath and subsequently for your bed. Better?

MISS MEACHAM: [*Off*] Red Robin in the three-thirty.

CHARLES: Much.

[*He blows her a kiss as she goes out into the hall with the pram, from which emerges a faint wail*]

JEAN: [*As she goes*] Oh. Did Mummy bring him out of 'ovely garden into nasty dark pace. Naughty Mummy. [*Her voice subsides.* CHARLES *returns to his book*]

MAJOR POLLOCK: [*Off*] Red Robin in the three-thirty? I'll remember that. Not that I can afford much these days, you know. Not like the old days when one would ring up the hall porter at White's, and get him to put on a couple of ponies. Lovely day, what?

MISS MEACHAM: [*Off*] Not bad.

[MAJOR POLLOCK *comes in. He is in the middle fifties, with a clipped military moustache and extremely neat clothes. In fact both in dress and appearance he is almost too exact a replica of the retired major to be entirely true*]

MAJOR POLLOCK: Hullo, Stratton. Still at it?

CHARLES: [*With only the most perfunctory look-up from his book*] Yes, Major.

MAJOR POLLOCK: Don't know how you do it. Really don't. Most praiseworthy effort, I think.

CHARLES: Thank you, Major.

[*Pause. The* MAJOR *sits*]

MAJOR POLLOCK: Of course when I was at Sandhurst—oh, so sorry—mustn't disturb you, must I?

CHARLES: [*Politely lowering his book*] That's all right, Major. When you were at Sandhurst?

MAJOR POLLOCK: Well, I was going to say that I was a bit like you. Off duty, while most of the other young fellers were gallivanting about in town, I used to be up in my room, or in the library there, cramming away like mad. Military history—great battles of the world—Clausewitz—that sort of stuff. I could have told you quite a lot about Clausewitz once.

CHARLES: Oh. And you can't now?

MAJOR POLLOCK: No. Afraid not. Everything goes, you know. Everything goes. Still I didn't regret all those hours of study at the time. I did jolly well at Sandhurst.

CHARLES: Did you get the Sword of Honour?

MAJOR POLLOCK: What? No. Came quite close to it, though. Passed out pretty high. Pretty high. Not that it did me much good later on—except that they made me battalion adjutant because I was good at paper work. Could have been brigade major, as it happens. Turned it down because I thought, if trouble came—well—you know—miles behind the line—away from one's own chaps. I suppose it was a bit foolish. I'd probably have been a general now, on full pay. Promotion was always a bit tight in the Black Watch. Should have chosen another regiment, I suppose.

CHARLES: [Plainly hoping to terminate the conversation] Yes.

MAJOR POLLOCK: Go on, my boy. Go on. So sorry. I talk too much. That's usually the trouble with old retired majors, what.

CHARLES: Not at all, sir. But I will go on, if you don't mind. I've rather a lot to do.

[There is a pause. CHARLES continues reading. The MAJOR gets up and, taking infinite pains not to make a sound, tiptoes to a table where he picks up a magazine, and tiptoeing back, sits down again. CHARLES has plainly been aware of the MAJOR's tactfully silent passage. MR. FOWLER comes through the french windows, holding a letter]

MR. FOWLER: Oh, hullo, Major. I've just had the most charming letter—

MAJOR POLLOCK: (Putting his fingers to his lips, and indicating CHARLES) Sh! [CHARLES gets up resignedly and goes to the door] Oh, I say. I do hope we're not driving you away.

CHARLES: No, that's quite all right. I can always concentrate much better in my room.

MAJOR POLLOCK: But you've got the baby up there, haven't you?

CHARLES: Yes, but it's a very quiet baby. It hasn't learnt to talk yet. [*He goes out*]

MAJOR POLLOCK: Well, Fowler, who's your letter from? An old flame?

MR. FOWLER: [*Chuckling happily*] Old flame? I haven't got any old flames. I leave that to you galloping majors.

MAJOR POLLOCK: Well, I used to do all right once, I must say. In the regiment they used to call me Bucko Pollock. Regency buck—you see. Still, those days are past and gone. *Eheu fugaces, Postume, Postume.*

MR. FOWLER: [*Correcting his accent*] *Eheu fugaces, Postume, Postume.* Didn't they teach you the new pronunciation at Wellington?

MAJOR POLLOCK: No. The old.

MR. FOWLER: When were you there?

MAJOR POLLOCK: Now let's think. It must have been nineteen eighteen I went up——

MR. FOWLER: But they were using the new pronunciation then, I know. Our head classics master was an old Wellingtonian, and I remember distinctly his telling me——

MAJOR POLLOCK: Well, perhaps they did and I've forgotten it. Never was much of a hand at Greek.

MR. FOWLER: [*Shocked*] Latin. Horace.

MAJOR POLLOCK: Horace, of course. Stupid of me. [*Plainly changing the subject*] Well, who *is* your letter from?

MR. FOWLER: It's a boy who used to be in my house and I haven't heard from for well over ten years. Brilliant boy he was, and done very well since. I can't think how he knew I was down here. Very good of him, I must say.

MAJOR POLLOCK: What happened to that other ex-pupil of yours—the painter feller?

MR. FOWLER: Oh. I still read about him in the newspapers occasionally. But I'm afraid I don't get much personal news of him. We've—rather lost touch, lately.

[MISS COOPER *comes in with a newspaper under her arm*]

MISS COOPER: Good afternoon, Major, we've managed to get your copy of the *West Hampshire Weekly News*.

MAJOR POLLOCK: [*Eagerly*] Good afternoon, Miss Cooper.

MISS COOPER: [*Handing him the newspaper*] Joe had to go to three places before he could find one.

MAJOR POLLOCK: Thank you very much.

MISS COOPER: What was the urgency?

MAJOR POLLOCK: Oh—I just wanted to have a look at it, you know. I've never read it—strange to say—although I've been here—what is it—four years?

MISS COOPER: I'm not surprised. There's never anything in it except parking offences and cattle shows.

[*The* MAJOR *opens the paper, turning away from her*]

MAJOR POLLOCK: Well, thanks anyway.

MR. FOWLER: I've had a charming letter, Miss Cooper, from someone I haven't seen or heard from in over ten years.

MISS COOPER: [*Brightly*] How nice. I'm so glad.

MR. FOWLER: I'm going to write to him and ask him if he'd care to come down for a day or two. Of course he probably won't—but just in case he does, will that room be vacant?

MISS COOPER: Not at the moment, I'm afraid, Mr. Fowler. We have so many casuals. But at the end of September—

MR. FOWLER: Good. I'll ask him for then.

[*During this interchange between* MISS COOPER *and* MR. FOWLER, MAJOR POLLOCK, *unseen by them, has turned the pages of his paper over quickly, as if he was searching for something. Suddenly his eye is evidently caught by what he reads, and he folds the paper back with a sharp sound.* MR. FOWLER *looks up at him*]

MR. FOWLER: You were with the Highland Division at Alamein, weren't you, Major?

[*There is no immediate reply. When the* MAJOR *does look up his eyes are glassy and staring*]

MAJOR POLLOCK: What? No. No, I wasn't. Not with the Highland Division.

MR. FOWLER: I thought you were.

MAJOR POLLOCK: [*Almost fiercely*] I never said so.

MR. FOWLER: I just wondered because this boy—Macleod his name is —James, I think, or John—anyway he was known at school as Curly—he says in this letter he was with the Highland Division. I just wondered if you'd run into him at all.

MAJOR POLLOCK: Macleod? No. No, I don't think so.

MR. FOWLER: Well, of course, it would have been very unlikely if you had. It was just possible, though. [*He goes to the door.* MISS COOPER *has been straightening cushions and tidying up.* MAJOR POLLOCK *sits down, holding his paper, and staring blankly into space. To himself*] Curly Macleod. He once elided a whole word in his Greek Iambics——

[*He chuckles to himself and goes out.* MAJOR POLLOCK *looks down again at his paper, and, as* MISS COOPER *straightens herself from her labours, pretends to be reading it casually*]

MAJOR POLLOCK: Yes. Pretty dull, I grant you.

MISS COOPER: What?

MAJOR POLLOCK: This paper. I don't suppose it's much read, is it?

MISS COOPER: Only by locals, I suppose. Farmers, estate agents— those sort of people.

MAJOR POLLOCK: I've never heard of anyone in the hotel reading it— have you?

MISS COOPER: Oh, yes. Mrs. Railton-Bell takes it every week.

MAJOR POLLOCK: Does she? Whatever for?

MISS COOPER: I don't know, I'm sure. There's not a lot that goes on in the world—even in West Hampshire—that she likes to miss. And she can afford fourpence for the information, I suppose.

MAJOR POLLOCK: [*Laughing jovially*] Yes, I suppose so. Funny, though—I've never seen her reading it.

MISS COOPER: Oh, she gets a lot of things sent in to her that she never reads. Most of the stuff on that table over there is hers——

MAJOR POLLOCK: Yes. Yes, I know. She'd have had hers this morning then, I suppose?

MISS COOPER: Yes. I suppose so.

MAJOR POLLOCK: Oh. Dash it all. Here I've gone and spent fourpence for nothing. I mean I could have borrowed hers, couldn't I?

[*He laughs heartily.* MISS COOPER *smiles politely and having finished her tidying up, goes to the door*]

MISS COOPER: I know you don't like venison, Major, so I've ordered you a chop for lunch tomorrow. Only I must ask you to be discreet about it, if you don't mind.

MAJOR POLLOCK: Yes, of course. Of course. Thank you so much, Miss Cooper.

[MISS COOPER *goes out.* MAJOR POLLOCK *opens the paper quickly and stares at it for some time, reading avidly. Then he suddenly rips out the whole page, crumpling it up and thrusting it into his pocket. Then he goes quickly to the table, and, after a feverish search, finds the* West Hampshire Weekly News. *He has turned it over to find the evidently offending page when* MRS. RAILTON-BELL *walks into the room from the hall, followed by her daughter* SIBYL. *The latter is a timid looking, wizened creature in the thirties, bespectacled, dowdy, and without make-up.*]

MRS. RAILTON-BELL: [*As she enters*] Well, if that's what you meant, you should have said so, dear. I wish you'd learn to express yourself a little bit better—Good afternoon, Major Pollock.

MAJOR POLLOCK: Good afternoon, Mrs. Railton-Bell. [*Jovially to* SIBYL] Afternoon, Miss R.B. [*He is holding the paper, unable to hide it, or put it back on the table. He sees that* MRS. RAILTON-BELL *has noticed it*] I'm so sorry. I was just glancing through your *West Hampshire News*. I wonder if you'd let me borrow it for a few moments. There's something I want to see.

MRS. RAILTON-BELL: Very well, Major. Only please return it.

MAJOR POLLOCK: Of course.

[*He goes to the door.* MRS. RAILTON-BELL *has moved to her seat. As she does so she picks up the other copy of the* West

Hampshire Weekly News from the floor where MAJOR POLLOCK *has dropped it*]

MRS. RAILTON-BELL: What's this? Here's another copy—

MAJOR POLLOCK: [*Feigning astonishment*] Of the *West Hampshire Weekly News?*

MRS. RAILTON-BELL: Yes.

MAJOR POLLOCK: Well, I'm dashed.

MRS. RAILTON-BELL: It was on the floor over here.

MAJOR POLLOCK: Must be one of the casuals, I suppose.

MRS. RAILTON-BELL: You'd better take it, anyway, and leave me mine.

MAJOR POLLOCK: [*Doubtfully*] You don't think, whoever owns it, might——

MRS. RAILTON-BELL: If it's been thrown down on the floor, it's plainly been read. I'd like mine back, if you don't mind, please, Major.

MAJOR POLLOCK: [*Conceding defeat*] Righty-oh. I'll put it back with the others. [*He does so, and takes the other copy from* MRS. RAILTON-BELL.] Think I'll just go out for a little stroll.

SIBYL: [*Shyly*] You don't happen to want company, do you, Major Pollock? I haven't had my walk yet.

MAJOR POLLOCK: [*Embarrassed*] Well, Miss R.B.—jolly nice suggestion and all that—the only thing is I'm going to call on a friend— you see—and——

SIBYL: [*More embarrassed than he*] Oh yes, yes. Of course. I'm so sorry.

MAJOR POLLOCK: No, no. I'm the one who's sorry. Well, cheerie-bye till dinner. [*He goes out*]

MRS. RAILTON-BELL: I wish he wouldn't use that revolting expression. It's so common. But then he *is* common——

SIBYL: Oh no, Mummy. Do you think so? He was in a very good regiment.

MRS. RAILTON-BELL: You can be in the Horse Guards and still be common, dear. [*Gently*] Sibyl, my dearest, do you mind awfully if your tactless old mother whispers something in your ear?

SIBLY: [*Resigned*] No.

MRS. RAILTON-BELL: I didn't think it was *terribly* wise of you to lay yourself open to that snub just now.

SIBYL: It wasn't a snub, Mummy. I'm sure he really *was* going to see a friend——[MRS. RAILTON-BELL *smiles understandingly and sympathetically, shaking her head ever so slightly*] Well, I often *do* go for walks with the Major.

MRS. RAILTON-BELL: I know you do, dear. What is more quite a lot of people have noticed it.

[*Pause.* SIBYL *stares at her mother*]

SIBYL: [*At length*] You don't mean—you can't mean—[*She jumps up and holds her cheeks with a sudden gesture*] Oh, no. How can people be so awful!

MRS. RAILTON-BELL: It's not being particularly awful when an unattached girl is noticed constantly seeking the company of an attractive older man.

SIBYL: [*Still holding her cheeks*] They think I chase him. Is that it? They think I run after him, they think I want—they think—no it *is* awful. It *is*. It *is*. It *is*.

MRS. RAILTON-BELL: [*Sharply*] Quieten yourself, my dear. Don't get into one of your *states*, now.

SIBYL: It's all right, Mummy. I'm not in a state. It's just—well—it's just so dreadful that people should believe such a thing is even possible. I hate that side of life. I hate it.

MRS. RAILTON-BELL: [*Soothingly*] I know you do, dear. But it exists, all the same, and one has to be very careful in this world not to give people the wrong impression. Quieter now?

SIBYL: Yes, Mummy.

MRS. RAILTON-BELL: Good. You must try not to let these things upset you so much, dear.

SIBYL: I only go for walks with the Major because I like hearing him talk. I like all his stories about London and the war and the regiment—and—he's seen so much of life and I haven't——

MRS. RAILTON-BELL: I don't know what you mean by that, dear, I'm sure.

SIBYL: I only meant——[*She checks herself*] I'm sorry.

MRS. RAILTON-BELL: [*Relentlessly pursuing her prey*] Of course I realise that you must occasionally miss some of the gaieties of life —the balls and cocktail parties and things—that a few other lucky young people can enjoy. I can assure you, dearest, if I could possibly afford it, you'd have them. But I *do* do my best, you know.

SIBYL: I know you do, Mummy.

MRS. RAILTON-BELL: There was Rome last year, and our Scandinavian cruise the year before——

SIBYL: I know, Mummy. I know. Don't think I'm not grateful. Please. It's only——[*She stops*]

MRS. RAILTON-BELL: [*Gently prompting*] Only what, dear?

SIBYL: If only I could *do* something. After all, I'm thirty-three——

MRS. RAILTON-BELL: Now, my dear. We've been over this so often. Dearest child, you'd never stand any job for more than a few weeks. Remember Jones & Jones?

SIBYL: But that was because I had to work in a basement, and I used to feel stifled and faint. But there must be something else.

MRS. RAILTON-BELL: [*Gently patting her hand*] You're not a very strong child, dear. You must get that into your head. Your nervous system isn't nearly as sound as it should be.

SIBYL: You mean my *states*? But I haven't had one of those for a long time——

MRS. RAILTON-BELL: No, dear—you've been doing very well. Very well, indeed. But there's quite a big difference between not having hysterical fits and being strong enough to take on a job [*Concluding the topic decisively*] Hand me that newspaper, would you, dear?

SIBYL: Which one?

MRS. RAILTON-BELL: The *West Hampshire Weekly News*. I want to see what the Major was so interested in. [SIBYL *hands her the paper*. MRS. RAILTON-BELL *fumbles in her pockets*] Oh, dear me, what a silly billy! I've gone and left my glasses and my book in the shelter at the end of Ragusa Road. Oh dear, I do hope they're not stolen. I expect they're bound to be. Now—doesn't that show how dependent I am on you, my dear. If you hadn't had that headache you'd have been with me this afternoon, and then you'd never have allowed me to——

SIBYL: I'll go and look for them.

MRS. RAILTON-BELL: Oh, would you, dear? That really is so kind of you. I hate you to fetch and carry for me, as you know—but my old legs are just a wee bit tired—it was the far end of the shelter, facing the sea.

SIBYL: Where we usually sit? I know.

[*She goes out.* MRS. RAILTON-BELL *opens the paper and scanning it very close to her eyes, she turns the pages to what she plainly knows, from past experience, to be the interesting section. Suddenly she stops moving the paper across her eyes. We do not see her face but the paper itself begins to shake slightly as she reads.* LADY MATHESON *comes in*]

LADY MATHESON: Oh, hullo dear. It's nearly time for the newsreel.

MRS. RAILTON-BELL: [*In a strained voice*] Gladys, have you got your glasses?

LADY MATHESON: Yes, I think so. [*She feels in her pocket*] Yes, here they are.

MRS. RAILTON-BELL: Then read this out to me.

[*She hands her the paper and points*]

LADY MATHESON: [*Unsuspecting*] Where, dear? Lorry driver loses licence?

MRS. RAILTON-BELL: No, no. Ex-officer bound over.

LADY MATHESON: [*Brightly*] Oh, yes. [*Reading*] "Ex-officer bound over. Offence in cinema." [*Looking up*] In cinema? Oh, dear—do we really want to hear this?

MRS. RAILTON-BELL: [*Grimly*] Yes, we do. Go on.

LADY MATHESON: [*Reading, resignedly*] "On Thursday last, before the Bournemouth Magistrates, David Angus Pollock, 55, giving his address as [*She starts violently*] the Beauregard Hotel, Morgan Crescent—" [*In a feverish whisper*] Major Pollock? Oh!

MRS. RAILTON-BELL: Go on.

LADY MATHESON: [*Reading*] "Morgan Crescent—pleaded guilty to a charge of insulting behaviour in a Bournemouth Cinema." Oh! Oh! "On the complaint of a Mrs. Osborn, 43 [*Breathlessly*] of 4 Studland Road." He must have been drinking——

MRS. RAILTON-BELL: He's a teetotaller.

LADY MATHESON: Perhaps just that one night.

MRS. RAILTON-BELL: No. Read on.

LADY MATHESON: "Mrs. Osborn, giving evidence, stated that Pollock, sitting next to her, persistently nudged her in the arm, and later attempted to take other liberties. She subsequently vacated her seat, and complained to an usherette. Inspector Franklin, giving evidence, said that in response to a telephone call from the cinema manager, Pollock had been kept under observation by police officers from three fifty-three P.M. until seven-ten P.M. by which time he had been observed to change his seat no less than five times, always choosing a seat next to a female person. There had, he admitted, been no further complaints, but that was not unusual in cases of this kind. On leaving the cinema Pollock was arrested and after being charged and cautioned stated: 'You have made a terrible mistake. You have the wrong man. I was only in the place half an hour. I am a colonel in the Scots Guards.' Later he made a statement. Appearing on behalf of the defendant, Mr. William Crowther, solicitor, stated that his client had had a momentary aberration. He was extremely sorry and ashamed of himself and would undertake never to behave in so stupid and improper a manner in future. He asked that his client's blameless record should be taken into account. He had enlisted in the army in 1925 and in 1939 was granted a commission as second lieutenant in the Royal Army Service Corps. During the war, he had held a responsible position in charge of an Army Supply Depot in the Orkney Islands, and had been discharged in 1946 with the rank of full lieutenant. Pollock was not called. The Chairman of the Bench, giving judgement, said: 'You have behaved disgustingly, but because this appears to be your first offence we propose to deal leniently with you.' The defendant was bound over for twelve months." [*She lowers the paper, disturbed and flustered to the core of her being*] Oh, dear. Oh, dear. Oh, dear.

MRS. RAILTON-BELL: [*Perfectly composed but excited*] Thursday. It must have happened on Wednesday. Do you remember—he missed dinner that night?

LADY MATHESON: Did he? Yes, so he did. Oh, dear. It's all too frightful! I can hardly believe it. Persistently. It's so dreadful.

MRS. RAILTON-BELL: On the Thursday he was terribly nervous and depressed. I remember now. And then on the Friday, suddenly as bright as a button. Of course he must have read the papers and thought he'd got away with it. What a stroke of luck that I get this weekly one sent to me.

LADY MATHESON: Luck, dear? Is it luck?

MRS. RAILTON-BELL: Of course it's luck. Otherwise we'd never have known.

LADY MATHESON: Wouldn't that have been better?

MRS. RAILTON-BELL: Gladys! What *are* you saying?

LADY MATHESON: I don't know, oh dear. I'm so fussed and confused. No, of course, it wouldn't have been better. One has to know these things, I suppose—although sometimes I wonder why.

MRS. RAILTON-BELL: Because if there's a liar and a fraudulent crook and a—I can't bring myself to say it—wandering around among us unsuspected, there could be—well—there could be the most terrible repercussions.

LADY MATHESON: Well, he's been wandering around among us for four years now and there haven't been any repercussions yet. [*With a faint sigh*] I suppose we're too old.

MRS. RAILTON-BELL: [*Coldly*] I have a daughter, you know.

LADY MATHESON: Oh. Poor Sibyl. Yes. And she's such a friend of his, isn't she? Oh, dear.

MRS. RAILTON-BELL: Exactly.

LADY MATHESON: [*After a moment's troubled reflection*] Maud, dear —it's not my business, I know, and of course you have a mother's duty to protect your child, that of course, I do see—and yet—well —she's such a strange girl—so excitable and shy—and so ungrownup in so many ways——

MRS. RAILTON-BELL: Come to the point, Gladys.

LADY MATHESON: Yes, I will. It's this. I don't think you ought to tell her this.

MRS. RAILTON-BELL: Not *tell* her?

LADY MATHESON: Well, not all of it. Not the details. Say he's a fraud, if you like, but not—please, Maud—not about the cinema. [*Suddenly distressed by the thought herself*] Oh, dear! I don't know how I shall ever look him in the face again.

MRS. RAILTON-BELL: You won't have to, dear. [*She has risen purposefully from her chair*] I'm going to see Miss Cooper now, and insist that he leaves this hotel before dinner tonight.

LADY MATHESON: Oh, dear. I wonder if you should?

MRS. RAILTON-BELL: Gladys, what *has* come over you this evening? Of course I should.

LADY MATHESON: But you know what Miss Cooper is—so independent and stubborn sometimes. She might not agree.

MRS. RAILTON-BELL: Of course she'll agree. She *has* to agree if we all insist.

LADY MATHESON: But we don't *all*. I mean it's just the two of us. Shouldn't we consult the others first? [*Suddenly realising the implication*] Oh, gracious! Of course that means we'll have to tell them all, doesn't it?

MRS. RAILTON-BELL: [*Delighted*] An excellent idea, Gladys. Where's Mr. Fowler?

LADY MATHESON: In his room, I think.

MRS. RAILTON-BELL: And the young people? Shall we have them? They count as regulars by now, I suppose. Yes. We'll have them, too.

LADY MATHESON: Oh, dear. I hate telling tales.

MRS. RAILTON-BELL: Telling tales? [*She points dramatically to the West Hampshire Weekly News*] The tale is told already, Gladys —to the world.

LADY MATHESON: Well, strictly speaking—only to West Hampshire.

MRS. RAILTON-BELL: Don't quibble, Gladys. [*At the french windows*] Miss Meacham's in the garden. I really don't think we need bother about Miss Meacham. She's so odd and unpredictable— and getting odder and more unpredictable every day. Here comes Sibyl. Go up and get the others down, dear. I'll deal with her.

LADY MATHESON: Maud, you won't——[SIBYL *comes in*] You'll remember what I said, won't you?

MRS. RAILTON-BELL: Yes, of course. Go on, dear. [LADY MATHESON *goes out. To* SIBYL] Clever girl. You found them, did you, darling? [*She takes the book and glasses from* SIBYL. *There is a pause. At length*] Sibyl, dear. I think you'd better go to your room if you don't mind.

SIBYL: Why, Mummy?

MRS. RAILTON-BELL: We're holding a meeting of the regulars down here to discuss a very urgent matter that has just cropped up.

SIBYL: Oh, but how exciting. Can't I stay? After all, I'm a regular, too——

MRS. RAILTON-BELL: I know, dear, but I doubt if the subject of the meeting is quite suitable for you.

SIBYL: Why, Mummy? What is it?

MRS. RAILTON-BELL: Oh, dear! You're such an inquisitive child. Very well, then. I'll tell you this much but only this much. We are going to discuss whether or not we think that Miss Cooper should be told to ask Major Pollock to leave this hotel at once and never come back.

SIBYL: [*Aghast*] What? But I don't understand. Why, Mummy? [MRS. RAILTON-BELL *does not reply*] Mummy, tell me, why?

MRS. RAILTON-BELL: I can't tell you dear. It might upset you too much.

SIBYL: But I must know, Mummy. I must. What has he done?

MRS. RAILTON-BELL: [*After only the slightest hesitation*] You really *insist* I should tell you?

SIBYL: Yes, I do.

MRS. RAILTON-BELL: Even after my strong warning?

SIBYL: Yes.

MRS. RAILTON-BELL: [*With a sigh*] Very well, then dear. I have no option, I suppose. [*With a quick gesture she hands the paper to* SIBYL] Read that. Middle column. Half way down. Ex-officer bound over.

[SIBYL *reads.* MRS. RAILTON-BELL *watches her. Suddenly* SIBYL *sits, her eyes staring, but her face blank.* LADY MATHESON *comes in. She sees* SIBYL *instantly*]

LADY MATHESON: [*Shocked*] Oh, Maud, you haven't——

MRS. RAILTON-BELL: I did my best, my dear, but she insisted. She absolutely insisted. [*Solicitiously bending over her daughter's chair*] I'm so sorry, my dear. It must be the most dreadful shock for you. It was for us too, as you can imagine. Are you all right? [SIBYL *takes her spectacles off and folding the paper meticulously, lays it down on the arm of her chair. She makes no reply. Slightly more sharply*] Are you all right, Sibyl?

SIBYL: [*Barely audible*] Yes, Mummy.

[JEAN *comes in, looking rather annoyed*]

JEAN: What is it, Mrs. Railton-Bell? I can only stay a moment. I must get back to the baby.

MRS. RAILTON-BELL: I won't keep you long, I promise you. Take a seat. [*Turning to* SIBYL, *sharply*] Sibyl, what have you done? [CHARLES *comes in. She takes* SIBYL'S *glasses from her hand*] Look, you've broken your glasses.

SIBYL: [*Murmuring*] How stupid.

CHARLES: Hullo, you've cut your hand, haven't you?

SIBYL: No.

CHARLES: Yes, you have. Let's see. [*With a rather professional air he picks up her limp hand and examines it*] Nothing much. No splinters. Here, you'd better have this. It's quite clean. [*He takes a clean handkerchief from his breast pocket and ties it neatly round her hand*] Iodine and a bit of plaster later.

[MR. FOWLER *has come in*]

MRS. RAILTON-BELL: Ah, Mr. Fowler, good. Would you take a seat, and then we can begin. The two young people are in a hurry. I'm afraid I have very grave news for you all.

CHARLES: The boiler's gone wrong again?

MRS. RAILTON-BELL: No. I only wish it were something so trivial.

CHARLES: I don't consider shaving in cold, brown water trivial.

MRS. RAILTON-BELL: Please, Mr. Stratton.

MR. FOWLER: [*Anxiously*] They're raising the prices again?

MRS. RAILTON-BELL: No. My news is graver even than that.

MR. FOWLER: I don't know what could be graver than that.

MRS. RAILTON-BELL: The news I have to give you, Mr. Fowler.

CHARLES: Look, Mrs. Railton-Bell, must we play twenty questions? Can't you just tell us what it is?

MRS. RAILTON-BELL: [*Angrily*] My hesitation is only because the matter is so painful and so embarrassing for me that I find it difficult to choose my words. However, if you want it baldly, you shall have it. [*After a dramatic pause*] Major Pollock—who is not a major at all but a lieutenant promoted from the ranks in the R.A.S.C.——

CHARLES: [*Excitedly*] No. You don't say! I knew it, you know. I always knew Sandhurst and the Black Watch was a phoney. Didn't I say so, Jean?

JEAN: Yes, you did, but I said it first—that night he made the boob about serviettes.

MR. FOWLER: [*Chipping in quickly*] I must admit I've always slightly suspected the public school education. I mean only to-day he made the most shocking mistake in quoting Horace—quite appalling.

MRS. RAILTON-BELL: [*Raising her voice*] Please, please, ladies and gentlemen. This is not the point. The dreadful, the really ghastly revelation is still to come. [*She gains silence, and once again pauses dramatically*] He was found guilty——

LADY MATHESON: Pleaded guilty——

MRS. RAILTON BELL: Please, Gladys. He was found or pleaded guilty —I don't really see that it matters which—to behaving insultingly to no less than six respectable women in a Bournemouth cinema.

[*There is an aghast silence*]

CHARLES: [*At length*] Good God! What a performance.

LADY MATHESON: Really, Maud, I must correct that. I must. We only know one was respectable—the one who complained—and even she seemed a little odd in her behaviour. Why didn't she just say straight out to the Major: 'I do wish you'd stop doing whatever it is that you are doing?' That's what I'd have done. About the other five we don't know anything at all. We don't even know if he nudged them or anything.

MRS. RAILTON-BELL: Of course he nudged them. He was in that cinema for an immoral purpose—he admitted it. And he was seen to change his seat five times—always choosing one next to female persons.

CHARLES: That could make ten nudges, really, couldn't it? If he had the chance of using both elbows.

JEAN: Eleven, with the original one. Or twelve, supposing——

MRS. RAILTON-BELL: Really, we seem to be losing the essential point in a welter of trivialities. The point is surely that the Major—the so-called Major—had pleaded guilty to a criminal offence of a disgusting nature, and I want to know what action we regular residents propose to take.

MR. FOWLER: What action do you propose, Mrs. Railton-Bell?

MRS. RAILTON-BELL: I propose, on your behalf, to go to Miss Cooper and demand that he leaves the hotel forthwith.

CHARLES: No.

MRS. RAILTON-BELL: You disagree, Mr. Stratton?

CHARLES: Yes, I do. Please don't think I'm making light of this business, Mrs. Railton-Bell. To me what he's done, if he's done it, seems ugly and repulsive. I've always had an intense dislike of the more furtive forms of sexual expression. So emotionally I'm entirely on your side. But logically I'm not.

MRS. RAILTON-BELL: [*Cuttingly*] Are you making a speech, Mr. Stratton? If so, perhaps you'd like to stand over there and address us.

CHARLES: No. I'm all right, where I am, thank you. I'm not making a speech either. I'm just saying that my dislike of the Major's offence is emotional and not logical. My lack of understanding of it is probably a short-coming in me. The Major presumably understands my form of lovemaking. I *should* therefore understand his. But I don't. So I am plainly in a state of prejudice against him, and must be very wary of any moral judgements I may pass in this matter. It's only fair to approach it from the purely logical standpoint of practical Christian ethics, and ask myself the question: "What harm has the man done?" Well, apart from possibly slightly bruising the arm of a certain lady, whose motives in complaining—I agree with Lady Matheson—are extremely questionable—apart from that, and apart from telling us a few rather pathetic lies about his past life, which most of us do anyway from time to time, I really can't see he's done anything to justify us chucking him out into the street.

JEAN: [*Hotly*] I don't agree at all. I feel disgusted at what he's done too, but *I* think I'm quite right to feel disgusted. I don't consider myself prejudiced at all, and I think that people who behave like that are a public menace and deserve anything they get.

CHARLES: Your vehemence is highly suspect. I must have you psychoanalysed.

JEAN: It's absolutely logical, Charles. Supposing next time it's a daughter——

CHARLES: [*Wearily*] I know. I know. And supposing in twenty or thirty years' time she sits next to a Major Pollock in a cinema——

JEAN: Exactly. [*He laughs*] It's not funny, Charles. How would you feel——

CHARLES: Very ashamed of her if she didn't use her elbows back, very hard, and in the right place.

JEAN: Charles, I think that's an absolutely monstrous——

MRS. RAILTON-BELL: Please, please, please. This is not a private argument between the two of you. I take it, Mr. Stratton, you are against any action regarding this matter? [CHARLES *nods*] Of any kind at all? [CHARLES *shakes his head*] Not even a protest?

CHARLES: I might give him a reproving glance at dinner.

MRS. RAILTON-BELL: [*Turning from him in disgust*] You, Mrs. Stratton, I gather, agree with me that I should see Miss Cooper?

JEAN: [*Firmly*] Yes.

CHARLES: [*Murmuring to her*] Book-burner.

JEAN: [*Furiously*] What's book-burning got to do with it?

CHARLES: A lot.

MRS. RAILTON-BELL: [*Imperiously*] Quiet, please. [*Turning to* MR. FOWLER] Mr. Fowler? What do you think?

MR. FOWLER: [*Confused*] Well, it's difficult. Very difficult. I can't say I see it like Stratton. That's the modern viewpoint, I know—nothing is really wrong that doesn't do actual and assessible harm to another human being. But he's not correct when he calls that Christianity. Christianity, surely, goes much further than that. Certain acts are wrong because they are, in themselves and by themselves, impure and immoral, and it seems to me that this terrible wave of vice and sexual excess which seems to have flooded this country since the war might well, in part, be due to the decline of the old standards, emotional and illogical though they may well seem to the younger generation. Tolerance is not necessarily a good, you know. Tolerance of evil may itself be an evil. After all it was Aristotle, wasn't it, who said——

[MISS MEACHAM *appears from the garden*]

MISS MEACHAM: Oh, really—you've all gone on far too long about it. And when you start quoting Aristotle, well, personally, I'm going to my room.

MRS. RAILTON-BELL: You heard, Miss Meacham?

MISS MEACHAM: I couldn't help hearing. I didn't want to. I was doing my system and you need to concentrate like billy-oh on that, but I had my chair against the wall to catch the sun, and I wasn't going to move into the cold just for you people.

MRS. RAILTON-BELL: Well, as you know the facts, I suppose we should canvass your opinion. What is it?

MISS MEACHAM: I haven't any.

MRS. RAILTON-BELL: You must have *some* opinion?

MISS MEACHAM: Why should I? I've been out of the world for far longer than any of you and what do I know about morals and ethics? Only what I read in novels, and as I only read thrillers, that isn't worth much. In Peter Cheyney the hero does far worse things to his girls than the Major's done, and no one seems to mind.

MRS. RAILTON-BELL: I don't think that it's quite the point what Peter Cheyney's heroes do to his girls, Miss Meacham. We want your views on Major Pollock.

MISS MEACHAM: Do you? Well, my views on Major Pollock have always been that he's a crashing old bore, and a wicked old fraud. Now I hear he's a dirty old man, too, well, I'm not at all surprised, and quite between these four walls, I don't give a damn.

[*She goes out. There is a pause, and then* MRS. RAILTON-BELL *turns to* MR. FOWLER]

MRS. RAILTON-BELL: Well, Mr. Fowler, I take you are on the side of action?

[*Pause*]

MR. FOWLER: I once had to recommend a boy for expulsion. Only once, in the whole of the fifteen years I was a housemaster. I was deeply unhappy about it. Deeply. And yet events proved me right. He was no good. He became a thief and a blackmailer, and—oh—horrible things happened to him. Horrible [*After a moment's pause*] Poor boy. He *had* a way with him——

MRS. RAILTON-BELL: [*Impatiently*] Are you in favour of action, Mr. Fowler?

MR. FOWLER: [*Unhappily*] Yes, I suppose so. Yes, I am.

MRS. RAILTON-BELL: [*To* LADY MATHESON] And you, Gladys? [*As* LADY MATHESON *hesitates*] You don't need to make a speech like the others, dear. Just say yes or no.

[*Pause*]

LADY MATHESON. [*At length*] Oh, dear!

MRS. RAILTON-BELL: Now don't shilly-shally, Gladys. You know perfectly well what you feel about all this dreadful vice that's going on all over the country. You've told me often how people like that should be locked up——

LADY MATHESON: [*At length*] Oh, dear!

MRS. RAILTON-BELL: [*Really impatient*] Oh, for heaven's sake, make up your mind, Gladys. Are you on the side of Mr. Stratton with his defence of vice, or are you on the side of the Christian virtues like Mr. Fowler, Mrs. Stratton and myself?

CHARLES: [*Quietly*] I have never in my life heard a question more disgracefully begged. Senator McCarthy could use your talents, Mrs. Railton-Bell.

MRS. RAILTON-BELL: Will you keep quiet! Well, Gladys, which is it to be?

LADY MATHESON: I'm on your side, of course. It's only——

MRS. RAILTON-BELL: [*To* CHARLES] Well, Mr. Stratton—apart from Miss Meacham, who might be said to be neutral, the count appears now to be five to one against you.

CHARLES: *Five* to one?

MRS. RAILTON-BELL: My daughter, of course, agrees with me.

CHARLES: How do you know?

MRS. RAILTON-BELL: I know her feelings in this matter.

CHARLES: May we hear them from herself? [SYBIL, *during the whole of this discussion, has not stirred in her chair. Her two hands, one bound with a handkerchief, have rested motionless in her lap, and she has been staring at the wall opposite her*] Miss Railton-Bell— could we hear your views?

[*There is no reply*]

MRS. RAILTON-BELL: Mr. Stratton is asking you a question, dear.

SIBYL: Yes, Mummy?

CHARLES: Could we hear your views?

SIBYL: My views?

MRS. RAILTON-BELL: [*Clearly, as to a child*] On Major Pollock, dear. What action should we take about him? [SYBIL *seems puzzled and makes no reply. To the others, in an aside*] It's the shock. [*To* SIBYL *again*] You know what you've just read in that paper, dear? What do you think of it?

SIBYL: [*In a whisper*] It made me sick.

MRS. RAILTON-BELL: Of course it did, dear. That's how we all feel.

SIBYL: [*Her voice growing louder in a crescendo*] It made me sick. It made me sick. It made me sick. It made me sick.

MRS. RAILTON-BELL: [*Going quickly to her and embracing her*] Yes, dear. Yes. Don't fuss now, don't fuss. It's all right.

SIBYL: [*Burying her face in her mother's arms*] I don't feel well, Mummy. Can I go and lie down?

MRS. RAILTON-BELL: Of course you can, dear. We can go into the writing-room. Such a nice comfy sofa, and there's never anyone there. [*She leads her to the hall door*] And don't fret any more, my dear. Try and forget the whole nasty business. Make believe it never happened—that there never was such a person as Major Pollock. That's the way.

[*They disappear together into the hall*]

LADY MATHESON: She should never have told her like that. It was such a mistake.

CHARLES: [*Angrily*] I agree. If that girl doesn't end as a mental case it won't be the fault of her mother.

LADY MATHESON: [*Loyally*] Mr. Stratton—I must say I consider that a quite outrageous way of twisting my remark. I used the word "mistake", and you have no right——

CHARLES: No, I haven't. I'm sorry. The comment was purely my own.

JEAN: It was *your* fault for asking her views.

CHARLES: She was sitting there quite peacefully, apparently listening. I wasn't to know she was in a state of high suppressed hysteria. I might, admittedly, have guessed, but anyway, I had an idiotic but well-meaning hope that I might get her—just this once just this once in the whole of her life—to disagree publicly with her mother. It could save her soul if she ever did.

MR. FOWLER: I didn't realise that modern psychiatry recognised so old-fashioned and sentimental a term as soul, Mr. Stratton.

CHARLES: Very well, for soul read mind, and one day when you have a spare ten minutes explain to me the difference.

MR. FOWLER: I will.

CHARLES: [*Getting up*] Not now, I'm afraid. It might muddle my anatomical studies. [*To* JEAN] Are you coming?

[JEAN *gets up, rather reluctantly*]

JEAN: I don't know what's the matter with you, this evening, Charles. You've behaving like an arrogant pompous boor.

CHARLES: You must forgive me. I suppose it's just that I'm feeling a little light-headed at finding myself, on an issue of common humanity, in a minority of one. The sin of spiritual pride, that's called—isn't it, Mr. Fowler?

[*He goes out.* JEAN *comes back from the door*]

JEAN: [*To the other two*] He's been overworking, you know. He'll be quite different about all this tomorrow. [*Confidently*] I'll see to that.

[MRS. RAILTON-BELL *comes in*]

MRS. RAILTON-BELL: She's quite all right, now. She always recovers from these little states very quickly. She's resting in the writing room.

LADY MATHESON: Oh, good.

JEAN: I was just apologising for my husband's behaviour, Mrs. Railton-Bell.

MRS. RAILTON-BELL: Thank you, my dear—but what I always say is— we're all of us entitled to our own opinions, however odd and dangerous and distasteful they may sometimes be. [*Briskly*] Now. Shall we all go and see Miss Cooper in a body, or would you rather I acted as your spokesman?

[*It is plain which course she would prefer. After a pause, they begin to murmur diffidently*]

LADY MATHESON: I think, perhaps, if *you* went, dear——

MR. FOWLER: I don't think a deputation is a good idea——

JEAN: You be our spokesman.

MRS. RAILTON-BELL: Very well [*She picks up the copy of the newspaper and goes to the door*] I hope you all understand it's a duty I hardly relish. [*She goes out*]

MR. FOWLER: [*To* LADY MATHESON] I would hardly call that a strictly accurate self-appraisal, would you?

LADY MATHESON: [*Doubtfully*] Well—after all—doing a duty can seem a pleasure, to some people, can't it? It never has done to me, I agree, but then I'm—well—so weak and silly about these things——

JEAN: [*At the door*] It would be a pleasure to me in this case. Horrid old man! [*To herself as she goes*] I hope the baby's not been crying——[*She goes out*]

MR. FOWLER: A ruthless young girl, that, I would say.

LADY MATHESON: So many young people are these days, don't you think?

MR. FOWLER: [*Meaningly*] Not only young people.

LADY MATHESON: [*Unhappily*] Yes—well. [*With a sigh*] Oh, dear! What a dreadful affair. It's made me quite miserable.

MR. FOWLER: I feel a little unhappy about it all myself. [*He sighs and gets up*] The trouble about being on the side of right, as one sees it, is that one sometimes finds oneself in the company of such very questionable allies. Let's go and take our minds off it all with television.

LADY MATHESON: [*Getting up*] Yes. Good idea. The newsreel will be nearly over now—but I think that dear Philip Harben is on, after. Such a pity I'll never have the chance of following any of his recipes.

MR. FOWLER: [*As they go out*] I agree. One suffers the tortures of Tantalus, and yet the pleasure is intense. Isn't that what is today called masochism?

> *They go out. The room is empty for a moment, and then*
> MAJOR POLLOCK *tentatively appears at the open french windows.*
> *He peers cautiously into the room, and, satisfying himself that it*
> *is empty, comes in. He goes quickly to the table on which are*
> MRS. RAILTON-BELL'S *journals. He sees at once that the West*
> *Hampshire Weekly News is no longer where he left it. Frantically he rummages through the pile, and then begins to search*
> *the room. He is standing, in doubt by the fireplace, when the*
> *door opens quietly and* SIBYL *comes in. As she sees him she*
> *stands stock still. He does not move either*]

MAJOR POLLOCK: [*At length, with pathetic jauntiness*] Evening, Miss R.B. And how's the world with you, eh?

SIBYL: Were you looking for Mummy's paper?

MAJOR POLLOCK: What? No, of course not. I've got the other copy——

SIBYL: Don't pretend any more, please. She's read it, you see.

MAJOR POLLOCK: Oh.

> [*There is a long pause. The* MAJOR'S *shoulders droop, and he*
> *holds the table for support*]

MAJOR POLLOCK: Did she show it to you?

SIBYL: Yes.

MAJOR POLLOCK: Oh.

SIBYL: And to all the others.

MAJOR POLLOCK: Miss Cooper, too?

SIBYL: Mummy's gone to tell her.

[*The* MAJOR *nods, hopelessly*]

MAJOR POLLOCK: [*At length*] Well—that's it, then, isn't it?

SIBYL: Yes.

MAJOR POLLOCK: Oh, God!

[*He sits down, staring at the floor. She looks at him steadily*]

SIBYL: [*Passionately*] Why did you do it? Why did you do it?

MAJOR POLLOCK: I don't know. I wish I could answer that. Why does anyone do anything they shouldn't? Why do some people drink too much, and other people smoke fifty cigarettes a day? Because they can't stop it, I suppose.

SIBYL: Then this wasn't—the first time?

MAJOR POLLOCK: [*Quietly*] No.

SIBYL: It's horrible.

MAJOR POLLOCK: Yes, of course it is. I'm not trying to defend it. You wouldn't guess, I know, but ever since school I've always been scared to death of women. Of everyone, in a way, I suppose, but mostly of women. I had a bad time at school—which wasn't Wellington, of course—just a Council school. Boys hate other boys to be timid and shy, and they gave it to me good and proper. My father despised me, too. He was a sergeant-major in the Black Watch. He made me join the Army, but I was always a bitter disappointment to him. He died before I got my commission. I only got that by a wangle. It wasn't difficult at the beginning of the war. But it meant everything to me, all the same. Being saluted, being called sir—I thought I'm someone, now, a real person. Perhaps some woman might even—[*He stops*] But it didn't work. It never has worked. I'm made in a certain way, and I can't change it. It has to be the dark, you see, and strangers, because——

SIBYL: [*Holding her hands to her ears*] Stop, stop! I don't want to hear it. It makes me ill.

MAJOR POLLOCK: [*Quietly*] Yes. It would, of course. I should have known that. It was only that you'd asked me about why I did such things, and I wanted to talk to someone about it. I never have, you see, not in the whole of my life. [*He gets up and gently touches her sleeve*] I'm sorry to have to upset *you*, of all people.

[*He goes to a table and collects two books*]

SIBYL: Why me, so especially? Why not the others?

MAJOR POLLOCK: Oh, I don't give a hang about the others. They'll all take it in their various ways, I suppose—but it won't mean much more to them than another bit of gossip to snort or snigger about. But it'll be different for you, Sibyl, and that makes me unhappy.

SIBYL: That's the first time you've ever called me Sibyl.

MAJOR POLLOCK: Is it? Well, there's not much point in all that Miss R.B. stuff now, is there?

SIBYL: What makes me so different from the others?

[*The* MAJOR *has gathered another book from a corner of the room, and a pipe. He turns now and looks at her*]

MAJOR POLLOCK: Your being so scared of—well—shall we call it life? It sounds more respectable than the word which I know you hate. You and I are awfully alike, you know. That's why I suppose we've drifted so much together in this place.

SIBYL: How can you say we're alike? *I* don't——[*She stops, unable to continue*]

MAJOR POLLOCK: I know you don't. You're not even tempted and never will be. You're very lucky. Or are you? Who's to say, really? All I meant was that we're both of us frightened of people, and yet we've somehow managed to forget our fright when we've been in each other's company. Speaking for myself, I'm grateful and always will be. Of course I can't expect *you* to feel the same way now.

SIBYL: What are you doing?

MAJOR POLLOCK: Getting my things together. Have you seen a pouch anywhere?

SIBYL: It's here.

[She goes to a table and collects it. He takes it from her]

MAJOR POLLOCK: *[With a wry smile]* Old Wellingtonian colours.

SIBYL: Why have you told so many awful lies?

MAJOR POLLOCK: I don't like myself as I am, I suppose, so I've had to invent another person. It's not so harmful, really. We've all got daydreams. Mine have gone a step further than most people's— that's all. Quite often I've even managed to believe in the Major myself. *[He starts]* Is that someone in the hall?

SIBYL: *[Listening]* No, I don't think so. Where will you go?

MAJOR POLLOCK: I don't know. There's a chap in London might put me up for a day or two. Only I don't so awfully want to go there——

SIBYL: Why not?

MAJOR POLLOCK: *[After a slight pause]* Well—you see—it's rather a case of birds of a feather.

SIBYL: Don't go to him. You mustn't go to him.

MAJOR POLLOCK: I don't know where else.

SIBYL: Another hotel.

MAJOR POLLOCK: It can't be Bournemouth or anywhere near here. It'll have to be London, and I don't know anywhere there I can afford——

SIBYL: I'll lend you some money.

MAJOR POLLOCK: You certainly won't.

SIBYL: I will. I have some savings certificates. You can have those. I can get more too, if you need it.

MAJOR POLLOCK: *[Holding her hand, gently]* No, Sibyl. No. Thank you—but no.

SIBYL: But you'll go to this man.

MAJOR POLLOCK: No, I won't. I'll find somewhere else.

SIBYL: Where?

MAJOR POLLOCK: Don't worry. I'll be all right.

[MISS COOPER comes in, and closes the door behind her]

MISS COOPER: [*Brightly*] There you are, Major Pollock. Can I see you in my office a moment?

MAJOR POLLOCK: We don't need to talk in your office, Miss Cooper. I know what you have to say. I'm leaving at once.

MISS COOPER: I see. That's your own choice, is it?

MAJOR POLLOCK: Of course.

MISS COOPER: Because I would like to make it perfectly plain to you that there's no question whatever of my requiring you to leave this hotel. If you want to stay on here you're at perfect liberty to do so. It's entirely a matter for you.

(*Pause*)

MAJOR POLLOCK: I see. That's good of you. But of course, I have to go.

MISS COOPER: I quite understand that you'd want to. I shan't charge the usual week's notice. When will you be going? Before dinner?

MAJOR POLLOCK: Of course.

MISS COOPER: Do you want me to help you find some place to stay until you can get settled?

MAJOR POLLOCK: I can hardly expect that, Miss Cooper.

MISS COOPER: Why on earth not? There are two hotels in London run by the Beauregard group. One is in West Kensington and the other in St. John's Wood. They're both about the same price. Which would you prefer?

MAJOR POLLOCK: [*After a pause*] West Kensington, I think.

MISS COOPER: I've got their card here somewhere. Yes, there's one here. [*She goes to the mantelpiece and takes a card from a small holder. She hands it to him*] Would you like me to ring them up for you?

MAJOR POLLOCK: Thank you, but I think perhaps I'd better ring them myself. In case of—further trouble, I don't want to involve you more than I need. May I use the phone in your office?

MISS COOPER: Certainly.

MAJOR POLLOCK: I'll pay for the call of course. [*He goes to the door and looks to see if anyone is about in the hall*] Sibyl, if I don't have a chance of seeing you again, I'll write and say goodbye.

[*He goes out.* MISS COOPER *turns to* SIBYL]

MISS COOPER: Your mother's gone up to dress for dinner, Miss Railton-Bell. She told me I'd find you in the writing room lying down and I was to tell you that you can have your meal upstairs tonight, if you'd rather.

SIBYL: That's all right.

MISS COOPER: [*Sympathetically*] How are you feeling now?

SIBYL: [*Brusquely*] All right.

[MISS COOPER *approaches her*]

MISS COOPER: [*Quietly*] Is there anything I can do to help you?

SIBYL: [*Angrily*] No. Nothing. And please don't say things like that. You'll make me feel bad again, and I'll make a fool of myself. I feel well now. He's going and that's good. I despise him.

MISS COOPER: Do you? I wonder if you should.

SIBYL: He's a vile, wicked man, and he's done a horrible beastly thing. It's not the first time, either. He admits that.

MISS COOPER: I didn't think it was.

SIBYL: And yet you told him he could stay on in the hotel if he wanted to? That's wicked, too.

MISS COOPER: Then I suppose I *am* wicked, too. [*She puts her hand on her arm*] Sibyl, dear——

SIBYL: Why is everyone calling me Sibyl this evening? Please stop. You'll only make me cry.

MISS COOPER: I don't mean to do that. I just mean to help you. [SIBYL *breaks down suddenly, but now quietly and without hysteria.* MISS COOPER *holds her*] That's better. Much better.

SIBYL: It's so horrible.

MISS COOPER: I know it is. I'm very sorry for you.

SIBYL: He says we're alike—he and I.

MISS COOPER: Does he?

SIBYL: He says we're both scared of life and people and sex. There— I've said the word. He says I hate *saying* it even, and he's right. I do. What's the matter with me? There must be something the matter with me.

MISS COOPER: Nothing very much, I should say. Shall we sit down?

[*She gently propels her on to the sofa and sits beside her*]

SIBYL: I'm a freak, aren't I?

MISS COOPER: [*In matter of fact tones*] I never know what that word means. If you mean you're different from other people, then, I suppose, you are a freak. But all human beings are a bit different from each other, aren't they? What a dull world it would be if they weren't.

SIBYL: I'd like to be ordinary.

MISS COOPER: I wouldn't know about that, dear. You see, I've never met an ordinary person. To me all people are extraordinary. I meet all sorts here, you know, in my job, and the one thing I've learnt in five years is that the word normal, applied to any human being, is utterly meaningless. In a sort of a way it's an insult to our Maker, don't you think, to suppose that He could possibly work to any set pattern.

SIBYL: I don't think Mummy would agree with you.

MISS COOPER: I'm fairly sure she wouldn't. Tell me—when did your father die?

SIBYL: When I was seven.

MISS COOPER: Did you go to school?

SIBYL: No. Mummy said I was too delicate. I had a governess some of the time, but most of the time Mummy taught me herself.

MISS COOPER: Yes. I see. And you've never really been away from her, have you?

SIBYL: Only when I had a job, for a bit. [*Proudly*] I was a salesgirl in a big shop in London—Jones & Jones. I sold lampshades. But I got ill, though, and had to leave.

MISS COOPER: [*Brightly*] What bad luck. Well, you must try again, some day, mustn't you?

SIBYL: Mummy says no.

MISS COOPER: Mummy says no. Well, then, you must just try and get Mummy to say yes, don't you think?

SIBYL: I don't know how.

MISS COOPER: I'll tell you how. By running off and getting a job on your own. She'll say yes quick enough then. [*She pats* SIBYL'*s knee sympathetically and gets up*] I have my menus to do. [*She goes towards the door*]

SIBYL: [*Urgently*] Will he be all right, do you think?

MISS COOPER: The Major? I don't know. I hope so.

SIBYL: In spite of what he's done, I don't want anything bad to happen to him. I want him to be happy. Is it a nice hotel—this one in West Kensington?

MISS COOPER: Very nice.

SIBYL: Do you think he'll find a friend there? He told me just now that he'd always be grateful to me for making him forget how frightened he was of people.

MISS COOPER: He's helped you too, hasn't he?

SIBYL: Yes.

MISS COOPER: [*After a pause*] I hope he'll find a friend in the new hotel.

SIBYL: So do I. Oh God, so do I.

[*The* MAJOR *comes in*]

MAJOR POLLOCK: [*Quickly, to* MISS COOPER] It's all right. I've fixed it. It might please you to know that I said *Mr.* Pollock, and didn't have to mention your name, or this hotel. I must dash upstairs and pack now. [*He turns to* SIBYL *and holds out his hand*] Goodbye, Sibyl.

[SIBYL *takes his hand, after a second's hesitation*]

SIBYL: Goodbye. [*She drops his hand and runs quickly to the door. Without looking back*] God bless you. [*She goes out*]

MAJOR POLLOCK: Very upset? [MISS COOPER *nods*] That's the part I've hated most, you know. It's funny. She's rather an odd one—almost a case—she's got a child's mind and hardly makes sense sometimes —and yet she means quite a lot to me.

MISS COOPER: I think you mean quite a lot to her, too.

MAJOR POLLOCK: I did, I think. Not now, of course. It was the gallant ex-soldier she was fond of—not——[*He stops*] I told her the whole story about myself. I thought it right. There's just a chance she might understand it all a bit better one day. I'm afraid, though, she'll never get over it.

MISS COOPER: No. I don't suppose she will.

MAJOR POLLOCK: One's apt to excuse oneself sometimes by saying: Well, after all, what I do doesn't do anybody much harm. But one does, you see. That's not a thought I like. Could you have a squint in the hall and see if anyone's around?

[MISS COOPER *half opens the door*]

MISS COOPER: Miss Meacham's at the telephone.

MAJOR POLLOCK: Damn.

MISS COOPER: What train are you catching?

MAJOR POLLOCK: Seven-forty-five.

MISS COOPER: You've got time.

MAJOR POLLOCK: I've got a tremendous lot of packing to do. Four years, you know. Hellish business. I'm dreading the first few days in a new place. I mean dreading, you know—literally trembling with funk at the thought of meeting new people. The trouble is I'll probably be forced by sheer terror to take refuge in all that Major stuff again.

MISS COOPER: Try not to.

MAJOR POLLOCK: Oh, I'll try all right. I'll try. I only hope I'll succeed. [*He goes cautiously to the door and turns*] Still there. Damn. [*Coming back*] Thank you for being so kind. God knows why you have been. I don't deserve it—but I'm grateful. Very grateful.

MISS COOPER: That's all right.

MAJOR POLLOCK: You're an odd fish, you know, if you don't mind my saying so. A good deal more goes on behind that calm managerial front of yours than anyone would imagine. Has something bad ever happened to you?

MISS COOPER: Yes.

MAJOR POLLOCK: Very bad?

MISS COOPER: I've got over it.

MAJOR POLLOCK: What was it?

MISS COOPER: I loved a man who loved somebody else.

MAJOR POLLOCK: Still love him?

MISS COOPER: Oh, yes. I always will.

MAJOR POLLOCK: Any hope?

MISS COOPER: [*Cheerfully*] No. None at all.

MAJOR POLLOCK: Why so cheerful about it?

MISS COOPER: Because there's no point in being anything else. I've settled for the situation you see, and it's surprising how cheerful one can be when one gives up hope. I've still got the memory, you see, which is a very pleasant one—all things considered.

MAJOR POLLOCK: [*Nodding*] I see. Quite the philosopher, what? [*To himself*] I must give up saying what. Well, Meacham or no Meacham, I'm going to make a dash for it, or I'll miss that train.

   [*He turns back to the door*]

MISS COOPER: Why don't you stay?

MAJOR POLLOCK: [*Turning, incredulously*] Stay? In the hotel, you mean?

MISS COOPER: You say you dread the new hotel.

MAJOR POLLOCK: I dread this one a damn sight more, now.

MISS COOPER: Yes, I expect you do. But at least you couldn't be forced by terror into any more Major stuff, could you?

   [*Pause*]

MAJOR POLLOCK: I might be forced into something a good deal more —conclusive—cleaning my old service revolver, perhaps—you know the form—make a nasty mess on one of your carpets and an ugly scandal in your hotel.

MISS COOPER: [*Lightly*] I'd take the risk, if you would.

MAJOR POLLOCK: My dear Miss Cooper, I'm far too much of a coward to stay on here now. Far too much.

MISS COOPER: I see. Pity. I just thought it would be so nice if you could prove to yourself that you weren't.

   [*Pause*]

MAJOR POLLOCK: [*At length*] You're thinking of her too, of course, aren't you?

MISS COOPER: Yes.

MAJOR POLLOCK: Reinstate the gallant ex-soldier in her eyes?

MISS COOPER: That's right.

MAJOR POLLOCK: Make her think she's helped me find my soul and all that.

MISS COOPER: Yes.

[*Another pause*]

MAJOR POLLOCK: [*With an eventual sigh*] Not a hope. Not a hope in the whole, wide, blinking world. I know my form, you see.

MISS COOPER: I wonder if you do.

MAJOR POLLOCK: [*Sadly*] Oh, I do. I do, only too well. Thanks for trying, anyway. [*He looks cautiously out into the hall*] Coast's clear. [*He turns round and looks at her for a long time. She stares back steadily at him. At length*] There's a nine-something train, isn't there?

MISS COOPER: Nine-thirty-two.

[*There is another pause as he looks at her in doubt. Then he gives a shamefaced smile*]

MAJOR POLLOCK: I expect I'll still catch the seven-forty-five.

[*He goes out*]

THE LIGHTS FADE

SCENE TWO

The dining room. It is small, rather bare and quite unpretentious. A door at back leads into the lounge, a swing door upstage right into the kitchen, and another downstage right into the

*hall and the rest of the hotel. Curtained windows are at the left.
Dinner is in full swing. The table by the window is now occupied by a pair of young "casuals"—much interested in each
other, and totally oblivious of everyone else. One table is unoc-
cupied and unlaid; otherwise all the tables are occupied by the
usual owners.*

*As the lights come on, conversation is general—which means,
more precisely, that the two casuals are murmuring together, the*
STRATTONS *are arguing,* LADY MATHESON *and* MR. FOWLER *are
talking between tables, and* MRS. RAILTON-BELL *is talking to*
SIBYL. MABEL, *a waitress, is hovering over* MISS MEACHAM *who is
absorbed in "Racing Up To Date."*

MABEL: [*Heard above the background*] Were you the fricassee or the
cambridge steak?

MISS MEACHAM: What? Oh, it doesn't matter. Both are uneatable.

MABEL: What about the cold chicken, then?

MISS MEACHAM: *Cold* chicken? But we haven't had it hot yet.

MABEL: If I were you I'd have the fricassee. It's all right. It's rabbit.

MISS MEACHAM: The fricassee then.

MR. FOWLER: Any cheese, Mabel?

MABEL: Afraid not.

MR. FOWLER: There's never any cheese.

[MABEL *serves* MISS MEACHAM *and stumps out to the kitchen.*
MRS. RAILTON-BELL *leans across to* LADY MATHESON]

MRS. RAILTON-BELL: I believe there's a new game on television tonight.

LADY MATHESON: Yes. I know, dear. I read all about it in the *Radio
Times*. It sounds quite fascinating—I shall certainly see it next
week.

MRS. RAILTON-BELL: Why not tonight, dear?

LADY MATHESON: I feel too tired. I'm going to go to bed directly after
dinner.

MRS. RAILTON-BELL: Of course. [*Lowering her voice*] What a really
nerve-racking day it's been, hasn't it? I don't suppose any of us will

ever forget it. Ever. I feel utterly shattered, myself. [*To* SIBYL] Pass the sauce dear.

[LADY MATHESON *nods.* MRS. RAILTON-BELL *takes a sip of wine.*
The MAJOR *has walked quietly into the dining room.* MRS.
RAILTON-BELL *turns and stares unbelievingly at him as he walks
slowly to his table and sits down. The conversation in the dining room has frozen into a dead silence, for even the casuals
seem affected by the electric atmosphere—though oblivious of
the cause—and have ceased talking. The silence is broken by*
DOREEN, *another waitress, entering the dining room and seeing
him*]

DOREEN: [*Calling through the kitchen door*] Mabel—Number Seven's in. You said he was out.

MABEL: [*Off*] Well, that's what Joe said. Joe said he was leaving before dinner.

DOREEN: Sorry, Major. There's been a muddle. I'll lay your table right away. [*She goes back into the kitchen. The silence remains unbroken, until* DOREEN *returns with a tray and begins quickly to lay the* MAJOR's *table*] What would you like? The fricassee's nice.

MAJOR POLLOCK: I'll have that. Thank you.

DOREEN: Soup first?

MAJOR POLLOCK: No, thank you.

DOREEN: [*Finally laying the table*] There we are. All cosy now. Fricassee you said?

MAJOR POLLOCK: That's right.

[*She goes into the kitchen.* SIBYL *is staring at the* MAJOR, *but he
does not meet her eyes. He is looking down at his table, as is
everyone else, aware of his presence, save* SIBYL *and* MRS.
RAILTON-BELL *who is glaring furiously in turn at him and at the
others. The silence is broken suddenly by a rather nervously
high-pitched greeting from* CHARLES]

CHARLES: [*To the* MAJOR] Hullo.

MAJOR POLLOCK: [*Murmuring*] Hullo.

CHARLES: Clouding over a bit, isn't it? I'm afraid we may get rain later.

[JEAN *is furiously glaring at her husband.* MRS. RAILTON-BELL *has turned fully round in her chair in an attempt to paralyse him into silence*]

MAJOR POLLOCK: Yes. I'm afraid we may.

MISS MEACHAM: We need it. This hard going's murder on form. [*To* MAJOR POLLOCK] You know Newmarket, don't you?

MAJOR POLLOCK: No, I don't.

MISS MEACHAM: But I remember your saying—[*She gets it*] Oh, I see. Well, it's a very tricky course in hard going. Still if they get some rain up there tomorrow, I think I'll be able to give you a winner on Tuesday.

MAJOR POLLOCK: Thank you. Thank you very much. The only thing is, I may not be here on Tuesday.

MISS MEACHAM: Oh, really? All right. Leave me your address then and I'll wire it to you. I'll need the money for the wire, though.

MAJOR POLLOCK: Thank you. That's very kind of you.

MISS MEACHAM: You won't think it so kind of me, if it loses.

[*She goes back to her* "Racing Up To Date." MISS COOPER *comes in*]

MISS COOPER: [*Brightly*] Good evening, Mrs. Railton-Bell. Good evening, Lady Matheson. Good evening, Mr. Pollock. [*The* "Mr." *is barely distinguishable from* "Major," *and her voice is as brightly* "managerial" *to him as to the others*] I hear they didn't lay your table tonight. I'm so sorry.

MAJOR POLLOCK: Quite all right.

MISS COOPER: I'd advise the fricassee, if I were you. It's really awfully nice.

MAJOR POLLOCK: I've ordered it.

MISS COOPER: Good, I'm so glad. [*She passes on*] Good evening, Mr. and Mrs. Stratton. Everything all right? [*They nod and smile*] Splendid.

[*She bows rather less warmly to "the casuals" and goes out.* MRS. RAILTON-BELL *pretends to feel an imaginary draft*]

MRS. RAILTON-BELL: [To LADY MATHESON] It's very cold in here suddenly, don't you think, dear? [LADY MATHESON *nods, nervously*] I'll think I'll turn my chair round a bit, and get out of the draft.

[*She does so, turning her back neatly on the* MAJOR. MR. FOWLER *gets up quietly from his table and walks to the door. To do this he has to pass the* MAJOR. *A step or so past him he hesitates and then looks back, nods and smiles*]

MR. FOWLER: Good evening.

MAJOR POLLOCK: Good evening.

[MRS. RAILTON-BELL *has had to twist her head sharply round in order to allow her eyes to confirm this shameful betrayal*]

MR. FOWLER: Hampshire did pretty well today, did you see? Three hundred and eighty-odd for five.

MAJOR POLLOCK: Very good.

MR. FOWLER: I wish they had more bowling. Well——

[*He smiles vaguely and goes on into the lounge. There is an audible and outraged "Well!" from* MRS. RAILTON-BELL. *Silence falls again. Suddenly and by an accident the* MAJOR's *and* LADY MATHESON's *eyes meet. Automatically she inclines her head and gives him a slight smile. He returns the salute*]

LADY MATHESON: [To MAJOR POLLOCK] Good evening.

MRS. RAILTON-BELL: [In a whisper] Gladys!

[LADY MATHESON, *who has genuinely acted from instinct, looks startled. Then she apparently decides to be as well hanged for a sheep as a lamb*]

LADY MATHESON: [*Suddenly very bold, and in a loud voice*] I advise the apple charlotte. It's very good.

MAJOR POLLOCK: Thank you. I'll have that.

[*She is instantly conscience-stricken at what she has done and hangs her head over her apple charlotte, eating feverishly. She refuses to look at* MRS. RAILTON-BELL, *who is staring at her with wide, unbelieving and furious eyes.* MRS. RAILTON-BELL, *getting no response from* LADY MATHESON, *deliberately folds her napkin and rises*]

MRS. RAILTON-BELL: [*Quietly*] Come, Sibyl.

SIBYL: [*Equally quietly*] I haven't finished yet, Mummy.

MRS. RAILTON-BELL: [*Looking puzzled at this unaccustomed response*] It doesn't matter, dear. Come into the lounge.

[SIBYL *makes no move to rise. She stares up at her mother. There is a pause*]

SIBYL: No, Mummy.

[*Pause*]

MRS. RAILTON-BELL: [*Sharply*] Sibyl, come with me at once——

SIBYL: [*With quiet firmness*] No, Mummy. I'm going to stay in the dining room, and finish my dinner. [MRS. RAILTON-BELL *hesitates, plainly meditating various courses of action. Finally she decides on the only really possible course left to her—the dignified exit. Before she has got to the door* SIBYL *has spoken to the* MAJOR] There's a new moon tonight, you know. We must all go and look at it afterwards.

MAJOR POLLOCK: Yes. We must.

[DOREEN *has bustled in with the* MAJOR'*s dish as* MRS. RAILTON-BELL, *her world crumbling, goes into the lounge.* DOREEN *serves* MAJOR POLLOCK]

DOREEN: Sorry it's been so long. You're a bit late, you see.

MAJOR POLLOCK: Yes. My fault.

DOREEN: What's the matter with you tonight? You always say "mea culpa."

[*She beats her breast in imitation of an obvious* MAJOR *bon mot*]

MAJOR POLLOCK: Do I? Well—they both mean the same, don't they?

DOREEN: I suppose so. [*Finishing the serving*] There you are. Now what about breakfast?

MAJOR POLLOCK: Breakfast?

DOREEN: Joe got it wrong about your going, didn't he?

[*There is a pause.* SIBYL *is looking steadily at the* MAJOR, *who now raises his eyes from his plate and meets her glance*]

MAJOR POLLOCK: [*Quietly, at length*] Yes, he did.

DOREEN: That's good. Breakfast usual time, then?

MAJOR POLLOCK: Yes, Doreen. Breakfast usual time.

[DOREEN *goes into the kitchen.* MAJOR POLLOCK *begins to eat his fricassee.* SIBYL *continues to eat her sweet. A decorous silence, broken only by the renewed murmur of "the casuals," reigns once more, and the dining room of the Beauregard Private Hotel no longer gives any sign of the battle that has just been fought and won between its four, bare walls.*]

CURTAIN

THE PRIMARY ENGLISH CLASS

Israel Horovitz

Israel Horovitz

With Diane Keaton as the inept, frenzied, and, finally, pathetic schoolteacher, Israel Horovitz' *The Primary English Class* was one of the highlights of the 1976 Off-Broadway season. Both play and performance were greeted with plaudits from the press. Clive Barnes described it in the New York *Times* as "a gem of an idea with a quite extraordinary flash of comic insight." Others termed it "an hilarious comedy of pathos by one of our most original playwrights" that provided "non-stop hilarity." Audiences agreed, and the comedy had a substantial run in New York while a Canadian company performed it for two seasons in Toronto, followed by a nationwide tour.

Mr. Horovitz won his first acclaim in 1968 with *The Indian Wants the Bronx*, a powerful and terrifying study of violence on a New York street. A striking Off-Broadway success with Al Pacino in the pivotal role, it also scored heavily in other major American cities, at the 1968 Spoleto Festival (Italy), the World Theatre Festival in England (1969), as well as in numerous other foreign countries. The play won a 1968 Drama Desk-Vernon Rice Award and three Obies, as well as a commendation from *Newsweek* magazine citing the author as one of the three most original dramatists of the year.

Israel Horovitz was born on March 31, 1939, in Wakefield, Massachusetts. After completing his domestic studies, he journeyed to London to continue his education at the Royal Academy of Dramatic Art and in 1965 became the first American to be chosen as playwright-in-residence with Britain's celebrated Royal Shakespeare Company.

His first play, *The Comeback*, was written when he was seventeen; it was produced in Boston in 1960. In the decade that followed, Mr. Horovitz' plays tenanted many stages of the world. Among them: *It's Called the Sugar Plum* (paired with *The Indian Wants the*

Bronx on the New York stage); *The Death of Bernard the Believer*; *Rats*; *Morning* (originally titled *Chiaroscuro*, it was initially performed at the Spoleto Festival and later on a triple bill, *Morning, Noon and Night*, Henry Miller's Theatre, New York, 1968); *Trees*; *Acrobats*; *Line* (now in its fifth season in a French-language production in Paris); *Leader*; and *The Honest-to-God Schnozzola* (for which he won a 1969 Off-Broadway Obie Award).

His other works for the stage include: *Shooting Gallery*; *Dr. Hero* (presented at Amherst and various other colleges as well as Off-Broadway by the Shade Company, 1973); *Turnstile*; *The Quanna-powitt Quartet* (four short plays designed to be performed on two double-bills: *Hopscotch, The 75th, Stage Directions, Spared*); and *The Reason We Eat*, which held its world premiere at the Hartman Theatre, Stamford, Connecticut, in November 1976 with Academy Award-winning actress Estelle Parsons in one of the principal roles.

Mr. Horovitz' most ambitious project to date is his full-length trilogy *The Wakefield Plays*. Set in Wakefield, Massachusetts, where he grew up, the three plays are *Alfred the Great, Our Father's Failing*, and *Alfred Dies*, and they are scheduled for a major Broadway production in the near future.

A collection of his plays, *First Season*, was published in 1968. His first novel, *Cappella*, was issued in 1973, followed by a novella, *Nobody Loves Me*, in 1975.

Twice the recipient of a Rockefeller Foundation Playwriting Fellowship, he also won a similar fellowship from the Creative Artists Program Service, funded by the New York State Council on the Arts. In 1972 he received an Award in Literature from the American Academy of Arts and Letters, and in 1973 he was honored with a National Endowment for the Arts Award.

The author, who divides his time between New York and Massachusetts, with frequent sojourns in France, also has written several major screenplays, notably *The Strawberry Statement*, which won the Prix de Jury, Cannes Film Festival, 1970.

THE PEOPLE OF THE PLAY

SMIEDNIK, *a Polish man*
PATUMIERA, *an Italian man*
LAPOUBELLE, *a French man*
MULLEIMER, *a German man*

MRS. PONG, *a Chinese woman*
YOKO KUZUKAGO, *a Japanese woman*
WASTBA, *an American woman*

THE PLACE: *Classroom.*

THE TIME: *Night.*

AUTHOR'S NOTE

Simultaneous translation is at times wanted.

These points of translation have been carefully selected to establish a vocabulary for the audience, as well as to sustain the presence of the translator's voice.

Such translation should be heard over speakers, in the auditorium. The translators must not be seen by the audience.

Translators' voices should reflect emotional reality of voice being translated, but should be subdued in tone: understated, slightly.

Whenever possible, both a male and female translator should be employed so that sex of translator might match sex of person being translated.

Action should never stop for translation, but should instead slow down, establishing rather a convention than a style.

Night. Square box classroom, white plaster walls, wainscoting white as well. Trim color orange. Room reminiscent of handball court: orange lines cut room in court pattern.

Twelve singular orange student desks, backs of five to upstage wall, four to stage-left wall, three downstage, between audience and center stage.

Small bright orange teacher's desk, stage-right wall. Straight-legged variety: teacher's legs and lower trunk constantly exposed to class. Orange wastebasket foot of desk. Wires on stage-left wall protrude from small circular cut: clock missing, taken from this spot. Circular shadow visible.

A janitor, SMIEDNIK, is upstage left, mopping the floor of the classroom. He is stout, uses regulation-size mop. In dark, we hear Bulgarina folk music. Then SMIEDNIK sings. Then lights up. SMIEDNIK sings "I Can't Give You Anything But Love . . . Baby . . ." in Polish. Uses the recognizable melody.

SMIEDNIK:
Nie mogę, ci dać niczego oprócz *baby*
To jest wszystko co mam, *baby*
Śuij troszeczkę, knuj tioszeczkę
Napewno znajdziesz . . .
Szczęścia i, myśle tak,
Wszystko czego kiedyś chciateś
Gee, bym cheiał cię widzieć
w bujlautach, *baby*
Tahidi któzych nie ma u Woolworta
Ale dokąd jeszcze nie mozemy, *Baby!*

[He stops mopping and gestures as though a nightclub performer in the throes of a big finish]

Nie mogę ci dać nic oprócz, mnie!
Nie mogę ci dać nic oprócz, *baby!*

[*In silence now, he straightens row of chairs.* SMIEDNIK *empties trash can and notices that the clock has been stolen from the wall. He mutters in Polish*]

Psaw krcw skradły by buty, gdybym nie uwigzat do nóg. [*He spits*] Pteww! [SMIEDNIK *gathers his mop into his pail now and goes to door. He opens door and sees that lights are out in the hall*] Gdzie do cholery swaitło? [*Pokes head out*] Ciemno! [*Looks at light in room*] Gównol [*Pokes head outside*] Jest tam kto???

[*No response. He gathers mop and pail again and moves into hallway. Ten count. There is no one on stage.* PATUMIERA *enters the room. He believes himself to be a movie-star type. IIis shirt is silk, open, with a silk ascot, loosely tied. His sunglasses are blue. He carries a black leather briefcase, barristers' variety, plus a second case of the attaché variety, black. He also carries a small black canvas duffel-bag. Several slips of paper are wedged between his teeth and lips. He spins twice in the center of the room, looking for a clock. He tries to lift his arm to look at his own wristwatch, but, due to the weight of his load, he cannot raise his wrist above his waist. He tries twice more and fails twice more. He finally stoops his face to his waist and reads his watch. He mutters, as he closes door to room. He is gasping for breath: winded*]

PATUMIERA: Chiami un' ambulanza.

TRANSLATOR'S VOICE: Call me an ambulance.

[PATUMIERA *falls into the center chair, downstage wall. Thus, he is alone on stage and his back is to the audience. He sits a moment, before muttering again*]

PATUMIERA: Chiama un dottore.

TRANSLATOR'S VOICE: Call me a doctor.

[*He throws his duffel-bag straight upstage. It lands at the feet of the second student-chair on the upstage wall. He throws his black attaché case to the same chair and then he throws his black briefcase to the same spot. He stands, papers still in mouth, and staggers to the chosen upstage wall chair, falls into it, exhausted. He removes his ascot and blue gabardine suitcoat and folds them into his black attaché case. He removes a tangerine from the black duffel-bag, peels it and tries to eat it, but the papers are still in his mouth. He removes them and eats the tangerine. The door opens and* PATUMIERA *wheels around to see who's come into the room. He smiles, assuming he's about to meet his teacher.* MONSIEUR LAPOUBELLE *enters. He is handsome, nearly bald, and diminutive. He wears extremely tight-fitting clothes: gray trousers and a black sweater with a silk scarf at the neck. He carries several papers in his mouth, but at the same time clenches a cigarette between his lips. He carries a cartable-type French book-satchel on his back and a brown leather briefcase in his left hand. In his right hand, he carries a sport coat and an overcoat and a smashed umbrella. He is also gasping air: winded. He collapses a moment on teacher's desk, causing* PATUMIERA *to believe that* LAPOUBELLE *is in fact the teacher.* PATUMIERA *stands and smiles.* LAPOUBELLE *mutters as he closes door]*

LAPOUBELLE: Appellez une ambulance.

TRANSLATOR'S VOICE: Call me an ambulance.

LAPOUBELLE: Appellez un medecin.

TRANSLATOR'S VOICE: Call me a doctor.

[LAPOUBELLE *staggers to exactly the same downstage chair first chosen by* PATUMIERA. *He drops his load and falls into it]*

LAPOUBELLE: Merde alors! Zut alors! Fi donc! Bordel!

TRANSLATOR: Crap! Bitch! Damn! Heck!

PATUMIERA: Parla Lei inglese?

TRANSLATOR: You speak English?

LAPOUBELLE: Quoi? . . . Répétez, s'il vous plaît.

PATUMIERA: [*Smiling*] Parla Lei Eengleesh?

[LAPOUBELLE *stands, drags his load across the room and sits beside* PATUMIERA]

LAPOUBELLE: Je comprends un peu.

TRANSLATOR: Yes, I understand a little.

PATUMIERA: Voi siete Francese? Io non parlo. Credo che sono l'unico Italiano nel mondo chi non parla Francese . . .

TRANSLATOR: You're French, right? That's a bad break. I must be the only Italian in the world who doesn't speak a word of French . . .

PATUMIERA: È straordinario quante lingue non parlo.

TRANSLATOR: It's amazing how many languages I don't speak.

PATUMIERA: Italiano è . . . come se dice . . . *tutta*.

TRANSLATOR: Italian is, you might say, *it*.

LAPOUBELLE: Je m'excuse, mais, je suis fatigué . . .

TRANSLATOR: Excuse me, but I'm a little tired . . .

PATUMIERA: [*Grabs* LAPOUBELLE's *hand, shakes it*] Piacere della Sua conoscenza. Il suo nome?

TRANSLATOR: It's a pleasure to meet you. Your name?

LAPOUBELLE: Quoi?

PATUMIERA: Signor Quoi?

LAPOUBELLE: Mister LaPoubelle.

PATUMIERA: Non capisco. Scusi.

LAPOUBELLE: Je m'appelle Jean-Michel LaPoubelle.

TRANSLATOR: My name is Jean Michel LaPoubelle.

PATUMIERA: [*Taking his hand again*] Come si chiama, signore?

LAPOUBELLE: Monsieur Chiama, alors?

PATUMIERA: Scusi?

LAPOUBELLE: Vous êtes Meester Chiama, n'est-ce-pas?

PATUMIERA: Meester . . . ? [*Laughs*] Heyyy! No, no, no . . . [*Speaks very slowly indeed*] Io suo nomo Meester Carlo Fredriko Rizzonini LaPatumiera . . .

TRANSLATOR: My name is Carlo Fredriko Rizzonini LaPatumiera . . .

LAPOUBELLE: Patooo . . . miera?

PATUMIERA: [*Adds with a bit of embarrassment*] La Patumiera.

LAPOUBELLE: [*Smiles*] Parlez-vous anglais?

PATUMIERA: [*Smiling as well*] Scusi?

LAPOUBELLE: Excusez-moi. [*Pauses, smiles*] J'ai complètement oublié
. . . [*Speaks in English with an extraordinarily thick accent*] Do
. . . yooo . . . speeks . . . in theee . . . Anglais? [PATUMIERA
smiles, but does not reply] Anglais? [*No reply. Suddenly*
LAPOUBELLE *slaps his own forehead*] Non pas Anglais . . . c'est
Eeengleesh, eh? [*Smiles and uses his hands now as he speaks, pan-
tomiming the pulling of each word from his own mouth*] Do . . .
yooo . . . speeks . . . in the Eengleesh?

PATUMIERA: [*Misunderstanding the hand signals for gestures of eating*] Una morte di fame Io. Qui mangiano solo roba da animali.
Roba che ti distrugge il cervello. Buona per porci, forse. Non di
certo per la gente!

TRANSLATOR: I'll say I'm hungry. All they eat here is animal food. It
destroys the brain. Fit for pigs not people.

PATUMIERA: Ho ordinato una pastasciutta, giu . . . Cosi spappolata
da restar tutta attaccata alla parete.

TRANSLATOR: I ordered a pasta downstairs . . . for snack . . . It was
so overcooked, it stuck to the wall.

PATUMIERA: Non credo che siano stati contenti del fatta che l'ho
sbattuta contro la parete ma . . .

TRANSLATOR: Hey, I don't think they appreciated me throwing it
against the wall, but . . .

LAPOUBELLE: [*After a long pause*] Dooo . . . yooo . . . speeks in the
Eeengleesh?

PATUMIERA: Eeengleesh?

LAPOUBELLE: C'est quoi? Ce n'est pas "Eeengleesh?" [*Slaps head,
laughs*] Ahhh-oui! [*Corrects himself*] C'est *Ahhngleesh* . . .

PATUMIERA: [*Smiling*] C'est? [*Confused*] Enngleesh? [*Recognizes
word, he laughs*] Ah! Si! Si si! Si si si! *Eeengleesh!*

[*Silence*]

LAPOUBELLE: I . . . habit . . . à . . . from . . . Paris . . . up unteel
. . . *Merde!*

PATUMIERA: Merda?

[LAPOUBELLE *opens briefcase, finds French/English dictionary,
begins to look for words*]

LAPOUBELLE: Excusez-moi, cher Monsieur Patchuli . . .

PATUMIERA: Patumiera!

LAPOUBELLE: [*Looking up, slightly annoyed*] Ah, oui, bien, sûr . . . Patoo . . .

PATUMIERA: . . . ccc—air—rah . . . Patumiera . . .

LAPOUBELLE: Oui. Bon.

PATUMIERA: Le piacciono le pellicole americane?

TRANSLATOR: Do you like American movies?

LAPOUBELLE: Qu'est-ce que vous avez dit?

TRANSLATOR: What did you say?

PATUMIERA: [*Pauses*] . . . non si preoccupi! [*He rushes to his desk, opens briefcase and grabs his Italian/English dictionary*]

LAPOUBELLE: [*Searching in his dictionary*] Une seconde . . . [*Reading*] Hibou . . . hic . . . hideux . . . ben, merde, alors! . . . [*Finds his words*] Alilili-oui! Hier! [*Reads*] Yez-ter-dai . . . [*Corrects himself*] Yester . . . dayii . . .

PATUMIERA: [*Smiling, doesn't look up from his own dictionary*] Aspeta momento . . .

LAPOUBELLE: [*Suddenly angry*] Merde alors! Fi donc! Zut alors! Bordel!

PATUMIERA: Che è successo?

LAPOUBELLE: [*Explaining, in French*] Ce n'est pas *yester*-quoi . . . vous savez . . .

PATUMIERA: Uno momento!

LAPOUBELLE: C'est avant hier . . .

PATUMIERA: Uno momento.

LAPOUBELLE: . . . non pas hier!

PATUMIERA: [*Looks up and smiles again*] Non si preoccupi, eh? [*Back into his dictionary again*]

LAPOUBELLE: [*Screams*] Regardez-moi! Je veux qu'on s'occupe de moi!

PATUMIERA: [*Angrily*] Basta!

LAPOUBELLE: Basta?

PATUMIERA: Basta!

LAPOUBELLE: [*Not laughing now, but instead quizzical*] Basta?

PATUMIERA: [*Simply, confused*] Si, basta.

LAPOUBELLE: Je connais le mot *basta*. C'est italien, alors!

TRANSLATOR: I know the word *basta*. It's Italian, right?

PATUMIERA: [*Ashamed of himself now*] Si, basta. [*Shrugs*] Scusi, eh?

LAPOUBELLE: C'est certainement italien . . . [*Smiles*] Vous êtes italien?

PATUMIERA: Italien?

LAPOUBELLE: Oui, oui. Vous. Italien?

PATUMIERA: [*Realizes he is finally understood. Very pleased*] Si. Si si. Si si si. [*Laughing and smiling. He shakes* LAPOUBELLE'S *hand again*] Mi chiamo Carlo Fredriko Rizzonini La Patumiera . . . [*Smiles, leans back. Smiles again*] Come si chiama, signor? [*There is a long pause*]

LAPOUBELLE: Incroyable. Je parle anglais mieux que je parle italien.

TRANSLATOR: Incredible. I speak English better than I speak Italian.

PATUMIERA: Scusi?

LAPOUBELLE: Scusi? Je fais trois mille kolometer pour me trouver en face d'un plat de ravioli.

TRANSLATOR: I have to travel three thousand miles to end up in a room with a plate of ravioli.

PATUMIERA: Scusi?

LAPOUBELLE: Je dois être le seul Français au monde qui ne parle aucune autre langue. Que la sienne—c'est notre tare familiale. Les langues . . .

TRANSLATOR: I must be the only Frenchman in the world who speaks absolutely no other language than French. Language is my family curse.

[PATUMIERA *is working at dictionary and phrasebook*]

LAPOUBELLE: Je suis désolé d'avoir crié. Vraiment. Ce n'est pas dans mes habitudes. Pas du tout. Je suis en fait un type tranquil.

TRANSLATOR'S VOICE: I'm sorry I yelled. I really am. It's not like me. Not at all. I'm really a quiet guy.

LAPOUBELLE: La vérité c'est que je suis plutôt bien connu . . . pour être tranquil.

TRANSLATOR'S VOICE: The fact of the matter is, I'm rather well known . . . for being quiet.

LAPOUBELLE: Je dois avoir des soucis.

TRANSLATOR'S VOICE: I must be anxious.

LAPOUBELLE: Evidement j'ai des soucis! Qui n'en aurait pas à ma place?

TRANSLATOR'S VOICE: Of course I'm anxious! Who wouldn't be?

LAPOUBELLE: Se taper six étages et dans le noir en plus! Mais qu'est-ce qu'elles ont, ces fichues lumières?

TRANSLATOR'S VOICE: Climbing a million stairs in pitch black. What the hell's the matter with the lights out there?

LAPOUBELLE: Je crois qu'on vient de m'empoisonner. En bas. J'ai commandé et mangé un petit bout de saucisson. Pour boucher un trou. Comme nourriture, ça avait l'air d'être destiné à notre ami le cochon plutôt que d'en provenir.

TRANSLATOR'S VOICE: I think I was poisoned just now. Downstairs. I ordered and ate a little drop of sausage . . . for a snack . . . It wasn't food *from* our friend, the pig, it was food *for* our friend the pig!

LAPOUBELLE: Mon estomas fait de ces bruits impardonables. Je suis absolument navré.

TRANSLATOR'S VOICE: My stomach is making unforgivable sounds. I am desperately sorry.

[PATUMIERA *suddenly throws down his dictionary after scratching forever on a piece of paper. He extends his arms, as if to say,* "Now, I understand." LAPOUBELLE *takes* PATUMIERA's *gesture to mean* "Now, I understand." LAPOUBELLE *smiles*]

PATUMIERA: [*With an enormous smile on his face and notes in hand*] Dooo . . . yooo . . . liiiike . . . Ahhmerican . . . moo-fies?

LAPOUBELLE: Je ne comprends pas?

PATUMIERA: [*Pulling each word from his mouth, speaks extraordinarily slowly*] Dooo . . . yooo . . . liiiike . . . Ahmerican moo-fies?

LAPOUBELLE: [*Still thinks* PATUMIERA *is commenting on his illness*] Oui, j'ai mai à l'estomac . . . C'est affreux . . .

TRANSLATOR: Yes, I've got an awful bellyache.

PATUMIERA: [*Tries again, still smiling. This time he offers* LAPOUBELLE *an* 8×10 *glossy resume photograph of himself, which* PATUMIERA *holds next to his own face, for comparison*] Dooo . . . yooo . . . liiiike . . . Ahmerican moofies? [*Smiles more than ever*] Ahhh dooo lotz. [LAPOUBELLE *takes* PATUMIERA's 8×10 *glossy photograph from him, comparing the man and the face.* PATUMIERA *takes* LA-POUBELLE's *pen*] Ha lei una penna?

LAPOUBELLE: La stylo . . . ? Oui, s'il vous plaît? [LAPOUBELLE *looks at photo, smiles.* PATUMIERA *takes back photo and autographs same and hands it back to* LAPOUBELLE *who looks at same and laughs.* PATUMIERA *pockets* LAPOUBELLE's *pen*] . . . mon cher Monsieur . . . Ah, ma stylo. [PATUMIERA *gives back pen to* LAPOUBELLE, *who is laughing out of control now*] C'est drôle!

PATUMIERA: [*Grabbing photograph away from* LAPOUBELLE] Che è successo?

TRANSLATOR: What's going on?

LAPOUBELLE: [*Laughing still out of control*] Mon Dieu! [*Doubled over*] Ma tête! [*Leaning on his desk*] Excusez-moi, cher monsieur . . . c'est drôle, *hein*?

PATUMIERA: [*Angrily*] Basta! Questa è la mia faccia a tu stai ridendo, biscotti.

TRANSLATOR: That's my face you're laughing at, cupcake.

LAPOUBELLE: Ça va, bien. Tien! [*Pauses*] Que j'ai mal à la tête! Mais mon Dieu! [*Turns to* PATUMIERA *again*] Il faut que nous speekons thee Eenglish now, hein? [*Thumbs through his dictionary*] Ecoutez! Yooo haf . . . how many . . . years?

PATUMIERA: Non capisco. Scusi. [*His feelings are hurt*]

LAPOUBELLE: [*Repeats himself, but slowly*] Yoo haf . . . how many years?

PATUMIERA: Non capisco. Scusi. [*Paces, refuses to answer. His feelings are still hurt*]

LAPOUBELLE: [*Angry now*] "Non capisco. Non capisco." C'est tout ce que vous savez dire? "Non capisco."

PATUMIERA: Calma, calma, Signor Pooblini . . .

LAPOUBELLE: Poubelle . . . LaPoubelle. Je m'appelle LaPoubelle. C'est facile, LaPoubelle! Vous voulez voir! [LAPOUBELLE *walks to the wastebasket that is positioned at front left leg of teacher's desk. He lifts wastebasket and waves it in* PATUMIERA's *face*] Regardez mon nom! LaPoubelle. Oui-oui, je sais. [*Shrugs. Set down wastebasket*] C'est exactment le même mot: LaPoubelle. C'est ne pas banal, hein?

PATUMIERA: [*Extremely confused now*] Scusi . . . [*Shrugs*] Non capisco . . . [*Holds up hands so as to not be yelled at by* LA-POUBELLE] I suo nome LAPOUBELLE? [*Smiles and picks up wastebasket*] Mi chiamo la Patumiera . . . [*No reply; louder*] Io sono Carlo Fredriko Rizzonini La Patumiera . . . [*Waves waste-baskot*] *La Patumiera!*

[LAPOUBELLE *begins to understand. Points to wastebasket*]

LAPOUBELLE: Patumier . . . quoi?

PATUMIERA: Patumiera. [*Begins to realize*] LaPoubelle?

LAPOUBELLE: Oui, LaPoubelle!

PATUMIERA: LaPoubelle?

LAPOUBELLE: Patumiera?

[*They both laugh now, understanding that they share the same name. They embrace, clapping each other's back.* LAPOUBELLE *sets wastebasket down again on its proper spot as they continue to laugh and point to wastebasket time and time again, stretching the moment out as long as they can before they fall again into embarrassed silence. They return to their seats. Each begins to thumb through his dictionary. Now man enters,* MULLEIMER. *He is dressed in grey slacks, black blazer with club patch, white shirt, striped tie, maroon sleeveless vest-sweater underneath jacket. He carries several briefcases and sacks. He wears incredibly thick eyeglasses. He holds papers in his mouth. Two cameras are strapped across his chest. He wears a raincoat over all, which he will soon try to remove without first removing cameras. He is totally breathless. He leans upon teacher's desk in state of near-collapse, attempting to regain normal breathing. Both* LA-POUBELLE *and* PATUMIERA *assume that* MULLEIMER *is the teacher, because he is at teacher's desk. They stand behind their desks and smile at* MULLEIMER, *who finally notices them and speaks, smiling as well*]

MULLEIMER: Ach du liebe Scheisse! [*Collapses into chair*] Ach du liebe heilige Scheisse! [*Throws his briefcase on floor*] Ich krieg noch einen Herzschlag! [*Heaves his chest*] Ich glaube ich hab' einen Herz Anfall!

TRANSLATOR: Holy crap! Holy jumping crap! I'm having a heart attack! I think I'm in coronary arrest!

MULLEIMER: Warum brennen denn die Lampen draussen nicht? Bin doch Kein Kananchen, ha, ha!

TRANSLATOR: Why the hell are the lights out out there? I'm not a rabbit!

MULLEIMER: [*Looks at other men*] Was ist denn für cinc beschissene Schule hier? Sechs Treppen hoch und Kein Fahrstuhl!

TRANSLATOR: What the hell kind of a school is this anyway? Six flights up and no elevator!

MULLEIMER: Für was halten die uns?

TRANSLATOR: What do they take us for?

MULLEIMER: Kancgeruhs? [*Laughs at his own joke*] Hah-hah-hah! [*Pauses; notices other men staring. Checks his fly zipper*] Was glotzen Sie mich denn so an?

TRANSLATOR: What are you staring at?

MULLEIMER: Haben Sie noch nie jemand mit einer Brille gesehen?

TRANSLATOR: Haven't you ever seen a man with eyeglasses before?

LAPOUBELLE: Qui êtes-vous?

TRANSLATOR: Who are you?

PATUMIERA: Credo di essere nella stanza sbagliata. [*Stands; smiles to* LAPOUBELLE]

TRANSLATOR: I think I'm in the wrong room.

PATUMIERA: Credo di essere nella classe sbagliata. [*Gathers his many briefcases and papers*] Fottiti, piscione! [*Walks to door. Looks at number on door. Looks at paper in teeth*] Il numero e' lo stesso.

TRANSLATOR: The number's the same.

MULLEIMER: Tut mir leid, aber ich spreche kein Englisch.

TRANSLATOR: Sorry, but I don't speak any English.

PATUMIERA: Che hai detto?

MULLEIMER: Das ist doch nicht Englisch.

TRANSLATOR: That's not English.

PATUMIERA: Credevo che questa fosse la classe per l'Inglese elementare.

TRANSLATOR: I thought that this was the Primary English Class.

MULLEIMER: Mir Klingt das mehr wie Spanisch.

TRANSLATOR: That sounds like Spanish to me.

PATUMIERA: Sono nella stanza sbagliata. Scusi.

TRANSLATOR: I'm in the wrong room. Excuse me.

[*It is here that* MULLEIMER *begins to entangle himself in his raincoat, which he has tried to remove without first removing the cameras that are strapped across his chest*]

MULLEIMER: Ich glaub' ich hab' mich in Zimmer geirrt. Entschuldigung.

TRANSLATOR: I'm in the wrong room. Excuse me.

LAPOUBELLE. [*Stands*] Ca m'étonne que ça m'arrive à moi, mais il me semble que je me suis trompé de salle. Sacre bleu!

TRANSLATOR: I'm in the wrong room. Excuse me.

[*They all crowd to the door. They all exit and the stage is absolutely empty for a count of ten.* LAPOUBELLE *is first to return*]

LAPOUBELLE: Moi, j'ai raison, eux, ils ont tort.

TRANSLATOR: I'm right, they're wrong.

PATUMIERA: [*Enters quickly; smiling*] Io ho ragione, loro hanno torto.

TRANSLATOR: I'm right, they're wrong.

MULLEIMER: [*Enters scratching head*] Ich hab'recht, Sie nicht.

TRANSLATOR: I'm right: you're wrong.

PATUMIERA: Alemno ci sta la luce. Un po basso ma la luce.

TRANSLATOR: At least the lights are on. Dim, but on.

MULLEIMER: Wenigstens brennen die Lampen wieder, Trübe, aber doch.

TRANSLATOR: At least the lights are on. Dim, but on.

LAPOUBELLE: Au moins il y a de la lumière. Pas beaucoup, mais enfin.

TRANSLATOR: At least the lights are on. Dim, but on.

LAPOUBELLE: Je m'excuse, mais je ne parle pas norvègien.

TRANSLATOR: Excuse me, I don't speak Norwegian.

PATUMIERA: Mi dispiace, ma non parlo olandese.

TRANSLATOR: Excuse me, I don't speak Dutch.

MULLEIMER: Tut mir leid, aber ich spreche weder Flamisch noch Portugiesisch . . . Spreche auch weder Franzoesisch, Englisch, Italienisch, Griechisch noch Hebraeisch.

TRANSLATOR: Excuse me, I don't speak either Flemish or Portuguese. I can't speak French, Italian, English, Greek or Hebrew, either.

MULLEIMER: Meine einzige Zunge ist und bleibt Deutsch.

TRANSLATOR: Actually, German's just about it for me.

[*They all sit. Smile. Silence*]

MULLEIMER: Mein Namme ist Mülleimer. [*He picks up and points to wastebasket as he says his name*]

TRANSLATOR: My name is Mülleimer.

MULLEIMER: Fritz Mülleimer.

LAPOUBELLE: [*Looks at wastebasket and then waves casually to* MULLEIMER] Oui, oui, je m'appelle LaPoubelle.

PATUMIERA: [*Looks at wastebasket at same time and also waves casually to* MULLEIMER] Si, si. Io sono la Patumiera . . . [*Smiles across to* LAPOUBELLE] Si, si, si, si si si. La Poubelle!

LAPOUBELLE: [*Smiles across to* PATUMIERA] Oui, oui, oui, oui oui oui. La Patumiera, aussi!

MULLEIMER: [*Smiling into his confusion*] Ja. Ja-ja. Ja-ja-ja. [*Pauses: sets basket down*] Wie, bitte?

LAPOUBELLE: Comment vous appellez-vous? Je m'appelle LaPoubelle.

[LAPOUBELLE *and* MULLEIMER *smile at one another. After a long pause,* PATUMIERA *speaks, English phrasebook in hands. Waving to indicate that the room is warm*]

PATUMIERA: [*In English*] I . . . canno breth. I . . . canno breth . . .
[*Smiles. He offers a raisin to* MULLEIMER *and* LAPOUBELLE *after
reading word on box*] Want uno ray-zeen?

MULLEIMER: Nein   danke,   bin   LAPOUBELLE: Non, Merci. J'en ai
satt.   jusque là . . .

TRANSLATOR: No thanks, stuffed.   TRANSLATOR: No,   thank   you.
                                              Stuffed.

PATUMIERA: [*He waves his arm again to indicate that it is warm in
the room. He repeats his newly learned English idiom*] I . . .
canno . . . breth . . . [*He is gaily popping raisins into his mouth.*
LAPOUBELLE *repeats his last word, in English*]

LAPOUBELLE: Breth? . . . [LAPOUBELLE *begins to look for word in his
French/English dictionary*] Breth? . . . Je chercherai . . .

TRANSLATOR: Breth? I'll look it up. [*A raisin lodges in* PATUMIERA's
*throat. He chokes. He will begin now to make incredible sounds,
wheezes, and groans. He will whack his own back, crawl about the
floor near his desk, flail his arms and his face will become bright
red in color. No one will pay close attention*]

MULLEIMER: [*Interrupting* LAPOUBELLE's *dictionary search*] Es tut
mir Leid, aber ich spreche kein Portugiesisch.

[LAPOUBELLE *looks up absently at* MULLEIMER, *who is standing
next to him, smiling broadly*]

LAPOUBELLE: Comment?

MULLEIMER: Es tut mir Leid, aber ich spreche kein Portugiesisch.

TRANSLATOR: I'm sorry, but I don't speak Portuguese.

LAPOUBELLE: [*Takes phrasebook*] Vous permettez, s'il vous plaît? I
. . . canno' breth, eh? Breth?

PATUMIERA: [*Reads as he chokes. Repeats in English*] I . . . canno
. . . breth . . .

LAPOUBELLE: Breth, eh? Ça va. D'accord. Je chercherai . . .

TRANSLATOR: "Breth," huh? Okay, then. I'll look it up . . .

MULLEIMER: Das ist doch die Anfängerklasse für Englisch hier, ja?

TRANSLATOR: This is the primary English class, right?

MULLEIMER: [*After no response*] Kann hier denn keiner sprechen?

TRANSLATOR: Well, how come nobody knows how to talk in here?

[*No response.* LAPOUBELLE *is busily looking up the word "Breth" in his dictionary.* PATUMIERA *is whacking himself on the back and dying.* MULLEIMER, *cleaning his glasses, sees nothing*]

MULLEIMER: Sie müssen wissen Ich habe fast zehn Jahre gespart, un hier herzukommen . . . in dieses Land.

TRANSLATOR: I'd like you to know that I saved my money nearly ten years to come here . . . to this country.

MULLEIMER: Und Unterwegs wäre ich beinahe umgebracht worden, im Flugzeug Von einem Luft-Piraten.

TRANSLATOR: And I nearly got killed on the airplane coming here. By a highjacker.

MULLEIMER: Auf der Untergrundbahn wär ich auch beinahe umgebracht worden [*Pauses*]

TRANSLATOR: I almost got killed on the subway, too.

[PATUMIERA *continues to choke and babble in Italian, calling for help*]

MULLEIMER: Auch von einem Piraten. [*Pauses*]

TRANSLATOR: Also by a highjacker.

MULLEIMER: In Hotel-Fahrstuhl wär ich auch beinahe umgebracht worden. [*Pauses*]

TRANSLATOR: I almost got killed in my hotel elevator, too.

MULLEIMER: Nicht von einem Luft-Piraten. Was zum Tuefel hätte auch ein Luft-Pirat in einem Hotel-Fahrstuhl zu suchen? [*Pauses*]

TRANSLATOR: Not by a highjacker. What the hell would a highjacker do with a hotel elevator?

MULLEIMER: Das war ein "Mugger" im Fahrstuhl. [*Pauses*]

TRANSLATOR: [*German accent on word "mugger"*] There was a "mugger" in the elevator.

MULLEIMER: Zu meinem Gluck war er unglaubich alt. [*Pauses, no reply*]

TRANSLATOR: Lucky for me, he was incredibly old.

MULLEIMER: Heiss hier drinnen. [*Pauses*]

TRANSLATOR: It's hot in here.

MULLEIMER: Ich krieg keine Luft.

TRANSLATOR: I can not breathe.

LAPOUBELLE: I canno . . . breathe?

PATUMIERA: Si. Si si. Si si si.

LAPOUBELLE: Comment?

PATUMIERA: Non posso respirare.

LAPOUBELLE: Je ne peux rien trouver de pareil dans mon dictionnaire.

TRANSLATOR'S VOICE: I can't find anything like that in my dictionary.

LAPOUBELLE: Tout ce que je trouve de semblable c'est le mot "respirer."

TRANSLATOR'S VOICE: All I can find that's close is the word "breathe."

LAPOUBELLE: Mais, si vous ne pouviez pas respirer depuis la première fois que vous avez dit "Je ne peux pas respirer" . . .

TRANSLATOR'S VOICE: But, if you couldn't breath since the first time you said "I cannot breathe" . . .

LAPOUBELLE: . . . vous seriez . . . *ben* . . . *mort*.

TRANSLATOR'S VOICE: . . . You'd be . . . well . . . dead.

[PATUMIERA *begins choking violently*]

LAPOUBELLE: Ca suffit cinema! Qu'est-ce qu'il y a?

TRANSLATOR: You're making a fool of yourself! What is it?

MULLEIMER: Sie machen sich ja laecherlich. Was haben Sie denn eigentlich?

TRANSLATOR: You're making a fool of yourself! What is it?

PATUMIERA: One canno . . . *breathe!* Non si respira un cavolo qui! [PATUMIERA *coughs violently and the raisin is released.* LAPOU-BELLE *and* MULLEIMER *whack him on the back several times until it looks as though they are killing him. Small old Chinese woman enters, watches, sits. She is absolutely silent*] Cosi e' maglio! [PATUMIERA *stops coughing, but men have now lifted him on to teacher's desk and continue whacking his back*] Basta! Basta! [*They stop.* PATUMIERA *is furious that they have overwhacked him.*

He first punches LAPOUBELLE's *arm, as he smiles and says "Gra-zie"*] Grazie! [*He now punches* MULLEIMER's *arm*] Grazie tanto! [MULLEIMER *rolls with the punch and is the first to notice the old Chinese woman,* MRS. PONG]

MULLEIMER: Ach! Guckt mal! Gutten Abend, gnädige Frau . . . [*He bows slightly, clicking his heels*]

LAPOUBELLE: Bonsoir, madame . . . [*He bows*]

PATUMIERA: Bouna sera, signora . . . [*He kisses her hand*]

MRS. PONG: Nay how mah?

LAPOUBELLE: Vous êtes japonaise?

MRS. PONG: M goi nā, ngoi m sät yĭt gä fŏn wah wä . . .

TRANSLATOR'S VOICE: Excuse me, but I don't even speak a word of English . . .

MRS. PONG: Gĭm mŏn hai ngoi gä ai yĭt ngĭt ŏw coi gä fai wä.

TRANSLATOR'S VOICE: This is my very first day in the city . . .

MRS. PONG: Ngoi dieng-ä loi may gŏk dŏm mŏn sē yä.

TRANSLATOR'S VOICE: I just got to this country yesterday . . .

MRS. PONG: Säle-lë . . .

TRANSLATOR'S VOICE: Sorry.

[*The three men have been standing, staring at* MRS. PONG *as she spoke. They are astonished.* LAPOUBELLE *is first to speak, as he goes to his desk and sits*]

LAPOUBELLE: Merde.

PATUMIERA: Merda.

MULLEIMER: Scheisse.

[*Silence. A beautiful young Japanese woman enters,* YOKO KUZU-KAGO. *She smiles and bows at everyone. Then she places a red apple on teacher's desk and giggles. She is breathing deeply, try-ing to catch her breath. She carries several small canvas bags, filled with books and papers. She has papers between her teeth*]

LAPOUBELLE: Bonjour, ma jolie . . . [LAPOUBELLE *bows and smiles*]

MULLEIMER: Guten Abend, mein Schatz. [MULLEIMER *bows and clicks heels and smiles*]

PATUMIERA: Ebbene, ciao, tesoro . . . [PATUMIERA *straightens his spine and sucks in his stomach and smiles.* YOKO *giggles copiously.* LAPOUBELLE *takes her hand and kisses it.* PATUMIERA *moves in as a movie star might and takes her hand. By mistake, he actually finds that he has taken* LAPOUBELLE's *hand and is about to kiss same.* PATUMIERA *hurls* LAPOUBELLE's *hand away and takes* YOKO's *hand, which he now kisses deeply, using his tongue for emphasis.* YOKO *giggles copious giggles*] Ah, tesoro . . . Tesoro mio . . .

YOKO: Daibu okure mashitaka? Ichijikan hodo maeni kitemimashi-taga makkura deshita. Sorede shitano chisana resutoran de karui shokuji o shite kimashita.

TRANSLATOR: Am I terribly late? I stopped here about an hour ago, but all the lights were out, so I stopped at the little restaurant downstairs and had a bite.

YOKO: I no choshi ga chotto hendesu.

TRANSLATOR: I feel a little sick to my stomach.

LAPOUBELLE: Excuscz-moi?

YOKO: Sukunakutomo akari ga tsuiteimasune. Kurai kedo tonikaku.

TRANSLATOR: At least the lights are on. Dim, but on.

PATUMIERA: [*Ushering* YOKO *to seat beside his*] Mia cara signorina, nelle poche ore da me vissute in America, ho gia' visto, letteral-mente, milioni di donne. Ma lei e chiaramente la pui belle di tutte. Che Dio la benedica.

TRANSLATOR: My dear young lady, in the scant thirty-six hours in which I've lived here in America, I have already looked at literally millions of women. But you are clearly the most beautiful of them all. God bless you.

YOKO: [*She turns to* PATUMIERA, *giggling*] Sumimasenga anatano osshatteiru kotoga wakarimasen.

TRANSLATOR: I'm sorry, but I don't understand you.

PATUMIERA: [*Confused*] Scusi?

MULLEIMER: [*Grabs* YOKO, *tries to lure her away from* PATUMIERA] Meine name ist Mülleimer.

YOKO: Hai. Hai hai. Hai hai hai. [*Pauses*] Moshiwake arimasenga eigoga hanasemasen. [*Smiles and bows*]

TRANSLATOR: Yes. Yes, yes. Yes, yes, yes. Sorry, but I don't speak a word of English.

MULLEIMER: [*Confused*] Gefällt ihnen denn mein Name nicht? Das wündert mich aber sehr.

TRANSLATOR: You think my name is funny? Well, who doesn't?

LAPOUBELLE: [*Smiling broadly*] Vous êtes chinoise?

[PATUMIERA *moves behind* YOKO *with air of great secrecy. He puts his fingers to his lips, as he whispers to her*]

PATUMIERA: Ho un segreto, Io!

TRANSLATOR: I have a secret!

PATUMIERA: Sono un membro del partito comunista.

TRANSLATOR: I am a member of the Communist Party.

MULLEIMER: [*Points to wastebasket*] Weiss schon, die Leute machen sich immer über meinen Namen lustig.

TRANSLATOR: People always laugh at the obvious, I know.

LAPOUBELLE: [*Sees* MULLEIMER *pointing at wastebasket*] C'est drôle, n'est-ce pas? Je sais, je sais.

TRANSLATOR: It's funny, isn't it? I know. I know.

MULLEIMER: Darf ich mich vorstellen, meine Fräulein . . . [*Extends his hand, leaning to her*] Meine name ist Mülleimer.

YOKO: Hajimemashite.

LAPOUBELLE: [*Leans in as well*] Je m'appelle LaPoubelle . . .

YOKO: Hajimemashite.

PATUMIERA: La Patumiera . . .

[*All are amazed to discover they all share common name*]

YOKO: Watashi no namaewa Kuzukago Yoko desu. [*She points to wastebasket*]

TRANSLATOR: My name is Yoko Kuzukago.

YOKO: Kuzukago Yoko. Kuzukago Yoko. [*All are smiling into each other's eyes as old Chinese woman moans, pitches forward out of her chair in a faint.* YOKO *is first to scream*] Ta-i-hen!

PATUMIERA: *Madonna mia!*

MULLEIMER: *Mein Gott!*

LAPOUBELLE: *Mon Dieu!* De l'eau! [*He exits the room*]

TRANSLATOR: Water!

MULLEIMER: Wasser! [*He exits the room*]

TRANSLATOR: Water!

PATUMIERA: Acqua! [*He exits the room*]

TRANSLATOR: Water!

YOKO: Ocha!

TRANSLATOR: Tea!

[YOKO *also exits the room and, for a moment, the old Chinese woman is alone, on the floor. Slowly, she pulls herself over to her chair and, holding it for support, stands. She shakes her head. She sits in the chair, composed again. An American woman,* DEBBIE WASTBA, *enters. She is laden with bookbags, shopping bags, handbags and briefcases; all hers. She has papers in her teeth. She is out of breath. She wears a long trenchcoat, British, with a colorful scarf, French. Her shoes are Italian and her bookbags a blend of Japanese, German and Chinese. Her clothing is probably a skirt and blouse, slightly subdued, perhaps with black tights worn under the skirt. Her clothing gives her an air of competence. She looks about the empty room, seeing the many bookbags, attaché cases, jackets, etc. Finally, she sees the old Chinese woman,* MRS. PONG, *and smiles broadly*]

WASTBA: Hi. I'm Ms. Wastba. [*Pronounced "Wah-stah-bah"*] Odd name, huh? Dates all the way back to Mesopotamia. Wastba. [*Spells it*] W-A-S-T-B-A. [*Pauses*] My great grandfather shortened it . . . after his . . . uh . . . trouble. [*Pauses*] Some muggy night, huh? I can't breathe. [*Pauses. Fanning the air*] I've never been able to take heat, which is ridiculous, when you consider my family background. Three thousand years of rotten luck. All we had to do was to stay put and we would have been swimming in gas and oil, but, no, we moved on and here I am. After six flights of climbing, I'd hate to be standing next to me on a bus. [*Laughs a bit at her own joke*] Ah, yes . . . [*Sets down a bag or two*] Wouldn't you know the elevator would be on the fritz? That's a slang word: fritz. [*Pauses*] You don't speak English at all, huh? [*Pauses, laughs*] I forgot. That's why you're here. [*She laughs again*] No English at all? [*No response*] That's okay, really. Listen, that's all the better. No rotten habits, you know what I mean? [*Pauses, smiles, unpacking her notebooks*] This is going to be total immersion. [*Smiles*] Total. [*Pauses; smiles again*] That means no speaking your base language. Which would certainly be Oriental in your case, right? [*Pauses, looks around room and sees men's bags and clothes in room*] You sure brought a lot of stuff, didn't you? [*Pauses*] There should be more of us. Maybe they're all late. [*Looks for clock, sees wires*] There must be a clock . . . Look at that! Clock's been stolen. [*Shakes her head to express "What's the use?", as she unpacks more books*] They'll steal anything nowadays, really. An old gentleman I know . . . quite well . . . he had his doorknobs taken. [*Pauses*] It's true. Hard to believe, isn't it? [*Pauses*] Listen, he was relieved they didn't get into his apartment altogether. [*Smiles*] Of course, neither did he . . . not for hours. [*Giggles a bit, explains*] No knobs. [*Pauses*] At the time, I thought it was kind of . . . well . . . kinky . . . You might say "inscrutable," right? [*She laughs. No response from* PONG. LAPOUBELLE *rushes into room carrying a take-out container of water. He rushes to* MRS. PONG]

LAPOUBELLE: Voici. De l'eau! Pour vous . . . Buvez un coup . . . Ça iar mieux . . . Buvez, buvez, etc. . . . . [PATUMIERA, *the same. Offers container*]

PATUMIERA: Acqua per lei, signora. [*And he bends near* MRS. PONG, *forcing her to drink as he babbles encouraging phrases.* MULLEIMER *rushes into room, carrying take-out container of water, as well. He forces* MRS. PONG *to drink same*]

MULLEIMER: Wasser, gnädige Frau. [YOKO *rushes into room. A teabag tag waves from her take-out container*]

YOKO: Ochao dozo. [YOKO *kneels near* MRS. PONG *and forces the old Chinese woman to drink tea. Each of them now pours liquid into the old Chinese woman, who squeals a lot, but seems nonetheless grateful. Each ad libs in his or her own language such phrases as "Drink up. You'll feel better, etc."*]

MULLEIMER: Trinken sie doch, meine Gute. Dann gehts ihnen gleich besser. Ja, ja. Ist schön gut.

[WASTBA *watches them a while before speaking*]

LAPOUBELLE: [*Pointing to* YOKO's *contribution*] Ca, c'est pas de l'eau, n'est-ce pas?

PATUMIERA: [*Also pointing to teabag*] Dev' essere qualcosa Oriental.

MULLEIMER: [*Slamming* MRS. PONG's *back*] Fühlen Sie sich besser? Ja?

[WASTBA *now stands poised, her hand outstretched to greet them all*]

WASTBA: Isn't that sweet of you all? Gifts for the Old Oriental! [*They all spin around and face her*] Hi! [*She moves forward with overstated confidence and friendliness, pumping their hands in greeting*] I'm your teacher. Debbie Wastba.

[*Each rushes forward to deal with her outstretched hand.* PATUMIERA *will again grab* LAPOUBELLE's *hand before finding* WASTBA's. *He will again use his tongue for emphasis, but this time will be shocked by* WASTBA's *reaction, which will be shock*]

MULLEIMER: Darf ich mich vorstellen, mein Name ist Fritz Mülleimer.

WASTBA: Fritz? [*Laughs*] Oh, the elevator . . . Yes.

MULLEIMER: Aber natürlich. Sie dürfen mich ruhig Fritz nennen.

WASTBA: Fritz?

MULLEIMER: Ja, Ja. Fritz. Ganz gewöhnlicher Deutscher Name. Bin Deutscher, aber ursprünglich stammen wir aus Mesopotamien. Während meine Vorfavern dort geblieben, so wäre ich jetzt Irake, ha, ha. Zum Gluck waren sie Nomaden.

WASTBA: I haven't understood a single word of what you've said. Do you know that?

MULLEIMER: [*Nonplussed. Chatty*] Aber naturlich. Bin Deutscher, von Kopf . . . bis Fuss.

WASTBA: Look at that: bowing. Aren't you the polite one, now? [*To* LAPOUBELLE] You? What's your name, hmmm?

LAPOUBELLE: Enchanté, Madame.

WASTBA: First or last?

LAPOUBELLE: [*Bows, takes her hand and kisses it*] Moi, je m'appelle Jean-Michel LaPoubelle.

WASTBA: [*Giggles*] Sheer poetry, I can tell you that.

PATUMIERA: [*It is here he executes his kiss*] Io sono Carlo Fredriko Rizzonini La Patumiera . . .

WASTBA: [*She recoils from him*] Just watch it, you!! [*She wipes her hand on her skirt.* YOKO *walks to the wastebasket and picks it up*]

YOKO: Watashi no namaewa Kuzukago Yoko desu.

WASTBA: Isn't that just simply one of the sweetest names you've ever heard?

YOKO: [*Picks up wastebasket*] Kuzukago Yoko. Kuzukago Yoko.

MRS. PONG: [*Pointing to wastebasket*] Ah, sē-lŏp-pŏng. Ngoi gwä lŏw Pŏng thlee dūk-ä sē-lŏp-pŏng, wa.

WASTBA: [*Sees wastebasket*] What's the matter with the wastebasket? [*Pronounced as her name:* WAH-STAH-BAH-SKET. YOKO *giggles. Puts wastebasket down. Giggles again*] Okay, folks, take your seats . . . [*Nobody moves. She talks louder*] Take . . . your . . . seats . . .

PATUMIERA: Take . . . you . . . zeets . . . [PATUMIERA *grabs his dictionary and starts looking for words. Smiling, he imitates* WASTBA, *calling to all. No response will follow*]

WASTBA: No, no, no. Sit down. [*She laughs nervously*] Doesn't anybody speak a *little* English? [*They all continue to mill about her*] Sit down. [*She laughs*] Watch me now. [*She drags her chair out from behind her desk and sets it in the middle of the classroom. She slowly, carefully, demonstrates an act of sitting, first lifting out her skirts, then sitting, then folding her skirts demurely and then folding her hands into her lap. All stand around her in circle, watching and smiling*] See what I did? [*Nobody responds, but* YOKO, *who giggles*] I sat. [*All smile and nod.* WASTBA *yells at them*] Sit down! [*Nobody sits*] Stay calm, everybody. [*She stands and walks the few steps to her desk. She turns away from the class. All watch, but for* PATUMIERA, *who is feverishly searching through his dictionary.* WASTBA *turns to class again, smiling competently now]* Class, this could be one of the worst nights of our lives. [*To* LAPOUBELLE] I want you to think seriously—deeply—about the following two words: sit down.

PATUMIERA: [*Suddenly screams*] Eye!

WASTBA: What's the matter? Your eye? Soot?

PATUMIERA: [*Struts happily to front of room, reading from his pad of paper*] Eye . . . have . . . eet! [*Turns and picks up his chair over his head, displaying same to* WASTBA] Eeet ees aye ki-eer.

WASTBA: Ki-air? Oh, no. No. It's *chair!* Chair. Good. It is a chair.

PATUMIERA: Alora, chair? Eeet ees a chair.

WASTBA: Good. Sit . . . in . . . it! [*She stands and takes chair from* PATUMIERA. *She places chair on floor and bends* PATUMIERA *into it. She fails. He will not bend. All, but for* MRS. PONG, *will soon assist* WASTBA] Sit! Sit! [*She motions to all to repeat word*] Sit! Sit!

MULLEIMER: Ach sitz! Komm sitz. [*He begins to help push* PATUMIERA *into chair*]

ALL: [*Repeat word*] Sit, Sitz, Seet! etc. [*They all understand, push* PATUMIERA *downward*]

PATUMIERA: [*He is panicked, as all are yelling at him. He stares at each with terror in his eyes*] Scusi. Non capisco.

YOKO: Seet! [*She pushes his head from the top*]

WASTBA and OTHERS: Sit! Sit! Sit!

[PATUMIERA *bends unwittingly and sits in chair, still confused*]

WASTBA: [*Thrilled*] Yes! He's sitting!

LAPOUBELLE: Seeting!

WASTBA: Right.

MULLEIMER: Zittsing!

WASTBA: Yes. [*To* PATUMIERA] You're *sitting!* [*She applauds* PATUMIERA. *All applaud as well.* PATUMIERA *is no less panicked, but is smiling*]

MULLEIMER: Zittsing!

WASTBA: [*To* MULLEIMER] Now you!

MULLEIMER: [*Sits with enormous grin of pride on face. He stretches legs way out in front of him, leans back, as though in a steam bath and "Zitzes"*] Zittsing!

WASTBA: Wonderful! [*To* LAPOUBELLE] Now you!

LAPOUBELE: Ah, oui. Mais, voilà. Seeting. [*He sits*]

PATUMIERA: Eet ees aye chair.

WASTBA: [*To* YOKO] And you.

YOKO: Sitty. [*She sits*]

WASTBA: [*Looks at* MRS. PONG] You did that on your own. Aren't you something?

[PATUMIERA *tries to save face and crosses to his seat, pointing a finger to and lecturing old* MRS. PONG]

PATUMIERA: Eeet ees aye chair.

WASTBA: Now then. Hello. I'm Debbie Wastba.

[*All are sitting, smiling now*]

PATUMIERA: Scusi?

WASTBA: Huh?

MULLEIMER: Was?

YOKO: Nani?

MRS. PONG: Häaaaaa?

LAPOUBELLE: Comment?

WASTBA: [*From her desk*] Listen, now, I'll just go really slow. [*Pauses, smiles*] My name is Debbie Wastba. [*She writes her name on blackboard. Each takes notebook and copies down name*] W-A-S-T-B-A. That's pronounced Wass-tah-bah: Wastba. [*She links each of the three syllables together on board, in the following way: WA ST BA*] Think of W*ah* as in wah-tah. Splash. Splash. *Stah* as in stah-bility. And *Bah* as in Bah-dum . . . as in [*Sings* Dragnet *theme*] Bum-tah-bum-bum. Well, listen. It was literally double its length in its ancient, biblical form. [*Pauses*] Actually, that tune was wrong. It would be much more like . . . [*Sings again, to tune of "My Funny Valentine"*] Bum bum-bum bum-bum-bum . . . bum bum-bum bum-bum-bum . . . bum bum-bum baaahhhmmmmmmmm . . . [*Pauses: sees they are confused*] Well, anyway, really, you can easily check your bibles if you want. [*Rummages through stack of papers on desk, holds up lesson plan*] This is our lesson plan. That's *lesson* . . . *plan*. Lesson plan. We're going to be together for several hours and I thought it would be highly professional and competent for me to make a plan. And I did. And here it is: [*She reads: smiling confidently*] One. A pleasant welcome and normal chatter. For two, I've planned your basic salutations, such as the goods—good morning, good afternoon, good night, good luck and good grief. [*She laughs*] That was a mildly amusing joke: "good grief." Later in the night —after we've learned a bit of English—you'll be able to, well, get the joke. [*Pauses*] Let's move along. Three will be basic customs: ours here. [*Reading again*] Four will be a short history of our English language. [*As the students take their notes, they, as we, begin to realize that* WASTBA *is only writing the numbers 1-6 on to the blackboard—no words. They raise their hands in question, but she waves them away, barging ahead*] Five will be the primary lesson of the primary English class, according to the book. And six will be the very essential verb "to be." At some point, we shall also inspect the very basic concept of silence. [*Smiles*] Now then, as you can see, there are only six points to cover and hours and hours ahead in which to cover them. [*All stare blankly at her smiling face*] Now then: Questions? [YOKO *sneezes*] God bless you.

MULLEIMER: Gesundheit!

PATUMIERA: Salute!

LAPOUBELLE: À vos souhaits!

[YOKO *sneezes again*]

MULLEIMER: Nochmals. Gesundheit!

PATUMIERA: Salute, ancora.

LAPOUBELLE: À vos souhaits!

WASTBA: God bless you again! [*Laughs*] That's a good one to learn. That's a basic custom, folks! [*Slowly: articulately*] God bless you. Everybody. God bless you . . . [*All stare at her*] God! . . . [*Waves arms above her head*]

ALL: [*Repeating, while looking up*] God . . .

WASTBA: God bless . . . [*Touching her breasts on word "Bless"*]

ALL: God bless . . .

YOKO: God breast . . .

WASTBA: God bless *you!*

ALL: God bless *you!* [*All point to* WASTBA *on word "you"*]

WASTBA: Thank you very much and I certainly hope He's paying attention, huh? [*Smiles to* LAPOUBELLE. *Points overhead to ceiling*] Him. [*All raise their hands to ask a question*]

YOKO: Shitsumon!

MULLEIMER: Duerfte ich Sie bitte etwas fragen!

[WASTBA *mumbles "Let's see . . ." and pretends to be about to call on each of them, tantalizing them*]

LAPOUBELLE: S'il vous plaît, mademoiselle . . .

[WASTBA *calls on* LAPOUBELLE]

WASTBA: I . . . choose . . . *you!*

LAPOUBELLE: Ah, merci, mademoiselle! Qu'est-ce que vous avez dit? Je ne comprends pas . . . Moi, je pense que personne ne comprend . . . [*Smiles*] Meme . . . enfin . . . meme moi. [*He smiles again*] Compris?

WASTBA: Huh?

LAPOUBELLE: [*Looking about class*] Y a-t-il quelqu'un qui parle français? [*All stare blankly at* LAPOUBELLE]

WASTBA: I'm sorry, sir, but I don't speak . . . what you're speaking . . . French would be my first guess. Actually, that's quite obvious, right? [*Pauses; smiles*] Right? [*No response*] Parlez-vous français?

LAPOUBELLE: [*Instantly animated; speaks rapidly*] Ou-ay! Français et seulement français! O la la! . . . je suis tellement heureux de vous entendre aussi parler français!

WASTBA: You're not French?

LAPOUBELLE: Comment?

WASTBA: Are you Swiss?

LAPOUBELLE: J'ai peur que je n'ai pas compris . . .

WASTBA: Don't the Swiss speak something like French?

LAPOUBELLE: Je ne comprends pas tout. Parlez plus lentement, s'il vous plait, chere mademoiselle . . .

WASTBA: Are you from Luxembourg?

LAPOUBELLE: Dîtes-le en français, s'il vous plaît.

WASTBA: It must be your accent . . .

LAPOUBELLE: *Comment?*

WASTBA: I'm a little anxious tonight . . .

LAPOUBELLE: Si vous le disiez en français, chère mademoiselle . . .

WASTBA: What?

LAPOUBELLE: Quoi?

WASTBA: Yes, thank you very much. [*To the class*] Listen, which of you speaks a little English?

PATUMIERA: [*After a long pause: a short silence*] Scusi?

WASTBA: Is that Greek?

PATUMIERA: Io . . . Non capisco . . .

WASTBA: Spanish, I'll bet.

PATUMIERA: Per piacere? Io . . .

WASTBA: [*She will tap out rhythm with her foot to Spanish words*] I used to know a little Spanish . . . let's see . . . Me voy a lavar un poco para quitarme la arena que tengo pegada.

PATUMIERA: Scusi?

WASTBA: Don't you get it? It's beach talk. It means, "I'm going to wash the sand from my body." If some greaseball-type bothers you at the beach, that's what you say. My friend Ramon Vasoro taught me that. [*They all stare at her, blankly*] Well, now, that's probably enough chatter. Do you have all your slips? [*No response*] Slips? [*No response*] Your slips. From the office. [*No response. She walks to* LAPOUBELLE *and begins rummaging through his brief-case*] Excuse me.

LAPOUBELLE: Qu'est-ce que vous faites là? [*She continues to rum-mage*] Pardoneez-moi, mademoiselle, mais qu'est-ce que vous vou-lez? [*She continues to rummage*] Si vous m'expliquez ce que vous cherchez, j'essayerai de la trouver! [*No response*] Mais, chère made-moiselle . . . Bordel! Quelle belle soirée!

WASTBA: [*She finds his slip*] This! [*She waves it to class*] Give me your slips. [*All smile and rummage about looking for their slips, which each finds and hands to* WASTBA. *As she collects each slip, she reads each name, mispronouncing each.*] LaPoo . . . Is this a name?

LAPOUBELLE: LaPoubelle. Je m'appelle Jean-Michel LaPoubelle. C'est cela? C'est mon nom que vous voudriez? C'est tout?

WASTBA: That's very unique. [*To* MULLEIMER] Where's yours? [*Takes slip, tries to read it*] Is this of Slavic persuasion? [*Squints. She moves to* MRS. PONG *and plucks the slip that has been stapled to* PONG's *sleeve, not looking away from* MULLEIMER's *slip*] Look at all these vowels. [*Hands slips to* PATUMIERA, *who is staring into* YOKO's *blouse, not paying attention to* WASTBA. *He takes the slip from her*] Can you pronounce this?

PATUMIERA: Grazie . . .

WASTBA: I don't think *that's* right. [*Squints. Looks again*] Maybe. How's your eye? [*Smiles at all*] I have new hard contacts. I hated the soft ones. Had to wash them every night. I went back to hard . . . [*Blank stares all around*] Contacts. [*Smiles*] Okay. There's a perfectly fine place to begin. [*She will walk to* MULLEIMER *and pluck his eyeglasses from his astonished face*]

MULLEIMER: Ah! [*He is nearly blind without glasses and will soon feel his way, looking for* WASTBA]

WASTBA: These are . . . [*She reaches out. Plucks glasses*] . . . eyeglasses.

MULLEIMER: Meine Brille!! [*He accidentally gropes* WASTBA, *grabbing her breast in one absolutely clean move. All see and are amazed.* PATUMIERA *stands. He is vaguely outraged*]

WASTBA: OH God!

PATUMIERA: EEEAYY!

WASTBA: [*Shocked and amazed*] I'm going to try to overlook that . . . [*Takes a deep breath*] God! Let's go on. [*To all*] These are eyeglasses. It's a new word. Learn it. Eyeglasses. [*Tries them on*] Oooooo. You must be blind as a bat. [*Smiles again*] Eyeglasses. Eye-glasses. Eyeee-glasssezzzz . . . [*Waves arms*] Everybody! Eyeee-glassezzz.

YOKO: Everiii—Eyeee-grasssezzz . . .

WASTBA: God! Eyeee-glasssessssszzz . . . [*Waves her arms*] Eyeeee-glassezzz . . .

LAPOUBELLE: Eye-glassée.

PATUMIERA: Eye-glasso.

WASTBA: Eye-glasses.

MRS. PONG: Eye . . . eye . . . gassieh.

WASTBA: [*Taps her foot to lead her students' chant of the word "eyeglasses"*] Everybody . . . eyeglasses . . . eyeglasses . . . etc. [*Smiling, but clearly in panic*] Wonderful. Really. I wouldn't kid you. You're all just really wonderful. [*She applauds her students, who are so pleased by her approval, they all scream the word "eyeglasses" at her again, each with his or her own indigenous accent*]

ALL: Eyee-glassy (zes) (o) (ée) etc.

[*N.B.:* MRS. PONG *has been totally silent, but is awake, staring at all that goes on, smiling deeply, nibbling food*]

WASTBA: Just really and sincerely terrific. Really. Terrific. Sincerely. [*Pauses*] Oh, God . . . [*Smiles*] Now watch. [*She points to her eye*] These are . . . contacts. [*No reply*] Contacts. [*No reply. She touches eye*] Contacts. [*Suddenly, she stiffens, blinking. A contact lens has popped out of her eye and fallen on to the floor*] Oh . . . my . . . dear . . . God! [*They all stare dumbly as* WASTBA *crawls around floor*] Help me! It's on the floor!

LAPOUBELLE: Floor!

[*He writes the word down. They look from one to the other, dumbly.* YOKO *and* PATUMIERA *move to her*]

WASTBA: Help me! I'm not insured! [*Suddenly, she stops them from stepping on lens*] Don't anybody move! [*They all look away from her. She falls back down on the floor*] I got it! [*She wets the tip of her index finger, right hand, with which she stabs at lens. When it sticks to the tip of her finger, she screams*] I really got it! Oh! Lucky break! [*She transfers lens to her mouth*] Thank God, huh? [*She takes it out of mouth, holds it to light, looks at it, places it back into her mouth. She squints at class. She stands, smiling*]

I said, "Thank God, huh?" [*She looks at it, holding the lens toward the light, squinting.* MULLEIMER, *blinded, has raised his hand, politely, but high in air. He holds his position*] I'll have to go wash it off. [*She walks to door*] I'll be right back.

[WASTBA *exits. There is silence in the room for a moment.* MULLEIMER *breaks the silence, smiling to all*]

MULLEIMER: Fräulein Lehrerin, hab ein kleines Problemchen! Bin ein bisschen schwer hörig. Gewöhlich bin ich ja Lippenleser, und das hilft schon, aber sie hat mir dock die Brille weggeschnappt, und jetzt kann ich nicht mehr sehen was ich nicht hören kann.

TRANSLATOR: Teacher, I've got a problem here. I'm a little hard of hearing, so usually I lip-read, which helps, but you took my glasses, so now I can't see what I don't hear.

[*There is a moment of silence in the room, as all stare at spot where once there was a transparent contact lens.* PATUMIERA *is the first to break the silence. He seems angry with* LAPOUBELLE]

PATUMIERA: [*To* LAPOUBELLE] Che Gazzi ai detta?

TRANSLATOR: What the hell did you say to her?

YOKO: [*Very confidently, takes center*] Kore wa akirakani totaru imashon no senjutsu desuyo.

TRANSLATOR: This is clearly a "total immersion" tactic.

PATUMIERA: Scusi?

YOKO: Konna hanashi o kiitakatoga arimasu. Otokono hito ga banana o te ni motte kyohitso ni haitee kitandesutte. Ban-ban to sakebinagara.

TRANSLATOR: I once heard of a man running into a classroom with a banana yelling "Bang-bang!"

YOKO: Konna funi. [YOKO *runs out of classroom*]

TRANSLATOR: Watch, I'll show you.

PATUMIERA: [*To* LAPOUBELLE] Scusi? Che Gazzi ai detta?

TRANSLATOR: Now, what do you say to her?

YOKO: [*Runs back into classroom*] Ban-ban. Tokyo deno dekigoto deshita. Amerikajin no bijinesuman no tame no nihongo no kurasu.

TRANSLATOR: It was in Tokyo. In a Japanese class for American businessmen.

YOKO: Kekkyoku Amerikajintachi wa sono hito o tatakinomeshite, motte ita banana o toriagechattan desutte.

TRANSLATOR: The way the story goes, the Americans beat the man up and took his banana.

PATUMIERA: Eh tu non vuoi rermare, eh?

TRANSLATOR: You're not going to stop, are you?

YOKO: Nani?

PATUMIERA: "Nani?" Se quella é inglese, tu' accenta è miserable . . . Un Orechio di stagno . . .

TRANSLATOR: "Nani?" If that's English, then your accent is intolerable. Language-wise, you've got a tin ear.

[PATUMIERA *moves to* WASTBA's *desk.* YOKO *begins copying down phrases from her phrasebook*]

MULLEIMER: Entschuldigen Sie, Fräulein Lehrerin, dürfte ich Sie bitte privat sprechen?

TRANSLATOR: Excuse me, teacher. May I have a private word with you?

LAPOUBELLE: Excusez-moi?

MULLEIMER: Fräulein Legrerin! Fräulein Lehrerin!

TRANSLATOR: Teacher! Teacher!

PATUMIERA: [*To* LAPOUBELLE] Ma, che hai fatto a lui adesso?

TRANSLATOR: Now, what did you do to him?

LAPOUBELLE: [*To* MULLEIMER] Que voulez-vous?

MULLEIMER: Entweder bringen Sie mir die Lehrerin oder lassen Sie mich in Ruhe, O.K.?

TRANSLATOR: Either get the teacher or get off my back, O.K.?

LAPOUBELLE: Une bonne classe, hein? Je suis très, très content. [LAPOUBELLE *has a small white paper bag filled with candies. He smiles and eats*]

TRANSLATOR: Quite a class, huh? I'm very pleased by the way things are going.

MULLEIMER: Kann nicht behäupten, dass ich die Amerikaner verstehe. Warm und Freundlich sind sie ja, aber sie nehmen man die Brille weg, und warum, wenn ich Fragen darf, warum?

TRANSLATOR: I can't pretend to understand Americans. They're warm and friendly, but they take your eyeglasses and why, I ask you, why?

MULLEIMER: Und was mich so masslos aergert ist dass niemand von Euch Schweinehunden mir hilft!

TRANSLATOR: And why, I keep wondering, won't any of you sons of bitches help me get them back?

MULLEIMER: Falls ich Ihnen sage ein Baum stuerzt im Walde, und kein Mensch hier spricht ein Wort Deutsch, stuerzt dann der Baum, oder nicht?

TRANSLATOR: If I tell you a tree falls in the forest and nobody in here speaks any German, then does the tree ever fall?

[LAPOUBELLE *offers candy to* MULLEIMER, *placing piece on* MULLEIMER's *desk.* MULLEIMER *stares down blindly. Angrily,* MULLEIMER *knocks the candy away*]

LAPOUBELLE: Est-ce que vous vous rendez compte combien vous êtes impoli?

TRANSLATOR: Do you have any idea how rude you're being?

[LAPOUBELLE *picks up candy and sits, sulks.* PATUMIERA *crosses to* YOKO *again; sits*]

YOKO: [*Taking over class as though teacher*] Ne. Minna kittekudasai. Hitotsu narai mashitayo. Eigo desuyo.

TRANSLATOR: Listen, everybody. I think I've learned something. I have some English here.

YOKO: [*In English; after checking her phrasebook and notes. Her accent is extremely heavy*] I am starbing to . . . dess. [*She giggles*]

TRANSLATOR: I am starving to death.

PATUMIERA: Si. Si, si. Si, si, si.

YOKO: [*In English; heavy accent*] I would like my check, my rolls and my orangeee . . . [YOKO *teaches words to all*]

MRS. PONG: Checoo . . .

PATUMIERA: Lolls . . .

YOKO: Lolls? Na. Rolls.

LAPOUBELLE: *Orange.*

YOKO: Watashiwa kotogakko de tomikakino seisekiga tottemo yokat-tandesuyo. Hontowa watashiwa kotobao umaku tsukaikonase-masu. [*Pauses; smiles at all*]

TRANSLATOR: I got really good grades in high school for creative writing and public speaking. I've got a way with words.

YOKO: Watashino ie wa mukashikara benjutsu ni taketeite, sono rekishi wa mesopotamia made sakanoborundesu. [*She giggles at a blank-faced* PATUMIERA]

TRANSLATOR: We have a history of oratory dating all the way back to Mesopotamia.

PATUMIERA: [*Frustrated by her incomprehensible language*] Non ho capito nemmena una parole che tu hai detta, mia stuzzicadente. Ma perche tu sei cosi magra? Non piàce a mangiare o sei stanca di mangiare il riso?

TRANSLATOR: I haven't understood word one of what you've just babbled, toothpick. How come you're so skinny, huh? Don't you like food or do you just pick at your rice?

LAPOUBELLE: [*To* YOKO] Je n'ai plus que douze heures et demie pour apprendre l'anglais, sinon je suis un homme mort. [LAPOUBELLE *grins as though his confession is totally unimportant*]

TRANSLATOR: I've got twelve and a half hours left in which to learn English or else I might as well be dead.

YOKO: Nani?

> [PATUMIERA *sees that* LAPOUBELLE *has moved in on* YOKO. *Sits on desk next to* YOKO, *squeezing* LAPOUBELLE *off desk completely.* YOKO *and* PATUMIERA *each take candy from* LAPOUBELLE, *which they dislike and discard*]

LAPOUBELLE: Demain matin de bonne, j'ai un rendez-vous extrème-ment important.

TRANSLATOR: I have an enormously important business meeting in the morning.

LAPOUBELLE: Si j'échoue, tout ma société d'assurance sera en faillite. Je perdrais mon job, ma jeune femme, mes enfants seraient obliges de quitter leur école privée . . .

[YOKO *and* PATUMIERA *turn away from* LAPOUBELLE]

TRANSLATOR: If I fail, my entire insurance company will bankrupt. Then I'll lose my job, my young wife and my children will have to drop out of private school . . . [LAPOUBELLE *stands at center, talking to no one in particular*]

LAPOUBELLE: Je n'aurai plus qu'à me tuer.

TRANSLATOR: I'll have to kill myself.

[LAPOUBELLE *sees that* YOKO *is no longer paying attention—is bored—and now smiling at* PATUMIERA. LAPOUBELLE *moves to* MRS. PONG, *as she nods to him, seeing that he is trapped and alone at center*]

MRS. PONG: Wa, wa.

LAPOUBELLE: [*To* MRS. PONG] Vous, vous êtes mariée, veuve ou di-vorcée?

TRANSLATOR: Are you married, widowed or divorced?

MRS. PONG: M goi nay. Ngoi n hiĕng gŏn nay mūn mwŭt wä. Nay gŏng mŏn-mŏn yä-ä yē. Ngoi ännäm gai wä.

LAPOUBELLE: Veuve! Je suis désolé. J'espère que la n'a pas trainé.

TRANSLATOR: I'm sorry to hear that. I hope it wasn't a lingering death.

MRS. PONG: Thlee mwŭt-ä. Yea thlee, toi mä siĕk-ä?

TRANSLATOR: Give me a clue: animal? vegetable? or mineral?

LAPOUBELLE: Oui, ça va mieux comma ça. Moi mème, j'ai perdu ma première femme . . .

TRANSLATOR: That's a relief. I myself lost my first wife . . .

MRS. PONG: Toi?

TRANSLATOR: Vegetable?

[MRS. PONG *has taken a piece of candy from* LAPOUBELLE's *bag during the above exchange*]

LAPOUBELLE: Non, elle m'a quitté.

TRANSLATOR: No. She ran away.

LAPOUBELLE: Elle m'a laissé un petit mot me disant qu'elle s'ennuyait avec moi.

TRANSLATOR: She left a note saying I was boring.

MRS. PONG: Haa?

LAPOUBELLE: Emmerdant, quoi.

TRANSLATOR: I said "boring."

MRS. PONG: Ahhhh.

LAPOUBELLE: Ma nouvelle femme est plutôt jeune. Elle aussi me trouve emmerdant.

TRANSLATOR: I have a young wife now. She finds me boring as well.

LAPOUBELLE: Heureusement, j'ai assez confiance en moi-même pourque ça ne m'ébranle pas.

TRANSLATOR: Luckily, I'm secure enough about my personality not to have to worry about such matters.

[MRS. PONG *throws her head back, snores loudly. Her head drops down to her chest. She is asleep, snoring loudly. She has, possibly, spat* LAPOUBELLE's *candy to floor.* PATUMIERA *and* YOKO *stare across to him.* LAPOUBELLE *is shocked and amazed and opens his suitcoat, trying to hide the sleeping* MRS. PONG *from his classmates*]

LAPOUBELLE: [To MULLEIMER] Elle est fatiguée, en plus elle est trés vieille. Alors, je lui ai conseillé de se reposer.

TRANSLATOR: She's very old and is obviously exhausted. I've convinced her to get some rest.

MULLEIMER: Bitte keine ploetzlichen Bewegungen! Kann nur Schatten sehen. Es ist einfach schrecklich.

TRANSLATOR: Try not to make any sudden moves. I can only see shadows, and it's terrifying.

MULLEIMER: Wenn ich ganz still sitze und die Augen schliesse, ist es doch viel weniger beaengstigend.

TRANSLATOR: It's a lot less scarey for me if I just sit here and close my eyes.

[MULLEIMER *does so, allowing his head to drop in sleeping position.* PATUMIERA *and* YOKO *stare at* LAPOUBELLE, *who stares at* MULLEIMER *and* MRS. PONG, *thinking he has put both of them to sleep.* LAPOUBELLE *sits; bows his head, silence*]

PATUMIERA: Ho nostalgico, Io.

TRANSLATOR: I am homesick.

YOKO: Uchi ga koishiiwa.

TRANSLATOR: I am homesick.

PATUMIERA: [*Moving toward* WASTBA's *desk*] Ma fortunamento per noi abbiamo una buona maestra . . . simpatico, riguardosa, gentile . . . [PATUMIERA *touches* WASTBA's *jacket on coat tree*]

TRANSLATOR: Lucky for us we've got ourselves a great little teacher . . . warm . . . considerate . . . gentle . . .

[*Suddenly we hear a bloodcurdling scream*—WASTBA's—*from offstage, beyond the door, somewhere deep in a dark corridor. There is a moment of silence before each stands and comments*]

MULLEIMER: Was war das? Unser kleiner kürbis vielleicht?

TRANSLATOR: What was that? Could that be our little pumpkin?

PATUMIERA: [*Also stands*] La madonna sta in un imbroglio.

TRANSLATOR: Sounds like that madonna's in trouble!

LAPOUBELLE: Notre adorable artichaut! Mon dieu!

TRANSLATOR: Our darling little artichoke! My God!

YOKO: [*Standing*] Sensei wa amerika de tatta hitorino watashino tomodachi nanoni.

TRANSLATOR: She's the only true friend I have in America!

[LAPOUBELLE *moves quietly to the door. Suddenly,* WASTBA *bursts into the room, slamming the door in* LAPOUBELLE'S *face. He disappears from our view, squashed behind door, into wall.* WASTBA *closes door now and presses her back against same. She holds* SMIEDNIK's *mop in her hand*]

LAPOUBELLE: Mademoiselle . . . [*He reaches for her and she screams, immediately handing mop to* LAPOUBELLE, *who places same behind coat tree, flat on floor, out of audience's view of same*]

WASTBA: Yaaa-iiiiii!!! GIT! [LAPOUBELLE *scoots back to his chair and sits.* WASTBA *continues to lean heavily against door, keeping it closed.* WASTBA *is incredibly frightened. She begins to speak. Her mouth moves, her lips form words, but there is no voice under them. Finally, the words are audible. All have been staring intently, wondering no doubt if this has all been part of an intensive study of primary English*] There's . . . there's a . . . there's a very dirty man . . . [*Rubs her face; looks down first*] There's a very dirty man out there . . . [*She giggles*] In the ladies' room. [*She waits for response. There is none*] There's a man in the ladies' room. [*Pauses*] He . . . touched . . . [*Pauses; then speaks in determined way*] He tried to hug me but, thank God, he was on his knees so he couldn't reach. [*Wipes brow*] I wouldn't want to tell you what he *did* reach, however.

PATUMIERA: Che successo?

WASTBA: I said I wouldn't tell you! What are you, a tell-me-a-story freak or something??

PATUMIERA: Scusi?

WASTBA: Yuh. Sure.

MULLEIMER: Ich kann weder hören noch sehen. Könnte mir Bitte jemand helfen???

TRANSLATOR: I can't hear or see. Could somebody help me?

LAPOUBELLE: Mais calmez-vous. Vous êtes affreusement tendue.

MULLEIMER: Wer ist das?

WASTBA: [*Completely panicked*] Oh . . . my . . . God . . . [*Screams*] Tranquility! [*Spins in circles*] Got . . . to . . . get . . . calm! [*Yells at class*] Calm down!

MULLEIMER: [*Stands in front of* WASTBA] Wo ist meine Brille?

WASTBA: I know you're upset, but can you imagine how *I* feel? [*She washes herself—her hands and arms—with "Wash-'n-Dri" napkins from her sack*] He . . . was . . . enormous. Eight or nine feet tall!

MULLEIMER: Wo ist meine Brille, Fräulein?

WASTBA: For God's sake, this is no time for foreign language problems! [*Pauses*] He couldn't have been eight or nine feet tall. I must be hysterical. Sit down. [*She sits, and they all sit, but for* MULLEIMER] I'm sitting. Why don't you whistle something? [*She whistles*] I'm whistling. [*She pauses*] I'm hysterical. Why don't you change the subject? Class. I'm changing the subject—[*She smiles*] We must move on. Whatever is happening is happening in the ladies' room and corridor and not in our room. [*Smiles, locks door again,* MULLEIMER *stands nearby*] Our door is locked. Our room is safe. [*Pauses*] Things make sense here.

MULLEIMER: [*In front of* WASTBA, *near door*] Meine Brille? Wo ist sie?

WASTBA: [*Pounds fist onto desk loudly*] Stop following me around, damn it. I said things make sense in here and now I really mean it!

MULLEIMER: [*Moves quickly, blindly, back to his desk. Students assist him—lead him*] Wie bitte?

WASTBA: We're going to just have to continue our class in a sane and orderly fashion. Otherwise, we perish. [*To* MULLEIMER] You want to perish?

MULLEIMER: Wie bitte?

WASTBA: Sit down.

LAPOUBELLE: Zeet! Zeet!

[MULLEIMER *finds his way back to his chair and sits*]

WASTBA: [*To* LAPOUBELLE] You! You want to perish?

LAPOUBELLE: [*Stands; recites the word, tentatively*] Per . . . per- . . . per-ashh . . .

WASTBA: "Ish," not "ash." There's a good word to learn. Perish.

[*Writes "Perish" on blackboard*]

PATUMIERA: Mia cara signorina . . .

WASTBA: [*Turns to him; angrily*] Sit down and learn the word "perish." [*Pauses.* PATUMIERA *stops, turns, rushes to his seat, sits*] I'm getting calm. If you were smart, you'd go for calm, too. See? If I were any calmer, I'd be boring.

LAPOUBELLE: Ma chere mademoiselle, il y a encore en petit probleme . . . encore . . .

WASTBA: I said "Boring."

YOKO: [*Stands suddenly; takes over. Points to her head in gesture of "I understand now"*] Ah! Bowling. [*She mimes bowling*]

MULLEIMER: Wo ist meine Brille?

WASTBA: I don't understand a word you're saying!

MULLEIMER: Ich verstehe kein Wort von dem was sie sagen.

LAPOUBELLE: Je ne comprends pas un mot de ce qu'ils disent.

PATUMIERA: Non capisco una parola di quel che dicono.

YOKO: Watashiwa ka rerano hanashiteru kotoga wakarimasen.

[*All at same time twice*]

WASTBA: [*Writes the word "English" beside the word "Perish" on the blackboard. Yells; stopping their words*] I'm afraid you're going to have to just get it through your heads that this is an *English* class and the language I'm afraid I must *insist* we all speak is . . . for the love of God . . . *English*. [*She points to the words*] Attention must be paid to these words: they both end in "i-s-h." [*Pauses*] Let's hear them. [*No response. Waves her arms*] English. Perish. [*No response*] English. Perish. English. Perish. I *demand* you follow! [*She points at* PATUMIERA] You! *English. Perish.*

[PATUMIERA *is again in panic. He smiles and shrugs and tries to repeat what she has said: tries to please her*]

PATUMIERA: [*Mimicking*] English. Perish.

WASTBA: Very good. [*Waves arms*] Everybody now: *Hit it!* [*Screams*] English! Perish.

LAPOUBELLE: English. Per-EESH.

WASTBA: *English! Perish!*

ALL: [*Each yells the words "English! Perish!" in an accent indigenous to his or her own particular country*] Iiingliish! Glishie! Anglish! (Etc.)

[MULLEIMER *leans forward trying to whisper in the direction of* WASTBA's *voice, but instead whispers in the clear*]

MULLEIMER: *Fräulein!* . . .

WASTBA: [*To all*] That was wonderful! See? You can get it if you really want . . . But you must try . . . Just like the song says . . .

MULLEIMER: [*Whispers again*] *Fräulein!*

WASTBA: Huh?

MULLEIMER: [*Whispers again; embarrassed to be without his glasses. Tries to appear as though all in his life is normal*] *Fräulein!*

WASTBA: [*Whispers across to him*] What do you want?

MULLEIMER: [*Whispers*] Wo ist meine Brille, Fräulein?

TRANSLATOR: [*Whispers*] Where are my glasses, lady?

WASTBA: [*Whispers*] Huh?

MULLEIMER: *Wo ist meine Brille, Fräulein?*

WASTBA: [*Whispers*] You will either get a goddamn English word out of that mouth of yours or just drop all talk! . . . [*Pauses; she still whispers*]

MULLEIMER: [*Whispers*] Verstehen Sie denn nicht dass ich nicht verstehe?

TRANSLATOR: [*Whispers*] Don't you understand that I don't understand?

WASTBA: [*Whispers*] Don't you understand that I don't understand? [MRS. PONG *stands and begins to walk to the closed door. She is holding her stomach and seems to be experiencing pain. She bows to* WASTBA, *who seems astonished to see the old woman's move to door. To old* MRS. PONG] What are you doing? [MRS. PONG *bows to* LAPOUBELLE *and* PATUMIERA, *who stand and return her bow*]

LAPOUBELLE: Bon soir, madame.

PATUMIERA: Bon sera . . .

WASTBA: Where are you going? [MRS. PONG *bows*] Where do you want to go to do what? [MRS. PONG *bows again*] Don't open that door! [WASTBA *leaps between* MRS. PONG *and the door*] Didn't you hear me? [WASTBA *shoves* MRS. PONG *back away from door and knocks her down.* MRS. PONG *squeals. All go to* MRS. PONG *and help her up*]

LAPOUBELLE: Elle lui fait mal!

TRANSLATOR: She hurt her!

PATUMIERA: Le ho fatto male!

TRANSLATOR: She hurt her!

YOKO: Sensei wa ranbo o shimashita!

TRANSLATOR: She hurt her!

WASTBA: I'm sorry. I didn't mean to shove that hard. Push always grows to shove, I swear to God!

LAPOUBELLE: Nom de Dieu, vous avez vu ça? Elle a frappé cette vieille vietnamienne.

WASTBA: I didn't mean to push this old Chinese lady around . . . or *certainly down!* [*Looks at all, who are each staring amazed at* WASTBA]

YOKO: [*Yells, as will all that follow*] Dou shitanodesuka?

PATUMIERA: Che è successo?

LAPOUBELLE: Qu'est-ce qui se passe?

MULLEIMER: Ich flehe Sie an meine Brille!

WASTBA: What the hell is happening in here anyway? [MRS. PONG *makes another run at the door, more confirmed this time. She succeeds in reaching the knob this time.* WASTBA *whacks at her hand on the knob*] Hey! [WASTBA *pulls* MRS. PONG *away from the door*] I told you once, damn it! Now get away from this door! [WASTBA *drags* MRS. PONG *back to her desk and seats her*] Now, damn it! I've told you there's a dirty man out there. [*She holds* MRS. PONG *by the back of her jacket*] At your age, what the hell are you looking for, anyway? [MRS. PONG *whimpers, pulling back. All are shocked, staring*] You could get hurt out there! [*Holding* MRS. PONG *still by back of her jacket*] Try to understand . . .

MRS. PONG: [*She breaks free and runs, screaming*] Ahhh-yiiiii . . .

WASTBA: Why are you screaming?

MRS. PONG: Ahhhh-yiiii!

WASTBA: Stop it!

MRS. PONG: Ooooo. [*She sits; whimpers. She eats*]

WASTBA: [*Leaning over* MRS. PONG] Did I hurt you, old Chinese woman?

MRS. PONG: [*Moving backwards as a crab*] Ahhh-yiiiiii-*ahhhh* . . .

YOKO: Kio ochitsukete! Kitto nani ka riyu ga arundesuwa.

WASTBA: [*To class*] I don't even know her name. [*To* YOKO] What's her name? [*No response*] Aren't you family? [*No response.* WASTBA *grabs large red tag from around* MRS. PONG's *neck*] There's a tag on her neck . . . [*Reads*] "Hi. My name is *Zink?*" [*Strains to read*] I can't read *this!* . . . [*To* MRS. PONG] What's your name? [*No reply*] Don't you even know your own name? [*Reads tag again*] "I don't speak English . . ." [*To all*] Oh, no need to be modest. [*Pats* MRS. PONG, *who moans*] "Mrs. Pong . . ." Is that your name: Mrs. Pong?

MULLEIMER: Meine Brille . . .

WASTBA: [*In panic; to* MULLEIMER] Hey, I've seen a lot worse on laundries and restaurants . . . Wing, Ling, Ding . . . [*Shrugs*] But, listen. Pong's no picnic either, I guess . . . [WASTBA *absently pats* MRS. PONG's *head, unintentionally scaring the old lady again*]

MRS. PONG: Yiiii—iiii . . .

WASTBA: [*To* MRS. PONG; *leaning in to her*] Don't you understand anything? [*No response*] What I did I did for your own good . . . [*N.B: Throughout above,* WASTBA *has been holding* MRS. PONG *erect in her chair*]

LAPOUBELLE: Je pense que vous devriez vraiment vous expliquer. Aprés tout, vous l'avez poussé parterre.

WASTBA: Everybody here is my witness, right?

PATUMIERA: Ho bisogno di un splegazione, adesso.

WASTBA: I know you're all upset. I'm upset, too . . . [MRS. PONG *whimpers*] Now *you're* upset, too . . . [WASTBA *smiles at all*] We're just going to have to drop our mutual differences for a while and learn some English. A common goal is always for the common good . . .

LAPOUBELLE: Chère mademoiselle . . . Personne ne comprend encore! Compris? Personne!

WASTBA: I said "common goal for common good." Don't you ever pay attention? [WASTBA *releases her hold on* MRS. PONG *and begins to move to the blackboard*] These distractions will have to stop. [*She picks up apple that* YOKO *brought to class for her.* WASTBA *smashes apple on desk.* YOKO *screams*] One rotten apple spoils a bunch. [WASTBA *throws apple into wastebasket*] One must resist temptation. Mrs. Pong has managed to distract us . . . She has, in short, managed to become our mutual rotten apple, *but* . . . I needn't remind you that the object of this class is clearly English and hardly some old Pong. [MRS. PONG *sings "I Can't Give You Anything But Love, Baby" very quietly; a hum. Reading from sheet at same time all babble questions about* MRS. PONG *and* WASTBA's *wrestling match*] . . . so if you'll kindly and politely pay a little attention here, I'm going to give you the history of English. [*Pauses; smiles*] I picked this sheet up in the office . . . early this morning. [WASTBA *has now written the words "The Great Vowel Shift" on the blackboard.* MRS. PONG *tries to calm herself down by singing more loudly now. The words are sometimes clear. "Baby" is sung in English*]

MRS. PONG: [*To the tune of "I Can't Give You Anything But Love."*] Bah, bah, bah, bah, bah, bah, bah, bah, bahhh . . . Ba-Bee Bah, bah, bah, bah, bah, bah, bah, bah, bahhh . . . Ba-bee.

WASTBA: "The Great Vowel Shift." [*Reading*] "Compared to Old English, in phonological terms, Middle English's č, c̄ . . . ī" . . . [*She writes the letters on blackboard as she lectures*]

YOKO: IIII . . .

PATUMIERA: Eeee . . .

WASTBA: Ī, ē, ū . . .

LAPOUBELLE: Ooooo . . .

WASTBA: Please just quietly take notes, okay. "ō and ē . . ."

MRS. PONG: [*Ill and faint*] Aaaaayyyyiiii . . .

WASTBA: Oh. [*Without looking up, continues reading*] ". . . and ā were raised in their articulation. Middle English's ā, which comes from Old English's short ă, in open syllables, was fronted as well." [*Looks up at class*] While this may seem to mean little to you, it means even less to me, and I was *born* speaking English perfectly! [*Reads again*] "The highest two Middle English front and back vowels, ī . . ."

YOKO: īīīī

WASTBA: "and ū respectively, became sounds traditionally known as diphthongs . . ."

MRS. PONG: [*Collapses in unconsciousness, her head crashing down forward on her desk*] Oooooo . . .

WASTBA: [*Continuing*] "These changes in the quality of the long or tense vowels constitute what is known as . . ." [*Underlining each word as she says it*] " . . . The Great Vowel Shift."

LAPOUBELLE: [*To* YOKO] Mon Dieu. Mais la vieille vietnamienne! Elle est tombée dans les pommes.

PATUMIERA: Forse è la vechiai. Mi sembra che questa vechia ha due centi anni.

YOKO: Toshi no seikamo shiremasenne. Nihyakusai gurai ni mierude-sho.

MULLEIMER: [*Head down; sulking*] Wo ist meine brille?

[*All gather around* MRS. PONG, *rubbing her hands and ad libbing encouraging remarks*]

YOKO: Shimpai shinakutemo daijobu desuyo.

LAPOUBELLE: Je vends les assurance de vie, et j'en ai vu de pires, croyez-moi!

PATUMIERA: Non fa paura, signora. Questa è una rechia. Ha bisogna di una riposa per un settimana e motto di medicazione. Conosca un dottore?

YOKO: Oisha san o shitte imasuka?

PATUMIERA: Conosca un dottore?

WASTBA: [*She now turns and faces them. For the first time in this sequence, she is aware that no one is paying any attention at all. She is furious. She throws the blackboard eraser and hits* LA-POUBELLE's *back. They all look up at her a bit frightened.* MRS. PONG *as well.* PATUMIERA *picks up eraser from floor. Silence*] Supposing I were to spring a little pop quiz right now, huh? Huh huh? Huh huh huh? Which one of you would even pass? [*She points to* PATUMIERA] You? Could you pass?

PATUMIERA: [*He has eraser and whacks himself on head with same for emphasis. Chalk dust flies*] Ho un dolore di testa.

LAPOUBELLE: Que j'ai mal à la tête.

MULLEIMER: Mir zerspringt der kopf.

YOKO: Atama ga itai wa.

MRS. PONG: Aaaii, ngoi gä hai tiĕk wah.

WASTBA: Okay, I'm now preparing the quiz . . . [*Turns to board, grabs forehead*] . . . You over there, you're giving me a headache. [*Looks at* PATUMIERA. PATUMIERA *smiles and then coughs*]

PATUMIERA: [*To* WASTBA] Ho una brutta tosse. [*Holds his chest*] Ho un dolore qui.

WASTBA: [*Turns and faces him, slowly*] Can I believe my ears? It sounds like an unwanted tongue . . .

PATUMIERA: [*Holds his stomach, in pain*] Ho un dolore di stomaco . . . [*Holds his thighs*] Mi fanno male le gambe . . . [*Grabs his back, suddenly*] Mi fa male le schiene!

WASTBA: And now lewd gestures, too!

PATUMIERA: Mi fa male il bracchio. Mi fa male l'orecchio. Ho i brividi. Ho febbre.

WASTBA: That does it, wop! I'm giving you a pop quiz!

PATUMIERA: Da ieri.

WASTBA: Take your pen and a piece of yellow lined paper and explain the Great Vowel Shift. Ten minutes, no open books.

PATUMIERA: [*Paying no attention*] Da ieri.

WASTBA: [*Screams*] *Are you taking this quiz or what?*

PATUMIERA: [*Humiliated to be yelled at in front of the others, he screams as well*] Non capisco un cavalo di quel che dici! [LAPOUBELLE *is still standing near* MRS. PONG. *He misunderstands the tension in the room, completely*]

LAPOUBELLE: [*In French*] On dirait qu'elle vit encore mais à peine. Et ce n'est pas grâce à vous . . . Quelle belle soirée!

PATUMIERA: *Non capisco un cavolo do quel che dici!* [*Screaming at* LAPOUBELLE] *Che cavolo dicono?*

LAPOUBELLE: [*Screams back at* PATUMIERA] *Qu'est-ce due vous dîtes, tireur de spaghetti? Hein? Sale macaroni?* [*To the world*] *Ben, merde, alors! Quelle belle soirée!*

[*All continue their complaints, as* MULLEIMER *chimes in as well*]

MULLIEMER: *Himmel! Herr Gott! Donnerwetternocheinmar! Ich will meine Brille???*

WASTBA: What the hell do you want?

MULLEIMER: [*Groping his way toward the sound of* WASTBA's *voice, his hands finds one of her breasts*] *Meine Brille!* [WASTBA *pulls back violently*]

WASTBA: *Oh . . . my . . . God!*

MULLEIMER: [*Reaches toward her again*] *Meine Brille, Fräulein!*

WASTBA: Goddammit, just keep your filthy little Dutch hands to yourself! Don't you think I've had enough sex for one night!

LAPOUBELLE: Sexe?

[MULLEIMER *reaches out toward her again and she slaps his face*]

WASTBA: I can't believe it! You're trying it again!

[*Silence in room as all stare amazed*]

MULLEIMER: [*Shocked and amazed, still blind without his eyeglasses. He staggers back*] Fräulein!

WASTBA: I'm sorry to have had to do that in front of everybody, but you did what you did in front of everybody.

[MULLEIMER *is not to be stopped now. He moves to* WASTBA *once more, reaches for her one final time*]

MULLEIMER: *Wo ist meine Brille?* [*He reaches out, she slaps*]

WASTBA: Now that is the goddamned limit! [*She slaps* MULLEIMER *again*]

MULLEIMER: Arghhh!

WASTBA: I've told you five or six times, Dutchie! This is the twentieth century, ya' know! I don't have to take that kind of crap from anybody anymore.

MULLEIMER: Was ist denn? Wo bin ich?

PATUMIERA: Che sta succedendo?

[N.B.: *Throughout the entire section,* MRS. PONG *has been watching, wide-eyed.* MRS. PONG *will soon make a break for the door again and will not, this time, be stopped. Her moves will be enormous in that she will leap from the floor, high into the air, several times, as she screams at* WASTBA *in rage.* MULLEIMER *has bowed his head now in shame and humiliation and* LAPOU-BELLE *is leading him back to his chair*]

WASTBA: If you ever . . . *ever!* . . . take such a horrid liberty again, I swear I will seek revenge . . . [*Pulls back, straightens herself*]

MULLEIMER: [*Whispered*] Fräulein? . . .

WASTBA: *If* you're getting my message! [*No response. She waits for an answer as she seats* MULLEIMER. MRS. PONG *begins her major move now. She leaps up, screams, and threatens to karate chop* WASTBA]

MRS. PONG: Eeiieewwwaamaaiiaaa!!!

WASTBA: Hey!

MRS. PONG: Nay kay kǐng wah! Nay kay kǐng mä ngoi dē jŏm lŏn-nä nay lieng-gä siew äng nay gä gieng wah!

TRANSLATOR'S VOICE: Stay back! Stay back or I'll break both of your arms and your neck, too!

MRS. PONG: How-lä. [*Stands straight now. Leans back and nods to* WASTBA, *who stands by the door, staring, astonished*] Ngoi chŭt coi gä mwŭn wah. [MRS. PONG *moves closer to* WASTBA *and points to* MULLEIMER, PATUMIERA, YOKO *and* LAPOUBELLE, *one at a time, angrily they try to calm* MRS. PONG *down*] Coi thlŏm gä gŏm ngoi ngǐm thlŏm boy sui äng cui dē gom ngoy ngim yit boy chä äng coi sē ngoi dē chut coi gä mwun hun thlee swa wah, how mah?

TRANSLATOR'S VOICE: I'm going out that door right now. Those three made me drink three glasses of water and she made me drink a cup of tea and now I'm going out the door and to the bathroom, okay?

MRS. PONG: Na hiew ngoi gŏng mah, hääää?

TRANSLATOR'S VOICE: Do you understand me?

MRS. PONG: [*Waves the terrified* WASTBA *away from the door and moves to it, stops, turns around, faces into room and yells at* WASTBA] Ngoy sä-lä ngoy m sät gŏng fŏn wa, lë, hī ngoy sät

gŏng fŏn wah, ngoi dē m loy coi yä! *Nay hiew ngoi gŏng mä?!
Hä?!*

TRANSLATOR'S VOICE: I'm sorry I don't speak English, but, if I did
speak English, I wouldn't be here! *Don't you understand that?!
Okay?!*

[*Making a final attempt to save* MRS. PONG, WASTBA *leans in and
pleads with her, as all surround* MRS. PONG]

WASTBA: Old Chinese woman, hear me. Don't go out there. I beg
you . . .

MRS. PONG: [*She chases* LAPOUBELLE, *screaming*] Ngoi coi lŏw yiek
mieng gŏn gwä nä cŏw thlay hŏn-nieh wä! A sui gŏw näy cow-a,
niek mä? Hä, hä-hä, hä-hä-hä?? [*In English to* LAPOUBELLE] Sit!
LAPOUBELLE *hides behind chair*]

WASTBA: My knee is bent to you. That's a beg. Please, Pong. Pong.
Pong. I'm pleading, Pong. Back up to your student desk. Just
throw it in reverse and back up. Please, Pong.

MRS. PONG: Nay hong huey lä-a. Ngoy chūt de chēt lë.

WASTBA: [*Moves to* MRS. PONG] I'll have to forcibly detain you. I
know it must rub your religion the wrong way, but what the hell
choice are you offering me, huh? [WASTBA *reaches for old* MRS.
PONG'S *sleeves*]

MRS. PONG: [*Raises her hand to chop. She screams*] Nay kay kung!
[WASTBA *leans silently against blackboard now, head bowed*]
Ngoy loy fŏn thlay ga fŏn jŭng yä . . . [MRS. PONG *holds up four
fingers*]

TRANSLATOR'S VOICE: I'll be back in four minutes . . . [MRS. PONG
waves her four fingers]

MRS. PONG: Thlay. Gä-wä.

TRANSLATOR'S VOICE: Four. Only. [*Repeating Chinese word and waving. She thinks* MRS. PONG *has said goodby*] Thlay, Pong, thlay
Gä-wä . . .

ALL: [*Waving*] Thlay, Gä-wä.

[MRS. PONG *stops, looks at* WASTBA, *shrugs, bows, opens door
and exits. As soon as* MRS. PONG *has negotiated her exit,* WASTBA

slams door closed tightly by hurling herself against same. There is silence in the room]

WASTBA: Well, listen . . . [*Smiles*] . . . maybe an old Oriental of her years just isn't cut out for a stiff class like ours . . . [*Walks to* MRS. PONG's *desk, finds her slip and walks back to wastebasket, where she throws slip away, after tearing it to bits. She moves to desk. She sits. Folds her hands, smiles*] Let's hope old Mrs. Pong finds another class . . . something more to her . . . well . . . fancy. [*Pause*] Here we are again; just us. [*Pauses, smiles*] Any questions?

PATUMIERA: Non ho capito nemmena una parola che tu hai detta!

TRANSLATOR: I haven't understood even one word of what you've said!

MULLEIMER: [*With overstated calm*] Okay . . . [*Smiles a big smile*] . . . Jetzt sitze ich und bin ruhiger . . .

TRANSLATOR: Okay . . . I'm sitting now and I'm calmer . . .

MULLEIMER: . . . also, wo ist meine Brille? [*He is now, as if to prove calmness, smiling rather idiotically*]

TRANSLATOR: Now, where are my glasses?

WASTBA: [*Calling back*] I'm not answering a single question until you're asking in English . . . [*Pauses*] Sorry . . .

MULLEIMER: Wo ist meine Brille?

WASTBA: Nope.

MULLEIMER: [*Through clenched teeth*] Wo ist meine Brille?

WASTBA: Uh uh . . .

MULLEIMER: Wo ist meine Brille? [*No response, as* WASTBA *crosses her arms on her chest and shakes her head.* MULLEIMER *stands now and screams*] In Ordnung! Dann eben nicht! Dann bin ich eben blind! [MULLEIMER *throws a tremendous temper tantrum. He screams. He throws his books. He breaks pencils and throws them onto the floor. He punches his desk. He beats the floor. Finally he sulks. Silence, as all stare in disbelief*]

WASTBA: Why did you do that?

LAPOUBELLE: De toute ma vie, je n'ai jamais vu une scene comme ça, jamais. Ça alors!

TRANSLATOR'S VOICE: In my entire life, I've never ever seen a scene like that! Wow!

PATUMIERA: Credi che abbia imparato qualcosa?

TRANSLATOR: Do you think he learned anything?

YOKO: [*She smiles and whispers to* PATUMIERA] Eigo wa omottayorimo taihendesune . . .

TRANSLATOR: English looks a lot tougher than I thought . . .

[WASTBA *at blackboard. She writes the word "Silence" on black-board. All stare at her. She stares back at them. There is silence*]

WASTBA: Silence. Can you hear it? [*Pauses, finger to word on black-board*] Silence.

LAPOUBELLE: Zi-lence?

WASTBA: Silence. That's what's wanted here: silence. Okay?

LAPOUBELLE: Ah, oui. C'est le même mot en francais: *silence*. [*Above "silence" in French*]

WASTBA: Si-lonce. Right. Now let's hear you say the word in English: silence . . .

LAPOUBELLE: Ouj, je comprends. [*Now in English*] Silence.

WASTBA: [*Smiles*] Perfect.

LAPOUBELLE: [*Put his fingers to his lips and repeats word*] Silence.

PATUMIERA: Silenco!

LAPOUBELLE: [*Looks sternly at* PATUMIERA] Shhh.

WASTBA: Silence.

PATUMIERA: Zi-*lence?*

LAPOUBELLE: Shhhh.

WASTBA: Silence.

YOKO: Silence? [*Giggles*]

LAPOUBELLE: Shhhh.

YOKO *and* PATUMIERA: Silence!

LAPOUBELLE: [*Angrily*] Shhh!

WASTBA: [*Smiling to* PATUMIERA *and* YOKO] That's much better . . . Silence.

YOKO *and* PATUMIERA: [*Happily*] Silence! Silence!

LAPOUBELLE: [*Angrily, to both. In French again. He stands*] Shhhh! Ecoutez! Silence, hein?

WASTBA: [*To* LAPOUBELLE: *Angrily*] Will you stop interrupting us?

LAPOUBELLE: Mais, mademoiselle . . .

WASTBA: [*Placing her finger to lips*] Shhh.

LAPOUBELLE: [*Angrily*] Bon. [*He sits. He is silent a moment*]

YOKO *and* PATUMIERA: [*In unison. Pointing to* LAPOUBELLE, *they begin laughing*] Silence. [YOKO *giggles*]

WASTBA: [*Moves to her desk, sits on it and* MULLEIMER's *glasses*] Now then . . . Ohhh! [*Finds glasses*] Look! I almost forgot! Not broken. Not broken. Didn't break them. [*She turns to* MULLEIMER] Your glasses . . . [*She puts them on his face*] Here you go. [*Mulleimer is shocked and amazed and thrilled*]

MULLEIMER: Meine Brille! [*He stands and looks at* WASTBA *and at class, overjoyed*] Ahhhh! Meine Brille! Ssank you.

WASTBA: [*Thrilled*] Ahhh!

MULLEIMER: Ssank you . . . veriii mich . . .

WASTBA: [*Pointing to his mouth*] English!

YOKO: Ahhh!

PATUMIERA: Ahhh!

MULLEIMER: Veri mich, yah!

WASTBA: [*Pointing to his lips*] English, class! English! Immersion is working! [*She applauds* MULLEIMER, *who bows*] Bless you, Mr. Mancini . . .

MULLEIMER: [*Laughing and bowing*] Veri mich, yahhh!

[*The rest of the class now applauds, wildly laughing. They are extremely happy to be succeeding. They are now applauding and cheering.* WASTBA *turns to them, delighted. She bows.* WASTBA *laughs anxiously, bows*]

WASTBA: Oh, my goodness. You're all expressing such approval! [MULLEIMER *stands and bows as well*] Oh, look at you! Excited . . . bowing, too . . . [WASTBA *straightens up*] Okay, now, let's settle. Settle, now, settle. [WASTBA *is laughing quite happily. She searches through her satchels of books. She smiles to the class*] I want you all to understand that while I have nothing . . . personally . . . against your tongues, I must teach this primary English class absolutely *by . . . the . . . book.* [*Smiles*] I'm sure you understand. [*Pauses*] Where's the book? [*Searches feverishly: finds book*] I got it! [*Looks up, smiling. Produces small book covered in orange fabric, which she waves at class*] I had to put ten dollars down on this. [*Smiles*] A deposit. [*Pauses*] In this country, it's assumed you're going to lose . . . something. Nor do I. Not at ten dollars a shot. [*Smiles*]

LAPOUBELLE: [*Recognizes a word and smiles as well*] Sum-zing!

WASTBA: Hmmm.

LAPOUBELLE: Je comprends un peu. *Sum-zing,* par example: c'est quelquechose, n'est-ce pas?

WASTBA: *Will you please and kindly pay some attenion! Sit down!*

LAPOUBELLE: [*Humiliated*] Enfin, merde! C'est quelquechose! Ce n'est pas compliqué! [*They all sit*]

ALL: Seetz . . . Sit dunn . . . Teetz . . . etc.

WASTBA: This is the book. Say it. Book. Book. Book.

ALL: Book. Book. Book.

WASTBA: [*Reads to them, clearly*] "The object of the primary English class will be to teach the negative form." [*To the class*] The negative should be right up your alleys. [*Reading again*] "You will reach the negative through the positive . . . ." [*To the class*] Pay attention. [*Reads again*] "You will reach the negative through the positive . . ." Okay . . . [*Reading*] "Touch the floor and announce to class 'I can touch the floor.'" [*Pause*] Once again, I learn to lower myself in the name of higher learning. [*She drops to the floor*] Okay. Here I am. Listen. [*She touches the floor and announces to class*] I can touch the floor. [*Reads again from book*] "Have they all said 'I can touch the floor!'?" [*Looks up*] Has *who* all said "I can touch the floor!?" This is just tawdry . . . If they think I'm going to make a life of this, they're barking up the wrong tree . . .

[LAPOUBELLE *suddenly drops out of his chair onto the floor, on all fours, as might a hound*]

LAPOUBELLE: Flo-er! Flo-er! [*He moves toward* WASTBU *grinning and yelping*] Flo-er! Flo-er!

WASTBA: What is it?

LAPOUBELLE: Flo-er! Flo-er! [*He moves closer to her, even more houndlike. She pulls away, frightened*]

WASTBA: What the hell are you doing? Get away from me! Sit! Scat! Heel! [*Screams*] Sit!!!

MULLEIMER: [*Sits on the floor, touching it with two hands*] Zeet? Zcct, fluur!

YOKO: [*Same*] Flory.

PATUMIERA: [*Same*] Scusi?

WASTBA: The floor! You're touching the floor! [*Demonstrates*]

PATUMIERA: [*Shocked and amazed and thrilled; on his knees*] Fleeer!

WASTBA: [*Flailing her arms about for them to follow*] I can touch the floor! I can touch the floor. I can touch the floor!

ALL: I can touch the floor! [*In unison, in their varying accents*]

WASTBA: [*Reading*] "If they can touch the floor and have said so, show them how to touch the desk." [*Looking up*] Okay, you sneaky devils, I can touch the desk.

LAPOUBELLE: Comment?

WASTBA: [*She runs to her desk, slaps same*] I can touch the *desk!*

LAPOUBELLE: [*Walks to her desk*] "I can tooooch le dest!"

WASTBA: [*Flailing her arms*] Everybody! [*Screaming and whacking the desk*] I CAN TOUCH THE DESK!

ALL: [*Screaming and whacking the desk as well*] I . . . Tooch . . . Desttie. [*Etc.*]

WASTBA: [*Reads from book*] "Simple parts of the body." What's simple, these days? [*She dances and slaps her feet*] Feet! I can touch my feet.

ALL: [*Imitate her as best they can*] Tooochhhh . . . Feetz . . . [*Etc.*]

WASTBA: This is working! Oh, my dear God! [*Laughs*] I can touch my knees!

ALL: I can touch my knees . . . [*Etc.*]

WASTBA: I can touch my nose!

ALL: I can touch my nose! [*Etc.*]

WASTBA: [*She stops them. They wait, fingers on noses*] Just hang on a minute . . . this is truly exciting. [*She looks at book again, reading*] "You will lead them to try to touch the ceiling. When they cannot, they will, of their own volition, offer: 'I cannot touch the ceiling.' And then you will have succeeded in teaching the primary English class." [*Looks up*] Do you understand that? [*Reading*] "Command them to touch the wall . . ." [*Looks up*] Touch the wall! I command you . . . [*No response. She reads again*] . . . "and then act on your own command, leading them." [*Looks up*] Okay. Touch the wall! [*She leads them to wall, waving arms for them to follow action and words*] I can touch the wall!

ALL: I can tooch wall . . . I toochy wall . . . Eye tooch vall . . . [*Etc.* WASTBA *will lead them around room, as group, screaming at them to touch various points and objects.* MULLEIMER *will follow, but always several beats behind rest of class*]

WASTBA: Touch the floor again! [*They do*]

ALL: [*But* LAPOUBELLE] I can touch floor again . . .

LAPOUBELLE: Ah, c'est facile. [*Swaggers*] Zee floor again. Voila!

WASTBA: Touch the corner!

ALL: [*Ganging together at corner*] I can tooch corner! . . . [*Etc.*]

WASTBA: Touch your elbow!

ALL: I can tooch my elbow! [*They do.* PATUMIERA *embraces* WASTBA *from behind, grasping her elbow*]

PATUMIERA: I can touch your elbow! [WASTBA *giggles*]

WASTBA: Stand by, my darling students, because here it comes! [*She staggers giggling, to center. She points to ceiling and screams to them*] Touch the ceiling! [*She pretends to try, stretching up high above her head toward ceiling. She wags her head "NO"*] Touch the ceiling! NAW-NAW-NAW . . . ceiling [*They all strain toward ceiling in attempt to please her, but none can touch ceiling, which is, of course, high above them. They all strain and moan*]

ALL:	WASTBA:
Arggghhh . . .	Touch the ceiling! Ooooo . . .
Ohhhh . . .	Touch the ceiling! Ooooo . . .
Zeiling . . .	Touch the ceiling! Ooooo . . . [*Etc.*]
Arghhh . . .	

[Etc. MULLEIMER, *silently, at front of room, has climbed to the top of* WASTBA's *desk. He reaches up and touches the ceiling]*

MULLEIMER: I . . . can . . . touch . . . zeeling . . . *[He stands, fingertips on ceiling, grinning broadly. Keeping his fingers on ceiling, he smiles down to* WASTBA *for approval. All others in class applaud* MULLEIMER's *success]*

ALL: Yayy . . . Ooooo . . . *[Etc.]*

WASTBA: *[Outraged; screams at* MULLEIMER*]* You rotten little son of a bitch!

MULLEIMER: Zeeling?

WASTBA: *[Screams]* Get down! *[He does; totally bewildered. She yells, as she slaps her textbook]* There's nothing in here about Germans!

YOKO: Doshite ikenaindesuka? Tenjo ni sawaretanoni.

WASTBA: *[Yells; cutting* YOKO's *line]* SHUT IT UP!!!

[There is silence in the room. PATUMIERA *smiles at* YOKO *and then at* WASTBA, *as if trying to explain the problem]*

PATUMIERA: Eeengleesh . . . Parla Eeengleesh.

WASTBA: Oh, yuh sure. You got it, champ!

PATUMIERA: *[Smiling even more broadly now]* Eeeengleesh, si?

WASTBA: Right. Now put a little cheese and tomato sauce on that!

PATUMIERA: *[Thinks he's succeeding]* Si?

WASTBA: *[Tight-lipped control]* Look, my dear *touristies,* we could really roll up our sleeves and get down to good hard work, or I could just send you back the word "English" and you could go on saying "Eeeeengliiish," just like we were playing ping-pong. *[Pauses. A knock is heard at door. Suddenly* WASTBA *stiffens]* Oh, my God! *[All watch her]* Pong! *[All look from one to the other.* WASTBA *goes to the door and, cautiously, she cracks open door.* WASTBA *slams the door and leans against it]* Him! Him! Him! Him! My heart! My God! *Him!*

ALL: *[Mimic her]* Him?

WASTBA: Out the door. In the hall. On his feet.

ALL: Feet!

WASTBA: Crap!

> [*They will each pick up her word "crap" in their own accents and pass the word from one to the other, as a small ball thrown, rapidly*]

MULLEIMER: [*Mimics her*] Crahrp?

LAPOUBELLE: [*Mimics* MULLEIMER] Crêpe?

PATUMIERA: [*Mimics* LAPOUBELLE] Cheptz?

MULLEIMER: [*Mimics* PATUMIERA] Grepz?

LAPOUBELLE: [*Mimics* MULLEIMER] Greque?

PATUMIERA: Grekzi?

WASTBA: Grekzi?

PATUMIERA: Grekzi?

YOKO: Grassi?

WASTBA: Grassy?

MULLEIMER: Was?

WASTBA: Huh?

LAPOUBELLE: Hein?

YOKO: Nani?

WASTBA: Huh?

MULLEIMER: Was?

WASTBA: Huh?

MULLEIMER: Was?

WASTBA: What?

MULLEIMER: Huh?

WASTBA: [*Stands; moves to her desk*] Listen, class, we've got to improve.

ALL: Improve!

WASTBA: If that old lady wants illicit sex, that's her business! We're here to learn English and that is, God damn it, precisely what I intend to do: so get ready to learn! [*All smile. Blank stares all around*] What did you all come here for if you don't speak any English? This is an English-speaking country!

YOKO: Ingrish.

WASTBA: Will you just shut it up, dopey!

YOKO: [*Correcting her*] Yoko.

WASTBA: Okay?

YOKO: [*Chirps happily*] O-kay . . . [*Giggles*]

WASTBA: [*Pauses*] I'm going to explain very slowly and carefully exactly what's going on here, so listen.

PATUMIERA: Non capisco un cavolo di quel che dici.

WASTBA: [*Furiously*] Sit down and put a belt on it, you! *Sit!*

ALL: Sit. Sitz. Seetz. [*Etc. There is a pause as all settle into their chairs*]

WASTBA: [*She sits now in the chair behind her desk and folds her hands demurely. She is trying desperately to be calm*] Class? [*All have notebooks and pencils poised now, thinking the lesson is finally coming*] In the simplest possible terms, here it is: there seems to be a maniac in the hall. [*Smiles*] Okay?

YOKO: O-kay. [*Giggles*]

WASTBA: You think a maniac is funny? [YOKO *giggles.* WASTBA *adds tersely*] If I were Oriental, I would be ashamed of you. [YOKO *takes her cue from* WASTBA's *tone of voice and is silent now*] Right. In this particular city, we have a perfect balance between maniacs and non-maniacs: one-to-one. [*Looks up quietly*] Here's the God's honest truth. [*Pauses*] My . . . well . . . cousin . . . My cousin was . . . well . . . How can I say it gently? Molested. Yup [*Looks up*] Did any of you know that? [*Smiles ironically*] Of course not. You want to know why not? Because *nobody* knew! Not for five years now! [*Pauses; adjusts her hands on desk to gain competent, serious posture. Smiles again, ironically*] Because she was too goddamn frightened to tell anybody. You *know* why??? . . . uhh . . . My cousin. [*Directly to class.* WASTBA *is anxious now; speaks quickly*] Here's why. On the night she was molested, she crawled out of the park . . . ripped and ravished . . . interfered with . . . Yuh, that's right! . . . She crawled out of the park and stopped the first passing man. A thin, ordinary-looking man. He was Caucasian, for Christ's sake! [*She is obviously overwrought now, fighting back her tears*] "Help!" she said. "I've been molested!"

she said. "Get a cop!" she said. "Hurry!" she said. "Please," she said. "For God's sakes," she said. "Hurry!" she said . . . [*Pauses*] He hurried all right. You know what he did? [*Leans back; smiles bravely*] He molested me. [*All are staring blankly at her*] No comments? No words of sympathy? No "Tough break, kiddo?" [*Pauses*] I could dial "Weather" and get a bigger response than I'm getting from you! [*All continue to stare blankly*]

LAPOUBELLE: [*Quietly. He is completely perplexed*] Chère mademoiselle . . . écoutez . . . Je suis absolument désolé d'avoir dire ça, mais il faut que vous . . .

WASTBA: [*To* LAPOUBELLE, *contemptuously*] I s'pose you think that's suave? Maybe that works in Brussels, froggy, but it's not cutting any ice with me, okay?

LAPOUBELLE: Personne ne comprend rien . . . *personne!*

WASTBA: Did it ever occur to any of you that your mothers were women?

PATUMIERA: Aspetta un momento. [*He has been studying his phrasebook and writing notes onto his pad of paper. He smiles proudly at* YOKO. *He smiles quietly at* WASTBA, *who is blowing her nose. All eyes on* PATUMIERA *now*] . . . un momento. Diro qualcosa . . . [*He holds his pad in front of him and studies it. He smiles again*] . . . Momento . . . [*Rummages through his phrasebook; smiles constantly to Yoko*]

TRANSLATOR: Wait just a minute. I'll say something.

PATUMIERA: Solo un secondo!

TRANSLATOR: Just a second.

PATUMIERA: [*Finds a phrase he likes*] Ne ho uno!

TRANSLATOR: I've got one! [PATUMIERA *slithers to* WASTBA, *using his most practiced movie-star walk. He has memorized something from his phrasebook.* WASTBA *is unhappy. She senses that* PATUMIERA *has some words of consolation, hence, she looks up at him*]

PATUMIERA: [*Reads slowly*] Signorina, may . . . I . . . smork?

WASTBA: Smork?

PATUMIERA: Posso fumare, signorina? [*Again, in English. Tries new pronunciation of word this time*] May . . . eye . . . schmork? [*He waves his cigarette pack*] Sigaretta!

WASTBA: Oh, sure, swell, smork. All of you go on! You want to have sets of malignant lungs: go on! Light up! Enjoy! Have your sigaretti . . .

PATUMIERA: [*Correcting her*] Sigaretta! [*Smiles to all*]

WASTBA: Sigaretta!

[PATUMIERA *smiles; shrugs; lights up a cigarette, drags on it deeply, blows smoke into the room. He will soon offer cigarettes to all, who will in turn begin to smoke. As each is quite anxious, quite a lot of smoke will be produced. Soon, in fact, the room will be filled with smoke and* WASTBA *will be coughing. At the moment,* WASTBA *is writing the words "Basic Salutations" on blackboard*]

PATUMIERA: [*Offers cigarettes to* YOKO] Sigaretta?

YOKO: Iie kekko desu. Watashinoga arimasukara. [*She lights a Japanese cigarette*]

PATUMIERA: [*To* MULLEIMER] Sigaretta?

MULLEIMER: Nein, danke. Ich habe meine eigenen. [*He lights a German cigarette*]

PATUMIERA: Si, Eigenen . . . [*To* LAPOUBELLE] Sigaretta?

LAPOUBELLE: Non merci, j'ai ma pipe. [*He lights a French pipe*]

YOKO: Ie kekko desu. Watashinoga arimasunode. [*She waves her Japanese cigarette*]

PATUMIERA: Giapponese, quella sigaretta? Vuole cambiare?

TRANSLATOR: Japanese, that cigarette? Let's exchange . . .

YOKO: Sorewa Itaria no tabako?

TRANSLATOR: Is that an Italian cigarette?

MULLEIMER: [*He offers* LAPOUBELLE *a drag of his cigarette*] Wollen Sie mal meine probieren? Vielleicht zu stark fuer Sie . . .

LAPOUBELLE: J'essaierai le vôtre, et vous le mien. Quoique le tabac francais sera probablement trop fort pour vous . . . [*He takes* MULLEIMER's *cigarette and puffs on it, exchanging his pipe for cigarette*]

TRANSLATOR: I'll try yours, you try mine. French tobacco's probably too strong for you though . . .

YOKO: Omoshiroi kedo. Yowai desune.

TRANSLATOR: Interesting, but too weak for my taste . . .

PATUMIERA: Interessante, ma un po leggiere per me. [*Puffing away happily*]

TRANSLATOR: Interesting, but too weak for my taste . . .

MULLEIMER: Ganz interessant, aber etwas schwach fuer meinen Geschmack. [*Puffing away happily*]

TRANSLATOR: Interesting, but too weak for my taste . . .

LAPOUBELLE: Interessant, mais pas assez fort à mon goût. [*Puffing away happily*]

TRANSLATOR: Interesting, but too weak for my taste . . .

[*The room is full of smoke.* WASTBA *is gasping and coughing.* PATUMIERA *walks to her, offers his packette of cigarettes*]

PATUMIERA: Sigaretta?

WASTBA: Oh, c'mon, will you? [*They all puff away, smiling*] I would like your . . . [*Coughs*] . . . attention . . . [*Coughs*] There is a slight problem. [*Coughs again. Room is full of smoke*] For Christ's sake! [*She slaps at the smoke in the air*] Open something, will you? [WASTBA *staggers to door and opens it, trying to add fresh air into room. She opens door fully, hiding herself behind door a moment,* MRS. PONG *is just outside door, smiling, re-entering room. She is puffing away on a Chinese cigarette. She takes step on to threshold. All class members see* MRS. PONG. WASTBA *does not, as she is behind door. Suddenly* WASTBA, *remembering that there is danger outside of door, slams door in* MRS. PONG's *face, knocking her out of threshold and sight. All are astonished*]

LAPOUBELLE: Elle vient de claquer la porte au nez de cette vieille Malasienne! [*He nervously puffs his pipe*]

PATUMIERA: Credo che sia stata lei ad uccidere la vecchia giapponese. [*To* WASTBA] Mi scusi, ma credo che lei ha appena ucciso la signora giapponese.

WASTBA: I know. I know. You must think I'm crazy to have opened the door with that maniac out there, but the smoke in here is so goddamned thick! [*Smiles; coughs*] Please stop smoking, okay?

YOKO: [*Puffing away on cigarette nervously*] Sensei wa toshiyorino gofu in o kizutsuke mashitayo.

WASTBA: Please, stop your smoking, okay, Yokè? [*YOKO smiles and puffs. Smoke hits WASTBA's face. WASTBA takes her cigarette and drops it on the floor. Angrily*] For God's sakes! I asked you politely!

YOKO: Toshiyori no gofujin o kizutsukete tabako o fumitsukete. Watashi wa seki ni modorimasu.

PATUMIERA: [*Confused*] Sigaretta? [*He offers cigarette to WASTBA*]

WASTBA: Oh, shove it, will you?

MULLEIMER: [*Puffing away on cigarette, he blows smoke right into WASTBA's face*] Ich lasse sie herein. [*WASTBA grabs his cigarette*] Hallo!

WASTBA: [*She stomps cigarette out on floor*] That's just about enough, okay?

MULLEIMER: Was ist denn?

[*WASTBA has begun to snap. She will scream at each of them, until she will suddenly say, in the sweetest of tones "good morning"*]

WASTBA: Sit down, Pilsner!

MULLEIMER: Wie, bitte?

WASTBA: *Down! Sit!* [*He sits*]

PATUMIERA: Non capisco nemmeno una parola di quel che sta dicendo.

WASTBA: Shut your mouth!

LAPOUBELLE: Excusez-moi, s'il vous plaît, mais . . .

WASTBA: [*Screams*] All of you: listen! [*Silence in room. N.B.: Change in her tone will be complete. She moves two steps into the center of the room, clasps her hands together and smiles demurely*] Good morning. [*No response. She nods to LAPOUBELLE*] Good morning. [*She rolls her arms at him, motioning for him to follow her words: to repeat them*] Good morning.

LAPOUBELLE: [*Stands; in disbelief*] Goood morr-ning.

WASTBA: Perfect. [*To MULLEIMER, who stands. LAPOUBELLE sits*] Now you. [*He stares dumbly at her*] Good morning.

MULLEIMER: Gud morgan . . .

WASTBA: Morning . . .

MULLEIMER: Morging . . .

WASTBA: Morning!

MULLEIMER: Morning!

WASTBA: You see? You got a will, you got a way. [To YOKO, *after* MULLEIMER *sits*] Right?

YOKO: [YOKO *stands for her turn. She turns to* PATUMIERA *and whispers*] Good morning, eh? [PATUMIERA *nods*]

WASTBA: Okay, let's start you right out on the other essential . . . according to my plan. [*Smiles to* YOKO] Good night.

PATUMIERA *and* YOKO: Ohh.

WASTBA: Good night!

YOKO: Good nightie.

WASTBA: Good nightie! Is that supposed to be cute? Good nightie! [*Smiles ironically*] It's not "Good nightie" but "Good night." [*Motions to her to repeat words*] Good night. [*No response. She speaks the words again, but with tremendous hostility*] Good night!

YOKO: [*Repeats tone*] Good night!

WASTBA: [*To* PATUMIERA] What's funny?

PATUMIERA: Good night.

WASTBA: What's funny? I asked what's funny?

PATUMIERA: [*Shyly now*] Good night?

LAPOUBELLE: [*Leans in correcting* PATUMIERA, *smiling to* WASTBA *for approval*] Goooood night. [*Smiles again. Nods smugly*] Goooood night.

WASTBA: You've got yourself a horrid oooo-sound. [*She squeezes his lips*] Gud, gud, gud. Gud night.

LAPOUBELLE: [*Repeats exactly*] Gud night.

MULLEIMER: [*Leans in to correct* LAPOUBELLE *at the same time* PATUMIERA *and* YOKO *try the same words*] Guden, guden, guden. Guden night.

YOKO: Good nightie . . .

PATUMIERA: God naght . . .

MULLEIMER: Guden, guden, guden . . . [*They each continue as* LAPOUBELLE *goes into a rage*] } [*Together—four times*]

LAPOUBELLE: C'est une catastrophe, cette leçon . . . et c'est de votre faute, je crois . . .

WASTBA: *Silence!*

MULLEIMER: [*Angrily now, to* WASTBA] Ich komme micht mit. Tut mir leid, aber ich verstehe nicht was Sie sagen . . .

WASTBA: [*Screams*] *I can't stand it!* [*All stop talking and look at her*] Stop your goddamn babble! Stop! Stop! Stop! [*She stands*] I *demand* you stop! [*She sits in* MRS. PONG's *chair*] I'm upset. [*She begins rocking* MRS. PONG's *desk back and forth, moaning*] Oh, dear God, I'm upset . . . My heart is filled with such loathing for all of you! [*Her body heaves as she sobs.* PATUMIERA *walks to her, cautiously*]

PATUMIERA: Come si sente? Sta bene?

WASTBA: [*On hearing his Italian language, sobs all the more*] It's hopeless, hopeless . . .

PATUMIERA: Che t' è successo? Diccelo per favore. [PATUMIERA *touches* WASTBA's *arm and she pulls back, violently, and screams*]

WASTBA: Don't you touch me! Oh, you would touch me! [*She is on her feet now*]

PATUMIERA: Per amor del cielo!

WASTBA: Don't you know? Can't you tell?? [*Pauses; no response*] Look at me! [*Nods ironically*] Don't pretend it doesn't show. [*No response*] Okay. Okay . . . [*Stands erect*] This is my first class, too . . . They just called me last night. [*Waits for reaction. Gets none. Smiles, nods*] Shocked, huh? Well . . . now you know . . . We must not fail here. [*Pauses*] You fail and I fail. I fail and you fail. You fail and I fail and we all fail. I fail and you don't get to speak English. You fail and I don't get to *teach* English. We all fail and . . . [*Pauses*] You see now, don't you? Language could be our mutual Waterloo! [*Pauses*] Have I made myself perfectly clear?

YOKO: [*Smiling*] Ware-ware wa ittai anataga doshte . . .

WASTBA: [*Screams*] *I'm gonna stuff an eggroll in that mouth of yours, butterfly!* [*Silence*] The next three words out of my mouth will be the most important words in the English language. [*She has been holding her lesson plan book and leafing through it. Her calmness at this moment is icy*] I certainly hope you'll have the decency to pay attention. [*She stares at her class. All look from one to another, wondering what it was they did that drove* WASTBA *crazy. Suddenly we hear three enormously loud raps at the door. The sound is quite terrifying*]

SMIEDNIK: [*Offstage. His lines are intercut with the pounding*] Daj mi moja miotłe, pani! Hey, Słodka, bez mej moitły nie moje pracowac! Nie zartuję, panno, dawaj, miotłe i dawaj ją szybkó. Wchodzę!! Otwieraj cholerne dzwi!

[*There is a sharp intake of breath from all and then silence.* WASTBA *looks at class, bows head, speaks softly*]

WASTBA: Poor, poor Pong. [*She walks to* MRS. PONG's *desk and gathers the four takeout containers together in a stack. She returns to the front of the room and drops the four takeout containers into the wastebasket*]

LAPOUBELLE: Nom de Dieu, qu'est-ce que c'est que-ça?

TRANSLATOR: What the hell is that?

PATUMIERA: Che é successo?

TRANSLATOR: What's happening?

YOKO: Dare ka hairitagatte irunjanaidesuka?

TRANSLATOR: I think somebody's trying to get into the room.

MULLEIMER: Was zum Teufel war das? [*Pauses; moves up from his seat*] Was zum *Teufel* war das? [*Moves to* WASTBA]

TRANSLATOR: What the devil was that?

PATUMIERA: [*Moves to* WASTBA] Che è successo, signorina?

LAPOUBELLE: [*Moves to* WASTBA] Qu'est-ce que c'est, mademoiselle?

WASTBA: Please, take your seats now . . . [*Smiles, calmly*] All of you: sit down. Come on, now . . . [*Calmly*] Please sit down.

MULLEIMER: Wir mussen die Tür aufmachen, and nachsehen, Fräulein. [MULLEIMER *moves to the door.* WASTBA *hurls her body between* MULLEIMER *and the door]* Heh! [MULLEIMER *hops away from her, moving backwards]*

WASTBA: Sit!

MULLEIMER: Fräulein, bitte . . .

WASTBA: *I* am the captain of this ship . . . not you! [*Backs him away from door by screaming and moving forward.* MULLEIMER *continues to hop]*

MULLEIMER: Fräulein!

WASTBA: *I'm* the one who killed the morning preparing . . . not you! [*Moves forward again]*

MULLEIMER: [*Hops backward again]* Fräulein!

WASTBA: *I'm* responsible here . . . not you!

YOKO: [*To* LAPOUBELLE] Ittai do shitandesuka?

LAPOUBELLE: [*To* YOKO *as he stands]* Qu'est-ce qu'elle fait?

PATUMIERA: [*Stands]* Che sta facendo?

LAPOUBELLE: [*To* WASTBA] Quand ce navire coulera, je serai le premier rat à se sauver.

WASTBA: We've got to stick together! [*Screams; panicked]* We've got to stick together. [*Yells at* MULLEIMER] Sit down and stick together.

MULLEIMER: Ich rühr mich nicht bis ich weiss was da draussen passiert ist!

WASTBA: [*Screams]* Take your seats!

PATUMIERA: [*He recognizes phrase and repeats same, screaming word aloud trying to be helpful]* Teetz . . .

WASTBA: I beg your pardon?

PATUMIERA: [*Pounds his desk; motions to all seats in room]* Goood teetz . . .

WASTBA: Mister, do you know that I am an educated woman? I may be Business Administration and not Language Arts, which is only to say that while words may not be my way . . . my field . . . I am nonetheless degree-certified and educated. Furthermore, this is not a goddamn Latin country! We are civilized people here! Now, goddammit, *sit down!* [*Suddenly there is the sound of pounding on the door again]*

SMIEDNIK: [*Screams offstage; screams are intercut with the pounding at the door*] Potreba mi mej miotły, kochanie. Pani, musze, iśc dp domu. Wchodzę! Otwieraj cholerne dzwi!

[*Silence in the room again.* LAPOUBELLE *speaks first, under his breath. He is quite obviously frightened*]

LAPOUBELLE: *Mais, enfin, merde, alors!* . . . *Qu'est-ce que c'est que ça??? La Guerre, Madame?* . . .

WASTBA: [*Intensely*] Don't you understand that there is more of us than there is of him?

MULLEIMER: *Was ist passiert, Fräulein? Kriegsausbruch vielleicht?*

PATUMIERA:*Che è successo, signorina? Una battaglia?*

WASTBA: He's probably only just another poor demented lunatic needing money for Godknowswhat kind of drug . . . That's all . . . It makes me want to spit. *Ptwew!* [*She actually spits on floor*]

PATUMIERA: Signorina . . . Vietato sputare, eh?

WASTBA: Money!

PATUMIERA: Money!

WASTBA: Money! That's it! Money!

YOKO: [*Repeats word as well*] . . . money . . . [*Giggles*]

WASTBA: [*Grabbing her pocketbook*] I'll chip in a dollar if you will . . . [*Looks up at them*] We can buy him off!

LAPOUBELLE: Mais, ma chère mademoiselle, il faut que vous nous donniez juste une petite chance, alors! . . . Nous sommes . . .

WASTBA: A dollar! [*To* PATUMIERA] A dollar, you!

PATUMIERA: [*With dollar, proudly*] Dollarr. [*She grabs his dollar*] Eyyy!

WASTBA: Thank you. [*To* LAPOUBELLE] C'mon, moustache, it's your life or a rotten dollar! What's to think about? Gimme' a dollar.

LAPOUBELLE: [*He takes out his wallet. She grabs it and takes a dollar*] Madame!

WASTBA: I'm only taking a dollar. One. See? [*To* YOKO] You paying attention? *Hello?*

YOKO: [*Has a dollar now*] Hello . . . Dolly.

WASTBA: To know you is to love you . . . Gimme' . . . [*Takes the dollar, counts people and then money*] Who's not in? [*To* MULLEIMER] You! A dollar. [*He takes out dollar*]

MULLEIMER: Dollar, ja . . .

WASTBA: Good boy.

MULLEIMER: [*Proudly*] Okay.

[WASTBA *walks carefully to the door. All are frozen to see what will happen. She puts her hand on the doorknob*]

WASTBA: Five lousy bucks. Let's hope he's got a sense of humor. Get the picture? [*She looks at* MULLEIMER] Hey! [*Grabs camera from him*] That'll help.

MULLEIMER: Äääh . . . Das ist meine Yashika, Fräulein . . .

WASTBA: [*To* YOKO] Okay, Yoko. [*Pauses; amazed*] Just wait a goddam minute . . . [*To* YOKO] Did you know that "Yoko" is "okay" spelled backwards. [*Pauses*] I'm wrong . . . [*Pauses*] . . . Okay is "yako." You're Yoko. ["*Yako*" *should be made to rhyme with* "*Jack-o.*" *Pauses; again in panic*] Something of value! I need something of value! [*See* YOKO's *gold make-up case*] Gimme' that! [*Grabs for it.* YOKO *resists*]

YOKO: Aiiii . . .

WASTBA: Gimme'! Make-up case!

YOKO: [*Resisting*] Aayyy-iiii . . .

WASTBA: Make-up casey!

YOKO: [*Suddenly giggles*] May cupcasey . . . [*Gives over make-up case to* WASTBA]

WASTBA: Six hundred million more of you, huh? That's just swell. [*Moves to door*] Well, let's hope, right? [*Cracks door open a bit.* LAPOUBELLE *grabs umbrella for protection. Stands by his desk with umbrella raised over his head*] I'll try what I assume is his tongue . . . Couldn't hurt. [*Yells out door*] Me voy a lavar un poco para quitarme la arena que tengo pegada! [*And with that she throws money, make-up case and camera out of door into the hallway. She instantly slams the door closed. All are shocked and amazed and scream at her*]

ALL: [*In own language*] Hey! What the hell did you do! That was my dollar! Have you lost your mind? [*Etc.* MULLEIMER *moves to the door. His attitude is "I'll take care of this"*]

MULLEIMER: [*To all*] Sit. [*To* WASTBA] Heute meine Brille und meine Yashika; morgen was? *Mein Schuhe? Meine Hosen?* Was, Fräulein, was?

WASTBA: Stay back, I'm telling you. [*Raises her fist*] I'm not above throwing a punch!

MULLEIMER: Das ist doch lacherlich.

WASTBA: I told you that we have to stick together and you GOD-DAMMIT! are going to have to *stick!* [*And with that, she punches his shoulder. Her fist is to* MULLEIMER'*s shoulder what a mosquito is to a grazing cow*]

MULLEIMER: Was machen Sie da, meine Dame?

WASTBA: My hand! [*She is bent in pain*] My poor hand. [*She moves to her desk*] I really hurt my hand on you.

MULLEIMER: Was it passiert?

YOKO: Doshitanodes'ka?

LAPOUBELLE: Mais. Qu'est-ce qui est arrivé?

PATUMIERA: Che è successo?

WASTBA: [*Crying*] I really hurt my hand on you . . .

MULLEIMER: Warum haben sie much geschlagen?

YOKO: Senseiwa naze Doitsujin o naguttan desuka?

LAPOUBELLE: Pourquoi elle lui a tapé dessus?

PATUMIERA: Perché gli ha dato quella botta?

WASTBA: I'm upset!

PATUMIERA: Sono sturbato, Io!

WASTBA: I'm so upset!

MULLEIMER: Bin ganz ausser mich. [*He paces, as a cat, the length of the room, holding eye-contact with* WASTBA]

YOKO: Iyani nacchau wa.

WASTBA: Am I ever upset!

YOKO: Honto ni iyani nacchau wa.

WASTBA: [*Sobbing*] Oh, God! I'm upset!

MULLEIMER: Mein Gott! Ich bin ausser mich!

WASTBA: This is truly upsetting. I want you to know that this is truly very upsetting.

MULLEIMER: [*He stands, throws notebooks on the floor, gathers his belongings*] Fräulein, ich geh' nach Hause. [MULLEIMER *moves to door, stops. He turns and faces* WASTBA]

TRANSLATOR: I'm going home now, Lady!

MULLEIMER: Aber bevor ich geh', will ich Ihnen noch was sagen . . .

TRANSLATOR'S VOICE: But before I go, I gotta' tell you something . . .

MULLEIMER: Frueher dachte ich, das Tod durch Ersticken das Schlimmste sie.

TRANSLATOR'S VOICE: I used to think that death by suffocation would be the worst.

MULLEIMER: Hab' mich geirrt.

TRANSLATOR'S VOICE: I was wrong.

MULLEIMER: [*He puts on his cap and coat*] Sie sind das Schlimmste.

TRANSLATOR'S VOICE: You are the worst.

MULLEIMER: Tod durch Ersticken ist ein Stueck Apfelstrudel verlichen zu einem abend mit Ihnen . . .

TRANSLATOR'S VOICE: Death by suffocation is a piece of apple strudel next to a night with you . . .

MULLEIMER: Ich verlasse diese klasse, bevor ich meinen Verstand und meine Schuhe verliere.

TRANSLATOR'S VOICE: I'm getting out of here while I still have my mind and my shoes.

MULLEIMER: Und wenn Ihr Freund der "mugger" sie haben will, kann er sie haben. [*He moves to her desk*]

TRANSLATOR: If your friend the "mugger" wants them, he can have them.

MULLEIMER: Was Ihr kostbares Englisch anbelangt . . . [*He rubs his hand through words written on blackboard*]

TRANSLATOR: As for your precious English . . .

MULLEIMER: . . . So platzieren Sie es auf einen kleinen, aber eleganten stuhl . . .

TRANSLATOR: . . . stick it on the center of a small but elegant chair . . .

MULLEIMER: [*He pulls her chair out and motions to seat, on his line*] . . . und *sit!* [*Pauses. Goes to door*] Fräulein . . . Auf Wiedersehn. [*He bows, clicks his heels. All freeze for a moment.* MULLEIMER *exits. He leaves door open. All stare a moment*]

WASTBA: [*Realizes, yells to* PATUMIERA] Close that door! [*She stands straight*] Close that door! [*She rushes to door*] Close that door! [*She slams it closed*] Oh, God! [*All stare, amazed*]

LAPOUBELLE: Elle a fermé la porte à l'Allemand!

PATUMIERA: Dov'e lo Svizzero?

YOKO: Sensei wa doitsujin o Shimedashimashita!

WASTBA: Okay, everybody, just settle!

PATUMIERA: Hai sbattuto fuori lo Svizzero!

WASTBA: [*To* PATUMIERA] Settle, you!

YOKO: [*Screams, to* WASTBA] Sensei wa doitsujin o shimedashimashita! [*Sound of knocking at the door*]

LAPOUBELLE: Écoutez!

WASTBA: Back to your seat.

LAPOUBELLE: Il a quelqu'un qui frappe à la porte, Madame!

WASTBA: Sit, will you? [*Knocking at the door again*]

PATUMIERA: Senti, forse e' lo Svizzero, no? [*Stands, looks to* WASTBA] Non dovremmo aprire la porta?

YOKO: Doitsujin wa hairitagatteirun ja nai desuka.

WASTBA: Settle, everybody, just settle!

LAPOUBELLE: [*Moving forward in room*] Vaut mieux aller voir. [*He carries his umbrella for protection. The sound of knocking at the door*] Écoutez!

WASTBA: Go back to your seat! [*The sound of pounding at the door*] I said "Back to your seat!" [*The sound of pounding at the door*]

LAPOUBELLE: Je vais ouvrir la porte.

WASTBA: It's your funeral. [*She steps back from the door, smiling and nodding magnanimously.* LAPOUBELLE *holds his umbrella as a club against door*]

LAPOUBELLE: Qui est là?

[*Suddenly we hear the sound of three enormous pounding sounds, joined by hard knocking.* LAPOUBELLE *jams his umbrella*

against door to hold it closed. YOKO *hides behind a frightened*
PATUMIERA. *The door rattles under the pounding*]

SMIEDNIK: [*Offstage, screaming. His screams are intercut with enor-*
mous knockings of the pail against the door] Pani, muszę iśc do
domu! Nie zaetuję, panno, dawaj moiłle i dawaj ją szybkó.
Wchodze! Otwieraj cholerne dżwi!

[LAPOUBELLE *is frozen in his tracks, there is silence.* LAPOUBELLE
finally backs away and hides near his desk]

WASTBA: Now, perhaps, you'll take me seriously. [*Pauses*] You're all
. . . well . . . new to this, while I'm . . . well . . . *not* new to this
[*Pauses. Smiles*] Please, everybody . . . sit down.

LAPOUBELLE: Ils sont dans de beaux draps . . . le Suisse et la vieille
Hawaienne, aussi. [*Bows head*] C'est certain maintenant . . . Mon
Dieu.

TRANSLATOR: The Swiss and the old Hawaiian lady are in big trouble.
My God, that's for sure.

WASTBA: [*Condescending tone*] Yes . . . I know . . . It's never what
our parents told us it would be. [*Touches* LAPOUBELLE's *shoulder*]
Please sit down now, okay?

LAPOUBELLE: No seet.

WASTBA: Sit!

LAPOUBELLE: Non!

WASTBA: Yes!

LAPOUBELLE: Non. No seet!

WASTBA: Damn you!

LAPOUBELLE: Ne me touchez pas! [*Shakes loose from her. Moves to*
his seat. Stops. Smiles at her ironically] Tu es dingue, cherie . . .
mais adorable . . . [*Waves*] Je t'embrasse . . . [*Pause*] Mon Dieu.
Ma tête. Mon cul . . .

WASTBA: You're going to have to stop wagging that tongue of
yours . . .

LAPOUBELLE: [*Suddenly screams*] Je n'ai plus confiance en vous, mademoiselle. *Je vous deteste!*

WASTBA: I'm going to have to treat you like a child. [*She walks to*

LAPOUBELLE] Every time you speak your tongue instead of English . . . [*She slaps his hand*] I'll slap you.

LAPOUBELLE: Pourquoi avez-vous fait ça? [WASTBA *slaps* LAPOUBELLE *again*]

PATUMIERA: Perche' t'ha preso a schiaffi?

WASTBA: [*To* PATUMIERA] There's that tongue of yours now!

PATUMIERA: Eh?

WASTBA: I'll have to slap you, too. [*She slaps* PATUMIERA] Okay?

PATUMIERA: [*He reacts as a movie star might for these lines*] Non picchio mai una donna. Anche se ti sorprende, essendo io Italiano . . .

WASTBA: You're not learning . . .

PATUMIERA: [*He moves now as a movie star might for these words*] Eh, Signora! . . . Io . . .

YOKO: Chotto kiite kudasai!

WASTBA: You, too? [*Walks to* YOKO] Sorry. [*Slaps* YOKO's *hand*]

YOKO: Cho-to!

PATUMIERA: E' pazza! [WASTBA *slaps* PATUMIERA's *face*]

LAPOUBELLE: Je m'en vais. [LAPOUBELLE *stands.* WASTBA *slaps him*] Elle est completement cinglée! [*She slaps him again, violently now*] Bordel! [*She slaps him again. He looks to* PATUMIERA] J'en ai assez! [LAPOUBELLE *begins to pack his belongings as rapidly as he can. He stuffs papers and notebooks and clothing into his briefcases and bookbags. He is now hysterical.* WASTBA, *equally hysterical, will slap him whenever she hears French language being emitted from* LAPOUBELLE's *lips*] Faites ce que vous voudrez, moi, je m'en vais.

TRANSLATOR'S VOICE: I couldn't care less what you're after here . . . I'm getting out! [WASTBA *slaps* LAPOUBELLE. N.B.: *He is now slapped both for his own words and for the* TRANSLATOR's *words*]

LAPOUBELLE: J'en ai assez!

TRANSLATOR'S VOICE: I've had enough! [WASTBA *slaps* LAPOUBELLE *again.* WASTBA *slaps* LAPOUBELLE *twice*]

LAPOUBELLE: Madame, votre anglais, vous n'avez qu'à vour en farcir. [WASTBA *slaps him*]

TRANSLATOR'S VOICE: Lady, you can take your English and eat it! [WASTBA *slaps him again*]

LAPOUBELLE: Maintenant, il faut absolument que je m'en aille. [WASTBA *slaps him again*]

TRANSLATOR'S VOICE: Now I'm *really* leaving!

LAPOUBELLE: Voilà! [*Slap.* LAPOUBELLE *places his hand on the door-knob.* WASTBA *pulls back from him, frightened. Silence, as all stare at* LAPOUBELLE'S *back as he faces door. Suddenly, he freezes*] Ça alors! Attendez, un petit moment . . .

TRANSLATOR'S VOICE: Uhhh, let's just wait a minute . . .

LAPOUBELLE: [*Turning back into position of facing* WASTBA *and classmates. He has a sick grin on his face*] Je m'en vais pas!

TRANSLATOR: I'm not gonna' leave . . .

LAPOUBELLE: Je perdrai mon boulot, ma jeune femme, mes enfants seraient obligés de quitter leur école privée . . .

TRANSLATOR: I'll lose my job, my young wife, and my children would have to drop out of private school . . .

LAPOUBELLE: En plus, ce con-là, il me tuerait.

TRANSLATOR: Also I'll be killed by the maniac out there.

LAPOUBELLE: [*He walks to* WASTBA *and offers his hand for her to hit*] S'il vous plaît, mademoiselle. [*She hits his hand sharply. He clenches hand into fist, considers punching her, does not. He smiles instead.* LAPOUBELLE *now returns to his chair and sits. He has joined the class. All sit quietly, attentive*]

WASTBA: Quiet, huh? [*Smiles*] You've learned, huh? [*Smiles again and makes a sudden pronouncement*] I have seen The Miracle Worker! [*She returns to her desk and sits. She smiles composed and erect now*] Calmness prevails and I am pleased. [*Smiles*] Now then, in accordance with our lesson plan, I would like to discuss the verb "to be." [*Pauses*] I hope this will fulfill and satisfy your foreign expectations. [*She stands and writes the words "To Be" on the blackboard next to the word "English." She has thus created the sentence "To Be English"*]

PATUMIERA: Che stai cercando di dire?

[WASTBA *turns and stares a moment at* PATUMIERA, *returns to blackboard. There is absolute silence in the room. Her hand-*

writing on blackboard is mere scribbles, almost more like Japanese characters than English]

WASTBA: *[Speaks words as she writes]* I am. You are. He, she, it is. We are. You are. They are. *[Smiles]* How many of you know this already? *[Absolute silence in the room]* Nobody. *[Stands; writes phrases on blackboard; turns to class after each and reads. She calls for the class to repeat her words, slapping each word with pointer for emphasis]* I am. You are. He, she, it is. We are. You are. They are. *[Motions with arms for them to follow]* Repeat after me, please. *[Smiles and points to blackboard]* I am.

ALL: I am.

WASTBA: You are.

ALL: You are.

WASTBA: He, she, it is.

ALL: He, she, it is.

WASTBA: We are.

ALL: We are.

WASTBA: You are.

ALL: You are.

WASTBA: They are.

ALL: They are.

WASTBA: Good.

ALL: Good.

WASTBA: Stop!

ALL: Stop!

WASTBA: *[Screams]* I said "Stop!"

[LAPOUBELLE, who is humiliated, screams and pounds his desk, out of control]

LAPOUBELLE: *I said stop!*

WASTBA: Do any of you have any questions?

[Suddenly LAPOUBELLE stands. Smashed umbrella held as sword, he charges to the front of the room]

LAPOUBELLE: [*Stands with his belongings in his arms. He nods to* PA-
TUMIERA] Bon soir, Monsieur Ravioli . . . [*Nods to* YOKO] Bon
Soir, ma petit Mademoiselle Sukiyaki . . . [*Bows to* WASTBA] . . .
et au revoir, Madame le Hot Dog . . . [*He unlocks door, turns
again to* WASTBA] . . . Au revoir, ma chère femme . . .

TRANSLATOR: Goodbye, my wife . . .

LAPOUBELLE: . . . et au revoir à mes petites enfants et vos leurs écoles
privées . . .

TRANSLATOR: . . . and goodbye my children and goodbye your private schools . . .

LAPOUBELLE: [*Prepares to leap out of door*] Salut, ange de la mort!

TRANSLATOR: Hello, Angel of Death!

[LAPOUBELLE *exits play.* WASTBA *goes to door, closes it, locks it*]

WASTBA: I repeat: do any of you have any questions?

YOKO: [*Stunned silence first*] Furansujin ga nigemashita! [*She
screams the same words again*] Furansujin ga nigemashita!

[PATUMIERA, *realizing* YOKO *will be slapped for speaking something other than English, leans in and whispers to her, using
hand gestures for emphasis*]

PATUMIERA: Sta zitto o quella ti prene a botte!

WASTBA: [*Thinking* PATUMIERA *is about to hit* YOKO] Hey!

PATUMIERA: Eh?

WASTBA: I'll do the slapping around here, okay? [*No response.* PA-
TUMIERA *just smiles*]

YOKO: [*Hides her hands behind her back*] Furansujin ga nigemashita!

WASTBA: [*To* PATUMIERA] Did you hear me?

YOKO: Furansujin!

WASTBA: Don't let me hear that tongue of yours again! [*Pauses,
raises hand*] You hear me?

YOKO: [*Head bowed in guilt and shame*] Sumimaszn.

WASTBA: Better. [*Rubbing her hands together, walking backwards to
her desk*] I am.

PATUMIERA: [*Repeats*] I am.

WASTBA: [To YOKO] You are. [No response] You are. *You are!* [YOKO looks up; quietly]

YOKO: [Pronounced perfectly] You . . . are.

WASTBA: [To PATUMIERA] He, she, it is.

PATUMIERA: [Repeats] He, she, it is.

WASTBA: [To YOKO] We are. [No response] We are. [No response] I said "We are!" *We are!* [YOKO turns around to WASTBA]

YOKO: [Quietly smiling] Watashi ga Amerika ni tatta hi ni wa nihyaku-hachijunin mono hito ga eki made miokurini kitekurema-shita. [She slaps her own hand, sharply]

TRANSLATOR: There were two hundred and eighty people gathered at the train station waving goodbye to me on the day I left for America.

YOKO: [She moves to position in front of WASTBA] Sonouchino nihyaku nanaju-nananin wa itoko deshita. [She slaps her own hand again]

TRANSLATOR: Two hundred and seventy-seven of them were cousins.

YOKO: [Sits in chair next to WASTBA so that WASTBA cannot avoid her eyes] Sonouchino hitori wa watashino haha, mo hitori wa wa-tashino chichi.

TRANSLATOR: One was my mother and one was my father.

YOKO: [Packing] Nokori no hitori was boi furendo no Jun deshita.

TRANSLATOR: The other one was my boyfriend, Jun.

YOKO: America ni kurutameni watashiwa minnato wakaretano desu.

TRANSLATOR: I gave up everybody to come here.

YOKO: Kono heya kara derukoto wa nijyu-nanadai tsuzuita watashino ie no meiyo o kegasukoto ni narimasu. [Goes to chair, collects her belongings]

TRANSLATOR: Walking out that front door represents more humilia-tion to me than the last twenty-seven generations of my family could even think about. [Gathers belongings; nods to PATUMIERA to join her. PATUMIERA shrugs a "No." YOKO does an Italian put-down gesture. She moves to door]

YOKO: [Opens door, after peeking out carefully] Mohito ban anatato issho ni irukurainara roka de kichigai to rumba o odotta hoga mada mashidesu. *Turns and faces WASTBA again]*

TRANSLATOR: Sugar, I would rather dance a rhumba with the lunatic in the hall than spend another night with you.

YOKO: Sayonara, Misu American Pie.

[YOKO *bows. She exits play.* SMIEDNIK *bursts into room. The knees of his trousers are visibly soaked. On seeing* SMIEDNIK, WASTBA *will recognize him and reach a near catatonic state of fear.* PATUMIERA *is confused and frightened*]

SMIEDNIK: Styszałaś teu kawat o Polaku i o śliwce, also teu o Polaku i ogòrku? Styszałaś o Polaku i stzajku smicciarzy?

TRANSLATOR: Heard the one about the Pollack and the prunes? Heard the one about the Pollack and the pickle? Heard the one about the Pollack and the garbage strike?

SMIEDNIK: Ty myślisz że to żarty??? Ty myślisz mnie imie Smienczne?

TRANSLATOR: You think we're all *jokes*??? Why? Just because I've got a funny name?

[SMIEDNIK *kicks wastebasket, violently*]

SMIEDNIK: Czegòs mi miotłe ukradła? Jamuzce podłoge myc, albo sie moge sie pojytce . . . gdzie jesta?

TRANSLATOR: Why'd you steal my mop? I gotta' mop floors, lady, that's how I put the food on the table. [*Pauses*] Where is it?

SMIEDNIK: Jednego godzina wdomu chiat bylem. Widzic sie! Na kolany I wrencc, podłoge wy mytem.

TRANSLATOR: I could'a' b'in home an hour ago, but for her. Look at me! I've b'in sponging the floor on my hands and knees 'cause'a' her.

SMIEDNIK: [*Sees mop at hatrack, goes to it. He grabs his mop*] Dawaj! Wy mytem podłoge wustepie kobiat I wtn samotny plazzek tutaj leci na schodach upada na palcach.

TRANSLATOR: I'm mopping the floor in the ladies' room and this maniac here comes running in all stooped over with her finger bent.

SMIEDNIK: Ona widzi mnie I zaczyna plakać. Ja chodzie de niej I chec uspokoic a una mnie voezy nad glowe z moje moitłe.

TRANSLATOR: She sees me and starts sobbing. I go and try to calm her down and she hits me over the head with my mop.

SMIEDNIK: I zamykà mnie wustepie, okolo jedna godzina asstara chinczyka kobieta przychodzie I otwiera dzwi.

TRANSLATOR: Then she locks me in the ladies' room for nearly an hour until an old Chinese woman comes and opens the lock . . .

SMIEDNIK: [*He moves to* WASTBA] Szytyry chas ja ukopnie twoj dzwi. I szytyry chas ty nie otwieraj. Wiedzirs ty jest sztrentny.

TRANSLATOR: Four times I come up here and bang on your door and four times you don't open your door. Don't you know that's nasty?

SMIEDNIK: [*At door*] Tys scienczie nie jest whop appresivne.

TRANSLATOR: Lucky for you I'm not a violent man. [*He exits, slamming door violently. A pause.* WASTBA *speaks to* PATUMIERA *who starts to pack his things*]

WASTBA: We are. C'mon, mister, please: we are. We really are. We are . . .

PATUMIERA: [*Repeats softly; gestures "you're nuts" to* WASTBA *first. Perhaps hums a tune, softly. He eyes his belongings, prepares to leave*] We are.

WASTBA: [*Quietly*] You are.

PATUMIERA: You are.

WASTBA: They are.

PATUMIERA: They are.

WASTBA: Good morning.

PATUMIERA: Good morning.

WASTBA: How are you?

PATUMIERA: How are you?

WASTBA: I am wonderful. [PATUMIERA's *flight bags and briefcases are packed. He goes for his jacket*]

PATUMIERA: I . . . wonderful.

WASTBA: Good.

PATUMIERA: Good.

WASTBA: Too bad . . .

PATUMIERA: Too bad . . .

WASTBA: What happens to women . . .

[PATUMIERA *puts on his suitcoat*]

PATUMIERA: Wha happens to women . . .
WASTBA: Like us . . .
PATUMIERA: Like us . . .
WASTBA: You are beautiful . . .
PATUMIERA: You . . . beautiful . . .
WASTBA: Debbie . . .
PATUMIERA: Deb . . .
WASTBA: So smart . . .
PATUMIERA: Smart . . .
WASTBA: Not wasting . . .
PATUMIERA: No wasting . . .
WASTBA: Time . . .

[WASTBA *bows her head and sobs.* PATUMIERA *stands, walks to five feet from her and watches, silently. She looks up and smiles*]

WASTBA: English . . .
PATUMIERA: English . . .
WASTBA: Is not difficult . . .
PATUMIERA: Is no difficult . . .
WASTBA: Anymore . . .
PATUMIERA: Anymore . . .
WASTBA: Why?
PATUMIERA: Why?
WASTBA: Because . . .
PATUMIERA: Because . . .
WASTBA: Of Debbie . . .
PATUMIERA: Of Debbie . . .
WASTBA: Because of Debbie . . .
PATUMIERA: Because of Debbie . . . [*He smiles at her*]

WASTBA: Because of Debbie Wastba . . .

PATUMIERA: [*Quietly; to her*] Because of Debbie Wastba . . .

WASTBA: My teacher . . .

PATUMIERA: My teacher . . .

WASTBA: Who is certainly . . .

PATUMIERA: [*Nearly embracing*] Who eeis certain . . .

WASTBA: . . . competent.

PATUMIERA: . . . compotentè.

WASTBA: . . . competent.

PATUMIERA: [*Softly; smiling*] . . . compotentè?

WASTBA: . . . compe*tent*.

PATUMIERA: . . . compe*tent?*

[WASTBA *smiles. Nods*]

WASTBA: Thank you. [*Pauses*] Good. [PATUMIERA *smiles*] It's hot, huh. [*She wipes her brow*] I can't breath . . . [*Smiles*]

PATUMIERA: [*Recognizing the idiom as an old friend*] Si. Si si. Si si si.

WASTBA: Huh?

PATUMIERA: [*Pulls at his shirt, mops brow, fans air*] I canno . . . breth. [*Smiles*] I canno breth.

WASTBA: Was that a negative I heard?

PATUMIERA: [*Confused*] I canno breth?

WASTBA: Mister, this could be the second chance to end all second chances . . .

PATUMIERA: Scusi?

WASTBA: [*Suddenly*] Touch the floor!

PATUMIERA: *Managa! l'America! Managa Christophe Columbe!* [*Makes "you're nuts" gesture*]

WASTBA: Touch the floor! [*She drops to her knees and touches the floor*] I can touch the floor!

PATUMIERA: [*Drops to his knees, touches floor*] Alora! I cain tooch the floor . . .

WASTBA: I can touch the desk!

PATUMIERA: Alora! I cain . . . tooch . . . the dest . . . [*She stands*]

WASTBA: [*She reaches up to ceiling above her head*] Can you touch the ceiling?

PATUMIERA: [*He looks at her desk and starts to climb onto it*] Si . . . é facile.

WASTBA: [*Moves quietly between* PATUMIERA *and her desk*] No, no, now . . . [*Reaches up again*] Touch the ceiling! Please mister, I'm begging you. This could be the most important moment of my life.

PATUMIERA: [*Reaches up to ceiling, but of course, cannot reach it. Confused, he apologizes, in Italian*] Signorina . . .

WASTBA: [*Screams; pleading*] English! Speak English! [*She reaches again for ceiling*] Touch the ceiling!

PATUMIERA: *Managa!* I canno . . .

WASTBA: *Say it!*

PATUMIERA: [*Reaching for ceiling, exasperated*] I canno . . . I canno tooch the ceiling . . .

[WASTBA *squeals with delight*]

WASTBA: [*She takes* PATUMIERA'S *face in her hands and pulls his face down to hers*] God bless you. [*They kiss. Going into the kiss,* PA- TUMIERA *is confused, thinking he has failed. After the kiss, he is changed, more confident somehow*]

PATUMIERA: Tesora . . . [*He reaches for her to kiss her again*] Tesorai, mia . . . [*She pulls away from him, realizing*]

WASTBA: Oh, oh . . .

PATUMIERA: Ey?

WASTBA: [*She grabs his hand and shakes it enthusiastically, carefully holding her body back from his*] I want to thank you. I really do. I'm really proud. English gets a lot easier, really. Just give it time. [*Pauses*] You've learned. [PATUMIERA *suddenly grabs his various bags and briefcases and moves to the door. She backs away. He grabs knob*] Where are you going? Don't! Don't go! No! No!!! Don't leave me!

PATUMIERA: [*Quietly*] Non ho capito nemmena una parola che tu hai detta.

> [PATUMIERA *exits the play, slamming door.* WASTBA *moves to door and leans her back against same. Turns. Locks door. She pauses a moment. She moves to desk and chair. Music in. She stands facing blackboard. She bows her head. She writes "The Primary English Class" on board and then returns to her desk. She tidies desk top, stacking notebooks, pencils, etc. She places apple center of desk, sits, folds hands on desk behind apple. She sits inordinately erect; a perfectly composed schoolteacher. Tableau. The lights fade to black*]

THE PLAY IS OVER

WAITING FOR LEFTY

Clifford Odets

Clifford Odets

Clifford Odets (1906-63) was the most gifted of the American play-wrights who developed a theatre of social protest during the 1930s. Born in Philadelphia, but growing up in New York, he tried his hand at writing and became an actor after graduation from high school. Making his debut in summer stock, he then appeared with various companies for the next five years, until 1931 when he joined the newly organized Group Theatre, which later was to produce most of his plays.

In 1935 Odets received world-wide attention with his powerful drama *Waiting for Lefty*. As Harold Clurman has recounted in his commendable history of the Group Theatre, *The Fervent Years*: "Sunday night, January 5, 1935, at the old Civic Repertory Theatre on Fourteenth Street, an event took place to be noted in the annals of the American theatre. . . . The first scene of *Lefty* had not played two minutes when a shock of delighted recognition struck the audience like a tidal wave. Deep laughter, hot assent, a kind of joyous fervor seemed to sweep the audience toward the stage. The actors no longer performed; they were being carried along as if by an exultancy of communication such as I had never witnessed in the theatre before. Audience and actors had become one. Line after line brought applause, whistles, bravos, and heartfelt shouts of kinship.

"When the audience at the end of the play responded to the militant question from the stage: 'Well, what's the answer?' with a spontaneous roar of 'Strike! Strike!' it was something more than a tribute to the play's effectiveness. . . . It was the birth cry of the thirties. Our youth had found its voice. It was a call to join the good fight for a greater measure of life in a world free of economic fear, falsehood, and craven servitude to stupidity and greed. . . . The audience, I say, was delirious. It stormed the stage [and] people went from the theatre dazed and happy; a new awareness and confidence had entered their lives."

After playing a series of Sunday benefits at the downtown playhouse, the Group Theatre brought *Waiting for Lefty* to Broadway for a regular run. Since its running time was approximately one hour, Odets supplied a companion piece, *Till the Day I Die,* a drama of the Nazi underground in Germany. The plays were an enormous success, and from then on the author was the Group's mainstay and poet laureate. During that same eventful year, they staged his *Awake and Sing* and *Paradise Lost;* in 1937 they presented *Golden Boy* and in the following season, *Rocket to the Moon.*

Subsequent Odets plays include: *Night Music* (1940); *Clash by Night* (1941); an adaptation, *The Russian People* (1942); *The Big Knife* (1949); *The Country Girl* (1950); and *The Flowering Peach* (1954).

Clifford Odets also spent some years in Hollywood, writing and, upon occasion, directing motion pictures.

NOTES FOR PRODUCTION

The background of the episodes, a strike meeting, is not an excuse. Each of the committeemen shows in his episode the crucial moment of his life which brought him to this very platform. The dramatic structure on which the play has been built is simple but highly effective. The form used is the old black-face minstrel form of chorus, end men, specialty men and interlocutor.

In Fatt's scenes before the "Spy Exposé," mention should again be made of Lefty's tardiness. Sitting next to Fatt in the center of the circle is a little henchman who sits with his back to the audience. On the other side of Fatt is Lefty's empty chair. This is so indicated by Fatt when he himself asks: "Yeah, where's your chairman?"

Fatt, of course, represents the capitalist system throughout the play. The audience should constantly be kept aware of him, the ugly menace which hangs over the lives of all the people who act out their own dramas. Perhaps he puffs smoke into the spotted playing space; perhaps during the action of a playlet he might insolently walk in and around the unseeing players. It is possible that some highly gratifying results can be achieved by the imaginative use of this character.

The strike committee on the platform during the acting out of the playlet should be used as chorus. Emotional, political, musical, they have in them possibilities of various comments on the scenes. This has been indicated once in the script in the place where Joe's wife is about to leave him. In the climaxes of each scene, slogans might very effectively be used—a voice coming out of the dark. Such a voice might announce at the appropriate moments in the "Young Interne's" scene that the USSR is the only country in the world where Anti-Semitism is a crime against the State.

Do not hesitate to use music wherever possible. It is very valuable in emotionally stirring an audience.

Characters:

Fatt
Joe
Edna
Miller
Fayette
Irv
Florrie
Sid
Clayton
Agate Keller
Henchman
Secretary
Actor
Reilly
Dr. Barnes
Dr. Benjamin
A Man

As the curtain goes up we see a bare stage. On it are sitting six or seven men in a semi-circle. Lolling against the proscenium down left is a young man chewing a toothpick: a gunman. A fat man of porcine appearance is talking directly to the audience. In other words he is the head of a union and the men ranged behind him are a committee of workers. They are now seated in interesting different attitudes and present a wide diversity of type, as we shall soon see. The fat man is hot and heavy under the collar, near the end of a long talk, but not too hot: he is well fed and confident. His name is HARRY FATT.

FATT: You're so wrong I ain't laughing. Any guy with eyes to read knows it. Look at the textile strike—out like lions and in like lambs. Take the San Francisco tie-up—starvation and broken heads. The steel boys wanted to walk out too, but they changed their minds. It's the trend of the times, that's what it is. All we workers got a good man behind us now. He's top man of the country looking out for our interests—the man in the White House is the one I'm referrin' to. That's why the times ain't ripe for a strike. He's working day and night—

VOICE FROM THE AUDIENCE: For who?

[*The* GUNMAN *stirs himself*]

FATT: For you! The records prove it. If this was the Hoover régime, would I say don't go out, boys? Not on your tintype! But things is different now. You read the papers as well as me. You know it. And that's why I'm against the strike. Because we gotta stand behind the man who's standin' behind us! The whole country——

ANOTHER VOICE: Is on the blink!

[*The* GUNMAN *looks grave*]

FATT: Stand up and show yourself, you damn red! Be a man, let's see what you look like! [*Waits in vain*] Yellow from the word go!

Red and yellow makes a dirty color, boys. I got my eyes on four or five of them in the union here. What the hell'll they do for you? Pull you out and run away when trouble starts. Give those birds a chance and they'll have your sisters and wives in the whore houses, like they done in Russia. They'll tear Christ off his bleeding cross. They'll wreck your homes and throw your babies in the river. You think that's bunk? Read the papers! Now listen, we can't stay here all night. I gave you the facts in the case. You boys got hot suppers to go to and——

ANOTHER VOICE: Says you!

GUNMAN: Sit down, Punk!

ANOTHER VOICE: Where's Lefty?

[*Now this question is taken up by the others in unison.* FATT *pounds with gavel*]

FATT: That's what I wanna know. Where's your pal, Lefty? You elected him chairman—where the hell did he disappear?

VOICES: We want Lefty! Lefty! Lefty!

FATT: [*Pounding*] What the hell is this—a circus? You got the committee here. This bunch of cowboys you elected. [*Pointing to man on extreme right end*]

MAN: Benjamin.

FATT: Yeah, Doc Benjamin. [*Pointing to other men in circle in seated order*] Benjamin, Miller, Stein, Mitchell, Phillips, Keller. It ain't my fault Lefty took a run-out powder. If you guys——

A GOOD VOICE: What's the committee say?

OTHERS: The committee! Let's hear from the committee!

[FATT *tries to quiet the crowd, but one of the seated men suddenly comes to the front. The* GUNMAN *moves over to center stage, but* FATT *says:*]

FATT: Sure, let him talk. Let's hear what the red boys gotta say!

[*Various shouts are coming from the audience.* FATT *insolently goes back to his seat in the middle of the circle. He sits on his raised platform and relights his cigar. The* GUNMAN *goes back to his post.* JOE, *the new speaker, raises his hand for quiet. Gets it quickly. He is sore*]

JOE: You boys know me. I ain't a red boy one bit! Here I'm carryin' a shrapnel that big I picked up in the war. And maybe I don't know it when it rains! Don't tell me red! You know what we are? The black and blue boys! We been kicked around so long we're black and blue from head to toes. But I guess anyone who says straight out he don't like it, he's a red boy to the leaders of the union. What's this crap about goin' home to hot suppers? I'm asking to your faces how many's got hot suppers to go home to? Anyone who's sure of his next meal, raise your hand! A certain gent sitting behind me can raise them both. But not in front here! And that's why we're talking strike—to get a living wage!

VOICE: Where's Lefty?

JOE: I honest to God don't know, but he didn't take no run-out powder. That Wop's got more guts than a slaughter house. Maybe a traffic jam got him, but he'll be here. But don't let this red stuff scare you. Unless fighting for a living scares you. We gotta make up our minds. My wife made up my mind last week, if you want the truth. It's plain as the nose on Sol Feinberg's face we need a strike. There's us comin' home every night—eight, ten hours on the cab. "God," the wife says, "eighty cents ain't money—don't buy beans almost. You're workin' for the company," she says to me, "Joe! you ain't workin' for me or the family no more!" She says to me, "If you don't start . . ."

I. JOE AND EDNA

The lights fade out and a white spot picks out the playing space within the space of seated men. The seated men are very dimly visible in the outer dark, but more prominent is FATT *smoking his cigar and often blowing the smoke in the lighted circle.*

A tired but attractive woman of thirty comes into the room, drying her hands on an apron. She stands there sullenly as JOE *comes in from the other side, home from work. For a moment they stand and look at each other in silence.*

JOE: Where's all the furniture, honey?

EDNA: They took it away. No installments paid.

JOE: When?

EDNA: Three o'clock.

JOE: They can't do that.

EDNA: Can't? They did it.

JOE: Why, the palookas, we paid three-quarters.

EDNA: The man said read the contract.

JOE: We must have signed a phony . . .

EDNA: It's a regular contract and you signed it.

JOE: Don't be so sour, Edna . . . [*Tries to embrace her*]

EDNA: Do it in the movies, Joe—they pay Clark Gable big money for it.

JOE: This is a helluva house to come home to. Take my word!

EDNA: Take MY word! Whose fault is it?

JOE: Must you start that stuff again?

EDNA: Maybe you'd like to talk about books?

JOE: I'd like to slap you in the mouth!

EDNA: No, you won't.

JOE: [*Sheepish*] Jeez, Edna, you get me sore some time . . .

EDNA: But just look at me—I'm laughing all over!

JOE: Don't insult me. Can I help it if times are bad? What the hell do you want me to do, jump off a bridge or something?

EDNA: Don't yell. I just put the kids to bed so they won't know they missed a meal. If I don't have Emmy's shoes soled tomorrow, she can't go to school. In the meantime let her sleep.

JOE: Honey, I rode the wheels off the chariot today. I cruised around five hours without a call. It's conditions.

EDNA: Tell it to the A & P!

JOE: I booked two-twenty on the clock. A lady with a dog was lit . . . she gave me a quarter tip by mistake. If you'd only listen to me—we're rolling in wealth.

EDNA: Yeah? How much?

JOE: I had "coffee and—" in a beanery. [*Hands her silver coins*] A buck four.

EDNA: The second month's rent is due tomorrow.

JOE: Don't look at me that way, Edna.

EDNA: I'm looking through you, not at you . . . Everything was gonna be so ducky! A cottage by the waterfall, roses in Picardy. You're a four-star-bust! If you think I'm standing for it much longer, you're crazy as a bedbug.

JOE: I'd get another job if I could. There's no work—you know it.

EDNA: I only know we're at the bottom of the ocean.

JOE: What can I do?

EDNA: Who's the man in the family, you or me?

JOE: That's no answer. Get down to brass tacks. Christ, gimme a break, too! A coffee cake and java all day. I'm hungry, too, Babe. I'd work my fingers to the bone if—

EDNA: I'll open a can of salmon.

JOE: Not now. Tell me what to do!

EDNA: I'm not God!

JOE: Jeez, I wish I was a kid again and didn't have to think about the next minute.

EDNA: But you're not a kid and you do have to think about the next minute. You got two blondie kids sleeping in the next room. They need food and clothes. I'm not mentioning anything else—But we're stalled like a flivver in the snow. For five years I laid awake at night listening to my heart pound. For God's sake, do something, Joe, get wise. Maybe get your buddies together, maybe go on strike for better money. Poppa did it during the war and they won out. I'm turning into a sour old nag.

JOE: [*Defending himself*] Strikes don't work!

EDNA: Who told you?

JOE: Besides that means not a nickel a week while we're out. Then when it's over they don't take you back.

EDNA: Suppose they don't! What's to lose?

JOE: Well, we're averaging six–seven dollars a week now.

EDNA: That just pays for the rent.

JOE: That is something, Edna.

EDNA: It isn't. They'll push you down to three and four a week before you know it. Then you'll say, "That's somethin'," too!

JOE: There's too many cabs on the street, that's the whole damn trouble.

EDNA: Let the company worry about that, you big fool! If their cabs didn't make a profit, they'd take them off the streets. Or maybe you think they're in business just to pay Joe Mitchell's rent!

JOE: You don't know a-b-c, Edna.

EDNA: I know this—your boss is making suckers outa you boys every minute. Yes, and suckers out of all the wives and the poor innocent kids who'll grow up with crooked spines and sick bones. Sure, I see it in the papers, how good orange juice is for kids. But dammit our kids get colds one on top of the other. They look like little ghosts. Betty never saw a grapefruit. I took her to the store last week and she pointed to a stack of grapefruits. "What's that!" she said. My God, Joe—the world is supposed to be for all of us.

JOE: You'll wake them up.

EDNA: I don't care, as long as I can maybe wake you up.

JOE: Don't insult me. One man can't make a strike.

EDNA: Who says one? You got hundreds in your rotten union!

JOE: The Union ain't rotten.

EDNA: No? Then what are they doing? Collecting dues and patting your back?

JOE: They're making plans.

EDNA: What kind?

JOE: They don't tell us.

EDNA: It's too damn bad about you. They don't tell little Joey what's happening in his bitsie witsie union. What do you think it is—a Ping-Pong game?

JOE: You know they're racketeers. The guys at the top would shoot you for a nickel.

EDNA: Why do you stand for that stuff?

JOE: Don't you wanna see me alive?

EDNA: [After a deep pause] No . . . I don't think I do, Joe. Not if you can lift a finger to do something about it, and don't. No, I don't care.

JOE: Honey, you don't understand what—

EDNA: And any other hackie that won't fight . . . let them all be ground to hamburger!

JOE: It's one thing to—

EDNA: Take your hand away! Only they don't grind me to little pieces! I got different plans. [*Starts to take off her apron*]

JOE: Where are you going?

EDNA: None of your business.

JOE: What's up your sleeve?

EDNA: My arm'd be up my sleeve, darling, if I had a sleeve to wear. [*Puts neatly folded apron on back of chair*]

JOE: Tell me!

EDNA: Tell you what?

JOE: Where are you going?

EDNA: Don't you remember my old boyfriend?

JOE: Who?

EDNA: Bud Hass. He still has my picture in his watch. He earns a living.

JOE: What the hell are you talking about!

EDNA: I heard worse than I'm talking about.

JOE: Have you seen Bud since we got married?

EDNA: Maybe.

JOE: If I thought . . . [*He stands looking at her*]

EDNA: See much? Listen, boyfriend, if you think I won't do this it just means you can't see straight.

JOE: Stop talking bull!

EDNA: This isn't five years ago, Joe.

JOE: You mean you'd leave me and the kids?

EDNA: I'd leave *you* like a shot!

JOE: No . . .

EDNA: Yes!

[JOE *turns away, sitting on a chair with his back to her. Outside the lighted circle of the playing stage we hear the other seated members of the strike committee. "She will . . . she will . . . it happens that way," etc. This group should be used throughout for various comments, political, emotional and as general chorus. Whispering . . . The fat boss now blows a heavy cloud of smoke into the scene*]

JOE: [*Finally*] Well, I guess I ain't got a leg to stand on.

EDNA: No?

JOE: [*Suddenly mad*] No, you lousy tart, no! Get the hell out of here. Go pick up that bull-thrower on the corner and stop at some cushy hotel downtown. He's probably been coming here every morning and laying you while I hacked my guts out!

EDNA: You're crawling like a worm!

JOE: *You'll* be crawling in a minute.

EDNA: You don't scare me that much! [*Indicates a half inch on her finger*]

JOE: This is what I slaved for!

EDNA: Tell it to your boss!

JOE: He don't give a damn for you or me!

EDNA: That's what I say.

JOE: Don't change the subject!

EDNA: This is the subject, the EXACT SUBJECT! Your boss makes this subject. I never saw him in my life, but he's putting ideas in my head a mile a minute. He's giving your kids that fancy disease called the rickets. He's making a jellyfish outa you and putting wrinkles in my face. This is the subject every inch of the way! He's throwing me into Bud Haas' lap. When in hell will you get wise——

JOE: I'm not so dumb as you think! But you are talking like a Red.

EDNA: I don't know what that means. But when a man knocks you down you get up and kiss his fist! You gutless piece of boloney.

JOE: One man can't——

EDNA: [*With great joy*] I don't say one man! I say a hundred, a thousand, a whole million, I say. But start in your own union. Get those hack boys together! Sweep out those racketeers like a pile of dirt! Stand up like men and fight for the crying kids and wives. Goddammit! I'm tired of slavery and sleepless nights.

JOE: [*With her*] Sure, sure! . . .

EDNA: Yes. Get brass toes on your shoes and know where to kick!

JOE: [*Suddenly jumping up and kissing his wife full on the mouth*] Listen, Edna. I'm goin' down to 174th Street to look up Lefty Costello. Lefty was saying the other day . . . [*He suddenly stops*] How about this Haas guy?

EDNA: Get out of here!

JOE: I'll be back! [*Runs out*]

[*For a moment* EDNA *stands triumphant. There is a blackout and when the regular lights come up,* JOE MITCHELL *is concluding what he has been saying.*]

JOE: You guys know this stuff better than me. We gotta walk out! [*Abruptly he turns and goes back to his seat and blackout*]

BLACKOUT

II. LAB ASSISTANT EPISODE

Discovered: MILLER, *a lab assistant, looking around; and* FAYETTE, *an industrialist.*

FAYETTE: Like it?

MILLER: Very much. I've never seen an office like this outside the movies.

FAY: Yes, I often wonder if interior decorators and bathroom-fixture people don't get all their ideas from Hollywood. Our country's extraordinary that way. Soap, cosmetics, electric refrigerators—just let Mrs. Consumer know they're used by the Crawfords and Garbos—more volume of sale than one plant can handle!

MILLER: I'm afraid it isn't that easy, Mr. Fayette.

FAY: No, you're right—gross exaggeration on my part. Competition is cut-throat today. Markets up flush against a stone wall. The astronomers had better hurry—open Mars to trade expansion.

MILLER: Or it will be just too bad!

FAY: Cigar?

MILLER: Thank you, don't smoke.

FAY: Drink?

MILLER: Ditto, Mr. Fayette.

FAY: I like sobriety in my workers . . . the trained ones, I mean. The Pollacks and niggers, they're better drunk—keeps them out of mischief. Wondering why I had you come over?

MILLER: If you don't mind my saying—very much.

FAY: [Patting him on the knee] I like your work.

MILLER: Thanks.

FAY: No reason why a talented young man like yourself shouldn't string along with us—a growing concern. Loyalty is well repaid in our organization. Did you see Siegfried this morning?

MILLER: He hasn't been in the laboratory all day.

FAY: I told him yesterday to raise you twenty dollars a month. Starts this week.

MILLER: You don't know how happy my wife'll be.

FAY: Oh, I can appreciate it. [He laughs]

MILLER: Was that all, Mr. Fayette?

FAY: Yes, except that we're switching you to laboratory A tomorrow. Siegfried knows about it. That's why I had you in. The new work is very important. Siegfried recommended you very highly as a man to trust. You'll work directly under Dr. Brenner. Make you happy?

MILLER: Very. He's an important chemist!

FAY: [Leaning over seriously] We think so, Miller. We think so to the extent of asking you to stay within the building throughout the time you work with him.

MILLER: You mean sleep and eat in?

FAY: Yes . . .

MILLER: It can be arranged.

FAY: Fine. You'll go far, Miller.

MILLER: May I ask the nature of the new work?

FAY: [*Looking around first*] Poison gas . . .

MILLER: Poison!

FAY: Orders from above. I don't have to tell you from where. New type poison gas for modern warfare.

MILLER: I see.

FAY: You didn't know a new war was that close, did you?

MILLER: I guess I didn't.

FAY: I don't have to stress the importance of absolute secrecy.

MILLER: I understand!

FAY: The world is an armed camp today. One match sets the whole world blazing in forty-eight hours. Uncle Sam won't be caught napping!

MILLER: [*Addressing his pencil*] They say twelve million men were killed in that last one and twenty million more wounded or missing.

FAY: That's not our worry. If big business went sentimental over human life there wouldn't be big business of any sort!

MILLER: My brother and two cousins went in the last one.

FAY: They died in a good cause.

MILLER: My mother says "no!"

FAY: She won't worry about you this time. You're too valuable behind the front.

MILLER: That's right.

FAY: All right, Miller. See Siegfried for further orders.

MILLER: You should have seen my brother—he could ride a bike without hands . . .

FAY: You'd better move some clothes and shaving tools in tomorrow. Remember what I said—you're with a growing organization.

MILLER: He could run the hundred yards in 9:8 flat . . .

FAY: Who?

MILLER: My brother. He's in the Meuse-Argonne Cemetery. Momma went there in 1926 . . .

FAY: Yes, those things stick. How's your handwriting, Miller, fairly legible?

MILLER: Fairly so.

FAY: Once a week I'd like a little report from you.

MILLER: What sort of report?

FAY: Just a few hundred words once a week on Dr. Brenner's progress.

MILLER: Don't you think it might be better coming from the Doctor?

FAY: I didn't ask you that.

MILLER: Sorry.

FAY: I want to know what progress he's making, the reports to be purely confidential—between you and me.

MILLER: You mean I'm to watch him?

FAY: Yes!

MILLER: I guess I can't do that . . .

FAY: Thirty a month raise . . .

MILLER: You said twenty . . .

FAY: Thirty!

MILLER: Guess I'm not built that way.

FAY: Forty . . .

MILLER: Spying's not in my line, Mr. Fayette!

FAY: You use ugly words, Mr. Miller!

MILLER: For ugly activity? Yes!

FAY: Think about it, Miller. Your chances are excellent . . .

MILLER: No.

FAY: You're doing something for your country. Assuring the United States that when those goddam Japs start a ruckus we'll have offensive weapons to back us up! Don't you read your newspapers, Miller?

MILLER: Nothing but Andy Gump.

FAY: If you were on the inside you'd know I'm talking cold sober truth! Now, I'm not asking you to make up your mind on the spot. Think about it over your lunch period.

MILLER: No . . .

FAY: Made up your mind already?

MILLER: Afraid so.

FAY: You understand the consequences?

MILLER: I lose my raise——

[*Simultaneously*] {

MILLER: And my job!

FAY: And your job!

MILLER: You misunderstand——

}

MILLER: Rather dig ditches first!

FAY: That's a big job for foreigners.

MILLER: But sneaking—and making poison gas—that's for Americans?

FAY: It's up to you.

MILLER: My mind's made up.

FAY: No hard feelings?

MILLER: Sure hard feelings! I'm not the civilized type, Mr. Fayette. Nothing suave or sophisticated about me. Plenty of hard feelings! Enough to want to bust you and all your kind square in the mouth! [*Does exactly that*]

BLACKOUT

III. THE YOUNG HACK AND HIS GIRL

Opens with girl and brother. FLORENCE *waiting for* SID *to take her to a dance.*

FLORRIE: I gotta right to have something out of life. I don't smoke, I don't drink. So if Sid wants to take me to a dance, I'll go. Maybe if you was in love you wouldn't talk so hard.

IRV: I'm saying it for your good.

FLORRIE: Don't be so good to me.

IRV: Mom's sick in bed and you'll be worryin' her to the grave. She don't want that boy hanging around the house and she don't want you meeting him in Crotona Park.

FLORRIE: I'll meet him anytime I like!

IRV: If you do, yours truly'll take care of it in his own way. With just one hand, too!

FLORRIE: Why are you all so set against him?

IRV: Mom told you ten times—it ain't him. It's that he ain't got nothing. Sure, we know he's serious, that he's stuck on you. But that don't cut no ice.

FLORRIE: Taxi drivers used to make good money.

IRV: Today they're makin' five and six dollars a week. Maybe you wanta raise a family on that. Then you'll be back here living with us again and I'll be supporting two families in one. Well . . . over my dead body.

FLORRIE: Irv, I don't care—I love him!

IRV: You're a little kid with half-baked ideas!

FLORRIE: I stand there behind the counter the whole day. I think about him—

IRV: If you thought more about Mom it would be better.

FLORRIE: Don't I take care of her every night when I come home? Don't I cook supper and iron your shirts and . . . you give me a pain in the neck, too. Don't try to shut me up! I bring a few dollars in the house, too. Don't you see I want something else out of life? Sure, I want romance, love, babies. I want everything in life I can get.

IRV: You take care of Mom and watch your step!

FLORRIE: And if I don't?

IRV: Yours truly'll watch it for you!

FLORRIE: You can talk that way to a girl . . .

IRV: I'll talk that way to your boy friend, too, and it won't be with words! Florrie, if you had a pair of eyes you'd see it's for your own good we're talking. This ain't no time to get married. Maybe later—

FLORRIE: "Maybe Later" never comes for me, though. Why don't we send Mom to a hospital? She can die in peace there instead of looking at the clock on the mantelpiece all day.

IRV: That needs money. Which we don't have!

FLORRIE: Money, money, money!

IRV: Don't change the subject.

FLORRIE: This is the subject!

IRV: You gonna stop seeing him? [*She turns away*] Jesus, kiddie, I remember when you were a baby with curls down your back. Now I gotta stand here yellin' at you like this.

FLORRIE: I'll talk to him, Irv.

IRV: When?

FLORRIE: I asked him to come here tonight. We'll talk it over.

IRV: Don't get soft with him. Nowadays is no time to be soft. You gotta be hard as a rock or go under.

FLORRIE: I found that out. There's the bell. Take the egg off the stove I boiled for Mom. Leave us alone, Irv.

[SID *comes in—the two men look at each other for a second.* IRV *exits*]

SID: [*Enters*] Hello, Florrie.

FLORRIE: Hello, Honey. You're looking tired.

SID: Naw, I just need a shave.

FLORRIE: Well, draw your chair up to the fire and I'll ring for brandy and soda . . . like in the movies.

SID: If this was the movies I'd bring a big bunch of roses.

FLORRIE: How big?

SID: Fifty or sixty dozen—the kind with long, long stems—big as that . . .

FLORRIE: You dope . . . .

SID: Your Paris gown is beautiful.

FLORRIE: [*Acting grandly*] Yes, Percy, velvet panels are coming back again. Madame La Farge told me today that Queen Marie herself designed it.

SID: Gee . . . !

FLORRIE: Every princess in the Balkans is wearing one like this. [*Poses grandly*]

SID: Hold it. [*Does a nose camera—thumbing nose and imitating grinding of camera with other hand. Suddenly she falls out of the posture and swiftly goes to him, to embrace him, to kiss him with love. Finally:*] You look tired, Florrie.

FLORRIE: Naw, I just need a shave. [*She laughs tremorously*]

SID: You worried about your mother?

FLORRIE: No.

SID: What's on your mind?

FLORRIE: The French and Indian War.

SID: What's on your mind?

FLORRIE: I got *us* on my mind, Sid. Night and day, Sid!

SID: I smacked a beer truck today. Did I get hell! I was driving along thinking of *us*, too. You don't have to say it—I know what's on your mind. I'm rat poison around here.

FLORRIE: Not to me . . .

SID: I know to who . . . and I know why. I don't blame them. We're engaged now for three years . . .

FLORRIE: That's a long time . . .

SID: My brother Sam joined the navy this morning—get a break that way. They'll send him down to Cuba with the hootchy-kootchy girls. He don't know from nothing, that dumb basketball player!

FLORRIE: Don't you do that.

SID: Don't you worry, I'm not the kind who runs away. But I'm so tired of being a dog, Baby, I could choke. I don't even have to ask what's going on in your mind. I know from the word go, 'cause I'm thinking the same things, too.

FLORRIE: It's yes or no—nothing in between.

SID: The answer is no—a big electric sign looking down on Broadway!

FLORRIE: We wanted to have kids . . .

SID: But that sort of life ain't for the dogs which is us. Christ, Baby!

I get like thunder in my chest when we're together. If we went off together I could maybe look the world straight in the face, spit in its eye like a man should do. Goddamit, it's trying to be a man on the earth. Two in life together.

FLORRIE: But something wants us to be lonely like that—crawling alone in the dark. Or they want us trapped.

SID: Sure, the big shot money men want us like that.

FLORRIE: Highly insulting us——

SID: Keeping us in the dark about what is wrong with us in the money sense. They got the power and means to be damn sure they keep it. They know if they give in just an inch, all the dogs like us will be down on them together—an ocean knocking them to hell and back and each singing cuckoo with stars coming from their nose and ears. I'm not raving, Florrie——

FLORRIE: I know you're not, I know.

SID: I don't have the words to tell you what I feel. I never finished school . . .

FLORRIE: I know . . .

SID: But it's relative, like the professors say. We worked like hell to send him to college—my kid brother Sam, I mean—and look what he done—joined the navy! The damn fool don't see the cards is stacked for all of us. The money man dealing himself a hot royal flush. Then giving you and me a phony hand like a pair of tens or something. Then keep on losing the pots 'cause the cards is stacked against you. Then he says, what's the matter you can't win —no stuff on the ball, he says to you. And kids like my brother believe it 'cause they don't know better. For all their education, they don't know from nothing.

But wait a minute! Don't he come around and say to you—this millionaire with a jazz band—listen, Sam or Sid or what's-your-name, you're no good, but here's a chance. The whole world'll know who you are. Yes sir, he says, get up on that ship and fight those bastards who's making the world a lousy place to live in. The Japs, the Turks, the Greeks. Take this gun—kill the slobs like a real hero, he says, a real American. Be a hero!

And the guy you're poking at? A real louse, just like you, 'cause they don't let him catch more than a pair of tens, too. On that foreign soil he's a guy like me and Sam, a guy who wants his baby like you and hot sun on his face! They'll teach Sam to point the guns the wrong way, that dumb basketball player!

FLORRIE: I got a lump in my throat, Honey.

SID: You and me—we never even had a room to sit in somewhere.

FLORRIE: The park was nice . . .

SID: In Winter? The hallways . . . I'm glad we never got together. This way we don't know what we missed.

FLORRIE: [*In a burst*] Sid, I'll go with you—we'll get a room somewhere.

SID: Naw . . . they're right. If we can't climb higher than this together—we better stay apart.

FLORRIE: I swear to God I wouldn't care.

SID: You would, you would—in a year, two years, you'd curse the day. I seen it happen.

FLORRIE: Oh, Sid . . .

SID: Sure, I know. We got the blues, Babe—the 1935 blues. I'm talkin' this way 'cause I love you. If I didn't, I wouldn't care . . .

FLORRIE: We'll work together, we'll—

SID: How about the backwash? Your family needs your nine bucks. My family——

FLORRIE: I don't care for them!

SID: You're making it up, Florrie. Little Florrie Canary in a cage.

FLORRIE: Don't make fun of me.

SID: I'm not, Baby.

FLORRIE: Yes, you're laughing at me.

SID: I'm not.

[*They stand looking at each other, unable to speak. Finally, he turns to a small portable phonograph and plays a cheap, sad, dance tune. He makes a motion with his hand; she comes to him. They begin to dance slowly. They hold each other tightly, almost as though they would merge into each other. The music stops, but the scratching record continues to the end of the scene. They stop dancing. He finally unlooses her clutch and seats her on the couch, where she sits, tense and expectant*]

SID: Hello, Babe.

FLORRIE: Hello.

[*For a brief time they stand as though in a dream*]

SID: [*Finally*] Good-by, Babe. [*He waits for an answer, but she is silent. They look at each other*] Did you ever see my Pat Rooney imitation? [*He whistles "Rosy O'Grady" and soft-shoes to it. Stops. He asks:*] Don't you like it?

FLORRIE: [*Finally*] No. [*Buries her face in her hands*]

[*Suddenly he falls on his knees and buries his face in her lap*]

BLACKOUT

IV. LABOR SPY EPISODE

FATT: You don't know how we work for you. Shooting off your mouth won't help. Hell, don't you guys ever look at the records like me? Look in your own industry. See what happened when the hacks walked out in Philly three months ago! Where's Philly? A thousand miles away? An hour's ride on the train.

VOICE: Two hours!!

FATT: Two hours . . . what the hell's the difference. Let's hear from someone who's got the practical experience to back him up. Fellers, there's a man here who's seen the whole parade in Philly, walked out with his pals, got knocked down like the rest—and blacklisted after they went back. That's why he's here. He's got a mighty interestin' word to say. [*Announces:*] TOM CLAYTON! [*As* CLAYTON *starts up from the audience,* FATT *gives him a hand which is sparsely followed in the audience.* CLAYTON *comes forward*] Fellers, this is a man with practical strike experience—Tom Clayton from little ole Philly.

CLAYTON: [*A thin, modest individual*] Fellers, I don't mind your booing. If I thought it would help us hacks get better living conditions, I'd let you walk all over me, cut me up to little pieces. I'm one of you myself. But what I wanna say is that Harry Fatt's right. I only been working here in the big town five weeks, but I know conditions just like the rest of you. You know how it is—don't take long to feel the sore spots, no matter where you park.

CLEAR VOICE: [*From audience*] Sit down!

CLAYTON: But Fatt's right. Our officers is right. The time ain't ripe. Like a fruit don't fall off the tree until it's ripe.

CLEAR VOICE: Sit down, you fruit!

FATT: [*On his feet*] Take care of him, boys.

VOICE: [*In audience, struggling*] No one takes care of me.

[*Struggle in house and finally the owner of the voice runs up on stage, says to speaker:*]

SAME VOICE: Where the hell did you pick up that name! Clayton! This rat's name is Clancy, from the old Clancys, way back! Fruit! I almost wet myself listening to that one!

FATT: [*Gunman with him*] This ain't a barn! What the hell do you think you're doing here!

SAME VOICE: Exposing a rat!

FATT: You can't get away with this. Throw him the hell outa here!

VOICE: [*Preparing to stand his ground*] Try it yourself . . . When this bozo throws that slop around. You know who he is? That's a company spy.

FATT: Who the hell are you to make—

VOICE: I paid dues in this union for four years, that's who's me! I gotta right and this pussy-footed rat ain't coming in here with ideals like that. You know his record. Lemme say it out——

FATT: You'll prove all this or I'll bust you in every hack outfit in town!

VOICE: I gotta right. I gotta right. Looka *him*, he don't say boo!

CLAYTON: You're a liar and I never seen you before in my life!

VOICE: Boys, he spent two years in the coal fields breaking up any organization he touched. Fifty guys he put in jail. He's ranged up and down the east coast—shipping, textiles, steel—he's been in everything you can name. Right now——

CLAYTON: That's a lie!

VOICE: Right now he's working for that Bergman outfit on Columbus Circle who furnishes rats for any outfit in the country before, during, and after strikes.

[*The man who is the hero of the next episode goes down to his side with other committee men*]

CLAYTON: He's trying to break up the meeting, fellers!

VOICE: We won't search you for credentials . . .

CLAYTON: I got nothing to hide. Your own secretary knows I'm straight.

VOICE: Sure. Boys, you know who this sonovabitch is?

CLAYTON: I never seen you before in my life!!

VOICE: Boys, I slept with him in the same bed sixteen years. HE'S MY OWN LOUSY BROTHER!!

FATT: [*After pause*] Is this true?

[*No answer from* CLAYTON]

VOICE *to* CLAYTON: Scram, before I break your neck!

[CLAYTON *scrams down center aisle*]

VOICE: [*Says watching him*] Remember his map—he can't change that—Clancy! [*Standing in his place says:*] Too bad you didn't know about this, Fatt! [*After a pause*] The Clancy family tree is bearing nuts!

[*Standing isolated clear on the stage is the hero of the next episode*]

BLACKOUT

V. THE YOUNG ACTOR

A New York theatrical producer's office. Present are a stenographer and a young actor. She is busy typing; he, waiting with card in hand.

STENOGRAPHER: He's taking a hot bath . . . says you should wait.

PHILIPS: [*The actor*] A bath did you say? Where?

STENOGRAPHER: See that door? Right through there—leads to his apartment.

PHILIPS: Through there?

STENOGRAPHER: Mister, he's laying there in a hot perfumed bath. Don't say I said it.

PHILIPS: You don't say!

STENOGRAPHER: An oriental den he's got. Can you just see this big Irishman burning Chinese punk in the bedroom? And a big old rose canopy over his casting couch . . .

PHILIPS: What's that—casting couch?

STENOGRAPHER: What's that? You from the sticks?

PHILIPS: I beg your pardon?

STENOGRAPHER: [*Rolls up her sleeves, makes elaborate deaf and dumb signs*] No from side walkies of New Yorkie . . . savvy?

PHILIPS: Oh, you're right. Two years of dramatic stock out of town. One in Chicago.

STENOGRAPHER: Don't tell him, Baby Face. He wouldn't know a good actor if he fell over him in the dark. Say you had two years with the Group, two with the Guild.

PHILIPS: I'd like to get with the Guild. They say——

STENOGRAPHER: He won't know the difference. Don't say I said it!

PHILIPS: I really did play with Watson Findlay in "Early Birds."

STENOGRAPHER: [*Withering him*] Don't tell him!

PHILIPS: He's a big producer, Mr. Grady. I wish I had his money. Don't you?

STENOGRAPHER: Say, I got a clean heart, Mister. I love my fellow man! [*About to exit with typed letters*] Stick around—Mr. Philips. You might be the type. If you were a woman——

PHILIPS: Please. Just a minute . . . please . . . I need the job.

STENOGRAPHER: Look at him!

PHILIPS: I mean . . . I don't know what buttons to push, and you do. What my father used to say—we had a gas station in Cleveland before the crash—"Know what buttons to push," Dad used to say, "and you'll go far."

STENOGRAPHER: You can't push me, Mister! I don't ring right these last few years!

PHILIPS: We don't know where the next meal's coming from. We——

STENOGRAPHER: Maybe . . . I'll lend you a dollar?

PHILIPS: Thanks very much: it won't help.

STENOGRAPHER: One of the old families of Virginia? Proud?

PHILIPS: Oh, not that. You see, I have a wife. We'll have our first baby next month . . . so . . . a dollar isn't much help.

STENOGRAPHER: Roped in?

PHILIPS: I love my wife!

STENOGRAPHER: Okay, you love her! Excuse me! You married her. Can't support her. No . . . not blaming you. But you're fools, all you actors. Old and young! Watch you parade in and out all day. You still got apples in your cheeks and pins for buttons. But in six months you'll be like them—putting on an act: Phony strutting "pishers"—that's French for dead codfish! It's not their fault. Here you get like that or go under. What kind of job is this for an adult man!

PHILIPS: When you have to make a living——

STENOGRAPHER: I know, but——

PHILIPS: Nothing else to do. If I could get something else——

STENOGRAPHER: You'd take it!

PHILIPS: Anything!

STENOGRAPHER: Telling me! With two brothers in my hair! [MR.

GRADY *now enters; played by* FATT] Mr. Brown sent this young man over.

GRADY: Call the hospital: see how Boris is. [*She assents and exits*]

PHILIPS: Good morning, Mr. Grady . . .

GRADY: The morning is lousy!

PHILIPS: Mr. Brown sent me. [*Hands over card*]

GRADY: I heard that once already.

PHILIPS: Excuse me . . .

GRADY: What experience?

PHILIPS: Oh, yes . . .

GRADY: Where?

PHILIPS: Two years in stock, sir. A year with the Goodman Theatre in Chicago . . .

GRADY: That all?

PHILIPS: [*Abashed*] Why, no . . . with the Theatre Guild . . . I was there . . .

GRADY: Never saw you in a Guild show!

PHILIPS: On the road, I mean . . . understudying Mr. Lunt . . .

GRADY: What part? [PHILIPS *can not answer*] You're a lousy liar, son.

PHILIPS: I did . . .

GRADY: You don't look like what I want. Can't understand that Brown. Need a big man to play a soldier. Not a lousy soldier left on Broadway! All in pictures, and we get the nances! [*Turns to work on desk*]

PHILIPS: [*Immediately playing the soldier*] I was in the ROTC in college . . . Reserve Officers' Training Corps. We trained twice a week . . .

GRADY: Won't help.

PHILIPS: With real rifles. [*Waits*] Mr. Grady, I weigh a hundred and fifty-five!

GRADY: How many years back? Been eating regular since you left college?

PHILIPS: [*Very earnestly*] Mr. Grady, I could act this soldier part. I could built it up and act it. Make it up——

GRADY: Think I run a lousy acting school around here?

PHILIPS: Honest to God I would! I need the job—that's why I could do it! I'm strong. I know my business! You'll get an A-1 performance. Because I need this job! My wife's having a baby in a few weeks. We need the money. Give me a chance!

GRADY: What do I care if you can act it! I'm sorry about your baby. Use your head, son. Tank Town stock is different. Here we got investments to be protected. When I sink fifteen thousand in a show I don't take chances on some youngster. We cast to type!

PHILIPS: I'm an artist! I can——

GRADY: That's your headache. Nobody interested in artists here. Get a big bunch for a nickel on any corner. Two flops in a row on this lousy street nobody loves you—only God, and He don't count. We protect investments: we cast to type. Your face and height we want, not your soul, son. And Jesus Christ himself couldn't play a soldier in this show . . . with all his talent. [*Crosses himself in quick repentance for this remark*]

PHILIPS: Anything . . . a bit, a walk-on?

GRADY: Sorry: small cast. [*Looking at papers on his desk*] You try Russia, son. I hear it's hot stuff over there.

PHILIPS: Stage manager? Assistant?

GRADY: All filled, sonny. [*Stands up; crumples several papers from the desk*] Better luck next time.

PHILIPS: Thanks . . .

GRADY: Drop in from time to time. [*Crosses and about to exit*] You never know when something—[*The* STENOGRAPHER *enters with papers to put on desk*] What did the hospital say?

STENOGRAPHER: He's much better, Mr. Grady.

GRADY: Resting easy?

STENOGRAPHER: Dr. Martel said Boris is doing even better than he expected.

GRADY: A damn lousy operation!

STENOGRAPHER: Yes . . .

GRADY: [*Belching*] Tell the nigger boy to send up a Bromo Seltzer.

STENOGRAPHER: Yes, Mr. Grady. [*He exits*] Boris wanted lady friends.

PHILIPS: What?

STENOGRAPHER: So they operated . . . poor dog!

PHILIPS: A dog?

STENOGRAPHER: His Russian wolfhound! They do the same to you, but you don't know it! [*Suddenly*] Want advice? In the next office, don't let them see you down in the mouth. They don't like it—makes them shiver.

PHILIPS: You treat me like a human being. Thanks . . .

STENOGRAPHER: You're human!

PHILIPS: I used to think so.

STENOGRAPHER: He wants a bromo for his hangover. [*Goes to door*] Want that dollar?

PHILIPS: It won't help much.

STENOGRAPHER: One dollar buys ten loaves of bread, Mister. Or one dollar buys nine loaves of bread and one copy of The Communist Manifesto. Learn while you eat. Read while you run . . .

PHIL: Manifesto? What's that? [*Takes dollar*] What is that, what you said . . . Manifesto?

STENOGRAPHER: Stop off on your way out—I'll give you a copy. From Genesis to Revelation, Comrade Philips! "And I saw a new earth and a new heaven; for the first earth and the first heaven were passed away; and there was no more sea."

PHILIPS: I don't understand that . . .

STENOGRAPHER: I'm saying the meek shall not inherit the earth!

PHILIPS: No?

STENOGRAPHER: The MILITANT! Come out in the light, Comrade.

BLACKOUT

VI. INTERNE EPISODE

DR. BARNES, *an elderly distinguished man, is speaking on the telephone. He wears a white coat.*

BARNES: No, I gave you my opinion twice. You outvoted me. You did this to Dr. Benjamin yourself. That is why you can tell him yourself. [*Hangs up phone, angrily. As he is about to pour himself a drink from a bottle on the table, a knock is heard*] Who is it?

BENJAMIN: [*Without*] Can I see you a minute, please?

BARNES: [*Hiding the bottle*] Come in, Dr. Benjamin, come in.

BENJAMIN: It's important—excuse me—they've got Leeds up there in my place—He's operating on Mrs. Lewis—the hysterectomy—it's my job. I washed up, prepared . . . they told me at the last minute. I don't mind being replaced, Doctor, but Leeds is a damn fool! He shouldn't be permitted——

BARNES: [*Dryly*] Leeds is the nephew of Senator Leeds.

BENJAMIN: He's incompetent as hell.

BARNES: [*Obviously changing subject, picks up lab. jar*] They're doing splendid work in brain surgery these days. This is a very fine specimen . . .

BENJAMIN: I'm sorry, I thought you might be interested.

BARNES: [*Still examining jar*] Well, I am, young man, I am! Only remember it's a charity case!

BENJAMIN: Of course. They wouldn't allow it for a second, otherwise.

BARNES: Her life is in danger?

BENJAMIN: Of course! You know how serious the case is!

BARNES: Turn your gimlet eyes elsewhere, Doctor. Jigging around like a cricket on a hot grill won't help. Doctors don't run these hospitals. He's the Senator's nephew and there he stays.

BENJAMIN: It's too bad.

BARNES: I'm not calling you down either. [*Plopping down jar suddenly*] Goddammit, do you think it's my fault?

BENJAMIN: [*About to leave*] I know . . . I'm sorry.

BARNES: Just a minute. Sit down.

BENJAMIN: Sorry, I can't sit.

BARNES: Stand then!

BENJAMIN: [*Sits*] Understand, Dr. Barnes, I don't mind being replaced at the last minute this way, but . . . well, this flagrant bit of class distinction—because she's poor—

BARNES: Be careful of words like that—"class distinction." Don't belong here. Lots of energy, you brilliant young men, but idiots. Discretion! Ever hear that word?

BENJAMIN: Too radical?

BARNES: Precisely. And some day like in Germany, it might cost you your head.

BENJAMIN: Not to mention my job.

BARNES: So they told you?

BENJAMIN: Told me what?

BARNES: They're closing Ward C next month. I don't have to tell you the hospital isn't self supporting. Until last year that board of trustees met deficits . . . You can guess the rest. At a board meeting Tuesday, our fine feathered friends discovered they couldn't meet the last quarter's deficit—a neat little sum well over $100,000. If the hospital is to continue at all, its damn—

BENJAMIN: Necessary to close another charity ward!

BARNES: So they say . . . [A wait]

BENJAMIN: But that's not all?

BARNES: [Ashamed] Have to cut down on staff too . . .

BENJAMIN: That's too bad. Does it touch me?

BARNES: Afraid it does.

BENJAMIN: But after all I'm top man here. I don't mean I'm better than others, but I've worked harder.

BARNES: And shown more promise . . .

BENJAMIN: I always supposed they'd cut from the bottom first.

BARNES: Usually.

BENJAMIN: But in this case?

BARNES: Complications.

BENJAMIN: For instance?

[BARNES is hesitant]

BARNES: I like you, Benjamin. It's one ripping shame.

BENJAMIN: I'm no sensitive plant—what's the answer?

BARNES: An old disease, malignant, tumescent. We need an anti-toxin for it.

BENJAMIN: I see.

BARNES: What?

BENJAMIN: I met that disease before—at Harvard first.

BARNES: You have seniority here, Benjamin.

BENJAMIN: But I'm a Jew!

[BARNES *nods his head in agreement.* BENJAMIN *stands there a moment and blows his nose*]

BARNES: [*Blows his nose*] Microbes!

BENJAMIN: Pressure from above?

BARNES: Don't think Kennedy and I didn't fight for you!

BENJAMIN: Such discrimination, with all those wealthy brother Jews on the board?

BENJAMIN: I've remarked before—doesn't seem to be much difference between wealthy Jews and rich Gentiles. Cut from the same piece!

BENJAMIN: For myself I don't feel sorry. My parents gave up an awful lot to get me this far. They ran a little dry goods shop in the Bronx until their pitiful savings went in the crash last year. Poppa's peddling neckties . . . Saul Ezra Benjamin—a man who's read Spinoza all his life.

BARNES: Doctors don't run medicine in this country. The men who know their jobs don't run anything here, except the motormen on trolley cars. I've seen medicine change—plenty—anesthesia, sterilization—but not because of rich men—in *spite* of them! In a rich man's country your true self's buried deep. Microbes! Less . . . Vermin! See this ankle, this delicate sensitive hand? Four hundred years to breed that. Out of a revolutionary background! Spirit of '76! Ancestors froze at Valley Forge! What's it all mean! Slops! The honest workers were sold out then, in '76. The Constitution's for rich men then and now. Slops! [*The phone rings. Angrily*] Dr. Barnes [*listens a moment, looks at* BENJAMIN] I see. [*Hangs up, turns slowly to the younger Doctor*] They lost your patient.

[BENJAMIN *stands solid with the shock of this news but finally hurls his operation gloves to the floor*]

BARNES: That's right . . . that's right. Young, hot, go and do it! I'm very ancient, fossil, but life's ahead of you, Dr. Benjamin, and when you fire the first shot say, "This one's for old Doc Barnes!" Too much dignity—bullets. Don't shoot vermin! Step on them! If I didn't have an invalid daughter—[BARNES *goes back to his seat, blows his nose in silence*] I have said my piece, Benjamin.

BENJAMIN: Lot of things I wasn't certain of. Many things these radicals say . . . you don't believe theories until they happen to you.

BARNES: You lost a lot today, but you won a great point.

BENJAMIN: Yes, to know I'm right? To really begin believing in something? Not to say, "What a world!" but to say, "Change the world!" I wanted to go to Russia. Last week I was thinking about it—the wonderful opportunity to do good work in their socialized medicine—

BARNES: Beautiful, beautiful!

BENJAMIN: To be able to work—

BARNES: Why don't you go? I might be able—

BENJAMIN: Nothing's nearer what I'd like to do!

BARNES: Do it!

BENJAMIN: No! Our work's here—America! I'm scared . . . What future's ahead, I don't know. Get some job to keep alive—maybe drive a cab—and study and work and learn my place—

BARNES: And step down hard!

BENJAMIN: Fight! Maybe get killed, but goddam! We'll go ahead! [BENJAMIN *stands with clenched fist raised high*]

BLACKOUT

AGATE: LADIES AND GENTLEMEN, and don't let anyone tell you we ain't got some ladies in this sea of upturned faces! Only they're wearin' pants. Well, maybe I don't know a thing; maybe I fell outa the cradle when I was a kid and ain't been right since—you can't tell!

VOICE: Sit down, cockeye!

AGATE: Who's paying you for those remarks, Buddy?—Moscow Gold? Maybe I got a *glass eye*, but it come from working in a factory at the age of eleven. They hooked it out because they didn't have a shield on the works. But I wear it like a medal 'cause it tells the world where I belong—deep down in the working class! We had delegates in the union there—all kinds of secretaries and treasurers . . . walkin' delegates, but not with blisters on their feet! Oh, no! On their fat little ass from sitting on cushions and raking in mazuma. [SECRETARY *and* GUNMAN *remonstrate in words and actions here*] Sit down, boys. I'm just sayin' that about unions in general. I know it ain't true here! Why no, our officers is all aces. Why, I seen our own secretary Fatt walk outa his way not to step on a cockroach. No, boys, don't think—

FATT: [*Breaking in*] You're out of order!

AGATE: [*To audience*] Am I outa order?

ALL: No, no. Speak. Go on, etc.

AGATE: Yes, our officers is all aces. But I'm a member here—and no experience in Philly either! Today I couldn't wear my union button. The damnedest thing happened. When I take the old coat off the wall, I see she's smoking. I'm a sonovagun if the old union button isn't on fire! Yep, the old celluloid was makin' the most god-awful stink: the landlady come up and give me hell! You know what happened?—that old union button just blushed itself to death! Ashamed! Can you beat it?

FATT: Sit down, Keller! Nobody's interested!

AGATE: Yes, they are!

GUNMAN: Sit down like he tells you!

AGATE: [*Continuing to audience*] And when I finish—

[*His speech is broken by* FATT *and* GUNMAN *who physically handle him. He breaks away and gets to other side of stage. The two are about to make for him when some of the committee men come forward and get in between the struggling parties.* AGATE's *shirt has been torn*]

AGATE: [*To audience*] What's the answer, boys? The answer is, if we're reds because we wanna strike, then we take over their salute, too! Know how they do it? [*Makes Communist salute*] What is it? An uppercut! The good old uppercut to the chin! Hell, some of us boys ain't even got a shirt to our backs. What's the boss class tryin' to do—make a nudist colony outa us?

[*The audience laughs and suddenly* AGATE *comes to the middle of the stage so that the other cabmen back him up in a strong clump*]

AGATE: Don't laugh! Nothing's funny! This is your life and mine! It's skull and bones every incha the road! Christ, we're dyin' by inches! For what? For the debutant-ees to have their sweet comin' out parties in the Ritz! Poppa's got a daughter she's gotta get her picture in the papers. Christ, they make 'em with our blood. Joe said it. Slow death or fight. It's war! [*Throughout this whole speech* AGATE *is backed up by the other six workers, so that from their activity it is plain that the whole group of them are saying these things. Several of them may take alternate lines out of this long last speech*] You Edna, God love your mouth! Sid and Florrie, the other boys, old Doc Barnes—fight with us for right! It's war! Working class, unite and fight! Tear down the slaughter house of our old lives! Let freedom really ring. These slick slobs stand here telling us about bogeymen. That's a new one for the kids—the reds is bogeymen! But the man who got me food in 1932, he called me Comrade! The one who picked me up where I bled—he called me Comrade, too! What are we waiting for . . . Don't wait for Lefty! He might never come. Every minute—

[*This is broken into by a man who has dashed up the center aisle from the back of the house. He runs up on stage, says:*]

MAN: Boys, they just found Lefty!

OTHERS: What? What? What?

SOME: Shhh . . . Shhh . . .

MAN: They found Lefty . . .

AGATE: Where?

MAN: Behind the car barns with a bullet in his head!

AGATE: [*Crying*] Hear it, boys, hear it? Hell, listen to me! Coast to coast! HELLO AMERICA! HELLO! WE'RE STORMBIRDS OF THE WORKING-CLASS. WORKERS OF THE WORLD . . . OUR BONES AND BLOOD! And when we die they'll know what we did to make a new world! Christ, cut us up to little pieces. We'll die for what is right! Put fruit trees where our ashes are! [*To audience*] Well, what's the answer?

ALL: STRIKE!

AGATE: LOUDER!

ALL: STRIKE!

AGATE *and* OTHERS: [*On stage*] AGAIN!

ALL: STRIKE, STRIKE, STRIKE!!!

CURTAIN

BLACK COMEDY

Peter Shaffer

Peter Shaffer

Peter Shaffer was born in Liverpool, England, on May 15, 1926. He attended St. Paul's School in London and spent three years at Trinity College, Cambridge. In 1951 he came to the United States, where he worked in a bookshop and in the acquisitions department of the New York Public Library while pressing on toward a writing career. He then returned to England for productions of several of his plays on British television.

Mr. Shaffer's extraordinary range as a playwright has enabled him to write in many different forms with consistent success. This versatility and fine craftsmanship have produced such diverse works as *Five Finger Exercise*, a serious probing of a neurotic family; *The Private Ear* and *The Public Eye*, a tandem bill of sharply contrasting comedies; and *The Royal Hunt of the Sun*, an impressive epic drama dealing with the confrontation between Atahuallpa, the sixteenth-century Inca sovereign of Peru, and the Spanish conquistador leader Pizarro. *The Royal Hunt of the Sun* had an overwhelming reception on the occasion of its première at the Chichester Festival on July 7, 1964. This success was repeated when the drama joined the National Theatre repertory at the Old Vic in London and, again, when it was presented in New York (1965), where it ran for 247 performances.

In 1970 Peter Shaffer once again was represented on the London stage with *The Battle of Shrivings*, starring Sir John Gielgud. This was followed by *Equus*, which opened at the Old Vic in 1973. With Alec McCowen and Peter Firth in the leads, it became an immediate hit. The drama was brought to New York on October 24, 1974, where it ran for almost three years and garnered a second New York Drama Critics' Circle Award for its author. (The first was presented in 1960 for *Five Finger Exercise*.)

Black Comedy originally was commissioned and produced by Lord

(Laurence) Olivier for the National Theatre during its 1965–66 season. In 1967 the comedy opened in New York, where it was hailed by the critics and ran for 337 performances. Its companion piece, *White Lies*, was written expressly for the New York stage and later was taken to London in revised form as *The White Liars* when *Black Comedy* was revived at the Lyric Theatre on February 21, 1968.

Characters:

BRINDSLEY MILLER: *A young sculptor (mid-twenties), intelligent and attractive, but nervous and uncertain of himself.*

CAROL MELKETT: *His fiancée. A young debutante; very pretty, very spoiled; very silly. Her sound is that unmistakable, terrifying deb quack.*

MISS FURNIVAL: *A middle-aged spinster. Prissy; and refined. Clad in the blouse and sack skirt of her gentility, her hair in a bun, her voice in a bun, she reveals only the repressed gestures of the middle-class spinster —until alcohol undoes her.*

COLONEL MELKETT: *CAROL's commanding father. Brisk, barky, yet given to sudden vocal calms which suggest a deep and alarming instability. It is not only the constant darkness which gives him his look of wide-eyed suspicion.*

HAROLD GORRINGE: *The camp owner of an antique china shop, and BRINDSLEY's neighbor, HAROLD comes from the North of England. His friendship is highly conditional and possessive: sooner or later, payment for it will be asked. A specialist in emotional blackmail, he can become hysterical when slighted, or (as inevitably happens) rejected. He is older than BRINDSLEY by several years.*

SCHUPPANZIGH: *A middle-class German refugee, chubby, cultivated, and effervescent. He is an entirely happy man, delighted to be in England, even if this means being employed full time by the London Electricity Board.*

CLEA: *BRINDSLEY's ex-mistress. Mid-twenties; dazzling, emotional, bright and mischievous. The challenge to her to create a dramatic situation out of the darkness is ultimately irresistible.*

GEORG BAMBERGER: *An elderly millionaire art collector, easily identifiable as such.*

THE SCENE: *The action of the play takes place in* BRINDSLEY's *apartment in South Kensington, London. This forms the ground floor of a large house, now divided into flats.* HAROLD GORRINGE *lives opposite;* MISS FURNIVAL *lives above.*

There are four ways out of the room. A door at the left leads directly across the passage to HAROLD's *room. A door to this, with its mat laid tidily outside, can clearly be seen. A curtain screens* BRINDSLEY's *studio; when it is parted we glimpse samples of his work in metal. To the right of this an open stair shoots steeply up to his bedroom above, reached through a door at the top. To the left, a trap in the floor leads down to the cellar.*

It is a gay room, when we finally see it, full of color and space and new shapes. It is littered with marvelous objects—mobiles, mannikins, toys, and dotty bric-a-brac—the happy paraphernalia of a free and imaginative mind. The total effect is of chaos tidied in honor of an occasion, and of a temporary elegance created by the furniture borrowed from HAROLD GORRINGE *and arranged to its best advantage.*

This consists of three elegant Regency chairs in gold leaf; a Regency chaise-longue to match; a small Queen Anne table bearing a fine opaline lamp with a silk shade; a Wedgwood bowl in black basalt; a good Coalport vase containing summer flowers; and a fine porcelain Buddha.

The only things which actually belong to BRINDSLEY *are a cheap square table bearing the drinks; an equally cheap round table in the middle of the room, shrouded by a cloth and decorated with the Wedgwood bowl; a low stool, improved by the Buddha; a record player; and his own artistic creations. These are largely assumed to be in the studio awaiting inspection; but one of them is visible in this room. On the dais stands a bizarre iron sculpture dominated by two long detachable metal prongs, and hung with metal pieces which jangle loudly if touched. On the wall hang paintings, some of them presumably by* CLEA. *All are nonfigurative: colorful geometric designs, splashes, splotches and splats of color; whirls and whorls and wiggles—all testifying more to a delight in handling paint than to an ability to achieve very much with it.*

THE TIME: 9:30 *on a Sunday night.*

THE LIGHT: *The stage is in complete darkness. On the few occasions when a lighter is lit, matches are struck or a torch is put on, the light onstage merely gets dimmer. When these objects are extinguished, the stage immediately grows brighter.*

[*Two voices are heard, those of* BRINDSLEY *and* CAROL. *They must give the impression of two people walking round a room with absolute confidence, as if in the light. We hear sounds as of furniture being moved. A chair is dumped down*]

BRINDSLEY: There! How do you think the room looks?

CAROL: [*Quacking*] Fabulous! I wish you could always have it like this. That lamp looks divine there. And those chairs are just the right color. I told you green would look well in here.

BRINDSLEY: Suppose Harold comes back?

CAROL: He is not coming back till tomorrow morning.

[BRINDSLEY *paces nervously*]

BRINDSLEY: I know. But suppose he comes tonight? He's mad about his antiques. What do you think he'll say if he goes into his room and finds out we've stolen them?

CAROL: Don't dramatize. We haven't stolen all his furniture. Just three chairs, the sofa, that table, the lamp, the bowl, and the vase of flowers, that's all.

BRINDSLEY: And the Buddha. That's more valuable than anything. Look at it.

CAROL: Oh, do stop worrying, darling.

BRINDSLEY: Well, you don't know Harold. He won't even let anyone touch his antiques.

CAROL: Look, we'll put everything back as soon as Mr. Bamberger leaves. Now stop being dreary.

BRINDSLEY: Well, frankly, I don't think we should have done it. I mean—*anyway*, Harold or no.

CAROL: Why not, for heaven's sake? The room looks divine now. Just look at it!

BRINDSLEY: Darling, Georg Bamberger's a multi-millionaire. He's lived all his life against this sort of furniture. Our few stolen bits aren't going to impress him. He's coming to see the work of an unknown sculptor. If you ask me, it would look much better to him if he found me exactly as I really am: a poor artist. It might touch his heart.

CAROL: It might—but it certainly won't impress Daddy. Remember, he's coming too.

BRINDSLEY: As if I could forget! Why you had to invite your monster father tonight, I can't think!

CAROL: Oh, not again!

BRINDSLEY: Well, it's too bloody much. If he's going to be persuaded I'm a fit husband for you just by watching a famous collector buy some of my work, he doesn't deserve to have me as a son-in-law!

CAROL: He just wants some proof you can earn your own living.

BRINDSLEY: And what if Bamberger *doesn't* like my work?

CAROL: He will, darling. Just stop worrying.

BRINDSLEY: I can't. Get me a whiskey. [*She does. We hear her steps, and a glass clinking against a bottle—then the sound of a soda syphon*] I've got a foreboding. It's all going to be a disaster. An A-one, copper-bottomed, twenty-four-carat disaster.

CAROL: Look, darling, you know what they say. Faint heart never won fair ladypegs!

BRINDSLEY: How true.

CAROL: The trouble with you is you're what Daddy calls a Determined Defeatist.

BRINDSLEY: The more I hear about your Daddy, the more I hate him. I loathe military men anyway . . . and in any case he's bound to hate me.

CAROL: Why?

BRINDSLEY: Because I'm a complete physical coward. He'll smell it on my breath.

CAROL: Look, darling, all you've got to do is stand up to him. Daddy's only a bully when he thinks people are afraid of him.

BRINDSLEY: Well, I am.

CAROL: You haven't even met him.

BRINDSLEY: That doesn't make any difference.

CAROL: Don't be ridiculous. [*Hands him a drink*] Here.

BRINDSLEY: Thanks.

CAROL: What can he do? To you?

BRINDSLEY: For one thing, he can refuse to let me marry you.

CAROL: Ah, that's sweetipegs.

[*They embrace*]

BRINDSLEY: I like you in yellow. It brings out your hair.

CAROL: Straighten your tie. You look sloppy.

BRINDSLEY: Well, you look divine.

CAROL: Really?

BRINDSLEY: I mean it. I've never seen you look so lovely.

CAROL: Tell me, Brin, have there been many before me?

BRINDSLEY: Thousands.

CAROL: Seriously!

BRINDSLEY: Seriously—none.

CAROL: What about that girl in the photo?

BRINDSLEY: She lasted about three months.

CAROL: When?

BRINDSLEY: Two years ago.

CAROL: What was her name?

BRINDSLEY: Clea.

CAROL: What was she like?

BRINDSLEY: She was a painter. Very honest. Very clever. And just about as cozy as a steel razor blade.

CAROL: When was the last time you saw her?

BRINDSLEY: [*Evasively*] I told you . . . two years ago.

CAROL: Well, why did you still have her photo in your bedroom drawer?

BRINDSLEY: It was just there. That's all. Give me a kiss . . . [*Pause*] No one in the world kisses like you.

CAROL: [*Murmuring*] Tell me something . . . did you like it better with her—or me?

BRINDSLEY: Like what?

CAROL: Sexipegs.

BRINDSLEY: Look, people will be here in a minute. Put a record on. It had better be something for your father. What does he like?

CAROL: [*Crossing to the record player*] He doesn't like anything except military marches.

BRINDSLEY: I might have guessed . . . Wait—I think I've got some! That last record on the shelf. The orange cover. It's called "Marching and Murdering with Sousa," or something.

CAROL: This one?

BRINDSLEY: That's it.

CAROL: [*Getting it*] "The Band of the Coldstream Guards."

BRINDSLEY: Ideal. Put it on.

CAROL: How d'you switch on?

BRINDSLEY: The last knob on the left. That's it . . . Let us pray! Oh God, let this evening go all right! Let Mr. Bamberger like my sculpture and buy some! Let Carol's monster father like me! And let my neighbor Harold Gorringe never find out that we borrowed his precious furniture behind his back! Amen. [*A Sousa march; loud. Hardly has it begun, however, when it runs down—as if there is a failure of electricity. Brilliant light floods the stage. The rest of the play, save for the times when matches are struck, or for the scene with* SCHUPPANZIGH, *is acted in this light, but as if in pitch darkness. They freeze:* CAROL *by the end of the sofa;* BRINDSLEY *by the drinks table. The girl's dress is a silk flag of chic wrapped round her greyhound's body. The boy's look is equally cool: narrow, contained, and sexy. Throughout the evening, as things slide into disaster for him, his crisp, detached shape degenerates progressively into sweat and rumple—just as the elegance of his room gives way relentlessly to its usual near-slum appearance. For the place, as for its owner, the evening is a progress through disintegration*] God! We've blown a fuse!

CAROL: Oh, no!

BRINDSLEY: It must be.

[*He blunders to the light switch, feeling ahead of him, trying to part the darkness with his hands. Finding the switch he flicks it on and off*]

CAROL: It is!

BRINDSLEY: Oh, no!

CAROL: Or a power cut. Where's the box?

BRINDSLEY: In the hall.

CAROL: Have you any candles?

BRINDSLEY: No. Damn!

CAROL: Where are the matches?

BRINDSLEY: They should be on the drinks table. [*Feeling round the bottles*] No. Try on the record player. [*They both start groping about the room, feeling for matches*] Damn, damn, damn, damn, damn, damn!

[CAROL *sets a maraca rattling off the record player*]

CAROL: There! [*Finding it*] No . . .

[*The telephone rings*]

BRINDSLEY: Would you believe it?! [*He blunders his way toward the sound of the bell. Just in time he remembers the central table— and stops himself from colliding into it with a smile of self-congratulation*] All right: I'm coming! [*Instead he trips over the dais, and goes sprawling—knocking the phone onto the floor. He has to grope for it on his knees, hauling the receiver back to him by the wire. Into receiver*] Hallo? . . . [*In sudden horror*] Hallo . . . No, no, no, no—I'm fine, just fine! . . . You? . . . [*His hand over the receiver; to* CAROL] Darling—look in the bedroom, will you?

CAROL: I haven't finished in here yet.

BRINDSLEY: Well, I've just remembered there's some fuse wire in the bedroom. In that drawer where you found the photograph. Go and get it, will you?

CAROL: I don't think there is. I didn't see any there.

BRINDSLEY: [*Snapping*] Don't argue. Just look!

CAROL: All right. Keep your hairpiece on.

[*During the following she gropes her way cautiously up the stairs—head down, arms up the banisters, silken bottom thrust out with the effort*]

BRINDSLEY: [*Controlling himself*] I'm sorry. I just know it's there, that's all. You must have missed it.

CAROL: What about the matches?

BRINDSLEY: We'll have to mend it in the dark, that's all. Please hurry, dear.

CAROL: [*Climbing*] Oh God, how dreary!

BRINDSLEY: [*Taking his hand off the receiver and listening to hear CAROL go*] Hallo? . . . Well, well, well, well! How are you? Good. That's just fine. Fine, fine! . . . Stop saying what?

[*CAROL reaches the top of the stairs—and from force of habit pulls down her skirt before groping her way into the bedroom*]

BRINDSLEY: [*Hand over the receiver*] Carol? . . . Darling? . . . [*Satisfied she has gone; in a rush into the telephone, his voice low*] Clea! What are you doing here? I thought you were in Finland . . . But you've hardly been gone six weeks . . . Where are you speaking from? . . . The Air Terminal? . . . Well, no, that's not a good idea tonight. I'm terribly busy, and I'm afraid I just can't get out of it. It's business.

CAROL: [*Calling from the bedroom door, above*] There's nothing there except your dreary socks. I told you.

BRINDSLEY: [*Calling back*] Well, try the other drawers . . . [*He rises as he speaks, turning so that the wire wraps itself around his legs. CAROL returns to her search. Low and rapid, into phone*] Look: I can't talk now. Can I call you tomorrow? Where will you be? . . . Look, I told you *no*, Clea. Not tonight. I know it's just around the corner, that's not the point. You can't come round . . . Look, the situation's changed. Something's happened this past month—

CAROL: [*Offstage*] I can't see anything. Brin, *please!*—

BRINDSLEY: Clea, I've got to go . . . Look, I can't discuss it over the phone . . . Has it got to do with what? Yes, of course it has. I mean you can't expect things to stay frozen, can you?

CAROL: [*Emerging from the bedroom*] There's nothing here. Haven't we any matches at all?

BRINDSLEY: Oh, stop wailing! [*Into phone*] No, not you. I'll call you tomorrow. Good-bye.

[*He hangs up sharply—but fails to find the rest of the telephone so that he bangs the receiver hard on the table first. Then he has to disentangle himself from the wire. Already* BRINDSLEY *is beginning to be fussed*]

CAROL: [*Descending*] Who was that?

BRINDSLEY: Just a chum. Did you find the wire?

CAROL: I can't find anything in this. We've *got* to get some matches!—

BRINDSLEY: I'll try the pub. Perhaps they'll have some candles as well.

[*Little screams are heard approaching from above. It is* MISS FURNIVAL *groping her way down in a panic*]

MISS FURNIVAL: [*Squealing*] Help! Help! . . . Oh please someone help me!

BRINDSLEY: [*Calling out*] Is that you, Miss Furnival?

MISS FURNIVAL: Mr. Miller? . . .

BRINDSLEY: Yes?

MISS FURNIVAL: Mr. Miller!

BRINDSLEY: Yes!

[*She gropes her way in.* BRINDSLEY *crosses to find her, but narrowly misses her*]

MISS FURNIVAL: Oh, thank God, you're there; I'm so frightened!

BRINDSLEY: Why? Have your lights gone, too?

MISS FURNIVAL: Yes!

BRINDSLEY: It must be a power cut. [*He finds her hand and leads her to a chair*]

MISS FURNIVAL: I don't think so. The street lights are on in the front. I saw them from the landing.

BRINDSLEY: Then it must be the main switch of the house.

CAROL: Where is that?

[MISS FURNIVAL *gasps at the strange voice*]

BRINDSLEY: It's in the cellar. It's all sealed up. No one's allowed to touch it but the electricity people.

CAROL: What are we going to do?

BRINDSLEY: Get them—quick!

CAROL: Will they come at this time of night?

BRINDSLEY: They've got to. [BRINDSLEY *accidentally touches* MISS FURNIVAL's *breasts. She gives a little scream.* BRINDSLEY *gropes his way to the phone*] Have you by any chance got a match on you, Miss Furnival?

MISS FURNIVAL: I'm afraid I haven't. So improvident of me. And I'm absolutely terrified of the dark.

BRINDSLEY: Darling, this is Miss Furnival, from upstairs. Miss Furnival—Miss Melkett.

MISS FURNIVAL: How do you do?

CAROL: [*Extending her hand into the darkness*] How do you do?

MISS FURNIVAL: Isn't this frightful?

[BRINDSLEY *picks up the phone and dials* "O"]

CAROL: Perhaps we can put Mr. Bamberger off.

BRINDSLEY: Impossible. He's dining out and coming on here after. He can't be reached.

CAROL: Oh, flip!

BRINDSLEY: [*Sitting on the dais, and speaking into the phone*] Hallo, Operator, can you give me the London Electricity Board, please? Night Service . . . I'm sure it's in the book, Miss, but I'm afraid I can't see . . . There's no need to apologize. No, I'm not blind!—I just can't see: we've got a fuse . . . No we *haven't* got any matches! [*Desperate*] Miss, *please:* this is an emergency . . . Thank you! . . . [*To the room*] London is staffed with imbeciles!

MISS FURNIVAL: Oh, you're so right, Mr. Miller.

BRINDSLEY: [*Rising, frantic; into the phone*] Miss, I *don't want* the number: I can't dial it! . . . Well, have *you* ever tried to dial a number in the dark? . . . [*Trying to keep control*] I just want to be connected . . . Thank you. [*To* MISS FURNIVAL] Miss Furnival, do you by any remote chance have any candles?

MISS FURNIVAL: I'm afraid not, Mr. Miller.

BRINDSLEY: [*Mouthing nastily at her*] "I'm afraid not, Mr. Miller" . . . [*Briskly, into phone*] Hallo? Look, I'd like to report a main fuse at Eighteen Scarlatti Gardens. My name is Miller [*Exasperated*] Yes, yes! All right! . . . [*Maddened; to the room*] Hold on! Hold bloody on!

MISS FURNIVAL: If I might suggest—Harold Gorringe opposite might have some candles. He's away for the weekend, but always leaves his key under the mat.

BRINDSLEY: What a good idea. That's just the sort of practical thing he would have. [*To* CAROL] Here—take this . . . I'll go and see, love. [*He hands her the telephone in a fumble; then makes for the door—only to collide smartly with his sculpture*] Bugger!

MISS FURNIVAL: Are you all right, Mr. Miller?

BRINDSLEY: I knew it! I bloody knew it. This is going to be the worst night of my life! . . .

[*He collides with the door*]

CAROL: Don't panic, darling. Just don't panic!

[*He stumbles out and is seen groping under* HAROLD's *mat for the key. He finds it and enters the room opposite*]

MISS FURNIVAL: You're so right, Miss Melkett. We must none of us panic.

CAROL: [*On the phone*] Hallo? Hallo? [*To* MISS FURNIVAL] This would have to happen tonight. It's just Brindsley's luck.

MISS FURNIVAL: Is something special tonight then, Miss Melkett?

CAROL: It couldn't be more special if it tried.

MISS FURNIVAL: Oh, dear. May I ask why?

CAROL: Have you ever heard of a German called Georg Bamberger?

MISS FURNIVAL: Indeed, yes. Isn't he the richest man in the world?

CAROL: Yes. [*Into phone*] Hallo? . . . [*To* MISS FURNIVAL] Well, he's coming here tonight.

MISS FURNIVAL: Tonight!

CAROL: In about twenty minutes, to be exact. And to make matters worse, he's apparently stone deaf.

MISS FURNIVAL: How extraordinary! May I ask why he's coming?

CAROL: He saw some photos of Brindsley's work and apparently got madly excited about it. His secretary rang up last week and asked if he could come and see it. He's a great collector. Brin would be absolutely *made* if Bamberger bought a piece of his.

MISS FURNIVAL: Oh, how exciting!

CAROL: It's his big break. Or was—till a moment ago.

MISS FURNIVAL: Oh, my dear, you *must* get some help. Jiggle that thing.

CAROL: [*Jiggling the phone*] Hallo? Hallo? . . . Perhaps the Bomb's fallen, and everyone's dead.

MISS FURNIVAL: Oh, please don't say things like that—even in levity.

CAROL: [*Someone answers her at last*] Hallo? Ah! This is Number Eighteen, Scarlatti Gardens. I'm afraid we've had the most dreary fuse. It's what's laughingly known as the Main Switch. We want a *little man* . . . Well, they can't all have flu . . . Oh, please try! It's screamingly urgent . . . Thank you. [*She hangs up*] Sometime this evening, they hope. That's a lot of help.

MISS FURNIVAL: They're not here to help, my dear. In my young days you paid your rates and you got satisfaction. Nowadays you just get some foreigner swearing at you. And if they think you're of the middle class, that only makes it worse.

CAROL: Would you like a drink?

MISS FURNIVAL: I don't drink, thank you. My dear father, being a Baptist minister, strongly disapproved of alcohol.

[*A scuffle is heard amongst milk bottles offstage, followed by a stifled oath*]

COLONEL MELKETT: [*Offstage*] Damn and blast! . . . [*Barking*] Is there anybody there?

CAROL: [*Calling*] In here, daddypegs!

COLONEL: Can't you put the light on, dammit? I've almost knocked meself out on a damn milk bottle.

CAROL: We've got a fuse. Nothing's working.

[COLONEL MELKETT *appears, holding a lighter which evidently is working—we can see the flame, and of course the lights go down a little*]

MISS FURNIVAL: Oh what a relief! A light!

CAROL: This is my father, Colonel Melkett, Miss Furnival. She's from upstairs.

COLONEL: Good evening.

MISS FURNIVAL: I'm taking refuge for a moment with Mr. Miller. I'm not very good in the dark.

COLONEL: When did this happen?

[MISS FURNIVAL, *glad for the light, follows it pathetically as the* COLONEL *crosses the room*]

CAROL: Five minutes ago. The main just blew.

COLONEL: And where's this young man of yours?

CAROL: In the flat opposite. He's trying to find candles.

COLONEL: You mean he hasn't got any?

CAROL: No. We can't even find the matches.

COLONEL: I see. No organization. Bad sign!

CAROL: Daddy, please. It could happen to any of us.

COLONEL: Not to me. [*He turns to find* MISS FURNIVAL *right behind and glares at her balefully. The poor woman retreats to the sofa and sits down.* COLONEL MELKETT *gets his first sight of* BRINDSLEY'S *sculpture*] What the hell's that?

CAROL: Some of Brindsley's work.

COLONEL: Is it, by Jove? And how much does that cost?

CAROL: I think he's asking fifty pounds for it.

COLONEL: My God!

CAROL: [*Nervously*] Do you like the flat, Daddy? He's furnished it very well, hasn't he? I mean it's rich, but not gaudipegs.

COLONEL: Very elegant—good: I can see he's got excellent taste. [*Seeing the Buddha*] Now that's what I understand by a real work of art—you can see what it's meant to be.

MISS FURNIVAL: Good heavens!

CAROL: What is it?

MISS FURNIVAL: Nothing . . . It's that Buddha—it so closely resembles the one Harold Gorringe has.

[CAROL *looks panic-stricken*]

COLONEL: It must have cost a pretty penny, what? He must be quite well off. . . . By Jove—it's got pretty colors.

[*He bends to examine it*]

CAROL: [*Sotto voce, urgently, to* MISS FURNIVAL] You know Mr. Gorringe?

MISS FURNIVAL: Oh, very well indeed. We're excellent friends. He has such lovely things . . . [*For the first time she notices the sofa on which she is sitting*] Oh . . .

CAROL: What?

MISS FURNIVAL: This furniture . . . [*Looking around her*] Surely—? My goodness!—

CAROL: [*Hastily*] Daddy, why don't you look in there? It's Brin's studio. There's something I particularly want you to see before he comes back.

COLONEL: What?

CAROL: It—it—er—it's a surprise, go and see.

COLONEL: Very well, Dumpling. Anythin' to oblige. [*To* MISS FURNIVAL] Excuse me.

[*He goes off into the studio, taking his lighter with him. The light instantly gets brighter onstage.* CAROL *sits beside the spinster on the sofa, crouching like a conspirator*]

CAROL: [*Low and urgent*] Miss Furnival, you're a sport, aren't you?

MISS FURNIVAL: I don't know. What is this furniture doing in here? It belongs to Harold Gorringe.

CAROL: I know. We've done something absolutely frightful. We've stolen all his best pieces and put Brin's horrid old bits into *his* room.

MISS FURNIVAL: But why? It's disgraceful!

CAROL: [*Sentimentally*] Because Brindsley's got nothing, Miss Furnival. Nothing at all. He's as poor as a church mouse. If Daddy had seen this place as it looks normally, he'd have forbidden our marriage on the spot. Mr. Gorringe wasn't there to ask—so we just took the chance.

MISS FURNIVAL: If Harold Gorringe knew that anyone had touched his furniture or his porcelain, he'd go out of his mind! And as for that Buddha—[*Pointing in the wrong direction*] it's the most precious piece he owns. It's worth hundreds of pounds.

CAROL: Oh, please, Miss Furnival—you won't give us away, will you? We're desperate! And it's only for an hour . . . Oh, please! *please!*

MISS FURNIVAL: [*Giggling*] Very well! I won't betray you!

CAROL: Oh, thank you!

MISS FURNIVAL: But it'll have to go back exactly as it was, just as soon as Mr. Bamberger and your father leave.

CAROL: I swear! Oh, Miss Furnival, you're an angel! Do have a drink. Oh no, you don't. Well, have a bitter lemon.

MISS FURNIVAL: Thank you. That I won't refuse.

[*The* COLONEL *returns, still holding his lighter. The stage darkens a little*]

COLONEL: Well, they're certainly a surprise. And that's supposed to be sculpture?

CAROL: It's not supposed to be. It is.

COLONEL: They'd make good garden implements. I'd like 'em for turnin' the soil.

[MISS FURNIVAL *giggles*]

CAROL: That's not very funny, Daddy.

[MISS FURNIVAL *stops giggling*]

COLONEL: Sorry, Dumpling. Speak as you find.

CAROL: I wish you wouldn't call me Dumpling.

COLONEL: Well, there's no point wastin' this. We may need it!

[*He snaps off his lighter.* MISS FURNIVAL *gives her little gasp as the stage brightens*]

CAROL: Don't be nervous, Miss Furnival. Brin will be here in a minute with the candles.

MISS FURNIVAL: Then I'll leave, of course. I don't want to be in your way.

CAROL: You're not at all. [*Hearing him*] Brin?—

[BRINDSLEY *comes out of* HAROLD's *room; returns the key to under the mat*]

BRINDSLEY: Hallo?

CAROL: Did you find anything?

BRINDSLEY: [*Coming in*] You can't find anything in this. If there's candles there, *I* don't know where they are. Did you get the electric people?

CAROL: They said they might send someone around later.

BRINDSLEY: How much later?

CAROL: They don't know.

BRINDSLEY: That's a lot of help. What a lookout! Not a bloody candle in the house. A deaf millionaire to show sculpture to—and your monster father to keep happy. Lovely!

COLONEL: [*Grimly lighting his lighter*] Good evenin'.

[BRINDSLEY *jumps*]

CAROL: Brin, this *is* my father—Colonel Melkett.

BRINDSLEY: [*Wildly embarrassed*] Well, well, well, well, well! . . . [*Panic*] Good evening sir. Fancy you being there all the time! I—I'm expecting some dreadful neighbors, some neighbor monsters, monster neighbors, you know . . . They rang up and said they might look round . . . Well, well, well . . .

COLONEL: [*Darkly*] Well, well.

MISS FURNIVAL: [*Nervously*] Well, well!

CAROL: [*Brightly*] Well!

[The COLONEL *rises and advances on* BRINDSLEY, *who retreats before him across the room*]

COLONEL: You seem to be in a spot of trouble.

BRINDSLEY: [*With mad nervousness*] Oh, not really! Just a fuse—nothing really, we have them all the time . . . I mean, it won't be the first fuse I've survived, and I daresay it won't be the last!

[He gives a wild, braying laugh]

COLONEL: [*Relentless*] In the meantime, you've got no matches. Right?

BRINDSLEY: Right.

COLONEL: No candles. Right?

BRINDSLEY: Right.

COLONEL: No basic efficiency, right?

BRINDSLEY: I wouldn't say that, exactly . . .

COLONEL: By basic efficiency, young man, I mean the simple state of being At Attention in life, rather than At Ease. Understand?

BRINDSLEY: Well, I'm certainly not at ease.

COLONEL: What are you goin' to do about it?

BRINDSLEY: Do?

COLONEL: Don't echo me, sir. I don't like it.

BRINDSLEY: You don't like it. . . . I'm sorry.

COLONEL: Now look you here. This is an emergency. Anyone can see that.

BRINDSLEY: No one can see anything: that's the emergency.

[*He gives his braying laugh again*]

COLONEL: Spare me your humor, sir, if you don't mind. Let's look at the situation objectively. Right?

BRINDSLEY: Right.

COLONEL: Good. [*He snaps off the lighter*] Problem: Darkness. Solution: Light.

BRINDSLEY: Oh, very good, sir.

COLONEL: Weapons: Matches—none! Candles—none! What remains?

BRINDSLEY: Search me.

COLONEL: [*Triumphantly*] Torches. Torches, sir! what?

BRINDSLEY: Or a set of early Christians.

COLONEL: What did you say?

BRINDSLEY: I'm sorry. I think I'm becoming unhinged. Very good. Torches—brilliant.

COLONEL: Routine. Well, where would you find one?

BRINDSLEY: The pub. What time is it?

[*The* COLONEL *lights his lighter, but now not at the first try. The stage light flickers up and down accordingly*]

COLONEL: Blasted thing. It's beginnin' to go. [*He consults his watch*] Quarter to ten. You can just make it, if you hurry.

BRINDSLEY: Thank you, sir. Your clarity of mind has saved the day.

COLONEL: Well, get on with it, man.

BRINDSLEY: Yes, sir! Back in a minute.

[*The* COLONEL *sits in the Regency chair*]

CAROL: Good luck, darling.

BRINDSLEY: Thank you, my sweet.

[*She blows him a kiss. He blows her one back*]

COLONEL: [*Irritated*] Stop that at once.

[BRINDSLEY *starts for the door—but as he reaches it,* HAROLD GORRINGE *is heard, offstage*]

HAROLD: [*Broad Lancashire accent*] Hallo? Hallo? Anyone there?

BRINDSLEY: [*Freezing with horror*] HAROLD!!

HAROLD: Brindsley?

BRINDSLEY: [*Meant for* CAROL] It's Harold. He's back!

CAROL: Oh, no!

BRINDSLEY: THE FURNITURE!!

HAROLD: What's going on here?

[HAROLD *appears. He wears a smart raincoat and carries a weekend suitcase. His hair falls over his brow in a flossy attempt at elegance*]

BRINDSLEY: Nothing, Harold. Don't go in there—come in here. We've had a fuse. It's dark—it's all over the house.

HAROLD: Have you phoned the electric? [*Reaching out*]

BRINDSLEY: [*Reaching out and grabbing him*] Yes. Come in here.

HAROLD: [*Grabbed*] Ohh! . . . [*He takes* BRINDSLEY's *hand and enters the room cozily on his arm*] It's rather cozy in the dark, isn't it?

BRINDSLEY: [*Desperately*] Yes! I suppose so . . . So you're back from your weekend then . . .

HAROLD: I certainly am, dear. Weekend! Some weekend! It rained the whole bloody time. I feel damp to my knickers.

BRINDSLEY: [*Nervously*] Well, have a drink and tell us all about it.

HAROLD: Us? [*Disengaging himself*] Who's here, then?

MISS FURNIVAL: [*Archly*] I am, Mr. Gorringe.

HAROLD: Ferny?

MISS FURNIVAL: Taking refuge, I'm afraid. You know how I hate the dark.

COLONEL: [*Attempting to light his lighter*] Blasted thing! . . . [*He succeeds*] There we are! [*Raising it to* GORRINGE's *face, with distaste*] Who are you?

BRINDSLEY: May I present my neighbor. This is Harold Gorringe—Colonel Melkett.

HAROLD: How do?

COLONEL: How d'ye do?

BRINDSLEY: And this is Miss Carol Melkett, Harold Gorringe.

CAROL: [*Giving him a chilly smile*] Hello! . . .

[HAROLD *nods coldly*]

BRINDSLEY: Here, let me take your raincoat, Harold.

[*He is wearing a tight, modish, gray suit and a brilliant straw-berry shirt*]

HAROLD: [*Taking it off and handing it to him*] Be careful, it's sopping wet.

[*Adroitly,* BRINDSLEY *drops the coat over the Wedgwood bowl on the table*]

COLONEL: You got no candles, I suppose?

HAROLD: Would you believe it, Colonel, but I haven't? Silly me!

[BRINDSLEY *crosses and blows out the* COLONEL's *lighter, just as* HAROLD *begins to look round the room. The stage brightens*]

COLONEL: What the devil did you do that for?

BRINDSLEY: I'm saving your wick, Colonel. You may need it later and it's failing fast.

[*The* COLONEL *gives him a suspicious look.* BRINDSLEY *moves quickly back, takes up the coat and drops it over the right end of the sofa, to conceal as much of it as possible*]

HAROLD: It's all right. I've got some matches.

CAROL: [*Alarmed*] Matches!

HAROLD: Here we are! I hope I've got the right end. [*He strikes one.* BRINDSLEY *immediately blows it out from behind, then moves swiftly to hide the Wedgwood bowl under the table and drops the tablecloth over the remaining end of the sofa.* MISS FURNIVAL *sits serenely unknowing between the two covers*] Hey, what was that?

BRINDSLEY: [*Babbling*] A draft. No match stays alight in this room. It's impossible. Cross currents, you know. Old houses are full of them. They're almost a permanent feature in this house . . .

HAROLD: [*Bewildered*] I don't know what you're on about.

[*He strikes another match.* BRINDSLEY *again blows it out as he nips over to sit in a chair, but this time is seen*] What's up with you?

BRINDSLEY: Nothing!

HAROLD: Have you got a dead body in here or something?

BRINDSLEY: NO!

[*He starts his maniacal laughter*]

HAROLD: Here, have you been drinking?

BRINDSLEY: No. Of course not.

[HAROLD *strikes another match.* BRINDSLEY *dashes up. All these strikings and blowings are of course accompanied by swift and violent alterations of the light*]

HAROLD: [*Exasperated*] Now look here! What's up with you?

BRINDSLEY: [*Inspired*] Dangerous!

HAROLD: What?

BRINDSLEY: [*Frantically improvising*] Dangerous! It's dangerous! . . . We can all die! Naked flames! Hideous accidents can happen with naked flames!

HAROLD: I don't know what you're on about—what's up with you?

[BRINDSLEY *clutches the bewildered* HAROLD *and backs him across to the center table*]

BRINDSLEY: I've just remembered! It's something they always warn you about. In old houses the fuse box and the gas meter are in the same cupboard. They are here!

COLONEL: So what about it?

BRINDSLEY: Well . . . electrical blowouts can damage the gas supply. They're famous for it. They do it all the time! And they say you've got to avoid naked flames till they're mended.

COLONEL: I've never heard of that.

HAROLD: Me neither.

BRINDSLEY: Well, take my word for it. It's fantastically dangerous to burn a naked flame in this room!

CAROL: [*Catching on*] Brin's absolutely right. In fact, they warned me about it on the phone this evening when I called them. They said, "Whatever you do, don't strike a match till the fuse is mended."

BRINDSLEY: There, you see!—it's terribly dangerous.

COLONEL: [*Grimly*] Then why didn't you warn me, Dumpling?

CAROL: I—I forgot.

COLONEL: Brilliant!

MISS FURNIVAL: Oh goodness, we must take care.

BRINDSLEY: We certainly must! . . . [*Pause*] Let's all have a drink. Cheer us up! . . .

CAROL: Good idea! Mr. Gorringe, would you like a drink?

HAROLD: Well, I must say, that wouldn't come amiss. Not after the journey I've had tonight. I swear to God there was thirty-five people in that compartment if there was one—babes in arms, toddlers, two nuns, three yapping poodles, and not a sausage to eat from Leamington to London. It's a bloody disgrace.

MISS FURNIVAL: You'd think they'd put on a restaurant car, Mr. Gorringe.

HAROLD: Not them, Ferny. They don't care if you perish once they've got your fare. Excuse me, I'll just go and clean up.

BRINDSLEY: [*Panic*] You can do that here.

HAROLD: Well, I must unpack anyway.

BRINDSLEY: Do it later.

HAROLD: No, I hate to keep clothes in a suitcase longer than I absolutely have to. If there's one thing I can't stand, it's a creased suit.

BRINDSLEY: Five more minutes won't hurt, surely?

HAROLD: Ooh, you aren't half bossy!

CAROL: What will you have? Winnie, Vera or Ginette?

HAROLD: Come again?

CAROL: Winnie Whiskey, Vera Vodka, or dear old standby Ginette.

HAROLD: [*Yielding*] I can see you're the camp one! . . . If it's all the same to you, I'll have a drop of Ginette, please, and a little lime juice.

COLONEL: Young man, do I have to keep reminding you that you are in an emergency? You have a guest arrivin' any second.

BRINDSLEY: Oh God, I'd forgotten!

COLONEL: Try the pub. Try the neighbors. Try who you damn well please, sir—but *get a torch!*

BRINDSLEY: Yes . . . Yes! . . . Carol, can I have a word with you, please?

CAROL: I'm here.

[*She gropes toward him and* BRINDSLEY *leads her to the stairs*]

COLONEL: What now?

BRINDSLEY: Excuse us just a moment, please, Colonel.

[*He pulls her quickly after him, up the stairs*]

MISS FURNIVAL: [*As they do this*] Oh, Mr. Gorringe, it's so exciting. You'll never guess who's coming here tonight.

HAROLD: Who?

MISS FURNIVAL: Guess.

HAROLD: The Queen!

MISS FURNIVAL: Oh, Mr. Gorringe, you are ridiculous!

[BRINDSLEY *arrives at the top of the stairs, then opens the bedroom door and closes it behind them*]

BRINDSLEY: What are we going to do?

CAROL: [*Behind the door*] I don't know!

BRINDSLEY: [*Behind the door*] Think!

CAROL: But—

BRINDSLEY: *Think!*

COLONEL: Is that boy touched or somethin'?

HAROLD: Touched? He's an absolute poppet.

COLONEL: A what?

HAROLD: A duck. I've known him for years, ever since he came here. There's not many secrets we keep from each other, I can tell you.

COLONEL: [*Frostily*] Really?

HAROLD: Yes, really. He's a very sweet boy.

[BRINDSLEY *and* CAROL *emerge from behind the bedroom door*]

BRINDSLEY: We'll have to put all Harold's furniture back in his room.

CAROL: *Now?!*

BRINDSLEY: We'll have to. I can't get a torch till we do.

CAROL: We can't!

BRINDSLEY: We must. He'll go mad if he finds out what we've done.

HAROLD: Well, come on, Ferny, don't be a tease. Who is it? Who's coming?

MISS FURNIVAL: I'll give you a clue. It's someone with money.

HAROLD: Money? . . . Let me think.

COLONEL: [*Calling out*] Carol!

CAROL: Look, can't you just tell him it was a joke?

BRINDSLEY: You don't know him. He can't bear anyone to touch his treasures. They're like children to him. He cleans everything twice a day with a special swansdown duster. He'd wreck everything. Would you like him to call me a thief in front of your father?

CAROL: Of course not!

BRINDSLEY: Well, he would. He gets absolutely hysterical. I've seen him.

COLONEL: [*Mildly*] Brindsley!

CAROL: Well, how the hell can we do it?

HAROLD: It's no good. You can't hear up there.

BRINDSLEY: [*Stripping off his jacket*] Look, you hold the fort. Serve them drinks. Just keep things going. Leave it all to me. I'll try and put everything back in the dark.

CAROL: It won't work.

BRINDSLEY: It's *got* to!

COLONEL: [*Roaring*] Brindsley!!

BRINDSLEY: [*Dashing to the door*] Coming, sir . . . [*With false calm*] I'm just getting some empties to take to the pub.

COLONEL: Say what you like. That boy's touched.

BRINDSLEY: [*To* CAROL, *intimately*] Trust me, darling.

[*They kiss*]

COLONEL: At the double, Miller.

BRINDSLEY: Yes, sir! Yes, sir! [*He rushes out, and in his anxiety he misses his footing and falls neatly down the entire flight of stairs. Picking himself up*] I'm off now, Colonel! Help is definitely on the way.

COLONEL: Well, hurry it up, man.

BRINDSLEY: Carol will give you drinks. If Mr. Bamberger arrives, just explain the situation to him.

HAROLD: [*Feeling for his hand*] Would you like me to come with you?

BRINDSLEY: No, no, no—good heavens, stay and enjoy yourself. [HAROLD *kisses his hand.* BRINDSLEY *pulls it away*] I mean, you must be exhausted after all those poodles. A nice gin and lime will do wonders. I shan't be a minute.

[*He reaches the door, opens it, then slams it loudly, remaining on the inside. Stealthily he opens it again, stands dead still for a moment, silently indicating to himself the position of the chairs he has to move—then he finds his way to the first of the Regency chairs, which he lifts noiselessly*]

CAROL: [*With bright desperation*] Well now, drinks! What's everyone

going to have? It's Ginette for Mr. Gorringe and I suppose Winnie for Daddy.

COLONEL: And how on earth are you going to do that in the dark?

CAROL: I remember the exact way I put out the bottles.

[BRINDSLEY *bumps into her with the chair and falls back, gored
by its leg*] It's very simple.

HAROLD: Oh, look, love, let me strike a match. I'm sure it's not that
dangerous, just for a minute.

[*He strikes a match*]

CAROL: Oh, no! . . . [BRINDSLEY *ducks down, chair in hand, and
blows out the match*] Do you want to blow us all up, Mr. Gorringe? . . . All poor Mr. Bamberger would find would be teensy
weensy bits of us. Very messypegs.

[*She snatches the box of matches, feels for the ice bucket, and
drops them into it.* BRINDSLEY *steals out, Felix-the-cat-like, with
the chair as* CAROL *fumbling starts to mix drinks. He sets it
down, opens* HAROLD's *door, and disappears inside it with the
chair*]

HAROLD: Bamberger? Is that who's coming? Georg Bamberger?

MISS FURNIVAL: Yes. To see Mr. Miller's work. Isn't it exciting?

HAROLD: Well, I never. I read an article about him last week in the
Sunday Pic. He's known as the mystery millionaire. He's almost
completely deaf—deaf as a post, and spends most of his time indoors alone with his collection. He hardly ever goes out, except to
a gallery or a private studio. That's the life! If I had money that's
what I'd do. Just collect all the china and porcelain I wanted.

[BRINDSLEY *returns with a poor, broken-down chair of his own
and sets it down in the same position as the one he has taken
out. The second chair presents a harder challenge. It sits right
across the room. Delicately he moves toward it—but he has
difficulty finding it. We watch him walk round it in desperately
narrowing circles till he touches it and with relief picks it up*]

MISS FURNIVAL: I've never met a millionaire. I've always wondered if they feel different to us. I mean their actual skins.

COLONEL: Their skins?

MISS FURNIVAL: Yes. I've always imagined they must be softer than ours. Like the skins of ladies when I was a girl.

CAROL: What an interesting idea.

HAROLD: Oh, she's very fanciful is Ferny. Real imagination, I always say.

MISS FURNIVAL: Very kind of you, Mr. Gorringe. You're always so generous with your compliments. [*As she speaks her next speech staring smugly into the darkness, hands clasped in maidenly gentility, the second Regency chair is being moved slowly across what should be her field of vision, two inches from her face. During the following,* BRINDSLEY *unfortunately misaims and carries the chair past the door, bumps into a wall, retreats from it, and inadvertently shuts the door softly with his back. Now he cannot get out of the room. He has to set down the chair, grope for the door handle, turn it, then open the door—then re-find the chair which he has quite lost. This takes a long and frantic time. At last he triumphs, and staggers from the room, nearly exhausted*] But this is by no means fancy. In my day, softness of skin was quite the sign of refinement. Nowadays, of course, it's hard enough for us middle classes to keep ourselves decently clothed, let alone soft. My father used to say, even before the bombs came and burnt our dear little house at Wendover: "The game's up, my girl. We middle classes are as dead as the dodo." Poor father, how right he was.

[*If the counter-point of face action goes well,* MISS FURNIVAL *may have to ad-lib a fair bit during all this, and not mind too much if nobody hears her. The essential thing for all four actors during the furniture-moving is to preserve the look of ordinary conversation*]

COLONEL: Your father was a professional man?

MISS FURNIVAL: He was a man of God, Colonel.

COLONEL: Oh. [BRINDSLEY *returns with a broken-down rocking chair of his own. He crosses gingerly to where the* COLONEL *is sitting*] How are those drinks coming, Dumpling?

CAROL: Fine, Daddy. They'll be one minute.

COLONEL: [*Speaking directly into* BRINDSLEY's *face*] Let me help you.

[BRINDSLEY *staggers back, startled*]

CAROL: You can take this bitter lemon to Miss Furnival if you want.

[BRINDSLEY *sets down the rocker immediately next to the* COLONEL's *chair*]

COLONEL: Very well.

[*He rises just as* BRINDSLEY's *hand pulls the chair from beneath him. With his other hand* BRINDSLEY *pulls the rocker into the identical position. The* COLONEL *moves slowly across the room, arms outstretched for the bitter lemon. Unknowingly* BRINDSLEY *follows him, carrying the third chair. The* COLONEL *collides gently with the table. At the same moment* BRINDSLEY *reaches it, and searches for the Wedgwood bowl. Their hands narrowly miss. Then the young man remembers the bowl is under the table. Deftly he reaches down and retrieves it—and carrying it in one hand and the chair in the other, triumphantly leaves the room through the arch unconsciously provided by the outstretched arms of* CAROL *and the* COLONEL, *giving and receiving a glass of Scotch—which they think is bitter lemon*]

CAROL: Here you are, Daddy. Bitter lemon for Miss Furnival.

COLONEL: Right you are, Dumpling. [*To* MISS FURNIVAL] So your father was a minister then?

MISS FURNIVAL: He was a saint, Colonel. I'm only thankful he never lived to see the rudeness and vulgarity of life today.

[*The* COLONEL *sets off to find her, but goes much too far to the right*]

HAROLD: [*He sits on the sofa beside her*] Oooh, you're so right, Ferny. Rudeness and vulgarity—that's it to a T. The manners of some people today are beyond belief. Honestly. Did I tell you what happened in my shop last Friday? I don't think I did.

MISS FURNIVAL: No, Mr. Gorringe, I don't think so.

[*Her voice corrects the* COLONEL'*s direction. During the following he moves slowly up toward her*]

HAROLD: Well, I'd just opened up—it was about quarter to ten and I was dusting off the teapots—you know, Rockingham collects the dust something shocking!—when who should walk in but that Mrs. Levitt, you know—the ginger-haired bit I told you about, the one who thinks she's God's gift to bachelors.

COLONEL: [*Finding her head with his hand and presenting her with the Scotch*] Here's your lemonade.

MISS FURNIVAL: Oh, thank you. Most kind.

[*Throughout* HAROLD'*s story,* MISS FURNIVAL *nurses the glass, not drinking. The* COLONEL *finds his way slowly back to the chair he thinks he was sitting on before, but which is now a rocker.* BRINDSLEY *re-appears, triumphantly carrying one of the original Regency chairs he took out. He moves slowly across the room getting his bearings*]

HAROLD: Anyway, she's got in her hand a vase I'd sold her last week —it was a birthday present for an old geezer she's having a bit of a ding dong with somewhere in Earls Court, hoping to collect all his lolly when he dies, as I read the situation. I'm a pretty good judge of character, Ferny, as you know—and she's a real grasper if ever I saw one.

[*The* COLONEL *sits heavily in the rocking chair, which over-balances backward, spilling him onto the floor*]

COLONEL: Dammit to hell!

CAROL: What's the matter, Daddy?

[*A pause.* BRINDSLEY *sits down panic-stricken on the chair he has carried in. The* COLONEL *feels the chair and sets it on its feet*]

COLONEL: [*Unbelieving*] It's a blasted rockin' chair! I didn't see a blasted rockin' chair here before! . . .

[*Astounded, the* COLONEL *remains on the floor.* BRINDSLEY *rises and moves the chair to the original position of the second chair he moved*]

HAROLD: Oh yes, you want to watch that. It's in a pretty ropey condition. I've told Brin about it several times. Anyway, this vase. It's a nice bit of Kang Tsi, blue and white with a good orange-peel glaze, absolutely authentic—I'd let her have it for twenty-five pounds, and she'd got infinitely the best of the bargain, no argument about that. [HAROLD *rises and leans against the center table to tell his story more effectively. The* COLONEL *seats himself again, gingerly*] Well, in she prances, her hair all done up in one of them bouffant hairdos, you know, tarty—French-like—it would have looked fancy on a girl half her age with twice her looks—

[BRINDSLEY *mistakenly lifts the end of the sofa.* MISS FURNIVAL *gives a little scream at the jolt*]

HAROLD: Exactly. You know the sort. [BRINDSLEY *staggers in the opposite direction onto the dais*] And d'you know what she says to me? "Mr. Gorringe," she says, "I've been cheated."

MISS FURNIVAL: No!

HAROLD: Her very words. "Cheated." [BRINDSLEY *collides with the sculpture. It jangles violently. To it*] Hush up, I'm talking!

CAROL: [*Covering up*] I'm frightfully sorry.

[HAROLD *whirls round, surprised*]

HAROLD: Anyway—"Oh, I say, and how exactly has that occurred, Mrs. Levitt?" "Well," she says, "quite by chance I took this vase over to Bill Everett in the Portobello, and he says it's not what you called it at all, Chinese and very rare. He says it's a piece of nineteenth-century trash." [BRINDSLEY *finds the lamp on the table and picks it up. He walks with it round the rocking chair, on which the* COLONEL *is now sitting again*] "Does he?" I say. "Does he?" I keep calm. I always do when I'm riled. "Yes," she says. "He does. And I'd thank you to give me my money back."

[The wire of the lamp has followed BRINDSLEY *round the bottom of the rocking chair. It catches.* BRINDSLEY *tugs it gently. The chair moves. Surprised, the* COLONEL *jerks forward.* BRINDSLEY *tugs it again, much harder. The rocking chair is pulled forward, spilling the* COLONEL *out of it, again onto the floor, and then falling itself on top of him. The shade of the lamp comes off. During the ensuing dialogue* BRINDSLEY *gets on his knees and crawls right across the room following the wire of the lamp. He finds the plug, pulls it out, and—still on his knees —retraces his steps, winding up the wire around his arm, and becoming helplessly entangled in it. The* COLONEL *remains on the floor, now really alarmed]*

MISS FURNIVAL: How dreadful, Mr. Gorringe. What did you do?

HAROLD: I counted to ten, and then I let her have it. "In the first place," I said, "I don't expect my customers to go checking up on my honesty behind my back. In the second, Bill Everett is ignorant as Barnsley dirt, he doesn't know Tang from Ting. And in the third place, that applies to you, too, Mrs. Levitt."

MISS FURNIVAL: You didn't!

HAROLD: I certainly did—and worse than that. "You've got in your hand," I said, "a minor masterpiece of Chinese pottery. But in point of fact," I said, "you're not even fit to hold a 1953 Coronation mug. Don't you ever come in here again," I said, "—don't you cross my threshold. Because if you do, Mrs. Levitt, I won't make myself responsible for the consequences."

CAROL: *[With two drinks in her hands]* My, Mr. Gorringe, how splendid of you. Here's your gin and lime. You deserve it.

[She hands him the bitter lemon]

HAROLD: *[Accepting it]* Ta. I was proper blazing, I didn't care.

CAROL: Where are you? Where are you, Daddy? Here's your Scotch.

COLONEL: Here, Dumpling!

[He gets up dazedly and fumbles his way to the glass of gin and lime. BRINDSLEY *meanwhile realizes he has lost the shade of the lamp. On his knees, he begins to look for it]*

HAROLD: Carrotty old bitch—telling *me* about pottery! *Oooh!!*

[*He shakes himself indignantly at the recollection of it*]

MISS FURNIVAL: Do you care for porcelain yourself, Colonel?

COLONEL: I'm afraid I don't know very much about it, madam. I like some of that Chinese stuff—you get some lovely colors, like on that statue I saw when I came in here—very delicate.

HAROLD: What statue's that, Colonel?

COLONEL: The one on the packing case, sir. Very fine.

HAROLD: I didn't know Brin had any Chinese stuff. What's it of then, this statue?

[BRINDSLEY *freezes*]

CAROL: [*Desperately*] Well, we've all got drinks, I'd like to propose Daddy's regimental toast. Raise your glasses everyone! "To the dear old Twenty-Fifth Horse. Up the British, and Death to All Natives!"

MISS FURNIVAL: I'll drink to that!

HAROLD: Up the old Twenty-Fifth!!

[*Quickly* BRINDSLEY *finds the Buddha, moves it from the packing case to the table, then gets* HAROLD's *raincoat from the sofa, and wraps the statue up in it, leaving it on the table*]

COLONEL: Thank you, Dumpling. That was very touchin' of you. Very touchin' indeed. [*He swallows his drink*] Dammit, that's gin!

HAROLD: I've got lemonade!

MISS FURNIVAL: Oh! Horrible! . . . Quite horrible! That would be alcohol, I suppose! . . . Oh dear, how unpleasant! . . .

HAROLD: [*To* MISS FURNIVAL] Here, love, exchange with me. No—you get the lemonade—but I get the gin. Colonel—

COLONEL: Here, sir.

[*Seizing her chance,* MISS FURNIVAL *downs a huge draft of Scotch. They all exchange drinks.* BRINDSLEY *resumes his frantic search for the shade*]

HAROLD: Here, Ferny.

[The COLONEL *hands her the gin and lime. He gets instead the bitter lemon from* HAROLD. HAROLD *gets the Scotch]*

MISS FURNIVAL: Thank you.

HAROLD: Well, let's try again. Bottoms up!

COLONEL: Quite. *[They drink. Triumphantly,* BRINDSLEY *finds the shade. Unfortunately at the same moment the* COLONEL *spits out his lemonade in a fury all over him, as he marches toward the* COLONEL *on his knees]* Look here—I can't stand another minute of this!

[He fishes his lighter out of his pocket and angrily tries to light it]

CAROL: Daddy, please!

COLONEL: I don't care, Dumpling. If I blow us up, then I'll blow us up! This is ridiculous . . . *[His words die in the flame. He spies* BRINDSLEY *kneeling at his feet, wound about with lamp wire]* What the devil are you doin' there?

BRINDSLEY: *[Blowing out his lighter]* Now don't be rash, Colonel! Isn't the first rule of an officer "Don't involve your men in unnecessary danger"?

[Quickly he steals, still on his knees, to the table]

COLONEL: Don't be impertinent. Where's the torch?

BRINDSLEY: Er . . . the pub was closed.

HAROLD: You didn't go to the pub in that time, surely? You couldn't have.

BRINDSLEY: Of course I did.

MISS FURNIVAL: But it's five streets away, Mr. Miller.

BRINDSLEY: Needs must when the devil drives, Miss Furnival. Whatever that means.

[Quickly he lifts the table, and steals out of the room with it and the wrecked lamp]

COLONEL: [*Who thinks* BRINDSLEY *is still kneeling at his feet*] Now look here: there's somethin' very peculiar goin' on in this room. I may not know about art, Miller, but I know men. I know a liar in the light, and I know one in the dark.

CAROL: Daddy!

COLONEL: I don't want to doubt your word, sir. All the same, I'd like your oath you went out to that public house. *Well?*

CAROL: [*Realizing he isn't there, raising her voice*] Brin, Daddy's talking to you!

COLONEL: What are you shoutin' for?

BRINDSLEY: [*Rushing back from* HAROLD's *room, still entangled in the lamp*] Of course. I know. He's absolutely right. I was—just thinking it over for a moment.

COLONEL: Well? What's your answer?

BRINDSLEY: I . . . I couldn't agree with you more, sir.

COLONEL: What?

BRINDSLEY: That was a very perceptive remark you made there. Not everyone would have thought of that. Individual. You know. Almost witty. Well, it *was* witty. Why be ungenerous? . . .

COLONEL: Look, young man, are you trying to be funny?

BRINDSLEY: [*Ingratiatingly*] Well, I'll try anything once . . .

HAROLD: I say, this is becoming a bit unpleasant, isn't it?

CAROL: It's becoming drearypegs.

COLONEL: Quiet, Dumpling. Let me handle this.

BRINDSLEY: What's there to handle, sir?

COLONEL: If you think I'm going to let my daughter marry a born liar, you're very much mistaken.

HAROLD: Marry!

CAROL: Well, that's the idea.

HAROLD: You and this young lady, Brin?

CAROL: Are what's laughingly known as engaged. Subject of course to Daddy's approval.

HAROLD: Well! [*Furious at the news, and at the fact that* BRINDSLEY *hasn't confided in him*] What a surprise! . . .

BRINDSLEY: We were keeping it a secret.

HAROLD: Evidently. How long's this been going on, then?

BRINDSLEY: A few months.

HAROLD: You old slyboots.

BRINDSLEY: [*Nervous*] I hope you approve, Harold.

HAROLD: Well, I must say, you know how to keep things to yourself.

BRINDSLEY: [*Placatingly*] I meant to tell you, Harold . . . I really did. You were the one person I was going to tell.

HAROLD: Well, why didn't you then?

BRINDSLEY: I don't know. I just never got around to it.

HAROLD: You saw me every day.

BRINDSLEY: I know.

HAROLD: You could have mentioned it at any time.

BRINDSLEY: I know.

HAROLD: [*Huffy*] Well, it's your business. There's no obligation to share confidences. I've only been your neighbor for three years. I've always assumed there was more than a geographical closeness between us, but I was obviously mistaken.

BRINDSLEY: Oh don't start getting huffy, Harold.

HAROLD: I'm not getting anything. I'm just saying it's surprising, that's all. Surprising and somewhat disappointing.

BRINDSLEY: Oh look, Harold, please understand—

HAROLD: [*Shrill*] There's no need to say anything! It'll just teach me in future not to bank too much on friendship. It's silly me again! Silly, stupid, trusting me!

[MISS FURNIVAL *rises in agitation and gropes her way to the drinks table*]

COLONEL: Good God!

CAROL: [*Wheedling*] Oh come, Mr. Gorringe. We haven't told anybody. Not one single soulipegs. Really.

COLONEL: At the moment, Dumpling, there's nothing to tell. And I'm not sure there's going to be!

BRINDSLEY: Look, sir, we seem to have got off on the wrong foot. If it's my fault, I apologize.

MISS FURNIVAL: [*Groping about on the drinks table*] My father always used to say, "To err is human: to forgive divine."

CAROL: I thought that was somebody else.

MISS FURNIVAL: [*Blithely*] So many people copied him.

[*She finds the open bottle of gin, lifts it and sniffs it eagerly*]

CAROL: May I help you, Miss Furnival?

MISS FURNIVAL: No, thank you, Miss Melkett. I'm just getting myself another bitter lemon. That is—if I may, Mr. Miller?

BRINDSLEY: Of course. Help yourself.

MISS FURNIVAL: Thank you, most kind!

[*She pours more gin into her glass and returns slowly to sit upstage on the edge of the dais*]

COLONEL: Well, sir, wherever you are—

BRINDSLEY: Here, Colonel.

COLONEL: I'll overlook your damn peculiar behavior this once, but understand this, Miller. My daughter's dear to me. You show me you can look after her, and I'll consider the whole thing most favorably. I can't say fairer than that, can I?

BRINDSLEY: No, sir. Most fair, sir. Most fair.

[*He pulls a hideous face one inch from the* COLONEL'*s*]

CAROL: Of course he can look after me, Daddy. His works are going to be world-famous. In five years I'll feel just like Mrs. Michelangelo.

HAROLD: [*Loftily*] There wasn't a Mrs. Michelangelo, actually.

CAROL: [*Irritated*] Wasn't there?

HAROLD: No. He had passionate feelings of a rather different nature.

CAROL: Really, Mr. Gorringe. I didn't know that.

[*She puts out her tongue at him*]

BRINDSLEY: Look, Harold, I'm sorry if I've hurt your feelings.

HAROLD: [*Loftily*] You haven't.

BRINDSLEY: I know I have. Please forgive me.

CAROL: Oh, do, Mr. Gorringe. Quarreling is so dreary. I hope we're all going to be great friends.

HAROLD: I'm not sure that I can contemplate a friendly relationship with a viper.

MISS FURNIVAL: Remember: to err is human, to forgive divine!

COLONEL: [*Irritated*] You just said that, madam.

[CLEA *enters, wearing dark glasses and carrying an air bag. She stands in the doorway, amazed by the dark. She takes off her glasses, but this doesn't improve matters*]

MISS FURNIVAL: [*Downing her gin happily*] Did I?

CAROL: Brin's not really a viper. He's just artistic, aren't you, darling?

BRINDSLEY: Yes, darling.

[CAROL *sends him an audible kiss across the astonished* CLEA. *He returns it, equally audibly*]

CAROL: [*Winningly*] Come on, Mr. Gorringe. It really is a case of forgive and forgettipegs.

HAROLD: Is it reallypegs?

CAROL: Have another Ginette and lime. I'll have one with you.

[*She rises and mixes the drink*]

HAROLD: [*Rising*] Oh, all right. I don't mind if I do.

CAROL: Let me mix it for you.

HAROLD: Ta. [*He crosses to her, narrowly missing* CLEA *who is now crossing the room to the sofa, and gets his drink*] I must say there's nothing nicer than having a booze up with a pretty girl.

CAROL: [*Archly*] You haven't seen me yet.

HAROLD: Oh, I just know it. Brindsley always had wonderful taste. I've often said to him, you've got the same taste in ladies as I have in porcelain. Ta.

[HAROLD *and* BRINDSLEY—*one from upstage, one from across the room—begin to converge on the sofa. On the word "modest" all three,* CLEA *in the middle, sit on it.* BRINDSLEY *of course imagines he is sitting next to* HAROLD]

BRINDSLEY: Harold!

CAROL: Oh don't be silly, Brin. Why be so modest? I found a photograph of one of his bits from two years ago, and I must say she was pretty stunning in a blowsy sort of way.

HAROLD: Which one was that, then? I suppose she means Clea.

CAROL: Did you know her, Mr. Gorringe?

HAROLD: Oh yes. She's been around a long time.

[BRINDSLEY *nudges* CLEA *warningly—imagining she is* HAROLD. CLEA *gently bumps* HAROLD]

CAROL: [*Surprised*] Has she?

HAROLD: Oh yes, dear. Or am I speaking out of turn?

BRINDSLEY: Not at all. I've told Carol all about Clea. [*He bangs* CLEA *again, a little harder—who correspondingly bumps against* HAROLD] Though I must say, Harold, I'm surprised you call three months "a long time."

[CLEA *shoots him a look of total outrage at this lie.* HAROLD *is also astonished*]

CAROL: What was she like?

BRINDSLEY: [*Meaningfully, into* CLEA's *ear*] I suppose you can hardly remember her, Harold.

HAROLD: [*Speaking across her*] Why on earth shouldn't I?

BRINDSLEY: Well, since it was two years ago, you've probably forgotten.

HAROLD: Two years?!

BRINDSLEY: *Two years ago!*

[*He punches* CLEA *so hard that the rebound knocks* HAROLD *off the sofa, drink and all*]

HAROLD: [*Picking himself up. Spitefully*] Well, now since you mention it, I remember her perfectly. I mean, she's not one you can easily forget!

CAROL: Was she pretty?

HAROLD: No, not at all. In fact, I'd say the opposite. Actually she was rather plain.

BRINDSLEY: She wasn't!

HAROLD: I'm just giving my opinion.

BRINDSLEY: You've never given it before.

HAROLD: [*Leaning over* CLEA] I was never asked! But since it's come up, I always thought she was ugly. For one thing, she had teeth like a picket fence—yellow and spiky. And for another, she had bad skin.

BRINDSLEY: She had nothing of the kind!

HAROLD: She did. I remember it perfectly. It was like new pink wall-paper, with an old gray crumbly paper underneath.

MISS FURNIVAL: Quite right, Mr. Gorringe. I hardly ever saw her, but I do recall her skin. It was a strange color, as you say—and very coarse . . . Not soft, as the skins of young ladies should be, if they are young ladies.

[CLEA *rises in outrage*]

HAROLD: Aye, that's right. Coarse.

MISS FURNIVAL: And rather lumpy.

HAROLD: Very lumpy.

BRINDSLEY: This is disgraceful.

HAROLD: You knew I never liked her, Brindsley. She was too clever by half.

MISS FURNIVAL: And so tiresomely Bohemian.

CAROL: You mean she was as pretentious as her name? [CLEA, *who has been reacting to this last exchange of comments about her like a spectator at a tennis match, now reacts to* CAROL, *open-mouthed*] I bet she was. That photograph I found showed her in a dirndl and a sort of a sultry peasant blouse. She looked like "The Bartered Bride" done by Lloyds Bank.

[*They laugh*, BRINDSLEY *hardest of all. Guided by the noise*, CLEA *aims her hand and slaps his face*]

BRINDSLEY: Ahh!

CAROL: What's wrong?

MISS FURNIVAL: What is it, Mr. Miller?

BRINDSLEY: [*Furious*] That's not very funny, Harold. What the hell's the matter with you?

[CLEA *makes her escape*]

HAROLD: [*Indignant*] With me?

BRINDSLEY: Well, I'm sure it wasn't the Colonel.

COLONEL: What wasn't, sir?

[BRINDSLEY, *groping about, catches* CLEA *by the bottom, and instantly recognizes it*]

BRINDSLEY: Clea! . . . [*In horror*] Clea!!

[CLEA *breaks loose and moves away from him. During the following he tries to find her in the dark, and she narrowly avoids him*]

COLONEL: What?

BRINDSLEY: I was just remembering her, sir. You're all talking the most awful nonsense. She was beautiful . . . And anyway, Harold, you just said I was famous for my taste in women.

HAROLD: Aye, but it had its lapses.

BRINDSLEY: [*Frantically moving about*] Rubbish! She was beautiful and tender and considerate and kind and loyal and witty and adorable in every way!

CAROL: You told me she was as cozy as a steel razor blade.

BRINDSLEY: Did I? Surely not! No. What I said was . . . something quite different . . . Utterly different . . . entirely different . . . As different as chalk from cheese. Although when you come to think of it, cheese isn't all that different from chalk.

[*He gives his braying laugh*]

COLONEL: Are you sure you know what you're talking about?

[*During this* CLEA *has reached the table, picked up a bottle of Scotch, and rejected it in favor of vodka, which she takes with her*]

CAROL: You said to me in this room when I asked you what she was like, "She was a painter. Very honest. Very clever, and just about as cozy—"

BRINDSLEY: [*Stopping, exasperated*] As a steel razor blade! Well then, I said it! So bloody what? . . .

CAROL: So nothing!

[*He throws out his hands in a gesture of desperate exhaustion and bumps straight into* CLEA. *They instantly embrace,* CLEA *twining herself around him, her vodka bottle held aloft. A tiny pause*]

COLONEL: If that boy isn't touched, I don't know the meaning of the word!

CAROL: What's all this talk about her being kind and tender, all of a sudden?

BRINDSLEY: [*Tenderly, holding* CLEA] She could be. On occasion. Very.

CAROL: Very rare occasions, I imagine.

BRINDSLEY: Not so rare. [*He kisses* CLEA *again*] Not so rare at all.

[*He leads her softly past the irritated* CAROL, *toward the stairs*]

CAROL: Meaning what, exactly? . . . [*Shouting*] Brindsley, I'm talking to you!

BRINDSLEY: [*Sotto voce, into* CLEA's *ear as they stand just behind* HAROLD] I can explain. Go up to the bedroom. Wait for me there.

HAROLD: [*In amazement, thinking he is being addressed*] Now? Do you think this is quite the moment?

BRINDSLEY: Oh God! . . . I wasn't talking to you.

CAROL: What did you say?

HAROLD: [To CAROL] I think he wants *you* upstairs. [*Slyly*] For what purpose, I can't begin to imagine.

COLONEL: They're going to do some more of that plotting, I daresay.

MISS FURNIVAL: Lover's talk, Colonel.

COLONEL: Very touching, I'm sure.

[BRINDSLEY *pushes* CLEA *ahead of him up the stairs*]

MISS FURNIVAL: "Journeys end in lovers meeting," as my father always used to say.

COLONEL: What a strikingly original father you seem to have had, madam.

[CAROL *joins the other two on the stairs. We see all three groping blindly up to the bedroom,* BRINDSLEY's *hands on* CLEA's *hips,* CAROL's *on* BRINDSLEY's]

CAROL: [*With a conspirator's stage whisper*] What is it, darling? Has something gone wrong? What can't you move?

[*This next dialogue sotto voce*]

BRINDSLEY: Nothing. It's all back—every bit of it—except the sofa, and I've covered that up.

CAROL: You mean, we can have lights?

BRINDSLEY: Yes . . . NO!!

CAROL: Why not?

BRINDSLEY: Never mind!

CAROL: Why do you want me in the bedroom?

BRINDSLEY: I don't. Go away!

CAROL: Charming!

BRINDSLEY: I didn't mean that.

COLONEL: There you are. They *are* plotting again. What the hell is going on up there?

BRINDSLEY: Nothing, Colonel. I've just remembered—there may be a torch under my bed. I keep it to blind the burglars with. Have another drink, Colonel!

[*He pushes* CLEA *into the bedroom and shuts the door*]

COLONEL: What d'you mean another? I haven't had one yet.

MISS FURNIVAL: Oh! Poor Colonel! Let me get you one.

COLONEL: [*Rising*] I can get one for myself, thank you. Let me get you another lemonade.

MISS FURNIVAL: [*Rising*] No, thank you, Colonel, I'll manage myself. It's good practice!

[*They grope toward the drinks table. Above,* CLEA *and* BRINDSLEY *sit on the bed*]

CLEA: So this is what they mean by a blind date. What the hell is going on?

BRINDSLEY: [*Sarcastic*] Nothing! Georg Bamberger is only coming to see my work tonight, and we've got a main fuse.

CLEA: Is that the reason for all this furtive clutching?

BRINDSLEY: Look, I can't explain things at the moment.

CLEA: Who's that—[*Debutante accent*] "frightful gel"?

BRINDSLEY: Just a friend.

CLEA: She sounded more than that.

BRINDSLEY: Well, if you must know, it's Carol. I've told you about her.

CLEA: The Idiot Deb?

BRINDSLEY: She's a very sweet girl. As a matter of fact we've become very good friends in the last six weeks.

CLEA: How good?

BRINDSLEY: Just good.

CLEA: And have you become friends with her father, too?

BRINDSLEY: If it's any of your business, they just dropped in to meet Mr. Bamberger.

CLEA: What was it you wanted to tell me on the phone tonight?

BRINDSLEY: Nothing.

CLEA: You're lying!

BRINDSLEY: Ah, here comes the inquisition! Look, Clea, if you ever loved me, just slip away quietly with no more questions, and I'll come round later and explain everything, I promise.

CLEA: I don't believe you.

BRINDSLEY: Please, darling . . . Please . . . Please . . . Please!!

[*They kiss, passionately, stretched out on the bed*]

COLONEL: [*Pouring*] At last . . . a decent glass of Scotch. Are you getting your lemonade?

MISS FURNIVAL: [*Cheerfully pouring herself an enormous gin*] Oh yes, thank you, Colonel!

COLONEL: I'm just wonderin' if this Bamberger fellow is goin' to show up at all. He's half an hour late already.

HAROLD: Oh! That's nothing, Colonel. Millionaires are always late. It's their thing.

MISS FURNIVAL: I'm sure you're right, Mr. Gorringe. That's how *I* imagine them. Hands like silk, and always two hours late.

CAROL: Brin's been up there a long time. What can he be doing?

HAROLD: Maybe he's got that Clea hidden away in his bedroom, and they're having a tête-à-tête!!

CAROL: What a flagrant suggestion, Mr. Gorringe.

BRINDSLEY: [*Disengaging himself*] No one in the world kisses like you.

CLEA: I missed you so badly, Brin. I had to see you. I've thought about nothing else these past six weeks. Brin, I made the most awful mistake walking out.

BRINDSLEY: Clea—*please!*

CLEA: I mean we've known each other for four years. We can't just throw each other away like old newspapers.

BRINDSLEY: I don't see why not. You know my politics, you've heard my gossip, and you've certainly been through all my entertainment section.

CLEA: Well, how about a second edition?

BRINDSLEY: Darling, we simply can't talk about this now. Can't you trust me just for an hour?

CLEA: Of course I can, darling. You don't want me down there?

BRINDSLEY: No.

CLEA: Then I'll get undressed and go quietly to bed. When you've got rid of them all, I'll be waiting.

BRINDSLEY: That's a terrible idea!

CLEA: [Reaching for him] I think it's lovely. A little happy relaxation for us both.

BRINDSLEY: [Falling off the bed] I'm perfectly relaxed!

CAROL: Brindsley!

CLEA: "Too solemn for day, too sweet for night. Come not in darkness, come not in light." That's me, isn't it?

BRINDSLEY: Of course not. I just can't explain now, that's all.

CLEA: Oh, very well, you can explain later . . . in bed!

BRINDSLEY: Not tonight, Clea.

CLEA: Either that or I come down and discover your sordid secret.

BRINDSLEY: There is no sordid secret!

CLEA: Then you won't mind my coming down!

CAROL, COLONEL: [Roaring together] BRINDSLEY!!!

BRINDSLEY: Oh God!! . . . All right, stay. Only keep quiet . . . Blackmailing bitch! [He emerges at the top of the stairs] Yes, my sweet?

CAROL: What are you doing up there? You've been an eternity!

BRINDSLEY: I . . . I . . . I'm just looking in the bathroom, my darling. You never know what you might find in that clever little cabinet.

COLONEL: [Moving to the stairs] Are you trying to madden me, sir? Are you trying to put me in a fury?

BRINDSLEY: Certainly not, sir!!

COLONEL: I warn you, Miller, it's not difficult! In the old days in the regiment I was known for my furies. I was famous for my furies . . . Do you hear?

CLEA: I may sing!

[She goes off into the bathroom]

BRINDSLEY: I may knock your teeth in!

COLONEL: What did you say?

CAROL: Brin! How dare you talk to Daddy like that!

BRINDSLEY: Oh!! I . . . I . . . I wasn't talking to Daddy like that . . .

CAROL: Then who *were* you talking to?

BRINDSLEY: I was talking to no one! Myself I was talking to! I was saying . . . "If I keep groping about up here like this, I might knock my teeth in!"

COLONEL: Mad! . . . Mad! . . . Mad as the south wind! It's the only explanation—you've got yourself engaged to a lunatic.

CAROL: There's something going on up there, and I'm coming up to find out what it is. Do you hear me, Brin?

BRINDSLEY: Carol—no!

CAROL: [*Climbing the stairs*] I'm not such a fool as you take me for. I know when you're hiding something. Your voice goes all deceitful —very, very foxipegs!

BRINDSLEY: Darling, please! That's not very ladylike . . . I'm sure the Colonel won't approve of you entering a man's bedroom in the dark!

[*Enter* SCHUPPANZIGH. *He wears the overcoat and peaked cap of the London Electricity Board and carries a large tool bag, similarly labeled*]

CAROL: I'm comin' up, Brindsley, I'm comin' up!!!

BRINDSLEY: [*Scrambling down*] I'm coming down . . . We'll all have a nice cozy drink . . .

SCHUPPANZIGH: 'Allo please? Mr. Miller? Mr. Miller? I've come as was arranged.

BRINDSLEY: My God . . . it's Bamberger!

CAROL: Bamberger?

BRINDSLEY: Yes, Bamberger.

[BRINDSLEY *rushes down the remaining stairs, pulling* CAROL *with him*]

SCHUPPANZIGH: You must have thought I was never coming!

[*He takes off his overcoat and cap*]

BRINDSLEY: Not at all. I'm delighted you could spare the time. I know how busy you are. I'm afraid we've had the most idiotic disaster. We've had a fuse.

HAROLD: You'll have to speak up, dear. He's stone deaf!

BRINDSLEY: [*Yelling*] We've had a fuse—not the best conditions for seeing sculpture.

SCHUPPANZIGH: Please not to worry. Here!

[*He produces a torch from his pocket and "lights" it. The light on stage dims a little, as usual, to indicate this. All relax with audible sighs of pleasure.* SCHUPPANZIGH *at once places his tool bag on the Regency chair, and puts his coat and cap on top of it, concealing that it is one of* HAROLD's *chairs*]

CAROL: Oh, what a relief!

BRINDSLEY: [*Hastily dragging the sheet over the rest of the sofa*] Do you always travel with a torch?

SCHUPPANZIGH: Mostly, yes. It helps to see details [*Seeing the others*] You are holding a private view?

MISS FURNIVAL: Oh, no! I was just going. I'd hate to distract you.

SCHUPPANZIGH: Please not on my account, dear lady. I am not as easily distracted.

MISS FURNIVAL: [*Charmed*] Oh! . . .

BRINDSLEY: [*Yelling in his ear*] May I present Colonel Melkett?

COLONEL: [*Yelling in his other ear*] A great honor, sir!

SCHUPPANZIGH: [*Banging his ear, to clear it*] No, no, mine—mine!

BRINDSLEY: Miss Carol Melkett.

CAROL: [*Screeching in his ear*] I say: hello. So glad you got here! It's terribly kind of you to take such an interest!

SCHUPPANZIGH: Not at all. *Vous êtes très gentil.*

CAROL: [*Yelling*] What would you like to drink?

SCHUPPANZIGH: [*Bewildered*] A little vodka, would be beautiful!

CAROL: Of course!

BRINDSLEY: Harold Gorringe—a neighbor of mine!

HAROLD: How do? Very honored, I'm sure.

SCHUPPANZIGH: Enchanted.

HAROLD: I must say it's a real thrill, meeting you!

BRINDSLEY: And another neighbor, Miss Furnival.

SCHUPPANZIGH: Enchanted.

MISS FURNIVAL: [*Hooting in his ear*] I'm afraid we've all been taking refuge from the *storm*, as it were. [*Exclaiming as she holds* SCHUPPANZIGH's *hand*] Oh! It *is* true! They *are* softer! Much, much softer!

SCHUPPANZIGH: [*Utterly confused as she strokes his hand*] Softer? Please?

[BRINDSLEY *and* HAROLD *pull her away, and she subsides onto the sofa*]

BRINDSLEY: Miss Furnival, please!

CAROL: [*At the drinks table*] Darling, where's the vodka?

BRINDSLEY: It's on the table.

CAROL: No, it isn't.

BRINDSLEY: It must be!

[*Above*, CLEA *reenters wearing the top half of* BRINDSLEY's *pajamas and nothing else. She gets into bed, still clutching the vodka bottle and carrying a plastic tooth-mug*]

CAROL: Well, see for yourself. There's Winnie and Ginette, and Vera has quite vanished, the naughty girl.

BRINDSLEY: She can't have done.

SCHUPPANZIGH: Please don't concern yourselves. I am pressed for time. If I might just be shown where to go.

BRINDSLEY: Of course. It's through the studio there. Darling, if you would just show our guest into the studio—*with his torch.*

CAROL: What?? . . .

BRINDSLEY: [*Sotto voce*] *The sofa!* . . . Get him out of here.

CAROL: Oh, yes!!

SCHUPPANZIGH: [*Sighting the sculpture*] Oh! Good gracious! What an extraordinary object!

BRINDSLEY: Oh, that's just a spare piece of my work I keep in here!

SCHUPPANZIGH: Spare, maybe, but fascinating!

BRINDSLEY: You really think so?

SCHUPPANZIGH: [*Approaching it*] I do! Ja!

BRINDSLEY: Well, in that case you should see my main collection. It's next door. My fiancée will show you!

[MISS FURNIVAL *sits on the sofa. She is now quite drunk*]

SCHUPPANZIGH: One amazement at a time, if you please! In this gluttonous age it is easy to get visual indigestion—hard to find visual Alka Seltzer . . . Permit me to digest this first!

BRINDSLEY: Oh, by all means . . . Good, yes . . . There's no hurry—no hurry at all . . . Only . . . [*Inspired*] Why don't you digest it *in the dark?*

SCHUPPANZIGH: I beg your pardon?

BRINDSLEY: You'll never believe it, sir, but I actually made that piece to be appreciated in the dark. I was working on a very interesting theory. You know how the Victorians said, "Children should be seen and not heard"? Well, I say, "Art should be felt and not seen."

SCHUPPANZIGH: Amazing.

BRINDSLEY: Yes, isn't it. I call it my theory of Factual Tactility. If it doesn't stab you to the quick—it's not art. Look! Why don't you give me that torch, and try for yourself?

SCHUPPANZIGH: Very well, I will!! [*He hands* BRINDSLEY *the torch*]

BRINDSLEY: Thank you! [*He turns off the torch and hands it to* CAROL. *At the same moment* MISS FURNIVAL *quietly lies down, her full length on the sofa*] Now just stretch out your arms and feel it all over, sir. [*He steals toward the studio*] Have a good long feel! [SCHUPPANZIGH *embraces the metal sculpture with a fervent clash. He pulls at the two metal prongs*] Do you see what I mean?

[*Silently he opens the curtains*]

SCHUPPANZIGH: Amazing! . . . Absolutely incredible! . . . It's quite true . . . Like this, the piece becomes a masterpiece at once.

BRINDSLEY: [*Astonished*] It does??

SCHUPPANZIGH: But of course! I feel it here—and here—the two needles of man's unrest! . . . Self love and self hate, leading to the same point! That's the meaning of the work, isn't it?

BRINDSLEY: Of course. You've got it in one! You're obviously a great expert, sir!

[*Quietly he pulls the sofa into the studio, bearing on it the supine* MISS FURNIVAL, *who waves good-bye as she disappears*]

SCHUPPANZIGH: Not at all. V*ous êtes très gentil*—but it is evident . . . Standing here in the dark, one can feel the vital thrust of the argument! The essential anguish! The stress and the torment of our times! It is simple but not simpleminded! Ingenious, but not ingenuous! Above all, it has real moral force! Of how many modern works can one say that, good people?

CAROL: Oh, none, none at all really.

SCHUPPANZIGH: I hope I do not lecture. It can be a fault with me.

CAROL: Not at all! I could listen all night, it's so profound.

HAROLD: Me, too. Really deep!

COLONEL: I don't know anything about this myself, sir, but it's an honor to listen to you.

[*He starts off upstage in search of the sofa, seating himself tentatively in the air, then moving himself along in a sitting position, trying to find it with his rear end. At the same moment* BRINDSLEY *emerges from the studio, closes the curtains behind him, and gropes his way to a corner where there stands a small packing-case. This he carries forward, hopefully to do duty for the missing sofa. Just as he places it on the ground the traveling* COLONEL *sits on it, trapping* BRINDSLEY's *hand beneath his weight. During the following,* BRINDSLEY *tries frantically to free himself*]

SCHUPPANZIGH: *Vous êtes très gentil!*

HAROLD: You mean to say you see all that in a bit of metal?

SCHUPPANZIGH: A *tiny* bit of metal, that's the point. A miracle of compression! You want my opinion, this boy is a genius. A master of the miniature. In the space of a matchbox he can realize anything he wants—the black virginity of Chartres! The white chorale of the Acropolis! *Wunderbar!*

CAROL: Oh, how super!

SCHUPPANZIGH: You should charge immense sums for work like this, Mr. Miller. They should be very very expensive! This one, for example, how much is this?

BRINDSLEY: Fifty.

CAROL: Five hundred guineas.

SCHUPPANZIGH: Ah so! Very cheap.

HAROLD: Cheap!

CAROL: I think so, Mr. Gorringe. Well . . . so will you have it then?

SCHUPPANZIGH: Me?

BRINDSLEY: Darling . . . aren't you rushing things just a little? Perhaps you would like to see the rest of my work.

SCHUPPANZIGH: Alas, I have no more time. To linger would be pleasant, but alas, I must work . . . Also, as Moses discovered, it is sufficient to glimpse milk and honey. One does not have to wolf them down!

BRINDSLEY: Well.

COLONEL: Well . . .

HAROLD: Well . . .

CAROL: Well . . . Would you like it then?

SCHUPPANZIGH: Very much.

COLONEL: [*Rising.* BRINDSLEY *is freed at last*] For five hundred guineas?

SCHUPPANZIGH: Certainly—if I had it!

HAROLD: According to the Sunday Pictorial, you must be worth at least seventeen million pounds.

SCHUPPANZIGH: The Sunday papers are notoriously ill-informed. According to my bank statement, I was worth one hundred pounds, eight shillings and fourpence.

HAROLD: You mean you've gone broke?

SCHUPPANZIGH: No. I mean I never had any more.

COLONEL: Now look, sir, I know millionaires are supposed to be eccentric, but this is gettin' tiresome.

CAROL: Daddy, ssh!—

SCHUPPANZIGH: Millionaires? Who do you think I am?

COLONEL: Dammit, man!—You must know who you are!

CAROL: Mr. Bamberger, is this some kind of joke you like to play?

SCHUPPANZIGH: Excuse me. That is not my name.

BRINDSLEY: It isn't?

SCHUPPANZIGH: No. My name is Schuppanzigh. Franz Schuppanzigh. Born in Weimar 1905. Student of Philosophy at Heidelberg 1934. Refugee to this country, 1938. Regular employment ever since with the London Electricity Board.

[*All rise*]

CAROL: Electricity?

MISS FURNIVAL: Electricity!

BRINDSLEY: You mean you're not?—

HAROLD: Of course he's not!

SCHUPPANZIGH: But who did you imagine I was?

HAROLD: [*Furious*] How dare you?

[*He snatches the electrician's torch*]

SCHUPPANZIGH: [*Retreating before him*] Please?—

HAROLD: Of all the nerve, coming in here, giving us a lecture about needles and virgins, and all the time you're simply here to mend the fuses!

COLONEL: I agree with you, sir. It's monstrous!

SCHUPPANZIGH: [*Bewildered*] It is?

[*The* COLONEL *takes the torch and shines it pitilessly in the man's face*]

COLONEL: You come in here, a public servant, and proceed to harangue your employers, unasked and uninvited.

SCHUPPANZIGH: [*Bewildered*] Excuse me. But I *was* invited.

COLONEL: Don't answer back. In my day you would have been fired on the spot for impertinence.

CAROL: Daddy's absolutely right! Ever since the Beatles, the lower classes think they can behave exactly as they want.

COLONEL: [*Handing the torch to* BRINDSLEY] Miller, will you kindly show this feller his work?

BRINDSLEY: The mains are in the cellar. There's a trap door. [*Indicating*] Do you mind?

SCHUPPANZIGH: [*Snatching the torch furiously*] Why should I mind? It's why I came, after all! [*He takes his coat, cap, and bag off* HAROLD's *Regency chair . . . Seeing it*] Now there is a really beautiful chair!

[BRINDSLEY *stares at the chair aghast—and in a twinkling seats himself in it to conceal it*]

BRINDSLEY: [*Exasperated*] Why don't you just go into the cellar?

SCHUPPANZIGH: How? Where is it?

BRINDSLEY: [*To* CAROL] Darling, will you open the trap, please.

CAROL: Me? [*Understanding—as he indicates the chair*] Oh—yes!

[*She kneels and struggles to open the trap*]

COLONEL: [*To* BRINDSLEY] Well, I must say, that's very gallant of you, Miller.

BRINDSLEY: I've got a sudden touch of lumbago, sir. It often afflicts me after long spells in the dark.

CAROL: [*Very sympathetic*] Oh, darling! Has it come back?

BRINDSLEY: I'm afraid it has, my sweet.

HAROLD: [*Opening the trap*] Here, let me. I'm not as frail as our wilting friend [*To* SCHUPPANZIGH] Well, down you go, you!

SCHUPPANZIGH: [*Shrugging*] So. Farewell. I leave the light of Art for the dark of Science.

HAROLD: Let's have a little less of your lip, shall we?

SCHUPPANZIGH: Excuse me.

[SCHUPPANZIGH *descends through the trap, taking the torch with him.* HAROLD *slams the trap door down irritably after him, and of course the lights immediately come up full. There is a long pause. All stand about embarrassed. Suddenly they hear the noise of* MISS FURNIVAL *singing "Rock of Ages" in a high drunken voice from behind the curtain. Above, attracted by the noise of the slam,* CLEA *gets out of bed, still clutching the vodka and tooth-mug, opens the door, and stands at the top of the stairs listening*]

BRINDSLEY: None of this evening is happening.

CAROL: Cheer up, darling. In a few minutes everything will be all right. Mr. Bamberger will arrive in the light—he'll adore your work and give you twenty thousand pounds for your whole collection.

BRINDSLEY: [*Sarcastic*] Oh, yes!

CAROL: Then we can buy a super Georgian house and live what's laughingly known as happily ever after. I want to leave this place just as soon as we're married.

[CLEA *hears this. Her mouth opens wide*]

BRINDSLEY: [*Nervously*] Sssh!

CAROL: Why? I don't want to live in a slum for our first couple of years—like other newlyweds.

BRINDSLEY: Sssh! Ssssh! . . .

CAROL: What's the matter with you?

BRINDSLEY: The gods listen, darling. They've given me a terrible night so far. They may do worse.

CAROL: [*Cooing*] I know, darling. You've had a filthy evening. Poor babykins. But I'll fight them with you. I don't care a fig for those naughty old Goddipegs. [*Looking up*] Do you hear? Not a single little fig! [CLEA *aims at the voice and sends a jet of vodka splashing down over* CAROL] *Ahh!!!*

BRINDSLEY: What is it?

CAROL: It's raining!

BRINDSLEY: Don't be ridiculous.

CAROL: I'm all wet!

BRINDSLEY: How can you be?

[CLEA *throws vodka over a wider area.* HAROLD *gets it*]

HAROLD: Hey, what's going on?

BRINDSLEY: What?

COLONEL: What the devil's the matter with you all? What are you hollerin' for? [*He gets a slug of vodka in the face*] Ahh!!

BRINDSLEY: [*Inspired*] It's a leak—the water mains must have gone now.

HAROLD: Oh good God!

BRINDSLEY: It must be!

[*Mischievously,* CLEA *raps her bottle on the top stair. There is a terrified silence. All look up*]

HAROLD: Don't say there's someone else here.

BRINDSLEY: Good Lord!

COLONEL: Who's there? [*Silence from above*] Come on! I know you're there!

BRINDSLEY: [*Improvising wildly*] I—I bet you it's Mrs. Punnet.

[CLEA *looks astonished*]

COLONEL: Who?

BRINDSLEY: [*For* CLEA'*s benefit*] Mrs. Punnet. My cleaning woman.

HAROLD: Cleaning woman?

BRINDSLEY: She does for me on Mondays, Wednesdays, and Fridays.

CAROL: Well, what would she be doing here now?

BRINDSLEY: I've just remembered—she rang up and said she'd look in about six to tidy up the place.

COLONEL: Dammit, man, it's almost eleven.

HAROLD: She's not that conscientious. She couldn't be!

CAROL: Not these days!

COLONEL: Well, we'll soon see. [*Calling up*] Mrs. Punnet?

BRINDSLEY: [*Desperately*] Don't interrupt her, sir. She doesn't like to be disturbed when she's working. Why don't we just leave her to potter around upstairs with her duster?

COLONEL: Let us first just see if it's her. Is that you, Mrs. Punnet? . . .

[CLEA *keeps still*]

COLONEL: [*Roaring*] MRS. PUNNET!

CLEA: [*Deciding on a cockney voice of great antiquity*] Hello! Yes?

BRINDSLEY: [*Weakly*] It is. Good heavens, Mrs. Punnet, what on earth are you doing up there?

CLEA: I'm just giving your bedroom a bit of a tidy, sir.

BRINDSLEY: At this time of night?

[*The mischief in* CLEA *begins to take over*]

CLEA: Better late than never, sir, as they say. I know how you like your bedroom to be nice and inviting when you're giving one of your parties.

BRINDSLEY: Yes, yes, yes, of course . . .

COLONEL: When did you come, madam?

CLEA: Just a few minutes ago, sir. I didn't like to disturb you, so I come on up 'ere.

HAROLD: Was it you pouring all that water on us, then?

CLEA: Water? Good 'eavens, I must have upset something. It's as black as Newgate's Knocker up 'ere. Are you playing one of your saucy games, Mr. Miller?

BRINDSLEY: No, Mrs. Punnet. We've had a fuse. It's all over the house.

CLEA: Oh! A *fuse!* I thought it might be one of them saucy games in the dark, sir: Sardines or Piccadilly. The kind that end in a general squeeze-up. I know you're rather partial to kinky games, Mr. Miller, so I just wondered.

[*She starts to come down the stairs*]

BRINDSLEY: [*Distinctly*] It is a fuse, Mrs. Punnet. The man's mending it now. The lights will be on *any minute!*

CLEA: Well, that'll be a relief for you, won't it?

[*She dashes the vodka accurately in his face, passes him by and comes into the room*]

BRINDSLEY: Yes, of course. Now why don't you just go on home?

CLEA: I'm sorry I couldn't come before, sir. I was delayed, you see. My Rosie's been taken queer again.

BRINDSLEY: I quite understand!

[*He gropes around trying to hide her, but she continuously evades him*] ·

CLEA: [*Relentlessly*] It's her tummy. There's a lump under her belly button the size of a grapefruit.

HAROLD: Oh, how nasty!

CLEA: Horrid. Poor little Rosie. I said to her this evening, I said, "There's no good your being mulish, my girl. You're going to the hospital first thing tomorrow morning and getting yourself ultra-violated!"

BRINDSLEY: Well, hadn't you better be getting back to poor little Rosie! She must need you, surely?—And there's really nothing you can do here tonight.

CLEA: [*Meaningfully*] Are you sure of that, sir?

BRINDSLEY: Positive, thank you.

[*They are close now*]

CLEA: I mean, I know what this place can be like after one of your evenings. A gypsy caravan, isn't it? Gin bottles all over the floor! Bras and panties in the sink! And God knows what in the——

[BRINDSLEY *muzzles her with his hand. She bites it hard, and he drops to his knees in silent agony*]

COLONEL: Please watch what you say, madam. You don't know it, but you're in the presence of Mr. Miller's fiancée.

CLEA: Fiancée?

COLONEL: Yes, and I am her father.

CLEA: Well, I never . . . Oh, Mr. Miller! I'm so 'appy for you! . . . Fiancée! Oh, sir! And you never told me!

BRINDSLEY: I was keeping it a surprise.

CLEA: Well, I never! Oh, how lovely! . . . May I kiss you, sir, please?

BRINDSLEY: [*On his knees*] Well, yes, yes, of course . . .

[CLEA *gropes for his ear, finds it and twists it*]

CLEA: Oh, sir, I'm so pleased for you! And for *you*, Miss, too!

CAROL: Thank you.

CLEA: [*To* COLONEL MELKETT] And for *you*, sir.

COLONEL: Thank you.

CLEA: You must be Miss Clea's father.

COLONEL: Miss Clea? I don't understand.

[*Triumphantly she sticks out her tongue at* BRINDSLEY, *who collapses his length on the floor, face down, in a gesture of total surrender. For him it is the end. The evening can hold no further disasters for him*]

CLEA: [*To* CAROL] Well, I never! So you've got him at last! Well done, Miss Clea! I never thought you would—not after four years . . .

BRINDSLEY: No—no—no—no. . . .

CLEA: Forgive me, sir, if I'm speaking out of turn, but you must admit four years is a long time to be courting one woman. Four days is stretching it a bit nowadays!

BRINDSLEY: [*Weakly*] Mrs. Punnet, *please!*

CAROL: Four years!

CLEA: Well, yes, dear. It's been all of that and a bit more really, hasn't it? [*In a stage whisper*] And of course it's just in time. It was getting a bit prominent, your little bun in the oven. [CAROL *screeches with disgust.* BRINDSLEY *covers his ears*] Oh, Miss, I don't mean that's why he popped the question. Of course it's not. He's always been stuck on you. He told me so, not one week ago, in this room. [*Sentimentally*] "Mrs. Punnet," he says, "Mrs. Punnet, as far as I'm concerned you can keep the rest of them—Miss Clea will always be on top of the heap for me." "Oh," I says, "then what about that debutante bit, Carol, the one you're always telling me about?" "Oh, 'er," he says, "she's just a bit of Knightsbridge candyfloss. A couple of licks and you've 'ad 'er."

[*There is a long pause.* CLEA *is now sitting on the table, swinging her vodka bottle in absolute command of the situation*]

COLONEL: [*Faintly; at last grappling with the situation*] Did you say four years, madam?

CLEA: [*In her own voice, quiet*] Yes, Colonel. Four years, in this room.

HAROLD: I know that voice. It's Clea!

MISS FURNIVAL: [*Surprised*] Clea!

CAROL: [*Horrified*] Clea!

BRINDSLEY: [*Unconvincingly surprised*] Clea!

CLEA: Surprised, Brin?

CAROL: [*Understanding*] Clea! . . .

COLONEL: I don't understand anything that's going on in this room.

CLEA: I know. It is a very odd room, isn't it? It's like a magic dark room, where everything happens the wrong way round. Rain falls indoors, the Daily comes at night and turns in a second from a nice maid into a nasty mistress.

BRINDSLEY: Be quiet, Clea!

CLEA: At last! One real word of protest! Have you finished lying, then? Have you eaten the last crumb of humble pie? Oh, you coward, you bloody coward! Just because you didn't want to marry me, did you have to settle for this lot?

CAROL: Marry!

COLONEL: Marry?

CLEA: Four years of meaning to end in this triviality! Miss Laughingly Known As and her Daddipegs!

CAROL: Stop her! She's disgusting.

COLONEL: How can I, for God's sake?

CAROL: Well, where's all that bloody resource you keep talking about?

[*The* COLONEL *goes to her but takes* CLEA's *hand by mistake*]

COLONEL: Now calm down, Dumpling. Keep your head . . . There—hold my hand, that's it, now Daddy's here. Everything is under control. All right?

CLEA: Are you sure that is your daughter's hand you're holding, Colonel?

COLONEL: What? Carol, isn't this your hand?

CAROL: No.

CLEA: You must have lived with your daughter for well over twenty years, Colonel. What remarkable use you've made of your eyes.

[*There is another pause. The* COLONEL *moves away in embarrassment*]

CLEA: [*Wickedly*] All right! Kinky game time! . . . Let's all play Guess the Hand.

HAROLD: Oh, good God!

CLEA: Or would you rather Guess the Lips, Harold?

CAROL: How disgusting!

CLEA: Well, that's me, dear. [CAROL's *accent*] I'm Queen Disgustipegs! [*She seizes* CAROL's *hand and puts it into* HAROLD's] Who's that?

CAROL: I don't know.

CLEA: Guess.

CAROL: I don't know, and I don't care.

CLEA: Oh, go on. Have a go!

CAROL: It's Brin, of course. You can't trick me like that! It's Brindsley's stupid hand.

HAROLD: I'm afraid you're wrong. It's me.

CAROL: [*Struggling*] It's not. You're lying.

HAROLD: [*Holding on*] I'm not. I don't lie.

CAROL: You're lying! . . . You're lying!

HAROLD: I'm not.

[CAROL *breaks away and blunders across the room. She is becoming hysterical*]

CLEA: You try it, Harold. Take the hand on your right.

HAROLD: I'm not playing. It's a bloody silly game.

CLEA: Go on . . . [*She seizes his hand and puts it into* BRINDSLEY'S] Well?

HAROLD: It's Brin.

BRINDSLEY: Yes.

CLEA: Well done!

[*She sits on the low stool*]

CAROL: [*Outraged*] How does he know that? How does *he* know your hand and I don't?

BRINDSLEY: Calm down, Carol.

CAROL: Answer me! I want to know!

BRINDSLEY: Stop it!

CAROL: I won't!

BRINDSLEY: You're getting hysterical!

CAROL: Leave me alone! I want to go home.

[*And suddenly* MISS FURNIVAL *gives a sharp short scream and blunders out through the curtains*]

MISS FURNIVAL: Prams! Prams! Prams—in the supermarket! . . . [*They all freeze. She is evidently out of control in a world of her own fears. She speaks quickly and strangely*] All those hideous wire prams full of babies and bottles—cornflakes over there, is all they say—and then they leave you to yourself. Biscuits over there—cat food over there—fish cakes over there—Airwick over there. Pink stamps, green stamps, free balloons—television dinners—pay as you go out—oh, Daddy, it's awful! And then the Godless ones, the heathens in their leather jackets—laughing me to scorn! But, not for long. Oh, no! Who shall stand when He appeareth? He'll strike them from their motorcycles! He'll dash their helmets to the ground! Yea, verily, I say unto thee—there shall be an end of gasoline! An end to cigarette puffing and jostling with hips . . . Keep off . . . Keep off! Keep off . . .

[*She runs drunkenly across the room and collides with* HAROLD]

HAROLD: Come on, Ferny, I think it's time we went home.

MISS FURNIVAL: [*Pulling herself together*] Yes. You're quite right . . . [*With an attempt at grandeur*] I'm sorry I can't stay any longer, Mr. Miller; but your millionaire is unpardonably late. So typical of modern manners . . . Express my regrets, if you please.

BRINDSLEY: Certainly. [*Leaning heavily on* HAROLD's *arms she leaves the room. He shuts the door after them*] Thank you, Clea. Thank you very much.

CLEA: Any time.

BRINDSLEY: You had no right.

CLEA: No?

BRINDSLEY: *You* walked out on *me*.

[*He joins her on the low stool*]

CLEA: Is that what I did?

BRINDSLEY: You said you never wanted to see me again.

CLEA: I never saw you at all—how could you be walked out on? You should live in the dark, Brindsley. It's your natural element.

BRINDSLEY: Whatever that means.

CLEA: It means you don't really want to be seen. Why is that, Brindsley? Do you think if someone really saw you, they would never love you?

BRINDSLEY: Oh, go away.

CLEA: I want to know.

BRINDSLEY: Yes, you always want to know. Pick-pick-pick away! Why is *that*, Clea? Have you ever thought why you need to do it? Well?

CLEA: Perhaps because I care about you.

BRINDSLEY: Perhaps there's nothing to care about. Just a fake artist.

CLEA: Stop pitying yourself. It's always your vice. I told you when I met you: you could either be a good artist, or a chic fake. You didn't like it, because I refused just to give you applause.

BRINDSLEY: God knows, you certainly did that!

CLEA: Is that what *she* gives you? Twenty hours of ego-massage every day?

BRINDSLEY: At least our life together isn't the replica of the Holy Inquisition you made of ours. I didn't have an affair with you: it was just four years of nooky with Torquemada!

CLEA: And don't say you didn't enjoy it!

BRINDSLEY: Enjoy it? I hated every second of it.

CLEA: Yes, I remember.

BRINDSLEY: Every second.

CLEA: I recall.

BRINDSLEY: When you left for Finland, it was the happiest day of my life.

CLEA: Mine, too!

BRINDSLEY: I sighed with relief.

CLEA: So did I.

BRINDSLEY: I went out dancing that very night.

CLEA: So did I. It was out with the lyre and the timbrel.

BRINDSLEY: Good. Then that's all right.

CLEA: Fine.

BRINDSLEY: Super!

CLEA: Duper!

BRINDSLEY: It's lovely to see you looking so happy.

CLEA: You, too. Radiant with self-fulfilment.

[A *pause*]

BRINDSLEY: If you felt like this, why did you come back?

CLEA: If *you* felt like this, why did you tell Mrs. Punnet I was still at the top of the heap?

BRINDSLEY: I never said that!

CLEA: You did.

BRINDSLEY: Never.

CLEA: You *did!*

BRINDSLEY: Of course I didn't. You invented that ten minutes ago, when you were *playing* Mrs. Punnet.

CLEA: I—Oh! So I did! . . .

[*They both giggle. She falls happily against his shoulder*]

BRINDSLEY: You know something—I'm not sure she's not right.

[*During this exchange the* COLONEL *and his daughter have been standing frozen with astonished anger. Now the father takes over*]

COLONEL: No doubt this is very funny to you two.

CLEA: It is, quite, actually.

COLONEL: I'm not so easily amused, however, madam.

BRINDSLEY: Now look, Colonel—

COLONEL: Hold your tongue, sir, I'm talking. Do you know what would have happened to a young man in my day who dared to treat a girl the way you have treated my Dumpling?

BRINDSLEY: Well, I assume, Colonel—

COLONEL: Hold your tongue, I'm talking.

CAROL: Oh, leave it, Daddy. Let's just go home.

COLONEL: In a moment, Dumpling. Kindly leave this to me.

BRINDSLEY: Look, Carol, I can explain—

CAROL: Explain what?

BRINDSLEY: It's impossible here.

COLONEL: You understate, sir.

BRINDSLEY: Carol, you don't understand.

CAROL: What the hell's there to understand? All the time you were going with me, she was in the background—that's all there is to it —What were you doing? Weighing us up? . . . Here!

[*She pulls off her engagement ring*]

BRINDSLEY: What?

CAROL: Your ring. Take the bloody thing back!

[*She throws it. It hits the* COLONEL *in the eye*]

COLONEL: My eye! My damned eye! [CLEA *starts to laugh again. In mounting fury, clutching his eye*] Oh, very droll, madam! Very droll indeed! Laugh your fill! Miller! I asked you a question. Do you know what would have happened to a young lout like you in my day?

BRINDSLEY: Happened, sir?

COLONEL: [*Quietly*] You'd have been thrashed, sir.

BRINDSLEY: [*Nervous*] Thrashed—

[*The man of war begins to go after him, feeling his way in the dark—like some furious robot*]

COLONEL: You'd have felt the mark of a father's horsewhip across your seducer's shoulders. You'd have gone down on your cad's bended knees, and begged my daughter's pardon for the insults you've offered her tonight.

BRINDSLEY: [*Retreating before the* COLONEL's *groping advance*] Would I, sir?

COLONEL: You'd have raised your guttersnipe voice in a piteous scream for mercy and forgiveness!

[*A terrible scream is heard from the hall. They freeze, listening as it comes nearer and nearer, then the door is flung open and*

HAROLD *plunges into the room. He is wild-eyed with rage: a lit and bent taper shakes in his furious hand*]

HAROLD: Ooooooh! You villain!

BRINDSLEY: Harold—

HAROLD: You skunky, conniving little villain!

BRINDSLEY: What's the matter?

HAROLD: [*Raging*] Have you seen the state of my room? My room? My lovely room, the most elegant and cared for in this entire district?—one chair turned absolutely upside down, one chair on top of another like a Portobello junk-shop! And that's not all, is it, Brindsley? Oh no, that's not the worst by a long chalk, is it, Brindsley?

BRINDSLEY: Long chalk?

HAROLD: Don't play the innocent with me. I thought I had a friend living here all these years. I didn't know I was living opposite a Light-fingered Lenny!

BRINDSLEY: Harold!—

HAROLD: [*Hysterical*] This is my reward, isn't it?—After years of looking after you, sweeping and tidying up this place, because you're too much of a slut to do it for yourself—to have my best pieces stolen from me to impress your new girl friend and her daddy. Or did she help you?

BRINDSLEY: Harold, it was an emergency.

HAROLD: Don't talk to me: I don't want to know! I know what you think of me now . . . "Don't tell Harold about the engagement. He's not to be trusted. He's not a friend. He's just someone to steal things from!"

BRINDSLEY: You know that's not true.

HAROLD: [*Shrieking—in one hysterical breath*] I know I was the last one to know—that's what I know! I have to find it out in a room full of strangers. Me, who's listened to more of your miseries in the small hours of the morning than anyone else would put up with! All your boring talk about women, hour after hour, as if no one's got troubles but you!—

CLEA: She's getting hysterical, dear. Ignore her.

HAROLD: It's you who's going to be ignored, Clea. [*To* BRINDSLEY] As for you, all I can say about your engagement is this: you deserve each other, you and that little nit.

[CAROL *gives a shriek*]

BRINDSLEY: Carol!

HAROLD: Oh, so you're there, are you?—Skulking in the shadows!

BRINDSLEY: Leave her alone!

HAROLD: I'm not going to touch her. I just want my things and I'll be off. Did you hear me, Brindsley? You give me my things now, or I'll call the police.

BRINDSLEY: Don't be ridiculous.

HAROLD: [*Grimly*] Item: One lyre-back Regency chair, in lacquered mahogany with Ormolu inlay and appliqué work on the cushions.

BRINDSLEY: In front of you.

[*He thrusts the taper at it*]

HAROLD: Ta. Item: One half-back sofa—likewise Regency—supported by claw legs and upholstered in a rich silk of bottle green to match the aforesaid chair.

BRINDSLEY: In the studio.

HAROLD: Unbelievable! Item: One Coalport vase, dated 1809, decorated on the rim with a pleasing design of daisies and peonies.

BRINDSLEY: On the floor.

HAROLD: Ta. [BRINDSLEY *hands it to him*] Ooooh! You've even taken the flowers! I'll come back for the chair and sofa in a minute. [*Drawing himself up with all the offended dignity of which a* HAROLD GORRINGE *is capable*] This is the end of our relationship, Brindsley. We won't be speaking again, I don't think. [*He twitches his raincoat off the table. Inside it, of course, is the Buddha, which falls on the floor and smashes beyond repair. There is a terrible silence. Trying to keep his voice under control*] Do you know what that statue was worth? Do you? More money than you'll ever see in your whole life, even if you sell every piece of that nasty, rusty rubbish. [*With the quietness of the mad*] I think I'm going to have to smash you, Brindsley.

BRINDSLEY: [*Nervously*] Now steady on, Harold . . . don't be rash . . .

HAROLD: Yes, I'm very much afraid I'll have to smash you . . . Smash for smash—that's fair do's. [*He pulls one of the long metal prongs out of the sculpture*] Smash for smash. Smash for *smash!*

[*Insanely he advances on* BRINDSLEY *holding the prong like a sword, the taper burning in his other hand*]

BRINDSLEY: [*Retreating*] Stop it, Harold. You've gone mad!

COLONEL: Well done, sir. I think it's time for the reckoning.

[*The* COLONEL *grabs the other prong and also advances*]

BRINDSLEY: [*Retreating from them both*] Now just a minute, Colonel. Be reasonable! . . . Let's not revert to savages! . . . Harold, I appeal to you—you've always had civilized instincts! Don't join the Army! . . .

CAROL: [*Grimly advancing also*] Get him, Daddy! Get him! Get him!

BRINDSLEY: [*Horrified at her*] Carol!

CAROL: [*Malevolently*] Get him! Get him! Get him! Get . . .

BRINDSLEY: *Clea!*

[CLEA *leaps up and blows out the taper. Lights up*]

COLONEL: Dammit! [CLEA *grabs* BRINDSLEY's *hand and pulls him out of danger. To* CLEA] Careful, my little Dumpling. Keep out of the way.

HAROLD: [*To* CAROL] Hush up, Colonel. We'll be able to hear them breathing.

COLONEL: Clever idea! Smart tactics, sir!

[*Silence. They listen.* BRINDSLEY *climbs carefully onto the table and silently pulls* CLEA *up after him.* HAROLD *and the* COLONEL, *prodding and slashing the darkness with their swords, grimly*]

hunt their quarry. Twenty seconds. Suddenly, with a bang
SCHUPPANZIGH *opens the trap from below. Both men advance on
it warily. The electrician disappears again below. They have almost reached it, on tiptoe, when there is another crash—this time
from the hall. Someone has again tripped over the milk bottles.*
HAROLD *and the* COLONEL *immediately swing round and start
stalking in the other direction, still on tiptoe. Enter* GEORG BAM-
BERGER. *He is quite evidently a millionaire. Dressed in the
Gulbenkian manner, he wears a beard, an eyeglass, a frock coat,
a top hat and an orchid. He carries a large deaf aid. Bewildered,
he advances into the room. Stealthily, the two armed men stalk
him as he silently gropes his way along and passes between
them*]

BAMBERGER: [*Speaking in a middle-aged German voice, as near to the
voice of* SCHUPPANZIGH *as possible*] Hello, please! Mr. Miller?

[HAROLD *and the* COLONEL *spin round in a third direction*]

HAROLD: Oh, it's the electrician!

BAMBERGER: Hello, please?

COLONEL: What the devil are you doing up here? [SCHUPPANZIGH *appears at the trap*] Have you mended the fuse?

HAROLD: Or are you going to keep us in the dark all night?

SCHUPPANZIGH: Don't worry. The fuse is mended.

[*He comes out of the trap.* BAMBERGER *goes round to the right*]

HAROLD: Thank God for that.

BAMBERGER: [*Still groping around*] Hallo, please? Mr. Miller—vere
are you? Vy zis darkness? Is a joke, yes?

SCHUPPANZIGH: [*Incensed*] Ah, no! That is not very funny, good people—just because I am a foreigner, to imitate my voice. You English can be the rudest people on earth!

BAMBERGER: [*Imperiously*] Mr. Miller! I have come here to give attention to your sculptures!

SCHUPPANZIGH: *Gott in himmel!*

BAMBERGER: *Gott in himmel!*

BRINDSLEY: God, it's him! Bamberger!

CLEA: He's come!

HAROLD: Bamberger!

COLONEL: Bamberger!

[*They freeze. The millionaire sets off, left, toward the open trap*]

BRINDSLEY: Don't worry, Mr. Bamberger. We've had a fuse, but it's mended now.

BAMBERGER: [*Irritably*] Mr. Miller!

CLEA: You'll have to speak up. He's deaf.

BRINDSLEY: [*Shouting*] Don't worry, Mr. Bamberger! We've had a fuse but it's all right now! . . . [*Standing on the table, he clasps* CLEA *happily.* BAMBERGER *misses the trap by inches*] Oh, Clea, that's true. Everything's all right now! Just in the nick of time!

[*But as he says this* BAMBERGER *turns and falls into the open trap door,* SCHUPPANZIGH *slams it to with his foot*]

SCHUPPANZIGH: So! Here's now an end to your troubles! Like Jehovah in the Sacred Testament, I give you the most miraculous gift of the Creation! Light!

CLEA: Light!

BRINDSLEY: Oh, thank God. *Thank God!*

[SCHUPPANZIGH *goes to the switch*]

HAROLD: [*Grimly*] I wouldn't thank Him too soon, Brindsley, if I were you!

COLONEL: Nor would I, Brindsley, if I were you!

CAROL: Nor would I, Brinnie Winnie, if I were you!

SCHUPPANZIGH: [*Grandly*] Then thank *me!* For I shall play God for this second! [*Clapping his hands*] Attend all of you. God said: "Let there be light!" And there was, good people, suddenly!—astoundingly! — instantaneously! — inconceivably — inexhaustibly — inextinguishably and eternally—LIGHT!

[SCHUPPANZIGH, *with a great flourish, flicks the light switch. Instant darkness. The turntable of the phonograph starts up again, and with an exultant crash the Sousa march falls on the audience—and blazes away in the black*]

END

BUS RILEY'S BACK IN TOWN

William Inge

William Inge

William Inge (1913–73) began his reign as one of America's leading dramatists in 1950, when the Theatre Guild introduced his compelling drama *Come Back, Little Sheba* to Broadway audiences. In 1953 he scored again with Joshua Logan's staging of *Picnic* and, although the author personally was discontented with the compromising "romantic" ending, the play won him both the New York Drama Critics' Circle Award and the Pulitzer Prize. At its Broadway opening, critic Richard Watts, Jr., wrote: "William Inge's new work revealed the power, insight, compassion, observation and gift for looking into the human heart that we all expected in him. . . . Here is a dramatist who knows how to set down how people behave and think and talk, who can create the feeling of a small Kansas town, and is able to write dramatic scenes that have vitality, emotional power and heartbreak. There is a true sense of the sadness and wonder of life in this new dramatist."

In 1955 he added another link to his chain of successes with *Bus Stop* and, two years later, *The Dark at the Top of the Stairs*—a revision of his very first play, *Farther Off from Heaven*, which Margo Jones produced in 1947 at her Dallas Theatre—was hailed by press and public as an exceptionally poignant study of family relationships. Although the latter was admittedly autobiographical, the author transferred the locale of the drama from his native Kansas, where he was born, to Oklahoma.

Rated as one of the mid-century's most perceptive and sensitive dramatists, Inge's close affiliation with the theatre originated with his tenure as stage and screen reviewer for the St. Louis *Star-Times*. In addition to the aforementioned plays, his other produced stage works included: *A Loss of Roses; Natural Affection;* and *Where's Daddy?* Though none of these was successful in New York, shortly before his untimely death, the author stated in a letter to this editor: "God knows, neither *Natural Affection* or *Where's Daddy?* ever won any kind of award. But *Natural Affection* was the first *black* comedy and no one knew how to react to it. I still feel that these two plays represent the best of my work. . . ."

William Inge also wrote more than a dozen short plays, two published novels, *Good Luck, Miss Wyckoff* and *My Son Is a Splendid Driver*, and in 1962 was the recipient of an Academy Award for his screenplay *Splendor in the Grass*.

A film version of *Bus Riley's Back in Town* (with Ann-Margret and Michael Parks) was released in 1965.

Characters:

Salesman
Howie
Jackie Loomis
Bernice Henry
Ralph Henry
Bus Riley

The scene of the play is the Fiesta Room of the Hotel Boomerang in a small town in middle Texas. The Fiesta Room is only the bar of the hotel, and as a bar not a very satisfactory one, being permitted to sell only beer. But the décor pretends, at least, to an air of festivity, with symbols of primitive Mexican culture. Mexican hats and serapes hang on the wall, there is a big poster of a bullfight, and the doors to the toilets are marked, one Señora, *the other* Señor. *But there is not much festivity in the Fiesta Room at present. Only one customer is in view, a* SALESMAN, *sitting at the bar, drinking a glass of beer and reading an evening paper.* HOWIE, *the bartender, an easygoing man of middle age, stays behind the bar, not even pretending to keep busy.*

SALESMAN: Used t'be I'd come into this town and sell maybe five thousand dollars' worth a merchandise in one day.

HOWIE: Bet ya don't do that now, do you?

SALESMAN: No. I'm doin' good now if I make my expenses in this town. I ain't kiddin'.

HOWIE: Yah. Things ain't what they used to be around here. That drought didn't help us any.

SALESMAN: Yah. That drought was bad.

HOWIE: But this little town really had it once.

SALESMAN: It sure did. [*He looks around the room*] This all the customers ya got, Howie?

HOWIE: It's early in the week. We don't do enough business to stay open, except on Friday and Saturday nights. There's always a crowd in here then.

SALESMAN: Things have sure changed. They sure have.

HOWIE: The business we do on weekends has to carry us through the week. It's the hotel's worry. Not mine. They wanta keep the room open just for the looks of things. When we have a losing week, I guess they make up for it with the dining room. The dining room does a pretty good business.

SALESMAN: Yah. It's about the only place in town you can get decent food. All you can get in these lunch stands around here is greaser food—chili and tamales. I can't eat it.

[*Now a young girl comes running into the room from the outside. She is* JACKIE LOOMIS, *a quite pretty girl of twenty-three or twenty-four, wearing a simple summer wash frock, spectator pumps and no stockings. There is something taut about her, a breathlessness that makes her seem to live every moment as though it were a crisis. She runs to the bar excitedly and speaks to* HOWIE]

JACKIE: [*In a somewhat private voice*] Howie, is it true Bus Riley's in town?

HOWIE: Yes, Jackie. At least, he was in town a day or so ago. His father, you know, has been real sick, and Bus had to come home to give him blood transfusions. Bus has been spending most of his time at the hospital, they say.

JACKIE: Has he been in here, Howie?

HOWIE: Yes, a few times. Usually comes in at night and has a few beers.

JACKIE: What's he like now, Howie?

HOWIE: Like? Well, I . . . uh . . .

JACKIE: Is he still a *god?*

HOWIE: [*Chuckles*] Well, I don't know I'd say he was a god. He looked pretty much like the same old Bus to me. The only difference I could see was he was wearing a sailor suit.

JACKIE: I've just *got* to see him, Howie. I've just *got* to.

HOWIE: [*At a loss for what to say*] Well, Jackie, I . . .

JACKIE: Don't tell anyone, Howie. Please don't tell anyone I asked about him. Will you promise?

HOWIE: No. I won't tell, Jackie.

JACKIE: Is he staying at home, do you know, Howie?

HOWIE: As far as I know, Jackie.

JACKIE: [*Digs into her purse for a piece of change*] Give me a dime, Howie.

HOWIE: You bet, Jackie.

[*She takes the dime from him and hurries into the telephone booth in a corner*]

SALESMAN: [*An observant man*] That was Del Loomis's daughter, wasn't it?

HOWIE: Yep!

SALESMAN: How is old Del these days?

HOWIE: The same, I guess. No one ever sees him.

SALESMAN: Dead drunk, I suppose.

HOWIE: I suppose. They keep a nurse with him mosta the time.

SALESMAN: Just think. He built this hotel, din he?

HOWIE: Built mosta the buildings in town.

SALESMAN: And now, they tell me, he don't have a nickel.

HOWIE: Dead drunk. Dead broke. Poor old Del.

SALESMAN: Yah. Well, he had it once, though.

HOWIE: Yah. Del had millions.

SALESMAN: Lived like a lord.

HOWIE: Had a whole fleet of automobiles, two ranches, swimming pool, fifty servants, several airplanes. Kept a yacht down in the Gulf.

SALESMAN: Yah. It just don't seem possible that a man can have as much as old Del did and then lose it.

HOWIE: Del Loomis just about made this town. He ran things here pretty much the way he wanted 'em. We all kowtowed to him.

SALESMAN: It was a one-man town.

HOWIE: Yah! When Del had it, all of us here were prosperous, working in his oil fields and at the ranches. He kept things humming. Then he lost it, and so did the rest of us. I guess we all owe a lot to Del, and he was a likable man, too, in a way. I mean he was always friendly when he met you on the street. But I guess all that money and all that power kinda went to his head. He was actin' kinda crazy around here, like he was Nero or one of those Roman emperors.

SALESMAN: Yah. I think Del was goin' off his rocker. That's what I think. [*He nods in the direction of* JACKIE, *who is still in the telephone booth*] That the daughter there was all the talk about? [HOWIE *nods a little reluctantly*] In love with some fellow Del didn't want her to marry, wasn't she?

HOWIE: That's it. The story got in all the papers. It all happened five or six years ago.

SALESMAN: This is the first time I ever saw her. She sure is a looker.

HOWIE: Del was crazy about her. He acted to me like he was jealous of the boy and in love with her himself.

[*Two young people come in:* RALPH *and* BERNICE HENRY, *a married couple, friends of* JACKIE. *A little mystified, they are looking for her*]

BERNICE: [*To* HOWIE] Did Jackie come in here?

HOWIE: [*Nodding to the telephone booth*] In there, Bernice.

BERNICE: Oh.

[JACKIE, *seeing* BERNICE *and* RALPH, *hurries out of the booth, a little embarrassed with a feeling of having been caught*]

JACKIE: Oh, I was just calling home, Bee. I . . . I just remembered that Daddy asked me to. He said maybe he'd want me to bring something home from town.

BERNICE: [*A little miffed*] Well, you might have told us. Ralph and I were looking all over for you after the movie let out. You made off in such a hurry. I thought we'd come over here together. We always do.

JACKIE: I . . . I'm sorry, Bee.

RALPH: What's the difference? Let's sit down and have a beer. [*He leads* BERNICE *to a booth on the side of the room opposite the bar, calling to* HOWIE *on the way*] Three beers, Howie!

BERNICE: [*Still a little peeved at* JACKIE] Maybe you want to get rid of Ralph and me.

JACKIE: No, Bee. Honest! It's just that I remembered suddenly that I'd promised Daddy to call. Honest!

BERNICE: [*Looking at her a little dubiously*] Well, I don't see why you had to go running off that way, without even saying a word.

[*She sits next to* RALPH *in the booth. Then* JACKIE *joins them, sitting opposite them*]

RALPH: [*To* BERNICE] It doesn't make any difference, Mama. We're not Jackie's guardians, or anything.

[HOWIE *goes over and sets down three beers for them*]

BERNICE: Oh, did you order beer for me? I'm not sure I want it. It makes me feel so logy in hot weather.

HOWIE: Want me to take it back?

BERNICE: No. I'll drink it. Darn! I wish you could order a Tom Collins in this town, or a gin and tonic. [HOWIE *returns to the bar*] Lord, that was a putrid movie. Now, when they try to make an ancient Egyptian princess out of Lana Turner, I just don't believe it. I don't care what you say, I don't believe it. She's about as Egyptian as our Scotty. Did you like the picture, Jackie?

JACKIE: I . . . I didn't pay much attention to it.

BERNICE: Jackie, you're so nervous these days, I don't know what to make of you.

JACKIE: I'm not usually, Bee. It's just tonight. I . . . I guess I *am* a little nervous tonight.

BERNICE: What about?

JACKIE: I . . . I don't know, Bee. Just nervous. That's all.

BERNICE: Now, Jackie honey, you wanta look after yourself, and when you find yourself getting nervous, go home and relax. Take it easy. Isn't that what you say, Ralph?

RALPH: Sure. Take it easy. That's my motto.

JACKIE: [*A little annoyed by* BERNICE's *assumed authority*] It's nothing to get worried about, Bee.

BERNICE: Did you like the movie, Ralph?

RALPH: I liked the photography. The color was pretty.

BERNICE: That's all you care about. The photography. I like a story that's *real*, that shows just how nasty people really are, and doesn't mince words about it.

RALPH: Can't a movie be real if it shows people being nice, too?

BERNICE: Maybe. But what's the point? I mean . . .

JACKIE: [*Suddenly jumping up from her seat*] Pardon me a minute, kids, will you?

BERNICE: Oh . . . sure. [JACKIE *disappears into the door marked* Señora. BERNICE *watches her and now reports to* RALPH] Do you know what she's going to do?

RALPH: Well, I take it for granted that when a girl pardons herself to go to the ladies' room, that she's going to do one of two things.

BERNICE: [*Shaking her head wisely*] Huh-uh. She's got you fooled. I know what she's going to do. She's going to take another of those pills.

RALPH: What pills?

BERNICE: Those sleeping pills she carries around with her.

RALPH: Honey, you keep telling me she takes sleeping pills, but if she does, why doesn't she ever go to sleep?

BERNICE: Ralph, don't you know anything about these things? She gets *high* on them, just like on liquor. Honest. I bet anything she's taking a pill now and just doesn't want us to know. You know why she ditched us after the movie, don't you?

RALPH: I'm perfectly willing to believe that she had to come over here to call her father.

BERNICE: Oh, you just don't know that girl. She came over here in hopes of finding Bus Riley. And she didn't want us to be around when she found him, either. And that wasn't her father she was calling when we came in. Huh-uh. She was calling Bus's house. I bet anything.

RALPH: Well, what if she was? What's it to you?

BERNICE: It just so happens that Jackie Loomis is my oldest, dearest friend. And I know all that she's been through. I just want to spare her from going through anything more . . . with that . . . that half-breed Bus Riley.

RALPH: You think she still loves him?

BERNICE: Of course she does. She's been jumpy as a cat, ever since she heard he was back. She's just been dying to find some excuse to see him.

RALPH: After . . . everything that happened?

BERNICE: Of course.

[JACKIE *comes out of the ladies' room now. She seems quite merry. She lingers by the juke box, studying the selections, then going to the open door to see if* BUS *can be seen anywhere down the street*]

RALPH: My God, the guy's been in prison since then . . .

BERNICE: I know, but she's still crazy about him. Besides, it was her father sent Bus to prison. She knows that. [*She makes sure that* JACKIE *cannot overhear her*] Bus wasn't really guilty of anything. I mean, Jackie was as much to blame for getting pregnant as Bus was. Even if he was a year older. It was just old man Loomis's way of getting revenge. He certainly wasn't going to let her marry Bus. Bus, half-Mexican, from the other side of the tracks.

RALPH: Bus was a pretty nice guy, though, honey. At least, when I knew him.

BERNICE: I'm not saying he wasn't. Still, he had a Mexican mother . . .

RALPH: But she's a very nice woman. I mean . . .

BERNICE: He lived out at the edge of town in that ugly little shanty full of kids.

RALPH: That's just because his old man wouldn't go to work.

BERNICE: All right. But what difference did that make to Del Loomis, when he was the richest man in middle Texas? He wouldn't have stood for Jackie marrying anyone like that. Why, Del Loomis was even trying to get Jackie married off to some European nobility.

RALPH: Del Loomis is a crackpot.

BERNICE: Maybe he is. But that doesn't keep the situation from being hopeless. It's just no good for Jackie to be getting excited all over again about Bus Riley. I don't know why he had to come back to town.

RALPH: His old man was about to die.

BERNICE: Yes, and you know why, don't you? Got stabbed in one of those Mexican joints he hangs out in, and lost almost all his blood.

RALPH: Well . . . you can't keep her from seeing Bus if she really wants to.

BERNICE: I can try.

[JACKIE *rejoins them at the booth*; BERNICE *becomes suddenly very silent*]

JACKIE: Oh, I don't want to go home tonight. I feel like I'd like to stay here until it closes. I don't want to go home.

BERNICE: Jackie, you can't stay here all alone. People would talk.

JACKIE: What difference would that make? People talk about me already.

BERNICE: That's not so, Jackie. You just imagine it.

JACKIE: [*With a quick little look at* BERNICE] Do I?

BERNICE: Yes. Of course you do.

JACKIE: Well . . . maybe I do.

RALPH: I'm about ready for bed now, aren't you, Mother?

BERNICE: Yes, and we've got to relieve the baby-sitter.

JACKIE: Oh, let's not go yet. Please, let's not go yet.

BERNICE: Jackie, there's no point in sitting in this dump all evening. Come on over to our house if you want to. You can have a beer there. Or Ralph could fix you something stronger.

JACKIE: No thanks, Bee. You'll be busy looking after the children. I . . . I won't bother you.

[*Now* BUS RILEY *enters.* JACKIE *is aware of him the moment he comes through the door, and* BERNICE *sees a look come into her eyes.* BUS *is a very handsome young man of twenty-four or twenty-five, with sleek black hair and just a suggestion of Latin features and coloring. He wears his Navy whites with splendor. He calls to* HOWIE *as soon as he enters, not noticing the people in the booth*]

BUS: Draw me a beer, Howie! [*He strides to the bar*] Well, the Old Man's on the way to recovery now. I'm clearin' outa here in the morning.

HOWIE: Leavin' us so soon, Bus?

BUS: Yah. I've had enough of this town, forever.

[*He drinks his beer.* BERNICE *and* RALPH *get up from the booth*]

BERNICE: Let's go, Jackie.

[JACKIE *sits almost as though wounded by the sight and sound of* BUS]

JACKIE: Well, I . . .

BERNICE: You can't stay here, Jackie. You know you can't.

RALPH: Come along, Jackie old girl.

JACKIE: [*Reluctantly rising to her feet*] Well . . . if you say so . . . I . . .

RALPH: [*To* BERNICE] I'll pay the bill. You and Jackie go on out to the car.

BERNICE: O.K., honey.

[*Like a protecting angel,* BERNICE *hovers about* JACKIE, *getting her out of the bar before* BUS *sees her. At the bar,* RALPH *lays down a bill for* HOWIE *and gives* BUS *a hearty slap on the back*]

RALPH: Hello, Riley! Good to see you back.

BUS: Oh . . . Ralph Henry! Hi ya, Ralph?

[*They shake hands*]

RALPH: How's your father?

BUS: Gettin' along O.K. now. Doc says he's outa danger.

RALPH: Good. Glad to hear it. Well . . . nice to've seen you, Bus.

BUS: Yah . . . thanks, Ralph. [RALPH *goes out now.* BUS *is still trying to identify him*] Let's see. He married Bernice Cain, didn't he?

HOWIE: Right. She just went out . . . with an old friend of yours.

BUS: Who? You mean . . . ?

HOWIE: Yah. She was sitting right over there when you came in.

BUS: I'll be damned. Well . . . maybe it's a good thing I din see her. Know anywhere I could get a bottle of whiskey, Howie? I been cooped up in that hospital room for so long, I feel like celebratin' a little before I leave town.

HOWIE: You can't buy hard liquor in this county, Bus. You'll have to drive over to the next county, buy it there.

BUS: It was Del Loomis had that law passed, wasn't it?

HOWIE: I guess so.

BUS: He stayed home getting plastered, but thought the county should stay dry. That hypocrite son of a bitch! [*He shows intense hatred and anger*] Well, I'm goin' from here to Galveston. Things are a li'l different down there.

HOWIE: I hear things are wide open in Galveston.

SALESMAN: I hear they got gambling down there, and women.

BUS: You can get anything you want there. *Anything.*

HOWIE: That where the Navy's been keepin' you all this time, Bus? Galveston?

BUS: Christ no! I've been everywhere there is to go. Around the world twice. I'm joining a new ship in Galveston. We sail for Hong Kong next week.

SALESMAN: [*His love of adventure stirred*] Hong Kong!

BUS: Howie, what's the situation with girls in this town? The same as with whiskey?

HOWIE: [*Laughs and begins to ponder the question*] Well, let me think, Bus.

BUS: How about Melba Freeman? She still around?

HOWIE: No. Melba got herself a job in Dallas. Left here a few years ago.

BUS: Oh. That's too bad. Well . . . how 'bout Maxine Tucker? Where's she?

HOWIE: Oh, she's married, Bus. Married Lyn Overton. Remember him? They got two kids now. Happy as can be.

BUS: Oh . . . that's great. Uh . . . whatever happened to Rosamund Skinner? There was a beauty.

HOWIE: Rose got killed in a auto accident, Bus. About a year ago. She and the boy she was with.

BUS: Oh, gee, that's too bad.

HOWIE: I'm afraid I can't think of anyone now, Bus. The town's pretty quiet now.

BUS: What the hell! I'll go down to the Mexican Quarter. I can pick up a chick there.

HOWIE: I can give you a shot to go with that beer, if you want it, Bus.

BUS: *Do* I?

HOWIE: I always keep a bottle back here to celebrate with. And this is an occasion, you being home.

[*He pours out a jigger which* BUS *grabs instantly and downs*]

BUS: Thanks, Howie.

HOWIE: How're things, Bus? I mean, on the level.

BUS: O.K. *now*, Howie. I mean . . . Well, they kept me in the cage for a year's all. I . . . I just don't think about it any more. The minute I got out, I made up my mind, I was never gonna think about it again. So . . . I'm in the Navy now and life is great. Sure. I get my kicks. Uh . . . Howie, how 'bout another shot of that stuff? That's the first real drink I've had since I got here; and man, I need it!

HOWIE: Sure, Bus.

[*He pours another, which* BUS *immediately downs*]

BUS: Thanks, Howie. You're a pal. If you could only find me a girl, you'd be a *real* pal.

HOWIE: I might do that. [BUS *looks at him questioningly*] Jackie's been asking me about you, Bus.

BUS: Has she?

HOWIE: She was calling you from here before Ralph and Bernice came in.

BUS: I guess I'd left the house.

HOWIE: I think she'd like to see you, Bus.

BUS: What's she like now, Howie?

HOWIE: Still the same sweet kid, Bus, and prettier'n ever.

BUS: Yah?

HOWIE: I bet she comes back here after she gets rid of Ralph and Bernice. I bet anything.

BUS: I'm not sure I'd know how to act around her now.

HOWIE: [*Looking out the front window*] I was right. There she is now, pulling up at the curb. She let Ralph and Bernice take her home, then got into her own car and came right back. I told you she wanted to see you.

BUS: [*This is a troubled moment for* BUS, *not knowing whether he can face her or not*] Howie, I don't know if I can . . .

HOWIE: What d'ya mean, Bus?

BUS: [*Making a start to get away*] I'm heading out the back way. I can't see Jackie again.

HOWIE: [*Catching* BUS *at the end of the bar*] Hold on, Bus. Hold on. She'll feel awful bad if you run off.

[BUS *says nothing. He just stays where he is, his back to the door, his head down, dreading to face her.* JACKIE *comes in. She is a little hesitant, a little uncertain of her welcome. She goes half the distance toward* BUS *before speaking. The* SALESMAN *watches with curiosity*]

JACKIE: Bus?

[BUS *turns to face her now. He has caught hold of himself and has a big smile for her*]

BUS: Jackie!

JACKIE: How are you, Bus?

BUS: Couldn't be better, Doll. Step right up here and have a beer. Long time no see. How ya doin'?

JACKIE: [*Joining him at the bar*] I'm all right, Bus.

[HOWIE *sets another beer before her*]

BUS: By God, you're still the best lookin' doll I ever saw.

JACKIE: Thank you, Bus. You look wonderful. Really!

BUS: It's the monkey suit. The girls always go for it.

JACKIE: [*More serious now*] Bus . . . I just had to see you. Why didn't you call me, Bus?

BUS: Well . . . I din know whether a call from me'd be very appreciated, Jackie.

JACKIE: Oh, Bus, it would have been. Honest, Bus, nothing that happened . . . was my fault. You know how Daddy is. It . . . it just made me sick, what happened.

BUS: Drink your beer, Doll.

JACKIE: I was praying you'd call me, Bus. I wanted so to hear your voice . . . to see you again . . .

BUS: I ran into trouble with your old man once, Jackie. I din want to again.

JACKIE: There's no reason to be afraid of him any more. He's changed.

BUS: Yah?

JACKIE: You know . . . he drinks. He . . . he doesn't know much that goes on any more. I . . . I do anything I want to now.

BUS: Well, that's great. You got your car outside? How 'bout drivin' over to the next county and pickin' up a bottle? We could stop at the Riverview, maybe, if it's still runnin'.

JACKIE: It is. My car's outside. Dance with me, Bus.

BUS: Dance? Here?

JACKIE: [*Running to the juke box to drop a nickel to play her favorite tune*] Yes. Please.

BUS: O.K. We'll dance.

[*The music starts, and he takes her in his arms. They dance slowly and softly to the love song, neither of them speaking for a while*]

SALESMAN: [*Softly to* HOWIE] That the boy . . . all the trouble was about?

HOWIE: Yah. That's him.

SALESMAN: And Del had him sent to prison?

HOWIE: Oh, it was a great big fluke. The boy was eighteen when it happened. The girl was seventeen. So, according to law, the girl was a minor and the boy wasn't. They sent him to some reform school, but they let him go after about a year. He's no criminal, and they knew it. If you ask me, Del's the one they shoulda sent to prison.

SALESMAN: Yah. Gimme another beer, Howie.

[HOWIE *gives him a glass of beer and then begins to wash and dry glasses. The* SALESMAN *is content to sit drinking his beer, just watching the two young people dance. Both* JACKIE *and* BUS *have been silent in each other's arms. Now* JACKIE, *as though rising out of a heavenly dream, speaks*]

JACKIE: Oh, Bus, I've been telling myself all day that maybe I'd see you tonight, and maybe be dancing with you again, after all these years.

BUS: Yah. It's great, Doll.

JACKIE: Bus . . . I missed you terribly after you'd gone.

BUS: Yah? Well . . . same here.

JACKIE: I was so afraid you'd think it was my fault . . . what happened.

BUS: No, Doll. I never blamed it on you.

JACKIE: Oh, Bus, I missed you so, I was afraid I'd go crazy. Honest. I wanted to talk to you, just to talk to you, and be with you. Why didn't you answer my letters, Bus?

BUS: Hell, Jackie. I didn't know what to say.

JACKIE: I know.

BUS: [*Trying to sound more cheerful*] Hey, I thought you'd be an old married woman by now.

JACKIE: No.

BUS: How come?

JACKIE: Oh, I've dated a few boys since you left, but they didn't seem to mean anything.

BUS: [*In a tone of inquiry*] Yah?

JACKIE: [*Daring to ask it*] How 'bout you, Bus? Have . . . have you fallen in love with anyone?

BUS: No. Not me. I don't fall in love any more.

[*They have stopped dancing now and stand far away from the bar, clinging to each other, talking in soft, repressed voices*]

JACKIE: Bus, I'll always remember when we first started going together.

BUS: [*A memory he has not tried to recall*] Oh . . . yah.

JACKIE: Remember how shy we were of each other for so long?

BUS: Yah. I remember.

JACKIE: You used to walk me home from school in the afternoon, and we'd sit together on my doorstep for *hours*, and not say a word.

BUS: [*Obviously not giving himself to the recall*] Sure, sure.

JACKIE: And the first time you kissed me. Oh, I'll never forget. Remember how scared we were when we made love, feeling so guilty and afraid. You used to tell me I was like some wonderful princess . . .

BUS: I'd forgotten I was so corny.

JACKIE: But we really felt those things, Bus. And when you really feel them, they're *not* corny. And I used to think of you as a god. I did. When we studied about Greece in Ancient History, and read about their gods and goddesses, I always visualized you, Bus, as Mercury, and Mars, and Apollo.

BUS: Well . . . I guess you had me wrong, Doll.

JACKIE: Oh, Bus, I was in love with you. I've been in love with you ever since, all these years. Every time I went out with another boy, I was mad because he wasn't you.

BUS: [*Turning it into a joke*] Hey, I guess I feel flattered.

JACKIE: All these years I've been wanting to tell you. I'm still in love with you, Bus. I guess I always will be.

BUS: Well . . . that's great. You know I think a lotta *you*, too, Doll. I sure as hell do.

JACKIE: Did you ever know what happened to me, Bus? Daddy took me to some doctor in Forth Worth, and I had an abortion. Oh, Bus, it was terrible. I almost died. I really wanted to die, Bus. I wanted the baby so bad.

[BUS *is not capable of dealing with this outpouring of sorrows. He is at a loss for words*]

BUS: Jackie, I . . . I just don't know what to say.

JACKIE: And then I came back here and heard what had happened to you. Oh Bus, I was despondent. I . . . I tried to kill myself, Bus. I did. Then Daddy sent me to a mental hospital in Kansas. I was there for about a year. For a long time, they wouldn't even let me out of my room without a guard.

BUS: [*Feeling more at a loss*] Yah . . . well, look, Doll, it's not doing any good, goin' over all this . . .

JACKIE: I've wanted to tell you, Bus. I wanted to tell you for so long now.

BUS: O.K., now you've told me. I been through bad times, too. Let's forget it. What d'ya say?

JACKIE: Kiss me, Bus [*There is a hesitant pause*] It's all right. I don't care if they see us. Kiss me.

BUS: Sure, Doll! [*Eagerly, he takes her in his arms and kisses her long and satisfyingly*] How was that, Doll?

JACKIE: [*Clinging to him*] Oh, Bus!

BUS: You still know how to cuddle, don't you, Doll?

JACKIE: Bus, don't make fun.

BUS: Who says I'm makin' fun? Look, Doll, you wait here a minute while I make a telephone call, will ya?

[*She stays planted as* BUS *hurries to the telephone booth.* HOWIE *and the* SALESMAN *have other things to talk about now*]

SALESMAN: Ya know, it always depresses me, kinda, to come back to this town now. It's so run-down now, compared with what it used to be. It used to be such a pretty town, with all them fine homes on Maple Street, a fine car settin' in every driveway, the lawns all trim and green.

HOWIE: Yah. Things change.

SALESMAN: They sure as hell do. Mosta them homes now are boarding houses, aren't they?

HOWIE: The Baker home is a funeral parlor.

SALESMAN: Yah. One of the finest houses in town and now it's a funeral parlor. This hotel's run-down, too. They don't even have a porter. It used to be a fine place to stay, but now it's the crummiest hotel on my route.

HOWIE: Wouldn't doubt it.

SALESMAN: Gimme one more beer, Howie. Then I'm goin' to bed.

[HOWIE *draws another beer and sets it before him.* BUS *now comes hurrying from the telephone booth to report to* JACKIE]

BUS: Look, Doll, they got a cabin for us at the Riverview. Why don't we pile in your car, drive into the next county and pick up a bottle, and then stop at the Riverview and throw a ball. What d'ya say, Doll?

JACKIE: [*Dumbly*] The Riverview?

BUS: Sure, Doll! Look, I've been cooped up with the Old Man all week now, and I wanta let off a little steam. Let's get goin', Doll.

JACKIE: [*Shattered with disillusionment, she sobs and runs to the door*] No. I don't want to go to the Riverview with you, or anywhere else.

BUS: Well, for cryin' out loud! [*He goes to her patiently*] Look, Doll, what's got into you all of a sudden?

JACKIE: Bus, you used to love me. I know you did. But you can't even pretend to now. You've just been making up polite answers to everything I've said. I'm just any other girl to you now that you can . . . can let off steam with, and then forget.

BUS: O.K., Doll. I'm not gonna talk you into it.

JACKIE: Oh, Bus, can't you remember the way we used to feel?

BUS: Maybe I don't want to.

JACKIE: [*Hurt*] Oh, Bus!

BUS: Come off it, Jackie. Come off it.

JACKIE: Goodbye, Bus.

[*She hurries outside now, and* BUS *mades a slow return to the bar.* HOWIE *is watching him, getting out his private bottle to pour him another shot*]

HOWIE: Thought you might need this.

BUS: You're a pal. What the hell am I gonna do with myself till morning?

HOWIE: How about goin' home and goin' to bed?

BUS: I couldn't get to sleep. I come back to this little town, and I remember too many things to sleep. I just keep wantin' to get away, to get away.

HOWIE: There's the Mexican Quarter. Some of those places stay open all night.

BUS: Yah. [*Picks up the shot of whiskey*] Gimme a beer to chase this down with, Howie.

HOWIE: O.K.

BUS: B'lieve me, when I clear outa this town tomorrow, it's for good.

[*He downs the whiskey and begins drinking his beer. By this time, the* SALESMAN *is asleep, his head lying in one arm, curved over the bar. He snores and* HOWIE *taps him on the shoulder. The* SALESMAN *stirs*]

SALESMAN: Huh? What . . . ? Oh, have I been asleep? What d'ya know? Well, I hope I'll be able to do that when I get into bed. What do I owe you, Howie?

HOWIE: One-ten.

SALESMAN: [*Taking money from his pocket*] There ya arc. [*Gets up from stool*] Ho hum! Gotta get up in the morning and see my customers. Wish business was better. I sure do.

HOWIE: Good night, Harry.

[*The* SALESMAN *goes off, wandering through the archway leading into the hotel lobby*]

BUS: I'll finish this up in a minute, Howie, and let you close.

[*He takes a long drink of beer*]

HOWIE: No hurry, Bus. Take your time, I gotta stay open till midnight, anyway, whether there's customers or not.

[BUS *wanders over to the juke box and drops a nickel, then wanders back to the bar. A slow, mean blues begins to play, full of a rasping trumpet*]

BUS: Did ya ever feel . . . like ya had to destroy something . . . in order to live?
HOWIE: No . . . no. I can't say that I ever felt that way, exactly.
BUS: I do. Maybe it's just a part of growin' up.

[*Now* JACKIE *wanders back into the Fiesta Room. There is a shyness, a hesitancy about her.* HOWIE *is the first to see her*]

HOWIE: You leave something behind, Jackie?

[*Now* BUS *turns around immediately to see her*]

BUS: Jackie!
JACKIE: Bus . . .

[*He hurries to her side, in the doorway*]

BUS: You makin' a return engagement?
JACKIE: Bus . . . I'll go with you.
BUS: You will?
JACKIE: Sure. I'll go.
BUS: Look, Jackie, maybe we better not.
JACKIE: I want to, Bus. I do.
BUS: How about all this love talk?

JACKIE: I won't say those things any more. I promise.

BUS: They just don't go any more, Jackie. They just don't go.

JACKIE: [*With a little laugh of deprecation*] I know . . .

BUS: Love, to me, is something they put you in jail for.

JACKIE: A doctor at the hospital told me . . . I was too sentimental about things.

BUS: I'm in this business now strictly for kicks, Doll.

JACKIE: I'll be . . . just an ordinary girl . . . you happen to pick up . . . and we'll throw a ball.

BUS: That's it, Doll. [*He grabs her to him hungrily and presses a sensual kiss against her lips. The music from the juke box makes mocking accompaniment. Then he throws a bill on the counter for* HOWIE] So long, Dad!

[BUS *wraps* JACKIE *in his arms and they hurry out together.* HOWIE *watches them, drying glasses*]

CURTAIN

THE DARK LADY OF THE SONNETS

Bernard Shaw

Bernard Shaw

Since there are enough volumes readily available to stock an ample library on the life and accomplishments of George Bernard Shaw (1856–1950), there seems little necessity to once again zero in on this fabled master of English drama and prose. Instead, we'll concentrate on the play at hand, *The Dark Lady of the Sonnets*.

The genesis of the play, which the author described as "An Interlude," has historical significance. According to one of Shaw's biographers, Archibald Henderson: "It was resolved (at a meeting of eminent and public-minded citizens) that the tercentenary of Shakespeare's death in 1916 should be the occasion for removing the reproach against Great Britain that it contained no adequate memorial of him. . . . Shaw almost from the beginning had been an active member of the General Committee of the Shakespeare Memorial National Theatre organization, and, later on, a member of the Executive Committee. Some favored a statue, others a 'Shakespeare Temple' or national theatre museum. Many leading figures in the arts and public life felt that the only appropriate memorial to Shakespeare would be a National Theatre."

At the time, Shaw expressed himself: "I want a National Theatre to do not only with Shakespear, but with everything that has proved itself worthy of survival in British drama."

Fund-raising schemes were formulated and one of these was to be a special charity matinee at the Haymarket Theatre in London. At the behest of Dame Edith Lyttelton (it was she who suggested a scene of jealousy between Queen Elizabeth I and the Dark Lady at the expense of the unfortunate Bard), Shaw put pen to paper and created *The Dark Lady of the Sonnets* and it was first performed on the afternoon of November 24, 1910.

The broad aims and purposes of the fund to be raised for such a theatre were set forth in the printed program of *The Dark Lady of the Sonnets:*

> This fund has been established to commemorate the Ter-centenary of Shakespeare's death by the erection and en-dowment of a Memorial Theatre to be used for the pur-poses of Drama in the best and widest sense of the term, so that we may have in England something corresponding to the great National Theatres on the Continent for the honor of Shakespeare's name and for the advance of that Art which his genius has glorified.

Objects of the Theatre

1. To keep the Plays of Shakespeare in its repertory.
2. To revive whatever is vital in English classical drama.
3. To prevent recent plays of great merit from falling into the oblivion to which the present theatrical system is apt to consign them.
4. To produce new plays and to further the development of the modern drama.
5. To produce translations of representative works of for-eign drama, ancient and modern.
6. To stimulate the art of acting through the various oppor-tunities which it will offer to the members of its com-pany.

When *The Dark Lady of the Sonnets* was broadcast on April 22, 1938, to commemorate the Bard's birthday, Shaw wrote and broad-cast himself a new prologue for the occasion. He said: "This play which you are going to hear is all about Shakespear [Note: He used that spelling throughout the play] and Queen Elizabeth; but it is re-ally only an appeal for the Shakespear Memorial National Theatre which we have been trying to make the English nation establish for thirty years past. Dame Edith Lyttelton invented the play in 1910; I wrote the dialogue; and we had a grand performance at the Haymar-ket Theatre with Mr. Granville-Barker in the part of Shakespear. But I am not going to talk to you about the National Theatre. Shake-spear does this so eloquently in the play, and Queen Elizabeth is so up-to-date with her reply to him, that if I anticipate them I shall spoil their speeches for you.

"And now, as there is nothing about either Will or Elizabeth in the title of the play, you may be wondering who on earth the dark lady was. Well, nobody knows; but there *was* a dark lady all the same. . . . In the play I have assumed that the dark lady was a maid of honor at Elizabeth's court. A friend of mine, the late Thomas Tyler, discovered that one of Elizabeth's maids of honor named Mary Fitton got into scrapes at court by her gallantries. Well, I had to get the dark lady in Whitehall Palace somehow; so let us pretend that she was Mary Fitton."

According to Shaw: "The appeal for a National Theatre with which the play concludes, and for the sake of which it was written, elicited applause but no subscriptions."

Some fifty-three years after *The Dark Lady of the Sonnets* had its première, the National Theatre finally became a reality with its 1963 inaugural production of *Hamlet*. Under the directorship of Lord (Laurence) Olivier and later, Peter Hall, the company held forth in its temporary quarters at the historic Old Vic, until 1976 when it moved into its own vast complex on the South Bank of the Thames.

In *The Dark Lady of the Sonnets*, Shakespeare begs Queen Elizabeth I to endow a national theatre for him and asks her to remember the theatre in her prayers, and she replies: "That is my prayer to posterity." It is therefore ironic and fitting that Britain's famed National Theatre was established and dedicated during the second Elizabethan Age.

Characters:

The Warder
William Shakespear
Queen Elizabeth
The Dark Lady

Fin de siècle 15–1600. *Midsummer night on the terrace of the Palace at Whitehall, overlooking the Thames. The Palace clock chimes four quarters and strikes eleven.*

A BEEFEATER *on guard. A* CLOAKED MAN *approaches.*

THE BEEFEATER: Stand. Who goes there? Give the word.

THE MAN: Marry! I cannot. I have clean forgotten it.

THE BEEFEATER: Then you cannot pass here. What is your business? Who are you? Are you a true man?

THE MAN: Far from it, Master Warder. I am not the same man two days together: sometimes Adam, sometimes Benvolio, and anon the Ghost.

THE BEEFEATER: [*Recoiling*] A ghost! Angels and ministers of grace defend us!

THE MAN: Well said, Master Warder. With your leave I will set that down in writing; for I have a very poor and unhappy brain for remembrance. [*He takes out his tablets and writes*] Methinks this is a good scene, with you on your lonely watch, and I approaching like a ghost in the moonlight. Stare not so amazedly at me; but mark what I say. I keep tryst here tonight with a dark lady. She promised to bribe the warder. I gave her the wherewithal: four tickets for the Globe Theatre.

THE BEEFEATER: Plague on her! She gave me two only.

THE MAN: [*Detaching a tablet*] My friend: present this tablet, and you will be welcomed at any time when the plays of Will Shakespear are in hand. Bring your wife. Bring your friends. Bring the whole garrison. There is ever plenty of room.

THE BEEFEATER: I care not for these new-fangled plays. No man can understand a word of them. They are all talk. Will you not give me a pass for The Spanish Tragedy?

THE MAN: To see The Spanish Tragedy one pays, my friend. Here are the means. [*He gives him a piece of gold*]

THE BEEFEATER: [*Overwhelmed*] Gold! Oh, sir, you are a better pay-master than your dark lady.

THE MAN: Women are thrifty, my friend.

THE BEEFEATER: Tis so, sir. And you have to consider that the most open handed of us must een cheapen that which we buy every day. This lady has to make a present to a warder nigh every night of her life.

THE MAN: [*Turning pale*] I'll not believe it.

THE BEEFEATER: Now you, sir, I dare be sworn, do not have an adventure like this twice in the year.

THE MAN: Villain: wouldst tell me that my dark lady hath ever done thus before? that she maketh occasions to meet other men?

THE BEEFEATER: Now the Lord bless your innocence, sir, do you think you are the only pretty man in the world? A merry lady, sir: a warm bit of stuff. Go to: I'll not see her pass a deceit on a gentleman that hath given me the first piece of gold I ever handled.

THE MAN: Master Warder: is it not a strange thing that we, knowing that all women are false, should be amazed to find our own particular drab no better than the rest?

THE BEEFEATER: Not all, sir. Decent bodies, many of them.

THE MAN: [*Intolerantly*] No. All false. All. If thou deny it, thou liest.

THE BEEFEATER: You judge too much by the Court, sir. There, indeed, you may say of frailty that its name is woman.

THE MAN: [*Pulling out his tablets again*] Prithee say that again: that about frailty: the strain of music.

THE BEEFEATER: What strain of music, sir? I'm no musician, God knows.

THE MAN: There is music in your soul: many of your degree have it very notably. [*Writing*] 'Frailty: thy name is woman!' [*Repeating it affectionately*] 'Thy name is woman.'

THE BEEFEATER: Well, sir, it is but four words. Are you a snapper-up of such unconsidered trifles?

THE MAN: [*Eagerly*] Snapper-up of—[*He gasps*] Oh! Immortal phrase! [*He writes it down*] This man is a greater than I.

THE BEEFEATER: You have my Lord Pembroke's trick, sir.

THE MAN: Like enough: he is my near friend. But what call you his trick?

THE BEEFEATER: Making sonnets by moonlight. And to the same lady, too.

THE MAN: No!

THE BEEFEATER: Last night he stood here on your errand, and in your shoes.

THE MAN: Thou, too, Brutus! And I called him friend!

THE BEEFEATER: Tis ever so, sir.

THE MAN: Tis ever so. Twas ever so. [He turns away, overcome] Two Gentlemen of Verona! Judas! Judas!!

THE BEEFEATER: Is he so bad as that, sir?

THE MAN: [Recovering his charity and self-possession] Bad? O no. Human, Master Warder, human. We call one another names when we are offended, as children do. That is all.

THE BEEFEATER: Ay, sir: words, words, words. Mere wind, sir. We fill our bellies with the east wind, sir, as the Scripture hath it. You cannot feed capons so.

THE MAN: A good cadence. By your leave. [He makes a note of it]

THE BEEFEATER: What manner of thing is a cadence, sir? I have not heard of it.

THE MAN: A thing to rule the world with, friend.

THE BEEFEATER: You speak strangely, sir: no offence. But, an't like you, you are a very civil gentleman; and a poor man feels drawn to you, you being, as twere, willing to share your thought with him.

THE MAN: Tis my trade. But alas! the world for the most part will none of my thoughts.

[Lamplight streams from the palace door as it opens from within]

THE BEEFEATER: Here comes your lady, sir. I'll to t'other end of my ward. You may een take your time about your business: I shall not return too suddenly unless my sergeant comes prowling round. Tis a fell sergeant, sir: strict in his arrest. Good een, sir; and good luck! [He goes]

THE MAN: 'Strict in his arrest'! 'Fell sergeant'! [*As if tasting a ripe plum*] O-o-o-h! [*He makes a note of them*]

[A CLOAKED LADY *gropes her way from the palace and wanders along the terrace, walking in her sleep*]

THE LADY: [*Rubbing her hands as if washing them*] Out, damned spot. You will mar all with these cosmetics. God made you one face; and you make yourself another. Think of your grave, woman, not ever of being beautified. All the perfumes of Arabia will not whiten this Tudor hand.

THE MAN: 'All the perfumes of Arabia'! 'Beautified'! 'Beautified'! a poem in a single word. Can this be my Mary? [*To* THE LADY] Why do you speak in a strange voice and utter poetry for the first time? Are you ailing? You walk like the dead. Mary! Mary!

THE LADY: [*Echoing him*] Mary! Mary! Who would have thought that woman to have had so much blood in her! Is it my fault that my counsellors put deeds of blood on me? Fie! If you were women you would have more wit than to stain the floor so foully. Hold not up her head so: the hair is false. I tell you yet again, Mary's buried: she cannot come out of her grave. I fear her not: these cats that dare jump into thrones though they be fit only for men's laps must be put away. Whats done cannot be undone. Out, I say. Fie! a queen, and freckled!

THE MAN: [*Shaking her arm*] Mary, I say: art asleep?

[THE LADY *wakes; starts; and nearly faints. He catches her on his arm.*

THE LADY: Where am I? What art thou?

THE MAN: I cry your mercy. I have mistook your person all this while. Methought you were my Mary: my mistress.

THE LADY: [*Outraged*] Profane fellow: how do you dare?

THE MAN: Be not wroth with me, lady. My mistress is a marvellous proper woman. But she does not speak so well as you. 'All the perfumes of Arabia'! That was well said: spoken with good accent and excellent discretion.

THE LADY: Have I been in speech with you here?

THE MAN: Why, yes, fair lady. Have you forgot it?

THE LADY: I have walked in my sleep.

THE MAN: Walk ever in your sleep, fair one; for then your words drop like honey.

THE LADY: [*With cold majesty*] Know you to whom you speak, sir, that you dare express yourself so saucily?

THE MAN: [*Unabashed*] Not I, nor care neither. You are some lady of the Court, belike. To me there are but two sorts of women: those with excellent voices, sweet and low, and cackling hens that cannot make me dream. Your voice has all manner of loveliness in it. Grudge me not a short hour of its music.

THE LADY: Sir: you are overbold. Season your admiration for a while with—

THE MAN: [*Holding up his hand to stop her*] 'Season your admiration for a while—'

THE LADY: Fellow: do you dare mimic me to my face?

THE MAN: Tis music. Can you not hear? When a good musician sings a song, do you not sing it and sing it again till you have caught and fixed its perfect melody? 'Season your admiration for a while': God! the history of man's heart is in that one word admiration. Admiration! [*Taking up his tablets*] What was it? 'Suspend your admiration for a space—'

THE LADY: A very vile jingle of esses. I said 'Season your—

THE MAN: [*Hastily*] Season: ay, season, season, season. Plague on my memory, my wretched memory! I must een write it down. [*He begins to write, but stops, his memory failing him*] Yet tell me which was the vile jingle? You said very justly: mine own ear caught it even as my false tongue said it.

THE LADY: You said 'for a space.' I said 'for a while.'

THE MAN: 'For a while' [*He corrects it*] Good! [*Ardently*] And now be mine neither for a space nor a while, but for ever.

THE LADY: Odds my life! Are you by chance making love to me, knave?

THE MAN: Nay: tis you who have made the love: I but pour it out at your feet. I cannot but love a lass that sets such store by an apt word. Therefore vouchsafe, divine perfection of a woman—no: I have said that before somewhere; and the wordy garment of my love for you must be fire-new—

THE LADY: You talk too much, sir. Let me warn you: I am more accustomed to be listened to than preached at.

THE MAN: The most are like that that do talk well. But though you spake with the tongues of angels, as indeed you do, yet know that I am the king of words—

THE LADY: A king, ha!

THE MAN: No less. We are poor things, we men and women—

THE LADY: Dare you call me woman?

THE MAN: What nobler name can I tender you? How else can I love you? Yet you may well shrink from the name: have I not said we are but poor things? Yet there is a power that can redeem us.

THE LADY: Gramercy for your sermon, sir. I hope I know my duty.

THE MAN: This is no sermon, but the living truth. The power I speak of is the power of immortal poesy. For know that vile as this world is, and worms as we are, you have but to invest all this vileness with a magical garment of words to transfigure us and uplift our souls til earth flowers into a million heavens.

THE LADY: You spoil your heaven with your million. You are extravagant. Observe some measure in your speech.

THE MAN: You speak now as Ben does.

THE LADY: And who, pray, is Ben?

THE MAN: A learned bricklayer who thinks that the sky is at the top of his ladder, and so takes it on him to rebuke me for flying. I tell you there is no word yet coined and no melody yet sung that is extravagant and majestical enough for the glory that lovely words can reveal. It is heresy to deny it: have you not been taught that in the beginning was the Word? that the Word was with God? nay, that the Word was God?

THE LADY: Beware, fellow, how you presume to speak of holy things. The Queen is the head of the Church.

THE MAN: You are the head of my Church when you speak as you did at first. 'All the perfumes of Arabia'! Can the Queen speak thus? They say she playeth well upon the virginals. Let her play so to me; and I'll kiss her hands. But until then, you are my Queen;

and I'll kiss those lips that have dropt music on my heart. [*He puts his arms about her*]

THE LADY: Unmeasured impudence! On your life, take your hands from me.

[THE DARK LADY *comes stooping along the terrace behind them like a running thrush. When she sees how they are employed, she rises angrily to her full height, and listens jealously*]

THE MAN: [*Unaware of* THE DARK LADY] Then cease to make my hands tremble with the streams of life you pour through them. You hold me as the lodestar holds the iron: I cannot but cling to you. We are lost, you and I: nothing can separate us now.

THE DARK LADY: We shall see that, false lying hound, you and your filthy trull. [*With two vigorous cuffs, she knocks the pair asunder, sending the man, who is unlucky enough to receive a righthanded blow, sprawling on the flags*] Take that, both of you!

THE CLOAKED LADY: [*In towering wrath, throwing off her cloak and turning in outraged majesty on her assailant*] High treason!

THE DARK LADY: [*Recognizing her and falling on her knees in abject terror*] Will: I am lost: I have struck the Queen.

THE MAN: [*Sitting up as majestically as his ignominious posture allows*] Woman: you have struck WILLIAM SHAKESPEAR!!!!!!

QUEEN ELIZABETH: [*Stupent*] Marry, come up!!! Struck William Shakespear quotha! And who in the name of all the sluts and jades and light-o'-loves and fly-by-nights that infest this palace of mine, may William Shakespear be?

THE DARK LADY: Madam: he is but a player. Oh, I could have my hand cut off—

QUEEN ELIZABETH: Belike you will, mistress. Have you bethought you that I am like to have your head cut off as well?

THE DARK LADY: Will: save me. Oh, save me.

ELIZABETH: Save you! A likely savior, on my royal word! I had thought this fellow at least an esquire; for I had hoped that even the vilest of my ladies would not have dishonored my Court by wantoning with a baseborn servant.

SHAKESPEAR: [*Indignantly scrambling to his feet*] Baseborn! I, a

Shakespear of Stratford! I, whose mother was an Arden! baseborn! You forget yourself, madam.

ELIZABETH: [*Furious*] S'blood! do I so? I will teach you—

THE DARK LADY: [*Rising from her knees and throwing herself between them*] Will: in God's name anger her no further. It is death. Madam: do not listen to him.

SHAKESPEAR: Not were it een to save your life, Mary, not to mention mine own, will I flatter a monarch who forgets what is due to my family. I deny not that my father was brought down to be a poor bankrupt; but twas his gentle blood that was ever too generous for trade. Never did he disown his debts. Tis true he paid them not; but it is an attested truth that he gave bills for them; and twas those bills, in the hands of base hucksters, that were his undoing.

ELIZABETH: [*Grimly*] The son of your father shall learn his place in the presence of the daughter of Harry the Eighth.

SHAKESPEAR: [*Swelling with intolerant importance*] Name not that inordinate man in the same breath with Stratford's worthiest alderman. John Shakespear wedded but once: Harry Tudor was married six times. You should blush to utter his name.

THE DARK LADY:) [*Crying out* (Will: for pity's sake—
ELIZABETH:)   *together*] (Insolent dog—

SHAKESPEAR: [*Cutting them short*] How know you that King Harry was indeed your father?

ELIZABETH: ⎧ Zounds! Now by—[*She stops to grind her teeth with rage*]
THE DARK LADY: ⎨ She will have me whipped through the streets. Oh, God! Oh, God!

SHAKESPEAR: Learn to know yourself better, madam. I am an honest gentleman of unquestioned parentage, and have already sent in my demand for the coat-of-arms that is lawfully mine. Can you say as much for yourself?

ELIZABETH: [*Almost beside herself*] Another word; and I begin with mine own hands the work the hangman shall finish.

SHAKESPEAR: You are no true Tudor: this baggage here has as good a right to your royal seat as you. What maintains you on the throne of England? Is it your renownéd wit? your wisdom that sets at nought the craftiest statesmen of the Christian world? No. Tis the mere chance that might have happened to any milkmaid, the caprice of Nature that made you the most wondrous piece of beauty the age hath seen. [ELIZABETH's *raised fists, on the point of striking him, fall to her side*] That is what hath brought all men to your feet, and founded your throne on the impregnable rock of your proud heart, a stony island in a sea of desire. There, madam, is some wholesome blunt honest speaking for you. Now do your worst.

ELIZABETH: [*With dignity*] Master Shakespear: it is well for you that I am a merciful prince. I make allowance for your rustic ignorance. But remember that there are things which be true, and are yet not seemly to be said (I will not say to a queen; for you will have it that I am none) but to a virgin.

SHAKESPEAR: [*Bluntly*] It is no fault of mine that you are a virgin, madam, albeit tis my misfortune.

THE DARK LADY: [*Terrified again*] In mercy, madam, hold no further discourse with him. He hath ever some lewd jest on his tongue. You hear how he useth me! calling me baggage and the like to your Majesty's face.

ELIZABETH: As for you, mistress, I have yet to demand what your business is at this hour in this place, and how you come to be so concerned with a player that you strike blindly at your sovereign in your jealousy of him.

THE DARK LADY: Madam: as I live and hope for salvation—

SHAKESPEAR: [*Sardonically*] Ha!

THE DARK LADY: [*Angrily*] —ay, I'm as like to be saved as thou that believest naught save some black magic of words and verses—I say, madam, as I am a living woman I came here to break with him for ever. Oh, madam, if you would know what misery is, listen to this man that is more than man and less at the same time. He will tie you down to anatomize your very soul: he will wring tears of blood from your humiliation; and then he will heal the wound with flatteries that no woman can resist.

SHAKESPEAR: Flatteries! [*Kneeling*] Oh, madam, I put my case at your royal feet. I confess to much. I have a rude tongue: I am unmannerly: I blaspheme against the holiness of anointed royalty; but oh, my royal mistress, AM I a flatterer?

ELIZABETH: I absolve you as to that. You are far too plain a dealer to please me. [*He rises gratefully*]

THE DARK LADY: Madam: he is flattering you even as he speaks.

ELIZABETH: [*A terrible flash in her eye*] Ha! Is it so?

SHAKESPEAR: Madam: she is jealous; and, heaven help me! not without reason. Oh, you say you are a merciful prince; but that was cruel of you, that hiding of your royal dignity when you found me here. For how can I ever be content with this black-haired, black-eyed, black-avised devil again now that I have looked upon real beauty and real majesty?

THE DARK LADY: [*Wounded and desperate*] He hath swore to me ten times over that the day shall come in England when black women, for all their foulness, shall be more thought on than fair ones. [*To* SHAKESPEAR, *scolding at him*] Deny it if thou canst. Oh, he is compact of lies and scorns. I am tired of being tossed up to heaven and dragged down to hell at every whim that takes him. I am ashamed to my very soul that I have abased myself to love one that my father would not have deemed fit to hold my stirrup—one that will talk to all the world about me—that will put my love and my shame into his plays and make me blush for myself there— that will write sonnets about me that no man of gentle strain would put his hand to. I am all disordered: I know not what I am saying to your Majesty: I am of all ladies most deject and wretched—

SHAKESPEAR: Ha! At last sorrow hath struck a note of music out of thee. 'Of all ladies most deject and wretched.' [*He makes a note of it*]

THE DARK LADY: Madam: I implore you give me leave to go. I am distracted with grief and shame. I—

ELIZABETH: Go. [THE DARK LADY *tries to kiss her hand*] No more. Go. [THE DARK LADY *goes, convulsed*] You have been cruel to that poor fond wretch, Master Shakespear.

SHAKESPEAR: I am not cruel, madam; but you know the fable of Jupiter and Semele. I could not help my lightnings scorching her.

ELIZABETH: You have an overweening conceit of yourself, sir, that displeases your Queen.

SHAKESPEAR: Oh, madam, can I go about with the modest cough of a minor poet, belittling my inspiration and making the mightiest wonder of your reign a thing of nought? I have said that 'not marble nor the gilded monuments of princes shall outlive' the words with which I make the world glorious or foolish at my will. Besides, I would have you think me great enough to grant me a boon.

ELIZABETH: I hope it is a boon that may be asked of a virgin Queen without offence, sir. I mistrust your forwardness; and I bid you remember that I do not suffer persons of your degree (if I may say so without offence to your father the alderman) to presume too far.

SHAKESPEAR: Oh, madam, I shall not forget myself again; though by my life, could I make you a serving wench, neither a queen nor a virgin should you be for so much longer as a flash of lightning might take to cross the river to the Bankside. But since you are a queen and will none of me, nor of Philip of Spain, nor of any other mortal man, I must een contain myself as best I may, and ask you only for a boon of State.

ELIZABETH: A boon of State already! You are becoming a courtier like the rest of them. You lack advancement.

SHAKESPEAR: 'Lack advancement.' By your Majesty's leave: a queenly phrase. [He is about to write it down]

ELIZABETH: [Striking the tablets from his hand] Your tables being to anger me, sir. I am not here to write your plays for you.

SHAKESPEAR: You are here to inspire them, madam. For this, among the rest, were you ordained. But the boon I crave is that you do endow a great playhouse, or, if I may make bold to coin a scholarly name for it, a National Theatre, for the better instruction and gracing of your Majesty's subjects.

ELIZABETH: Why, sir, are there not theatres enow on the Bankside and in Blackfriars?

SHAKESPEAR: Madam: these are the adventures of needy and desperate men that must, to save themselves from perishing of want, give the sillier sort of people what they best like; and what they best like, God knows, is not their own betterment and instruction, as we well see by the example of the churches, which must needs compel men to frequent them, though they be open to all without charge. Only when there is a matter of a murder, or a plot, or a pretty youth in petticoats, or some naughty tale of wantonness, will your subjects pay the great cost of good players and their finery, with a little profit to boot. To prove this I will tell you that I have written two noble and excellent plays setting forth the advancement of women of high nature and fruitful industry even as your Majesty is: the one a skilful physician, the other a sister devoted to good works. I have also stole from a book of idle wanton tales two of the most damnable foolishnesses in the world, in the one of which a woman goeth in man's attire and maketh impudent love to her swain, who pleaseth the groundlings by overthrowing a wrestler; whilst, in the other, one of the same kidney sheweth her wit by saying endless naughtinesses to a gentleman as lewd as herself. I have writ these to save my friends from penury, yet shewing my scorn for such follies and for them that praise them by calling the one As You Like It, meaning that it is not as I like it, and the other Much Ado About Nothing, as it truly is. And now these two filthy pieces drive their nobler fellows from the stage, where indeed I cannot have my lady physician presented at all, she being too honest a woman for the taste of the town. Wherefore I humbly beg your Majesty to give order that a theatre be endowed out of the public revenue for the playing of those pieces of mine which no merchant will touch, seeing that his gain is so much greater with the worse than with the better. Thereby you shall also encourage other men to undertake the writing of plays who do now despise it and leave it wholly to those whose counsels will work little good to your realm. For this writing of plays is a great matter, forming as it does the minds and affections of men in such sort that whatsoever they see done in show on the stage, they will presently be doing in earnest in the world, which is but a larger stage. Of late, as you know, the Church taught the people by means of plays; but the people flocked only to such as were full of superstitious miracles and bloody martyrdoms; and so the Church, which also was just then brought into straits by the policy of your royal father, did abandon and discountenance the art of playing; and thus it fell into the hands of poor players and greedy merchants that had their pockets to look to and not the greatness of this your kingdom. Therefore now must your Majesty take up that good work that your Church hath abandoned, and restore the art of playing to its former use and dignity.

ELIZABETH: Master Shakespear: I will speak of this matter to the Lord Treasurer.

SHAKESPEAR: Then am I undone, madam; for there was never yet a Lord Treasurer that could find a penny for anything over and above the necessary expenses of your government, save for a war or a salary for his own nephew.

ELIZABETH: Master Shakespear: you speak sooth; yet cannot I in any wise mend it. I dare not offend my unruly Puritans by making so lewd a place as the playhouse a public charge; and there be a thousand things to be done in this London of mine before your poetry can have its penny from the general purse. I tell thee, Master Will, it will be three hundred years and more before my subjects learn that man cannot live by bread alone, but by every word that cometh from the mouth of those whom God inspires. By that time you and I will be dust beneath the feet of the horses, if indeed there be any horses then, and men be still riding instead of flying. Now it may be that by then your works will be dust also.

SHAKESPEAR: They will stand, madam: fear not for that.

ELIZABETH: It may prove so. But of this I am certain (for I know my countrymen) that until every other country in the Christian world, even to barbarian Muscovy and the hamlets of the boorish Germans, have its playhouse at the public charge, England will never adventure. And she will adventure then only because it is her desire to be ever in the fashion, and to do humbly and dutifully whatso she seeth everybody else doing. In the meantime you must content yourself as best you can by the playing of those two pieces which you give out as the most damnable ever writ, but which your countrymen, I warn you, will swear are the best you have ever done. But this I will say, that if I could speak across the ages to our descendants, I should heartily recommend them to fulfil your wish; for the Scottish minstrel hath well said that he that maketh the songs of a nation is mightier than he that maketh its laws; and the same may well be true of plays and interludes. [*The clock chimes the first quarter.* THE WARDER *returns on his round*] And now, sir, we are upon the hour when it better beseems a virgin queen to be abed than to converse alone with the naughtiest of her subjects. Ho there! Who keeps ward on the queen's lodgings tonight?

THE WARDER: I do, an't please your majesty.

ELIZABETH: See that you keep it better in future. You have let pass a most dangerous gallant even to the very door of our royal chamber. Lead him forth; and bring me word when he is safely locked out; for I shall scarce dare disrobe until the palace gates are between us.

SHAKESPEAR: [*Kissing her hand*] My body goes through the gate into the darkness, madam; but my thoughts follow you.

ELIZABETH: How! to my bed!

SHAKESPEAR: No, madam, to your prayers, in which I beg you to remember my theatre.

ELIZABETH: That is my prayer to posterity. Forget not your own to God; and so goodnight, Master Will.

SHAKESPEAR: Goodnight, great Elizabeth. God save the Queen!

ELIZABETH: Amen.

[*Exeunt severally: she to her chamber: he, in custody of* THE WARDER, *to the gate nearest Blackfriars*]

HAPPY ENDING

Douglas Turner Ward

Douglas Turner Ward

A man of multiple theatrical talents, Douglas Turner Ward was born on a plantation in Burnside, Louisiana, on May 5, 1930. He was educated at Wilberforce University and the University of Michigan. After a spell as a journalist, he turned to acting and first appeared on the New York stage in 1957 in the Circle-in-the-Square revival of Eugene O'Neill's *The Iceman Cometh*. Subsequently, he performed in a succession of plays including: *A Raisin in the Sun*; *Lost in the Stars*; *The Blacks*; *One Flew over the Cuckoo's Nest*; *The Blood Knot*; and *Coriolanus*.

As a dramatist, he made his professional debut at the Off-Broadway St. Marks Playhouse on November 15, 1965, with two short plays, *Happy Ending* (performed by an exceptional cast: Esther Rolle, Frances Foster, Robert Hooks, and Mr. Ward) and *Day of Absence*. The double bill ran for 504 performances and won for Mr. Ward both a Drama Desk-Vernon Rice Award and an Obie Award for outstanding Off-Broadway achievement.

In March 1970 *Day of Absence* was presented once again at the St. Marks Playhouse, this time with a new companion piece, *Brotherhood*, also written by Mr. Ward. The production was presented by the newly established Negro Ensemble Company, which was cofounded by Robert Hooks, Gerald S. Krone, and Mr. Ward, who continues to serve as its artistic director. The Negro Ensemble Company is one of the cornerstones of the flourishing black theatre movement and it stresses "relevant plays and players for tomorrow's black cultural welfare." Since its first production in 1968, the organization has emerged as a vital force in contemporary American theatre and has toured extensively both in the United States and in Europe.

In 1969 Douglas Turner Ward appeared in a prominent role in

Ceremonies in Dark Old Men, by Lonne Elder III, and in 1972 he directed and appeared in Joseph A. Walker's Tony Award drama, *The River Niger.* Two years later, he directed and acted in another notable Negro Ensemble Company production, *The First Breeze of Summer,* by Leslie Lee.

According to a recent newspaper account, the author has just completed his first play in seven years. It's part of a Haitian trilogy and it concludes with the rise of Toussaint, the eighteenth-century Haitian military and political leader.

Characters:

Ellie
Vi
Junie
Arthur

TIME: *The present, an early weekday evening around five or six* P.M.

PLACE: *The spotless kitchen of a Harlem tenement apartment. At stage left is a closed door providing entry to the outside hallway. On the opposite side of the stage is another door leading into the interior of the railroad flat. Sandwiched between this door and a window facing the brick walls of the apartment's inner shaft is a giant, dazzling white refrigerator. Positioned center stage is a gleaming, porcelain-topped oval table. Directly behind is a modern stove-range. To the left of the stove, another window looks out upon a backyard court. The window is flanked on its left by a kitchen sink. Adjacent to the refrigerator, upstage right, a bathroom door completes the setting.*

As the curtain rises, waning rays of daylight can be seen streaming through the courtyard window. Two handsome women, both in their late thirties or early forties, are sitting at opposite ends of the kitchen table. They are dressed as if recently entered from work. Hats and coats are still worn, handbags lie on floor propped against legs of respective chairs. They remain in dejected poses, weeping noiselessly.

ELLIE: Let me have your handkerchief, Vi . . .

[VI *hands it to her absently.* ELLIE *daubs eyes, then rests hankie on table. It lies there until* VI *motions for it to be handed back*]

VI: What we go'n' do, Ellie?

ELLIE: Don' know . . . Don't seem like there's much more we kin do . . .

VI: This time it really might happen . . .

ELLIE: I know . . .

VI: Persons kin go but just so far . . .

ELLIE: Lord, this may be the limit . . .

VI: End of the line . . .

ELLIE: Hear us, Savior!

VI: . . . Think it might help if I prayed a novena to him first thing tomorrow morning?

ELLIE: . . . Certainly couldn't do no harm . . .

[*They lapse into silence once again, passing hankie back and forth on request. Suddenly,* JUNIE, *a tall, slender, sharply handsome, tastefully dressed youth in his early twenties, bursts upon the scene, rushing through hallway door*]

JUNIE: [*Rapidly crossing, shedding coat in transit*] Hey, Vi, Ellie . . . [*Exits through interior door, talking offstage*] Ellie, do I have any more pleated shirts clean . . . ? Gotta make fast impression on new chick tonight . . . [*Thrusting head back into view*] One of them foxy, black "Four-Hundred" debutantes, you dig! All class and manners, but nothing underneath but a luscious, V-8 chassis! —Which is A-O-reeet wit' me since that's all I'm after. You hear me talking to ya! Now, tell me what I say! Hah, hah, hah! [*Withdraws head back offstage*] . . . Sure got them petty tyrants straight at the unemployment office today. [*Dripping contempt*] Wanted me to snatchup one of them jive jobs they try to palm off on ya. I told 'em no, thanks!—SHOVE IT! [*Reentering, busily buttoning elegantly pleated shirt*] If they can't find me something in my field, up to my standards, forgit it! . . . Damn, act like they paying you money out their own pockets . . . Whatcha got to eat, Ellie? . . . I'm scarfy as a bear. In fact—with little salt 'n' pepper, I could devour one of you—or both between a double-decker! [*Descends upon them to illustrate playfully. Pulls up short on noticing their tears for the first time*] Hey? . . . What'sa matter . . . ? What's up? [*They fail to respond*] Is it the kids? [*They shake heads negatively*] Somebody sick down home? [*Fearfully*] Nothing's wrong wit' mother?!!! [*They shake heads again*] Roy or Jim in jail? . . . Arthur or Ben lose their jobs? [*Another double headshake*] Tell me, I wanta know! Everything was fine this morning. Som'um musta happened since. Come on, what is it?!

ELLIE: Should we tell him, Vi?

VI: I don't know . . . No use gitting him worried and upset . . .

ELLIE: [*Sighing heavily*] Maybe we better. He's got to find out sooner or later.

JUNIE: What are you crying for?

ELLIE: . . . Our bosses—Mr. and Mrs. Harrison, Junie . . .

JUNIE: ???Mr. and Mrs. Harrison . . . ? [*Suddenly relieved, amused and sardonic*] What happened? They escaped from a car wreck—UNHURT?

ELLIE: [*Failing to grasp sarcasm*] No.

JUNIE: [*Returning to shirt-buttoning*] Did you just git disappointing news flashes they go'n' live forever?

VI: [*Also misreading*] No, Junie.

JUNIE: Well, what then? . . . I don't get it.

ELLIE: They's getting a divorce . . .

JUNIE: ???A what—?

VI: A divorce.

JUNIE: ???Why?

ELLIE: 'Cause Mr. Harrison caught her wit' a man.

JUNIE: Well, it's not the first time 'cording to you.

ELLIE: The other times wasn't wit' his best friend.

JUNIE: His best friend?! WHEEE! Boy, she really did it up this time . . . Her previous excursions were restricted to his casual acquaintances! . . . But why the hell should he be so upset? He's put up wit' all the rest. This only means she's gitting closer to home. Maybe next time it'll be him, ha, ha, ha . . .

ELLIE: [*Reprimandingly*] It's no joke, Junie.

JUNIE: [*Exiting into bathroom*] How'd it happen?

ELLIE: [*Flaring at the memory*] Just walked in and caught 'em in his own bedroom!

VI: [*Even more outraged*] Was that dirty dog, Mr. Heller, lives on the 19th floor of the same building!

ELLIE: [*Anger mounting*] I warned her to be careful when she first started messing with him. I told her Mr. Harrison was really gon' kick her out if he found out, but she'd have the snake sneak in sometimes soon as Mr. Harrison left! Even had nerve to invite him to chaperone his wife back later in the evening for a li'l' after-dinner snack!

JUNIE: [*Reentering, merrily*] What's a little exchange of pleasantries among rich friends, bosom buddies? Now, all Harrison has to do is return the favor and even things up.

VI: She really cooked her goose this time.

JUNIE: Good for her.

ELLIE: Good . . . ?

JUNIE: Sure—what'd she 'spect? To wait till she hauled some cat into bed right next to her old man befo' he got the message?

VI: They is gitting a *divorce*, Junie!

JUNIE: [*Sauntering over to fruit bowl atop refrigerator*] That's all? . . . I'm surprised I didn't read headlines 'bout a double murder and one suicide . . . But I forgot!—that's our colored folk's method of clearing up little gummy problems like that— that is, MINUS the suicide bit.

ELLIE: *They's breaking up their home, Junie!*

JUNIE: [*Biting into apple selected from bowl*] They'll learn to live wit' it . . . Might even git to like the idea.

VI: And the chillun?

JUNIE: Delicate li'l' boobies will receive nice fat allowances to ease the pain until they grow up to take over the world.

ELLIE: ???Is that all you feel at a time like this, boy?

VI: Disastrous, that's what it is!

ELLIE: Tragicall 'n' unfair!

JUNIE: Is this what you boohooing 'bout?!!!

ELLIE: Could you think of anything worser?

JUNIE: But, why?! [*Exits into interior*]

ELLIE: 'Cause this time we KNOW HE MEANS BUSINESS, JUNIE! Ain't no false alarm like them other times. We were there, right there! . . . Had a feeling somp'um was go'n' happen soon as I answered the door and let Mr. Heller in! Like chilly pneumonia on top a breeze . . . Miss Harrison told me she didn't wanta be dusturbed for the rest of the afternoon. Well, she was disturbed all right! They musta fell asleep 'cause Mr. Harrison even got home late and still caught 'em . . .

JUNIE: [*Returns with tie, etc., to continue dressing*] Couldn't you have interrupted their togetherness and sounded a timely danger warning?

ELLIE: We didn't hear him. I was in the kitchen, Vi down in basement ironing. I didn't know Mr. Harrison had come in 'till I
heard screaming from the bedroom. But soon as I did, I called Vi
and me and her tipped down the hall and heard Mr. Harrison
order Mr. Heller to put his clothes back on and stop considering
hisself a friend for the rest of his life! " 'N' you—slut! Pack up and
git out soon as you find a suitable apartment." . . . Then he invited me and Vi into the room and told us he was divorcing
her. . . . That man was hurt, Junie, hurt deep! Could see it in his
eyes . . . Like a little boy, so sad he made you wanta grab hold his
head and rock him in your arms like a baby.

VI: Miss Harrison looked a sight herself, po' thing! Like a li'l' girl
caught stealing crackers out the cookie jar.

ELLIE: I almost crowned old back-stabber Heller! Come brushing up
'gainst *me* on his way out!

JUNIE: [*Almost cracking up with laughter*] Shoulda pinned medal on
him as he flew by. Escaping wit' head still on shoulder and no
bullet-holes dotting through his chest.

ELLIE: [*Once again taking him literally*] The skunk really left us all
too high and dry for that, Junie . . . Oh, don't think it wouldn't
broke your heart, too, nephew . . . Sneaky rascal gone, rest of us
in sorrow, tears pouring down our faces 'n' me and Vi jist begging
and begging . . . [*As if to Harrisons*] "Y'all please think twice befo'
you do anything you'll be sorry for. You love each other—and
who's in better position than Vi and me to know how much you
love each other—"

[JUNIE *ceases dressing to listen closely*]

VI: 'Course she love him, just can't help herself.

ELLIE: "—When two hearts love each other as much as we know
y'all do, they better take whole lots of time befo' doing something
so awful as breaking up a marriage—even if it ain't hunert-percent
perfect. Think about your reputation and the scandal this will
cause Mr. Harrison. Jist 'bout kill your po' mother—her wit' her
blood pressure, artritis, gout, heart tickle 'n' everything. But most
of all, don't orphan the kids! Kids come first. Dear li'l' angels! Just
innocents looking on gitting hurt in ways they can't understand."

JUNIE: [*Incredulous*] You told 'em this, Ellie?

ELLIE: Love conquers all, Junie!

JUNIE: Wit' your assistance, Vi?

VI: As much as I could deliver, Junie.

JUNIE: And what impression did your tender concern have on the bereaved couple?

ELLIE: Mr. Harrison said he understood 'n' appreciated our feelings and was very grateful for our kindly advice—but he was sorry, his mind was made up. She'd gone too far and he couldn't forgive her not EVER! . . . We might judge him a harsh, vindicty man, he said, but he couldn't bring hisself to do it. Even apologized to us for being so cruel.

JUNIE: [*Continuing his slow boil*] You accepted his apology, Vi?

VI: I should say not. I pleaded wit' him agin to think it over for sake of home, family and good name!

JUNIE: Well, of all the goddamn things I ever heard!

ELLIE: [*Heartened by his misread support*] I'm telling ya!

VI: I knew it was go'n' happen if she kept on like she did!

ELLIE: Just wouldn't listen!

JUNIE: It's a disgrace!

ELLIE: Ain't the word!

VI: Lot worse than that!

JUNIE: Did you both plop down on your knees begging him to give her another chance?

VI: NO!—But we woulda if we'd thought about it! Why didn't we, Ellie?!

ELLIE: Things happened so fast—

JUNIE: Never have I been so humiliated in all my life—!

VI: [*Self-disgusted by their glaring omission*] No excuse not thinking 'bout it, Ellie!

ELLIE: Certainly ain't.

JUNIE: What about your pride—!?

VI: You right! Musta been false pride kept us from dropping to our knees!

JUNIE: Acting like imbeciles! Crying your heart out 'cause Massa and Mistress are go'n' break up housekeeping!!! Maybe I oughta go beat up the adulterous rat crawling in between the sheets!!! [*Pacing up and down in angry indignation as they sit stunned*] Here we are—Africa rising to its place in the sun wit' prime ministers and other dignitaries taking seats around the international conference table—us here fighting for our rights like never before, changing the whole image, dumping stereotypes behind us and replacing 'em wit' new images of dignity and dimension—and I come home and find my own aunts, sisters of my mother, daughters of my grandpa who never took crap off no cracker even though he did live on a plantation—DROWNING themselves in tears jist 'cause boss man is gonna kick bosslady out on her nose . . . !!! Maybe *Gone With The Wind* was accurate! Maybe we jist can't help "Miss Scarrrrrrlet-ing" and "Oh Lawdying" every time mistress white gets a splinter in her pinky. That's what *I'm* talking about.

VI: Ain't you got no feelings, boy?

JUNIE: Feelings?!!! . . . So you work every day in their kitchen, Ellie, and every Thursday you wash their stinky clothes, Vi. But that don't mean they're paying you to bleed from their scratches! . . . Look—don't get me wrong—I'm not blaming you for being domestics. It's an honorable job. It's the only kind available sometimes, and it carries no stigma in itself—but that's all it is, A JOB! An exchange of work for pay! BAD PAY AT THAT! Which is all the more reason why you shouldn't give a damn whether the Harrisons kick, kill or mangle each other!

ELLIE: You gotta care, Junie—

JUNIE: "Breaking up home and family!"—Why, I've seen both of you ditch two husbands apiece and itching to send third ones packing if they don't toe the line. You don't even cry over that!

ELLIE: Don't have time to—

JUNIE: Boy, if some gray cat was peeping in on you, he'da sprinted back home and wrote five Uncle Tom Cabins and ten Old Black Joes!

ELLIE: Wait a minute, now—

JUNIE: I never heard you shedding such tragic tears when your own li'l' crumbcrushers suffered through fatherless periods! All you grumbled was "good riddance, they better off wit'out the sons-abitches!" . . . Maybe Harrison tots will make out just as well. They got puny li'l' advantages of millions of dollars and slightly less parched skins!

VI: Show some tenderness, boy. Ain't human not to trouble over our bosses' sorrows—

JUNIE: That's what shames me. I gave you credit for more integrity. Didn't figger you had chalk streaks in ya. You oughta be shamed for *yourselves!*

ELLIE: And done what?

JUNIE: NOTHING!—Shoulda told 'em their sticky mess is their own mud puddle. You neutrals. Just work there. Aren't interested in what they do!

ELLIE: That wouldn't be expressing our deepest sentiments—

JUNIE: I'm ashamed you even had any "sentiments!" . . . Look, it's hopeless, I'm not getting anywhere trying to make you understand . . . I'm going out for a whiff of fresh air! [*Rushes to exit*]

ELLIE: COME BACK HERE, BOY!

JUNIE: [*Stopping at door*] What? To watch you blubber over Massa? No, thanks!

ELLIE: I said come here, you hear me talking to you!

VI: You still ain't too big to git yourself slapped down!

ELLIE: Your ma gave us right any time we saw fit! [*He returns reluctantly. Stands aside. An uneasy silence prevails. They commence a sweet, sly, needling attack*] . . . Better git yourself somp'um to eat. [*Rises, taking off coat*]

JUNIE: [*Sulking*] I lost my appetite.

ELLIE: [*Hanging coat up*] What you want?

JUNIE: I told you I'm not hungry anymore.

VI: We made you lose your appetite . . . ?

[*He doesn't reply*]

ELLIE: What did you crave befo' you lost it?

JUNIE: Anything you had cooked. Didn't have anything special in mind . . .

ELLIE: [*Off-handedly*] Steak? . . . T-Bone? . . . Porterhouse? . . . Filet . . . ?

JUNIE: No. . . . I didn't particularly have steak in mind.

VI: Been eating too many lately, huh? [*Stands at table exchanging goods from* ELLIE's *shopping bag into her own*]

JUNIE: Just kinda tired of 'em, that's all.

ELLIE: How 'bout some chicken then . . . ? Roast beef? . . . Lobster? . . . Squab? Duck, or something?

JUNIE: [*Nettled*] All I wanted was some food, Ellie! . . . In fact, I really had a hankering for some plain ole collard greens, neck bones or ham hocks . . .

ELLIE: Good eatin', boy. Glad to hear that. Means that high-class digestion hasn't spoiled your taste buds yet . . . But if you want that rich, choice food, you welcome to it—

JUNIE: I know that, Ellie!

ELLIE: It's in the freezer for you, go and look.

JUNIE: I don't hafta, Ellie, I know—

ELLIE: Go look anyway.

JUNIE: [*Goes and opens refrigerator door*] It's there, Ellie, I didn't need look.

VI: Come here for a second, Junie, got something on your pants leg. [*He obeys. She picks a piece of lint off trousers, then rubs material admiringly*] Pants to your suit, ain't they? . . . Sure is a fine suit to be trotting off to the unemployment office . . . Which one-'r the other you gon' wear tonight when you try to con that girl out her virginity—if she still got it?—The gray one? Brown one? The tweed? Or maybe you go'n' git sporty and strut that snazzy plaid jacket and them tight light pants? If not—which jacket and which pants?

ELLIE: Slept good last night, nephew? Or maybe you gitting tired of that foam rubber mattress and sheep-fur blanket?

VI: How do them fine college queens and snooty office girls like the furniture they half-see when you sneak 'em in here late at night? Surprised to see such fancy stuff in a beat-up ole flat, ain't they? But it helps you put 'em at ease, don't it? I bet even those sweet li'l' white ones are impressed by your class?

JUNIE: [*Indignantly*] That's not fair, Vi—

ELLIE: When last time you bought any food in this house, boy?

JUNIE: Ellie, you know—

ELLIE: When, Junie?

JUNIE: Not since I been here, but—

VI: And your last piece of clothes?

JUNIE: [*More indignant*] I bought some underwear last week, Vi!

VI: I mean clothes you wear on top, Junie. Shirts, pants, jackets, coats?

JUNIE: [*Squirming*] You—you know I haven't, Vi—

ELLIE: [*Resists*] Buy anything else in your room besides that tiny, midget frame for your ma's picture?

JUNIE: All right. I know I'm indebted to ya. You don't have to rub it in. I'll make it up to you when I git on my feet and *fulfill* my potential . . . But that's not the point!

ELLIE: You ain't indebted to us, Junie.

JUNIE: Yes, I am, I know it, I thank you for it.

ELLIE: Don't hafta thank us—

JUNIE: But that's not the issue! Despite your benevolence, I refuse to let you blackmail my principle, slapping me in the face wit' how good you been to me during my temporary outta work period! I'm talking to you now, 'bout something above our personal relationship. Pride—Race—Dignity—

ELLIE: What's go'n' happen to me and Vi's dignity if Mr. Harrison throws Mrs. Harrison out on her nose as you put it?

JUNIE: Git another job! You not dependent on them. You young, healthy, in the prime of life . . . In fact—I've always wondered why you stagnate as domestics when you're trained and qualified to do something better and more dignified.

ELLIE: Glad you brought that up. Know why I'm not breaking my back as a practical nurse and Vi's not frying hair—'cept on the side? . . . 'Cause the work's too hard, the money ain't worth it and there's not much room for advancement—

JUNIE: Where kin you advance as a domestic? From kitchen to closet?!

[VI *has moved to fridge to deposit meats etc.*]

ELLIE: [*Refusing to be provoked, continuing evenly*] Beside, when I started working for the Harrisons, Junie, Mr. Harrison vowed that he would support me for life if I stayed with 'em until his daughter Sandy, his oldest child, reached ten years old.

JUNIE: Bully for him! He'll build ya a little cottage backa the penthouse garage!

ELLIE: [*Still unruffled*] Mr. Harrison is strictly a man of his word, Junie. Which means that even if I left one day after Sandy made ten, he owes me some money every week or every month as long as I live . . . Sandy is *nine*, Junie, EN-EYE-EN-EE! If I don't last another year, the deal is off.

JUNIE: Don't need no handouts! Even hearing you say you want any, makes me shame!

ELLIE: Done used that word quite a lot, boy. You shamed of us? . . . Well, git slapped in the face wit' this? How shame you go'n' be when you hafta git outta here and hustle yourself a job?—ANY JOB?!!!

JUNIE: Huh?

ELLIE: How shame you go'n' be when you start gitting raggedy and all them foxy girls are no longer impressed 'bout how slick, smooth and pretty you look? When you stop being one-'r the best-dressed black boys in New York City?

JUNIE: Don't get you, Ellie?

ELLIE: I know you went to college for a coupler years, boy, but I thought you still had some sense, or I woulda told you . . .

VI: [*Standing at* JUNIE's *right as* ELLIE *sits to his left*] Every time you bite into one of them big tender juicy steaks and chaw it down into your belly, ever think where it's coming from?

ELLIE: The Harrisons.

VI: Every time you lay one of them young gals down in that plush soft bed of yours and hear her sigh in luxury, ever think 'bout who you owe it to?

ELLIE: The Harrisons.

VI: When you swoop down home to that rundown house your ma

and pa rent, latch eyes on all that fine furniture there, you ever think who's responsible?

ELLIE: The Harrisons.

VI: You ain't bought a suit or a piece of clothes in five years and none of the other four men in this family have . . . Why not?

ELLIE: Mr. Harrison.

VI: Junie, you is a fine, choice hunk of chocolate pigmeat, pretty as a new-minted penny and slick 'nuff to suck sugar outta gingerbread wit'out it losing its flavor—but the Harrisons ain't hardly elected you no favorite pin-up boy to introduce to Santa Claus. Took a heap of pow'ful coaxing to win you such splendid sponsorship and wealthy commissions, 'cause waiting for the Harrisons to voluntarily *donate* their Christian charity is one sure way of landing head-first in the poor-house dungeon . . . Who runs the Harrisons' house, Junie? [*Moves to sit at table*]

JUNIE: ??? . . . Ellie . . . I guess . . . ?

ELLIE: *From top to bottom.* I cook the food, scrub the floor, open the doors, serve the tables, answer the phones, dust the furniture, raise the children, lay out the clothes, greet the guests, fix the drinks and dump the garbage—all for bad pay as you said . . . You right, Junie, money I git in my envelope ain't worth the time 'n' the headache . . . *But—God Helps Those Who Help Themselves* . . . I also ORDER the food, estimate the credit, PAY the bills and BALANCE the budget. Which means that each steak I order for them, befo' butcher carves cow, I done reserved TWO for myself. Miss Harrison wouldn't know how much steak cost and Mr. Harrison so loaded, he writes me a check wit'out even looking . . . Every once in a full moon they git so good-hearted and tell me take some left-overs home, but by that time my freezer and pantry is already fuller than theirs . . . Every one of them high price suits I lay on you haven't been wore more than once and some of 'em not at all. You lucky to be same size as Mr. Harrison, Junie. He don't know how much clothes he got in his wardrobe, which is why *yours* is as big as *his*. Jim, Roy, Arthur and Ben can't even fit into the man's clothes, but that still don't stop 'em from cutting, shortening, altering and stretching 'em to fit. Roy almost ruined his feet trying to wear the man's shoes . . . Now, I've had a perfect record keeping y'all elegantly dressed and stylishly—fashion-plated—'cept that time Mr. Harrison caught me off-guard asking: "Ellie, where's my brown suit?" "In the cleaners," I told him and had to snatch it off your hanger and smuggle it back—temporarily.

VI: If y'all warn't so lucky and *Mrs. Harrison* so tacky flashy Ellie and I would also be best dressed domestics of the year.

ELLIE: Which, if you didn't notice, is what your Aunt Doris was—rest her soul—when we laid her in her grave, decked out in the costliest, ritziest, most expensest nightgown the good Lord ever waited to feast his eyes on . . . As for furniture, we could move out his whole house in one day if we had to.

VI: Which is what we did when they moved from the old penthouse and we hired us a moving van to haul 'nuff pieces to furnish both our own apartments and still had enough to ship a living room set down home to your ma. Mr. Harrison told us to donate the stuff to charity. We did—US!

ELLIE: Add all *our* bills I add on to *their* bills—Jim even tried to git me to sneak in his car note, but that was going too far—all the deluxe plane tickets your ma jets up here on every year, weekly prescriptions filled on their tab, tons of laundry cleaned along wit' theirs and a thousand other services and I'm earning me quite a bonus along with my bad pay. It's the BONUS that counts, Junie. Total it up for nine years and I'd be losing money on any other job. Now Vi and I, after cutting cane, picking rice and shucking corn befo' we could braid our hair in pigtails, figure we just gitting back what's owed us . . . But, if Mr. Harrison boots Mrs. Harrison out on her tocus, the party's over. He's not go'n' need us. Miss Harrison ain't got a copper cent of her own. Anyway, the set-up won't be as ripe for picking. My bonus is suddenly cut off and out the window go my pension.

VI: Suppose we did git us another job wit' one-'r them penny-pinching old misers hiding behind cupboards watching whether you stealing sugar cubes? Wit' our fringe benefits choked off, we'd fall down so quick to a style of living we ain't been used to for a long time, it would make your head swim. I don't think we could stand it . . . Could you?

ELLIE: So when me and Vi saw our pigeons scampering out the window for good today, tears started flowing like rain. The first tear trickle out my eyes had a roast in it.

vi: Mine was a chicken.

ELLIE: Second had a crate of eggs.

vi: Mine a whole pig.

ELLIE: Third an oriental rug.

vi: A continental couch.

ELLIE: An overcoat for Arthur.

vi: A bathrobe for Ben.

ELLIE: My gas, electric and telephone bills in it.

vi: Three months' rent, Lord!

ELLIE: The faster the stream started gushing, the faster them night-
mares crowded my eyes until I coulda flooded 'em 'nuff water to
swim in. Every time I pleaded "Think of your love!—"

vi: She meant think 'bout our bills.

ELLIE: Every time I begged "Don't crack up the home!—"

vi: It meant please keep *ours* cemented together!

ELLIE: "Don't victim the chillun!—"

vi: By all means insure the happiness of *our* li'l' darlings!

ELLIE: They didn't know 'bout these eyeball visions—they only see
what they see 'n' hear what they hear—and that's okey-doke wit'
me—but I was gitting these watery pictures in my mind 'n' feeling
a giant-size sickness in my gut! Few seconds longer and I woulda
been down on my knees wit'out even thinking 'bout it!

vi: If I didn't beat ya to the floor!

ELLIE: Junie—maybe we shoulda given a little more thought to that
—watchamacallit?—"image" of yours. Maybe we did dishonor
Africa, embarrass the NAACP, are hopelessly behind time and
scandalously outdated. But we didn't have too much time to think
. . . Now that you know the whole truth, you have a right to
disown us. We hardly worthy of your respect . . . But when I
thought 'bout that new topcoat wit' the velvet-trimmed collar I
just packed to bring you . . . [*Tears begin to re-form*] . . . coupler
new cashmere sweaters, brand-new slacks, a shiny new attache
case for your appointments, and a scrumptious new collapsible
swimming pool I promised your ma for her backyard—I couldn't
help but cry. [vi *has joined her in a double torrent*]

JUNIE: [*Who has been standing stoically throughout, says:*] . . . Vi?

VI: . . . What?

JUNIE: . . . Pass me the handkerchief. . . . [*He receives it and joins the table—a moist-faced trio.* ARTHUR, ELLIE'*s husband, walks in, finding them thus*]

ARTHUR: [*Beelining for bathroom*] Even', everybody . . . [*Hearing no response, stops before entering john*] Hey, what's the matter? What you three looking like somebody died for?

ELLIE: It's the Harrisons, Arthur. Mr. Harrison gitting a divorce.

ARTHUR: Aww, not ag'in!

VI: He really means it this time, Arthur.

ARTHUR: . . . He does?

ELLIE: Yes, Jesus.

ARTHUR: You sure?

VI: Caught her dead to rights.

ARTHUR: [*Indignant*] But he can't do that!

VI: He is.

ARTHUR: What 'bout us?!

JUNIE: What you think we grieving 'bout?

ARTHUR: Well, just don't sit there! What we go'n' do?

ELLIE: Done it, didn't work.

ARTHUR: Not at all?

ELLIE: Nope.

ARTHUR: Not even a little bit?

ELLIE: Not one lousy inch.

ARTHUR: [*Crestfallen*] Make room for me.

[*They provide space. He sits, completing the depressed quartet*]

JUNIE: [*Suddenly jolted with an idea*] Ellie! Wait! Why don't you tell him to take her on a private ocean cruise, just the two of 'em, so they kin recapture the thrill for one another!

ELLIE: He did that already, until somebody told him she was cuddling up with the ship stoker in the engine room.

JUNIE: [*Undaunted*] Advise him to spend less time wit' his business and more with her. She wouldn't need look outside for satisfaction!

ELLIE: Tried that too, but his business like to fell apart and he caught her making eyes at the messenger bringing him the news.

JUNIE: [*Desperate*] Convince him she's sick! It's not her fault, he should send her to a psychiatrist!

ELLIE: Already did . . . till he found out she was doing more than talking on the couch.

JUNIE: What 'bout a twenty-four hour guard on her? That won't give her so many opportunities?!

ELLIE: What about guards? They men, too.

JUNIE: [*In angry frustration*] Well, damn, git her a chastity belt and lock her up!

ELLIE: Locks, also, have been known to be picked.

ARTHUR: [*Inspired by a brilliant solution*] WAIT! *I GOT IT! I GOT IT!* . . . Tell him you know of some steady ready goofer dust . . . or jooger-mooger saltpeter to cool her down. And you'll slip it in her food every day!

ELLIE: Wouldn't work . . . Way her glands function, probably jazz her up like a Spanish fly.

VI: Let's face it, it's all over. We just gotta tuck in our belts, stare the future square in the eye and git ready for a depression. It's not go'n' do us no good to whine over spilt clabber . . . You jist better start scrounging 'round for that job, Junie. Befo' you git chance to sneeze, we will have had it. And call up —NO! Write your ma and tell her not to come up this year.

ELLIE: Arthur, best you scrape up another job to moonlight wit' the one you got. We facing some scuffling days 'head us.

VI: Well . . . I better git out of here and go warn my own crew 'bout Satan's retribution . . . Well . . . it was good while it lasted, Ellie . . .

ELLIE: Real good.

[*They glance at each other and another deluge starts. The phone interrupts, but no one bothers to answer. Finally,* ARTHUR

*rises and exits in the direction of peals. During his absence, the
disconsolate trio remains silent]*

ARTHUR: [*Reentering slowly, treading each step with the deliber-
ateness of a man fearful of cracking eggs*] That—was—Mr. Harrison—he said—thank both of you for desperately trying to
shock him to his senses—pry open his eyes to the light—and res-
cue his house from collapsing—he and Mrs. Harrison, after
stren'ous consideration, are gonna stick it out together! [*A stunned
moment of absolute silence prevails, finally broken by an ear-split-
ting, exultant whoop which erupts simultaneously from each
member of the quartet. They spring to feet, embracing and pranc-
ing around the room, crying through laughter.* ARTHUR *simmers
down first, shhushes to recapture their attention*] ELLIE . . .
Ellie, Mr. Harrison requests if it's not too much trouble, he'd like
for you to come over and stay wit' Sandy and Snookie while he
and Mrs. Harrison go out and celebrate their reunion and it's too
late to git a baby-sitter.

ELLIE: If it's all right?!!!! . . . Tell him I'm climbing on a broom-
stick, then shuttling to a jet! [ARTHUR *starts to exit*] Wait a minute! Waaaait a minute! Hold on!—I must be crazy! Don't tell him
that . . . Tell him he knows very well it's after my working hours
and I'm not paid to baby-sit and since I've already made plans for
the evening, I'll be glad to do it for double-overtime, two extra
days' pay and triple-time off to recuperate from the imposition
. . . And, Arthur! . . . Kinda suggest that *you* is a little peeved
'cause he's interrupting me from taking care of something important for you. He might toss in a day for your suffering.

ARTHUR: He'll swear he was snatching you away from my deathbed,
guarding my door 'gainst Lucifer busting through! [*Exits*]

ELLIE: I'd better throw on some more clothes. [*Exits*]

JUNIE: Vi, what you s'pose grandpa would say 'bout his chillun if he
got a breathing-spell in between dodging pitchforks and side-step-
ping the fiery flames?

VI: Shame on you, boy, Papa ain't near'bouts doing no ducking 'n'
dodging. Why, he's right up there plunked down safe, snuggled up
tight beside the good Lord's righteous throne.

ARTHUR: [*Reentering*] He was real sorry. "If it wasn't such a special occasion, he wouldn't bother us!"

[*They guffaw heartily*]

JUNIE: This IS a special occasion! . . . [*Grandly*] Arthur, break out a flagon of the latest champagne Ellie brought us.

ARTHUR: At your service, massa Junie.

JUNIE: The nineteen-forty-seven! That was a good year. Not the fifty, which was bad!

ARTHUR: No kidding?!

[ARTHUR *moves to refrigerator.* ELLIE *returns, ready to depart*]

JUNIE: Wait for a drink, auntie. We've gotta celebrate OUR resurrection. A Toast of Deliverance. [ARTHUR *presents* JUNIE *with champagne, points out '47 label, then gets goblets from shelf.* JUNIE *pours, they lift goblets*] First! . . . To the victors and the vanquished, top-dog and the bottom-dog! Sometimes it's hard to tell which is which . . . !

VI: If nothing else, boy, education did teach you how to sling around some GAB.

ARTHUR: Ain't hardly the way I heard the slinging described.

[*They all laugh*]

JUNIE: Second! . . . To my two cagey aunts. May they continue to prevail in times of distress!

ARTHUR: May they!

JUNIE: . . . Third! . . . To the Harrisons! . . . May they endure forever in marital bliss! Cheers to 'em! [*All cheer. After finishing drink,* ELLIE *moves to exit through hallway door.* JUNIE *stops her*] Oh, Ellie . . . why don't you start fattening Mr. Harrison up? Please slip some more potatoes and starch onto his menu. I've gained a few pounds and the clothes are gitting a little tight. Don't you think it's time for him to plumpen up a bit, stick on a little weight? . . .

ELLIE: Would ten pounds do?

JUNIE: Perfect! [*Another round of laughter. Again she moves to exit*]

. . . AND ELLIE! . . . Kinda hint 'round to him that fashions is changing. I wouldn't want him to fall behind in the latest styles . . .

VI: [*Lifting goblet, along with* ARTHUR *and* ELLIE, *in a final toast*] There's hope, Junie. You'll make it, boy, you'll make it . . .

[*Laughter rings as lights fade*]

CURTAIN

HELLO OUT THERE

William Saroyan

William Saroyan

William Saroyan was born of Armenian parentage in Fresno, California, on August 3, 1908. He began working as a newsboy at eight, became a telegraph boy at thirteen; at fifteen he left public school and pruned vines alongside Japanese and Mexican laborers in his uncle's vineyards in Northern California.

Largely self-educated, the avant-courier of mid-century drama and the irrepressible *enfant terrible* of the literary milieu, he was determined to write at an early age: "I began to send stuff to magazines soon after I paid thirteen dollars for an Underwood typewriter in Fresno in 1921 when I was just thirteen. . . ." As personal curriculum, he digested most of the works of the great writers during his moments away from his menial chores. At the age of seventeen, he settled in San Francisco, where he began to write in earnest. According to legend, the youthful author wrote a story a day in an unheated room, bundled up in woolens, the floor around him littered with discarded or torn sheets of manuscript.

When his first short story, *The Daring Young Man on the Flying Trapeze*, was published in *Story* magazine in 1934, it created something of a sensation among the literati. That same year, the story was issued in book form and from then on, his success was assured.

Two of Mr. Saroyan's prime characteristics as a writer have continued undiminishingly through the years: his intense love affair with life and his remarkably prolific output. The author of more than fifty books and plays, he has declared: "I wrote in a hurry for many reasons, the best of which was the simplest and I think the truest: I was impatient to reach the best in me, and I knew there was no short cut, I had to work to reach it." And reach it he did with several major novels (*The Human Comedy*; *My Name Is Aram*; *The Adventures of Wesley Jackson*), scores of short stories (some of which have become modern classics), essays, poems, and above all, his plays.

William Saroyan met with almost instant success in the theatre. After making a striking debut as a dramatist with *My Heart's in the Highlands* (1939), he scored doubly with *The Time of Your Life*, the first play ever to win both the New York Drama Critics' Circle Award and the Pulitzer Prize, 1939–40. According to the author, the much-lauded comedy-drama was written in six days, and as he later told a newspaper interviewer, "After all, the stuff in the play has been gathering ever since I was old enough to see and feel life. This isn't a 'play' in the accepted sense of the word. I think there isn't enough 'play' in plays. Something ought to be done about it, and that's what I'm trying to do. You might just as well call plays 'mechanical,' because that's what most of them have become."

The Time of Your Life was anything but "mechanical." It fostered a new style of drama, one that undeniably has influenced many of our latter-day avant-gardists. At its 1939 Broadway première, the New York *Times'* drama critic, Brooks Atkinson, hailed the play as "something worth cherishing—a prose poem in ragtime with a humorous and lovable point of view." Critic Richard Watts, Jr., in his columnar paean, wrote: "Mr. Saroyan's new play is a delight and joy. A sort of cosmic vaudeville show, formless, plotless and shamelessly rambling, it is a helter-skelter mixture of humor, sentimentalism, philosophy and melodrama, and one of the most enchanting theatrical works imaginable." Precisely thirty years later, the Repertory Theatre of Lincoln Center opened its season with a highly successful revival of the play. In covering the 1969 presentation for *Variety*, Hobe Morrison termed it "an enjoyable, satisfying and astonishingly timely play now. *The Time of Your Life* is a provocative item in American Theatre history and, it's good to see, still a vastly entertaining show."

Since 1939, Mr. Saroyan's dramatic works have been performed in every conceivable corner of the world. To list some, in nonchronological order: *The Beautiful People; My Heart's in the Highlands; Love's Old Sweet Song; Across the Board on Tomorrow Morning; Hello Out There; Sweeney in the Trees; Get Away Old Man; Jim Dandy; The Violin Messiah; Once Around the Block; Talking to You;* and *The Cave Dwellers*.

Versatile as well as prolific, he also wrote the scenario for a popular ballet, *The Great American Goof*, initially presented in 1940 by the Ballet Theatre and, in 1943, won Hollywood's Academy Award for his original screen play *The Human Comedy*.

During the past decade, Mr. Saroyan has published at least a half-dozen new books, including *I Used to Believe I Had Forever Now I'm Not So Sure* (fifty-two short pieces written over a period of thirty-four years) and *Days of Life and Death and Escape to the Moon*, "a very personal journal" that records the author's thoughts on an assortment of subjects.

An ardent disciple of the short play, Mr. Saroyan wrote to this editor: "The short story has flourished with incredible variety and freshness and successful experiment—it is an easy form to read. Well, I think the short play can be made just as effective and popular as the short story. *All* writers have written in the short play form, some unintentionally of course. When it *is* intentional, the writer is simply thinking in terms of the theatre in one or another of its contemporary forms. And he is thinking of people acting out character parts in front of an audience."

Hello Out There was first produced in 1941 at the Lobero Theatre, Santa Barbara, as the curtain raiser to *The Devil's Disciple* by George Bernard Shaw, to whom the play is dedicated. On September 29, 1942, it opened at the Belasco Theatre, New York, with Eddie Dowling and Julie Haydon in the two principal roles.

Characters:

Young Man
The Girl
A Man
Second Man
Third Man
A Woman

SCENE: *A little jailhouse in Matador, Texas.*

There is a fellow in a small-town prison cell, tapping slowly on the floor with a spoon. After tapping half a minute, as if he were trying to telegraph words, he gets up and begins walking around the cell. At last he stops, stands at the center of the cell, and doesn't move for a long time. He feels his head, as if it were wounded. Then he looks around. Then he calls out dramatically, kidding the world.

YOUNG MAN: Hello—out there! [*Pause*] Hello—out there! Hello—out there! [*Long pause*] Nobody out there. [*Still more dramatically, but more comically, too*] Hello—out there! Hello—out there!

[A GIRL'S VOICE *is heard, very sweet and soft*]

THE VOICE: Hello.

YOUNG MAN: Hello—out there.

THE VOICE: Hello.

YOUNG MAN: Is that you, Katey?

THE VOICE: No—this here is Emily.

YOUNG MAN: Who? [*Swiftly*] Hello out there.

THE VOICE: Emily.

YOUNG MAN: Emily who? I don't know anybody named Emily. Are you that girl I met at Sam's in Salinas about three years ago?

THE VOICE: No—I'm the girl who cooks here. I'm the cook. I've never been in Salinas. I don't even know where it is.

YOUNG MAN: Hello out there. You say you cook here?

THE VOICE: Yes.

YOUNG MAN: Well, why don't you study up and learn to cook? How come I don't get no jello or anything good?

THE VOICE: I just cook what they tell me to. [*Pause*] You lonesome?

YOUNG MAN: Lonesome as a coyote. Hear me hollering? Hello out there!

THE VOICE: Who you hollering to?

YOUNG MAN: Well—nobody, I guess. I been trying to think of some-body to write a letter to, but I can't think of anybody.

THE VOICE: What about Katey?

YOUNG MAN: I don't know anybody named Katey.

THE VOICE: Then why did you say, "Is that you, Katey?"

YOUNG MAN: Katey's a good name. I always did like a name like Katey. I never *knew* anybody named Katey, though.

THE VOICE: I did.

YOUNG MAN: Yeah? What was she like? Tall girl, or little one?

THE VOICE: Kind of medium.

YOUNG MAN: Hello out there. What sort of a looking girl are *you*?

THE VOICE: Oh, I don't know.

YOUNG MAN: Didn't anybody ever tell you? Didn't anybody ever talk to you that way?

THE VOICE: What way?

YOUNG MAN: You know. Didn't they?

THE VOICE: No, they didn't.

YOUNG MAN: Ah, the fools—they should have. I can tell from your voice you're O.K.

THE VOICE: Maybe I am and maybe I ain't.

YOUNG MAN: I never missed yet.

THE VOICE: Yeah, I know. That's why you're in jail.

YOUNG MAN: The whole thing was a mistake.

THE VOICE: They claim it was rape.

YOUNG MAN: No—it wasn't.

THE VOICE: That's what they claim it was.

YOUNG MAN: They're a lot of fools.

THE VOICE: Well, you sure are in trouble. Are you scared?

YOUNG MAN: Scared to death. [*Suddenly*] Hello out there!

THE VOICE: What do you keep saying that for all the time?

YOUNG MAN: I'm lonesome. I'm as lonesome as a coyote. [A *long one*] Hello—out there!

[THE GIRL *appears, over to one side. She is a plain girl in plain clothes*]

THE GIRL: I'm kind of lonesome, too.

YOUNG MAN: [*Turning and looking at her*] Hey— No fooling? Are you?

THE GIRL: Yeah— I'm almost as lonesome as a coyote myself.

YOUNG MAN: Who *you* lonesome for?

THE GIRL: I don't know.

YOUNG MAN: It's the same with me. The minute they put you in a place like this you remember all the girls you ever knew, and all the girls you didn't get to know, and it sure gets lonesome.

THE GIRL: I bet it does.

YOUNG MAN: Ah, it's awful. [*Pause*] You're a pretty kid, you know that?

THE GIRL: You're just talking.

YOUNG MAN: No, I'm not just talking—you *are* pretty. Any fool could see that. You're just about the prettiest kid in the whole world.

THE GIRL: I'm not—and you know it.

YOUNG MAN: No—you are. I never saw anyone prettier in all my born days, in all my travels. I knew Texas would bring me luck.

THE GIRL: Luck? You're in jail, aren't you? You've got a whole gang of people all worked up, haven't you?

YOUNG MAN: Ah, that's nothing. I'll get out of this.

THE GIRL: Maybe.

YOUNG MAN: No, I'll be all right—*now*.

THE GIRL: What do you mean—now?

YOUNG MAN: I mean after seeing you. I got something now. You know for a while there I didn't care one way or another. Tired. [*Pause*] Tired of trying for the best all the time and never getting it. [*Suddenly*] Hello out there!

THE GIRL: Who you calling now?

YOUNG MAN: You.

THE GIRL: Why, I'm right here.

YOUNG MAN: I know. [*Calling*] Hello out there!

THE GIRL: Hello.

YOUNG MAN: Ah, you're sweet. [*Pause*] I'm going to marry *you*. I'm going away with *you*. I'm going to take you to San Francisco or some place like that. I *am*, now. I'm going to win myself some real money, too. I'm going to study 'em real careful and pick myself some winners, and we're going to have a lot of money.

THE GIRL: Yeah?

YOUNG MAN: Yeah. Tell me your name and all that stuff.

THE GIRL: Emily.

YOUNG MAN: I know that. What's the rest of it? Where were you born? Come on, tell me the whole thing.

THE GIRL: Emily Smith.

YOUNG MAN: Honest to God?

THE GIRL: Honest. That's my name—Emily Smith.

YOUNG MAN: Ah, you're the sweetest girl in the whole world.

THE GIRL: Why?

YOUNG MAN: I don't know why, but you are, that's all. Where were you born?

THE GIRL: Matador, Texas.

YOUNG MAN: Where's that?

THE GIRL: Right here.

YOUNG MAN: Is this Matador, Texas?

THE GIRL: Yeah, it's Matador. They brought you here from Wheeling.

YOUNG MAN: Is that where I was—Wheeling?

THE GIRL: Didn't you even know what town you were in?

YOUNG MAN: All towns are alike. You don't go up and ask somebody what town you're in. It doesn't make any difference. How far away is Wheeling?

THE GIRL: Sixteen or seventeen miles. Didn't you know they moved you?

YOUNG MAN: How could I know, when I was out—cold? Somebody hit me over the head with a lead pipe or something. What'd they hit me for?

THE GIRL: Rape—that's what they *said*.

YOUNG MAN: Ah, that's a lie. [*Amazed, almost to himself*] She wanted me to give her money.

THE GIRL: Money?

YOUNG MAN: Yeah, if I'd have known she was a woman like that—well, by God, I'd have gone on down the street and stretched out in a park somewhere and gone to sleep.

THE GIRL: Is that what she wanted—money?

YOUNG MAN: Yeah. A fellow like me hopping freights all over the country, trying to break his bad luck, going from one poor little town to another, trying to get in on something good somewhere, and she asks for money. I thought she was lonesome. She *said* she was.

THE GIRL: Maybe she was.

YOUNG MAN: She was *something*.

THE GIRL: I guess I'd never see you, if it didn't happen, though.

YOUNG MAN: Oh, I don't know—maybe I'd just mosey along this way and see you in this town somewhere. I'd recognize you, too.

THE GIRL: Recognize me?

YOUNG MAN: Sure, I'd recognize you the minute I laid eyes on you.

THE GIRL: Well, who would I be?

YOUNG MAN: Mine, that's who.

THE GIRL: Honest?

YOUNG MAN: Honest to God.

THE GIRL: You just say that because you're in jail.

YOUNG MAN: No, I mean it. You just pack up and wait for me. We'll high-roll the hell out of here to Frisco.

THE GIRL: You're just lonesome.

YOUNG MAN: I been lonesome all my life—there's no cure for that—but you and me—we can have a lot of fun hanging around together. You'll bring me luck. I know it.

THE GIRL: What are you looking for luck for all the time?

YOUNG MAN: I'm a gambler. I don't work. I've *got* to have luck, or I'm a bum. I haven't had any decent luck in years. Two whole years now—one place to another. Bad luck all the time. That's why I got in trouble back there in Wheeling, too. That was no accident. That was my bad luck following me around. So here I am, with my head half busted. I guess it was her old man that did it.

THE GIRL: You mean her father?

YOUNG MAN: No, her husband. If I had an old lady like that, I'd throw her out.

THE GIRL: Do you think you'll have better luck, if I go with you?

YOUNG MAN: It's a cinch. I'm a good handicapper. All I need is somebody good like you with me. It's no good always walking around in the streets for anything that might be there at the time. You got to have somebody staying with you all the time—through winters when it's cold, and springtime when it's pretty, and summertime when it's nice and hot and you can go swimming—through *all* the times—rain and snow and all the different kinds of weather a man's got to go through before he dies. You got to have somebody who's right. Somebody who knows you, from away back. You got to have somebody who even knows you're wrong but likes you just the same. I know I'm wrong, but I just don't want anything the hard way, working like a dog, or the *easy* way, working like a dog—working's the hard way and the easy way both. All I got to do is beat the price, always—and then I don't feel lousy and don't hate anybody. If you go along with me, I'll be the finest guy anybody ever saw. I won't be wrong any more. You know when you get enough of that money, you *can't* be wrong any more —you're right because the money says so. I'll have a lot of money and you'll be just about the prettiest, most wonderful kid in the whole world. I'll be proud walking around Frisco with you on my arm and people turning around to look at us.

THE GIRL: Do you think they will?

YOUNG MAN: Sure they will. When I get back in some decent clothes, and you're on my arm—well, Katey, they'll turn around and look, and they'll see something, too.

THE GIRL: Katey?

YOUNG MAN: Yeah—that's your name from now on. You're the first girl I ever called Katey. I've been saving it for you. O.K.?

THE GIRL: O.K.

YOUNG MAN: How long have I been here?

THE GIRL: Since last night. You didn't wake up until late this morning, though.

YOUNG MAN: What time is it now? About nine?

THE GIRL: About ten.

YOUNG MAN: Have you got the key to this lousy cell?

THE GIRL: No. They don't let me fool with any keys.

YOUNG MAN: Well, can you get it?

THE GIRL: No.

YOUNG MAN: Can you *try*?

THE GIRL: They wouldn't let me get near any keys. I cook for this jail, when they've got somebody in it. I clean up and things like that.

YOUNG MAN: Well, I want to get out of here. Don't you know the guy that runs this joint?

THE GIRL: I know him, but he wouldn't let you out. They were talking of taking you to another jail in another town.

YOUNG MAN: Yeah? Why?

THE GIRL: Because they're afraid.

YOUNG MAN: What are they afraid of?

THE GIRL: They're afraid these people from Wheeling will come over in the middle of the night and break in.

YOUNG MAN: Yeah? What do they want to do that for?

THE GIRL: Don't *you* know what they want to do it for?

YOUNG MAN: Yeah, I know all right.

THE GIRL: Are you scared?

YOUNG MAN: Sure I'm scared. Nothing scares a man more than ignorance. You can argue with people who ain't fools, but you can't argue with fools—they just go to work and do what they're set on doing. Get me out of here.

THE GIRL: How?

YOUNG MAN: Well, go get the guy with the key, and let me talk to him.

THE GIRL: He's gone home. Everybody's gone home.

YOUNG MAN: You mean I'm in this little jail all alone?

THE GIRL: Well—yeah—except me.

YOUNG MAN: Well, what's the big idea—doesn't anybody stay here all the time?

THE GIRL: No, they go home every night. I clean up and then I go, too. I hung around tonight.

YOUNG MAN: What made you do that?

THE GIRL: I wanted to talk to you.

YOUNG MAN: Honest? What did you want to talk about?

THE GIRL: Oh, I don't know. I took care of you last night. You were talking in your sleep. You liked me, too. I didn't think you'd like me when you woke up, though.

YOUNG MAN: Yeah? Why not?

THE GIRL: I don't know.

YOUNG MAN: Yeah? Well, you're wonderful, see?

THE GIRL: Nobody ever talked to me that way. All the fellows in town—[*Pause*]

YOUNG MAN: What about 'em? [*Pause*] Well, what about 'em? Come on—tell me.

THE GIRL: They laugh at me.

YOUNG MAN: Laugh at *you?* They're fools. What do they know about anything? You go get your things and come back here. I'll take you with me to Frisco. How old are you?

THE GIRL: Oh, I'm of age.

YOUNG MAN: How old are you?—Don't lie to me! Sixteen?

THE GIRL: I'm seventeen.

YOUNG MAN: Well, bring your father and mother. We'll get married before we go.

THE GIRL: They wouldn't let me go.

YOUNG MAN: Why not?

THE GIRL: I don't know, but they wouldn't. I know they wouldn't.

YOUNG MAN: You go tell your father not to be a fool, see? What is he, a farmer?

THE GIRL: No—nothing. He gets a little relief from the government because he's supposed to be hurt or something—his side hurts, he says. I don't know what it is.

YOUNG MAN: Ah, he's a liar. Well, I'm taking you with me, see?

THE GIRL: He takes the money I earn, too.

YOUNG MAN: He's got no right to do that.

THE GIRL: I know it, but he does it.

YOUNG MAN: [*Almost to himself*] This world stinks. You shouldn't have been born in this town, anyway, and you shouldn't have had a man like that for a father, either.

THE GIRL: Sometimes I feel sorry for him.

YOUNG MAN: Never mind feeling sorry for him. [*Pointing a finger*] I'm going to talk to your father some day. I've got a few things to tell that guy.

THE GIRL: I know you have.

YOUNG MAN: [*Suddenly*] Hello—out there! See if you can get that fellow with the keys to come down and let me out.

THE GIRL: Oh, I couldn't.

YOUNG MAN: Why not?

THE GIRL: I'm nobody here—they give me fifty cents every day I work.

YOUNG MAN: How much?

THE GIRL: Fifty cents.

YOUNG MAN: [*To the world*] You see? They ought to pay money to *look* at you. To breathe the *air* you breathe. I don't know. Sometimes I figure it never is going to make sense. Hello—out there! I'm scared. You try to get me out of here. I'm scared them fools are going to come here from Wheeling and go crazy, thinking they're heroes. Get me out of here, Katey.

THE GIRL: I don't know what to do. Maybe I could break the door down.

YOUNG MAN: No, you couldn't do that. Is there a hammer out there or anything?

THE GIRL: Only a broom. Maybe they've locked the broom up, too.

YOUNG MAN: Go see if you can find anything.

THE GIRL: All right. [*She goes*]

YOUNG MAN: Hello—out there! Hello—out there! [*Pause*] Hello—out there! Hello—out there! [*Pause*] Putting me in jail. [*With con-*

tempt] Rape! Rape? *They* rape everything good that was ever born. His side hurts. They laugh at her. Fifty cents a day. Little punk people. Hurting the only good thing that ever came their way. [*Suddenly*] Hello—out there!

THE GIRL: [*Returning*] There isn't a thing out there. They've locked everything up for the night.

YOUNG MAN: Any cigarettes?

THE GIRL: Everything's locked up—all the drawers of the desk, all the closet doors—everything.

YOUNG MAN: I ought to have a cigarette.

THE GIRL: I could get you a package maybe, somewhere. I guess the drug store's open. It's about a mile.

YOUNG MAN: A mile? I don't want to be alone that long.

THE GIRL: I could run all the way, and all the way back.

YOUNG MAN: You're the sweetest girl that ever lived.

THE GIRL: What kind do you want?

YOUNG MAN: Oh, any kind—Chesterfields or Camels or Lucky Strikes —any kind at all.

THE GIRL: I'll go get a package. [*She turns to go*]

YOUNG MAN: What about the money?

THE GIRL: I've got some money. I've got a quarter I been saving. I'll run all the way. [*She is about to go*]

YOUNG MAN: Come here.

THE GIRL: [*Going to him*] What?

YOUNG MAN: Give me your hand. [*He takes her hand and looks at it, smiling. He lifts it and kisses it*] I'm scared to death.

THE GIRL: I am, too.

YOUNG MAN: I'm not lying—I don't care what happens to me, but I'm scared nobody will ever come out here to this God-forsaken broken-down town and find you. I'm scared you'll get used to it and not mind. I'm scared you'll never get to Frisco and have 'em all turning around to look at you. Listen—go get me a gun, because if they come, I'll kill 'em! They don't understand. Get me a gun!

THE GIRL: I could get my father's gun. I know where he hides it.

YOUNG MAN: Go get it. Never mind the cigarettes. Run all the way [*Pause, smiling but seriously*] Hello, Katey.

THE GIRL: Hello. What's *your* name?

YOUNG MAN: Photo-Finish is what they *call* me. My races are always photo-finish races. You don't know what that means, but it means they're very close. So close the only way they can tell which horse wins is to look at a photograph after the race is over. Well, every race I bet turns out to be a photo-finish race, and my horse never wins. It's my bad luck, all the time. That's why they call me Photo-Finish. Say it before you go.

THE GIRL: Photo-Finish.

YOUNG MAN: Come here. [THE GIRL *moves close and he kisses her*] Now, hurry. Run all the way.

THE GIRL: I'll run. [THE GIRL *turns and runs. The* YOUNG MAN *stands at the center of the cell a long time.* THE GIRL *comes running back in. Almost crying*] I'm afraid. I'm afraid I won't see you again. If I come back and you're not here, I—

YOUNG MAN: Hello—out there!

THE GIRL: It's so lonely in this town. Nothing here but the lonesome wind all the time, lifting the dirt and blowing out to the prairie. I'll stay *here*. I won't *let* them take you away.

YOUNG MAN: Listen, Katey. Do what I tell you. Go get that gun and come back. Maybe they won't come tonight. Maybe they won't come at all. I'll hide the gun and when they let me out you can take it back and put it where you found it. And then we'll go away. But if they come, I'll kill 'em! Now, hurry—

THE GIRL: All right. [*Pause*] I want to tell you something.

YOUNG MAN: O.K.

THE GIRL: [*Very softly*] If you're not here when I come back, well, I'll have the gun and I'll know what to do with it.

YOUNG MAN: You know how to handle a gun?

THE GIRL: I know how.

YOUNG MAN: Don't be a fool. [*Takes off his shoe, brings out some currency*] Don't be a fool, see? Here's some money. Eighty dollars. Take it and go to Frisco. Look around and find somebody. Find somebody alive and halfway human, see? Promise me—if I'm not here when you come back, just throw the gun away and get the hell to Frisco. Look around and find somebody.

THE GIRL: I don't *want* to find anybody.

YOUNG MAN: [*Swiftly, desperately*] Listen, if I'm not here when you come back how do you know I haven't gotten away? Now, do what I tell you. I'll meet you in Frisco. I've got a couple of dollars in my other shoe. I'll see you in San Francisco.

THE GIRL: [*With wonder*] San Francisco?

YOUNG MAN: That's right—San Francisco. That's where you and me belong.

THE GIRL: I've always wanted to go to *some* place like San Francisco —but how could I go alone?

YOUNG MAN: Well, you're not alone any more, see?

THE GIRL: Tell me a little what it's like.

YOUNG MAN: [*Very swiftly, almost impatiently at first, but gradually slower and with remembrance, smiling, and* THE GIRL *moving closer to him as he speaks*] Well, it's on the Pacific to begin with —ocean water all around. Cool fog and seagulls. Ships from all over the world. It's got seven hills. The little streets go up and down, around and all over. Every night the fog-horns bawl. But they won't be bawling for you and me.

THE GIRL: What else?

YOUNG MAN: That's about all, I guess.

THE GIRL: Are people different in San Francisco?

YOUNG MAN: People are the same everywhere. They're different only when they love somebody. That's the only thing that makes 'em different. More people in Frisco love somebody, that's all.

THE GIRL: Nobody anywhere loves anybody as much as I love you.

YOUNG MAN: [*Shouting, as if to the world*] You see? Hearing you say that, a man could die and still be ahead of the game. Now, hurry. And don't forget, if I'm not here when you come back, get the hell to San Francisco where you'll have a chance. Do you hear me? [THE GIRL *stands a moment looking at him, then backs away, turns and runs. The* YOUNG MAN *stares after her, troubled and smiling. Then he turns away from the image of her and walks about like a lion in a cage. After a while he sits down suddenly and buries his head in his hands. From a distance the sound of several automo-*

biles approaching is heard. He listens a moment, then ignores the implications of the sound, whatever they may be. Several automobile doors are slammed. He ignores this also. A wooden door is opened with a key and closed, and footsteps are heard in a hall. Walking easily, almost casually and yet arrogantly, a MAN *comes in. The* YOUNG MAN *jumps up suddenly and shouts at the* MAN, *almost scaring him]* What the hell kind of a jail-keeper are you, anyway? Why don't you attend to your business? You get paid for it, don't you? Now, get me out of here.

THE MAN: But I'm not the jail-keeper.

YOUNG MAN: Yeah? Well, who are you, then?

THE MAN: I'm the husband.

YOUNG MAN: What husband you talking about?

THE MAN: You know what husband.

YOUNG MAN: Hey! *[Pause, looking at* THE MAN] Are you the guy that hit me over the head last night?

THE MAN. I am.

YOUNG MAN: *[With righteous indignation]* What do you mean going around hitting people over the head?

THE MAN: Oh, I don't know. What do you *mean* going around—the way you do?

YOUNG MAN: *[Rubbing his head]* You hurt my head. You got no right to hit anybody over the head.

THE MAN: *[Suddenly angry, shouting]* Answer my question! What do you mean?

YOUNG MAN: Listen, you—don't be hollering at me just because I'm locked up.

THE MAN: *[With contempt, slowly]* You're a dog!

YOUNG MAN: Yeah. Well, let me tell you something. You *think* you're the husband. You're the husband of nothing. *[Slowly]* What's more, your wife—if you want to call her that—is a tramp. Why don't you throw her out in the street where she belongs?

THE MAN: *[Draws a pistol]* Shut up!

YOUNG MAN: Yeah? Go ahead, shoot—*[Softly]* and spoil the fun. What'll your pals think? They'll be disappointed, won't they. What's the fun hanging a man who's already dead? *[*THE MAN *puts* *the gun away*] That's right, because now you can have some fun yourself, telling me what you're going to do. That's what you came here for, isn't it? Well, you don't need to tell me. I *know* what you're going to do. I've read the papers and I know. They have fun. A mob of 'em fall on one man and beat him, don't they? They tear off his clothes and kick him, don't they? And women and little children stand around watching, don't they? Well, before you go on *this* picnic, I'm going to tell you a few things. Not that that's going to send you home with your pals —the other heroes. No. You've been outraged. A stranger has come to town and violated your women. Your pure, innocent, virtuous women. You fellows have got to set this thing right. You're men, not mice. You're home-makers, and you beat your children. [*Suddenly*] Listen, you—I didn't know she was your wife. I didn't know she was anybody's wife.

THE MAN: You're a liar!

YOUNG MAN: Sometimes—when it'll do somebody some good—but not this time. Do you want to hear about it? [THE MAN *doesn't answer*] All right, I'll tell you. I met her at a lunch counter. She came in and sat next to me. There was plenty of room, but she sat next to me. Somebody had put a nickel in the phonograph and a fellow was singing *New San Antonio Rose*. Well, she got to talking about the song. I thought she was talking to the waiter, but *he* didn't answer her, so after a while *I* answered her. That's how I met her. I didn't think anything of it. We left the place together and started walking. The first thing I knew she said, "This is where I live."

THE MAN: You're a dirty liar!

YOUNG MAN: Do you want to hear it? Or not? [THE MAN *does not answer*] O.K. She asked me to come in. Maybe she had something in mind, maybe she didn't. Didn't make any difference to me, one way or the other. If she was lonely, all right. If not, all right.

THE MAN: You're telling a lot of dirty lies!

YOUNG MAN: I'm telling the truth. Maybe your wife's out there with your pals. Well, call her in. I got nothing against her, or you—or any of you. Call her in, and ask her a few questions. Are you in love with her? [THE MAN *doesn't answer*] Well, that's too bad.

THE MAN: What do you mean, too bad?

YOUNG MAN: I mean this may not be the first time something like this has happened.

THE MAN: [*Swiftly*] Shut up!

YOUNG MAN: Oh, you know it. You've always known it. You're afraid of your pals, that's all. She asked me for money. That's all she wanted. I wouldn't be here now if I had given her the money.

THE MAN: [*Slowly*] How much did she ask for?

YOUNG MAN: I didn't ask her how much. I told her I'd made a mistake. She said she would make trouble if I didn't give her money. Well, I don't like bargaining, and I don't like being threatened, either. I told her to get the hell away from me. The next thing I knew she'd run out of the house and was hollering. [*Pause*] Now, why don't you go out there and tell 'em they took me to another jail—go home and pack up and leave her. You're a pretty good guy, you're just afraid of your pals. [THE MAN *draws his gun again. He is very frightened. He moves a step toward the* YOUNG MAN, *then fires three times. The* YOUNG MAN *falls to his knees.* THE MAN *turns and runs, horrified*] Hello—out there! [*He is bent forward.* THE GIRL *comes running in, and halts suddenly, looking at him*]

THE GIRL: There were some people in the street, men and women and kids—so I came in through the back, through a window. I couldn't find the gun. I looked all over but I couldn't find it. What's the matter?

YOUNG MAN: Nothing—nothing. Everything's all right. Listen. Listen, kid. Get the hell out of here. Go out the same way you came in and run—run like hell—run all night. Get to another town and get on a train. Do you hear me?

THE GIRL: What's happened?

YOUNG MAN: Get away—just get away from here. Take any train that's going—you can get to Frisco later.

THE GIRL: [*Almost sobbing*] I don't want to go any place without you.

YOUNG MAN: I can't go. Something's happened. [*He looks at her*] But I'll be with you always—God damn it. Always!

[*He falls forward.* THE GIRL *stands near him, then begins to sob softly, walking away. She stands over to one side, stops sobbing, and stares out. The excitement of the mob outside increases.*

THE MAN, *with two of his pals, comes running in.* THE GIRL
watches, unseen]

THE MAN: Here's the son of a bitch!

ANOTHER MAN: O.K. Open the cell, Harry.

[*The* THIRD MAN *goes to the cell door, unlocks it, and swings it
open. A* WOMAN *comes running in*]

THE WOMAN: Where is he? I want to see him. Is he dead? [*Looking
down at him, as the* MEN *pick him up*] There he is. [*Pause*] Yeah,
that's him. [*Her husband looks at her with contempt, then at the
dead man*]

THE MAN: All right—let's get it over with.

THIRD MAN: Right you are, George. Give me a hand.

[*They lift the body*]

THE GIRL: [*Suddenly, fiercely*] Put him down!

THE MAN: What's this?

SECOND MAN: What are you doing here? Why aren't you out in the
street with the others?

THE GIRL: Put him down and go away. [*She runs toward the* MEN.
THE WOMAN *grabs her*]

THE WOMAN: Here—where do you think *you're* going?

THE GIRL: Let me go! You've no right to take him away.

THE WOMAN: Well, listen to her, will you? [*She slaps* THE GIRL *and
pushes her to the floor*] Listen to the little slut, will you?

[*They all go, carrying the* YOUNG MAN's *body.* THE GIRL *gets up
slowly, no longer sobbing. She looks around at everything, then
looks straight out, and whispers*]

THE GIRL: Hello—out—there! Hello—out there!

NEXT

Terrence McNally

Terrence McNally

A notable Off-Broadway success, *Next* (paired with Elaine May's *Adaptation*) opened at the Greenwich Mews Theatre on February 10, 1969. Clive Barnes of the New York *Times* proclaimed the presentation as "just plain marvelous—funny, provocative and touching" while his Sunday colleague Walter Kerr counseled, "You mustn't miss it!" *The New Yorker*, in a somewhat rare moment of accord with most of the newspaper contingent, reported that it was "the funniest evening imaginable. . . . Terrence McNally is in top form."

The dual bill became an instant smash hit, and within months of its Manhattan premiere, companies were dispatched to present the show in Boston (Kevin Kelly of the Boston *Globe* called it "the highlight of the year") and Los Angeles, where dedicated readers of the *Hollywood Reporter* were enjoined to "hasten immediately to this rare and precious evening of theatre."

Ideally performed by James Coco and Elaine Shore, the play ran for 707 performances in New York.

Born in 1939 and raised in Corpus Christi, Texas, Terrence McNally came to New York to attend Columbia University, where he earned his B.A. degree in English in 1960. On graduation he was awarded the Harry Evans Traveling Fellowship for work in creative writing.

In 1963 Mr. McNally made his Broadway debut as playwright with a new adaptation of *The Lady of the Camellias*, designed and directed by Franco Zeffirelli. Two years later, the author again was represented on Broadway, this time with an original work that had had its première (1964) at the Tyrone Guthrie Theatre, Minneapolis—*And Things That Go Bump in the Night*. The New York presentation (1965) was directed by Michael Cacoyannis and starred Eileen Heckart.

During the 1968–69 season, Mr. McNally was represented on New York stages by six short plays: *Sweet Eros; Witness; ¡Cuba Si!; Tour; Noon;* and *Next.*

The author also enjoyed wide praise for his 1968 television production, *Apple Pie.* The New York *Times* lauded the three short plays in the over-all work as "a bitingly original look at some American attitudes toward the war in Vietnam." Mr. McNally continued his exploration of the same theme in *Bringing It All Back Home,* which was introduced in this editor's collection, *The Best Short Plays* 1969.

In October 1971 his full-length play *Where Has Tommy Flowers Gone?* was produced at the Eastside Playhouse, and in 1973 his *Whiskey* was performed at Theatre at St. Clement's, New York City, and was welcomed as a "hilarious commentary on contemporary society and its standards."

Bad Habits, comprised of two thematically related short plays, both set in curative homes with opposing philosophies, opened Off-Broadway in February 1974, and after 96 showings was transferred to Broadway, where it ran for an additional 177 performances.

The author's most recent Broadway success was the 1975 production *The Ritz,* which entertained audiences for 398 performances, and later was converted into a film with its Tony Award-winning star, Rita Moreno.

Mr. McNally has been the recipient of two Guggenheim Fellowships and a citation from the American Academy of Arts and Letters.

Characters:

Marion Cheever
Sergeant Thech

SCENE: *An examination room decorated in neutral colors; anonymous-looking. Stage left there is an examination table, a scale and a cabinet filled with medical equipment. Stage right there is a desk and two chairs. The only bright color in the room is the American flag, center stage.*

As the curtain rises, the room is empty.

SGT. THECH: [*Offstage*] Next!

[MARION CHEEVER *enters. He is a fat man in his late forties and he is nattily dressed. He carries a brief case*]

MARION: Hello? I'm next!

[*He looks around, puts down his brief case, takes out a cigarette case, lights one up, sits in front of the desk and waits somewhat impatiently*]

SGT. THECH: [*Entering*] No smoking.

MARION: [*Rising*] Good morning. Good morning! [*Briskly*] Well! I think we can get this over with rather quickly.

SGT. THECH: No smoking.

MARION: [*Snuffing out his cigarette*] I'm sorry. Filthy habit. [*He's put his hat on her desk.* SGT. THECH *hands it back to him*] Oh, my hat! I'm sorry!

[*He looks for a place to put it. There is none, so he puts it on the floor*]

SGT. THECH: [*Already busy at her desk with papers and forms*] Your card and bottle, please.

MARION: [*Rummaging in his brief case*] As I was starting to say, I think we can get this over with rather quickly. There's obviously been a mistake. [*He laughs*] I mean I—

SGT. THECH: The government does not make mistakes. If your country has called you it has its reasons. May I have your card and bottle, please?

MARION: [*Still going through his brief case*] I thought to myself, "My God! They can't mean me."

SGT. THECH: That's it.

MARION: Is that it? [*Hands her the card. She begins to type*] I thought to myself there must be someone else in my building with the same name because why else would I get a card to come down here?

SGT. THECH: Is your name Marion Cheever?

MARION: Yes, it is. But you know I just had a fortieth birthday and I thought to myself nobody sends a card like this to a man like me.

SGT. THECH: They're taking older men.

MARION: How old exactly?

SGT. THECH: It's inching up all the time. May I have your bottle, please?

MARION: [*Looking in brief case*] Inching up all the time, is it? The bottle, yes, here it is!

[*He hands her his urine specimen*]

SGT. THECH: Strip.

MARION: I didn't know that . . . the inching up all the time.

SGT. THECH: Remove all articles of clothing including your shoes and socks.

MARION: Who are you?

SGT. THECH: Your examining officer, Sergeant Thech. And by the authority vested in me by this government, I order you to strip.

MARION: A lady examining officer! Oh, that's funny! They must be pretty hard up these days.

SGT. THECH: And if you have not begun to strip in the next ten seconds I will complete these forms without further examination and report you to the board of examiners as fit for duty.

MARION: [*As if coming out of a trance*] Oh, my God, I'm sorry. I didn't hear one word you said. I don't know what I was thinking of. What did you say? That if I hadn't . . .

SGT. THECH: Begun to strip in the next ten seconds . . .

MARION: You will complete those forms . . .

SGT. THECH: Without further examination . . .

MARION: And report me to the board of examiners? . . .

SGT. THECH: As fit for duty.

MARION: [*Biting his lip*] Do you think that's fair?

SGT. THECH: Would you prefer not to strip?

MARION: Indeed I would!

SGT. THECH: Very well, then I will stamp these forms . . .

MARION: No, don't do that!

SGT. THECH: Then you have ten seconds. [*Timing him*] One one-thousand, two one-thousand . . .

MARION: I'm going to strip! [*While* SGT. THECH *counts*] I'm going to let you do it because not only am I over forty, I am not a healthy over forty and . . .

SGT. THECH: Seven one-thousand.

MARION: [*To make her stop*] Where do I go?

SGT. THECH: [*Points to the center of the room*] Right over there.

MARION: Right over there. Well! Everybody else is doing it, why not?

SGT. THECH: [*Filling out a questionnaire*] Your name.

MARION: Do you have a little hanger?

SGT. THECH: Use the stool. Your name.

MARION: Cheever. Marion Cheever.

SGT. THECH: Do you spell Marion with an *o*?

MARION: I do, yes.

SGT. THECH: Age.

MARION: Forty . . . eight! Forty-eight.

SGT. THECH: Sex.

MARION: Did you put that down? I'm forty-eight years old.

SGT. THECH: Sex.

MARION: Well, what do you think I am?

SGT. THECH: Color of hair.

MARION: Brown. Black. Blackish brown.

SGT. THECH: Eyes.

MARION: Two.

SGT. THECH: Color of eyes . . .

MARION: I'm sorry! Blue. Blue-green. Aqua.

SGT. THECH: Occupation.

MARION: [*Still apologizing for the eyes*] You rattled me.

SGT. THECH: Occupation.

MARION: I don't know what's the matter with me.

SGT. THECH: Your occupation, Mr. Cheever.

MARION: I'm a dancer.

SGT. THECH: Toe or tap.

MARION: Oh, really! Toe or tap! I'm the assistant manager of the Fine Arts Theatre, 58th Street and Park Avenue. You've probably heard of us. Toe or tap! I was funning!

SGT. THECH: How long.

MARION: Is what?

SGT. THECH: How long have you been the assistant manager of the Fine Arts Theatre?

MARION: I'm sorry. How long have I been assistant manager of the Fine Arts Theatre? About twelve years.

[*He has removed his shirt by now. His undershirt is torn and dirty. He's trying to find something to hide behind*]

SGT. THECH: Marital status.

MARION: [*Eying the American flag*] Single. Single now. Divorced I guess is what I'm supposed to say.

[*He will use the flag to cover himself as he continues to strip* SGT. THECH *doesn't see all this, as he is behind her and she is busy typing in the questionnaire*]

SGT. THECH: How many times.

MARION: Twice.

SGT. THECH: Number of dependents.

MARION: Three girls.

SGT. THECH: Sex.

MARION: I said three girls!

SGT. THECH: Ages.

MARION: Fourteen, twelve and two. Two with my first wife and one with my second.

SGT. THECH: Did you finish grammar school?

MARION: I certainly did.

SGT. THECH: High school.

MARION: You bet.

SGT. THECH: College.

MARION: No, I never got to college. I meant to but I never . . .

SGT. THECH: Do you belong to a church?

MARION: I just never got there. You know what I mean?

SGT. THECH: Do you belong to a church?

MARION: Oh, yes!

SGT. THECH: Which denomination.

MARION: The Sacred Heart of Jesus.

SGT. THECH: Which denomination.

MARION: Roman Catholic. What do you think with a name like that? It's a temple?

SGT. THECH: Do you attend church?

MARION: You bet.

SGT. THECH: Regularly or occasionally.

MARION: Yes, unh-hunh, unh-hunh!

SGT. THECH: Regularly or occasionally.

MARION: Yes, regularly on occasion.

SGT. THECH: Is your father living or deceased?

MARION: Living.

SGT. THECH: His age.

MARION: Seventy-two.

SGT. THECH: Is your mother living or deceased?

MARION: Deceased.

SGT. THECH: Age of death.

MARION: Thirty-one.

SGT. THECH: Cause of death.

MARION: Natural causes.

SGT. THECH: Be specific.

MARION: Heart.

SGT. THECH: Any brothers.

MARION: Yes.

SGT. THECH: How many?

MARION: One. He's alive.

SGT. THECH: Sisters.

MARION: Two. They're both alive. Both living.

SGT. THECH: Do you live alone?

MARION: At the present time I do. I get a lot of company, of course, but unh, officially, for the record, I live alone.

SGT. THECH: Do you own your own home?

MARION: No. It's a . . . you know . . . residential hotel for . . . unh . . . men. Single men.

[MARION *has undressed now and is sitting on a low stool. The flag is draped across him*]

SGT. THECH: [*Turning to a new page*] Measles.

MARION: What?

SGT. THECH: Have you ever had the measles?

MARION: Oh, measles! No, no I haven't.

SGT. THECH: Chicken pox.

MARION: No, I never had chicken pox.

SGT. THECH: Whooping cough.

MARION: I think it *might* have been. I was coughing an awful lot and I was very sick.

SGT. THECH: Yes or no.

MARION: No. It wasn't *exactly* whooping cough but . . .

SGT. THECH: Rheumatic fever.

MARION: [*Thinking hard*] Unh! Did I have rheumatic fever? Is that what it was? No, no, I don't think so.

SGT. THECH: Mumps.

MARION: [*Jumping at this*] Yes! Yes, yes, yes! Now just a minute on the mumps.

SGT. THECH: Tuberculosis.

MARION: They weren't your ordinary mumps!

SGT. THECH: Jaundice.

MARION: Will you please let me tell you about my mumps! I was in bed for months. I practically had last rites!

SGT. THECH: Venereal disease.

MARION: I don't think you realize how serious my mumps were.

SGT. THECH: Venereal disease.

MARION: Not yet! I just wish you'd let me tell you about my mumps.

SGT. THECH: Allergies.

MARION: What about allergies?

SGT. THECH: Are you allergic to anything?

MARION: Yes, yes, as a matter of fact I am.

SGT. THECH: Go on, explain.

MARION: I know this sounds silly but I'm allergic to peach fuzz. I swell up like a balloon.

SGT. THECH: Anything else?

MARION: No, but I can't even go *near* a fruit stand. All I have to do is look at a peach and . . .

SGT. THECH: Any history of epilepsy.

MARION: Me and peach fuzz is no joke!

SGT. THECH: Have you a family history of diabetes?

MARION: Diabetes? Well, why not. Somebody must have had it.

SGT. THECH: Heart attacks.

MARION: I told you about that.

SGT. THECH: Cancer.

MARION: Bite your tongue!

SGT. THECH: Nervous or mental disorders.

MARION: I'm a nervous wreck!

SGT. THECH: Do you smoke?

MARION: You saw me. Remember? When you came in here, the first thing you said . . .

SGT. THECH: How much.

MARION: Three packs a day. Twenty cigarettes to a pack, that's sixty cigarettes. That's a lot of smoking.

SGT. THECH: Do you drink?

MARION: That, too, oh yes!

SGT. THECH: How much?

MARION: Whenever I smoke. Smoking makes me want to drink, and drinking makes me want to smoke. It's a vicious circle.

SGT. THECH: Do you take any drugs?

MARION: Anything! Give it to me and I'll take it.

SGT. THECH: Name the drugs.

MARION: Aspirins and Bromo Seltzers for the hangovers, Nikoban for the smoking. And Miltown! I take lots of Miltown.

SGT. THECH: For what purpose?

MARION: Because I am a nervous wreck. For what purpose!

SGT. THECH: All right, Mr. Cheever, on the scale now, please. [*She turns and sees him draped in the American flag*] Drop that flag.

MARION: I was just admiring it! I have one just like it at home. [SGT. THECH *returns the flag to its proper place.* MARION *all the while walks along with it, unwilling to give up its protection*] The same colors, the same shape. It's amazing how similar they are! [SGT. THECH *is pulling the flag away from him*] Then could I have a little robe or something? I mean I don't know if it's of any interest to you, but I'm right on the verge of another bad cold. [SGT. THECH *salutes the flag, then makes ready to examine* MARION] I'm going to write somebody a letter about this.

SGT. THECH: On the scale.

MARION: [*Wrapping the sheet around himself*] I'll refuse to go, you know. You're just wasting your time, I hope you understand.

SGT. THECH: On the scale, Mr. Cheever.

[MARION *gets on the scale and plays with the weights*]

MARION: You know something? It's wrong. At least ten pounds off. Easily that.

SGT. THECH: Don't tamper. [*She is washing her hands*]

MARION: What are you going to do? Operate? [SGT. THECH *comes to the scale and weighs him. Next, she makes ready to measure him. When she raises up the measuring pole,* MARION *starts and backs off the scale*] Would you warn someone before you do that? You know you could put someone's eye out with that thing.

SGT. THECH: Step back onto the scale.

[MARION *gets back onto scale while* SGT. THECH *measures him. When she swings the pole back into place* MARION *jumps off again*]

MARION: You missed me by *that* much!

SGT. THECH: [*At the examining table*] Sit at the edge of the table.

MARION: [*Under his breath*] I hate this whole day! It's goddamn humiliating, that's what it is. Calling a man in here and . . .

SGT. THECH: On the table, Mr. Cheever.

MARION: [*Trying a new approach*] I'm sorry I'm not cooperating. You have your job to do, and I'll try to help in every way I can.

SGT. THECH: [*At his back, listening with a stethoscope*] Breathe. In, out. In, out.

MARION: In, out. See when you ask me how simple it is? [SGT. THECH's *stethoscope is at his chest now.* MARION *is very ticklish*] Don't do that!

[*He laughs while* SGT. THECH *listens to his heart*]

SGT. THECH: Unh-hunh!

MARION: What did that mean? "Unh-hunh?" You heard something you didn't like?

SGT. THECH: Open.

[She has a tongue depressor down his throat]

MARION: Just ask me and I'll open! You don't have to lunge at me like that! [SGT. THECH *checks his eyes with a light*] It's on, it's on! [SGT. THECH *looks into his ears with a light*] I hate this. I hate it a lot. [*While* SGT. THECH *checks his ears*] When you were examining my heart, did you hear something I should know about? It wasn't very subtle, going "unh-hunh" like that. It's my ticker, so if there's anything wrong I'd like to know about it. [SGT. THECH *has crossed the room. She turns to face him and speaks very softly. We just see her lips moving*] What? What did you say?

SGT. THECH: Your hearing is perfect.

MARION: Now just a minute. I will not be railroaded.

SGT. THECH: [*Holding up an eye chart*] Read this chart.

MARION: All of it?

SGT. THECH: The third line.

MARION: [*Running all the letters together*] TOZDY!

SGT. THECH: The second line.

MARION: The second line's a little fuzzy.

SGT. THECH: Try the top line, Mr. Cheever.

MARION: [*With much squinting*] The top line's a real problem. Let's see . . . it's a . . . no . . . Z!

SGT. THECH: Excellent.

MARION: Now just a minute. It's an E. I said it was a Z. Now I failed that test. You give me credit for failing.

SGT. THECH: Failure is relative in any case, private.

MARION: Private?

SGT. THECH: [*Back at the examining table*] Lie down.

MARION: You called me private.

SGT. THECH: Lie down.

MARION: You've got me inducted already when I haven't even been given a full opportunity to fail yet.

SGT. THECH: This is your opportunity, Mr. Cheever, don't pass it up. [*Timing him until he obeys*] One one-thousand, two one-thousand . . .

MARION: [*Getting onto the table*] All right, I'm lying! Just stop all that counting. [SGT. THECH *begins to take his blood pressure*] I've heard of shanghaiing but this little episode is really a lulu. It's white slavery if you think I'm passing this test. Out and out kidnapping. I simply won't go. You can't just take a man out of civilian life and plop him into the army. So there's a war on, I didn't start it. [*Lifts his head up a moment*] I think you'll find I have a labile blood pressure. It can rocket at a moment's notice.

SGT. THECH: Keep your head down.

MARION: What do they want with me anyway? I'm on the verge of my big break. Do you know what that means to a civilian? I've stood in the back of that lousy theatre for eleven years, and they are going to promote me next winter. I am going to be *the* manager at quite a substantial raise in salary, thank you. Unh-hunh, sergeant, I'm not going into any army, war or peace!

SGT. THECH: [*While she makes ready to take a blood sample*] I want you to close your eyes and count to ten slowly and then touch the tip of your nose with your left index finger.

MARION: Oh, all right, that sounds easy. I don't mind this part at all. One, two, three, four . . . this is very restful . . . five, six—[*Suddenly sitting up*] Wait! Wait, wait, wait, wait, wait! I saw it. [SGT. THECH *is holding a syringe*] I hate needles. I'm not afraid of them, I just don't like them.

SGT. THECH: Shall I complete the forms, Mr. Cheever, or will you let me continue with the examination?

MARION: I know you must do your job, but please be very careful. I have very small veins. Don't be nervous.

SGT. THECH: Lie down.

MARION: You have all the time in the world. And no air bubbles! [SGT. THECH *is drawing blood*] Oh, my God! I'm going to have a heart attack right on this table. [SGT. THECH *finishes, empties his blood from the syringe into a test tube*] I'm bleeding. Look at this,

I'm bleeding. [SGT. THECH's *hands go under the sheet as she checks his spleen, liver, kidney, etc.*] Just tell me what it is you're looking for and I'll tell you where it's at!

SGT. THECH: In.

MARION: In!

SGT. THECH: Out.

MARION: It's out!

SGT. THECH: In.

MARION: In! In! Oh, my God, oh!

SGT. THECH: On your feet.

MARION: On my feet! Bleed someone to death and tell him on his feet. Sure, why not? Here I go, sergeant, on my feet!

SGT. THECH: Drop your shorts.

MARION: What?

SGT. THECH: You heard me. [*Timing him*] One one-thousand, two one-thousand . . .

MARION: Drop my shorts? Oh no, sergeant, that I flatly refuse.

SGT. THECH: You are a candidate for national service. I am your examining officer and I am ordering you to drop your shorts.

MARION: [*While* SGT. THECH *counts*] Now wait just a minute. Let me explain something. I'm not wearing shorts. I have this . . . well, *problem* . . . and I have to wear this . . . well sort of a *girdle* and . . .

SGT. THECH: Drop your girdle.

MARION: [*As* SGT. THECH *is nearing the count of ten*] Yes! Yes, of course, I'll drop it. I just thought I should explain about my back problem and the abdominal muscles. I thought you'd want to know about them. [MARION *has worked off the girdle. It drops to the floor.* SGT. THECH *is approaching him*] It's off! I swear to God it's off!

[SGT. THECH *has her hand under sheet and at his groin*]

SGT. THECH: Turn your head and cough.

MARION: Oh, really!

SGT. THECH: Cough.

MARION: Cough!

SGT. THECH: Again.

MARION: Cough!

SGT. THECH: Again.

MARION: How many hernias are you checking for? Two's about average, you know. Cough!

SGT. THECH: Well done, Cheever. Now sit.

MARION: [*Sits on the edge of the examining table while* SGT. THECH
checks him for reflexes] You're terrific you are! You and Pegeen
ought to team up. She was my first wife. Talk about your lady
wrestlers and roller-derby queens! But next to you, she was Snow
White. But I foxed her. Just when she thought she had me where
she wanted me, I sprang the divorce on her. "On what grounds,
may I ask?" she growled, fat hands on her fat hips . . . Dutch
Cleanser I used to call her. "On exactly what grounds?" [SGT.
THECH *is busy completing some forms*] "Mental cruelty," I smiled,
and boy did that answer ever throw her for a loop! She begged
me to change it to adultery but I held firm. You should have seen
the look on that judge's face in Juarez when I dropped that little
bombshell. Mental cruelty!

SGT. THECH: All right, Mr. Cheever, you can get dressed now. Your
physical examination is over.

MARION: [*Caught in midair*] Oh. It's over. Well, that wasn't so bad.
How did I do? Am I 4-F?

SGT. THECH: You have nothing to worry about. I found no evidence
of physical abnormality.

MARION: [*Aghast*] You found no evidence of physical abnormality?
Now wait a minute. What about my labile blood pressure? Oh no,
sergeant, I'm not done in here. Not yet. I want more testing.
You're not convinced. I'm not leaving until I get a better verdict.
What about my sinus condition? Did you know I had one? Of
course not, you didn't look up my nose. What kind of examina-
tion is it without looking up a person's nose? A lot of things could
be wrong up there. I can't breathe seven months out of the year.
Would you write that down, please? And what about my eye test?
I know I failed my eye test!

SGT. THECH: [*Busy at her desk tabulating the examination results*] If you won't cooperate, I have to judge you on the basis of objective evidence. You do not squint, you do not wear glasses and you saw my lips moving at a distance of over fifteen feet away. We have ways of evaluating the condition of a subject whether the subject cooperates or not. You'd have to be a lot smarter and better rehearsed than you are to fool an examining officer.

MARION: [*Triumphant*] All right, then what about my feet? You didn't even make me take my socks off. That's all right, I'll do it myself. Here. Now look at this. They're flat. I'm not ashamed. See how flat they are? Do you see any arch? Of course you don't. You call that normal? And see, see all those corns? My feet are covered with corns. And I'll tell you something, something highly abnormal: I was born with all these corns. That's right, sergeant, I was born with corns. They are hereditary. Ask yourself, is that normal? [SGT. THECH *continues working at desk*] And look! [*He shakes his arms in front of her*] No muscle tone. All flab! See how the skin just hangs there? And it's not a question of diet. I've dieted all my life. I simply don't burn fat! [*Now showing her his teeth*] And teeth! My teeth. They're full of decay. If I have a candy bar I have to have an inlay. I swear to God I do. My gums are very spongy. I mean I'll probably have a coronary in five years . . . if I live very carefully. [*Desperately trying to attract* SGT. THECH's *attention*] And sergeant, here, watch this, look now, sergeant, over here, see this? . . . [*He removes his toupee*] You didn't know that, did you? It fools lots of people but there it is. I lost all of my hair in a period of thirteen months after my last divorce. It just went! Right out by the roots it came. Is that normal, to lose so much hair in thirteen months? And that's not hereditary, sergeant. My father still has every hair in his head. You know what my kind of hair loss is? Nerves, sergeant, plain old-fashioned nerves! It's highly irregular he should have all his and I don't have mine! And what about my mind? You haven't asked me one single question about my mind. For all you know I could be a raving lunatic. I could be a . . .

SGT. THECH: [*She's into the psychological and intelligence tests*] I have twelve apples.

MARION: [*Thrown*] You have what?

SGT. THECH: You have twelve apples. Together we have . . .

MARION: [*Involuntarily*] Twenty-four apples.

[*He realizes what he's done and groans*]

SGT. THECH: I have a pie which I wish to divide as follows: one-fourth of the pie to Fred, one-fourth of the pie to Phyllis, one-fourth of the pie to you. How much pie will I have left for myself?

MARION: [*Thinks a moment*] Who are Fred and Phyllis? I mean maybe Phyllis didn't finish all her piece and then there'd be more for you. A quarter and a half!

SGT. THECH: You are on a train going sixty miles an hour. Your destination is a hundred and twenty away. How many hours will it take you to get to your destination?

MARION: I would say three days. But then I don't take trains. I really wouldn't swear to that answer.

SGT. THECH: Who was the first President of the United States?

MARION: George Washington. Was that right?

SGT. THECH: Who were the allies of the United States in the Second World War?

MARION: The good people.

SGT. THECH: Who were its enemies?

MARION: No one. We had no enemies.

SGT. THECH: Who are the allies of the United States now?

MARION: Just about everyone.

SGT. THECH: Who are its enemies?

MARION: Who can tell?

SGT. THECH: Name three of the twelve Apostles.

MARION: Joseph . . . and his brother . . . and his sister!

SGT. THECH: In what year did Columbus discover America?

MARION: 1776. No, wait, it was 1775!

SGT. THECH: What is the great pox and how does it differ from the small pox?

MARION: The great pox is greater than the small pox. However, both are poxes.

SGT. THECH: If you found an unopened letter lying on the sidewalk, fully addressed and stamped, what would you do?

MARION: I would probably step on it. I mean who wouldn't? You're walking along, you'd be surprised what you step on!

SGT. THECH: If you were seated in a theatre and you saw a fire break out nearby before the rest of the audience noticed it—what would you do?

MARION: That one's right up my alley. As a theatre manager I know about this. The main thing is I wouldn't want to start a panic. So I'd very quietly leave and go home.

SGT. THECH: If you found a wallet lying on the sidewalk—what would you do?

MARION: I'd be delighted. I never find anything.

SGT. THECH: What is the similarity between a chair and a couch?

MARION: A chair and a couch? You can sit on them.

SGT. THECH: A rabbit and a squirrel.

MARION: [Reasonably] You could sit on a rabbit and a squirrel. The rabbit might even like it.

SGT. THECH: What is the difference between a giant and a dwarf?

MARION: The difference? I see the similarity all right but the difference is tricky.

SGT. THECH: A profit and a loss.

MARION: A profit is when the loss is greater than the sum. It's exactly like giants and dwarfs.

SGT. THECH: A man and a gorilla.

MARION: Hair. Lots of hair.

SGT. THECH: Complete the following sentences. People obey the law because . . .

MARION: Because! Because they have to obey it.

SGT. THECH: I am happiest when my family is . . .

MARION: Yes! I think we all are. Well, aren't you?

SGT. THECH: What is the meaning of the following proverbs. He who laughs last laughs best.

MARION: Yes . . . well . . . that means that *he* who laughs *last* laughs *best*.

SGT. THECH: A rolling stone gathers no moss.

MARION: That's one of my favorites. It means that a rolling *stone* . . . gathers no *moss!*

SGT. THECH: I am going to say a word.

MARION: Did I get that one right?

SGT. THECH: After I say it I want you to say the first word that comes to your mind without thinking.

MARION: Are you sure?

SGT. THECH: You have one second. Tree. Tree!

MARION: I'm sorry. I was thinking. I couldn't help myself.

SGT. THECH: House.

MARION: House. The first word that comes to mind when you say house is house.

SGT. THECH: Father.

MARION: [*Drawing a blank*] Father . . . father . . .

SGT. THECH: Grass.

MARION: Green. There, I got one!

SGT. THECH: Shower.

MARION: Tree. When it showers you stand under a tree with your father.

SGT. THECH: Snake.

MARION: Juicy. Juicy snake.

SGT. THECH: House.

MARION: Whores. No, no! That's not right.

SGT. THECH: Mother.

MARION: None. I mean . . .

SGT. THECH: Green.

MARION: Colors. Green colors.

SGT. THECH: Floor.

MARION: Me. Really! I'm on my feet all day.

SGT. THECH: Purse.

MARION: Snatch. Purse snatcher.

SGT. THECH: Have you ever suffered from night terrors?

MARION: Terribly.

SGT. THECH: Insomnia.

MARION: Of course insomnia! Because of the night terrors.

SGT. THECH: Sleepwalking.

MARION: Absolutely! In the morning my ankles are so swollen!

SGT. THECH: Anxiety states.

MARION: This is so good in here this part! Keep on.

SGT. THECH: Hallucinations.

MARION: Of grandeur. Of course terrible grandeur!

SGT. THECH: Delusions.

MARION: They're not the same thing? Listen, can't we go back to the anxiety states?

SGT. THECH: Compulsive eating.

MARION: No, I've never been bothered by that. About my anxiety states . . . !

SGT. THECH: Have you ever indulged in homosexual activities.

MARION: They have been very good to me.

SGT. THECH: When did you stop?

MARION: Who said anything about stopping? They're a small but vital minority. The Fine Arts Theatre welcomes them.

SGT. THECH: Did you have a normal relationship with your mother?

MARION: I'm sure she thought so!

SGT. THECH: Did you have a normal relationship with your father?

MARION: After we stopped dating the same girl, everything was fine.

SGT. THECH: Do you have any history of bedwetting?

MARION: Even my top sheet is rubber.

SGT. THECH: Have you ever attempted suicide?

MARION: No, but I've thought of murder.

SGT. THECH: Are you now or have you ever been a member of the Communist party?

MARION: I wouldn't be surprised. I mean you join anything nowadays and next thing you know it's pinko.

SGT. THECH: What is your responsibility to your community?

MARION: Unh . . . to shovel the snow.

SGT. THECH: What is your responsibility to your family?

MARION: To be there.

SGT. THECH: What is your responsibility to your country?

MARION: To be there.

SGT. THECH: [*Abruptly*] All right, Mr. Cheever, you may go now. The examination is over.

MARION: The whole thing?

SGT. THECH: That's right.

MARION: Well? How did I do? Am I 4-F yet?

SGT. THECH: I don't think you have anything to worry about. I doubt if they would find someone like you acceptable.

MARION: [*Stung, but hiding it*] Oh well, good. Good. Based on what? The last two answers?

SGT. THECH: The entire psychological examination.

MARION: I see. Well, then I *am* 4-F?

SGT. THECH: You'll get your classification in the mail.

MARION: I can hardly wait.

SGT. THECH: You may go now. I'm through with you.

[SGT. THECH *turns her back to him and begins typing up his test results*]

MARION: [*Beginning to dress*] Oh, don't worry, I'm going. Nothing in the world could make me stay here. Granted, I've enjoyed all this. I mean you've been just wonderful. It must be difficult examining someone while they're still alive and breathing! And your attention has been so flattering. I'm not used to so much fuss. You're great, just great. The way you concentrated on me. I never distracted you from me once. I'm sure you have a big future ahead of you. [SGT. THECH *types*] Now you're through with me and would like me to go. You have taken my time, you have taken my blood, you have taken my urine, you have taken my secrets and now you would like me out of here so you can digest them in private. Isn't that right? Well, I'm not going. If I go I take *all* of me with me. I'd like my blood and my urine back! I mean I'm 4-F, you can't have any use for them. [SGT. THECH *types*] You know I am not simply the sum total of my parts. I am someone. I am a citizen. I have my rights. I pay my taxes, I serve my jury duty, I buy American. I don't make trouble. I support the administration. I keep my mouth shut. I believe everything I read. I do all that and that gives me rights! I want my blood and my urine back and I . . . I demand an apology! I have given everything to everyone and now I want something back! Don't tell me about responsibilities. I visit my kids, I bring them presents; I visit my father, I bring him presents; I visit my sisters, their kids get presents, too. I pay my rent; I pay my alimony; I meet my car payments—a hot red Mustang I can hardly fit behind the wheel of, but I'm meeting those payments! I do everything I'm supposed to do . . . I'm never late for work . . . and now I demand a reward! I want a reward. You owe me something. My country owes me something. Somebody owes me something. Because I have nothing! My big break? A lousy twenty-bucks raise. Big deal, crap! My children don't give a damn. What do I get on Father's Day? A lot of crap from Woolworth's their mothers picked out. My father doesn't recognize my voice on the telephone. My mother is dead. I've been married twice. You think it's fun, a man my age going home alone at night? Who looks at men like me after a while? I know what I look like! I'm no fool! [SGT. THECH *continues typing*] You know what the ushers at the theatre call me behind my back? Fatso. Yeah! that hurts. But when I become *the* manager I am going to fire those ushers and hire new ushers and *they* will call me Fatso behind my back. Because that is exactly what I am. A fatso. I am nothing but what I eat. But I feed myself. Nobody feeds me. And I eat everything I want. When I want candy, I eat candy. When I want a pizza at two A.M., I call up and order pizza. I'm going to get older and fatter and someday I'm going to die from overweight and smoking. But when I go, I'm paying for my own funeral and I'm going to give myself the best funeral that money can buy. Because dead or alive I pay my own way! Those niggers on relief, can they say that? They cannot! And they get to do everything. They get to riot, they get to loot, they get to yell, they get to hate, they get to kill! They

get in the papers, they get on television and everybody pays attention. Everybody cares. And what do I get? There's nothing on television about me. My name's not in the Sunday papers. And I'm
the one who does everything he should. I'm the one who never
makes trouble. I'm the good citizen. But everybody else gets to do
everything! You see those teen-age girls with their skirts up to here
strutting around with their hair all piled up and driving a man
crazy. And those men all like fags with that hair and those pants.
They do anything they want. They have anything they want. And
I get shit! [*He bangs on* SGT. THECH's *desk with his fist.* SGT. THECH
goes on typing] How dare you call me in here, examine me, ignore
me, dismiss me and tell me I'm not acceptable. *You* are not acceptable! I want my orange juice. You took my blood and I want
my orange juice. I know my rights. I want my radiator fixed. I
want those people next door to turn their radio down when I bang
on the wall. I want quiet. I want my sleep. I want them to stop all
those parties upstairs. I want people to listen to me when I call up
and make complaints. Not just sit there and type. Stop it! And listen to me! [SGT. THECH *has finished typing up her report*] I said
stop! [*He puts his hands over the typewriter keys*] Good. Very
good! [*Now* MARION *will describe everything* SGT. THECH *does while
she is doing it—as if he were giving her the orders to do it*] That's
right. Fold the paper. Open the drawer. Put it away. Close it. Now
you're doing exactly as you're told. Get up. Fold the sheet. Check
the instruments. Make sure you've got everything. One final check
now. Excellent. Now out you go. Close the door. There! [SGT.
THECH *has left the room, closing the door behind her*] All right, on
the scale now, Cheever! Do I have to? Why not? There's nothing
to be afraid of. [MARION *gets on the scale*] You're the perfect
weight, just right for your height. You're an excellent physical
specimen, Cheever. Am I? You're in very good shape. You're very
acceptable. [MARION *steps off the scale*] On the table now.
[MARION *crosses to the examination table*] Lie down. [MARION
obeys] Give me your arm. Will it hurt? Not you, Cheever. You're
very brave. [MARION *moves his lips silently: "Can you hear what
I'm saying?"*] Yes, you said, "Can you hear what I'm saying?"
Your hearing is perfect. I know. Now read the chart. The last line,
the smallest letters. "A-W-G-H-L." Excellent, you have perfect vision. Rest now. Thank you. [MARION *lets his head drop on the
table*] Tell me about it. I was thirteen years old. Yes, go on. I

came home and she wasn't there. Yes. It was so sudden. None of us knew. We all thought she would always be there and then when she wasn't . . . [*His voice trails off in tears*] You must have been very sad. I was, I was. I felt so cold. Didn't you tell anyone how you felt? Nobody asked me. I'm asking you. I never got to say good-bye. I understand. [*Short pause*] On your feet now. I don't think I can. Yes, Cheever, you can do it. You're very strong now and very brave and very acceptable. [MARION *gets up off the table*] Up now, shoulders back, walk tall. That's it. You're doing fine. [MARION *goes to* SGT. THECH's *desk, puts on her white examination coat which she has left over her chair, sits, types a moment, then looks up*] You have ten seconds to strip. By the power vested in me by the United States government I order you to remove all articles of clothing. One one-thousand, two one-thousand, three one-thousand, four one-thousand. Sorry. You are not acceptable. [*His head spins around as he looks straight ahead into the audience*] NEXT!

[*The lights snap off*]

CURTAIN

BOUND EAST FOR CARDIFF

Eugene O'Neill

Eugene O'Neill

Eugene O'Neill (1888–1953) was born in New York City, the son of the well-known romantic actor James O'Neill. He was exposed to the theatre at an early age for he spent a good portion of his formative years backstage and on tour with his parents. His primary education, though fragmentary, was received at various private schools. After a year at Princeton and a brief period as a gold prospector, he signed on as a seaman for several voyages to South America and elsewhere, all the while assimilating impressions that later he was to utilize in his sea plays. Then came short sojourns as an actor and reporter for a newspaper in New London, Connecticut. After a few months' apprentice work there, his health broke down. He wrote in 1919: "My lungs being affected, I spent six months in a sanatorium thinking it over. It was in this enforced period of reflection that the urge to write first came to me. The next fall, I began my first play—*The Web*. In 1914–15, I was a student in Professor [George Pierce] Baker's English '47 at Harvard. The summer of 1916 I spent at Provincetown, Massachusetts. It was during that summer the Provincetown Players, who have made the original productions of nearly all my short plays in New York, were first organized."

It was in that same year that the group staged the initial production of *Bound East for Cardiff* at Provincetown, and in the autumn presented it at the Playwrights' Theatre in Greenwich Village, New York.

One of the original members of the Provincetown Players, Susan Glaspell, recalled in 1927: "I may see it through memories too emotional, but it seems to me I have never sat before a more moving production than our *Bound East for Cardiff*, when Eugene O'Neill was produced for the first time on any stage. . . . The sea has been good to him. It was there for his opening. There was a fog, just as the script demanded, fog bell in the harbor. The tide was in, and it washed under us and around, spraying through the holes in the floor, giving us the rhythm and the flavor of the sea while the big dying sailor talked to his friend Drisc of the life he had always wanted deep in the land, where you'd never see a ship or smell the sea. . . . It is not merely figurative language to say the old wharf shook with applause."

Bound East for Cardiff was the first of O'Neill's memorable S.S. *Glencairn* cycle. The others that were to follow: *In the Zone; The Long Voyage Home;* and *The Moon of the Caribbees.*

In 1920 O'Neill came to Broadway with *Beyond the Horizon,* which won him his first Pulitzer Prize. He was to receive three more: for *Anna Christie; Strange Interlude;* and, posthumously, *A Long Day's Journey into Night.* In 1936 he was awarded the Nobel Prize for Literature, the only American dramatist to be so honored.

Among the great dramatist's other works are *The Emperor Jones; The Hairy Ape; All God's Chillun Got Wings; Desire Under the Elms; The Great God Brown; Lazarus Laughed; Marco Millions; Mourning Becomes Electra; Ah, Wilderness!; Days Without End; The Iceman Cometh; A Moon for the Misbegotten; A Touch of the Poet; Hughie;* and *More Stately Mansions.*

Characters:

Yank
Driscoll
Cocky
Davis
Scotty
Olson
Paul
Smitty
Ivan
The Captain
The Second Mate

SCENE: *The seamen's forecastle of the British tramp steamer Glencairn on a foggy night midway on the voyage between New York and Cardiff. An irregularly shaped compartment, the sides of which almost meet at the far end to form a triangle. Sleeping bunks about six feet long, ranged three deep with a space of three feet separating the upper from the lower, are built against the sides. On the right above the bunks three or four portholes can be seen. In front of the bunks, rough wooden benches. Over the bunks on the left, a lamp in a bracket. In the left foreground, a doorway. On the floor near it, a pail with a tin dipper. Oilskins are hanging from a hook near the doorway.*

The far side of the forecastle is so narrow that it contains only one series of bunks.

In under the bunks a glimpse can be had of seachests, suit cases, seaboots, etc., jammed in indiscriminately.

At regular intervals of a minute or so the blast of the steamer's whistle can be heard above all the other sounds.

Five men are sitting on the benches talking. They are dressed in dirty patched suits of dungaree, flannel shirts, and all are in their stocking feet. Four of the men are pulling on pipes and the air is heavy with rancid tobacco smoke. Sitting on the top bunk in the left foreground, a Norwegian, PAUL, is softly playing some folk song on a battered accordion. He stops from time to time to listen to the conversation.

In the lower bunk in the rear a dark-haired, hard-featured man is lying apparently asleep. One of his arms is stretched limply over the side of the bunk. His face is very pale, and drops of clammy perspiration glisten on his forehead.

It is nearing the end of the dog watch—about ten minutes to eight in the evening.

COCKY: [*A wizened runt of a man. He is telling a story. The others are listening with amused, incredulous faces, interrupting him at the end of each sentence with loud derisive guffaws*] Makin' love to me, she was! It's Gawd's truth! A bloomin' nigger! Greased all over with cocoanut oil, she was. Gawd blimey, I couldn't stand 'er. Bloody old cow, I says; and with that I fetched 'er a biff on the ear wot knocked 'er silly, an'——[*He is interrupted by a roar of laughter from the others*]

DAVIS: [*A middle-aged man with black hair and mustache*] You're a liar, Cocky.

SCOTTY: [*A dark young fellow*] Ho-ho! Ye werr neverr in New Guinea in yourr life, I'm thinkin'.

OLSON: [*A Swede with a drooping blond mustache—with ponderous sarcasm*] Yust tink of it! You say she wass a cannibal, Cocky?

DRISCOLL: [*A brawny Irishman with the battered features of a prizefighter*] How cud ye doubt ut, Ollie? A quane av the naygurs she musta been surely. Who else wud think herself aqual to fallin' in love wid a beauthiful, divil-may-care rake av a man the loike av Cocky? [*A burst of laughter from the crowd*]

COCKY: [*Indignantly*] Gawd strike me dead if it ain't true, every bleedin' word of it. 'Appened ten year ago come Christmas.

SCOTTY: 'Twas a Christmas dinner she had her eyes on.

DAVIS: He'd a been a tough old bird.

DRISCOLL: 'Tis lucky for both av ye ye escaped; for the quane av the cannibal isles wad 'a died av the belly ache the day afther Christmas, divil a doubt av ut. [*The laughter at this is long and loud*]

COCKY: [*Sullenly*] Blarsted fat 'eads!

[*The sick man in the lower bunk in the rear groans and moves restlessly. There is a hushed silence. All the men turn and stare at him*]

DRISCOLL: Ssshh! [*In a hushed whisper*] We'd best not be talkin' so loud and him tryin' to have a bit av a sleep. [*He tiptoes softly to the side of the bunk*] Yank! You'd be wantin' a drink av wather, maybe? [YANK *does not reply.* DRISCOLL *bends over and looks at him*] It's asleep he is, sure enough. His breath is chokin' in his throat loike wather gurglin' in a poipe. [*He comes back quietly and sits down. All are silent, avoiding each other's eyes*]

COCKY: [*After a pause*] Pore devil! It's over the side for 'im, Gawd 'elp 'im.

DRISCOLL: Stop your croakin'! He's not dead yet and, praise God, he'll have many a long day yet before him.

SCOTTY: [*Shaking his head doubtfully*] He's bod, mon, he's verry bod.

DAVIS: Lucky he's alive. Many a man's light woulda gone out after a fall like that.

OLSON: You saw him fall?

DAVIS: Right next to him. He and me was goin' down in number two hold to do some chippin'. He puts his leg over careless-like and misses the ladder and plumps straight down to the bottom. I was scared to look over for a minute, and then I heard him groan and I scuttled down after him. He was hurt bad inside for the blood was drippin' from the side of his mouth. He was groanin' hard, but he never let a word out of him.

COCKY: An' you blokes remember when we 'auled 'im in 'ere? Oh, 'ell, 'e says, oh, 'ell—like that, and nothink else.

OLSON: Did the captain know where he iss hurted?

COCKY: That silly ol' josser! Wot the 'ell would 'e know abaht anythink?

SCOTTY: [*Scornfully*] He fiddles in his mouth wi' a bit of glass.

DRISCOLL: [*Angrily*] The divil's own life ut is to be out on the lonely sea wid nothin' betune you and a grave in the ocean but a spindle-shanked, gray-whiskered auld fool the loike av him. 'Twas enough to make a saint shwear to see him wid his gold watch in his hand, tryin' to look as wise as an owl on a tree, and all the toime he not knowin' whether 'twas cholery or the barber's itch was the matther wid Yank.

SCOTTY: [*Sardonically*] He gave him a dose of salts, na doot?

DRISCOLL: Divil a thing he gave him at all, but looked in the book he had wid him, and shook his head, and walked out widout sayin' a word, the second mate afther him no wiser than himself, God's curse on the two av thim!

COCKY: [*After a pause*] Yank was a good shipmate, pore beggar. Lend me four bob in Noo Yark, 'e did.

DRISCOLL: [*Warmly*] A good shipmate he was and is, none better. Ye said no more than the truth, Cocky. Five years and more ut is since first I shipped wid him, and we've stuck together iver since through good luck and bad. Fights we've had, God help us, but 'twas only when we'd a bit av drink taken, and we always shook hands the nixt mornin'. Whativer was his was mine, and many's the toime I'd a been on the beach or worse, but for him. And now ——[*His voice trembles as he fights to control his emotion*] Divil take me if I'm not startin' to blubber loike an auld woman, and he not dead at all, but goin' to live many a long year yet, maybe.

DAVIS: The sleep'll do him good. He seems better now.

OLSON: If he wude cat something——

DRISCOLL: Wud ye have him be eatin' in his condishun? Sure it's hard enough on the rest av us wid nothin' the matther wid our insides to be stomachin' the skoff on this rusty lime-juicer.

SCOTTY: [*Indignantly*] It's a starvation ship.

DAVIS: Plenty o' work and no food—and the owners ridin' around in carriages!

OLSON: Hash, hash! Stew, stew! Marmalade, py damn! [*He spits disgustedly*]

COCKY: Bloody swill! Fit only for swine is wot I say.

DRISCOLL: And the dishwather they disguise wid the name av tea! And the putty they call bread! My belly feels loike I'd swalleyed a dozen rivets at the thought av ut! And sea-biscuit that'd break the tecth av a lion if he had the misfortune to take a bite at one! [*Unconsciously they have all raised their voices, forgetting the sick man in their sailor's delight at finding something to grumble about*]

PAUL: [*Swings his feet over the side of his bunk, stops playing his accordion, and says slowly*] And rot-ten po-tay-toes! [*He starts in playing again. The sick man gives a groan of pain*]

DRISCOLL: [*Holding up his hand*] Shut your mouths, all av you. 'Tis a hell av a thing for us to be complainin' about our guts, and a sick man maybe dyin' listenin' to us. [*Gets up and shakes his fist at the Norwegian*] God stiffen you, ye squarehead scut! Put down that organ av yours or I'll break your ugly face for you. Is that banshee schreechin' fit music for a sick man?

[*The Norwegian puts his accordion in the bunk and lies back and closes his eyes.* DRISCOLL *goes over and stands beside* YANK. *The steamer's whistle sounds particularly loud in the silence*]

DAVIS: Damn this fog! [*Reaches in under a bunk and yanks out a pair of seaboots, which he pulls on*] My lookout next, too. Must be nearly eight bells, boys.

[*With the exception of* OLSON, *all the men sitting up put on oilskins, sou'westers, seaboots, etc., in preparation for the watch on deck.* OLSON *crawls into a lower bunk on the right*]

SCOTTY: My wheel.

OLSON: [*Disgustedly*] Nothin' but yust dirty weather all dis voyage. I yust can't sleep when weestle blow. [*He turns his back to the light and is soon fast asleep and snoring*]

SCOTTY: If this fog keeps up, I'm tellin' ye, we'll no be in Carrdiff for a week or more.

DRISCOLL: 'Twas just such a night as this the auld Dover wint down. Just about this toime ut was, too, and we sittin' round in the fo'castle, Yank beside me, whin all av a suddint we heard a great slitherin' crash, and the ship heeled over till we was all in a heap on wan side. What came afther I disremimber exactly, except 'twas a hard shift to get the boats over the side before the auld teakittle sank. Yank was in the same boat wid me, and sivin morthal days we drifted wid scarcely a drop of wather or a bite to chew on. 'Twas Yank here that held me down whin I wanted to jump into the ocean, roarin' mad wid the thirst. Picked up we were on the same day wid only Yank in his senses, and him steerin' the boat.

COCKY: [*Protestingly*] Blimey but you're a cheerful blighter, Driscoll! Talkin' abaht shipwrecks in this 'ere blushin' fog.

[YANK *groans and stirs uneasily, opening his eyes.* DRISCOLL *hurries to his side*]

DRISCOLL: Are ye feelin' any betther, Yank?

YANK: [*In a weak voice*] No.

DRISCOLL: Sure, you must be. You look as sthrong as an ox. [*Appealing to the others*] Am I tellin' him a lie?

DAVIS: The sleep's done you good.

COCKY: You'll be 'avin your pint of beer in Cardiff this day week.

SCOTTY: And fish and chips, mon!

YANK: [*Peevishly*] What're yuh all lyin' fur? D'yuh think I'm scared to——[*He hesitates as if frightened by the word he is about to say.*]

DRISCOLL: Don't be thinkin' such things!

[*The ship's bell is heard heavily tolling eight times. From the forecastle head above the voice of the lookout rises in a long wail:* Aaall's welll. *The men look uncertainly at* YANK *as if undecided whether to say good-by or not*]

YANK: [*In an agony of fear*] Don't leave me, Drisc! I'm dyin', I tell yuh. I won't stay here alone with every one snorin'. I'll go out on deck. [*He makes a feeble attempt to rise, but sinks back with a sharp groan. His breath comes in wheezy gasps*] Don't leave me, Drisc! [*His face grows white and his head falls back with a jerk*]

DRISCOLL: Don't be worryin', Yank. I'll not move a step out av here —and let that divil av a bosun curse his black head off. You speak a word to the bosun, Cocky. Tell him that Yank is bad took and I'll be stayin' wid him a while yet.

COCKY: Right-o.

[COCKY, DAVIS, *and* SCOTTY *go out quietly*]

COCKY: [*From the alleyway*] Gawd blimey, the fog's thick as soup.

DRISCOLL: Are ye satisfied now, Yank? [*Receiving no answer, he bends over the still form*] He's fainted, God help him! [*He gets a tin dipper from the bucket and bathes* YANK's *forehead with the water.* YANK *shudders and opens his eyes*]

YANK: [*Slowly*] I thought I was goin' then. Wha' did yuh wanta wake me up fur?

DRISCOLL: [*With forced gayety*] Is it wishful for heaven ye are?

YANK: [*Gloomily*] Hell, I guess.

DRISCOLL: [*Crossing himself involuntarily*] For the love av the saints don't be talkin' loike that! You'd give a man the creeps. It's chippin' rust on deck you'll be in a day or two wid the best av us.

[YANK *does not answer, but closes his eyes wearily. The seaman who has been on lookout,* SMITTY, *a young Englishman, comes in and takes off his dripping oilskins. While he is doing this the man whose turn at the wheel has been relieved enters. He is a dark burly fellow with a round stupid face. The Englishman steps softly over to* DRISCOLL. *The other crawls into a lower bunk*]

SMITTY: [*Whispering*] How's Yank?

DRISCOLL: Better. Ask him yourself. He's awake.

YANK: I'm all right, Smitty.

SMITTY: Glad to hear it, Yank. [*He crawls to an upper bunk and is soon asleep*]

IVAN: [*The stupid-faced seaman who came in after* SMITTY *twists his head in the direction of the sick man*] You feel gude, Jank?

YANK: [*Wearily*] Yes, Ivan.

IVAN: Dot's gude. [*He rolls over on his side and falls asleep immediately*]

YANK: [*After a pause broken only by snores—with a bitter laugh*] Good-by and good luck to the lot of you!

DRISCOLL: Is ut painin' you again?

YANK: It hurts like hell—here. [*He points to the lower part of his chest on the left side*] I guess my old pump's busted. Ooohh! [*A spasm of pain contracts his pale features. He presses his hand to his side and writhes on the thin mattress of his bunk. The perspiration stands out in beads on his forehead*]

DRISCOLL: [*Terrified*] Yank! Yank! What is ut? [*Jumping to his feet*] I'll run for the captain. [*He starts for the doorway*]

YANK: [*Sitting up in his bunk, frantic with fear*] Don't leave me, Drisc! For God's sake, don't leave me alone! [*He leans over the side of his bunk and spits.* DRISCOLL *comes back to him*] Blood! Ugh!

DRISCOLL: Blood again! I'd best be gettin' the captain.

YANK: No, no, don't leave me! If yuh do I'll git up and follow you. I ain't no coward, but I'm scared to stay here with all of them asleep and snorin'. [DRISCOLL, *not knowing what to do, sits down on the bench beside him. He grows calmer and sinks back on the mattress*] The captain can't do me no good, yuh know it yourself. The pain ain't so bad now, but I thought it had me then. It was like a buzz-saw cuttin' into me.

DRISCOLL: [*Fiercely*] God blarst ut!

[*The* CAPTAIN *and the* SECOND MATE *of the steamer enter the forecastle. The* CAPTAIN *is an old man with gray mustache and whiskers. The* MATE *is clean-shaven and middle-aged. Both are dressed in simple blue uniforms*]

THE CAPTAIN: [*Taking out his watch and feeling* YANK's *pulse*] And how is the sick man?

YANK: [*Feebly*] All right, sir.

THE CAPTAIN: And the pain in the chest?

YANK: It still hurts, sir, worse than ever.

THE CAPTAIN: [*Taking a thermometer from his pocket and putting it into* YANK's *mouth*] Here. Be sure and keep this in under your tongue, not over it.

THE MATE: [*After a pause*] Isn't this your watch on deck, Driscoll?

DRISCOLL: Yes, sorr, but Yank was fearin' to be alone, and—

THE CAPTAIN: That's all right, Driscoll.

DRISCOLL: Thank ye, sorr.

THE CAPTAIN: [*Stares at his watch for a moment or so; then takes the thermometer from* YANK's *mouth and goes to the lamp to read it. His expression grows very grave. He beckons the* MATE *and* DRISCOLL *to the corner near the doorway.* YANK *watches them furtively. The* CAPTAIN *speaks in a low voice to the* MATE] Way up, both of them. [*To* DRISCOLL] Has he been spitting blood again?

DRISCOLL: Not much for the hour just past, sorr, but before that—

THE CAPTAIN: A great deal?

DRISCOLL: Yes, sorr.

THE CAPTAIN: He hasn't eaten anything?

DRISCOLL: No, sorr.

THE CAPTAIN: Did he drink that medicine I sent him?

DRISCOLL: Yes, sorr, but it didn't stay down.

THE CAPTAIN: [*Shaking his head*] I'm afraid—he's very weak. I can't do anything else for him. It's too serious for me. If this had only happened a week later we'd be in Cardiff in time to——

DRISCOLL: Plaze help him some way, sorr!

THE CAPTAIN: [*Impatiently*] But, my good man, I'm not a doctor. [*More kindly as he sees* DRISCOLL'*s grief*] You and he have been shipmates a long time?

DRISCOLL: Five years and more, sorr.

THE CAPTAIN: I see. Well, don't let him move. Keep him quiet and we'll hope for the best. I'll read the matter up and send him some medicine, something to ease the pain, anyway. [*Goes over to* YANK] Keep up your courage! You'll be better tomorrow. [*He breaks down lamely before* YANK'*s steady gaze*] We'll pull you through all right—and—hm—well—coming, Robinson? Dammit! [*He goes out hurriedly, followed by the* MATE]

DRISCOLL: [*Trying to conceal his anxiety*] Didn't I tell you you wasn't half as sick as you thought you was? The Captain'll have you out on deck cursin' and swearin' loike a trooper before the week is out.

YANK: Don't lie, Drisc. I heard what he said, and if I didn't I c'd tell by the way I feel. I know what's goin' to happen. I'm goin' to—— [*He hesitates for a second—then resolutely*] I'm goin' to die, that's what, and the sooner the better!

DRISCOLL: [*Wildly*] No, and be damned to you, you're not. I'll not let you.

YANK: It ain't no use, Drisc. I ain't got a chance, but I ain't scared. Gimme a drink of water, will yuh, Drisc? My throat's burnin' up. [DRISCOLL *brings the dipper full of water and supports his head while he drinks in great gulps*]

DRISCOLL: [*Seeking vainly for some word of comfort*] Are ye feelin' more aisy loike now?

YANK: Yes—now—when I know it's all up. [*A pause*] You mustn't take it so hard, Drisc. I was just thinkin' it ain't as bad as people think—dyin'. I ain't never took much stock in the truck them sky-pilots preach. I ain't never had religion; but I know whatever it is what comes after it can't be no worser'n this. I don't like to leave you, Drisc, but—that's all.

DRISCOLL: [*With a groan*] Lad, lad, don't be talkin'.

YANK: This sailor life ain't much to cry about leavin'—just one ship after another, hard work, small pay, and bum grub; and when we git into port, just a drunk endin' up in a fight, and all your money gone, and then ship away again. Never meetin' no nice people; never gittin outa sailor town, hardly, in any port; travellin' all over the world and never seein' none of it; without no one to care whether you're alive or dead. [*With a bitter smile*] There ain't much in all that that'd make yuh sorry to lose it, Drisc.

DRISCOLL: [*Gloomily*] It's a hell av a life, the sea.

YANK: [*Musingly*] It must be great to stay on dry land all your life and have a farm with a house of your own with cows and pigs and chickens, 'way in the middle of the land where yuh'd never smell the sea or see a ship. It must be great to have a wife, and kids to play with at night after supper when your work was done. It must be great to have a home of your own, Drisc.

DRISCOLL: [*With a great sigh*] It must, surely; but what's the use av thinkin' av ut? Such things are not for the loikes av us.

YANK: Sea-farin' is all right when you're young and don't care, but we ain't chickens no more, and somehow, I dunno, this last year has seemed rotten, and I've had a hunch I'd quit—with you, of course —and we'd save our coin, and go to Canada or Argentine or some place and git a farm, just a small one, just enough to live on. I never told yuh this cause I thought you'd laugh at me.

DRISCOLL: [*Enthusiastically*] Laugh at you, is ut? When I'm havin' the same thoughts myself, toime afther toime. It's a grand idea and we'll be doin' ut sure if you'll stop your crazy notions—about —about bein' so sick.

YANK: [*Sadly*] Too late. We shouldn'ta made this trip, and then—— How'd all the fog git in here?

DRISCOLL: Fog?

YANK: Everything looks misty. Must be my eyes gittin' weak, I guess. What was we talkin' of a minute ago? Oh, yes, a farm. It's too late. [*His mind wandering*] Argentine, did I say? D'yuh remember the times we've had in Buenos Aires? The moving pictures in Barracas? Some class to them, d'yuh remember?

DRISCOLL: [*With satisfaction*] I do that; and so does the piany player. He'll not be forgettin' the black eye I gave him in a hurry.

YANK: Remember the time we was there on the beach and had to go to Tommy Moore's boarding house to git shipped? And he sold us rotten oilskins and seaboots full of holes, and shipped us on a skysail yarder round the Horn, and took two months' pay for it. And the days we used to sit on the park benches along the Paseo Colon with the vigilantes lookin' hard at us? And the songs at the Sailor's Opera where the guy played ragtime—d'yuh remember them?

DRISCOLL: I do, surely.

YANK: And La Plata—phew, the stink of the hides! I always liked Argentine—all except that booze, caña. How drunk we used to git on that, remember?

DRISCOLL: Cud I forget ut? My head pains me at the menshun av that divil's brew.

YANK: Remember the night I went crazy with the heat in Singapore? And the time you was pinched by the cops in Port Said? And the time we was both locked up in Sydney for fightin'?

DRISCOLL: I do so.

YANK: And that fight on the dock at Cape Town——[*His voice betrays great inward perturbation*]

DRISCOLL: [*Hastily*] Don't be thinkin' av that now. 'Tis past and gone.

YANK: D'yuh think He'll hold it up against me?

DRISCOLL: [*Mystified*] Who's that?

YANK: God. They say He sees everything. He must know it was done in fair fight, in self-defense, don't yuh think?

DRISCOLL: Av course. Ye stabbed him, and be damned to him, for the skulkin' swine he was, afther him tryin' to stick you in the back, and you not suspectin'. Let your conscience be aisy. I wisht I had nothin' blacker than that on my sowl. I'd not be afraid av the angel Gabriel himself.

YANK: [*With a shudder*] I c'd see him a minute ago with the blood spurtin' out of his neck. Ugh!

DRISCOLL: The fever, ut is, that makes you see such things. Give no heed to ut.

YANK: [*Uncertainly*] You don't think He'll hold it up agin me—God, I mean.

DRISCOLL: If there's justice in hiven, no! [YANK *seems comforted by this assurance*]

YANK: [*After a pause*] We won't reach Cardiff for a week at least. I'll be buried at sea.

DRISCOLL: [*Putting his hands over his ears*] Ssshh! I won't listen to you.

YANK: [*As if he had not heard him*] It's as good a place as any other, I s'pose—only I always wanted to be buried on dry land. But what the hell'll I care then? [*Fretfully*] Why should it be a rotten night like this with that damned whistle blowin' and people snorin' all round? I wish the stars was out, and the moon, too; I c'd lie out on deck and look at them, and it'd make it easier to go—somehow.

DRISCOLL: For the love av God don't be talkin' loike that!

YANK: Whatever pay's comin' to me yuh can divvy up with the rest of the boys; and you take my watch. It ain't worth much, but it's all I've got.

DRISCOLL: But have ye no relations at all to call your own?

YANK: No, not as I know of. One thing I forgot: You know Fanny the barmaid at the Red Stork in Cardiff?

DRISCOLL: Sure, and who doesn't?

YANK: She's been good to me. She tried to lend me half a crown when I was broke there last trip. Buy her the biggest box of candy yuh c'n find in Cardiff. [*Breaking down—in a choking voice*] It's hard to ship on this voyage I'm goin' on—alone! [DRISCOLL *reaches out and grasps his hand. There is a pause, during which both fight to control themselves*] My throat's like a furnace. [*He gasps for air*] Gimme a drink of water, will yuh, Drisc? [DRISCOLL *gets him a dipper of water*] I wish this was a pint of beer. Oooohh! [*He chokes, his face convulsed with agony, his hands tearing at his shirt front. The dipper falls from his nerveless fingers*]

DRISCOLL: For the love av God, what is ut, Yank?

YANK: [*Speaking with tremendous difficulty*] S'long, Drisc! [*He stares straight in front of him with eyes starting from their sockets*] Who's that?

DRISCOLL: Who? What?

YANK: [*Faintly*] A pretty lady dressed in black. [*His face twitches and his body writhes in a final spasm, then straightens out rigidly*]

DRISCOLL: [*Pale with horror*] Yank! Yank! Say a word to me for the love av hiven! [*He shrinks away from the bunk, making the sign of the cross. Then comes back and puts a trembling hand on* YANK's *chest and bends closely over the body*]

COCKY: [*From the alleyway*] Oh, Driscoll! Can you leave Yank for arf a mo' and give me a 'and?

DRISCOLL: [*With a great sob*] Yank! [*He sinks down on his knees beside the bunk, his head on his hands. His lips move in some half-remembered prayer*]

COCKY: [*Enters, his oilskins and sou'wester glistening with drops of water*] The fog's lifted. [COCKY *sees* DRISCOLL *and stands staring at him with open mouth.* DRISCOLL *makes the sign of the cross again*]

COCKY: [*Mockingly*] Sayin' 'is prayers! [*He catches sight of the still figure in the bunk and an expression of awed understanding comes over his face. He takes off his dripping sou'wester and stands, scratching his head. In a hushed whisper*] Gawd blimey!

THE CURTAIN FALLS

THE TYPISTS

Murray Schisgal

Murray Schisgal

Murray Schisgal was born in the East New York section of Brooklyn, on November 25, 1926. He attended Thomas Jefferson High School, but left when he was seventeen to serve in the United States Navy during World War II. After his discharge in 1946, he worked at a number of odd jobs (including playing saxophone and clarinet with a small jazz band) and pursued his education at night. He earned his high school diploma, took classes at Long Island University, and studied law at Brooklyn Law School. In 1953 he received his LL.B. degree and went into law practice in an office on Delancey Street in lower Manhattan. He relinquished the legal profession in 1956 and turned to teaching in New York City's public school system. While teaching, he worked for his B.A. degree at the New School for Social Research. Between classroom activities, Mr. Schisgal also devoted much time to writing, first fiction, then plays. As he once explained in an interview: "I write because I need to. I've written four novels and many short stories, all unpublished. I seem to write more effectively for the stage. I write about things that disturb me and which only can be placated by my writing of them."

In 1960, after completing five short plays, Mr. Schisgal quit teaching and set off for Spain "to do nothing but write." En route, he stopped in London and, at the suggestion of a friend, took his plays to the British Drama League. The ruling powers of that organization were duly impressed and decided to produce two of the plays, *The Typists* and *The Postman* (later renamed *The Tiger*). The double bill opened in December 1960, and its reception prompted the staging of his full-length work, *Ducks and Lovers*, at the Arts Theatre, London, in October 1961.

The Typists and *The Tiger* opened at the Off-Broadway Orpheum Theatre on February 4, 1963, with Eli Wallach and Anne Jackson as the principals in both plays. Well received, the production ran for 200 performances and won several awards including the Drama Desk-Vernon Rice Award for outstanding achievement in the Off-Broadway theatre. *The Typists* later was presented on television with Mr. Wallach and Miss Jackson, and *The Tiger* was made into a film under the title *The Tiger Makes Out*, with the original stars re-creating their stage roles.

Mr. Schisgal's greatest success came on November 11, 1964, when his comedy *Luv* opened at the Booth Theatre, New York. Directed by Mike Nichols, and with Eli Wallach, Anne Jackson, and Alan Arkin comprising the cast, it ran for 901 performances on Broadway, had two national tours, and was translated into nineteen languages for presentation in twenty-six countries. It was subsequently filmed with Jack Lemmon, Peter Falk, and Elaine May.

In 1967 the author was represented once again Off-Broadway by the double bill of *Basement* and *Fragments* (with James Coco and Gene Hackman), and this was followed in 1968 with the Broadway engagement of his comedy *Jimmy Shine*, which starred Dustin Hoffman.

Subsequent New York productions included: *A Way of Life* (1969); *The Chinese* and *Dr. Fish* (1970); *An American Millionaire* (1974); and *All Over Town* (1974).

Frequently described as an avant-garde author with black comedy tendencies, Mr. Schisgal has readily conceded that he has been enormously influenced by the works of Antonin Artaud, Luigi Pirandello, Jean Genet, and Eugene Ionesco, among others. His plays seem, on the surface, to be "a sort of pop-art theatre of the absurd," but beneath the comic surface, there is always pathos and compassion. And in *The Typists*, as he amuses us, he also reminds us of the sadness, self-delusion, and reconciliation that underlie and infuse the human condition.

Characters:

Sylvia
Paul

THE TIME: *At twenty-odd years of age.*

THE SCENE: *An office: forward, center, a pair of simple metal typewriter tables, with leaves extended, on which there are two old standard typewriters, stacks of postcards, and a bulky telephone directory on each; rear, a large window, two tall green steel file cabinets, a desk between them on which there are a great many telephone directories and a telephone, a door to the restroom; at the right wall, forward, a water cooler, a wooden coat hanger, the entrance door; in the left wall, the door to the employer's office.*

The sun streams through the window; as the play progresses it fades imperceptibly until, at the end, the room is almost in complete darkness.

The same clothes are worn throughout by the actors, although altered to suit the physical changes—subtle, almost unnoticed when they occur—that take place during the course of the play.

SYLVIA PAYTON *enters from right. She is late for work. She throws her coat on the hanger, rushes across the room, deposits her lunch bag in the top drawer of a cabinet, removes cover from her typewriter and begins typing rapidly, glancing anxiously at the employer's door. In a moment she relaxes; she types slowly and hums to herself; she takes her comb and mirror from her pocketbook and fixes her hair. The front door opens. She puts everything away and without turning to see who has entered she starts to type rapidly again.* PAUL CUNNINGHAM *approaches, passing his lunch bag from hand to hand.*

PAUL: Good morning. I'm Paul Cunningham. I was hired yesterday by . . . [*Laughing uneasily*] That's funny. I forgot his name. You'll have to excuse me. First day on the job . . . I'm a little nervous. It was the boss who hired me, though; at least that's what he said.

SYLVIA: I know. He told me. [*Rising, shaking his hand*] Sylvia. Miss Sylvia Payton. Glad to meet you, Mr. Cunningham. If you'll hang up your coat I'll show you what you have to do.

PAUL: I'm sorry I'm late, Miss Payton. I got on the wrong train by mistake. Generally you'll find that I'm a pretty prompt person.

SYLVIA: Oh, that's all right. Just make sure it doesn't happen too often. He's very strict when it comes to being here on time. And now that he's made me responsible for this whole department . . . Of course I won't say anything to him about this morning.

PAUL: I'd appreciate that a lot.

SYLVIA: Don't even mention it. Believe me, I didn't ask him to be made a supervisor. I don't like telling anyone what to do; that's part of my nature, I guess. You give me your lunch bag, Mr. Cunningham. I'll put it in the file cabinet; that's where I keep mine.

PAUL: Thanks. I was sure lucky to get this job. I go to school at night and a lot of firms don't hire you if they know that.

SYLVIA: You must be a very ambitious person. What are you studying?

PAUL: [Proudly] Law. Another three years and I should get my degree. Boy, that's one day I'm looking forward to.

SYLVIA: It must be extremely difficult to have a job and go to school at the same time.

PAUL: It's been real rough so far. But it has its advantages. When I get out, I'm going to have the satisfaction of knowing I did it myself, with my own sweat and my own money; that's more than most fellows my age can say.

SYLVIA: How true that is.

PAUL: Listen, I have an uncle who's a lawyer, a pretty darn famous lawyer, too. Francis T. Cunningham. You ask anybody in the legal field about Francis T. Cunningham and they'll tell you how much he's worth. Well, if I wanted to, I just have to pick up that phone, give him a ring and my worrying days would be over. But that's not for me; no, sir. I'll do it alone or I'm not doing it at all.

SYLVIA: [Uncovers PAUL's typewriter, opens directory for him] I think you're a hundred percent right. You know, I once went with a boy —it was nothing serious, it could have been, but . . . I won't go into that now. Anyway, his father was helping him through medical school. He didn't have to earn a penny of his own. Do you think he finished? What happened was that his father remarried and stopped giving him money. He fell completely apart; you never saw anything like it.

PAUL: There's no substitute for character.

SYLVIA: That's exactly the point. Well, we'd better get to work before he starts screaming. We're on a promotion campaign now and it's a very important job. I suppose that's why you were hired. What we do is type out the names and addresses of prospective customers on these postcards. The advertisement is printed on the back. We get the information we want straight from the telephone book. Don't leave out any names; go right down the line. He checks everything and he can be awfully mean if he wants to. I've just started on the A's, so you'll start with the . . .

PAUL: B's.

SYLVIA: Right. That way we'll be sure to get everyone.

PAUL: It sounds easy enough.

SYLVIA: It is. And after awhile you can do it without even thinking.
    [*They are both seated, typing*]

PAUL: Ooops! My first card and my first mistake. I'm afraid I'm a little rusty. I haven't been doing much typing lately. [*He is about to throw card into basket*]

SYLVIA: No, don't throw it away. If he sees it, he'll raise the roof. At the beginning you ought to type more slowly. Lean back in your chair. Posture's very important. And strike each key with the same steady rhythm.

PAUL: Like this?

SYLVIA: Better, much better; don't move your head; keep your eyes on the material you're typing.

PAUL: [*Sitting rigidly, uncomfortably*] It's really nice of you to help me this way.

SYLVIA: I'm only too glad to, Mr. Cunningham.

PAUL: Paul.

SYLVIA: [*Staring at him, warmly*] Paul. [*The buzzer rings once*] That's for me. [*Quickly tidying herself*] He doesn't usually call me in this early. You go on with your work, Paul. He gets furious when he doesn't hear these typewriters going. He probably wants to know why it took us so long to get started this morning. Don't worry. I'll cover up for you.

PAUL: [*Holding her arm*] Thanks for everything, Sylvia.

SYLVIA: You're welcome . . . Paul. [PAUL *watches her as she swings her hips self-consciously and exits to employer's office. He then starts to type, makes an error, crumples card and is about to throw it into basket, on second thought he slips the card into his pocket. Again he types and makes an error, looks guiltily toward the employer's office and slips card into his pocket. All the while he whistles to the tune of "Way Down Upon The Swanee River. . . ."* SYLVIA *re-enters, angrily*] He's got some goddamn nerve! What does he think I am, a child? I see it doesn't pay to be nice to people. Well, he can just go and look for someone else to do his dirty work. I'm leaving! [*Gathers her things together*]

PAUL: What happened?

SYLVIA: Bawling me out for being five minutes late; that's nerve, believe me.

PAUL: [*Laughing*] So you were late this morning, too?

SYLVIA: There's nothing funny about it, Paul. When you've devoted as much time and energy as I have to this firm, giving them the best you're capable of, then maybe you'll see things differently. Where are my gloves?

PAUL: [*Rising, gives them to her*] Here they are. Listen, Sylvia; you're excited. Why don't you think about it, huh?

SYLVIA: There's nothing to think about. When he asks you where I went, you just tell him for me that I don't care to associate with a firm that has no feelings for its employees. [*She struggles with coat, he helps her put it on*]

PAUL: It's not easy finding a job now, I can tell you that.

SYLVIA: With my experience? You must be joking. I've been made many many offers in the past that I've refused out of a sense of loyalty to that . . . to that sex maniac in there. This is my reward.

PAUL: I wouldn't give him the satisfaction; no, sir.

SYLVIA: What satisfaction?

PAUL: Well, it stands to reason that he wanted you to quit, doesn't it? He knows you're a sensitive girl. By leaving you're doing just what he wants.

SYLVIA: You think he deliberately . . .

PAUL: Why else would he have bawled you out?

SYLVIA: [*Slight pause; takes off coat, puts it on hanger*] I'd die before I gave him the satisfaction. If that's what he has in mind, he's got another guess coming. I'm leaving at my convenience, not his.

PAUL: Now you're talking.

SYLVIA: Believe me, there'll come a day when he'll really need me. "Miss Payton, won't you please help me get this job through in time?" Then it'll be my turn. I'll just laugh right in his stupid face and walk out.

PAUL: Boy, I'd like to be here to see it. Is he married?

SYLVIA: Who would marry him? Ugly as sin, that's what he is. [*They type, laugh over the noise of their typing, then suddenly stop*] We had a girl working here once, she was a riot. She used to draw these caricatures and mail them to him; anonymously, of course. But you should have seen them; they were the funniest thing.

   [*They type, laugh, stop suddenly*]

PAUL: The last job I had was for this woman, Mrs. Jameson. She was as blind as a bat without her glasses. You know what we used to do? Whenever we got the chance we hid her glasses somewhere in the office. For two or three days until she'd find them, we didn't have to do anything, not a single piece of work. We just sat around talking all day.

SYLVIA: I was with an insurance company when I graduated from high school. There was this man in charge there, Mr. Williams, his name was, and he used to have loose hands, if you know what I mean.

PAUL: I know.

SYLVIA: Well, one day he was telling me how to type a policy and he let his hands fall—very, very casually—on my shoulder. So I turned around and looked up at him and spat right in his face.

PAUL: You were fired, I bet.

SYLVIA: As a matter of fact we got along very well after that.

   [*They type; stop suddenly; turn to one another*]

PAUL: Have you read any good books lately?

SYLVIA: I read a very good detective novel last week. It was called *Murder in Bombay.*

PAUL: I'm a science fiction man myself.

[*They type; stop suddenly; turn to one another*]

SYLVIA: Can I ask you something?

PAUL: Sure. What is it?

SYLVIA: If you had to choose between getting a million dollars or losing a leg which would you take?

PAUL: Right leg or left leg?

SYLVIA: Any leg.

PAUL: [*Pause*] I'd take the million dollars.

SYLVIA: I wouldn't. I'd keep my legs.

[*They type; stop suddenly. They both stare at the audience,* PAUL *leaning forward,* SYLVIA *back in her chair, her face expressionless, her hands in her lap*]

PAUL: I was born in a poor section of Brooklyn. My parents were at each other's throat most of the time. It was a miserable childhood. I had no brothers or sisters; there was only the three of us living in this old run-down house, with cats crying and screaming all night in the alley. Why my parents ever got married, I don't know, and why they stayed together for as long as they did I don't know that either. They're separated now. But it doesn't much matter any more. They were as unlike as any two people could be. All my father wanted was to be left alone to smoke his pipe and listen to the radio. My mother—she was a pretty woman, she knew how to dress, all right—she liked to go out and enjoy herself. I was stuck between the two of them and they pulled on both sides. I couldn't talk to one without the other accusing me of being ungrateful; I couldn't touch or kiss one of them without being afraid that the other one would see me and there would be a fight. I had to keep my thoughts to myself. I had to grow up wishing for some kind of miracle. I remember coming home from school one afternoon. I must have been twelve or thirteen. There was this man in the living room with my mother. They weren't doing anything; they were just sitting and talking. But I felt that something was going on. I seemed to stop breathing and I ran out of the house and threw up on the curbstone. Later on I swore to myself that I would make a miracle happen; that I wouldn't ever have to be where I didn't want to be and I wouldn't have to do what I didn't want to do; that I could be myself, without being afraid. But it's rough. With a background like mine you're always trying to catch up; it's as if you were born two steps behind the next fellow.

[*They type; stop suddenly. They both stare at the audience,* SYLVIA *leaning forward,* PAUL *back in his chair, etc.*]

SYLVIA: My family never had money problems. In that respect we were very fortunate. My father made a good living, while he was alive, that is. He passed away when I was seventeen. You could say he and my mother had a fairly happy marriage. At least we never knew when they were angry with one another, and that's a good thing for children. I have a sister. Charlotte. She's older than I am. She's married now and we don't bother much with each other. But when we were younger you wouldn't believe what went on. Every time we quarreled, according to my parents she was right; I was always wrong. She got everything she wanted, no matter what, and I had to be content with the leftovers. It was just unbearable. Anyway, my father was sick for a long time before he passed away. He had this ring, it was a beautiful ring, with a large onyx stone in it, and when I was a girl I used to play with it. I'd close one eye and I'd look inside of it and I'd see hundreds and hundreds of beautiful red and blue stars. My father had always promised me that ring; he always said it belonged to me. I thought for certain he'd give it to me before he passed away, but he didn't say anything about it; not a word. Well, afterward, I saw it. You know where I saw it? On my sister's finger. He had given it to her. Now I don't think that's a background that leaves many possibilities for development. I don't forgive my father; definitely not. And I don't forgive my sister. My mother, whom I now support with my hard work, still says I'm wrong.

[*They type; stop suddenly; turn to one another*]

PAUL: Do you go to the movies?

SYLVIA: Not too often.

PAUL: Me neither.

SYLVIA: Do you like to watch television?

PAUL: I never get the chance. Don't forget I go to school five nights a week. But my wife watches it a lot; that's all she does.

SYLVIA: [*Surprised*] I didn't know you were married.

PAUL: [*Types*] This machine's full of errors. I'm getting nowhere fast. [*He is about to crumple card*]

SYLVIA: [*Rising*] Let me see that please. [*Examines card, incommensurate anger*] Now this could be erased. We don't approve of wasting material when it can be saved. That isn't the policy of this office.

PAUL: Okay. You don't have to be mad. I'll do it.

SYLVIA: I'm not mad. But I am responsible for what goes on in this department. I'm sick and tired of covering up for your mistakes. Everyone must think I'm a piece of rag to be stepped on. First him and now you.

PAUL: Do you mind telling me what you're talking about!

SYLVIA: You know very well what I'm talking about. This is my thanks; this is what I get for trying to be helpful and nice to people. I'm wrong I know. I'm always wrong. Everything I do is wrong. Well, Mr. Cunningham, I've had enough, quite enough, and I won't take any more from you or anyone else. I won't! I won't! [*She flees upstage to the restroom.* PAUL *slaps the typewriter, goes to telephone, dials*]

PAUL: [*Loudly*] Let me speak to Mr. Francis T. Cunningham, please. Who's calling? Paul Cunningham! [*Softly*] Hello, Uncle Frank. It's me again. Paul. How . . . how are you? Everything all right? That's good. Oh, everything's fine with me; still plugging away. I got a new job; yeah, typing, office work; just enough for bread. Uhuh. Uncle, can't you give me a hand? It's too rough for me. I can't hold down a job and go to school five nights a week; it's killing me. I know, I know. But I thought if you could give me a part-time job in your office, or maybe one of your friends, if you spoke to them . . . Yeah, sure. I understand. It's okay. Yeah. Send my regards.

[PAUL *returns to typewriter.* SYLVIA *enters, exchanges her directory. Her appearance is that of a woman in her thirties*]

SYLVIA: I'm sorry for losing my temper, Paul. It won't happen again.

PAUL: Forget it. [*He types*]

SYLVIA: You've become an expert at that machine.

PAUL: [*Glumly*] At least I am an expert at something.

SYLVIA: Is anything the matter?

PAUL: No, but I was just thinking. What am I knocking myself out for? School almost every night, weekends I'm home studying, I can't remember the last time I took a decent vacation. What for? You're young only once; this is the time to enjoy yourself.

SYLVIA: [*At typewriter*] I don't know how true that is. You probably could enjoy yourself a great deal more if you were a lawyer; that's why some sacrifices have to be made now.

PAUL: That's the kind of logic that leads nowhere. By your reasoning all lawyers should be happy men. No, sir; that isn't the way life is. You could be a ditch-digger and be happy if you know how to live. I tell you, I've had it. A fellow in my position has to take advantage of what's offered to him. He's got to be practical and look the facts right in the eye. [*Tapping table*] This here is what's offered to me. This is my chance and from now on I start concentrating on this job. I'll show him I'm on the ball and maybe he'll find something else for me, give me a promotion, a better salary. Why not? An outfit this big always needs men who aren't afraid to work. Listen, I've got two kids at home. I've got to start thinking of them, too.

SYLVIA: [*Stiffly*] You have two children?

PAUL: Sure. I don't waste any time. Look, I've got their pictures here. We took these last summer. [*He shows her photographs inside wallet*] Well, what do you think?

SYLVIA: [*Coldly*] They're beautiful, Paul. What's their names?

PAUL: Frank and Sally. But we call the boy Buddy; he hates it when we call him Frank; funny rascal. They're not bad for a character like me, are they? You know what I'm going to do, Syl? I'm going right in to him and ask him what my chances for advancement are. I might as well get all this settled now. Frankly I can use a little more money, too. The expenses are killing me. If we had a union in this place, we'd get some action. I may do something about that yet. [*He heads for employer's office, turns*] What . . . what would you say is the best way to approach him?

SYLVIA: I honestly don't know, Paul. He changes from one minute to the next. But if he isn't wearing his glasses, that's a bad sign; I know that much.

PAUL: Glasses . . . I got it. Wish me luck?

SYLVIA: I hope you get something good. [*After* PAUL *exits, she goes to phone, dials*] Ma? Sylvia. No, I'm all right. Did the lamp come? Well, just make sure when it comes that it isn't damaged; you'll have to sign for it and that means you inspected it. Look at it carefully; if there isn't any damage you can sign, but if there's anything wrong with it, the smallest thing, refuse to sign and tell the man to take it back. Do you understand? I hope so. Did I . . . get any calls? I didn't say I was expecting any, don't put words in my mouth, I merely asked you if I got any. Never mind. It's not important. Did Charlotte call? How is she? [PAUL *enters left. He has the appearance of a man in his thirties.* SYLVIA *carries on the remainder of her call as though talking to a boyfriend*] Oh, stop being silly. I really couldn't. I have something this Saturday. I mean it. [*Laughing*] No, no. Well, perhaps Sunday. Call me at home. All right. Bye.

PAUL: [*At typewriter*] It looks good, real good. He's considering it. He says they may need someone on the sales staff. I'm first on the list.

SYLVIA: That does sound good. What about the raise?

PAUL: I'll have to wait awhile, he said. But I'll get it. He was impressed, especially when I told him I had some legal experience. You should have seen his eyes open up. It's only a question of time, and once I start moving, you watch, it's going to take a pretty fast man to keep up with me.

SYLVIA: You certainly have ambition, Paul.

PAUL: [*Rises to exchange directory*] Listen, I don't intend to spend the rest of my life working here or any place else. I'll make my bundle and that's it. There's a world outside that window, a world with a thousand different things to see and do, and I'm going to see and do every last one of them; you watch.

SYLVIA: There's a million different things to do in the world.

PAUL: Lie in the sun . . .

SYLVIA: Dance . . .

PAUL: Travel . . .

SYLVIA: Wear pretty clothes.

PAUL: Visit places . . .

SYLVIA: Meet interesting people . . .

PAUL: Mountains. A place with mountains . . .

SYLVIA: [*Grabs* PAUL's *lapels, her emotions soaring*] Oh, Paul, I'm so filled with the desire to live, to experience things, to laugh . . . Oh, I want to laugh, Paul!

[*Silence.* PAUL *stares dumbly at her, clears his throat. Stiffly they return to their chairs, type energetically*]

PAUL: [*In a moment, calmly*] When do we have lunch?

SYLVIA: We can have it any time we want. But I usually have it at one. The later you have it the shorter the afternoon is.

PAUL: How about waiting until one-thirty?

SYLVIA: That isn't easy.

PAUL: I know, but then we'd only have a couple of more hours to go. The afternoon would fly. What do you say?

SYLVIA: I'm willing, if you are.

PAUL: It's a deal, then. One-thirty lunch. [*They shake hands*]

SYLVIA: One-thirty.

PAUL: Right.

[*They both type*]

SYLVIA: You know, I'm getting hungry already.

PAUL: So am I. I didn't have any breakfast.

SYLVIA: I had a cup of coffee, that's all.

PAUL: What have you got for lunch?

SYLVIA: A tuna-fish sandwich with tomatoes and mayonnaise, an orange and a piece of layer cake. What did you bring?

PAUL: Two turkey sandwiches and an apple, I think.

SYLVIA: One-thirty. [*They shake hands*]

PAUL: That's the deal. [*They both type*] We went down to China-town last weekend. What a meal we had.

SYLVIA: I'm crazy about Chinese food. I once went with a fellow who knew how to speak Chinese and you should have seen the things he ordered; the most fantastic dishes, with chicken livers and mushrooms and almonds . . .

PAUL: The Chinese people can cook, all right, but when it comes to *real* cooking you can't beat the Italians. There's a place we go to on the West Side; you should taste their veal parmesan or their chicken cacciatore. And they make a spaghetti sauce, you could . . .

SYLVIA: [*Goes to file cabinet*] I think I'll eat now.

PAUL: [*Rising, furiously*] We made a deal, didn't we?

SYLVIA: Don't be childish. If I want to eat now, I'll eat now, and that's all there is to it.

PAUL: You women are all alike. No backbone. No self-discipline. Go ahead and eat, I'm not going to stop you. But I'm sticking to my word.

SYLVIA: I didn't say I was going to eat, Mr. Cunningham. I merely said I was thinking of eating; listen before you speak. [*She waves at him blank postcards which she has taken from cabinet*] And if you want to know something else, I could probably wait longer than you; I could probably go without lunch, which is more than some people can say.

PAUL: [*At typewriter*] Is that so?

SYLVIA: [*At typewriter*] That's so exactly.

PAUL: We'll see, Miss Supervisor.

SYLVIA: You're jealous. It's coming out all over you. I am supervisor . . .

PAUL: [*Waving his arm*] Of this whole department. Boy, I'll never forget that as long as I live. [*Mimicking her in a small voice*] "Believe me, Mr. Cunningham, I didn't ask him to be made supervisor. I don't like telling anyone what to do; that's part of my nature . . ." [*He falls on typewriter in a fit of laughter*]

SYLVIA: You just keep that up and you won't be working here much longer, I assure you of that, Mr. Cunningham.

PAUL: Tell him. Go ahead and tell him. You'd be doing me a favor!

SYLVIA: What? You mean a man with your legal experience, with your plans and ambitions, requires a favor from me?

PAUL: Miss Payton, I loathe you!

SYLVIA: That, Mr. Cunningham, would be a gross understatement to describe my feelings for you. You make me sick!

PAUL: Why don't you quit, then?

SYLVIA: Why don't you?

PAUL: I wouldn't give you the satisfaction.

SYLVIA: And I wouldn't give you the satisfaction!

[*They both type, loudly, rapidly*]

PAUL: [*Slaps keys*] What the hell am I doing? This isn't what I want. No, goddamn it!

SYLVIA: [*Without looking at him*] I wonder if the man knows what he wants.

PAUL: [*Almost ominously*] You bet I do. And do you know what it is? You know what I'd really like to do? Now, right here in this office? [*Rises, moves around* SYLVIA's *chair*] I'd like to rip the clothes right off your back, piece by piece. I'd like to dig my fingers into your flesh and feel your body break and sweat under mine. Do you understand me, Miss Payton?

SYLVIA: [*Rises; softly*] Paul.

PAUL: It's been eating me up, ever since I first saw you. I want you, Miss Payton. Now! Now! This minute! Here, on the floor, screaming your lungs out and with your legs kicking up in the air. That's all I've been thinking of at that stupid typewriter; that's all that's been on my mind. [*Pause*] Now you know.

SYLVIA: And what do you think I've been thinking of? My body aches with wanting you, Paul. [*Turning, pointing to his typewriter*] How many times have I closed my eyes, just hoping you'd do something instead of sitting there like a stone statue! [*She falls back into him; he embraces her around the waist, standing behind her*]

PAUL: Sylvia.

SYLVIA: I'll have to tell my mother, Paul. And you should tell your wife. Oh, I'll be good to the children. I promise you that.

PAUL: [Stunned] Tell my wife?

SYLVIA: We will get married, won't we?

PAUL: Sylvia, listen . . .

SYLVIA: [Turning to face him] We will get married, won't we?

PAUL: Aw, the hell with it! I'm going to eat. [Gets lunch bag, throws coat over arm]

SYLVIA: [At typewriter] It's my fault, I know; you don't have to tell me.

PAUL: It's nobody's fault. It's . . . the way things are. [At door right] Can I get you anything?

SYLVIA: I'm not eating.

PAUL: Suit yourself. [PAUL exits. SYLVIA runs to cabinet, takes out lunch bag; she eats her sandwich ravenously. The door is suddenly thrown open. Quickly SYLVIA turns, clutching the sandwich to her chest, hiding it] Are you sure you don't want anything?

SYLVIA: [With a mouthful of food] Positive.

PAUL: All right.

[PAUL exits. SYLVIA goes to the phone, slowly, lethargically, dials]

SYLVIA: Ma? Sylvia. Nothing's wrong. I'm having my lunch now. The sandwich is fine. Did the table come? How is it? Are you sure? Sometimes they get damaged in shipping. Did you look carefully? Well, I hope so. Yes. Did I get any calls? No, I wasn't expecting any; I just asked. [Pause] What did Charlotte say? That's just like her. She could come at least once a week to see how you are. All right, have it your own way. I'm too tired to argue with you. How are the children? That's nice. [Pause] An eighty-five average doesn't mean he's a genius; no, not by any stretch of the imagination. I'm not saying she has stupid children; that isn't what I said, but I can't stand it when you raise them to the sky. I repeat, an eighty-five average is not in the genius class, and if you want proof ask anyone in the educational field. Oh, all right, all right; let's just drop it. I'll see you later. Of course I'm coming home. Where do you think I'd go? Fine. Good-bye. [SYLVIA *throws the remainder of her sandwich into basket, reluctantly sits down at typewriter. As she types and swings the carriage across—for want of something to do—she sings the material she is typing with the lilting intonation of a small girl bouncing a ball on the sidewalk while reciting doggerel. Typing*] Mrs. Anna Robinson, of 4 East 32nd Street, in the city and state of New York. [*Taking card out, putting new card in; forlornly*] How are you today, Mrs. Anna Robinson? It has been so nice talking to you. Who have we here? Oh, it's [*Typing*] Mr. Arnold Robinson, of 1032 Lexington Avenue, in the city and state of New York. [*Taking card out, putting new card in*] It was so pleasant talking to you, Mr. Robinson. Send my regards to the family. Why, if it isn't [*Typing*] Mrs. Beatrice Robinson, who lives no less on Park Avenue, in the city and state of New York. [*Taking card out, putting new card in*] Must you leave so soon, Mrs. Robinson?

[SYLVIA *takes a gumdrop from a bag of candy, continues typing.* PAUL *enters. He is now in his forties. He carries a container of coffee*]

PAUL: [*Referring to her candy*] Up to your old tricks again, Sylvia? You'll never keep your figure that way.

SYLVIA: Don't worry about my figure; just worry about your own.

PAUL: [*Pulling his stomach in*] You've got a point there. Here, I brought you some coffee.

SYLVIA: Thanks. [*Gets newspaper*] How is it outside?

PAUL: A little chilly, but the sun's strong; nice. I took a walk up to the park. You never saw so many characters sitting on the benches and sunning themselves. I sure would like to know how they do it.

SYLVIA: Half of them are probably on relief.

PAUL: We work and they sun themselves.

SYLVIA: You should see the cars some of them have.

PAUL: You don't have to tell me. I know.

SYLVIA: I read in the newspapers that by the year 2000 people will work only three hours a day and have a three-day week.

PAUL: That's not going to help me.

SYLVIA: [At *typewriter; opens newspaper*] We could try to get into a union.

PAUL: Do you know one that isn't crooked?

SYLVIA: How I wish this day was over.

PAUL: It'll feel good getting these shoes off.

SYLVIA: I'll wash my hair and do a little ironing.

PAUL: No date tonight?

SYLVIA: Don't be funny.

PAUL: [*At typewriter*] You know, I was thinking, Syl. Ever since I was a kid I always thought I would like to be independent, to live my own life, without getting involved with responsibilities and families. Inside of me I suppose I always was afraid of that. But, you know, everything I've done in my life has taken me away from what I thought I'd like to be when I was a kid. I got married as soon as I could; I had children right away; I made it so tough for myself I couldn't get through law school. I couldn't live the kind of life I thought I wanted. I've been asking myself lately, what is it I really wanted? You know what the answer to that is, Syl? You know what it has to be? What I got. What I am. Maybe all I really wanted was to be sorry for myself.

SYLVIA: Does anyone know what they want, Paul?

PAUL: Don't you?

SYLVIA: Not any more. I thought I knew, just as you did. But if that's what I wanted, why am I where I am today?

PAUL: It doesn't make sense, does it?

SYLVIA: I swore that at the first opportunity I'd break away from my mother and my sister; I'd have nothing more to do with them and that would be happiness for me. But here I am still living with my mother and every day I ask how my sister is, what she's doing, how her husband is, the children . . . And I don't give a damn. Not a damn.

PAUL: The things I don't give a damn about . . . Syl, let's look into it. This is important.

SYLVIA: I've always said there's nothing more important than getting to know yourself. When you realize that people can live their whole lives without knowing themselves, without really getting to understand themselves, it . . . it reaches the ridiculous.

PAUL: [*Rising*] You're absolutely right.

SYLVIA: [*Rising*] Let's see what's behind it all. Let's study it a moment.

PAUL: All right, let's get to it. Why?

SYLVIA: Why?

PAUL: Why do you say that leaving your family would make you happy? If that's all there was to it, you could have left them years ago. No, there's something you're hiding.

SYLVIA: You're not telling the truth. If all you wanted was to feel sorry for yourself, all you'd have to do is sit in a corner and feel sorry for yourself; that's all there is to it. But, no; that isn't it.

PAUL: Then what is it?

SYLVIA: What are you hiding?

[*As one speaks, wagging a finger, the other paces back and forth, nodding without listening, following a separate train of thought*]

PAUL: The fact remains that you do care what happens to your family, you care a lot, an awful lot; that's why you phone every day, that's why you're always asking about your sister. You have to keep them together; you need them more than they need you because you never developed emotionally enough to forget the past and start a new life for yourself.

SYLVIA: You deliberately put yourself in situations in which you had to fail. Why is it I never heard you say you loved your wife? What was behind your marriage at such an early age? Why didn't you wait until you finished school so that you'd have a fair chance of getting ahead?

PAUL: Simply because you wanted something from them. It had nothing to do with your father's ring; you use that for a smoke screen.

SYLVIA: Now we're coming closer to the truth. You had to rush into marriage, have children and become burdened with impossible responsibilities, the very things you were afraid of; you had to fail because it wasn't that you wanted to feel sorry for yourself, but you wanted other people to feel sorry for you.

PAUL: That's it! They alone could give you what you wanted; no one else, not even a husband; that's why you never got married. Now we're coming closer to it . . .

SYLVIA: So that they would pity and pamper you like a child; you mistook that for love, which was what you really wanted from them, the love which you couldn't get from your parents.

[*They suddenly stand face-to-face*]

PAUL: There it is! You wanted love!

SYLVIA: You wanted love, of course!

PAUL: Don't you see it now, Syl?

SYLVIA: It's all so clear.

PAUL: When you know something about yourself, then you can start doing something about it.

[*They march back to their typewriters*]

SYLVIA: This has been one of the most pleasant conversations I've ever had, Paul.

PAUL: I enjoyed it myself. [*Glancing at wristwatch*] And the afternoon's going pretty fast.

SYLVIA: Thank God for that.

[*They both type*]

PAUL: You know, thinking about it, I'm sure a lot better off than you are.

SYLVIA: Why's that?

PAUL: Well, I've got a place of my own; I did marry, have children. You could say I fulfilled a pretty important part of my life.

SYLVIA: That's nonsense. Do you think it requires any special ability to get married and have children?

PAUL: All I'm saying is that there are some people who would be awfully glad if they could have gotten married.

SYLVIA: Are you referring to me, Mr. Cunningham?

PAUL: I didn't mention any names, did I? But if the shoe fits, wear it, Miss Payton!

SYLVIA: [*Grimly*] Don't make me laugh. If I had to make the choice —and I assure you I don't—I would much prefer being single than being forced to continue an unhappy marriage.

PAUL: An unhappy marriage? Where do you get that from? Did you ever hear me say that?

SYLVIA: I can put one and one together, Mr. Cunningham. We both know that if you had your way about it you would have left her long ago.

PAUL: Is that right?

SYLVIA: That's exactly right.

PAUL: Well, for your information, Miss Payton, my wife is the finest [*Rising*], do you hear me? The finest, the most decent woman I ever had the good fortune to meet.

SYLVIA: Please, Mr. Cunningham.

PAUL: And for your further information, I wouldn't trade her for a dozen like you.

SYLVIA: You couldn't possibly. [*The buzzer rings; she fixes her hair, etc.*] Thank God, at last I'll have a moment away from you.

PAUL: I bet you think I don't know what goes on in there?

SYLVIA: What is he raving about now?

PAUL: Go ahead in. I can hear your boyfriend panting behind the door.

SYLVIA: Jealous?

PAUL: Of you?

SYLVIA: It's happened before.

PAUL: [*Turning away from her, loud undertone*] You bitch!

SYLVIA: [*Turning, flaring*] What did you say? [*No answer*] You'd better be quiet.

[*She exits.* PAUL *goes to hanger and without unwrapping or removing the whiskey bottle from his coat pocket pours a drink into a water cup, swallows it, then fills the cup again. He dials the phone*]

PAUL: Barbara. Paul. How're the kids? That's good. Oh, pretty much the same. Listen, Barb, I'm . . . I'm sorry about last night. I had a little too much to drink. No, no, don't go excusing it. I just want you to know I didn't mean any of it. I think an awful . . . an awful lot of you, you know that, and I respect you, I always have. It's when I'm drinking, it's the whiskey that does the talking. I'm going to stop, I promise you. Barb, you forgive me, don't you? Well, say it; I want to hear you say it; please. [*Pause*] Thank you. I'll try to get home early and we'll do something, we'll do something different, something . . . different, I promise you. All right. Don't forget. So long.

[*He finishes his drink, crumples cup and slips it into his pocket.* SYLVIA *enters, carrying several sheets of paper, which she places on* PAUL's *typewriter. She is now in her forties*]

SYLVIA: He wants you to type copies of these. He's waiting for them.

PAUL: What's that?

SYLVIA: [*At typewriter*] You heard me.

PAUL: Well, you hear me now. You can go right in there and tell him to go to hell. I'm not his secretary.

SYLVIA: Why don't you tell him yourself?

PAUL: That's a good idea! [*Moves to employer's office, grabbing papers from typewriter, turns*] That's a damn good idea! [*Exits*]

SYLVIA: [*Typing, singsong, as before*] Mr. Thomas Weaver, of 424 Harley Street, in the Bronx, New York. [*Taking card out, putting card in*] I hope that you're having a pleasant day, Mr. Thomas Weaver. Now who is this coming along? Oh, it's [*Typing*] Miss Tina Lee Weaver, of number 78 Monroe Avenue, in the Bronx, New York. How are you . . .

[PAUL *enters. He shouts at employer's door as he rips papers in half and throws them in the air*]

PAUL: There, there, that's what I think of you and your job, you old bastard!

SYLVIA: Paul!

PAUL: Why don't you go in and see your boyfriend now? You'll see him hiding behind the desk. If he stayed on his feet like a man I would have punched him right in the nose.

SYLVIA: Did you . . . quit?

PAUL: What the hell do you think I did? Trying to pull that stuff on me. I'm not his secretary and I never was. [*Shouting at employer's door*] Do you hear me, you old bastard! I'm not your secretary and I never was!

SYLVIA: [*Rising, with concern*] Please, Paul, be quiet; you're in enough trouble.

PAUL: Trouble? Me? Ha! That's the funniest thing I heard yet. You're looking at a free man, Miss Payton; a free and independent man. Yes, sir. I haven't felt this good in years.

SYLVIA: [*Following him to coat hanger*] But what will you do?

PAUL: [*Removing whiskey bottle from coat, throwing wrapper away*] Start living for one thing; start being myself; start being a man again. You know what it means to be a man, Miss Payton? You don't meet men any more; they're all afraid of losing their jobs, afraid of spending a dollar, afraid of their own shadows. But not this man. No, sir. I don't lick anybody's boots. What are you staring at? This? It's an old custom of mine. Care to join me? No, I didn't think so. [*He drinks from bottle*]

SYLVIA: Paul, don't; this isn't like you.

PAUL: How do you know what I'm like? How does anybody know? We all live alone, Miss Payton; we all live alone in a cruel and lonely world. [*He drinks*]

SYLVIA: How true that is.

PAUL: You know what I'm going to do? Yes, sir. The hell with it. I'm dropping everything, leaving everything. The first bus heading west tomorrow you know who's going to be on it? I am. You bet. [*He raises bottle to mouth*]

SYLVIA: [*Tries to take bottle from him*] Paul, you've had enough of that.

PAUL: [*Pulls bottle away from her*] Listen, this is no spur-of-the-minute thing with me, and it's not the whiskey doing the talking either. I've been thinking of it for a long long time. This city stinks for my money; there's nothing here but a lot of smoke, noise and corruption. I don't know where that bus is going to take me, but I'm not getting off until I find a place where there's plenty of fresh air, lots of room, that's what I want, lots of room, and mountains, mountains as high as you can see. Yes, sir. When I find that place I'm getting off and that's where I'm staying.

SYLVIA: I always dreamt of going somewhere like that, ever since I was a girl; some place away from everyone and everything I know.

PAUL: Do you mean that?

SYLVIA: I'd give anything.

PAUL: [Puts bottle on typewriter table] Syl.

SYLVIA: Yes, Paul?

PAUL: Listen, we . . . we get along pretty well, don't we?

SYLVIA: We get along extremely well.

PAUL: [Standing behind her] The times I thought of taking you in my arms and holding you . . .

SYLVIA: Oh, if you only had, Paul.

PAUL: It's not too late, is it?

SYLVIA: No, no, it's not.

PAUL: The two of us, together. [He holds her about the waist; she clasps his hands]

SYLVIA: Oh, Paul. I'm so happy. I'll call my mother. And you call your wife. I don't want there to be any hard feelings. Let's make it as pleasant as possible for everyone.

PAUL: [Stunned] You want me to call my wife?

SYLVIA: Of course, silly; we're getting married, aren't we?

PAUL: But you don't understand . . .

SYLVIA: We are getting married, aren't we?

PAUL: Aw, what's the use.

SYLVIA: I know; it's my fault; no matter what I do or say it's my fault.

PAUL: No, my fault; it's my fault. I'm no good, Sylvia. I never was. I never had the guts to do anything but feel sorry for myself. I've been a lazy selfish son-of-a-bitch all my life. I never did a damn thing that amounted to a bag of beans. And now . . . Oh, my God! [Leaning on typewriter, he sobs loudly]

SYLVIA: Paul, stop it; what are you doing? What's wrong?

PAUL: I don't care for myself; it's not for me. My life's over. My wife . . . [*Shouting*] That bitch can go to hell! But the kids, Sylvia. I love those kids. Now what's going to happen to them? I don't have a job; there's no money put away, nothing. What did I do? What was I trying to prove?

SYLVIA: Why don't you go in and speak to him? Apologize, tell him anything. You're one of the best typists he's ever had; don't forget that.

PAUL: Do you think there's a chance? I can type; no one can say I can't. That's one thing I can do. Look, Sylvia. Look. [*He stands with his back to the typewriter and with his hands behind him types*] Check that. Go ahead. You'll find there isn't a single mistake. And this, look at this. [*He stands between both typewriters, spreads his arms out and types on both machines simultaneously*]

SYLVIA: I know, Paul; you're very good.

PAUL: There. Perfect. Check it. Check it. And this, Sylvia, look at this.

SYLVIA: That's enough, Paul. I believe you. I know you can . . . [*He stands on the chair at his typewriter, removes one shoe, gives it to* SYLVIA, *and types with his stockinged foot, swings carriage across with his large toe, then slumps down in chair*] Come down from there. You are good, you're very good.

PAUL: They deserve everything I can give them, Syl. I love those kids. [*He lifts up his foot;* SYLVIA *puts on his shoe*]

SYLVIA: I know. Now let's get you fixed up so you'll look presentable when you see him. [*Straightens his tie, brushes his jacket, etc.*] Stand still. Stop moving around.

PAUL: He'll never give me another chance, not after what I said to him.

SYLVIA: You just walk in and speak to him. There. Now you look fine. I'll fix things up out here. And we'd better get rid of this bottle. [*She takes it away from him as he raises it to his mouth*]

PAUL: No more of that for me. I learned my lesson.

SYLVIA: I hope so. Well, go ahead in.

PAUL: Syl, I just want you to know this: if I get my job back, you're going to see some changes. Paul Cunningham has grown up at last.

SYLVIA: Go ahead in.

PAUL: No, not until I thank you for . . . for everything you've done.

SYLVIA: I didn't do a thing.

PAUL: Yes, you did; more than I can thank you for. Did you ever think, Syl, what would have happened if the two of us had met before I married Barbara?

SYLVIA: [*Wistfully*] Yes, I thought of it, many times.

PAUL: [*Moving toward her*] Syl, listen to me . . .

SYLVIA: [*Raising her hands, moving away from him*] Not that again. Please. Go in. Go on in.

[PAUL *exits to employer's office.* SYLVIA *empties whiskey bottle in drain of water cooler, then drops bottle into basket; she picks paper from floor; sits at typewriter, puts eyeglasses on, and types.* PAUL *enters. He is now in his fifties*]

PAUL: It's all right; it's all right. He's taken me back.

SYLVIA: I'm so glad for you.

PAUL: He was darn nice about it, too. He just listened to me and then he said, "It's understandable, Mr. Cunningham. We all have our problems."

SYLVIA: He can be nice when he wants to.

PAUL: "We all have our problems." He's not a stupid man.

SYLVIA: On the contrary, he understands a great many things.

PAUL: You know, we should buy him something; a little gift from the staff, something to show our appreciation. [*Rubbing hands, sits at typewriter*] Well, let's get to it. There's not much left to the day now.

SYLVIA: Yes, soon it'll be over. [*They type in silence. Suddenly* PAUL *breaks out in forced laughter*] What's so amusing?

PAUL: Miss Supervisor . . . I'll never forget that as long as I live. "Believe me, Mr. Cunningham, I didn't ask him to be made a supervisor. I don't like telling anyone what to do."

SYLVIA: We all have our pretensions, Paul.

PAUL: [*Clearing his throat*] That's very true. [*They type.* SYLVIA *starts to laugh*] What is it? What . . . what is it? What?

SYLVIA: I was just thinking of a boy I once went with.

PAUL: The Chinese fellow?

SYLVIA: No, no. I don't know any Chinese fellow. This boy was an entertainer. He could make you laugh by just looking at you.

PAUL: Did I ever tell you, Sylvia, that I used to take singing lessons?

SYLVIA: No?

PAUL: I did. When I was eight, nine . . .

SYLVIA: [*Rises, collects typed cards*] I didn't know that.

PAUL: [*Sings*] "Way down upon the Swanee River . . . Far, far from home . . ."

SYLVIA: You do have a voice.

PAUL: [*Sings monosyllabically*] Da, *da*, da, da, da, *da*, *da* . . .

SYLVIA: [*At employer's door*] Shh, not too loudly.

[SYLVIA *exits, without tidying herself, to employer's office.* PAUL *types and sings monosyllabically, using his typewriter as if it were a musical instrument. On the card he has just typed he notices an error, crumples it and slips it into his pocket; he continues singing.* SYLVIA *enters. They are now in their middle-sixties, aged, slow-moving, but not gray-wigged, not senile*]

PAUL: [*Looking at his watch*] Sylvia, it's twelve minutes to five.

SYLVIA: We don't generally stop until ten minutes to, Paul.

PAUL: I know. But I thought . . .

SYLVIA: That wouldn't be fair.

PAUL: You're right, as always. [*They type*] Now, Sylvia? [*Without looking at timepiece*]

SYLVIA: There's still . . . I would say a minute.

[*They type*]

PAUL: Now, Sylvia?

SYLVIA: Yes . . . Now.

PAUL: Thank God.

SYLVIA: I am tired. A good hot bath and then to bed with me.

[*Rising he inadvertently brushes a card off the table; he picks it up, reads*]

PAUL: "All wool knickers. From factory to you. At a tremendous saving." Knickers. We've been selling knickers.

SYLVIA: [*Covering typewriters*] Come, come, let's put everything away.

PAUL: [*Going to coat hanger*] Not many people wear knickers nowadays, do they? Knickers. They're warm, though; and practical, they're very practical.

SYLVIA: [*As* PAUL *struggles with his coat*] Here, let me help you with that. Isn't it too early yet?

PAUL: Just getting ready. [*He helps her put on her coat*]

SYLVIA: What time is it, Paul? It doesn't feel like five.

PAUL: [*Looking at wristwatch*] Another . . . two minutes. [*They sit down at typewriters, in their coats, immobile, expressionless, waiting for the two minutes to pass. Then* PAUL *looks at his watch. Rising*] It's time.

SYLVIA: [*As they move toward the employer's office*] I have such a bad recollection. What is this new man's name, Paul?

PAUL: Smith or Stone or . . . I never could remember names.

SYLVIA: We'll give him a friendly good-bye just the same.

[*They stand on the threshold of the office, wave and cry shrilly*]

PAUL: Good night. Good night in there.

SYLVIA: Have a pleasant evening. Good night.

PAUL: I'll walk you to the subway, Sylvia.

SYLVIA: That would be very nice.

[SYLVIA *stands by the door, buttoning her coat.* PAUL *removes some crumpled cards from his pocket, he looks at them, forlornly, lets them fall from his hands to the floor. He starts to-*]

ward SYLVIA *but changes his mind, returns, gets down on his haunches and picks up some crumpled cards; he looks around the office for a place to put them; finding none he slips them back into his pockets and exits with* SYLVIA]

CURTAIN

POOR AUBREY

George Kelly

George Kelly

George Kelly (1887–1974), a leading dramatist of the twenties and thirties, brought to the stage some of the period's most telling and incisive social satires.

Born in Philadelphia, he began his theatrical career as an actor and for five years played juvenile roles with various road companies. He then turned to vaudeville, where his brother Walter had already gained headline status as "The Virginia Judge." While playing on the Keith and Orpheum circuits, he began writing his own sketches; one of these was *Poor Aubrey*, which originally was presented at the celebrated Palace Theatre in New York City. As Kelly later wrote on the occasion of the first publication of the play: "The form of the present manuscript is exactly that in which this comedy was presented for two years in the principal Keith and Orpheum Theatres of the United States of America and the Dominion of Canada, and it was from its central character, Aubrey Piper, that the three-act comedy, *The Show-Off*, was developed."

Kelly's first full-length play, *The Torchbearers* (1922), was a highly successful satire on the pretentiousness of amateur theatricals. This was followed in 1924 by *The Show-Off*, which had a Broadway run of 571 performances and still remains a leading staple of stock and community theatres. On the heels of Aubrey Piper came another memorable George Kelly character, Harriet Craig in *Craig's Wife*, which opened in 1925, spanned the season, and won the Pulitzer Prize for drama.

During the two decades that followed, the theatre was to be enlivened by a procession of Kelly plays. To name some: *Daisy Mayme*; *Behold the Bridegroom*; *Maggie the Magnificent*; *Philip Goes Forth*; *Reflected Glory*; *The Deep Mrs. Sykes*; and *The Fatal Weakness*.

The author was equally noted for his meticulous direction of his plays. As James Cagney recounted in his autobiography: "George Kelly was one of America's best playwrights and one of the few really first-rate directors in my life."

In addition to *Poor Aubrey*, he wrote a number of popular and widely performed short plays, including: *The Flattering Word; The Weak Spot; One of Those Things;* and *Finders-Keepers*.

After *The Fatal Weakness* (1946), Kelly was no longer active in the theatre, but the family's theatrical tradition was upheld, and quite strikingly, by his actress niece, now Princess Grace of Monaco.

Characters:

Aubrey Piper
Amy, *his wife*
Mrs. Fisher, *Amy's mother*
Mrs. Cole (Marion Brill), *a friend of Amy's*

SCENE: *The sitting room in Fisher's house,
about four o'clock of a Saturday afternoon
in February.*

AMY *enters briskly through the portières at the right, carrying a fancy cushion, which she sets in the armchair at the back of the room; then continues on over to an arched doorway at the left and draws the curtains together. She is a dark-haired, trim-looking woman, in her late twenties, dressed in black—a very pretty dress, of black crêpe, with a graceful side sash of the goods, piped with buff-colored silk. She has on black slippers and stockings, and wears a string of buff-colored beads—quite large. Her general manner suggests a quality of intelligent definiteness; something of which is even evident in the arrangement of her hair. While she is engaged at the curtains, the portières over at the right are brushed aside, and her husband swings into the room, and stands preening himself near the table. He is fearfully and wonderfully gotten up!—a perfect flash of cross-barred gray and brilliantine. Poor* AUBREY! *He is painfully arrayed, even to the toupee; a feature that, as Dickens remarked of Sairey Gamp's transformation, could scarcely be called false, it is so very innocent of anything approaching to deception. And the quantities of brilliantine that have obviously been employed upon it only serve to heighten its artificiality. He is wearing a glistening white vest and a shiny gold watch-chain, a necktie of living green, with a rather large horsehoe tie-pin of imitation diamonds, and a very high collar. He has a flashily bordered silk handkerchief set forth in the breast pocket of his coat, and there is a pair of heavy-rimmed nose-glasses depending from his neck on a black tape.*

AUBREY: [*Touching his toupee gingerly*] Does this thing look all right?

AMY: What?

AUBREY: This toupee. [*She glances over her right shoulder indifferently*] I put some of that brilliantine on it.

AMY: [*Resuming her arrangement of the curtains*] It's all right.

AUBREY: [*Turning to the little wall mirror just below the portières at the right*] You don't seem very enthusiastic about it.

AMY: [*Turning from the curtains and crossing quickly to the table— an oblong table, in the middle of the room, and towards the back*] Because I don't think you need it. [*She picks up a small folded cover from the table, shakes it out, and tosses it across her left shoulder; then commences to gather up the scattered books and put them into the little table-rack*]

AUBREY: [*Settling the toupee at the mirror*] What do you want your friend to think, that you married an old man?

AMY: Why, a man doesn't look old simply because he hasn't a big head of hair.

AUBREY: Well, mine's pretty thin here on top.

AMY: Well, that's nothing; lots of young men haven't much.

AUBREY: [*Turning to her*] Why, it was you that suggested my getting a toupee in the first place!

AMY: [*Stopping, and resting her hands on the table; and speaking directly to him*] I know very well it was; because I knew I'd never have a minute's peace till you'd get one. All I heard morning, noon and night was something about your hair coming out. You might think nobody ever heard of anybody being baldheaded.

AUBREY: [*Turning back to the mirror*] Well, a man's got to make the most of himself.

AMY: Well, if you think that thing's adding anything to *your* appearance, you've got another think. [*She starts towards the tabourette in front of the bay window over at the left*] Lift up this plant here for me, I want to put this cover on. [*She picks up a dead leaf or two from the floor and tosses them out the window. He remains standing at the mirror, looking at the toupee very critically from various angles*] Aubrey!

AUBREY: [*Without moving, and with a touch of irritation*] All right, all right!

AMY: Well, hurry up!—I want to change these covers. [*He withdraws lingeringly from the mirror*] You'll keep fooling with that wig till there isn't a hair left on it.

AUBREY: [*Crossing to her*] It isn't a wig, now, Amy! I've told you that half a dozen times!

AMY: [*Raising her hand quietly, to silence him*] Well, a toupee then, dearie,—don't get excited.

AUBREY: I'm not getting excited at all!

AMY: [*Indicating the plant with an authoritative gesture*] Lift up this plant and shut up. [*He lifts up the plant and holds it, till she has changed the covers*] There.

[*He sets the plant down again, and she settles it more precisely*]

AUBREY: [*Starting back across the room*] You just call it a wig because you know it makes me mad!

AMY: [*Straightening up and looking after him, with one hand on her hip*] I don't know why it should make you so mad, to have it called a wig.

AUBREY: [*Turning to her sharply*] Because it *isn't* a wig! It's a toupee!

AMY: [*Turning to the plant again and giving it a final touch*] Well, it's pretty, whatever it is.

AUBREY: It isn't even a toupee; it's just a patch!

AMY: It's a young *wig*, that's what it is. [*He turns and glares at her*] And if it were only half as big as it is, anybody that'd look at it a mile away'd know that it never grew on you.

[*She goes quickly out through the portières at the right, and he returns to the mirror and preens himself generally. Immediately she comes back into the room again, carrying a big, dark dust-cloth, with which she commences to dust the center table; while he struts across the room in front of the table, settling his cuffs and whistling the opening bars of the chorus of "I'm Forever Blowing Bubbles"*]

AUBREY: [*As he approaches the bay window*] What do you say about putting a couple of these plants out on the front porch?

AMY: What for?

AUBREY: I think it adds a lot to the appearance of the house as you come up the street.

AMY: Oh, don't be silly, Aubrey!

AUBREY: [*Wheeling around and looking at her in astonishment*] What do you mean, don't be silly?

AMY: [*Pausing in her dusting*] Why, who ever heard of anybody putting plants on a front porch in February!

AUBREY: I don't mean to leave them out there! We could bring them in again as soon as she goes.

AMY: [*Starting for the little corner table*] Yes, and she'd go away thinking we were both crazy. [*She arranges the few magazines on the table, and then commences to dust it*]

AUBREY: [*Sauntering back to the center table, where he proceeds to take the books which she has just arranged out of the little rack, and stand them on their ends*] Oh, everybody's thinking you're crazy, with you!

AMY: [*Turning to him and speaking emphatically*] Well, I know that's exactly what I'd think, if I were to come along and see plants on an open porch in the middle of winter.

AUBREY: [*Occupied with the book arrangement, and without looking up*] Well, I've seen *lots* of plants on front porches in the winter.

AMY: [*Returning to her work of dusting the table*] Well, if you did, they were *enclosed* porches. [*She finishes the dusting, and starts back towards the center table; but comes to a dead stop upon seeing the arrangement of the books, and her husband's intense absorption in it. There is a slight pause*] What are you doing with those books?

AUBREY: [*Still busy*] I'm just standing them up this way, so you can see what they are.

AMY: Can't you see what they are in the rack?

AUBREY: Certainly you can; but I think they show up better this way.

AMY: [*Stepping towards him and pushing him out of the way*] Go away! and let them alone! [*She hurriedly commences to gather them up and restore them to the rack*]

AUBREY: [*Wandering towards the arched doorway*] That's the way they have them in all the store windows. [*He proceeds to push the curtains back*]

AMY: Well, this isn't a store window. [*She glances at what he's doing, and starts towards him*] And don't push those curtains back that way, Aubrey! I just fixed them. [*She pushes him towards the back of the room*]

AUBREY: They cover up the Victrola, that way.

AMY: [*Settling the curtains*] That doesn't matter. These doors look too bare with the curtains pushed back. [*She starts back towards the center table to complete her rearrangement of the books*] Now, let things alone, for Heaven's sake! She can see the Victrola when she goes in there.

AUBREY: She may not go in there.

AMY: [*Addressing him, as she crosses to the portières, taking the dust cloth with her*] Well, I guess she's seen Victrolas before, even if she *doesn't* go in there. [*She goes out through the portières. He stands for a second fixing himself, then breaks into "I'm Forever Blowing Bubbles" again. The detection of a speck of dust on his left shoe brings his whistling to a close; and, whipping out the elegant handkerchief from his breast pocket, he leans over to flick it off. The effort dislodges the toupee, which drops to the floor in front of him. He snatches it up frantically, and claps it back upon his head; thrusts his handkerchief back into his pocket, and, with a panic-stricken glance over his right shoulder, in the direction of the portières, bolts to the bay window, holding the toupee in place with his left hand. AMY hurries in from the right carrying a small vase, which she takes to the little stand down at the right*] Any sign of her?

AUBREY: [*Adjusting the toupee, and pretending to look out the window*] I don't see any sign of her yet.

AMY: Maybe her train's late. [*She glances about the room, to see that everything is all right*]

AUBREY: I don't know why it *should* be; there wasn't any hold-up along the line to-day that *I* heard of.

AMY: [*Settling her sash*] She said in her telegram that she'd get into Broad Street at three o'clock sharp, and that she'd come right out here—Because she had to leave again on the Bridge train at four-fourteen.

AUBREY: [*Turning from the window and coming towards her*] Too bad she didn't know, she could have gotten right off here at North Philadelphia—And then she could have gotten that Bridge train right there again at—a—four-twenty-seven.

[*He finishes his remarks with an explanatory gesture, and stands looking at his wife. She is still settling her sash. There is a fractional pause. Then she finishes and looks up at him. Then there is another pause, during which her eyes shift to his toupee, which is on askew,—a bit over the left eye]*

AMY: [*With a kind of wearied impatience*] Fix your toupee.

AUBREY: [*Putting his hand to it, and with a note of challenge in his voice*] What's the matter with it?

AMY: Why, it's all over the place.

AUBREY: Is that so!

AMY: Well, look at it!

AUBREY: Well, I fixed it that way! [*He emphasizes the remark with a little bob of his head, and starts towards the mirror*]

AMY: Well, it's pretty.

AUBREY: To let the air get to my scalp.

AMY: Well, for Heaven's sake, don't have it fixed that way when Marion comes! [*Fixing the lace at her left cuff*] You look as though your head were lopsided.

[*He turns from the mirror, and gives her a withering look. But she is occupied with her cuff*]

AUBREY: [*Turning back to the mirror*] How is it you didn't put on your other dress?

AMY: What other dress?

AUBREY: The one with all the beads.

AMY: [*Looking at him*] Why, this is my good dress.

AUBREY: I think that other one's more of a flash.

AMY: [*Turning away again and settling the front of her dress*] Oh, don't be such a show-off, Aubrey!

AUBREY: [*Turning sharply and looking at her*] Show-off!

AMY: That's what I said.

AUBREY: I don't know how you figure *that's* showing off!—Because I want you to *look* good.

AMY: [*Looking at him stonily, and speaking in a level key*] You want me to look good because I'm *your* wife. And you want this friend of mine to *see* me looking good; just as you want her to see that

Victrola in there—[*She indicates the arched door with a slight nod*] that isn't half paid for. [*She looks out*]

AUBREY: [*Coming towards her a step or two*] I suppose *you'd* rather have her think you married some poor thing!

AMY: Listen, Aubrey—It won't make the least bit of difference *what* we want her to think—She's a very smart girl; and all she'll have to do is glance around this room, and she'll know *exactly* what I married. [*She looks straight out again*]

AUBREY: [*Mimicking her tone*] Is that so! [*She simply emphasizes his remarks with a slow and very positive nod*] Well, now, you listen to me for a minute, Amy! You know I can beat it right over to the barber shop [*She breaks into a rather tired little laugh*] and stay there, till this friend of yours has gone, [*He moves over towards the little stand*] if you're so awfully afraid that I'm going to show up so badly in front of her!

AMY: [*Looking after him with a very knowing expression*] No fear of your beating it over to the barber shop.

AUBREY: No?

AMY: You'll be strutting around here in front of her if she stays till midnight.

AUBREY: [*Very nettled, and securing his tie and tie-pin*] All right.

AMY: [*Taking a step or two towards him*] And, by the way, Aubrey— When Marion comes—I want you to do me a little favor; and don't be giving her a lot of big talk,—the way you were doing to that insurance man the other night; [*He turns and looks at her in astonished indignation*] for I don't want her to think you're silly.

AUBREY: When was I doing any big talk to any insurance man?

AMY: The other night when you were talking to that man about the price of a fifty-thousand-dollar policy.

AUBREY: Well, what about it?

AMY: Nothing; only that he was just laughing up his sleeve at you.

AUBREY: Is that so!

AMY: Well now, what else *could* he do, Aubrey? He knew you hadn't the slightest intention of taking any such policy.

AUBREY: How do you know he did?

AMY: Because he knows you're only a clerk. And that you don't get enough salary in six months to pay one year's premium on a policy like that. So when Marion comes, please don't be trying to impress her; [*She turns away from him rather slowly and moves up to the center table*] for she's a very sensible woman.

AUBREY: [*Turning and going up to the mirror*] I won't have anything to say to the woman at all.

AMY: [*Glancing through a magazine*] Oh, yes, you will, dearie.

AUBREY: She's not coming to see me.

AMY: That doesn't make any difference to you.

AUBREY: No reason why I should stand around *gabbing* to her.

AMY: Well, you'll stand around gabbing, if you can get anybody to listen to you.

AUBREY: Well, now, you watch me.

AMY: I've been watching you; and listening to you, too; for nearly four years.

AUBREY: [*Turning to her from the mirror, very peevishly, and holding up his right hand*] All right, I'll raise my hand,—if I want to say anything.

AMY: I know what you'll do, if you get the chance; I've heard you before.

[*There is a slight pause, during which he frets a bit. Then his mood shifts and he breaks into whistling his familiar "I'm Forever Blowing Bubbles." But this dies gradually as he becomes conscious of the little vase which Amy brought in for the stand at his right. He tilts his head a bit to one side and looks at it with critical disapproval*]

AUBREY: You know, it's too bad we haven't got something flashier for this stand here.

AMY: [*Just lifting her eyes over the top of the magazine*] There's that vase up in Mother's room.

AUBREY: Is she up there now?

AMY: She was when I came down.

AUBREY: [*With a gesture of finality*] Well, *that's* out.

AMY: Why, she wouldn't mind my taking it.

AUBREY: [*Speaking emphatically*] It isn't that! But if she sees you taking anything out of her room, she'll get an idea there's something going on down here, and she'll be right down for the rest of the night and you won't be able to chase her! [*He turns and looks out the bay window*]

AMY: Why, she knows that Marion Brill is coming here this afternoon.

AUBREY: [*Turning to her sharply, with a distressed expression*] Did you tell her?

AMY: Certainly I told her.

AUBREY: [*Despairingly*] Good night!

AMY: Why, I want her to *meet* Marion! She's never *met* her!

AUBREY: Well, if your mother ever gets *talking*, this friend of yours'll know everything from *your* age to *my* salary! [*He turns away*] Now, I'm telling you!

AMY: [*With a glance towards the portières, and speaking in an emphatic but subdued manner*] I don't care whether she does or not.

AUBREY: Well, I *do*.

[AMY *glances quickly towards the bay window; then, dropping the magazine, she steps eagerly towards it*]

AMY: There's a taxi, now. [*She draws the curtain aside and looks keenly out*]

AUBREY: [*Whirling round and striding towards the bay window,— holding on to his toupee with his left hand*] Is it stopping?

AMY: [*Suddenly, and in a tone of suppressed excitement*] There she is! [*She runs to the door at the back of the room and vanishes into the hallway*] She's looking for the number!

[AUBREY *peers eagerly through the bay window, then steps quickly up to the door at the back*]

AUBREY: Don't stand out there talking, now, Amy, without something around you!

[*He rushes across, still holding on to the toupee and, after a fleeting glance through the portières, reaches the mirror, where he gives himself a hasty and critical survey. Then the laughter and greetings of his wife and* MRS. COLE *reach him from the front door; so, with a glance in that direction, he struts forward and strikes a pose,—swinging his nose-glasses carelessly back and forth, and looking away off*]

AMY: [*Off*] I knew you through the window of the taxi!

MRS. COLE: [*Off*] Well, you know, I was thinking all the way out, "Now, I wonder if Amy got my wire."

AMY: I got it yesterday morning.

MRS. COLE and AMY: [*Together*]
  { [MRS. COLE] Because, you know, I couldn't wait to hear from you.
  { [AMY] But I said to Aubrey, "There's no use in my sending any word now, for she's already left Chicago by this time."

[*The front door closes*]

MRS. COLE: Well, you see, dear, I didn't know *definitely*—

MRS. COLE and AMY: [*Together*]
  { [MRS. COLE] Up until Thursday night that I was coming.
  { [AMY, *appearing in the hall door*] Oh, well, it doesn't matter! [*Coming into the room*] Just so long as I get to see you.

[*She glances at her husband, then turns and faces the hall door. There is a second's pause; then* MRS. COLE *enters the room; and, glancing about, stops just inside the door. She is a bit older than* AMY,—*probably three or four years, and considerably lighter in coloring. And very smart.* AMY *said she was, and she is—extremely so. It's in the clearness of her eye, and the peculiarly deft coördination of her general movement. Her clothes are smart, too; and by the looks of them, she must have married rather well; they are quite gorgeous. A fine seal coat, full length, with a cape effect, and an enormous muff made of black fox; rather large hat of black lace over black satin, faced with pale coral, and black slippers and stockings. She doesn't remove her coat, but when she opens it, there is a glimpse of a light coral-colored dress, heavily trimmed with steel beads, a long neck-scarf in steel silk, and a lovely-looking necklace of pale jade. She is wearing white kid gloves and carries a fancy bag made of jade and coral beads on her left wrist]*

MRS. COLE: What an attractive house you have, Amy.

AMY: [*Smiling, and indicating her husband*] There's the principal attraction, over there.

[AUBREY *acknowledges the compliment by melting slightly*]

MRS. COLE: [*Smiling graciously and going towards* AUBREY] Is this *him?*

[*He advances*]

AMY: That's him.

MRS. COLE: I'm *so* glad to meet you, Mr. Piper.

AUBREY: [*With a touch of condescension*] How do you do?

[*They shake hands*]

MRS. COLE: You know, I've always been enormously *curious* to see Amy's husband.

AUBREY: That so?

AMY: [*Looking straight out, and securing a hairpin in the right side of her head*] There he is.

MRS. COLE: [*Tilting her head a bit and looking at* AUBREY *with a smile*] He's terribly good-looking.

AMY: [*Turning away*] Oh!

[MRS. COLE *turns her head sharply and looks at her, still smiling*]

AUBREY: [*Addressing his wife*] You hear *that?*

[MRS. COLE *turns again to* AUBREY]

AMY: Please don't tell him that, Marion! He's bad enough as it is.

MRS. COLE: I don't know how you managed it, Amy. I could never do it. You should see *my* husband, Mr. Piper. I don't suppose he's any *older* than Mr. Piper, but, my dear, he *looks* old enough to be your father. [AMY *gives a little laugh of incredulity, and* MRS. COLE *turns suddenly to her*] Really! [*Then she turns suddenly again to* AUBREY] He's almost bald!

[AUBREY'*s smile freezes*]

AMY: Let me take your coat, Marion.

[AUBREY *turns quietly around, touching his toupee with his right hand, and moves up to the mirror, where he takes a reassuring peep at it, unobserved*]

MRS. COLE: I don't think I'll bother, dear, really; that taxicab's waiting out there for me. You see, I've got to get that Bridge train out of Broad Street at four-fourteen.

AUBREY: I was just saying to Amy, it's too bad you didn't know, you could have gotten right off here at North Philadelphia, and wouldn't have had to go downtown at all.

AMY: You know, that Bridge train makes a stop here, Marion, at North Philadelphia, on the way to Atlantic City.

MRS. COLE: Oh, does it!

AMY: Get's there at four-twenty-seven.

MRS. COLE: Isn't it too bad I didn't know that.

AUBREY: Well, you won't have to go back downtown now, as it is, will you, Mrs. Cole?

MRS. COLE: Yes, I've checked my grip at Broad Street.

AMY: Oh, isn't that too bad!

MRS. COLE: Well, it doesn't matter! Just so long as I got to see you.

AMY: That's about all you'll be able to do.

MRS. COLE: Well, sometime I'm going to invite myself to spend a few days with you, and then we'll have lots of time to talk.

AMY: I wish you could spend them now.

MRS. COLE: So do I, dear child; but what can a poor woman do with a sick husband on her hands.

AMY: How is he, Marion?

MRS. COLE: Why, he's pretty good, now.

AMY: Sit down. [*She picks up the cushion from the right end of the sofa to make a place for* MRS. COLE]

MRS. COLE: [*Stepping over to the sofa and unfastening her coat*] I must unfasten this coat. [AMY *sits at the left end of the sofa; then* MRS. COLE *sits down*] You know he had quite an attack of the flu last winter; and, I don't know, he never seemed to really get over it.

[AUBREY *has assumed a position over at the right of the center table, and is listening with a general expression of heavy consequence*]

AMY: So many people didn't.

AUBREY: One of the bookkeepers down at my office was telling me the other day that the flu has left him with a weak heart.

MRS. COLE: Yes, I've heard of that, too. But with my husband, it all seems to be in his nerves. That's the reason he's at Atlantic City now.

AMY: How long has he been there, Marion?

MRS. COLE: Since the week after New Year's.

AUBREY: They say Atlantic City's a great place for the nerves.

MRS. COLE: Well, Ralph says he feels ever so much better. I had a letter from him on Tuesday, and he said he was only going to stay another week. So I thought I'd better just run down there myself and see how he is before he starts that long trip back to Chicago.

AMY: That flu was a dreadful thing, wasn't it?

MRS. COLE: Dreadful! My dear, you've never seen anything change a person the way it has changed my husband. [*She turns suddenly to* AUBREY] He's even lost his hair.

[*She coughs a little, and uses her handkerchief; while* AUBREY *glides to the mirror again, touching his toupee discreetly*]

AMY: [*Picking up the muff from* MRS. COLE's *lap*] I love this muff, Marion.

MRS. COLE: Do you know how long I've had that?

AMY: How long?

MRS. COLE: Three years last Christmas.

AMY: Really!

MRS. COLE: Ralph gave it to me the first Christmas we were married.

AMY: [*Holding it out on her left arm*] It's beautiful!

[AUBREY *comes forward again*]

AUBREY: What kind of fur *is* that, Mrs. Cole?

MRS. COLE: Fox.

AUBREY: Makes a nice looking fur.

MRS. COLE: [*Turning and looking at it*] It was pretty when I first got it. [*Turning again to* AUBREY] But it's getting old now; [*Looking back to the muff*] the hair's commencing to fall out. [*He turns and drifts to the back of the room*] I was so sorry to hear about your father, Amy.

AMY: Yes, it was so sudden.

MRS. COLE: How is your mother, Amy?

[AUBREY *turns and looks towards his wife*]

AMY: She keeps pretty well.

MRS. COLE: That's good.

AMY: She's here with us, you know.

[AUBREY *makes a despairing gesture*]

MRS. COLE: Oh, is she?

AMY: Yes.

MRS. COLE: Living with you, you mean?

AMY: [*Getting up*] Hum-hum. I must tell her you're here.

MRS. COLE: Well, now, don't bother her, Amy, if she's doing any-thing.

AMY: Not a thing—She's crazy to see you.

MRS. COLE and AMY: [*Together*]

{ [MRS. COLE] I don't want to bother her.

{ [AMY] I told her I'd call her as soon as you came. [*Going out through the portières*] I'll be down in a second.

[AUBREY, *standing up at the back of the room, glances after his wife, then turns and looks at* MRS. COLE. *She is settling her muff beside her on the sofa. He glances at himself in the mirror, and then comes forward, rather grandly, flipping the nose-glasses back and forth*]

MRS. COLE: Isn't it nice that Amy can have her mother here with her.

AUBREY: Yes; I've had her here ever since Mr. Fisher died.

MRS. COLE: She must be so much company for you.

AUBREY: Yes; a person'd never be lonesome.

MRS. COLE: I often say to *my* husband, I wish there were some one like that with us; I get so lonesome sometimes in the house during the day.

AUBREY: Well, when my father-in-law died, I thought Amy's mother might just as well come here with us. She was alone; and we had plenty of room; so I said, "Come ahead! [*He makes a rather magnificent gesture with his right hand*] The more the merrier!"

MRS. COLE: This *is* rather a large house, isn't it?

AUBREY: Yes, it is. Quite a wonderfully made house, too. They were put up by the McNeil people out here at Jenkintown. They're considered to build the best dwelling-house of anybody in the country. They just put up the twenty of them, as kind of sample houses— ten on that side, and ten on this. Of course, these on this side have the southern exposure; so a person's got to have quite a little pull to get hold of one of these. [*He catches his thumbs in the armholes of his vest, and, tilting his head a bit to the left side, looks away out and off, tapping his fingers on his chest*] But I have a friend—that's one of the biggest real estate men here in town, and he was able to fix it for me.

MRS. COLE: You were very lucky, weren't you?

AUBREY: Yes, I *was* pretty lucky in a way. Although I'd like to have gotten hold of one of the corner ones.

MRS. COLE: Are they a much larger house than these?

AUBREY: They're a fifteen-thousand-dollar house; these are only ten. [*He moves across in front of her, with ever so slight a suggestion of strut*]

MRS. COLE: I see.

AUBREY: [*With a casual glance out of the bay window*] I'm very anxious to get hold of one of them. I told this friend of mine to keep his eye open, and if there's a chance, I'll go as high as twenty thousand. Then, of course, I could always rent this.

MRS. COLE: It's an awfully nice street.

AUBREY: Nice in summer.

MRS. COLE: I was so surprised when I saw it, because the taxicab driver didn't know where it was when I asked him.

[AUBREY *looks at her, with a quick movement of his head*]

AUBREY: Didn't know where Cresson Street was?

MRS. COLE: He said not.

AUBREY: [*Shaking his head from side to side and smiling with heavy amusement*] He must be an awful rube.

MRS. COLE: He had to ask the traffic officer down on Broad Street.

AUBREY: Well, I'll tell you—I don't suppose they *have* many calls for taxis out this way. You see, most everybody in through here has his own car.

MRS. COLE: Oh, I see.

AUBREY: Some of them have a half a dozen, for that matter. [*He laughs consequentially, and she reflects his amusement faintly*] I was saying to Amy, when we got your wire yesterday, it was too bad *my* car was laid up, I could have picked you up at the station today.

MRS. COLE: Oh, that didn't matter.

AUBREY: But I've been working it pretty hard lately, and I had to turn it in Thursday to have the valves ground.

MRS. COLE: There's always something to be done to them, isn't there?

AUBREY: I should say so. Funny thing, too,—people have an idea if they get hold of a high-priced car their trouble's over. [*She smiles and shakes her head from side to side in appreciation of that illusion*] I swear, I've had just as much trouble with my *Pierce Arrow* as I ever had with my Buick.

[*They both laugh, and* AUBREY *looks out the window*]

AMY:[*Coming in through the portières*] Mother says she was just coming down to inquire how it was you hadn't come. [AUBREY *turns and looks at his wife, then turns around and moves towards the back of the room.* MRS. FISHER *comes in through the portières, and* MRS. COLE *rises*] This is Mrs. Cole, Mother—Marion Brill that you've heard so much about.

MRS. FISHER: [*Coming forward*] Well, indeed I have.

MRS. COLE: [*Advancing*] I'm *so* glad to meet you, Mrs. Fisher.

MRS. FISHER: [*Shaking hands with her*] How do you do. I'm certainly pleased to meet you, too.

MRS. COLE: Thank you.

MRS. FISHER: For I think I've heard your name more than any other girl's name I ever heard in this house.

MRS. COLE: Well, Amy and I worked beside each other so long.

MRS. FISHER: All I used to hear morning, noon and night was, "Marion Brill said so and so" [MRS. COLE *and* AMY *laugh*] or, "Marion Brill is going to do so and so." [MRS. FISHER *laughs*]

AMY: I'm afraid that's about all we did was talk, wasn't it, Marion? [*She laughs again*]

MRS. COLE: It's about all *I* used to do. [*She laughs*]

MRS. FISHER: [*Indicating the sofa*] Won't you sit down, Mrs. Cole?

MRS. COLE: Thanks.

AMY: [*Indicating the armchair*] Sit here, Mother.

MRS. FISHER: Amy, why didn't you ask Mrs. Cole to take off her coat?

MRS. COLE: She did, Mrs. Fisher.

[MRS. FISHER *sits down*]

AMY: Marion can't stay, Mother.

MRS. COLE: I've got to go almost immediately, Mrs. Fisher.

MRS. FISHER: It's too bad you can't stay for a cup of tea, anyway.

MRS. COLE: I'd love it, Mrs. Fisher, but I really haven't time.

MRS. FISHER: You're going to Atlantic City, aren't you?

MRS. COLE: Yes.

MRS. FISHER: [*As though admitting a weakness in herself*] I wish I was going with you. [*She laughs shyly. And when she laughs she's pretty. She must have been a rather pretty girl; for there are traces of it yet; even after nearly thirty years as the wife of a poor man. Her husband was a wage-earner, always; and it was only by dint of vigilance and excessive scrimping that they were able to purchase and pay for the house in which she now lives. But the economic strain has told upon her, in many ways; perhaps, most obviously, in the developing of a certain plainness of personal quality,—a simplicity that is at once pathetic and, in a way, quaint. And her manner of dressing and the arrangement of her hair rather heighten this impression. She looks old-fashioned. But her hair is quite lovely; it's thick and silvery, with the loveliest wave in it; and she has it simply parted in the middle and drawn back over her ears. She must have been a decided blonde. Her dress, which looks as though she might have made it herself, a long time ago, has no particular pattern; simply a plain, brown poplin dress, without a bit of trimming except a little ruffle of the goods, about two inches deep, around the hem of the skirt. This skirt is one of the old-fashioned, full kind,—touching all the way round. She is wearing a deep lace collar, probably to relieve the almost basque-like tightness of the body, and an enormous breastpin, featuring a very vague likeness of a delicate-looking gentleman in a straw hat; presumably,* MR. FISHER]

MRS. COLE: Do you like Atlantic City, Mrs. Fisher?

[*She nods, still smiling*]

AMY: Yes, Mother's always been crazy about Atlantic City.

MRS. FISHER: I like the bathing.

MRS. COLE: Yes, wonderful, isn't it?

MRS. FISHER: I used to go in sometimes twice a day. [*She laughs a little again*]

MRS. COLE: You must have liked it.

MRS. FISHER: [*With an instant change to seriousness of expression and voice*] Of course, that was before my operation.

[AUBREY, *who has been standing at the back of the room watching her with an expression of contemptuous pity, makes an impatient gesture and turns to the bay window.* AMY *feels the movement, and, under the pretext of touching her hair, glances towards him*]

MRS. COLE: It certainly is a wonderful place.

MRS. FISHER: I haven't been there now since my husband died.

MRS. COLE: Is that so?

MRS. FISHER: Yes; it'll be four years the seventeenth of next October. He died the day Amy was twenty-five. [AUBREY *turns from the bay window and looks daggers at her*] Died on her birthday. Didn't he, Amy?

AMY: Yes. [*She glances towards* AUBREY *again, and he says voicelessly to her, but with very eloquent gestures,* "Didn't I tell you!" *and goes towards the back of the room again*]

MRS. COLE: And you haven't been to Atlantic City *since* then?

MRS. FISHER: No, not since then. But before that, we used to spend two days there every single summer. [AUBREY *turns and looks at her stonily*] Go down on Saturday morning, and come up Sunday night. Of course, it didn't cost us anything, you know, 'cept our fares; because we used to carry our lunch with us. [AUBREY *begins to boil*] And in those days, they used to allow the excursionists to sleep under the boardwalk, if you remember.

[AUBREY *raises his hand in the hope of attracting her attention and silencing her; but she is oblivious of him. He's away up in the left-hand corner of the room, out of the range of* MRS. COLE'S *eye*]

MRS. COLE: Yes, I remember.

MRS. FISHER: Dear me, I used to look forward to those two days the whole year round. [*She laughs a little*] I was just saying to Amy the other day, that if I could see my way clear to do it, I believe I'd enjoy a day down there now, just as much as ever I did.

MRS. COLE: Well, I don't see why you shouldn't, Mrs. Fisher.

MRS. FISHER: [*With another instantaneous shift to seriousness*] Well, of course, since my operation,

[AUBREY *makes a movement of excessive irritation, and* AMY *gets it; and thinks it wise to interrupt her mother*]

MRS. FISHER and AMY: [*Together*]

   [MRS. FISHER] I've got to be more careful. I can't do the things—that—I—

   [AMY, *turning suddenly to* MRS. COLE] You haven't been in Atlantic City since you were married, have you, Marion?

MRS. COLE: No, it's five years since I've been there.

MRS. FISHER: Are you going to stay there for any length of time, Mrs. Cole?

MRS. COLE: No, I'm not, Mrs. Fisher; I just want to see how my husband is.

MRS. FISHER: Has he consumption?

[AUBREY *snaps with irritation*]

MRS. COLE: No-o, he had the flu last winter; [MRS. FISHER *folds her lips in, shakes her head slowly from side to side, and looks at the floor in front of her*] and he's never been exactly himself since.

MRS. FISHER: They never do much good after that flu.

[AMY *rises and crosses towards the left*]

AMY: I suppose it depends upon how bad a person's had it, Mother. [*As soon as she passes out of the range of* MRS. COLE's *vision,* AUBREY *appeals to her to know if there isn't something she can do to shut her mother up. She simply dismisses him with a deft gesture; and, with a sharp nod of her head, indicates the immediate presence of* MRS. COLE]

MRS. FISHER: [*Unaware of the situation*] Well, now, this doctor that tended me during my operation [AUBREY *whirls round and goes to the hall door, at the back, and* AMY *comes around and sits down on the sofa, to* MRS. COLE'S *left*] Doctor Stainthorpe—she's a lady doctor—she was telling me that the flu is like scarlet fever; if it don't leave you with one thing, it'll leave you with something else.

MRS. COLE: Well, Mr. Cole seems pretty good, most of the time, but occasionally he has a spell of sort of—nervous exhaustion.

[AUBREY *wanders over and stands resting his right hand on the center table, listening to* MRS. COLE]

MRS. FISHER: Maybe he works too hard.

MRS. COLE: No, I don't think it's that; [*Speaking directly to* AUBREY] his work is easy enough. [*Shifting her eyes again to* MRS. FISHER] He's just a wig-maker. [AUBREY *drifts towards the mirror*] Makes all kinds of hair goods, you know.

MRS. FISHER: Oh, yes.

AMY: I don't think I ever knew your husband's business, Marion.

MRS. COLE: Didn't I ever tell you?

AMY: You *may* have, but I've forgotten.

[*With a glance at his toupee in the mirror,* AUBREY *glides down at the right of* MRS. FISHER]

MRS. COLE: That's what he does—Makes all these toupees that you see,—[AUBREY *turns quietly away and glides up again towards the back of the room*] and switches and—patches—All that kind of thing.

MRS. FISHER: Did you have any trouble finding the house, Mrs. Cole?

MRS. COLE: No, not very much.

AMY: Marion came out in a taxi.

MRS. FISHER: [*As though coming out in a taxi were quite an experience*] Oh, *did* you!

MRS. COLE: [*Dropping her handkerchief*] Yes, I came right out Broad Street.

AMY: [*Handing her the handkerchief*] Here's your handkerchief, Marion.

MRS. COLE and MRS. FISHER: [*Together*]

  { [MRS. COLE] Oh, thanks. Did I drop that?
  { [MRS. FISHER] Have you any children, Mrs. Cole?

MRS. COLE: What did you say, Mrs. Fisher?

MRS. FISHER: I say, have you any children?

MRS. COLE: No, I haven't, Mrs. Fisher.

MRS. FISHER: Didn't you ever have any?

[AUBREY *looks helplessly at his wife, then back to his mother-in-law*]

MRS. COLE: No.

MRS. FISHER: Well, maybe you're just as well off.

MRS. COLE: Yes, I suppose I am, in a way.

MRS. FISHER: [*Looking at the floor in front of her, and shaking her head philosophically*] If they never make you laugh, they'll never make you cry.

MRS. COLE: That's true.

MRS. FISHER: I buried a boy, when he was eight years old; and, dear me, it seemed as though I never in this *world* would get over it. But when I read in the newspapers now about all these bandits, and moving-picture people,—I'm kind of glad he went when he did. He might have gotten in with bad company and turned out just as bad as any of the others.

MRS. COLE: It's hard to tell how they'll turn out.

MRS. FISHER: Well, you see, this is such a terrible neighborhood in through here, to bring a boy *up* in. [AUBREY *makes a movement of controlled desperation.* AMY *glances at him, and he gives her a speaking look*] So many foreigners.

MRS. COLE: Is that so?

MRS. FISHER: Oh, it's just dreadful. [AUBREY *tries to signal her with divers shakes and waves of his hands. But it is utterly lost upon* MRS. FISHER. *She is all set for a good chat; and it will require more than the gesticulations of* MR. PIPER *to distract her. So she goes serenely on; never even casting a glance in his direction*] A body'd be afraid to put their nose outside the door, after dark. Why, right across the street here [*She extends her arm and hand towards the right*] in two-twenty-eight, there's a big *Polish* family; and I don't believe there's a soul in that house speaks a word of English. And there's a *colored* organization of some kind has just bought two-forty-nine—[AUBREY *has passed into a state of desperate unconsciousness, and stands glaring at his mother-in-law*] that's the corner property on this side. [*She points to the right*] Paid three thousand dollars cash for it, too. So you can see what the neighborhood's coming to.

AMY: [*Tactfully*] Aubrey,—I wish you'd go down and close the heater; the house is getting cold again, I think.

[*He starts for the portières immediately, and* MRS. COLE *turns and says something to* AMY. *As* AUBREY *crosses the back of the room, he fixes* MRS. FISHER *with an icy glare, which he holds until he passes through the portières. Not knowing wherein she has offended, she turns and looks over her right shoulder after him with an expression of puzzled resentment. Then she turns to* AMY]

MRS. FISHER: Amy, you'd better go down, too; he'll be locking those grates again, the way he did last week.

AMY: [*Rising*] He doesn't need to touch those grates; that fire's all right. [*She goes out*]

MRS. FISHER: We have one of those old-fashioned heaters; and when you're raking it, unless you turn it just a certain way, the grates'll lock. It's a perfect nuisance. I often say, I don't wonder people want to live in apartments; where they won't have to be bothered with all this heater business.

MRS. COLE: It is a bother.

MRS. FISHER: Oh, it's a pest.

MRS. COLE: Although I had the hardest time getting used to an apartment when I was first married.

MRS. FISHER: Oh, do you live in an apartment in Chicago, Mrs. Cole?

MRS. COLE: Yes, I've lived in one ever since I've been out there.

MRS. FISHER: Well, you ought to be glad of it.

MRS. COLE: Well, really, it was the only place we could get—there have been so few houses go up in Chicago in the last few years.

MRS. FISHER: That's just the way it's been here. Why, when Amy was married four years ago, she couldn't get a house for love or money. That is, I mean, one that she could afford the rent, you know.

MRS. COLE: Yes, I know.

MRS. FISHER: Of course, she could have gotten plenty at fancy rents; but as I said to her, "How are you going to pay it on his wages?" [*She turns carefully in her chair and glances over her right shoulder towards the portières, for fear* AUBREY *might be within hearing distance. Then she turns back to* MRS. COLE, *and, leaning towards her a bit, speaks in a rather subdued tone*] He's only a clerk, you know,—down here in the Pennsylvania Freight Office. But she couldn't get a thing. Of course, I'd have liked to have her stay here; because there was only Mr. Fisher and myself; but—a—[*She turns again and glances over her right shoulder, then back again to* MRS. COLE; *this time with even more confidence*] my husband never liked him. [*She indicates* AUBREY *with a nod towards the portières. Then to emphasize the fact, she looks straight at* MRS. COLE *and gives her head a little shake from side to side. But evidently she feels that she hasn't stated the circumstance sufficiently; or that, having mentioned it at all, it implies some measure of elucidation; for she rises gingerly, and, tiptoeing over to the center table, rests her left hand upon it and leans towards* MRS. COLE *in an attitude of extreme caution and confidence*] Said he was kind of a blatherskite, you know—[*She tiptoes towards the portières, but stops halfway and turns again*] Very big ideas and very little brains. [*She continues on to the portières and glances out; then returns to the table*] So—a—finally, they had to take two little rooms over here on Lehigh Avenue. Nine dollars a month, so you can imagine what they were like. But you couldn't tell them anything. As I said to them, the night they first told me they were going to be married—I said, "How do you two ever expect to make ends meet on thirty-two dollars a week?" "Oh," he says, "that's only temporary," he says,—"I'll *own* the Pennsylvania Railroad within the next five years." This is the way he's owning it. [*She looks towards the portières; then turns back and says emphatically*] He's never even gotten a raise. He's been getting thirty-two dollars a week for the last four years. [*She moves stealthily towards the portières again; far enough over to enable her to glance through them; then comes back to the table*] But—a—as soon as Mr. *Fisher* died, I told Amy she could come here, and I'd take my rent out in board. And then she makes me different things to wear—she's very handy, you know.

MRS. COLE: Yes, she's a wonderful *girl*.

MRS. FISHER: But, you know, you'd think *he* was doing me a favor to *live* here. [MRS. COLE *doesn't know exactly what to say, so she simply shakes her head from side to side and smiles*] He doesn't like me, you know. Hardly ever speaks to me. I suppose you noticed it, didn't you?

MRS. COLE: No, I didn't, Mrs. Fisher.

MRS. FISHER: He's been *furious* ever since last spring. [*She turns away again and glances towards the portières; then turns hurriedly back, as though she had a particularly incredible item of information to communicate*] Wanted *me* to put a *mortgage* on this house to get him an automobile. Can you imagine that! He's *crazy* about automobiles. And, Mrs. Cole, I know just as well as I'm standing here, that if he *got* one, he'd only kill himself—for he has no more brains than a rabbit. So I told him. I sez—[AMY'*s voice, out at the right, interrupts her*]

AMY: Be sure and close this cellar door, Aubrey; there's a draught here if you don't.

MRS. FISHER: [*Tiptoeing back to her chair, with a significant gesture to* MRS. COLE] Well, I hope you find your husband all right, Mrs. Cole. [*She sits down*]

MRS. COLE: I hope so, thanks, Mrs. Fisher. He *seems* pretty good, from his letters.

AMY: [*Coming through the portières*] I'm sorry, Marion, but I seem to be the only one around here that knows how to tend to that heater.

MRS. COLE: [*Rising*] Well, you know, you were always able to do everything, Amy. [*She moves a little towards the center table, fastening her glove*]

AMY: You don't have to go already, do you, Marion?

MRS. COLE: I'm afraid so, dear; [MRS. FISHER *rises*] it's getting on to four o'clock. [AUBREY *sways in through the portières, flicking imaginary ashes from himself with the fancy handkerchief*]

MRS. FISHER: Couldn't you take a later train, Mrs. Cole?

[AUBREY *comes forward*]

MRS. COLE: Why, I suppose I could, Mrs. Fisher; but I've wired Mr. Cole that I'll be on *that* one.

MRS. FISHER: Oh, I see.

MRS. COLE: And he's so nervous and worrisome since he's been sick, that I'm afraid if I'm *not* on it, he'll be tearing his hair out. [*She turns, laughing a little, which* AMY *and her mother reflect, and goes back to the sofa for her muff.* AUBREY *is feigning a profound absorption in an examination of his finger nails.* AMY *goes up towards the bay window*]

MRS. FISHER: Are you going to the station on the trolley, Mrs. Cole?

MRS. COLE: No, I told the taxi to wait, Mrs. Fisher. I hope he's still out there. Is he, Amy?

AMY: [*At the window*] Yes, he's still there.

MRS. FISHER: [*Hurrying across in front of* MRS. COLE] Oh, I must see it! Pardon me.

MRS. COLE: Certainly. [*Going up towards the hall door*] Now, Amy, I *do* hope you're going to write to me occasionally.

AMY: [*Coming away from the window, towards her*] You're the one who never writes.

MRS. COLE: [*Laughing guiltily*] I know, darling; but I'm going to reform, really.

AMY: Well, now, I'm going to wait and see.

MRS. COLE: But, really, I've been so terribly busy since Mr. Cole's been ill, that I don't seem to be able to—[*She becomes confidential*]

MRS. FISHER: [*Turning, at the window, and addressing* AUBREY, *who is standing directly opposite her, and who happens to be the first one her eye lights upon*] Seems so funny to see an automobile in this street. [AUBREY *is paralyzed; and before he can recover the use of his arm sufficiently to try to silence her, she has turned again to the window; and he stands watching her, frozen with the fear that she may turn again, and sustained only by the hope that* MRS. COLE *did not hear her. His agony is very brief, however, for almost immediately,* MRS. FISHER *turns again and addresses him*] I don't think I've ever *seen* one in this street be-fore. [AUBREY *makes a frantic gesture to her, and, turning around to his left, strides up to the back of the room, pointing vigorously at* MRS. COLE. MRS. FISHER *is bewildered—She simply stares blankly at the goings-on of her son-in-law; and it is not until he strides forward again at the right, glowering at her savagely, that it oc-curs to her to speak*] Why, what's the matter with you!

[AUBREY *suddenly raises his left arm and hand as though he'd like to sweep her from the earth, but the opportune turning of* MRS. COLE *to say good-by to* MRS. FISHER, *restores order*]

MRS. COLE: Good-by, Mrs. Fisher.

MRS. FISHER: [*Shaking hands with her*] Good-by, Mrs. Cole.

MRS. COLE: I'm sorry to have to run away like this.

MRS. FISHER: Well, I know how you feel.

MRS. COLE: [*Turning and chucking* AMY *under the chin*] But I *did* want to see my child here. And her husband—probably the *best*-looking man I've seen in Philadelphia so far.

[AMY, *with an exclamation of deprecation goes laughing out into the hallway.* MRS. FISHER *laughs a little, out of courtesy*]

AUBREY: [*Swaggering, excessively self-satisfied, and pointing after his wife*] Tell *her* that!

MRS. FISHER: I hope the next time you come this way you'll be able to stay a little longer, Mrs. Cole.

MRS. COLE: Thanks; I hope so, too, Mrs. Fisher. [*She turns to* AUBREY] Good-by, Mr. Piper.

AUBREY: Good-by, Mrs. Cole.

[*They shake hands*]

MRS. COLE: [*Dropping her glove*] I'm *so* glad to have met you.—Oh!

AUBREY: [*Stooping*] I'll get it.

[*The toupee glides off and falls on to the black, fur rug on which they're standing; but he doesn't observe the circum-stance, and restores the glove with a touch of flourish*]

MRS. COLE: Thanks.

[*She simply takes the glove, without the slightest evidence of an appreciation of the situation. But old* MRS. FISHER *is in a state of siege; and, taking advantage of her position behind* MRS. COLE, *endeavors to communicate to her son-in-law, by means of funny little pointings and movements with her head, some knowledge of his condition. But* AUBREY *is mercifully oblivious of everything, save that he is in the presence of a very attractive woman, who has admitted that she considers him probably the best-looking man she has seen in Philadelphia*]

AUBREY: Sorry you have to go so soon.

MRS. COLE: I'm sorry, too, Mr. Piper. But if I'm not on that train, [*She turns to* MRS. FISHER] I'm afraid I'll get scalped. [*She goes out into the hallway*]

MRS. FISHER: [*Stepping to the hall door*] Don't let her stand out there in the cold with nothing around her, Mrs. Cole.

MRS. COLE: No, I'll send her right in, Mrs. Fisher.

MRS. FISHER: Good-by.

MRS. COLE: Good-by.

AUBREY: [*Standing immediately behind* MRS. FISHER, *looking out into the hallway*] Good-by.

MRS. COLE: Amy, your mother says you mustn't stand out here in the cold with nothing around you.

[MRS. FISHER *turns, and, with a glance at* AUBREY, *steps to the bay window, to watch* MRS. COLE *get into the taxi.* AUBREY *follows her and takes up his position just back of her, looking out*]

MRS. FISHER: [*After a slight pause*] Good-by. [*She waves to* MRS. COLE; *and so does* AUBREY,—*perhaps with a trifle more dignity than the occasion implies. Then the taxi moves away, and they watch it, smiling, down the street. Suddenly* MRS. FISHER *looks sharply in the opposite direction*] There's the boy with the paper. [*Turning from the window, folding her arms tightly together*] I've got to get my little woolen shawl; this room's too chilly for me.

[*She goes out through the portières. The front door closes; and* AUBREY *turns from the window to the hall door*]

AMY: [*Entering briskly through the hall door, carrying the evening paper*] Here's the *Ledger*.

AUBREY: You ought to have something around you.

AMY: [*Stepping to the bay window*] I'm not cold. Where's Mother?

AUBREY: [*Opening the paper*] She's gone up for her shawl.

[*He sits in the armchair and* AMY *peers through the bay window, as though trying to catch a last glimpse of the departing taxi*]

AMY: [*Suddenly turning from the window*] Isn't Marion nice?

AUBREY: Yes, she's very pleasant.

AMY: [*Looking at herself in the mirror*] She's an awfully smart girl, too. She had charge of our entire department when I worked at the bank.

[*There is a slight pause*]

AUBREY: [*Half-turning, and very significantly*] Say, Amy.

AMY: What?

AUBREY: Listen.

[*She turns her head sharply and looks at him. He beckons her to him with a rather mysterious nod, and she comes to him*]

AMY: What?

AUBREY: [*In a subdued, level tone*] Did you get your mother telling her your age?

AMY: That's nothing; Marion knows my age.

AUBREY: I *told* you what she'd do.

AMY: [*Starting towards the portières*] Well, now, it doesn't make the least bit of difference; so don't start anything. [*She glances through the portières*]

AUBREY: It's a good thing she didn't have any longer to stay.

MRS. FISHER: [*Off*] You know, Amy,—

AMY: [*Turning suddenly to him with a deft gesture*] Sh—sh—[*She steps to the mirror and pretends to be fixing her hair*]

AUBREY: Or she'd have told her a whole lot more.

MRS. FISHER: [*Coming through the portières wearing a rather skimpy-looking white shoulder-shawl and carrying some pale-pink knitting*] I always pictured that girl as a much bigger woman than she is, when you used to talk about her. [*She walks over to the sofa. She appears to be having difficulty in disentangling her yarn*]

AMY: Don't you think she's a big girl?

MRS. FISHER: Well, *stouter,* I mean.

AMY: No, she never was stout.

MRS. FISHER: [*Sitting on the sofa, and settling herself*] I'd never know her in the world from that picture you have of her upstairs.

AMY: [*Turning from the mirror*] Don't you think she's nice?

MRS. FISHER: Very nice.

AMY: [*Standing at her husband's right*] Give me a piece of that paper.

MRS. FISHER: And very stylish, too.

AMY: Any part'll do.

[*He detaches a section of the paper and gives it to her. She moves a step or two forward and commences to read. AUBREY resumes his reading; and MRS. FISHER knits*]

MRS. FISHER: [*After a pause*] I'll bet there was five hundred dollars right on her back there today if there was a penny. And that's not counting her hat nor her shoes, either. [*There is another little pause*] That wig business must be a very good business. [*AUBREY looks over at her stonily; but she's occupied with her knitting*] I saw a piece in the *North American* the other morning, that a lot of people were wearing wigs now that don't need them at all. [*She looks over at AMY, to find AUBREY glaring at her*] That's what it said. [*He snaps his head round and continues reading*] She was telling me, Amy, that she lives in an apartment there in Chicago. Sez they couldn't get a house when they first went there. Sez there hasn't been a house go up in Chicago since before the war.

[*She laughs faintly to herself*] I was telling her about the time you and Aubrey had, when you were first married—[*He looks over at her, with a dangerous squint*] trying to get even a couple of rooms somewhere. And the kind they were, when you *did* get them. [*She laughs a little more, at the recollection of them*] But they had the nerve to charge you nine dollars a month for them, just the same. [*She smiles and looks at* AUBREY]

AUBREY: [*Explosively*] I suppose you told her *that*, too, didn't you!

[AMY *is startled out of her interest in the newspaper*]

MRS. FISHER: [*After a second's amazement*] Told her what?

AUBREY: When were you handing out all this information?

AMY: Now, Aubrey, don't start, please!

AUBREY: [*Jumping to his feet*] It's enough to *make* [*He slams the piece of newspaper down on the chair violently*] a fellow start! [*He thrusts his hands into his trousers' pockets and strides towards the back of the room*] Trying to make me look like a poor *sap!* [*He crosses to the hall door and right back again*]

MRS. FISHER: [*Looking in bewilderment at* AMY] Why, what's the matter with *him!*

AMY and AUBREY: [*Together*]
{ [AMY] Nothing at all, Mother.
{ [AUBREY] You know very *well* what's the matter with me!

MRS. FISHER: What?

AUBREY: Handing out a line of *gab* about my *business!* Every time you can get anybody to *listen* to you.

MRS. FISHER: Who was handing out any line of gab about your business?

AUBREY: *You* were!—and you're always doing it!

MRS. FISHER: Why, you haven't got any line of business for anybody to hand out any line of gab about—that I ever heard of. [*She turns away*]

AUBREY: It doesn't matter whether I have any line of business or not! It isn't necessary for you to be gabbing to perfect strangers about it.

MRS. FISHER: What did you want me to do, sit there lookin' at the woman, like a cow?

AMY: Mother, please.

AUBREY: You don't have to talk about my affairs!

MRS. FISHER: [*With vast amusement*] Your affairs—

AUBREY: That's what I said, my affairs! [MRS. FISHER *laughs derisively, and* AUBREY *turns to his wife, desperately*] You hear her!

MRS. FISHER: That's funny.

AMY: She wasn't talking about you, Aubrey.

AUBREY: She *was* talking about me! That's all she ever *does*, is talk about me!

[MRS. FISHER *whirls around*]

MRS. FISHER: I was talkin' about houses!—that ain't you, is it?

AUBREY: I know what you were talking about, you needn't tell me.

MRS. FISHER: I had to talk about something, didn't I?

AMY: Keep quiet, Aubrey!

AUBREY and MRS. FISHER: [*Together*]

{ [AUBREY, *whirling around and going towards the hall door*] No, I won't keep quiet!

{ [MRS. FISHER] You two were down in the cellar fixing the fire! And you can't sit there with your two hands as long as each other when a person's visiting in your house!

AUBREY: [*Stopping abruptly*] I suppose you mentioned *that*, too, didn't you!

MRS. FISHER: [*Half-turning and listening narrowly*] Mentioned what?

AUBREY: That it was *your* house!

[MRS. FISHER *turns her whole body round to him in a literal bounce*]

MRS. FISHER: [*Shrilly*] Well, whose house *would* I mention that it was!

AUBREY: [*Turning to* AMY *with a broad gesture*] You see! Didn't I tell you!

AMY and AUBREY: [*Together*]

> ([AMY] Well, what of it, Aubrey! What of it!
> { [AUBREY] Every opportunity she gets she's trying to make me look
> like a poor thing!

[*He brings his right hand down thunderously upon the center
table. Then, thrusting his hands into his trousers' pockets again,
strides over to the arched door and back again to the portières*]

MRS. FISHER: [*After a strained pause*] Why, what's the matter with
the crazy Jack!

AMY: Pay no attention to him, Mother.

MRS. FISHER: I suppose I won't be able to say this house *is* my own
after a while.

AUBREY: [*Stopping above the center table and rapping his fist upon
it*] It isn't necessary for you to be gabbing to perfect strangers
about *whose* house it is!

MRS. FISHER: [*Keenly*] I guess it'd have been all right if I'd told her it
was yours, wouldn't it?

AUBREY: [*Repudiating her remark with a sharp gesture*] You don't
have to tell anybody *anything!*

[MRS. FISHER *springs to her feet*]

MRS. FISHER: I suppose that's what's the matter with you, isn't it?

AUBREY and MRS. FISHER: [*Together*]

> ([AUBREY] There's nothing at all the matter with me! [*He touch
> { his handkerchief to his forehead*]
> ([MRS. FISHER] He's very likely been telling this friend of yours,
> Amy, that this is *his* house! And I guess with a lot of big talk about
> taking *me* in, and giving *me* a home! Trying to make *me* look like
> a poor thing!

AMY: [*Trying to pacify her mother*] Now, he didn't tell her anything
of the kind, Mother!

MRS. FISHER: [*Shaking with wrath*] He did if he got the chance! I
know him.

AMY: Well, he didn't *get* the chance; I was only out of the room two minutes.

MRS. FISHER: [*Returning to the sofa*] Well, that's long enough for him! I've heard *him* before. [*She gathers up her knitting, preparatory to sitting down*] Blowing his bubbles! [*She sits down, fuming*] The big blatherskite! [*There is a pause.* AMY *and* AUBREY *look at each other, then at* MRS. FISHER, *who knits violently*] I'm very glad now I *did* tell her this was my house!—[*She knits a little more*] For I know he'd very soon tell her it was *his*, if he got my back turned long enough! [*She draws some yarn from the ball*] And it wouldn't be mine long, either, if I listened to all his silly blather about stocks, and bonds, and automobiles, and every other thing! —On his thirty-two dollars a week. [AUBREY *looks stonily at her for a second; then she turns sharply and leans on the arm of the sofa towards him*] I told her *that*, too!

AUBREY: [*Turning to* AMY] You see! Didn't I tell you!

MRS. FISHER: [*Resuming her knitting*] So she'd know how much brains you had!

AMY: It wasn't at all necessary, Mother, for you to tell Marion that.

MRS. FISHER: [*Without looking up from her work*] Well, I told her; whether it was necessary or not. [*She looks at* AMY *and speaks emphatically*] It was the truth, anyway. And I guess that's more than can be said for a whole lot that *he* told her.

[*She indicates* AUBREY *with a nod; then resumes her work. There is a pause.* AUBREY *is standing fuming.* AMY *picks up the piece of the paper that he threw on the chair, then extends the piece that she has been reading towards him*]

AMY: Do you want this?

AUBREY: [*Half-turning, and with a shade of hauteur*] What is it?

AMY: Why, it's the newspaper of course! What do you think it is?

[*He deigns to take it. She gives him a long look, then opens the other half of the paper and reads*]

AUBREY: [*Opening his part of the paper*] A man'd certainly have a swell chance trying to make anything of himself around this *hut!*

MRS. FISHER: I don't see that anybody's trying to *stop* you from making something of yourself.

AUBREY: No, and I don't see that anybody's trying to *help* me any, either. Only trying to make me look like a *pinhead* every chance they get.

MRS. FISHER: Nobody'll have to try very hard to make *you* look like a pinhead. Your own silly talk'll do *that* for you, any time at all.

AUBREY: [*Turning to her sharply*] I suppose it's silly talk to try to make a good impression.

MRS. FISHER: [*Looking over at him, and inclining her head conclusively*] Yes—It's silly to try to make an impression of *any* kind; for the only one that'll be made'll be the *right* one; and that'll make itself. [*She reverts to her work*]

AUBREY: Well, if you were out in the world as much as I am, you'd very soon see how much easier it is for a fellow to get along if people think he's *got* something.

MRS. FISHER: Well, anybody listen to you very long'd know you *couldn't* have very much.

AUBREY: Is that so!

MRS. FISHER: [*Quietly*] You heard me. [AUBREY *steps over to the armchair and sits down, looking bitterly at his mother-in-law*] People that are smart enough to be able to make it easier for anybody, are not interested in what you've *got*. [*Looking over at him*] It's what you've got in your *brains* that they're interested in. And nobody has to tell them that, either. They'll know all about it, if you never opened your mouth.

AMY: Oh, stop talking, Mother.

[*She turns, with a movement of wearied impatience, then continues to read. There is a quiet pause; AMY and AUBREY reading, and MRS. FISHER knitting. Then AUBREY looks up from his paper, thinks for a second, and half turns to his wife*]

AUBREY: Did you get that remark your friend made, as she was going out?

AMY: What remark?

[MRS. FISHER *looks over*]

AUBREY: [*With a self-satisfied smile*] About the best-looking man in Philadelphia?

MRS. FISHER: [*Rearranging her knitting*] Oh, dear!

[AUBREY *gives her a narrow look; then turns back to his wife*]

AUBREY: She made it twice, too.

AMY: I suppose I'll never hear the end of that now.

AUBREY: No, but it made an awful hit with me, after all the talk you made about putting on the toupee.

AMY: Oh, it wasn't the toupee that made her say it; don't flatter yourself.

AUBREY: I don't think it hurt any.

AMY: No, and I don't think you're so crazy about the toupee yourself.

AUBREY: It's better than being baldheaded.

AMY: I notice you got rid of it very quickly, as soon as she went.

[MRS. FISHER *listens*]

AUBREY: What?

AMY: [*Without looking up from the paper*] You heard me. [MRS. FISHER *can't resist a glance at* AUBREY; *but realizing that her expression might precipitate another row, she turns away quietly and continues with her knitting.* AUBREY *hasn't grasped the significance of his wife's remark. He turns and looks at her with a puzzled expression; but she is reading; so he turns back again and looks straight out, baffled. Then a thought occurs to him. He reaches up and touches his head. The toupee is off. His brows lift and his mouth falls open, and he sits staring straight ahead for a second. Then he glances furtively at his mother-in-law, but she is studiously avoiding the situation. He gets up, very quietly; and, with a little glance over his right shoulder at his wife, turns and gives a quick look on the armchair and under it. No sign of the toupee. He feels all over his head and around the back of his neck; puts his hand up under his coat, and looks on the floor back of the armchair. All very quietly, and with a pathetic attempt at noncha-*]

lance. But the toupee is not to be seen. He saunters up towards the back of the room, steps over and glances at himself in the mirror, then stands looking about the floor in a quandary. His wife observes him out of the corner of her eye, and turns to him] What are you looking for?

[*He glances at* MRS. FISHER, *then goes very close to his wife and speaks in a confidential tone*]

AUBREY: My toupee. Did you see anything of it?

AMY: Where'd you put it?

AUBREY: [*With a shade of impatience*] I didn't put it anywhere.

AMY: Well, where did you have it?

AUBREY: [*Becoming more impatient*] I had it on my head, of course! Where'd you think I had it!

AMY: I thought you took it off, when Marion went.

AUBREY: No, I didn't take it off!

AMY: Well, where is it?

AUBREY: [*Throwing discretion to the winds*] I don't know *where* it is! That's why I'm asking *you!* [MRS. FISHER *can no longer contain herself, and bursts into unrestrained laughter. They both turn sharply and look at her,* AUBREY *glaring*] Funny! Isn't it!

[AMY *crosses quickly to the center table, in front of her husband*]

AMY: Did you see anything of it, Mother?

MRS. FISHER: [*Bursting out afresh*] I saw it *fall off,* that's all *I* know about it.

[*They stand looking at her*]

AUBREY: You see that! She'd let me walk around here all day with it off, and never tip me off that it was off!

MRS. FISHER: What good was it to tip you off that it was off after it was off! [*Turning back to her knitting*] The cat was out of the bag, then.

AMY: Where'd it fall off, Mother?

MRS. FISHER: When he was picking that woman's glove up, up there at the hallway. [AMY *turns quickly towards the hall door, glancing about the floor; and* MRS. FISHER *turns to* AUBREY] It isn't *my* fault if his old *wig* doesn't fit him.

[*He is looking at her with murder in his eye; but she doesn't flinch. If anything, there is a glint of challenge in her look. And it's quite as steady as his own.* AMY *finds the toupee where it fell, and holds it up towards* AUBREY *by one hair*]

AMY: Is this it?

[*But the duel of eyes is still on between* AUBREY *and his mother-in-law, and he is oblivious of both his wife and her question. So the toupee, looking very much like a dead cat, depends from* AMY'*s uplifted fingers. Then, suddenly,* AUBREY *snatches it, with a whirling movement, and goes towards the mirror to adjust it*]

MRS. FISHER: [*Following him with her eyes*] It just serves him right! That's what he gets for showing off!

AUBREY: [*Whirling at the mirror, and literally shouting at her*] Shut up, will you!

[*The violence of his turning sends the toupee flying off his head on to the floor, and causes* MRS. FISHER *to start so that her ball of yarn flies four feet into the air*]

AMY: [*Taking a step towards her husband and lifting her hand to enjoin silence*] Sh—sh—sh—

AUBREY: [*Looking at her with an eye of fire*] I won't stand much more of this, Amy! Now, I'm telling you!

AMY: Keep quiet, Aubrey! Marion probably never noticed it at all.

MRS. FISHER: I don't know how she could *help* noticing it. *I* noticed it; and I don't think my eyesight's as good as hers.

AUBREY: Then, why didn't you say something!

MRS. FISHER: Because I knew if I did I'd very likely get snatched baldheaded! [AUBREY *starts violently, and* MRS. FISHER *snaps back to her knitting*]

AUBREY: [*Appealing to his wife*] You hear that! Is it any wonder my nerves are the way they are!

AMY: Oh, keep quiet, Aubrey! For Heaven's sake! [*Pointing to the toupee on the floor*] And pick up your wig.

[*This is too much for* AUBREY. *He literally sways against the portières*]

AUBREY: [*Recovering himself*] It isn't a wig, now, Amy! I've told you that a half-dozen times!

AMY: [*Looking up from the paper which she has commenced to read, and in an exhausted tone*] Well, then, pick up your toupee!

[*He picks it up and simply slaps it back on to his head. The effect is weird; for it is quite disheveled from its recent experiences, and, in his temper, he has put it on backwards. He swings forward and sits in the armchair, very sulkily.* AMY *continues to read the evening paper.* MRS. FISHER *knits, and* AUBREY *sits sulking, looking straight ahead. There is a pause. Then, possibly at the recollection of certain of the remarks that his mother-in-law made earlier in the battle,* AUBREY *darts a sudden glare in her direction; only to find that she has been the victim of similar memories. So they sit and scowl at each other; then turn away. Then turn back again, and away again. Then* AUBREY *becomes conscious of his wife; and of the fact that she is reading the evening newspaper; and, by the association of ideas, his thought is diverted into more becoming channels. He half-turns to* AMY, *with something of the self-importance that characterized his earlier manner, and, after a slight pause, addresses her*]

AUBREY: Have you got the—a—financial page there?

[AMY *hands it to him; and the curtain commences to descend very slowly*]

MRS. FISHER: Hum!

[*He glares over at her, but she's knitting; so, withdrawing his eyes, he reaches into his vest pocket and brings forth the rimmed nose-glasses, which he settles rather authentically upon his nose. Then he takes a silver pencil from the other vest pocket, and, turning to his wife, accepts the newspaper. Then he crosses his knees, and, spreading the newspaper upon them, proceeds to figure profits in the margin.* AMY *stands looking at him, and* MRS. FISHER *knits*]

THE CURTAIN IS DOWN

INFANCY

Thornton Wilder

Thornton Wilder

Thornton Wilder (1897–1975) was one of this century's most distinguished literary figures. Born in Madison, Wisconsin, he won three Pulitzer Prizes—one for his first novel, *The Bridge of San Luis Rey* (1928), and for his two most stimulating and provocative plays, *Our Town* (1938) and *The Skin of Our Teeth* (1943).

One of the few writers who successfully combined careers as novelist and dramatist, he initially came to the theatre with *The Trumpet Shall Sound*, a play about the Civil War, performed at the American Laboratory Theatre, New York, in 1926.

Thereafter, he was to contribute to the Broadway stage a translation of André Obey's *Lucrèce* (1932), a new version of *A Doll's House* (1937), and an adaptation of a German farce, *The Merchant of Yonkers* (1938). Despite a lustrous cast and an elaborate production by Max Reinhardt, the latter ran for about forty performances, but the author remained undaunted. In 1954 he offered the comedy again—this time with a new title, *The Matchmaker*—at the Edinburgh Festival. With Ruth Gordon in the title role and Sir Tyrone Guthrie's vigorous staging, the play later became a solid hit in both London and New York. Its ultimate success, however, came in its third transformation, as one of the most successful musicals of all time, *Hello, Dolly!* (1964).

Infancy had its première at the Off-Broadway Circle-in-the-Square in January 1962, as part of a triple bill with the over-all title of *Plays for Bleecker Street*. The first of a projected cycle of fourteen short plays covering the Seven Ages of Man and the Seven Deadly Sins, its companion pieces were *Childhood* and *Someone from Assisi*.

Wilder's other short plays include *The Happy Journey to Trenton and Camden; The Long Christmas Dinner;* and *Pullman Car Hiawatha*.

Thornton Wilder was an original and unconventional dramatist, who aroused controversy, but whose works form a permanent contribution to the American theatre.

Characters:

Officer Avonzino
Miss Millie Wilchick
Tommy
Mrs. Boker
Moe

Central Park, New York. In the Twenties. One or more large park benches. Some low stools at the edges of the stage to indicate bushes.

Enter PATROLMAN AVONZINO, *a policeman from the Keystone comic movies with a waterfall moustache, thick black eyebrows and a large silver star. Swinging his billy-club jauntily, he shades his eyes and peers down the paths for trouble. Reassured, he extracts a small memorandum book from an inner pocket of his jacket and reads:*

AVONZINO: "Wednesday, April 26 . . ." Right "Centra' Park, Patrol Section Eleven, West, Middle." Right! "Lieutenant T. T. Avonzino." Correct. Like Tomaso Tancredo Avonzino. "Eight to twelve; two to six. Special Orders: Suspect mad dog, black with white spots. Suspect old gentleman, silk hat, pinches nurses." *[Reflects]* Pinch babies okay; pinch nurses, nuisance. *[Puts the book away, strolls, then takes it out again for further instructions]* Probable weather: late morning, percipitation—percipitation like rain. *[Strolls]* Seven to eight-thirty, no nuisances. Millionaires on horses; horses on millionaires. Young gents running in underwear; old gents running in underwear. *[Reflects]* Running in underwear, okay; *walking* in underwear, nuisance. Eight-thirty to nine-thirty, everybody late for working, rush-rush, no time for nuisances. Nine-thirty to twelve: babies. One thousand babies with ladies. Nuisances plenty: old gents poisoning pigeons; ladies stealing baby carriages. Nuisances in bushes: young gents and young girls taking liberties. *[Hotly]* Why can't they do their nuisances at home? That's what homes are for: to do your nuisances in. *[He shields his eyes and peers toward the actors' entrance at the back of the stage; emotionally]* Here she comes! Miss'a Wilchick! *Baby!*— prize baby of Centra' Park. *[He extracts a handbook from another pocket of his jacket]* "Policeman's Guide. Lesson Six: Heart Attacks and Convulsions." No. No. "Lesson Sixteen: Frostbite." No!

"Lesson Eleven": . . . Ha! "An officer exchanges no personal remarks wid de public." Crazy! [*In dreamy ecstasy*] Oh, personal re-marks. It's personal remarks dat make-a de world go round; dat make-a de birds sing. [*Indignantly*] Nobody, *nobody* wid flesh and blood can live widout'a personal re-marks. Ha! She comes . . . ! [*He steals off by the aisle through the audience*]

[*Enter from the back* MISS MILLIE WILCHICK, *pushing* TOMMY'*s baby carriage.* TOMMY, *now invisible in the carriage, is to be played by a full-grown man.* MILLIE *brings the carriage to rest by a bench. She peers up the various paths in search of* OFFICER AVONZINO. *Disappointed, she prepares to make herself comfortable. From the foot of the carriage she brings out a box of chocolates, another of marshmallows and a novel. Before sitting down she talks into the carriage*]

MILLIE: . . . lil sweet lovums. Miss Millie's lil lover, aren't you? Yes, you are. I could squeeze lil Tommy to death, yes. I could. Kiss-kiss-kiss, yes, I could. [*Again peering down the paths*] Don't know where Mr. Policerman is! Big handsome Officer Avonzino. He take care of Miss Millie and lil lover-boy Tommy . . . Hm . . . Maybe he come by and by. [*She sits on the bench and selects a candy*] . . . Peppermint . . . strawb'ry? . . . Well, and a marshmallow. [*She opens the novel at the first page and reads with great deliberation*] "Doris was not strictly beautiful, but when she passed men's heads turned to gaze at her with pleasure." Doris was not strictly beautiful, but . . . [*A squeal of joy*] Oh, they don't write like that any more!! Oh, I'm going to enjoy this book. Let's see how it ends. First, there must be one of those chawclut cream centers. [*She turns to the last page of the novel*] "He drew her to him, pressing his lips on hers. 'Forever,' he said. Doris closed her eyes. 'Forever,' she said. The end." [*Delighted cry*] They *don't* write like that any more. "For e . . . e . . . ever." Could I say 'forever,' if his lips . . . 'e-e-v' . . . were pressed on mine? [*She closes her eyes and experiments*] . . . e . . . ver . . . for . . . e . . . Yes, I guess it could be done. [*She starts dreaming*] Oh, I *know* I could write a novel. [*She dreams*]

[*Slowly* TOMMY'*s hands can be seen gripping the side of his carriage. With great effort he pulls himself up until his head appears. He is wearing a lace-trimmed cap*]

TOMMY: Fur . . . evvah . . . Do-rus . . . nah . . . strigly boo-toody . . . [*Fretfully*] I can't say it . . . bloody-fill . . . Why don't they *teach* me to say it? I want to LEARN and they won't teach me. Do-rua nah stackly . . . boody . . . Fur evvah . . . [*Near to wailing*] Time's going by. I'm getting owe-uld. And nobody is showing me *anything*. I wanta make a house. I wanta make a house. I wanta make a bay-bee. Nobody show-ow-ow-s me how-ta.

MILLIE: [*Waking up*] Tommy! What are you crying about? Has 'a got a little stummyache? Has 'a got a foot caught? No. [*Leaning over him, suddenly severe*] Has Tommy wet his bed?!! No. No. Then's what's a matter?

TOMMY: Wanta make a house!

MILLIE: Wants to be petted, yes.

TOMMY: [*Violently*] Wanta make a baybeee!

MILLIE: Miss Millie's lil lover wants a little attention.

TOMMY: [*Fortissimo*] Chawclut. Chawclut. Wanta eat what you're eating. Wanta eat what you smell of . . . chawclut.

MILLIE: Now don't you climb up. You'll fall out. It's terrible the way you're growing.

TOMMY: Put me on the ground. I wanta learn to walk. I wanta walk. I wanta walk. I wanta find things to *eat*.

MILLIE: [*Sternly*] Now Miss Millie's going to spank you. Crying for nothing. You ought to be ashamed of yourself. [*She stands joggling the baby carriage with one hand and holding the opened novel with the other*] "This little pig went to *mar-ket*." There! "This little pig . . ." Sh-sh-sh! "Doris was not strictly beautiful, but . . ." Oh, I read that. "This little pig stayed at home." [*She looks into the carriage with great relief*] God be praised in his glory, babies get tired soon . . . Asleep. [*She walks across the stage; then suddenly stops*] I don't know what I'm going to do. My life is hell. Here I am, a good looking girl almost thirty and *nothing ever happens*. Everybody's living, except me. Everybody's happy, except ME!! [*She returns, sobbing blindly to the baby carriage*] Those silly novels—I hate them—just gab-gab-gab. Now I'm crying so I can't see which is pineapple. [*She chances to look in the direction of the aisle through the audience*] Oh, my God, there comes Officer Avonzino. [*She clasps her hands in fervent prayer*] Oh, my God, help a girl! If you ever helped a girl, help her now! [*She rapidly hides novel and candy under* TOMMY's *blankets, and takes out another book. She arranges herself at one end of the bench and pretends to fall into a reverie*]

[*Enter* PATROLMAN AVONZINO *through the audience. He steals behind her and puts his hands over her eyes. The following passage is very rapid*]

AVONZINO: You've got one guessing coming to you! Who is in Centra' Park? Maybe who?

MILLIE: Oh, I don't know. I really don't.

AVONZINO: You've got two guessings. Maybe the Mayor of Newa-York, maybe him, you think? Now you got one guessing. Maybe T. T. Avonzino—like somebody you know, somebody you seen before.

MILLIE: Oh! Officer Avonzino!!

[*He leaps on the bench beside her. She is kept busy removing his hands from her knees*]

AVONZINO: Somebody you know. Somebody you seen before.

MILLIE: Officer, you must behave. You really must behave.

AVONZINO: Action! I believe in a action! Personal remarks and da action.

[TOMMY *has raised himself and is staring enormous-eyed and with great disapproval at these goings-on*]

TOMMY: [*Loudly*] Ya! Ya! Ya! Ya! Ya!

[OFFICER AVONZINO *is thunderstruck. He jumps up as though caught out of order by his superior. He stands behind the bench adjusting his tie and coat and star*]

MILLIE: Why, what's the matter, Mr. Avonzino?

AVONZINO: [*Low and terse*] Him. Looka at him. Looka at him, *looking.*

TOMMY: Ya. Ya. Ya

MILLIE: Go to sleep, Tommy. Just nice policeman. Tommy's friend. Go to sleep.

TOMMY: [*One last warning, emphatically*] Ya! [*He disappears*]

MILLIE: But, Officer, he's just a *baby*. He doesn't understand one little thing.

AVONZINO: [*Blazing, but under his breath*] Oh no, oh no, ho no, oh no—he got *thoughts*. Turn-a de carriage around. I no wanta see that face.

MILLIE: [*Turning the carriage*] I'm surprised at you. He's just a dear little baby. A dear little . . . animal.

AVONZINO: Miss Wilchick, I see one thousand babies a day. They got *ideas*.

MILLIE: [*Laughing girlishly*] Why, Mr. Avonzino, you're like the author of this book I've been reading.—Dr. Kennick. He says babies are regular geniuses in their first fourteen months. He says: you know why babies sleep all the time? Because they're learning all the time, they get tired by learning. Geniuses, he says, imagine!

AVONZINO: *What* he say?

MILLIE: They learn more than they'll ever learn again. And faster. Like hands and feet; and to focus your eyes. And like walking and talking. He says their brains are exploding with power.

AVONZINO: What he say?

MILLIE: Well,—after about a year they stop being geniuses. Dr. Kennick says the reason why we aren't geniuses is that we weren't brought up right: we were stopped.

AVONZINO: That's a right. He gotta the right idea. Miss Wilchick, I see one thousand babies a day. And what I say is: stop 'em. That's your business, Miss Wilchick; that's my business. There's too many ingeniouses in Centra' Park right now: stop 'em. [TOMMY *begins to howl.* AVONZINO *points at him with his billy-club*] What did I tell you? They all understand English. North'a Eighth Street they all understand English.

MILLIE: [*Leaning over* TOMMY's *carriage*] There, there. Nice policeman don't mean *one* word of it.

AVONZINO: [*Looking at the actors' entrance; they are both shouting to be heard*] Here comes another brains. I go now.

MILLIE: Oh, that must be Mrs. Boker—I'm so sorry this happened, Mr. Avonzino.

AVONZINO: I see you later, maybe—when you get permission from the professor—permission in writing, Miss Wilchick. [*He goes out through the audience*]

[*Enter* MRS. BOKER *pushing* MOE's *carriage.* MOE *starts crying in sympathy with* TOMMY. *Both women shout*]

MRS. BOKER: What's the matter with Tommy, good morning, on such a fine day?

MILLIE: [*Leaning over* TOMMY] What's a matter?

TOMMY: CHAWCLUT!! STRAWBRY!! I'm hungreee.

MILLIE: Really, I don't know what ails the child.

MRS. BOKER: [*Leaning over* MOE's *carriage; beginning loud but gradually lowering her voice as both babies cease howling*] . . . K . . . L . . . M . . . N . . . O . . . P . . . Q . . . R . . . S . . . T . . . Have you ever noticed, Miss Wilchick, that babies get quiet when you say the alphabet to them? . . . W . . . X . . . Y . . . A . . . B . . . C . . . D . . . I don't understand it. Moe is mad about the alphabet. Same way with the multiplication table. [*To* MOE, *who is now silent*] Three times five are fifteen. Three times six are eighteen. When my husband has to keep Moe quiet: the multiplication table! Never fails! My husband calls him Isaac Newton.—Seven times five are thirty-five. Eight times five are forty. Never fails.

MILLIE: [*Intimidated*] Really?

MRS. BOKER: [*Pointing to the silent carriages*] Well, look for yourself! Isn't silence grand? [*She sits on a bench and starts taking food out of* MOE's *carriage*] Now, dear, have some potato chips. Or pretzels. What do you like?

MILLIE: Well, you have some of my marshmallows and candy.

MRS. BOKER: Marshmallows! Oh, I know I shouldn't!—Have you noticed that being around babies makes you think of eating all the time. I don't know why that is. [*Pushing* MILLIE *in raucous enjoyment of the joke*] Like, being with babies makes us like babies. And you know what *they* think about!!

MILLIE: [*Convulsed*] Oh, Mrs. Boker, what will you say next!—How is Moe, Mrs. Boker?

MRS. BOKER: [*Her mouth full*] How *is* he!! Sometimes I wish he'd be sick for *one* day—just to give me a present. [*Lowering her voice*] I don't have to tell you what life with a baby is. [*Looking around circumspectly*] It's *war—one long war.*—Excuse me, I can't talk while he's listening. [*She rises and wheels* MOE's *carriage to a distance; returning, she continues in a lowered voice*] My husband believes that Moe understands every word we say.

MILLIE: Mrs. Boker!

MRS. BOKER: I don't know what to believe, but one thing I do know: that baby lies on the floor and listens to every word we say. At first my husband took to spelling out words you know—but Albert Einstein, there—in two weeks he got them all. He would *look* at my husband, *look* at him with those big eyes! And then my husband took to talking in Yiddish—see what I mean?—but no! In two weeks Albert Einstein got Yiddish.

MILLIE: But, Mrs. Boker!! It's just a baby! He don't understand *one word.*

MRS. BOKER: *You* know that. *I* know that. But—[*Pointing to the carriage*] does *he* know that? It's driving my husband crazy. "Turn it in and get a dog," he says. "I didn't ask for no prodigy," he says, "All I wanted was a baby—" [*Lowering her voice*] Of course, most of the time my husband worships Moe . . . only . . . only we don't know what to do with him, as you might say.

MILLIE: Oh, you imagine it, Mrs. Boker!

MRS. BOKER: Listen to me!—Have some of these pretzels; they'll be good after those sweets. Listen to me, Junior's at the crawling stage. He does fifty miles a day. My husband calls him Christopher Columbus.—My husband's stepped on him five times.

MILLIE: Mrs. Boker! You've got a play-pen, haven't you?

MRS. BOKER: PLAY-PEN!! He's broke two, hasn't he? We can't afford to buy no lion's cage, Miss Wilchick,—besides, Macy's don't sell them. Now listen to me: Christopher Columbus follows us wherever we go, see? When I get supper—There he is! He could make a gefilte fish tomorrow. That child—mad about the bathroom! Know what I mean? My husband says he has a "something" mind—you know: d. i. r. t. y.

MILLIE: Mrs. Boker!

MRS. BOKER: Sometimes I wish I had a girl—only it'd be just my luck to get one of those Joans of Arcs. [MOE *starts to howl*] There he goes! Like I said: understands *every* word we say. Now watch this: [*She leans over* MOE's *carriage, holding a handkerchief before her mouth*] You mustn't let them smell what you've been eating, *or else*—Listen, Moe; like I was telling you: New York City is divided into five boroughs. There's the Bronx, Moe, and Brooklyn and Queens—[MOE *quiets almost at once*] See how it works?— Richmond and Manhattan.—It's crazy, I know, but what can I do about that?—Yes, Manhattan, the largest, like I told you, is Manhattan. Yes, Manhattan. [*She looks in the carriage. Silence*] Isn't it a blessing that they get tired so soon? He's exhausted by the boroughs already.

MILLIE: But he doesn't understand a word of it!!

MRS. BOKER: What has understanding got to do with it, Miss Wilchick? I don't understand the telephone, but I *telephone*.

[TOMMY *has raised his head and is listening big-eyed*]

TOMMY: N'Yak Citee divi fife burrs. Manha . . . Manha . . . Manha . . . [*He starts crying with frustration*] I can't *say* it. I can't *say* it.

MRS. BOKER: Now yours is getting excited.

TOMMY: I can't talk and nobody'll teach me. I can't talk . . .

MRS. BOKER: [*Loud*] Go over and put him to sleep.

MILLIE: [*Loud*] But I don't know the boroughs. Please, Mrs. Boker, just once, you show me.

MRS. BOKER: I'll try something else. Watch this! Listen, Tommy, are you listening? "I pledge legions to my flag and to the republic in which it stands." You were a girl scout, weren't you? "Something something invisible with liberty and justice for all." [TOMMY *has fallen silent*] "I pledge legions to my flag . . ."

MILLIE: [*Awed*] Will anything work?

MRS. BOKER: [*Lowering her voice*] They don't like those lullabies and "this little pig went to market." See, they like it *serious*. There's nothing in the world so serious like a baby.—Well, now we got a little quiet again.

MILLIE: Mrs. Boker, can I ask you a question about Moe? . . . Take one of these; it's pineapple inside . . . Is Moe, like they say, house-broken?

MRS. BOKER: Moe?! Gracious sakes! Moe makes a great show of it. I guess there isn't a thing in the world that interests Moe like going to his potty. [*She laughs*] When he wants to make us a present: *off* he goes! When he's angry at us . . . oh, no! He plays it like these violinists play their violin . . . which reminds me! . . . [*Looking about her speculatively*] Do you suppose . . . I could just . . . slip behind these bushes a minute? . . . is that police officer around?

MILLIE: Well-ah . . . Officer Avonzino is awfully particular about nuisances, what he calls nuisances. Maybe you could go over to the avenue there—there's a branch library . . .

MRS. BOKER: Will you be an angel and watch Moe for me? If he starts to cry, give him the days of the week and the months of the year. He *loves* them.—Now where's this library?

MILLIE: Why, the Museum of National History's right over there.

MRS. BOKER: [*Scream of pleasure*] Museum of Natural History!! How could I have forgotten that! Just full of animals. Of *course*! I won't be a minute, dear . . . !

[*They exchange good-byes.* MRS. BOKER *goes out.* MILLIE *eyes* MOE's *carriage apprehensively, then seats herself and resumes her novel at the last page*]

MILLIE: "Roger came into the room. His fine strong face still bore the marks of the suffering he had experienced." Oh! I imagine his wife died. Isn't that wonderful! He's *free*! "He drew her to him, pressing his lips on hers. 'For ever,' he said." Oh! "For ever." [*In a moment, she is asleep*]

[TOMMY *pulls himself up and stares at* MOE's *carriage*]

TOMMY: Moe! . . . Moe!

MOE: [*Surging up furiously*] Don't make noises at me! Don't look at me! Don't do anything. [*Telephone business, swiftly*] Hello, g'bye! [*He disappears*]

TOMMY: Moe! . . . Moe! . . . Talk to me something! . . . Moe, why are you thatway at me?

MOE: [*Surging up again, glaring*] My daddy says I'm stupid. He says, "Stupid, come here!" He says, "All right, stupid, fall down!" I don't want to talk. I don't want to look. G'bye! [*He disappears*]

TOMMY: What does "stupid" mean?

MOE: [*Invisible*] I won't tell. [*Surging up, showing his fingers; a rapid-fire jumble*] Do you know what these are? Sometimes you call them fingers; sometimes you call them piggies. One, two, six, five, four, two, ten. This little piggie stayed at home, I don't know why that is. Do you know what you do when the loud bell rings? You do this: [*Telephone business*] "Hello . . . jugga . . . jugga . . . jugga," and when you don't like it any more you say, "G'bye!" Maybe I am stupid—But that's because MY MOUTH HURTS ALL THE TIME and they don't give me enough to eat and I'm hungry all the time and that's the end of it, that's the end of it. [*He disappears*]

TOMMY: Moe, tell me some more things.

MOE: [*Surging up again*] "Stupid, come here!" "Stupid, get your god-damn tail out of here!" [*Shaking his carriage*] I hate him. I hate him. But I watch him and I learn. *You see*: I learn. And when I get to walk I'm going to do something so that he won't *be* any more. He'll be away—away where people can walk on him.— Don't you hate your father?

TOMMY: Well . . . I don't see him much. Like, once a year.

MOE: You mean: once a day.

TOMMY: Moe, what does "year" mean?

MOE: Year is when it's cold.

TOMMY: [*Brightening*] Yes, I know.

MOE: Sometimes he holds out his hands and says: "How's the little fella? How's the little champ?" And I give him a look! I wasn't born yesterday. He hasn't got anything to sell to me.

TOMMY: Moe—where's your Mommy? [*Silence*] Moe, she's not here. Where's your Mommy? You don't hate your Mommy, do you?

MOE: [*Turning his face sideways, cold and proud*] I don't care about her. She's always away. She goes away for years. She laughs at me . . . with that *man*. He says: "All right, fall down, stupid," and she laughs. I try to talk to her and she goes away all the time and does, "Hello—jugga—jugga—jugga—goo-*bye!*" If she don't care about me any more, I don't care about her any more. Goo-*bye!* [*Silence*]

TOMMY: Say some more, Moe; say some more things.

MOE: [*Low and intense*] Maybe I am stupid. Maybe I'll never be able to walk or make talk. Maybe they didn't give me good feet or a good mouth.—You know what I think? I think they don't want us to walk and to get good and get better. They want us to *stop.* That's what I think. [*His voice has risen to a hysterical wail*] Goddam! Hell! [*He starts throwing cloth elephants and giraffes out of the carriage*] I'm not going to try. Nobody wants to help me and lots of time is passing and I'm not getting bigger, and . . . and . . . [*Anti-climax*] I'm sleepeee . . . [*He continues to whimper*]

[MILLIE *wakes up. She goes gingerly to* MOE's *carriage and joggles it*]

MILLIE: Moe! What's the matter, Moe? "Rockabye, baby, in the tree-top—" [MOE *wails more loudly*] Oh, goodness, gracious me. [*In desperation*] Moe! Do you know that *that* street is called Central Park West? And then there's Columbus Avenue? And then there's Amsterdam Avenue? And then there's Broadway? [MOE *has hushed*] And then there's West End Avenue. [*She can hardly believe her luck; she whispers*] And then there's Riverside Drive. [*She peers into the carriage a long time, then tiptoes to the other end of the stage, with clenched fists*] I hate babies. [*Toward* TOMMY] I hate you—sticking your crazy face into my business,—frightening Officer Avonzino, the only man I've talked to in six months. I hate you—always butting in. I have a right to my own life, haven't I? *My own life!* I'm sick to death of squalling, smelling, gawking babies . . . I'd be a stenographer only I don't know anything; nobody ever taught me anything . . . "Manhattan, the Bronx,"—what do I care what keeps you quiet? You can yell your heads off for all I care! I don't know why nature didn't make it so that people came into the world already grownup—instead of a dozen and more years of screaming and diapers and falling down and breaking everything . . . and *asking questions!* "What's that?" "Why-y-y?" "Why-y-y?" . . . Officer Avonzino will never

come back, that's certain! . . . Oh, what do I care? You're going
to grow up to be *men*—nasty, selfish men. You're all alike. [*Drying
her eyes, she picks up her novel from* MOE's *carriage and strolls off
the stage at the back*]

[MOE's *head, now solemn and resolute, rises slowly*]

MOE: Tommy! . . . Tommy!

TOMMY: [*Appearing*] I'm tired.

MOE: You know what I'm going to do, do you?

TOMMY: No—what, Moe?

MOE: I'm just going to lie still.

TOMMY: What do you mean, Moe?

MOE: I'll shut my eyes and do nothing. I won't eat. I'll just go away-
away. Like I want Daddy to do.

TOMMY: [*Alarm*] No, Moe! Don't go where people can walk on you!

MOE: Well, I *will* . . . You know what I think? I think people aren't
SERIOUS about us. "Little piggie went to market, cradle will fall,
Manhattan, The Bronx"—that's not serious. They don't want us
to get better.

TOMMY: *Maybe* they do.

MOE: Old people are only interested in old people. Like kiss-kiss-kiss;
that's all they do; that's all they think about.

TOMMY: [*Eagerly*] Ye-e-es! Miss'a Millie, all the time, kiss-kiss-kiss,
but she don't mean me; she means the policeman.

MOE: We're in the way, see? We're too little, that's how. I don't
want to be a man,—it's too hard! [*He disappears*]

TOMMY: [*With increasing alarm*] Moe! . . . Moe! . . . Don't stop
talking, Moe! . . . MOE!

[MILLIE *returns hastily*]

MILLIE: Now what's the matter with you? I'll spank you. Always crying and making a baby of yourself.

TOMMY: [*At the same time; frantic*] Moe's going away-away. He's
not going to eat any more. Go look at Moe . . . *Do* something.
Do something!

MILLIE: What is the matter with you? Why can't you be quiet like Moe? [*She goes and looks in* MOE's *carriage and is terrified by what she sees*] Help! . . . Hellllp! The baby's turned purple! Moe! Have you swallowed something—[*She dashes to the audience-exit*] Officer Avonzino! Officer! Hellllp!—Oh, they'll kill me. What'll I do?

[OFFICER AVONZINO *rushes in from the audience*]

AVONZINO: What'a matter, Miss Wilchick; you gone crazy today?

MILLIE: [*Gasping*] . . . look . . . he's turned black, Officer Avonzino . . . His mother's over at the Museum. Oh . . . I don't know what to do.

[OFFICER AVONZINO, *efficient but unhurried, opens his tunic and takes out his handbook. He hunts for the correct page*]

AVONZINO: First, don't scream, Miss Wilchick. Nobody scream. Babies die every day. Always new babies. Nothing to scream about . . . Babies turn black,—so! Babies turn blue, black, purple, all the time. Hmph: "Turn baby over, lift middle . . . [*He does these things*] "Water" . . . [*To* MILLIE] Go to nurses over there . . . twenty nurses . . . Bring back some ippycack.

MILLIE: Oh, Officer . . . help me. I'm fainting.

AVONZINO: [*Furious*] Faintings on *Sundays*,—not workdays, Miss Wilchick.

MILLIE: [*Hand to head*] Oh . . . oh . . .

[AVONZINO *catches her just in time and drapes her over bench like a puppet*]

AVONZINO: Lesson Thirty-Two: Let mother die. Save baby. I get water. [*He dashes off*]

[TOMMY *raises his head*]

TOMMY: Moe! Don't be black. Don't be black. You're going to walk soon. And bye and bye you can go to school. And even if they don't teach you good, you can kind-of teach yourself. [MOE *is sob-*

bing] Moe, what's that noise you're making? Make a crying like a baby, Moe.—Soon you can be big and shave. And be a policerman. And you can make kiss-kiss-kiss . . . and make babies. And, Moe,—

MOE: [*Appearing*] Don't talk to me. I'm tired. I'm tired.

TOMMY: And you can show your babies how to walk and talk.

MOE: [*Yawning*] I'm . . . tire' . . . [*He sinks back*]

TOMMY: [*Yawning*] I'm tired, tooooo. [*He sinks back*]

[AVONZINO *returns with a child's pail of water. He leans over* MOE]

AVONZINO: [*Astonished*] What'a matter with you!! You all red again. You not sick. Goddam! Tricks. Babies always doing tricks. [*Shakes* MILLIE] Miss Wilchick! Wake up! Falsa alarm. Baby's okay.

MILLIE: [*Coming to, dreamily*] Oh, Officer . . . [*Extending her arms amorously*] Oh you're so . . . handsome . . . Officer . . .

AVONZINO: [*Sternly*] Lesson Eleven: no personal remarks with public. [*Shouts*] It's going to rain: Better take George Washington home . . . and Dr. Einstein, too.

MILLIE: Oh! How *is* the Boker baby?

AVONZINO: Boker baby's a great actor. Dies every performance. Thousands cheer.

MILLIE: [*Pushes* TOMMY *toward exit*] Oh, I can't go until Mrs. Boker comes back.—[*Peers out*] Oh, there she comes, running. See her?

AVONZINO: You go. I take care of baby til a'momma comes. [*At exit* MILLIE *turns for a heart-felt farewell; he points billy-stick and commands her*] Go *faint*, Miss Wilchick! [*She goes out.* AVONZINO *addresses* MOE] I'd like to make your damn bottom red. I know you. All you babies want the whole world. Well, I tell you, you've got a long hard road before you. Pretty soon you'll find that you can cry all you want and turn every color there is—and nobody'll pay *no* attention at all. Your best days are over; you've had'm. From now on it's all up to you,—George Washington, or whatever your name is.

[*Enters* MRS. BOKER, *breathless*]

MRS. BOKER: Oh!

AVONZINO: I sent Miss Wilchick home. [*Pointing toward rain*] You better start off yourself.

MRS. BOKER: [*Pushing the carriage to the exit*] Has everything been all right, Officer?

AVONZINO: Just fine, lady, just fine. Like usual: babies acting like growed-ups; growed-ups acting like babies.

MRS. BOKER: *Thank* you, Officer. [*She goes out*]

[OFFICER AVONZINO, *shading his eyes, peers down the aisle through the audience. Suddenly he sees something that outrages him. Like a Keystone Cop he does a double-take and starts running through the audience, shouting*]

AVONZINO: Hey there!! You leave that baby-carriage alone! Don't you know what's inside them baby-carriages . . . ?

CURTAIN

THE OTHER SON

Luigi Pirandello

(Translated by William Murray)

Luigi Pirandello

Awarded the Nobel Prize in 1934, Luigi Pirandello was, and still remains, a dominant force in the development of the modern theatre. The position he occupies at the crossroads of dramatic evolution and the impact his works have had upon succeeding generations of playwrights rank him as one of the giants of the theatre, comparable in status and influence with Ibsen, Strindberg, Chekhov, Shaw, and O'Neill.

Pirandello radically reformed the Italian theatre by giving it the power and substance to challenge the period's enervating supremacy of opera. More saliently, he revolutionized the presentation of human character on the stage with his masterly fusion of illusion and reality. His dramatic explorations of man's innate multiple identity and its concomitant "mask and face" technique have led directly into the antinaturalistic styles of much of our contemporary theatre.

How man appears to others, and above all to himself, in an indifferent, insecure world is a major and recurring theme in most of Pirandellos plays. As a principal and lifelong concern of the author, he wrote: "We believe ourselves one person, but it is true to say that we are many persons, many according to the possibilities of being which exist within us. We are one for this and another for that person—always diverse and yet filled with the illusion that our personality is always the same for all."

Sicilian by birth (June 28, 1867), Luigi Pirandello began his literary career as a poet, and by the time he turned to the stage, he had already established himself as a major novelist (*The Late Mattia Pascal*), short-story writer, and critic.

It was in December 1910 that Pirandello had his first encounter with the professional theatre when two of his short plays, *The Vice* and *Sicilian Limes*, were successfully presented in Rome. It was a significant and prophetic beginning of a new career for the forty-three-year-old author who, possibly unaware of it at the time, was to devote most of the rest of his life to writing plays.

An intensive writer, he seemed to have discovered in drama the perfect cathartic outlet for the turmoil of his own personal life. After the family's sulphur mines had collapsed along with their fortune, Pirandello's wife, for some years afflicted by hysteria, developed a mental illness bordering on insanity, and until her death in 1918, Pirandello devoted himself to her care.

From 1918 onward, he sought pacification from his domestic tragedies by dedicating himself to a prodigious output of plays, but it wasn't until 1921 that he became an international celebrity with the production of *Six Characters in Search of an Author*. During the years that followed, he wrote thirty full-length and thirteen short plays, of which the best known in this country are *Six Characters in Search of an Author*; *Right You Are If You Think You Are*; *The Man with the Flower in His Mouth*; *As You Desire Me*; and *Enrico IV*.

Respected by his actors and associates as a born craftsman with an acute and remarkable awareness of the demands of the stage, Pirandello had an abiding and practical love for the theatre that never diminished. In 1925 he established (in association with his eldest son) his own art theatre in Rome at the Teatro Odescalchi and, later, undertook extensive and vigorous tours with his company in Europe and America. The venture was an artistic success but a financial disaster in which Pirandello himself lost a large sum of money. Yet this did not lessen his dedication to the theatre, and he continued to write plays until his death in 1936.

Although scores of professional critics, theatre historians, and academicians have attempted to characterize Pirandello's style of drama, it is most effectively defined, perhaps, in his own words: "A serious theatre, mine. It demands the complete participation of the moral-human entity. It is certainly not a comfortable theatre. A difficult theatre, a dangerous theatre. Nietzsche said that the Greeks put up white statues against the black abyss, in order to hide it. I, instead, topple them in order to reveal it. . . . It is the tragedy of the modern spirit."

By coincidence or historic design, Luigi Pirandello, master dramatist, entered the realm of the theatre in 1910 with two short plays; in

1937, the last of his works to be premièred in his native land also happened to be a short play, *I'm Dreaming, but Am I?*

William Murray, translator of two volumes of Pirandello plays, was born in New York City in 1926. He was educated in Italy and France before returning to the United States to continue his studies at Phillips Exeter Academy and Harvard University. He is the author of several novels and also has contributed short stories and articles to *The New Yorker* and many other periodicals.

The Other Son (*L'altro figlio*) originally was published as a short story in *La lettura* in 1905. The dramatization was first presented in Rome in 1923.

Characters:

Maragrazia
Ninfarosa
Rocco Trupia
A Young Doctor
Jaco Spina
Tino Ligreci
Gialluzza
Aunt Marassunta
Mrs. Tuzza La Dia
Marinese

In Sicily, in the early 1900s.

*A row of huts on the outskirts of the Sicilian village of Farnia,
at a turn in a dreary little street leading off into the countryside.
The one-story clay houses are set apart from each other, with
vegetable gardens behind, and are windowless. The light from
the street is admitted through dingy open doorways, each set
above a short flight of worn steps. At left, directly opposite and
off by itself, stands* NINFAROSA's *house, not quite so wretched
and old as the others.*

*At curtain, four women of the neighborhood are sitting in
their doorways, mending clothes, cleaning vegetables, sewing or
otherwise occupied. They have been talking.* GIALLUZZA *is thin,
about thirty, with faded blonde hair worn low on her neck in a
bun.* AUNT MARASSUNTA *is an old woman of about sixty, attired
in mourning in a faded black cotton dress, with a black kerchief
over her head and knotted under her chin.* MRS. TUZZA LA DIA *is
about forty, her eyes always fixed on the ground and her voice a
permanent lament.* MARINESE *is red-haired and flashily dressed.*
JACO SPINA, *an old peasant in a black stocking-cap and shirt-
sleeves, is stretched out on the ground at the end of the road,
his head resting on a donkey saddle. He is smoking his pipe and
listening to the conversation. A few very dark, sun-baked children
wander about here and there.*

GIALLUZZA: And at sunset tonight, more of them leaving!

TUZZA: [*Whining*] Good luck to them, poor things!

MARINESE: They say more than twenty are going this time!

[*Through the houses at right comes* TINO LIGRECI, *a young peasant who has just completed his military service. He's a cocky
type, wears bell-shaped trousers and a cap tilted jauntily to one
side*]

TINO: [*To* MARASSUNTA] Evening, Aunt Marassù. Do you know if the
doctor's come by here yet? I know he was on his way to Rocco
Trupia's, the house with the column.

MARASSUNTA: No, Sonny, he hasn't been here. At least I haven't seen him.

MARINESE: Why? Who's sick?

TINO: No one, thank God. I wanted to tell him to keep an eye on my mother. [*He hesitates a bit, looking at them, then, in a worried voice*] And you, too, keep an eye on her for me. She'll be all alone, poor thing.

[*Meanwhile,* MARAGRAZIA *appears from behind* NINFAROSA's *house. She is over seventy and her face is a network of wrinkles. Her eyes are red from prolonged weeping and her thin, wispy hair hangs in two small knots over her ears. She looks like a bundle of rags, stained and filthy, worn constantly winter and summer, torn and patched, colorless and reeking of all the dirt of the streets. On her feet she wears shapeless, worn shoes and heavy blue cotton socks*]

MARINESE: [*To* TINO] So you're leaving?

TINO: Tonight, with the rest of them. But not for San Paolo, like the others. I'm going to Rosario de Santa Fe.

MARAGRAZIA: [*From behind him*] You're leaving, too?

TINO: Sure I'm going. I'm going so I won't have to look at you or hear you cry any more, you old crone!

MAGAGRAZIA: [*Staring into his eyes*] To Rosario, you said? Rosario de Santa Fe?

TINO: That's what I said, to Rosario. What are you looking at me like that for? Want me to go blind?

MARAGRAZIA: No, I envy you! Because you'll be seeing—[*She breaks into a silent sobbing, her chin trembling*] My boys! They're both there! Tell them how you left me, that they'll never see me again if they don't come home soon!

TINO: Sure, you can count on it! As soon as I get there. Things get done over there: you call and they come running! Now I've got to go and find the doctor.

MARAGRAZIA: [*Holding him by one arm*] Wait. If I give you a letter for them, will you take it?

TINO: Give it to me.

MARAGRAZIA: I haven't got it yet. I'll have Ninfarosa write it for me right away and I'll bring it to your house, all right?

TINO: Fine, bring it to me. And meanwhile, good-by to all of you. And if we never see each other again—[*Suddenly moved*]—Aunt Marassù, give me your blessing!

MARASSUNTA: [*Rising and making the sign of the Cross over him*] God bless you and keep you, my son! And may the good Lord go with you by land and by sea!

TINO: [*To the others, smiling to disguise his real feelings*] And so long to all of you, then! [*He shakes hands with all three*]

TUZZA: Have a good trip, Tinù.

MARINESE: Good luck! And don't forget us!

GIALLUZZA: And come back soon, in good health, with a sackful of money!

TINO: Thanks, thanks. Stay well and good luck to all of you! [*Exits at left*]

MARASSUNTA: Just back from the army and he leaves his mother here all alone!

TUZZA: Asks the rest of us to keep an eye on her!

MARAGRAZIA: [*After having watched him go, turning to the others*] Is Ninfarosa in?

GIALLUZZA: She's home. Knock. [*The old woman does so*]

NINFAROSA: [*From inside the house*] Who is it?

MARAGRAZIA: Me, Maragrazia.

NINFAROSA: [*Off*] All right, I'm coming.

[MARAGRAZIA *quietly sits down on the steps of* NINFAROSA'S *house. As she listens to the conversation of the other women, she nods her head and weeps*]

GIALLUZZA: They told me Saro Scoma was going, too, and him with a wife and three kids!

TUZZA: [*In her usual whine*] And a fourth on the way!

MARINESE: [*Unable to stand it any longer*] Jesus, what a voice! It's hard on the nerves, neighbor! Turns my stomach! Three and one is four, and if they had them, then it means they wanted to have them and I'll bet they had a good time doing it! So stop your whining, let them worry about it!

JACO SPINA: [*Sitting up and crossing his hands over his chest*] If I was king—[*And he spits*]—if I was king of this country, not one letter—a letter, I said?—not even a postcard would I let them send from over there!

GIALLUZZA: A fine idea, Jaco Spina! And what would they do, these poor mothers, these wives, without news and no one to help them?

JACO SPINA: Yes, a fine lot of help they get! [*Spits again*] The mothers have to go and work like dogs and the wives just go to hell! Over some houses I can see the horns growing right up to the sky! Why don't they ever write about the bad things over there? Everything's rosy, according to them. And every letter that gets here is like a hen clucking to her chicks, as far as these ignorant lunkheads are concerned. Cluck, cluck, cluck, and off they all go! There's no one left in Farnia to do the hoeing or prune the trees. Old people, women, children. I have to sit and watch my piece of land go to waste. [*Holding out his arms*] What good is one pair of arms? And still they go and they go! Rain on their faces and wind up their backs, say I! I hope they all break their fool necks, damn them!

[NINFAROSA *emerges from her house. She is dark but has a ruddy complexion, with black, shining eyes, red lips, and a trim, solid-looking figure. She is proud and gay, wears a large cotton kerchief, red with yellow moons, over her breast and two heavy gold bands in her ears*]

NINFAROSA: What's the sermon today? Oh, so it's you, Uncle Jaco? Listen, it's better here with only the women! The fewer the men, the better the women! We'll work the land by ourselves!

JACO SPINA: You women are good for just one thing!

NINFAROSA: What's that, Uncle Jaco? Out with it!

JACO SPINA: For crying. And one other thing.

NINFAROSA: So that's two things we're good for! Not bad! But I'm not crying, am I?

JACO SPINA: I know you, girl! Not even when your first husband died!

NINFAROSA: Right. And if it had been me instead of him, wouldn't he have married someone else? So there you are! [*Indicating* MARAGRAZIA] Anyway, look at her. She cries enough for all of us.

JACO SPINA: That's because the old woman has water to spare and likes to squirt it from her eyes! [*So saying, he rises, picks up his saddle, and exits*]

MARAGRAZIA: Two boys I lost, beautiful like the sun, and I'm not supposed to cry?

NINFAROSA: They were beautiful, all right! And worth crying for! Swimming in luxury over there and they leave you to die here like a beggar!

MARAGRAZIA: [*Shrugging*] They're only boys. How can you expect them to understand what a mother feels?

NINFAROSA: And anyway, why so many tears, so much suffering, when everyone says it was you who drove them away in the first place?

MARAGRAZIA: [*Beating her breast and getting to her feet, astounded*] Me? Me? Who said that?

NINFAROSA: It doesn't matter who, somebody did.

MARAGRAZIA: It's a lie! Me? Drove them away, when I—

MARASSUNTA: Oh, let her alone!

MARINESE: Can't you see she's joking?

NINFAROSA: I'm joking, I'm joking, take it easy! Now what do you want? You knocked, didn't you?

MARAGRAZIA: Oh, yes. The usual favor. If you can.

NINFAROSA: Another letter?

MARAGRAZIA: If you can. I'm giving it to Tino Ligreci. He's leaving tonight for Rosario de Santa Fe.

NINFAROSA: So Tino's going, too, eh? Then good luck to him! Quick now, hurry up! I'm sewing something and I ran out of thread. I have to go and buy some.

MARAGRAZIA: Yes, listen: I want you to write about the little house, just the way you did last time.

NINFAROSA: You mean those four walls of mud and straw you call a house?

MARAGRAZIA: Yes, I was thinking about it all last night. Listen: "My dear boys! You must remember, I'm sure, the four walls of our house. They are still standing. Well, your mother will give them to you for life if you'll only come home to her very soon."

NINFAROSA: Oh, that's sure to send them flying back, especially if it's true they're both rich! Maybe they'll come back so fast the house will blow over before they can get into it!

MARAGRAZIA: Oh, Daughter, a single stone of your old home is worth a whole kingdom anywhere else! Write, write! [*And she produces from the bosom of her dress a single sheet of cheap letter paper and an envelope*]

NINFAROSA: Give it to me. You wait there, please. [*Indicates the steps*] You'd dirty the whole room. [*Exits into the house*]

MARAGRAZIA: [*Sitting down again*] Yes, you're right. I'll stay here. Your house is clean. I walk the fields and roads. You'll wonder where I am one day and you'll find me back there, in my little house, eaten by the rats.

NINFAROSA: [*Off*] I've already written about the house. Anything else you want me to add?

MARAGRAZIA: Just this: "My darling sons, now that winter is coming on, your poor mother's afraid of the cold. Please send her—it's not much—a ten-lire note so she can buy herself—

NINFAROSA: [*Emerging from the house with her shawl over her shoulders and stuffing the folded letter into the envelope*] All done, all done! Here you are! Take it! [*Offering her the letter*]

MARAGRAZIA: [*Amazed*] What? So fast? Already done? But how?

NINFAROSA: It's all in here. Even the stuff about the ten lire, don't worry. I have to go now. [*She exits at left*]

MARAGRAZIA: But how did she write it all down so fast, without even knowing what I wanted to buy with the ten lire?

MARINESE: Oh, we all know that! Your dress! You've made her write that at least twenty times!

[*Unconvinced and puzzled,* MARAGRAZIA *pauses, still holding the letter. Meanwhile, from the end of the street, a young* DOCTOR *enters*]

DOCTOR: [*To* GIALLUZZA] Excuse me, but can you tell me where the house with the column is, the one belonging to Rocco Trupia?

GIALLUZZA: What, Doctor, you just came from up there and you didn't see it?

MARINESE: It's right on the edge of town. You can't miss it. There's a piece of an old column, some kind of old ruin, stuck in a corner of the wall.

DOCTOR: I didn't see any column.

MARASSUNTA: That's because the wall is hidden from the road by a bunch of cactus. Unless you know the place, you're liable to miss it.

DOCTOR: Well, I'm not going back there now and eat myself another ton of dust. Do me a favor, one of you: send one of your kids to tell this Rocco Trupia the doctor wants to talk to him.

MARASSUNTA: Is it about his aunt? Ah, the poor woman! Is she worse?

DOCTOR: About the same. He'll have to persuade her, or force her if necessary, to go to the hospital. She'll never get well at home. I've already filled out the application for her.

GIALLUZZA: [*To one of the boys*] You go, Calicchio. Go on, up to the house with the column, you know the one. Tell Uncle Rocco Trupia he's wanted here, that the doctor wants to see him. Go on now.

[*The boy nods assent and exits on the run up the road*]

DOCTOR: Thanks. Send him to my house. I'm going home. [*Starts to go*]

MARAGRAZIA: Excuse me, Doctor, would you do me a favor and read me this letter?

MARASSUNTA: [*Quickly, to* MARAGRAZIA, *in an effort to prevent the* DOCTOR *from reading the letter*] No, no! Don't bother the doctor now, he's in a hurry!

MARINESE: [*To the* DOCTOR] Pay no attention to her, Doctor!

DOCTOR: Why not? I've got time. [*To* MARAGRAZIA] Give it to me. [*He takes the envelope, removes the letter, and opens it. After glancing at it, he looks up at the old woman as if suspecting her of trying to play a joke on him. The neighbor women laugh]* What is this?

MARAGRAZIA: You can't read it?

DOCTOR: What is there to read? There's nothing written here.

MARAGRAZIA: [*Amazed and indignant*] Nothing? What do you mean, nothing?

DOCTOR: Just a couple of scribbles, scratched any which way. Look!

MARAGRAZIA: Ah, I knew it! She didn't write anything? Why? Why would she do that to me?

DOCTOR: [*Indignantly, to the laughing women*] Who did this? And what's so funny?

MARASSUNTA: Because she finally caught on.

TUZZA: It took her long enough.

MARINESE: Ninfarosa, the dressmaker, fools her every time like that.

GIALLUZZA: To get rid of her.

MARAGRAZIA: So that's why, Doctor, that's why my boys don't answer my letters! She never wrote any of them, not even the other ones! That's why! They have no idea how I am, what's happened to me, not even that I'm dying just to see them! And I put the blame on them, when all the time it was her, her tricking me! [*She begins to cry again*]

MARASSUNTA: But it wasn't just out of spite, believe me, Doctor.

DOCTOR: [*To* MARAGRAZIA] Come on now, don't cry like that. Come to my house later and I'll write the letter for you. Go on, go on now. [*He gently urges her off*]

MARAGRAZIA: [*Still crying as she disappears behind* NINFAROSA's *house*] Oh, God! How could she do that to a poor suffering mother? What a thing to do, what a thing to do!

[*She exits. At this point,* NINFAROSA *returns. She witnesses the old woman's departure and notices the penitent, embarrassed expressions on her friends' faces*]

NINFAROSA: Don't tell me she found out!

DOCTOR: Oh, so it's you, is it!

NINFAROSA: Hello, Doctor.

DOCTOR: Never mind that. Aren't you ashamed of yourselves, treating that poor old woman like that?

NINFAROSA: Before you jump to any conclusions, you'd better hear me out first.

DOCTOR: So what have you got to say for yourself?

NINFAROSA: She's crazy, Doctor. Don't get all upset on her account.

DOCTOR: And what if she is? What fun is there in playing a joke on a lunatic?

NINFAROSA: No fun, Doctor, no fun at all. It's what you do with children to keep them happy. She went crazy, Doctor, when those two sons of hers left for America. She won't face the fact that they've forgotten all about her. For years she's been sending them letter after letter. I pretend to write them for her. This way, a couple of scribbles on a sheet of paper. People going there pretend to take them and forward them for her. And she, poor woman, believes it. Ah, Doctor, if we all acted like her, you know what we'd have here? A sea of tears, that's what, and all of us drowning in it. Take me, for instance: that jumping jack of a husband of mine, you know what he did? Sent me a picture of him and his girl over there, with their heads close together, cheek to cheek, and holding hands—here, give me yours—like this! And laughing, laughing right in my face! Me they sent it to! But you see that hand of mine? See how white and soft and gentle it is? That's me. I take the world as it is.

GIALLUZZA: Lucky you, Ninfarò!

NINFAROSA: Lucky? You could all be like me. If you were, nothing would bother you.

MARASSUNTA: You're too fast for us.

NINFAROSA: And you're too slow. But say anything you like about me. It goes in one ear and out the other, you know that.

DOCTOR: You all have your lives still to live, but that poor old woman—

NINFAROSA: What are you talking about? Her? She could have anything she wanted, be waited on hand and foot. If she wanted to. She doesn't want it. Ask anyone here.

ALL: Yes! She's right! It's true!

NINFAROSA: In her own son's house!

DOCTOR: What do you mean? She has another son?

MARINESE: Yes, sir. That same Rocco Trupia you want to see.

DOCTOR: Really? She's the sister of that other crazy woman who doesn't want to go to the hospital?

GIALLUZZA: Her sister-in-law, Doctor.

NINFAROSA: But don't mention it to her! She won't hear a word of it! Not about her son or any of the relatives on the father's side.

DOCTOR: Maybe he treated her badly.

NINFAROSA: I don't think so. But here's Rocco Trupia now. You can ask him.

[*In fact,* ROCCO TRUPIA *now enters down the road, accompanied by the boy sent to fetch him. He walks like a typical peasant, heavily and slowly, on bow legs, one hand behind his back. He is red-haired, pale, and freckled. His deep-set eyes glance fiercely, fleetingly about from time to time. He goes up to the* DOCTOR, *pushing his black stocking cap to the back of his head as a form of greeting*]

ROCCO: I kiss your hands, Your Excellency. What can I do for you?

DOCTOR: I want to talk to you about your aunt.

ROCCO: You want to send her to the hospital? Forget it, Your Excellency. Let her die in peace in her own bed.

DOCTOR: As usual, like everyone else, you think it's shameful for her to be cured in a hospital. Is that it?

ROCCO: Cured? Doctor, the poor don't get cured in hospitals. She'd only die of despair, without the comfort of her own things around her. She won't go and I'm not going to force her, not even if you paid me in gold. She's been like a mother to me, so you can imagine—

DOCTOR: And while we're on the subject of your mother—

ROCCO: [*Interrupting him sullenly*] Doctor, is that all you wanted to see me about? I'm always at your service, but if Your Excellency wishes to talk to me about my mother, I'll say good-by. I have work to do. [*He starts to go*]

DOCTOR: [*Detaining him*] Wait a minute! I know you're well off!

ROCCO: [*Heatedly*] Want to come home with me and see? It's a poor man's house, but you're a doctor and I suppose you've been in a lot of them. Maybe you'd like to see the bed I keep always made up just for her, that—that kind old woman! Yes, she's my mother! I can't deny it! You can ask these women here if it isn't true that I've always insisted my wife and children respect that old woman as if she were the Madonna Herself—[*Making the sign of the Cross, then adding more softly*]—and me not even worthy to mention Her name! What have I done to this mother of mine that she should shame me like this before the whole town? Right from my birth I was brought up by my father's relatives, because she wouldn't spare me a drop of milk, not even to relieve the pain in her breasts! And still I always treated her like my mother! And when I say mother, I mean—[*He suddenly removes his cap and falls to his knees*]—that's what I mean, Doctor, because to me a mother is sacred! [*He rises*] When those damn sons of hers left for America, I immediately went to bring her home, where she'd have been mistress of my house, me and everyone in it. No, sir! She has to go begging through the streets, making a spectacle of herself and bringing shame on me! Doctor, I swear to you that if one of those damn sons of hers ever comes back to Farnia, I'll kill him for the shame and all the poison I've had to swallow for fourteen years on their account! I'll kill him, just as sure as I'm talking to you now in front of these women and these innocents here! [*His eyes flaming and his face contorted with rage, he wipes his mouth on his sleeve*]

DOCTOR: Now I know why your mother doesn't want to come and stay with you! It's because you hate your brothers!

ROCCO: Hate them? Me? Yes, now I hate them! But when they were here, they were closer to me than my own sons and I respected them as my older brothers, while they, instead, were a couple of Cains to me. They wouldn't work and I worked for all of us. They'd come and tell me they had nothing to eat, that my mother would have to go hungry, and I'd give. They'd get drunk and play around with whores, and I'd pay. When they left for America, I bled myself white for them. The whole town can tell you that.

WOMEN: It's true, it's true! Poor man! He took the bread out of his own mouth for them!

DOCTOR: But then why?

ROCCO: [*With a snicker*] Why? Because my mother says I'm not her son!

DOCTOR: [*Stunned*] What? Not her son?

ROCCO: Doctor, get these women here to explain it to you. I have no time to waste. The men are waiting for me and the mules are loaded up with manure. There's work to do and—look at me—you've got me all worked up. I kiss your hands, Doctor. [*And he leaves the way he came*]

NINFAROSA: He's right, poor man. So ugly and sullen-looking, from his eyes you'd think he was bad, but he isn't.

TUZZA: And he's a worker, too!

MARINESE: On that score—work, wife, and children, that's all he knows! And he never has a bad word to say about anyone.

GIALLUZZA: He's got a nice piece of land up there, by the house with the column, and it pays well.

MARASSUNTA: That old lunatic could live like a queen! But here she comes again, still crying.

[MARAGRAZIA *reappears from behind* NINFAROSA's *house, holding another sheet of letter paper in her hand*]

MARAGRAZIA: I bought another sheet of paper for the letter, if Your Excellency will be so kind.

DOCTOR: Yes, all right. But meanwhile I've been talking to your son. Now why didn't you tell me you had another son here?

MARAGRAZIA: [*Terrified*] No, no, for God's sake, don't talk about it, don't talk about it! It makes my blood run cold just to think about him! Don't even mention him to me!

DOCTOR: But why? What's he done to you? Out with it!

MARAGRAZIA: Nothing. He hasn't done anything, Doctor. I have to admit that. Nothing. Ever.

NINFAROSA: [*Who had gone to get the* DOCTOR *a chair, now offering it to him*] Here, sit down, Doctor. You must be tired of standing.

DOCTOR: [*Sitting down*] Yes, thank you. I really am tired. [*To* MARAGRAZIA] Well? If he hasn't done anything—

MARAGRAZIA: I'm trembling all over, you see? I can't—I can't talk about it. Because he—he isn't my son, Doctor!

DOCTOR: What do you mean, he isn't your son? What are you saying? Are you stupid or really crazy? Did you give birth to him or didn't you?

MARAGRAZIA: Yes, sir. I did. And maybe I am stupid. But crazy, no. I wish to God I were! Then I wouldn't be suffering like this. But there are some things Your Excellency can't understand, because you're too young. My hair is white. I've suffered here a long time. And I've gone through a lot, too much! I've seen things, things you can't even imagine!

DOCTOR: What have you seen? Speak up!

MARAGRAZIA: You'll have read about it in books, maybe, about how, many years ago, cities and whole countrysides rose up against all the laws of man and God!

DOCTOR: You mean the time of the Revolution?

MARAGRAZIA: That's when, yes, sir. They threw open all the jails, Doctor, all the jails in all the towns and villages. And you can imagine what kind of hell broke loose all over! The worse crooks, the worst murderers—savage, bloodthirsty beasts—mad from having been cooped up for so many years! And one of them was a certain Cola Camizzi. The worst of all. A bandit chief. He killed God's poor creatures like this, for the fun of it, like flies. To try out his gunpowder, he'd say, or to make sure his gun aimed straight. This man took to the hills, not far from where we were. He came through Farnia. He already had a gang with him, but he wasn't satisfied. He wanted others. And he'd kill anyone who wouldn't join him. I'd been married only a few years and I'd already had those two boys of mine who are now in America, blood of my blood! We had some land around Pozzetto that my husband, that dear soul, worked as a sharecropper. Cola Camizzi came by there and forced my husband to go with him. Two days later he came back, looking like a corpse. I hardly recognized him. He couldn't talk. His eyes were full of what he'd seen and he kept his hands hidden out of sight, poor man, because of the horror of what he'd been forced to do. Ah, good sir, my heart turned over when I saw him like that! "Nino, darling, what did you do?" I shouted at him. He couldn't answer. "You ran away? And what if they catch you again? They'll kill you!" From the heart, from the heart I was speaking to him. But him—not a word—sitting there by the fire, keeping his hands out of sight, like this, under his coattails, and his eyes staring straight ahead and seeing nothing. All he said was, "Better dead!" That's all. He stayed in hiding three days and on the fourth he went out. We were poor, he had to work. So he went out to work. Night came. He didn't come back. I waited and waited. Oh, God! I knew already, I'd foreseen it all! But I couldn't help thinking, "Who knows, maybe they haven't killed him, maybe they've only taken him away again!" I found out six days later that Cola Camizzi and his gang were staying near Montelusa, in an old abandoned monastery. I went there, I was half-crazy. It was more than six miles from Pozzetto. The wind was blowing that day, blowing like I'd never seen it before or since. Can you see the wind? Well, that day you could *see* it! It was as if all the souls of the people they'd murdered were screaming to God and men for vengeance. I went with the wind, all disheveled I was, and it swept me along. I was screaming, screaming louder than the wind itself! I flew! It didn't take me more than an hour to reach the monastery, which was high up, high up in a grove of black trees. Next to the monastery there was a big courtyard with a wall all around it. You went in through a tiny little door, almost hidden—I still remember—hidden by a big stump growing right out of the wall. I picked up a rock to bang as loud as I could on the door. I banged and I banged, but they wouldn't open. I kept on banging until they finally let me in. Oh, what I saw! In their hands—their hands—those murderers . . . [*Overcome by the memory, she is unable to continue. She raises a hand as if about to throw something*]

DOCTOR: [*Turning pale*] Well?

MARAGRAZIA: They were playing—there, in the courtyard—they were bowling—but with heads—the heads of men—all black, covered with dirt—they held them by the hair—and—and one of them was Nino's—he had it—Camizzi—and—and he held it up so I could look at it! [*She screams and hides her face*] They were all trembling, those murderers trembling so hard that when Cola Camizzi put his hands around my throat to shut me up, one of them jumped him. Then four, five, ten of them threw themselves at him and tore him apart, like so many dogs. They'd had enough, fed up even then with the way he used to bully them and make them do things. And I had the satisfaction of seeing him torn apart right there, under my very eyes, by his own friends!

WOMEN: [*Crying out spontaneously*] Good! Good! Tore him apart! The murderer! The vulture! God's vengeance!

DOCTOR: [*After a pause*] And what about this son of yours?

MARAGRAZIA: The man who first went for Camizzi, the man who came to my defense was a man named Marco Trupia.

DOCTOR: Ah, so this Rocco—

MARAGRAZIA: His son. But, Doctor, you don't think I could have become that man's wife, after what I had just seen? He took me by force, kept me tied up for three months, and gagged, because I used to scream. Whenever he came for me, I'd bite him. After three months they caught him and put him in jail, where he died not long after. But I had to bear his son. I swear to you I'd have torn out my guts to avoid having his baby! I couldn't even bear to hold him in my arms. At the mere thought of having to give him my breast, I'd scream like a madwoman. I wanted to die. My mother, bless her, wouldn't even let me see him. They took him away and he was raised by his father's relatives. Now what do you think, Doctor? Aren't I right to say he isn't my son?

DOCTOR: Perhaps. But how is he to blame?

MARAGRAZIA: He isn't. And when, in fact, have my lips ever spoken a word against him? Never, Doctor! In fact—But what can I do if every time I see him, even from far away, I begin to tremble? He's exactly like his father, even his voice. It's not me, it's my blood that denies him! [*Timidly indicating the sheet of paper in her hand*] If Your Excellency would please do me the favor you promised . . .

DOCTOR: [*Rising*] Oh, yes. Come, come with me, to my house.

MARASSUNTA: If only it would do some good, poor woman . . .

MARAGRAZIA: [*Quickly, heatedly*] It will, it will! Because it's her fault —[*Indicating* NINFAROSA]—her fault if my boys haven't come home yet!

DOCTOR: Come on now, let's go!

MARAGRAZIA: [*Quickly*] Yes, sir! I'm ready! A nice long, long letter . . . [*And as she follows the* DOCTOR *out, her hands joined as if in prayer*] "My darling boys, your loving mother . . . !"

CURTAIN

AMICABLE PARTING

George S. Kaufman and
Leueen MacGrath

George S. Kaufman and Leueen MacGrath

George S. Kaufman (1889–1961) was one of the leading figures of the American theatre. Born in Pittsburgh, Pennsylvania, he began his professional writing career by conducting a daily humorous column for the Washington *Times*. This was followed by a stint on the New York *Evening Mail*; from there he moved on to the drama department of the New York *Tribune* and, subsequently, the New York *Times*.

His first Broadway success came in 1921 with the comedy *Dulcy*, written in collaboration with Marc Connelly. It ran for 246 performances and established not only the reputations of the authors but also that of its leading lady, Lynn Fontanne.

Known as "the great collaborator" during his long career in the theatre, Kaufman coauthored (along with Marc Connelly, Morrie Ryskind, Ring Lardner, Edna Ferber, Alexander Woollcott, Katherine Dayton, and John P. Marquand) dozens of plays and musicals. These include: *Merton of the Movies*; *To the Ladies*; *Minick*; *The Royal Family*; *Beggar on Horseback*; *Animal Crackers*; *June Moon*; *The Band Wagon*; *Of Thee I Sing* (the first musical ever to be awarded the Pulitzer Prize, 1932); *Let 'Em Eat Cake*; *Dinner at Eight*; *First Lady*; *Stage Door*; *The Land Is Bright*; and *The Late George Apley*.

His most convivial writing partnership began in 1930 when he worked with Moss Hart on a devastating satire of Hollywood, *Once in a Lifetime*. It entertained audiences for 406 performances and later was made into a film, one of the first lampoons of itself produced by the industry. Thereafter, the team was to enliven the Broadway sector with *You Can't Take It with You* (which won the Pulitzer Prize in 1937); the musical *I'd Rather Be Right*; *The Fabu-*

lous Invalid; The American Way; Merrily We Roll Along; George Washington Slept Here; and *The Man Who Came to Dinner.*

Kaufman's final two Broadway successes as a dramatist were *The Solid Gold Cadillac* (written with Howard Teichmann, 1953) and the book for the 1955 Cole Porter musical *Silk Stockings* (coauthored with Leueen MacGrath and Abe Burrows).

Oddly enough, he only wrote one play without a collaborator during his more than thirty years in the theatre: *The Butter and Egg Man,* produced in 1925, which had an engagement of 243 performances.

Not only was George S. Kaufman a master of play construction and comic and biting satiric dialogue, but he also was a masterful director who piloted more than a score of plays and musicals to outstanding Broadway success.

An internationally known actress as well as playwright, Leueen MacGrath (the second Mrs. George S. Kaufman) collaborated with her husband on several stage works, including *Silk Stockings; The Small Hours;* and *Fancy Meeting You Again.*

Born in London, and trained for the stage at the Royal Academy of Dramatic Art, she made her first appearance in 1933 at the Garrick Theatre in *Beggars in Hell.* From then onward, she was seen in dozens of plays both in London and on tour. In 1948 she made her Broadway debut in *Edward, My Son* with Robert Morley and Dame Peggy Ashcroft. (She subsequently appeared in the film version opposite Spencer Tracy.)

Her success in *Edward, My Son* prompted many other offers from Broadway managements and she was prominently cast in, among others, *The Enchanted; The High Ground;* and *The Love of Four Colonels.*

In 1955 she reappeared on the English stage as Cassandra in the highly acclaimed production of *Tiger at the Gates* opposite Sir Michael Redgrave, and later in that same year returned to these shores to repeat her role at the Plymouth Theatre, New York.

Miss MacGrath continues to divide her professional activities between the two countries. Her most recent appearances in the West End were in Terence Rattigan's *A Bequest to the Nation* and John Mortimer's *A Voyage Round My Father,* while in New York she won considerable praise for her portrayals of Mrs. Alving in Ibsen's *Ghosts* and as Irina Arkadina in Chekhov's *The Seagull.*

Characters:

Bill Reynolds
Alicia Reynolds
Their Dog

FOREWORD

This is meant to be high comedy.
It should be played lightly, gayly.
Never heavily. Never emotionally. Thank you.

—THE AUTHORS

The scene is the living room of BILL *and* ALICIA REYNOLDS. *Its distinguishing features are two ceiling-high bookshelves, packed with books. Otherwise one finds the customary sofa, chairs, tables, a Hi-Fi set, a desk, and several paintings on the walls.*

BILL REYNOLDS *is at a small bar, mixing a cocktail shaker full of drinks.* ALICIA *is moving from one piece of furniture to another, carrying rather large pieces of cardboard, on which are scrawled either* BILL *or* ALICIA.

ALICIA: [*Distributing the tags among the furniture*] Let's see—this sofa is yours—Bill——[*A Bill tag*] This chair's mine—*Alicia*——[*An Alicia tag*] You did say I could have it, didn't you?

BILL: Help yourself.

ALICIA: This table is yours—Bill—this small sofa is mine—Alicia—that chair is yours—Bill. Oh, I've already tagged that—this chair is mine—Alicia's—somehow it's more feminine. That pretty well divides up the furniture . . . Now the paintings. [*She goes to an interesting painting—is about to tag it with her name*] I would like to have this one, if you don't mind, Bill.

BILL: Suits me.

ALICIA: Now, Bill, you're sure?—I mean, that you don't want it? Of course I love it, but then you love it, too.

BILL: No, Sweetie, you saw it first—I remember very clearly. Paris, '53. What was the name of that restaurant? Chez Something.

ALICIA: Nico.

BILL: Chez Nico. Too much to eat, too much to drink, too much for this painting.

ALICIA: Listen, I wanted to go back to the hotel and sleep. It was you that wanted to go to art galleries.

BILL: Yes, but you never can just look. You always have to buy, don't you? That acquisitive streak of yours.

ALICIA: If it weren't for that acquisitive streak of mine we wouldn't have so many lovely things.

BILL: And by the same token we wouldn't have to pin on so many lovely labels.

ALICIA: I didn't exactly collect things for that purpose, you know. In my naïve way I thought we were going to spend our lives together.

BILL: Oh, you poor little abandoned bride!

ALICIA: Really! You have the most extraordinary way of——[*She gains control of herself*] Bill, we agreed we're not going to argue. This whole thing is to be what is known as amicable—a civilized divorce. Up to now we've divided everything fairly, and avoided argument . . . Now! Do you want the picture? Because if you do, take it.

BILL: Look, Alicia, it's yours. I never liked it anyhow. You must have realized that.

ALICIA: You never—but it was the first painting we ever bought.

BILL: It may have been the first, but it's also the dreariest. All those black shadows.

ALICIA: I remember you talking at great, and, if I may say so, boring length about the "mood content" of those black shadows.

BILL: I was just explaining it to you.

ALICIA: Oh, thank you so much, Mr. Reynolds. To think I've always wanted to meet Berenson, when I had you all the time.

BILL: I'm entitled to my judgment, and I never liked it.

ALICIA: But this is fantastic. I remember so clearly—we came out of the gallery, and we couldn't get a taxi, and I stood with it under my coat because it was raining. We got it back to the hotel, and put it up, and just sat there and looked at it, and you agreed with me that we owned the most beautiful painting in the world. And now it turns out you never liked it.

BILL: Look—what's the use of all this? You like it and you're getting it. Now let's get on to the books.

ALICIA: It's just that it's so terrifying, suddenly. I get the feeling I haven't known what you've liked, all the time we've been married. Did you ever like *me*, for instance?

BILL: Yes, I liked you . . . Now, come on—the books.

ALICIA: But not enough to live with me.

BILL: [*Taking the top off the shaker*] We'd better empty this so we can put a label on it. [*Pouring*]

ALICIA: You can have it. I like to stir things.

BILL: [*Muttering to himself*] You sure do, Baby.

ALICIA: There's something so frightfully common about shakers. Like a terrible bartender.

BILL: Oh, pardon me, Duchess. [*Shakes the shaker right in her ear*]

ALICIA: [*Another remembered irritation*] And whistling through your teeth—that's another thing. That's attractive, too.

BILL: [*Heavy sarcasm*] Oh, do go on. If we're making lists, let's clean things up. I think I'd better sit down for this. [*He does so, elaborately*] I've always liked it when you comb your hair in a restaurant, just as we're sitting down to eat. But since you've always shaken your powder-puff in the soup beforehand, I don't suppose it matters very much.

ALICIA: If we're going to play this sort of scene I wish you'd ring up Noël Coward and get some good dialogue . . . Come on—we'll do the books.

BILL: Yes, let's get it over with. [*They look at the two enormous bookshelves*] So many! Dear heaven! Suppose you take all the books in this one, and I'll take those in that one.

ALICIA: Oh, no. There are books in that section that mean a great deal to me.

BILL: [*Looking at the nearest shelves*] "Wild Birds of the Antarctic." . . . "Collected Speeches of Thomas E. Dewey." . . . I'm sure you'll want those.

ALICIA: You know what I mean. My Kafka, my Rilke, Baudelaire . . . [*And she is off*]

"Mon enfant, ma soeur,
Songe a la douceur
D'aller la-bas vivre ensemble!
La, tout n'est qu'ordre et beaute,
Luxe, calme et volupte.
Aimer a loisir" . . .

How does it go?

BILL: Look! He's your poet. Give me a poet I can hum. [*He takes a book from the shelf*] Here's your Baudelaire—you can cuddle up with him on a cold night. [*Opens the volume, lightly*] Only you'd better take something to bed with you to cut the pages.

ALICIA: [*Loftily*] I read him in another edition. Years ago—before I ever knew you.

BILL: In your literary days.

ALICIA: Well, at least I was in a group of people who minded about that sort of thing.

BILL: I see—I dragged you down. From that high intellectual level.

ALICIA: Not at all. It's just that some people are interested in things like that and other people are not. They prefer "Wild Birds of the Antarctic."

BILL: [*With great definiteness*] That is not mine. [*He tosses "Wild Birds" over to her*]

ALICIA: [*Opening it*] "To William J. Reynolds, Jr., for finding the best birds' nest at Winnetonka Camp. Second Prize." . . . Oh, bad luck. Who got first?

BILL: If you must know, a dirty sneak named Kenneth Prentice. [*Staunchly*] As a matter of fact, I'm very proud of this book. [*Puts it aside, purposefully*] I've always wanted to read it.

ALICIA: I do hope you can get around to it . . . And what did you win Thomas E. Dewey's speeches for?

BILL: [*Tossing Dewey aside*] We'd better make three piles. The ones you want, and the ones I want, and the Salvation Army.

ALICIA: Let's hope we can send 'em anonymously.

BILL: [*Facing the shelves again*] Now, here are the Russians . . . Dostoievsky, Tolstoi, Maxim Gorki—Edna Ferber! What's *she* doing here?

ALICIA: Oh, I want that. That's inscribed to me.

BILL: [*Opening it*] It's inscribed to both of us.

ALICIA: Well, I remember she gave it to me.

BILL: "The Brothers Karamazoff"—I suppose that's inscribed to you, too. [*No answer—just Alicia's icy face*] Now, there are two copies of that, I know, so we can each have one. We bought one when we went to Cuba. I remember you said that was a good time to read it.

ALICIA: And I know we bought one in the South of France—remember?—for the same reason. Only you read all the Henry Miller books instead, because they were sexy. Whatever became of those, anyhow? You can't buy them here, and I want to read them.

BILL: I told you they weren't suitable for you. I gave them to Sam Carter—he was writing a thing on them.

ALICIA: You gave them to Sam Carter! After all the trouble we had smuggling them in, wrapped in my underwear. Really! You and Sam Carter! Like two smutty little boys, giggling in corners.

BILL: We were not giggling in corners or anywhere else. Henry Miller is not just a pornographic writer, as you well know.

ALICIA: [*Back to the shelves*] Oh! "Little Women!" Did you ever read it?

BILL: I've always meant to.

ALICIA: It's not quite the same as Henry Miller, I must say. [*A sip of her drink, then back to the shelves*] "How Not to Write a Play," by Walter Kerr.

BILL: What play was it he *wrote*?

ALICIA: Oh, here it is! My French cookbook! It's got the most gorgeous recipes in it.

BILL: I thought you must have mislaid it. Several years ago.

ALICIA: Since you completely ruined your palate by smoking and drinking, I didn't see any point in giving you good food.

BILL: And why do you think I took up smoking and drinking? The palate requires *some* stimulation.

ALICIA: [*Busy at the shelves*] Aldous Huxley! I suppose we'll just have to divide him in half.

BILL: He'll never notice, with all that mescaline inside him.

ALICIA: "Tarzan of the Apes!" That is certainly yours.

BILL: Oh, certainly.

ALICIA: "Moby Dick?"

BILL: I've seen it.

ALICIA: "A Thousand and One Funny Stories." [*She tosses it over to him*]

BILL: [*Tossing it right back*] Why don't you give it to your friend Tom Bender? It'll help to while away the evenings with him. Because as I remember Tom they'll need quite some whiling away.

ALICIA: You don't have to worry about Tom's ability to entertain me.

BILL: Well, it could be that my interest in him is not quite the same as yours.

ALICIA: It could indeed.

[*For a moment they alternately drink and work on the books, laying a volume aside now and then*]

BILL: [*As she tosses a book onto his pile*] What's that?

ALICIA: Longfellow.

BILL: Oh, no! [*He tosses it back. She returns it with a little more definiteness; it goes back and forth about four times, each time with a little more force. Finally tossing it into neutral territory*] Salvation Army.

ALICIA: Oh! Here's another "Brothers Karamazoff."

BILL: I knew we had another one.

ALICIA: How many brothers were there, anyhow?

BILL: Not as many as we have copies.

ALICIA: Anyhow, that leaves two for you and two for me. That ought to see us through.

BILL: You know, somebody would be glad to have one of these.

ALICIA: All right—we'll make four piles. Yours, and mine, and the Salvation Army, and somebody . . . Give me another drink. [*He fills her glass. They both drink*] Now! I'm offering a very fine set of Sir Walter Scott. I never like any author whose books are in a set. They go on and on—it's so boring.

BILL: According to you every author should write one book and then quit.

ALICIA: Not a bad idea . . . Now, what bids do I hear on Scott? Beautiful Morocco binding—look fine on any shelf. There's only one trouble—you can't read 'em.

BILL: And here's Dickens! I want these. I've always wanted to read "Vanity Fair" again.

ALICIA: Oh, yes. It has that very funny character, Sam Pickwick, in it.

BILL: You know I meant Thackeray. I want him, too.

ALICIA: You're never going out of the house again after we separate, are you? Just curl up with your books and your music. [A *thought*] Oh! What are we going to do about the records?

BILL: Same as the books—you take the good ones and leave me the others. Quite simple.

ALICIA: I'll tell you what I do insist on! This! [*Puts on a record— something on the sentimental side*]

BILL: Oh, no! That's not fair! [*They listen together for a moment— plainly, the music strikes a note that recalls the past. For a moment they look at each other, embarrassed. Breaking the mood*] Come on—we've got a lot to do. [*He switches off the music*]

ALICIA: All right, we'll finish the books first and do the records tomorrow.

BILL: We're going to finish the whole darned job, NOW! If it takes all night.

ALICIA: You can take all night if you want to. *I've* got a date.

BILL: Who with?

ALICIA: None of your business.

BILL: You'll go out with just anyone, won't you?

ALICIA: Give me a hand. [*Drink in hand, she essays a small four-step ladder to reach a higher shelf. A little unsteady by this time*] "How to Be Happy in Marriage," by Havelock Ellis. Well, *that's* one we seem to have missed out on.

BILL: [*Tossing it aside*] Somebody at the Salvation Army must be married.

ALICIA: On second thought I think I'll keep it for later on.

BILL: Shall I inscribe it for you? "To Alicia: A wife who never lost her amateur standing."

ALICIA: If I may say so, it takes two to make a marriage.

BILL: Yes, Mary Margaret McBride?

ALICIA: [*In a snarl*] Oh, shut up! [*She turns back to the shelves for a moment, then faces him again*] That's one of the reasons we never got on. Whenever I've tried to discuss anything, you turned it aside with a flip remark.

BILL: Just my defense, because I'm misunderstood. [*Holds out the shaker to fill her glass*] Here!

ALICIA: [*He is three feet below her*] I know you're afraid of heights, but could you take a small chance?

BILL: Sorry. [*Comes up a step or two. As he pours the drink he absently strokes her leg. Just as absently, she touches the top of his head with a fond gesture. Suddenly they both realize what they are doing. They draw away*]

ALICIA: Here's that dictionary that's always getting lost.

BILL: It only got lost when we played scrabble and you claimed that a "quonk" was a small Eurasian animal.

ALICIA: [*Deep in the dictionary*] How interesting! Did you know there was an Emperor of China until 1912?

BILL: [*Phony politeness*] No, I didn't. Please go on.

ALICIA: That's all it says. "Born 1906"—"last Emperor of China until his abdication in 1912." Poor little fellow! Six years old and they kicked him out.

BILL: You've got a heart as big as all outdoors, haven't you?

ALICIA: [*One drink too many, and a little maudlin*] It just doesn't seem fair. How could they know if he was going to be a good Emperor or not? Tiny little boy like that!

BILL: You realize you're showing more sympathy for that boy Emperor of China, who you never knew existed before, than you've shown me for the past year and a half?

ALICIA: At least I have some human feelings, and that's something I didn't pick up around *this* house.

BILL: If you want a really good cry there's a copy of "Black Beauty" up there.

ALICIA: [*Genuinely pleased*] Oh, wonderful! Where?

BILL: [*Handing it to her*] Here you are! I've found out what touches you, anyhow—Chinamen and horses!

ALICIA: Do you remember that terribly moving scene where they took the other horse away from her? I used to cry and cry.

BILL: Would you like some mood music while you re-read it? [*He puts on a sentimental record*]

ALICIA: [*Perched up on the step, drink in the other hand. Reads*] "Whilst I was young I lived upon my mother's milk, as I could not eat grass. In the daytime I ran by her side, and at night I lay down close to her."

[BILL *adopts an attitude of exaggerated attention*]

BILL: I have an idea. Why don't you take a theatre and give one of those Charles Laughton readings?

ALICIA: [*Really maudlin now*] You just don't mind. You don't mind at all. That's the story of our life together. [*Another sip of her drink*]

BILL: What is? "Black Beauty"? I'm the old brown horse that's led away, of course, and you're the beautiful Black Beauty.

ALICIA: You're horrid, aren't you? . . . Come on—we'd better get on with our work . . . "Lanny Budd." One—two—three—four—five nine volumes. Mr. Sinclair really worked at that, didn't he? [*Opens one of them*] From your bookmark it appears you got to page 11 of Volume 1. [*She piles all nine in her arms*] Well, added to Dickery and Thackens——

BILL: Who?

ALICIA: [*Very clearly*] I say that added to Dickery and Thackens these ought to keep you busy. [*Posed on the small ladder, she is loaded with books, plus her martini glass*] Now, will you help me down, please?

BILL: No, I don't think so.

ALICIA: Please, Bill. I don't want to upset my drink.

[*He lifts her down. The books scatter, but she saves her martini and holds it up triumphantly. At all events, they wind up rather breathless, and with their faces close together. Their looks meet for a second—there is a sudden kiss, followed by an embrace*]

BILL: Where do you want to go? On your sofa or mine?

ALICIA: Oh, no! Do you think I have no will power at all? It's only because you ply me with drink, and give me "Black Beauty," and put on sloppy music——[*She becomes suddenly very busy, picking up about four books at once*] This is for you, this is for me, this is Salvation Army . . . "Journey to the Aegean." Oh, I want Tom to read this.

BILL: Why don't you do just that thing? Give him "Journey to the Aegean," and let him go to the Aegean.

ALICIA: It just happens that I am very fond of Tom.

BILL: So am I, if he's in the Aegean. Think of the trouble it'll save. [*A wave of the hand that takes in the room, the books, everything*]

ALICIA: You're so lazy, you are.

BILL: I never wanted you to go, and it wasn't true about the painting. I love it. Yes, and I love this apartment, and everything in it.

ALICIA: And "Black Beauty"?

BILL: Don't push me too far . . . If I knew you better, I'd tell you that I love you, too.

ALICIA: You would tell me now, when it's too late.

BILL: Look—you were the one who wanted to go.

ALICIA: Because we decided we didn't love each other.

BILL: You decided.

ALICIA: But the whole point is you let me decide. You didn't seem to care whether I stayed or not.

BILL: You're very stupid, aren't you?

ALICIA: Yes.

BILL: All right, then. [*He kisses her, soundly*] Now, do you agree to love, honor and obey me, and to start pulling these labels off the furniture?

ALICIA: With pleasure. [*Starts pulling off labels*] "He loves me, he loves me not."

BILL: [*Also pulling labels*] At least this has postponed all that reading I'd have to do. "She loves me" . . . [*He has absently pulled an* ALICIA *label off a desk, then stops to look at it in his hand. A change of manner*] What did you put your name on this for?

ALICIA: On what?

• BILL: On what? This desk of mine.

ALICIA: Well, it *became* your desk, but I bought it.

BILL: Exactly. You bought it, and gave it to me as a present.

ALICIA: Oh, the meanness of you! You stand there half a minute ago, persuading me to make a fool of myself and come back to you, and then you start quibbling—worse than quibbling—*haggling*— over an imitation, reproduction Louis the Seize desk.

BILL: Well, that was a fine present to give me. Some awful reproduction of a Louis de Something desk.

ALICIA: If you hadn't been so ignorant about furniture you'd have known it. And if you hadn't been so ignorant about me our life together wouldn't have been such a disaster. [*Furiously, she goes to work putting the labels back on the furniture. He does the same, in his lazier way. A dog crosses the room and goes out, if he can be made to do that. We see the faces of* BILL *and* ALICIA. *Plainly, they had forgotten about the dog*] Now, don't you go and put a label on Augustus. He's always been my dog, as you well know.

BILL: Of *course*. You feed him all the time.

ALICIA: I've fed *you* too, and what's that got me?

BILL: You gave him better stuff.

ALICIA: I'll tell you what we'll do. He's unquestionably mine, but you can visit him when you want to.

BILL: Any particular visiting hours?

ALICIA: A dog's place is with the woman.

BILL: Man's best friend is his dog. It doesn't say anything about women.

ALICIA: But if you want him three months a year, you can have him in the summer, when I go to Europe.

BILL: By all means. We can enjoy the New York humidity together, he and I. Both of us with our tongues hanging out.

ALICIA: Only remember to give *him* a drink too once in a while.

BILL: Look! Which one of us has taken him out for his walk late every night, in all kinds of weather?

ALICIA: You didn't have to walk him far. Only around the corner to Moriarity's Bar.

BILL: Remember you told how he pined, that time I had to go to Canada. You looked fine when I got back, but he was skinny as a whippet.

ALICIA: Oh, now the dog and I are coming in for comparison.

BILL: Look! You can have every stick of furniture, and every book and every record, but I'm keeping Augustus.

ALICIA: Oh, no you're not. If it comes to that I'd rather *stay* with you.

BILL: Well, thank you. I think you're really one of the most gracious ladies I ever met. *That's* a reason for staying with me if I ever heard one.

ALICIA: Listen—I can't talk about this now—it's quarter to seven and I've got a date.

BILL: Surely you can keep your date waiting—we have a very important decision to make.

ALICIA: How can we make any decisions when as usual you just don't understand? Have you stopped to think how lonely I'm going to be? I need Augustus—I need him to protect me.

BILL: Well, it's no go. I mind about him more than you do, and that's all there is to it. He's part of my life.

ALICIA: He's part of *both* of our lives, together. And I've just realized something else. That's why you've stayed with me all this time—because of the dog.

BILL: Oh, sure, sure.

ALICIA: Well, it's true and you can't deny it . . . Fine thing to find out after five years of marriage.

BILL: [*Spilling over*] *All right!* Take Augustus, and the books, and the paintings, and the ironing board, and the Waring Mixer, and my old socks. They're all yours!—take them all!

ALICIA: Thank you. I will . . . Good-bye. [*She goes out of the room. BILL goes back to the phonograph—puts on the sentimental record. He sips at his drink and listens to the music, and presently he is lost in the recollections that the music brings. There is perhaps an impetuous gesture in the direction in which ALICIA has gone— then he pulls himself back to reality. But the music continues to do its work—he is plainly a man who wishes that the divorce were not about to take place. Then ALICIA, her coat and hat on, reappears in the doorway. She catches a glimpse of his face, and she too is caught up in the emotion. Then suddenly she picks up one of the discarded tags—this one reads BILL'S. It is attached to a loop of string. Her eyes still on* BILL, *she slips the string over her neck so that she herself is clearly tagged as BILL'S. She then comes slowly toward him]*

CURTAIN

MISS JULIE

August Strindberg

(Translated from the Swedish by Michael Meyer)

August Strindberg

Author of more than sixty plays (as well as poems, novels, stories, and autobiographical works), August Strindberg (1849–1912) is the Swedish theatre's best known dramatist and one of the most influential figures in modern drama.

He was born in Stockholm, the son of a shipping merchant and a former maidservant. Four years after his birth, his father went bankrupt, and his mother died when he was thirteen; the following year, his father married his housekeeper. At the age of eighteen he went to Upsala University, but poverty forced him to interrupt his studies, though he was able to resume his education in 1870. In the interim, he tried teaching, acting, and journalism.

After leaving Upsala for good, he obtained a position on the staff of the Royal Library in Stockholm and remained there for eight years. His initial recognition as a writer came in 1879 when he published his novel *The Red Room*, which dealt with life among the young artists and writers of Stockholm.

From 1883 to 1889, Strindberg and his family lived mostly abroad; in 1889 he returned to Stockholm and thenceforth made that city his home. In the middle 1890s, he suffered a serious mental breakdown due to overwork and marital unhappiness. By 1897 he had recovered and was once more in full creative activity. Strindberg was married three times, but each matrimonial venture proved unsatisfactory and ended in divorce.

Strindberg's plays have had a profound influence upon the development of European and American drama and he is the acknowledged ancestor of some of this century's greatest dramatists. According to translator Michael Meyer, "he perfected, in such plays as *Miss Julie* and *Creditors*, a terse, nervous dialogue, less deliberate and more fragmentary than Ibsen's, the shorthand of speech. Ibsen had reduced dialogue from poetic verbosity to a taut and spare colloquial prose, but Strindberg reduced it even further. Structurally, too, he achieved an economy beyond Ibsen's; he proudly pointed out that the plots of *Miss Julie* and *Creditors* would each have sufficed for a five-act play but that he had reduced each of them to a single act of less than ninety minutes. 'Take a lamb cutlet,' he said, 'it looks large, but three-quarters of it is bone and fat, containing a kernel of meat. I strip off the bone and fat and give you the kernel.' "

In *Miss Julie*, written in 1888, he exposes an upper-class woman who is tormented by her hatred and contempt of men and her intense physical desire for them. Its power and remarkable character depiction render this short drama one of the finest examples of this play-form.

The admirable translation which appears here was initially performed by Britain's National Theatre Company at the Festival Theatre, Chichester, in 1965, with Maggie Smith in the title role and Albert Finney as Jean.

Michael Meyer was educated at Wellington College and Christ Church, Oxford. He is the author of a novel, *The End of the Corridor*; a widely acclaimed biography of the great Norwegian dramatist Ibsen; a play, *The Ortolan*; and a number of radio and television dramas.

Internationally known as a translator of Ibsen and Strindberg, Mr. Meyer was awarded the Gold Medal of the Swedish Academy in 1964 for his definitive Strindberg translations.

Characters:

Miss Julie, twenty-five.
Jean, *her father's valet*, thirty.
Christine, *her father's cook*, thirty-five.

The action takes place in the Count's kitchen, on midsummer night.

A large kitchen, the roof and side walls of which are concealed by drapes and borders. The rear wall rises at an angle from the left; on it, to the left, are two shelves with utensils of copper, iron and pewter. The shelves are lined with scalloped paper. Over to the right we can see three-quarters of a big, arched exit porch, with twin glass doors, through which can be seen a fountain with a statue of Cupid, lilac bushes in bloom, and tall Lombardy poplars.

On the left of the stage is visible the corner of a big tiled stove, with a section of an overhead hood to draw away fumes. To the right, one end of the kitchen table, of white pine, with some chairs. The stove is decorated with birch-leaves; the floor is strewn with juniper twigs. On the end of the table is a big Japanese spice-jar containing flowering lilacs. An ice-box, a scullery table, a sink. Above the door is a big old-fashioned bell, of the alarm type. To the left of this emerges a speaking-tube.

[CHRISTINE *is standing at the stove, frying in a pan. She is dressed in a light cotton dress, with apron.* JEAN *enters, dressed in livery and carrying a pair of big riding boots, with spurs. He puts them down on the floor where we can see them*]

JEAN: Miss Julie's crazy again tonight. Completely crazy!

CHRISTINE: Oh, you're here at last?

JEAN: I went with his lordship to the station, and as I passed the barn on my way back I went in for a dance, and who do I see but Miss Julie leading the dance with the gamekeeper? But as soon as she sees me, she rushes across and offers her arm for the ladies' waltz. And then she danced like—I've never known the like! She's crazy.

CHRISTINE: She always has been. Especially this last fortnight, since the engagement got broken off.

JEAN: Yes, what about that? He was a gentleman, even if he wasn't rich. Oh, they're so full of caprices. [*Sits down at the table*] It's odd, though, that a young lady should choose to stay at home with the servants, eh? rather than go off to her relations with her father.

CHRISTINE: Oh, I expect she doesn't feel like seeing anyone after that hullaballoo she had with her young man.

JEAN: Very likely! He knew how to stand up for himself, though. Know how it happened, Christine? I saw it, you know, though I took care not to let on I had.

CHRISTINE: No! You saw it?

JEAN: Indeed I did. They were down at the stable yard one evening, and Miss Julie was putting him through his paces, as she called it —do you know what that meant? She made him leap over her riding whip, the way you teach a dog to jump. He leaped twice, and each time she gave him a cut; but the third time, he snatched the whip out of her hand and broke it across his knee. And that was the last we saw of him.

CHRISTINE: Was that what happened? You can't mean it.

JEAN: Yes, that's the way it was. Now, what have you got to tempt me with this evening, Christine?

CHRISTINE: [Serves from the pan and lays a place] Oh, just a bit of kidney I cut from the joint.

JEAN: [Smells the food] Lovely! Cel-ci est mon grand délice! [Feels the plate] You might have warmed the plate, though.

CHRISTINE: You're fussier than his lordship himself, once you start. [Pulls his hair affectionately]

JEAN: [Angrily] Don't pull my hair. You know how sensitive I am.

CHRISTINE: Now, now. It's only love, you know.

[JEAN eats. CHRISTINE brings a bottle of beer]

JEAN: Beer—on midsummer eve? No, thank you. I can do better than that. [Opens a drawer in the table and takes out a bottle of red wine with yellow sealing-wax on the cork] See that? Yellow seal! Give me a glass, now. A wine glass, I'm drinking this pur.

CHRISTINE: [Goes back to the stove and puts a small saucepan on] God have mercy on whoever gets you for a husband. I never met such a fusspot.

JEAN: Oh, rubbish. You'd be jolly pleased to get a gentleman like me. And I don't think you've lost anything through people calling you my fiancée [*Tastes the wine*] Good! Very good! Just not quite sufficiently *chambré*. [*Warms the glass with his hands*] We bought this one in Dijon. Four francs a litre it cost—and then there was the bottling—and the duty. What are you cooking now? The smell's infernal.

CHRISTINE: Oh, some filthy mess Miss Julie wants for Diana.

JEAN: Please express yourself more delicately, Christine. But why should you have to cook for that confounded dog on midsummer eve? Is it ill?

CHRISTINE: It's ill all right! It managed to slip out with the gate-keeper's pug, and now it's in trouble—and *that* Miss Julie won't allow.

JEAN: Miss Julie is stuck-up about some things, in others she demeans herself, exactly like her ladyship when she was alive. She was most at home in the kitchen or the stables, but one horse wasn't enough to pull her carriage. She went around with dirty cuffs, but there had to be a crest on every button. Miss Julie, now, to return to her—she doesn't bother about herself and her person. To my mind, she is not what one would call a lady. Just now, when she was dancing in the barn, she grabbed the gamekeeper from Anna and made him dance with her. We'd never do that— but that's how it is when the gentry try to lower themselves—they become really common. But she's a magnificent creature! What a figure! What shoulders! and—etcetera, etcetera!

CHRISTINE: No need to overdo it. I've heard what Clara says, and she dresses her.

JEAN: Oh, Clara! You women are always jealous of each other. I've been out riding with her—and the way she dances——!

CHRISTINE: Well, aren't you going to dance with me, when I'm ready?

JEAN: Yes, of course.

CHRISTINE: Promise?

JEAN: Promise? When I say I'll do a thing, I do it. Thank you for that, it was very nice. [*Corks the bottle*]

MISS JULIE: [*In the doorway, talking to someone outside*] I'll be back immediately. Don't wait for me.

[JEAN *hides the bottle in the drawer of the table and gets up respectfully*]

MISS JULIE: [*Enters and goes up to* CHRISTINE *by the stove*] Well, is it ready?

[CHRISTINE *indicates that* JEAN *is present*]

JEAN: [*Gallantly*] Have you ladies secrets to discuss?

MISS JULIE: [*Flips him in the face with her handkerchief*] Don't be inquisitive!

JEAN: Ah! Charming, that smell of violets.

MISS JULIE: [*Coquettishly*] Saucy fellow! So you know about perfumes, too? You certainly know how to dance—stop looking, now, go away!

JEAN: [*Boldly, yet respectfully*] Is this some magic brew you ladies are preparing on midsummer eve, which will reveal the future and show whom fate has in store for you?

MISS JULIE: [*Sharply*] You'd need sharp eyes to see him. [*To* CHRISTINE] Pour it into a bottle, and cork it well. Come now, and dance a schottische with me, Jean.

JEAN: [*Slowly*] I don't wish to seem disrespectful, but this dance I had promised to Christine——

MISS JULIE: Well, she can have another dance with you, can't you, Christine? Won't you lend me Jean?

CHRISTINE: That's hardly up to me. If Miss Julie condescends, it's not his place to refuse. Go ahead, Jean, and thank madam for the honour.

JEAN: To be frank, without wishing to offend, I wonder if it would be wise for Miss Julie to dance twice in succession with the same partner. These people soon start talking——

MISS JULIE: [*Flares up*] Talking? What kind of talk? What do you mean?

JEAN: [*Politely*] If madam doesn't understand, I must speak more plainly. It looks bad if you show a preference for one of your servants while others are waiting to be similarly honoured——

MISS JULIE: Preference! What an idea! I am astounded. I, the lady of the house, honour my servants by attending their dance, and when I take the floor I want to dance with someone who knows how to partner a lady. I don't want to be made ridiculous——

JEAN: As madam commands. I am at your service.

MISS JULIE: [*Softly*] Don't regard it as a command. Tonight we are ordinary people trying to be happy, and all rank is laid aside. Come, give me your arm! Don't worry, Christine! I won't steal your lover!

[JEAN *offers* MISS JULIE *his arm, and escorts her out*]

PANTOMIME

This should be played as though the actress were actually alone. When the occasion calls for it she should turn her back on the audience. She does not look towards them; and must not hasten her movements as though afraid lest they should grow impatient.

CHRISTINE *alone. A violin can be faintly heard in the distance, playing a schottische.* CHRISTINE *hums in time with the music; clears up after* JEAN, *washes the plate at the sink, dries it and puts it away in a cupboard. Then she removes her apron, takes a small mirror from a drawer, lights a candle and warms a curling-iron, with which she then crisps the hair over her forehead. Goes out into the doorway and listens. Returns to the table. Finds* MISS JULIE's *handkerchief, which the latter has forgotten; picks it up and smells it; then spreads it out, as though thinking of something else, stretches it, smooths it, folds it into quarters, etc.*

JEAN: [*Enters alone*] No, she really *is* crazy! What a way to dance! Everyone was grinning at her from behind the doors. What do you make of it, Christine?

CHRISTINE: Oh, it's that time of the month for her, and then she always acts strange. Well, are you going to dance with me now?

JEAN: You're not angry with me for leaving you like that——?

CHRISTINE: No, a little thing like that doesn't bother me. Besides, I know my place——

JEAN: [*Puts his arm round her waist*] You're a sensible girl, Christine. You'd make a good wife——

MISS JULIE: [*Enters; is disagreeably surprised; speaks with forced lightness*] Well, you're a fine gentleman, running away from your partner like that!

JEAN: On the contrary, Miss Julie. As you see, I have hastened to return to the partner I forsook!

MISS JULIE: [*Changes her tone*] Do you know, you dance magnificently. But why are you wearing uniform on midsummer eve? Take it off at once.

JEAN: Then I must ask madam to go outside for a moment. I have my black coat here——[*Goes right with a gesture*]

MISS JULIE: Does my presence embarrass you? Can't you change a coat with me here? You'd better go into your room, then. Or stay, and I'll turn my back.

JEAN: With your permission, Miss Julie. [*Goes right. We see his arm as he changes his coat*]

MISS JULIE: [*To* CHRISTINE] Christine, Jean is very familiar with you. Are you engaged to him?

CHRISTINE: Engaged? If you like. We call it that.

MISS JULIE: Call——?

CHRISTINE: Well, you've been engaged yourself, madam——

MISS JULIE: We were properly engaged.

CHRISTINE: Didn't come to anything, though, did it?

[*JEAN enters in black tails and a black bowler hat*]

MISS JULIE: *Très gentil, monsieur Jean! Très gentil!*

JEAN: *Vous voulez plaisanter, madame!*

MISS JULIE: *Et vous voulez parler francais!* Where did you learn that?

JEAN: In Switzerland. I was wine waiter at the biggest hotel in Lucerne.

MISS JULIE: You look quite the gentleman in those tails. *Charmant!*
[*Sits at the table*]

JEAN: Oh, you're flattering me.

MISS JULIE: [*Haughtily*] Flattering *you?*

JEAN: My natural modesty forbids me to suppose that you would pay
a truthful compliment to one so humble as myself, so I assumed
you were exaggerating, for which I believe the polite word is flattering.

MISS JULIE: Where did you learn to talk like that? You must have
spent a lot of your time at the theatre.

JEAN: Yes. And I've been around a bit, too.

MISS JULIE: But you were born here, weren't you?

JEAN: My father worked on the next farm to yours. I used to see you
when I was a child, though you wouldn't remember me.

MISS JULIE: No, really?

JEAN: Yes. I remember one time especially—no, I oughtn't to mention that.

MISS JULIE: Oh, yes! Tell me. Come on! Just this once.

JEAN: No, I really couldn't now. Some other time, perhaps.

MISS JULIE: Some other time means never. Is it so dangerous to tell
it now?

JEAN: It isn't dangerous, but I'd rather not. Look at her! [*Indicates*
CHRISTINE, *who has fallen asleep in a chair by the stove*]

MISS JULIE: A charming wife she'll make. Does she snore, too?

JEAN: She doesn't do that, but she talks in her sleep.

MISS JULIE: [*Cynically*] How do you know?

JEAN: [*Coolly*] I've heard her.

[*Pause. They look at each other*]

MISS JULIE: Why don't you sit?

JEAN: I wouldn't permit myself to do that in your presence.

MISS JULIE: But if I order you to?

JEAN: Then I shall obey.

MISS JULIE: Sit, then. No, wait. Can you give me something to drink first?

JEAN: I don't know what we have in the ice-box. Only beer, I think.

MISS JULIE: What do you mean, only beer? My taste is very simple. I prefer it to wine.

[JEAN *takes a bottle of beer from the ice-box, opens it, gets a glass and plate from the cupboard and serves her*]

MISS JULIE: Thank you. Won't you have something yourself?

JEAN: I'm not much of a drinker, but if madam orders me——

MISS JULIE: Orders? Surely you know that a gentleman should never allow a lady to drink alone.

JEAN: That's perfectly true. [*Opens another bottle and pours a glass*]

MISS JULIE: Drink my health, now! [JEAN *hesitates*] Are you shy?

JEAN: [*Kneels in a parody of a romantic attitude, and raises his glass*] To my mistress's health!

MISS JULIE: Bravo! Now kiss my shoe, and the ceremony is complete.

[JEAN *hesitates, then boldly takes her foot in his hands and kisses it lightly*]

MISS JULIE: Excellent. You ought to have been an actor.

JEAN: [*Gets up*] We mustn't go on like this, Miss Julie. Someone might come in and see us.

MISS JULIE: What then?

JEAN: People would talk, that's all. And if you knew how their tongues were wagging up there just now——

MISS JULIE: What kind of thing were they saying? Tell me. Sit down.

JEAN: [*Sits*] I don't want to hurt you, but they were using expressions which—which hinted that—well, you can guess! You aren't a child, and when people see a lady drinking alone with a man—let alone a servant—at night—then——

MISS JULIE: Then what? Anyway, we're not alone. Christine is here.

JEAN: Asleep.

MISS JULIE: Then I shall wake her. [*Gets up*] Christine! Are you asleep?

[CHRISTINE *mumbles to herself in her sleep*]

MISS JULIE: Christine! My God, she is asleep!

CHRISTINE: [*In her sleep*] Are his lordship's boots brushed? Put on the coffee. Quickly, quickly, quickly! [*Laughs, then grunts*]

MISS JULIE: [*Takes her by the nose*] Will you wake up?

JEAN: [*Sharply*] Don't disturb her!

MISS JULIE: [*Haughtily*] What!

JEAN: People who stand at a stove all day get tired when night comes. And sleep is something to be respected——

MISS JULIE: A gallant thought, and one that does you honour. [*Holds out her hand to* JEAN] Come outside now, and pick some lilac for me.

[*During the following dialogue,* CHRISTINE *wakes and wanders drowsily right to go to bed*]

JEAN: With you?

MISS JULIE: With me.

JEAN: Impossible. I couldn't.

MISS JULIE: I don't understand. Surely you don't imagine——?

JEAN: I don't, but other people might.

MISS JULIE: What? That I have fallen in love with a servant?

JEAN: I'm not being conceited, but such things have happened—and to these people, nothing is sacred.

MISS JULIE: Quite the little aristocrat, aren't you?

JEAN: Yes, I am.

MISS JULIE: If I choose to step down——

JEAN: Don't step down, Miss Julie, take my advice. No one will believe you did it freely. People will always say you fell——

MISS JULIE: I have a higher opinion of people than you. Come and see! Come! [*She fixes him with her eyes*]

JEAN: You know, you're strange.

MISS JULIE: Perhaps. But so are you. Everything is strange. Life, people, everything, is a scum which drifts, drifts on and on across the water until it sinks, sinks. I have a dream which recurs every so often, and I'm reminded of it now. I've climbed to the top of a pillar, and am sitting there, and I can see no way to descend. When I look down, I become dizzy, but I must come down—but I haven't the courage to jump. I can't stay up there, and I long to fall, but I don't fall. And yet I know I shall find no peace till I come down, down to the ground. And if I could get down, I should want to burrow my way deep into the earth . . . Have you ever felt anything like that?

JEAN: No. I dream that I'm lying under a high tree in a dark wood. I want to climb, up, up to the top, and look round over the bright landscape where the sun is shining—plunder the bird's nest up there where the gold eggs lie. And I climb and climb, but the trunk is so thick and slippery, and it's so far to the first branch. But I know that if I could only get to that first branch, I'd climb my way to the top as though up a ladder. I haven't reached it yet, but I shall reach it, even if it's only in a dream.

MISS JULIE: Why do I stand here prattling with you about dreams? Come, now! Just into the park!

[*She offers him her arm, and they go*]

JEAN: We must sleep with nine midsummer flowers under our pillow tonight, Miss Julie, and our dreams will come true!

[*They turn in the doorway.* JEAN *puts a hand to one of his eyes*]

MISS JULIE: Have you something in your eye?

JEAN: It's nothing. Only a speck of dust. It'll be all right soon.

MISS JULIE: My sleeve must have brushed it. Sit down and I'll take it out. [*Takes him by the arm, makes him sit, takes his head and pushes it backwards, and tries to remove the dust with the corner of her handkerchief*] Sit still now, quite still! [*Slaps his hands*] Come, obey me! I believe you're trembling, you great, strong lout! [*Feels his biceps*] What muscles you have!

JEAN: [*Warningly*] Miss Julie!

MISS JULIE: Yes, monsieur Jean?

JEAN: *Attention! Je ne suis qu'un homme!*

MISS JULIE: Sit still, will you! There! Now it's gone. Kiss my hand and thank me.

JEAN: [*Gets up*] Miss Julie, listen to me. Christine's gone to bed now—will you listen to me!

MISS JULIE: Kiss my hand first.

JEAN: Listen to me!

MISS JULIE: Kiss my hand first.

JEAN: All right. But you've only yourself to blame.

MISS JULIE: For what?

JEAN: For what? Are you a child? You're twenty-five. Don't you know it's dangerous to play with fire?

MISS JULIE: Not for me. I am insured.

JEAN: [*Boldly*] No, you're not. And if you are, there's inflammable material around that isn't.

MISS JULIE: Meaning you?

JEAN: Yes. Not because I'm me, but because I'm a young man——

MISS JULIE: Of handsome appearance! What incredible conceit! A Don Juan, perhaps? Or a Joseph! Yes, upon my word, I do believe you're a Joseph!

JEAN: Do you?

MISS JULIE: I almost fear it.

[JEAN *moves boldly forward and tries to take her round the waist to kiss her*]

MISS JULIE: [*Slaps him*] Stop it!

JEAN: Are you joking or serious?

MISS JULIE: Serious.

JEAN: Then you were being serious just now, too. You play games too seriously, and that's dangerous. Well, now I'm tired of this game and must ask your permission to get back to my work. His lordship's boots must be ready in time, and it's long past midnight.

MISS JULIE: Forget the boots.

JEAN: No. They're part of my job, which doesn't include being your playmate. And never will. I flatter myself I'm above that.

MISS JULIE: Aren't we proud!

JEAN: In some respects. In others, not.

MISS JULIE: Have you ever been in love?

JEAN: We don't use that word. But I've been fond of a lot of girls, and once I was sick because I couldn't get the one I wanted. Yes, sick, do you hear, like those princes in the Arabian Nights, who couldn't eat or drink because of love.

MISS JULIE: Who was she? [JEAN *is silent*] Who was she?

JEAN: You cannot order me to answer that.

MISS JULIE: If I ask you as an equal? As a friend! Who was she?

JEAN: You.

MISS JULIE: [*Sits*] How absurd!

JEAN: Yes, if you like. It was absurd. Look, this was the story I didn't want to tell you just now—but now I will tell you. Do you know how the world looks from down there? No, you don't. Like hawks and eagles, whose backs one seldom sees because most of the time they hover above you! I lived in a hut with seven brothers and sisters and a pig, out in the grey fields where never a tree grew. But from the window I could see the wall of his lordship's park, with apple trees rising above it. It was the Garden of Paradise, and there stood many evil angels with flaming swords to guard it. But despite them I and other boys found a way in to the tree of life— You despise me now?

MISS JULIE: Oh, I suppose all boys steal apples.

JEAN: You can say that now, but you do despise me. However. One day I entered the garden with my mother, to weed the onion beds. On one side of the garden stood a Turkish pavilion in the shadow of jasmine trees and overgrown with honeysuckle. I didn't know what it could be for, but I'd never seen such a beautiful building. People went in and came out again; and, one day, the door was left open. I crept in and saw the walls hung with pictures of kings and emperors, and there were red curtains on the windows with tassels—ah, now you understand! I——[*Breaks a flower from the lilac and holds it beneath* MISS JULIE's *nose*] I'd never been into the palace itself, never seen anything except the church—but this was more beautiful—and however my thoughts might stray, they always returned there. And gradually I began to long just once to experience the full ecstasy of actually—*enfin*, I crept inside, saw and marvelled. But then—someone's coming! There was only one exit—for the lords and ladies. But for me—there was another—and I had no choice but to take it. [MISS JULIE, *who has taken the lilac blossom, lets it fall on the table*] Then I ran, broke through a raspberry bush, charged across a strawberry patch, and found myself on a terrace with a rose garden. There I saw a pink dress and a pair of white stockings. You. I lay down under a pile of weeds— *under*, can you imagine that?—under thistles that pricked me and wet earth that stank. And I looked at you as you walked among the roses, and I thought: "If it is true that a thief can enter heaven and dwell with the angels, then it's strange that a peasant's child here on earth cannot enter the great park and play with the Count's daughter."

MISS JULIE: [*Romantically*] Do you suppose all poor children have had the same ideas as you about this?

JEAN: [*At first hesitant, then with conviction*] Have all poor——? Yes! Of course! Of course!

MISS JULIE: It must be a terrible misfortune to be poor.

JEAN: [*Deeply cut, speaks with strong emotion*] Oh, Miss Julie! Oh! A dog may lie on the Countess's sofa, a horse may have its nose patted by a young lady's hand, but a servant——! [*Changes his tone*] Oh, now and then a man has strength enough to hoist himself up in the world, but how often does it happen? But do you know what I did? I ran down into the millstream with my clothes on. They dragged me out and beat me. But the following Sunday, when my father and all the others had gone to visit my grandmother, I managed to fix things so that I stayed at home. And then I scrubbed myself with soap and hot water, put on my best clothes, and went to church, in order that I might see you. I saw you, and returned home, determined to die. But I wanted to die beautifully, and pleasantly, without pain. Then I remembered it was dangerous to sleep under an elder bush. We had a big one, in flower. I plundered it of everything it held, and then I lay down in the oat-bin. Have you ever noticed how beautiful oats are? Soft to the touch like human skin. Well, I shut the lid and closed my eyes. I fell alseep, and woke up feeling really very ill. But I didn't die, as you can see. What did I want? I don't know. I had no hope of winning you, of course—but you were a symbol to me of the hopelessness of my ever climbing out of the class in which I was born.

MISS JULIE: Do you know you're quite a *raconteur*? Did you ever go to school?

JEAN: A bit. But I've read a lot of novels, and gone to theatres. And I've heard gentlefolk talk. That's where I've learned most.

MISS JULIE: Do you listen to what we say?

JEAN: Certainly! And I've heard plenty, too, sitting on the coachman's box or rowing the boat. One time I heard you and a lady friend——

MISS JULIE: Indeed? What did you hear?

JEAN: Oh, I wouldn't care to repeat it. But it surprised me a little. I couldn't imagine where you'd learned all those words. Maybe at bottom there isn't as big a difference as people suppose between people and—people.

MISS JULIE: Oh, nonsense. We don't act like you do when we're engaged.

JEAN: [*Looks at her*] Are you sure? Come, Miss Julie, you don't have to play the innocent with me——

MISS JULIE: The man to whom I offered my love was a bastard.

JEAN: That's what they always say—afterwards.

MISS JULIE: Always?

JEAN: I've heard the expression several times before on similar occasions.

MISS JULIE: What occasions?

JEAN: Like the one in question. The last time——

MISS Julie: [*Rises*] Be quiet! I don't wish to hear any more.

JEAN: *She* didn't want to, either. Strange. Well, have I your permission to go to bed?

MISS JULIE: [*Softly*] Go to bed? On midsummer eve?

JEAN: Yes. Dancing with that pack up there doesn't greatly amuse me.

MISS JULIE: Get the key of the boat and row me out on the lake. I want to see the sun rise.

JEAN: Is that wise?

MISS JULIE: You speak as though you were frightened of your reputation.

JEAN: Why not? I don't want to make myself a laughing-stock, and maybe get sacked without a reference, now that I'm beginning to make my way. And I think I have a certain responsibility towards Christine.

MISS JULIE: Oh, I see, it's Christine now——

JEAN: Yes, but you too. Take my advice. Go back to your room and go to bed.

MISS JULIE: Am *I* to obey *you?*

JEAN: For once. For your own sake. I beg you! It's late, drowsiness makes one drunk, one's head grows dizzy. Go to bed. Besides—if my ears don't deceive me—the other servants are coming here to look for me. And if they find us together here, you are lost!

[*Approaching voices are heard, singing:*]

> VOICES: One young girl in a big dark wood!
> Tridiridi-ralla, tridiridi-ra!
> Met a boy she never should!
> Tridiridi-ralla-ra!
>
> O lay me down in the grass so soft!
> Tridiridi-ralla, tridiridi-ra!
> And her m-m-m she lost!
> Tridiridi-ralla-ra!
>
> O thank you sir, but I must go!
> Tridiridi-ralla, tridiridi-ra!
> Another loves me now, so—
> Tridiridi-ralla-la!

MISS JULIE: I know these people, and I love them, as I know they love me. Let them come here, and I'll prove it to you.

JEAN: No, Miss Julie, they don't love you. They take your food, but they spit at you once you've turned your back. Believe me! Listen to them, listen to what they're singing! No, don't listen!

MISS JULIE: [*Listens*] What are they singing?

JEAN: It's a filthy song. About you and me.

MISS JULIE: How vile! Oh! The little traitors——!

JEAN: The mob is always cowardly. One can't fight them. One can only run away.

MISS JULIE: Run away? But where? We can't go out—or into Christine's room!

JEAN: No. Into my room, then. We can't bother about conventions now. And you can trust me. I am your true, loyal and respectful—friend.

MISS JULIE: But suppose—suppose they look for you in there?

JEAN: I'll bolt the door. And if anyone tries to break in, I'll shoot. Come! [*Drops to his knees*] Come!

MISS JULIE: [*Urgently*] You promise——

JEAN: I swear.

[MISS JULIE *runs out right.* JEAN *hastens after her*]

BALLET

The peasants stream in, wearing their best clothes, with flowers in their hats and a fiddler at their head. A barrel of beer and a keg of schnapps decorated with greenery are set on a table, glasses are produced, and they drink. They form a ring and dance, singing: "Two girls crept out of a big, dark wood!" When this is finished, they go out, singing.

[MISS JULIE *enters, alone. She sees the chaos in the kitchen, clasps her hands, then takes out a powder puff and powders her face*]

JEAN: [*Enters, agitated*] There—you see! And you heard them. Do you think you can possibly stay here now?

MISS JULIE: No. I don't. But what can we do?

JEAN: Go away—travel—far away from here——

MISS JULIE: Travel? Yes, but where?

JEAN: To Switzerland, the Italian lakes! Have you never been there?

MISS JULIE: No. Is it beautiful there?

JEAN: Ah! An eternal summer! Oranges, laurel trees—ah!

MISS JULIE: But what shall we do there?

JEAN: I'll start a hotel. *De luxe*—for *de luxe* people.

MISS JULIE: Hotel?

JEAN: Ah, that's a life, believe me! New faces all the time, new languages! Never a minute for worry or nerves, or wondering what to do. There's work to be done every minute, bells ringing night and day, trains whistling, buses coming and going, and all the time the golden sovereigns roll into the till. Yes, that's a life!

MISS JULIE: It sounds exciting. But—I——?

JEAN: Shall be the mistress of the house; the pearl of the establishment. With your looks—and your style—why, we're made! It'll be terrific! You'll sit at your desk like a queen, setting your slaves in motion by pressing an electric bell. The guests will defile before your throne, humbly laying their tribute upon your table—you've no idea how people tremble when they get a bill in their hand. I shall salt the bills, and you shall sugar them with your prettiest smile! Oh, let's get away from here! [*Takes a timetable from his pocket*] Now, at once, by the next train! We'll be in Malmö by 5.30, Hamburg 8.40 tomorrow morning, Frankfurt to Basel will take a day, through the Gothard Pass—we'll be in Como in, let me see, three days. Three days!

MISS JULIE: It sounds wonderful. But, Jean—you must give me courage. Tell me you love me. Come and kiss me.

JEAN: [*Hesitates*] I'd like to—but I daren't. Not in this house—not again. I love you—never doubt that—can you doubt it, Miss Julie?

MISS JULIE: [*Shy, feminine*] Miss! Call me Julie! There are no barriers between us now. Call me Julie!

JEAN: [*Tormented*] I can't! There are still barriers between us—there always will be, as long as we're in this house. There's the past, there's his lordship—I've never met anyone I respected as I do him—I only have to see his gloves on a chair and I feel like a small boy—I only have to hear that bell ring and I jump like a frightened horse—and when I see his boots standing there, so straight and proud, I cringe. [*Kicks the boots*] Superstition—ideas shoved into our heads when we're children—but we can't escape them. Come to another country, a republic, and others will cringe before my porter's livery—yes, they'll cringe, I tell you, but I shan't! I wasn't born to cringe—I'm a man, I've got character, just let me get my fingers on that first branch and watch me climb! Today I'm a servant, but next year I'll own my own hotel, in ten years I'll be a landed gentleman! Then I'll go to Rumania, get a decoration—why, I might—might, mind you—end up with a title.

MISS JULIE: How wonderful!

JEAN: Oh, in Rumania I could buy myself a title. I'd be a Count, and you'd be a Countess. My Countess!

MISS JULIE: What do I care about all that? That's what I'm giving up now. Tell me you love me, otherwise—yes, otherwise—what am I?

JEAN: I'll tell you a thousand times—later. Only—not here. Above all, no emotional scenes, or it'll be all up with us. We must think this over coolly, like sensible people. [*Takes a cigar, cuts and lights it*] Sit down there now, and I'll sit here and we'll talk as though nothing had happened.

MISS JULIE: [*In despair*] Oh, my God! Have you no feelings?

JEAN: I? No one has more feelings than I. But I can control them.

MISS JULIE: A moment ago you could kiss my shoe—and now——!

JEAN: [*Harshly*] Yes, that was a moment ago. Now we've something else to think about.

MISS JULIE: Don't speak so harshly to me.

JEAN: I'm not speaking harshly. I'm talking sense. One folly has been committed, don't let's commit any more. His lordship may be here any moment, and by then we've got to decide what we're going to do with our lives. What do you think of my plans for our future? Do you approve of them?

MISS JULIE: They seem to me quite sensible, but—just one question. A big project like that needs a lot of capital. Have you that?

JEAN: [*Chews his cigar*] I? Certainly. I have my professional expertise, my experience, my knowledge of languages. We've adequate capital, I should say.

MISS JULIE: But all that doesn't add up to the price of a railway ticket.

JEAN: That's perfectly true; which is why I need a backer to advance me the money.

MISS JULIE: Where are you going to find one quickly?

JEAN: You'll find one, if you come with me.

MISS JULIE: I couldn't. And I haven't any money of my own.

[*Pause*]

JEAN: Then our whole plan collapses.

MISS JULIE: And——?

JEAN: Things must stay as they are.

MISS JULIE: Do you suppose I'm going to remain under this roof as your whore? With *them* sniggering at me behind their fingers? Do you think I can look my father in the face after this? No! Take me away from here, from the shame and the dishonour—oh, what have I done, my God, my God! [*Sobs*]

JEAN: Come, don't start that. What have you done? The same as many others before you.

MISS JULIE: [*Screams convulsively*] Oh, now you despise me! I'm falling—I'm falling——!

JEAN: Fall down to me, and I'll lift you up again.

MISS JULIE: What dreadful power drew me to you? The attraction of the weak to the strong? Of the faller to the climber? Or was it love? Was this love? Do you know what love is?

JEAN: I? Yes, of course. Do you think I've never had a woman before?

MISS JULIE: How can you think and talk like that?

JEAN: That's life as I've learned it. And that's me. Now don't get nervous and act the lady. We're both in the same boat now. Come here, my girlie, and I'll give you another glass of wine. [*Opens drawer, takes out the bottle of wine and fills two used glasses*]

MISS JULIE: Where did you get that wine from?

JEAN: The cellar.

MISS JULIE: My father's burgundy!

JEAN: Is it too good for his son-in-law?

MISS JULIE: And I drink beer! I!

JEAN: That only proves you have an inferior palate to mine.

MISS JULIE: Thief!

JEAN: Going to tell?

MISS JULIE: Oh, oh! Accomplice to a sneakthief! Was I drunk, was I dreaming? Midsummer night! The night of innocent festival——

JEAN: Innocent? Hm!

MISS JULIE: [*Paces to and fro*] Is there anyone on this earth as miserable as I?

JEAN: Why should you be miserable after such a conquest? Think of Christine in there. Don't you suppose she has feelings, too?

MISS JULIE: I thought so just now, but I don't any longer. Servants are servants——

JEAN: And whores are whores.

MISS JULIE: [*Kneels and clasps her hands*] Oh, God in Heaven, end my miserable life! Save me from this mire into which I'm sinking! Save me, save me!

JEAN: I can't deny I feel sorry for you. When I lay in the onion bed and saw you in the rose garden—I might as well tell you now—I had the same dirty thoughts as any small boy.

MISS JULIE: You—who wanted to die for me?

JEAN: The oat-bin? Oh, that was just talk.

MISS JULIE: A lie?

JEAN: [*Begins to get sleepy*] More or less. I once read a story in a paper about a sweep who curled up in a wood-chest with some lilacs because he'd had a paternity order brought against him——

MISS JULIE: I see. You're the kind who——

JEAN: Well, I had to think up something. Women always fall for pretty stories.

MISS JULIE: Swine!

JEAN: *Merde!*

MISS JULIE: And now you've managed to see the eagle's back——

JEAN: Back?

MISS JULIE: And I was to be the first branch——

JEAN: But the branch was rotten——

MISS JULIE: I was to be the signboard of the hotel——

JEAN: And I the hotel——

MISS JULIE: I was to sit at the desk, attract your customers, fiddle your bills——

JEAN: No, I'd have done that——

MISS JULIE: Can a human soul become so foul?

JEAN: Wash it, then!

MISS JULIE: Servant, lackey, stand up when I speak!

JEAN: Servant's whore, lackey's bitch, shut your mouth and get out of here! You dare to stand there and call me foul? None of my class ever behaved the way you've done tonight. Do you think any kitchen-maid would accost a man like you did? Have you ever seen any girl of my class offer her body like that? I've only seen it among animals and prostitutes.

MISS JULIE: [Crushed] You're right. Hit me, trample on me, I've deserved nothing better. I'm worthless—but help me, help me out of this—if there is a way out.

JEAN: [More gently] I don't want to disclaim my share in the honour of having seduced you, but do you imagine a man in my position would have dared to so much as glance at you if you hadn't invited him? I'm still dumbfounded——

MISS JULIE: And proud.

JEAN: Why not? Though I must confess I found the conquest a little too easy to be really exciting.

MISS JULIE: Hurt me more.

JEAN: [Gets up] No. Forgive me for what I've said. I don't hit defenceless people, least of all women. I can't deny it gratifies me to have found that it was only a gilt veneer that dazzled our humble eyes, that the eagle's back was as scabbed as our own, that the whiteness of those cheeks was only powder, that those polished fingernails had black edges, that that handkerchief was dirty though it smelt of perfume——But on the other hand, it hurts me to have discovered that what I was aspiring towards was not something worthier and more solid. It hurts me to see you sunk so low, to find that deep down you are a kitchen slut. It hurts me, like seeing the autumn flowers whipped to tatters by the rain and trodden into the mud.

MISS JULIE: You speak as though you were already above me.

JEAN: I am. You see, I could make you into a Countess, but you could never make me into a Count.

MISS JULIE: But I am of noble blood, and you can never be that.

JEAN: That's true. But my children could be noblemen, if——

MISS JULIE: But you're a thief. That's something I am not.

JEAN: There are worse things than being a thief. Besides, when I work in a house I regard myself more or less as a member of the family, a child of the house, and people don't call it stealing when a child takes a berry from a bush heavy with fruit. [*His passion rises again*] Miss Julie, you're a fine woman, much too good for someone like me. You've been the victim of a drunken folly, and you want to cover it up by pretending to yourself that you love me. You don't, unless perhaps physically—and then your love is no better than mine—but I can never be content with being just your animal, and I can never make you love me.

MISS JULIE: Are you sure of that?

JEAN: You mean it might happen? I could love you, easily—you're beautiful, you're refined——[*Approaches her and takes her hand*] Educated, lovable when you want to be, and once you have awoken a man's passion, it could never die. [*Puts his arm round her waist*] You are like hot wine, strongly spiced, and a kiss from you——! [*Tries to lead her towards his room, but she tears herself free*]

MISS JULIE: Let me go! You won't win me like that!

JEAN: How, then? Not like that. Not by flattery and fine words. Not by thinking of your future, rescuing you from what you've done to yourself. How, then?

MISS JULIE: How? How? I don't know. There is no way. I detest you as I detest rats, but I cannot run away from you.

JEAN: Run away with me!

MISS JULIE: [*Straightens herself*] Run away? Yes, we must run away.

But I'm so tired. Give me a glass of wine. [JEAN *pours her some. She looks at her watch*] But we must talk first. We have a little time. [*Drains the glass and holds it out for more*]

JEAN: Don't drink so much, you'll get drunk.

MISS JULIE: What does that matter?

JEAN: What does it matter? It's stupid to get drunk. What were you going to say to me just now?

MISS JULIE: We must run away! But first we must talk—that is, I must talk—so far you've been doing all the talking. You've told me about your life, now I want to tell you about mine, so that we know all about each other before we go away together.

JEAN: One moment. Forgive me, but—consider—you may later regret having revealed your private secrets to me.

MISS JULIE: Aren't you my friend?

JEAN: Yes—sometimes. But don't rely on me.

MISS JULIE: You're only saying that. Anyway, everyone else knows. You see, my mother was a commoner, of quite humble birth. She was brought up with ideas about equality, freedom for women and all that. And she had a decided aversion to marriage. So when my father proposed to her, she replied that she would never become his wife, but—well, anyway, she did. I came into the world, against my mother's wish as far as I can gather. She wanted to bring me up as a child of nature, and into the bargain I was to learn everything that a boy has to learn, so I might stand as an example of how a woman can be as good as a man. I had to wear boy's clothes, and learn to look after horses—though I was never allowed to enter the cowshed. I had to groom and saddle them, and hunt—and even learn to slaughter. That was horrible. Meanwhile, on the estate, all the men were set to perform the women's tasks, and the women the men's—with the result that the estate began to fail, and we became the laughing-stock of the district. In the end my father came to his senses and put his foot down, and everything was changed back to the way he wanted it. My mother fell ill—what illness, I don't know—but she often had convulsions, hid herself in the attic and the garden, and sometimes stayed out all night. Then there was the great fire which you have heard about. The house, the stables and the cowshed were all burned down, under circumstances suggesting arson—for the accident happened the very day our quarterly insurance had expired, and the premium my father sent had been delayed through the inefficiency of the servant carrying it, so that it hadn't arrived in time. [*Fills her glass and drinks*]

JEAN: Don't drink any more.

MISS JULIE: Oh, what does it matter? So we were left penniless, and had to sleep in the carriages. My father couldn't think where he would be able to find the money to rebuild the house. Then mother advised him to ask for a loan from an old friend of hers, a brick merchant who lived in the neighbourhood. Father got the money free of interest, which rather surprised him. So the house was rebuilt. [*Drinks again*] Do you know who burned the house down?

JEAN: Your mother!

MISS JULIE: Do you know who the brick merchant was?

JEAN: Your mother's lover!

MISS JULIE: Do you know whose the money was?

JEAN: Wait a moment. No, that I don't know.

MISS JULIE: It was my mother's.

JEAN: His lordship's too, then. Unless he'd made a marriage settlement.

MISS JULIE. No, there wasn't any marriage settlement. My mother had had a little money of her own, which she didn't want my father to have the use of. So she entrusted it to her—friend.

JEAN: Who kept it!

MISS JULIE: Exactly. He kept it. All this came to my father's knowledge—but he couldn't start an action, repay his wife's lover, or prove that the money was his wife's. It was my mother's revenge on him, for taking control of the house out of her hands. He was on the verge of shooting himself—the rumour was that he had done so, but had failed to kill himself. Well, he lived; and he made my mother pay for what she had done. Those five years were dreadful for me, I can tell you. I was sorry for my father, but I took my mother's side, because I didn't know the circumstances. I'd learned from her to distrust and hate men—she hated men, as I've told you. And I promised her that I would never be a slave to any man.

JEAN: And then you got engaged to that young lawyer?

MISS JULIE: So that he should be my slave.

JEAN: And he wasn't willing?

MISS JULIE: He was willing enough, but he didn't get the chance. I tired of him.

JEAN: I saw it. In the stable.

MISS JULIE: Saw what?

JEAN: How he broke off the engagement.

MISS JULIE: That's a lie! It was I who broke it off! Has he been saying he did it, the little wretch?

JEAN: He wasn't a wretch. You hate men, Miss Julie.

MISS JULIE: Yes. Most of the time. But sometimes—when the weakness comes—when nature burns—! Oh, God! Will the fire never die?

JEAN: You hate me, too?

MISS JULIE: Immeasurably! I'd like to shoot you like an animal——

JEAN: "The woman gets two years penal servitude and the animal is shot." That's the law for that, isn't it? But you've nothing to shoot with. So what shall we do?

MISS JULIE: Go away!

JEAN: To torment each other to death?

MISS JULIE: No. To be happy—for two days—a week—as long as one can be happy—and then—die——

JEAN: Die? Don't be stupid. I'd rather start the hotel than do that.

MISS JULIE: [Not hearing him]——on the Lake of Como, where the sun always shines, where the laurels are green at Christmas, and the orange-trees flame!

JEAN: The Lake of Como is about as beautiful as a puddle, and I never saw any oranges there except in the grocers' shops. But it's a good spot for tourists, there are a lot of villas to hire out to loving couples, and that's a profitable industry—you know why? Because they lease them for six months, and then leave after three weeks.

MISS JULIE: [Naïvely] Why after three weeks?

JEAN: They quarrel, of course! But they have to pay the full rent, and then you hire it out again. So it goes on, couple after couple. For love must go on, if not for very long.

MISS JULIE: You don't want to die with me?

JEAN: I don't want to die at all. Partly because I like life, and partly because I regard suicide as a crime against the Providence which gave us life.

MISS JULIE: You believe in God—*you?*

JEAN: Certainly I do. And I go to church every other Sunday. Quite frankly now, I'm tired of all this, and I'm going to bed.

MISS JULIE: I see. And you think I'm going to rest content with that? Don't you know what a man owes to a woman he has shamed?

JEAN: [*Takes out his purse and throws a silver coin on the table*] Here. I always pay my debts.

MISS JULIE: [*Pretends not to notice the insult*] Do you know what the law says——?

JEAN: Unfortunately the law doesn't demand any penalty from a woman who seduces a man.

MISS JULIE: Can you see any other solution than that we should go away, marry, and part?

JEAN: And if I refuse to enter into this *mésalliance?*

MISS JULIE: *Mésalliance?*

JEAN: Yes—for me! I've got a better heritage than you. None of my ancestors committed arson.

MISS JULIE: How do you know?

JEAN: You couldn't prove it, because we don't have any family records—except with the police. But I've studied your pedigree in a book I found on the table in the drawing-room. Do you know who the first of your ancestors to get a title was? He was a miller who let the King sleep with his wife one night during the Danish war. I haven't any noble ancestors like that—I haven't any noble ancestors at all. But I could become one myself.

MISS JULIE: This is my reward for opening my heart to a servant, for giving my family's honour——!

JEAN: Dishonour! Don't say I didn't tell you. One shouldn't drink, it loosens the tongue. And that's fatal.

MISS JULIE: Oh God, how I regret it, how I regret it! If you at least loved me——!

JEAN: For the last time—what do you want? Shall I burst into tears, shall I jump over your riding crop, shall I kiss you, lie to you for three weeks on Lake Como, and then—what? What shall I do? What do you want me to do? This is beginning to get tiresome. It's always like this when one gets involved with women. Miss Julie! I see you are unhappy, I know you are suffering, but I do not understand you! We don't fool around like you do—we don't hate—love is a game we play when we have a little time free from work, but we aren't free all day and all night like you! I think you're ill. Yes, undoubtedly, you're ill.

MISS JULIE: You must be kind to me. Now at last you're speaking like a human being.

JEAN: Act like one yourself, then. You spit at me, and won't let me wipe it off—on you.

MISS JULIE: Help me, help me! Just tell me what to do. Where shall I go?

JEAN: For God's sake! If I only knew!

MISS JULIE: I've been out of my mind, I've been mad, but isn't there some way out?

JEAN: Stay here, and keep calm. No one knows.

MISS JULIE: Impossible. The servants know. And Christine.

JEAN: They don't know for sure. They wouldn't really believe it could happen.

MISS JULIE: [*Hesitantly*] But—it could happen again.

JEAN: That is true.

MISS JULIE: And—then?

JEAN: [*Frightened*] Then? My God, why didn't I think of that? Yes, there's only one answer—you must go away. At once. I can't come with you—then we'd be finished—you must go alone—far away anywhere.

MISS JULIE: Alone? Where? I can't!

JEAN: You must! And before his lordship returns. If you stay, you know what'll happen. Once one has made a mistake one wants to go on, because the damage has already been done. Then one gets more and more careless and—in the end one gets found out. So go! You can write to his lordship later and tell him everything—except that it was me! He'll never guess that. And I don't suppose he'll be over-keen to find out who it was.

MISS JULIE: I'll go, if you'll come with me.

JEAN: Are you mad, woman? Miss Julie ran away with her servant! It'd be in the newspapers in a couple of days, and his lordship'd never live that down.

MISS JULIE: I can't go. I can't stay. Help me! I'm so tired, so dreadfully tired. Order me! Make me do something! I can't think, can't act——

JEAN: Now you see what a contemptible creature you are! Why do you prink yourselves up and stick your noses in the air as though you were the lords of creation? Very well, I shall order you. Go up to the house, get dressed, get some money for the journey and come back here.

MISS JULIE: [Half-whispers] Come with me.

JEAN: To your room? Now you're being crazy again. [Hesitates for a moment] No! Go, at once! [Takes her hand and leads her out]

MISS JULIE: [As she goes] Speak kindly to me, Jean!

JEAN: An order always sounds unkind. Now you know how it feels!

[JEAN, left alone, heaves a sigh of relief, sits at the table, takes out a notebook and pencil, and makes some calculations muttering occasionally to himself. Dumb mime, until CHRISTINE enters, dressed for church, with a man's dickey and white tie in her hand]

CHRISTINE: Blessed Jesus, what a mess! What on earth have you been up to?

JEAN: Oh, it was Miss Julie—she brought the servants in. You must have been fast asleep—didn't you hear anything?

CHRISTINE: I slept like a log.

JEAN: Dressed for church already?

CHRISTINE: Yes. You promised to come with me to Communion this morning.

JEAN: So I did. And I see you've brought my uniform. O.K., then. [*Sits.* CHRISTINE *dresses him in his dickey and white tie. Pause*]

JEAN: [*Sleepily*] What's the lesson today?

CHRISTINE: Execution of John the Baptist, I expect. [*Makes a cutting motion across her throat*]

JEAN: Oh God, that's a long one. Hi, you're strangling me! Oh, I'm so tired, so tired.

CHRISTINE: Yes, what have you been doing, up all night? You're quite green in the face.

JEAN: Sitting here, talking with Miss Julie.

CHRISTINE: She doesn't know what's right and proper, that one.

[*Pause*]

JEAN: I say, Christine.

CHRISTINE: Mm?

JEAN: It's strange, you know, when you think of it. Her.

CHRISTINE: What's strange?

JEAN: Everything.

[*Pause*]

CHRISTINE: [*Sees the glasses, half empty, on the table*] Have you been drinking together, too?

JEAN: Yes.

CHRISTINE: For shame! Look me in the eyes!

JEAN: Yes?

CHRISTINE: Is it possible? Is it *possible?*

JEAN: [*After a moment*] Yes.

CHRISTINE: Ugh! *That* I'd never have believed! No! Shame on you, shame!

JEAN: You aren't jealous of her, are you?

CHRISTINE: No, not of her! If it had been Clara or Sophie—then I'd have torn your eyes out. But her—no—I don't know why. Ah, but it's disgusting!

JEAN: Are you angry with her, then?

CHRISTINE: No, with you! It's a wicked thing to have done, wicked! Poor lass! No, I don't care who hears it, I don't want to stay any longer in a house where people can't respect their employers.

JEAN: Why should one respect them?

CHRISTINE: Yes, you're so clever, you tell me! But you don't want to work for people who lower themselves, do you? Eh? You lower yourself by it, that's my opinion.

JEAN: Yes, but it's a comfort for us to know they aren't any better than us.

CHRISTINE: Not to my mind. If they're no better than we are, there's no point our trying to improve ourselves. And think of his lordship! Think of him and all the misery he's had in his time! No, I don't want to stay in this house any longer. And with someone like you! If it'd been that young lawyer fellow—if it'd been a gentleman——

JEAN: What's wrong with me?

CHRISTINE: Oh, you're all right in your way, but there's a difference between people and people. No, I'll never be able to forget this. Miss Julie, who was always so proud, so cool with men—I never thought she'd go and give herself to someone—and to someone like you! She, who all but had poor Diana shot for running after the gatekeeper's pug! Yes, I'm not afraid to say it! I won't stay here any longer. On the 24th of October I go!

JEAN: And then?

CHRISTINE: Yes, since you've raised the subject, it's time you started looking round for something, seeing as we're going to get married.

JEAN: What kind of thing? I can't have a job like this once I'm married.

CHRISTINE: No, of course not. Still, you might get something as a porter, or maybe a caretaker in some factory. A bird in the hand's worth two in the bush; and there'll be a pension for your wife and children.

JEAN: [Grimaces] Yes, that's all very fine, but I don't intend to die to oblige my wife and children just yet, thank you. I've higher ambitions than that.

CHRISTINE: Ambitions? What about your responsibilities? Think of them.

JEAN: Oh, shut up about responsibilities, I know my duty. [*Listens towards the door*] But we've plenty of time to think about that. Go inside now and get yourself ready, and we'll go to church.

CHRISTINE: Who's that walking about upstairs?

JEAN: I don't know. Probably Clara.

CHRISTINE: [*Going*] It surely can't be his lordship. He couldn't have come back without our hearing him.

JEAN: [*Frightened*] His lordship? No, it can't be, he'd have rung.

CHRISTINE: [*Goes*] Well, God help us. I've never been mixed up in the likes of this before.

[*The sun has now risen and is shining on the tops of the trees in the park. Its beams move gradually until they fall at an angle through the windows.* JEAN *goes to the door and makes a sign*]

MISS JULIE: [*Enters in travelling clothes with a small birdcage, covered with a cloth, which she places on a chair*] I'm ready now.

JEAN: Ssh! Christine is awake!

MISS JULIE: [*Very nervous throughout this dialogue*] Does she suspect anything?

JEAN: She knows nothing. But, my God—what a sight you look!

MISS JULIE: What's wrong——?

JEAN: You're as white as a sheet, and—forgive me, but your face is dirty.

MISS JULIE: Let me wash, then. Here. [*Goes to the washbasin and washes her face and hands*] Give me a towel. Oh the sun's rising!

JEAN: And then the Devil loses his power.

MISS JULIE: Yes, the Devil's been at work tonight. But Jean, listen. Come with me! I've got some money now.

JEAN: [*Doubtfully*] Enough?

MISS JULIE: Enough to start with! Come with me! I can't go alone today. Think—midsummer day, on a stuffy train, squashed among crowds of people staring at me—having to stand still on stations, when one longs to be flying away! No, I can't, I can't! And then— memories—memories of midsummers in childhood, the church garlanded with birch-leaves and lilac, dinner at the long table, the family, friends—the afternoons in the park, dancing, music, flowers, games! Oh, one runs, one runs away, but memories follow in the baggage-wagon—and remorse—and guilt!

JEAN: I'll come with you—but it must be now, at once, before it's too late. Now, this minute!

MISS JULIE: Get dressed, then. [*Picks up the birdcage*]

JEAN: No luggage, though. That'd give us away.

MISS JULIE: No, nothing. Only what we can have in the compartment with us.

JEAN: [*Has taken his hat*] What have you got there? What is it?

MISS JULIE: It's only my greenfinch. I don't want to leave him.

JEAN: For heaven's sake! We can't take a birdcage with us now. You're crazy. Put that cage down.

MISS JULIE: My one memory of home—the only living thing that loves me, since Diana was unfaithful to me. Don't be cruel! Let me take her with me!

JEAN: Put that cage down, I tell you. And don't talk so loud, Christine will hear us.

MISS JULIE: No, I won't leave her for strangers to have. I'd rather you killed her.

JEAN: Bring the little beast here then, and I'll wring its neck.

MISS JULIE: All right—but don't hurt her. Don't—no, I can't!

JEAN: Bring it here. I can.

MISS JULIE: [*Takes the bird out of its cage and kisses it*] Ah, poor little Serina, are you going to die now and leave your mistress?

JEAN: Please don't make a scene. Your life and your happiness are at stake. Here, quickly! [*Snatches the bird from her, takes it to the chopping block and picks up the kitchen axe. MISS JULIE turns away*] You ought to have learned how to wring chickens' necks instead of how to fire a pistol. [*Brings down the axe*] Then you wouldn't have been frightened of a drop of blood.

MISS JULIE: [*Screams*] Kill me, too! Kill me! You, who can slaughter an innocent bird without a tremor! Oh, I hate and detest you! There is blood between us now! I curse the moment I set eyes on you, I curse the moment I was conceived in my mother's womb!

JEAN: What's the good of cursing? Come!

MISS JULIE: [*Goes towards the chopping block, as though drawn against her will*] No, I don't want to go yet. I can't—I must see—ssh! There's a carriage outside! [*Listens, but keeps her eyes fixed all the while on the chopping block and the axe*] Do you think I can't bear the sight of blood? You think I'm so weak—oh, I should like to see your blood, your brains, on a chopping block—I'd like to see all your sex swimming in a lake of blood—I think I could drink from your skull, I'd like to bathe my feet in your guts, I could eat your heart, roasted! You think I'm weak—you think I loved you, because my womb wanted your seed, you think I want to carry your embryo under my heart and feed it with my blood, bear your child and take your name! By the way, what is your name! I've never heard your surname—you probably haven't any. I'd have to be "Mrs. Kitchen-boy," or "Mrs. Lavator"—you dog, who wear my collar, you lackey who carry my crest on your buttons—am I to share with my own cook, compete with a scullery slut? Oh, oh, oh! You think I'm a coward and want to run away? No, now I shall stay. Let the storm break! My father will come home—find his desk broken open—his money gone! He'll ring—this bell—twice, for his lackey—then he'll send for the police and I shall tell everything. Everything. Oh, it'll be good to end it all—if only it could be the end. And then he'll have a stroke and die. Then we shall all be finished, and there'll be peace—peace—eternal rest! And the coat of arms will be broken over the coffin—the title extinct—and the lackey's line will be carried on in an orphanage, win laurels in the gutter, and end in a prison!

JEAN: That's the blue blood talking! Bravo, Miss Julie! Just give the miller a rest, now——!

[CHRISTINE *enters, dressed for church, with a prayer-book in her hand.* MISS JULIE *runs towards her and falls into her arms, as though seeking shelter*]

MISS JULIE: Help me, Christine! Help me against this man!

CHRISTINE: [*Motionless, cold*] What kind of a spectacle's this on a Sunday morning? [*Looks at the chopping block*] And what a pigsty you've made here. What does all this mean? I never heard such shouting and bawling.

MISS JULIE: Christine! You're a woman, and my friend. Beware of this vile man!

JEAN: [*Somewhat timid and embarrassed*] While you ladies discuss the matter, I'll go inside and shave. [*Slips out right*]

MISS JULIE: You must understand! You must listen to me!

CHRISTINE: No, this kind of thing I don't understand. Where are you going in those clothes? And what's he doing with his hat on—eh? —eh?

MISS JULIE: Listen to me, Christine. Listen, and I'll tell you everything——

CHRISTINE: I don't want to know anything——

MISS JULIE: You must listen to me——

CHRISTINE: About what? What you've done with Jean? That doesn't bother me—that's between you and him. But if you're thinking of trying to fool him into running away, we'll soon put a stop to that.

MISS JULIE: [*Very nervous*] Now try to be calm, Christine, and listen to me. I can't stay here, and Jean can't stay here—so we have to go——

CHRISTINE: Hm, hm!

MISS JULIE: [*Becoming brighter*] Listen, I've just had an idea—why don't we all three go away—abroad—to Switzerland—and start a hotel together—I've money, you see—and Jean and I could run it —and you, I thought you might take charge of the kitchen—isn't that a good idea? Say yes, now! And come with us, and then everything'll be settled! Say yes, now!

CHRISTINE: [*Coldly, thoughtfully*] Hm, hm!

MISS JULIE: [*Speaks very rapidly*] You've never been abroad, Christine—you must get away from here and see the world. You've no idea what fun it is to travel by train—new people all the time— new countries—we'll go through Hamburg and look at the zoo— you'll like that—and then we'll go to the theatre and listen to the opera—and when we get to Munich there'll be all the museums, Christine, and Rubens and Raphael, those great painters, you know—you've heard of Munich—where King Ludwig lived, you know, the King who went mad. And we'll see his palaces—they've still got palaces there, just like in the fairy tales—and from there it isn't far to Switzerland—and the Alps, Christine—fancy, the Alps, with snow on them in the middle of summer—and oranges grow there, and laurel trees that are green all the year round——

[JEAN *can be seen in the wings right, whetting his razor on a strop which he holds between his teeth and his left hand. He listens contentedly to what is being said, every now and then nodding his approval*]

MISS JULIE: [*More rapidly still*] And we'll start a hotel there—I'll sit at the desk while Jean stands in the doorway and receives the guests—I'll go out and do the shopping—and write the letters—oh, Christine, what a life it'll be! The trains will whistle, and then the buses'll arrive, and bells will ring on all the floors and in the restaurant—and I'll write out the bills—and salt them, too—you can't imagine how timid tourists are when they have to pay the bill! And you—you'll be in charge of the kitchen—you won't have to do any cooking yourself, of course—and you'll wear fine clothes, for the guests to see you in—and you, with your looks, I'm not flattering you, Christine, you'll get yourself a husband one fine day, a rich Englishman, you'll see—English people are so easy to—[*Slowing down*]—catch—and we'll become rich—and build ourselves a villa on Lake Como—it rains there sometimes, of course, but—[*Slows right down*]—the sun must shine there too, sometimes—though it looks dark—and—so—if it doesn't we can come home again—back to—[*Pause*] Back here—or somewhere——

CHRISTINE: Now listen. Do you believe all this?

MISS JULIE: [*Crushed*] Do I believe it?

CHRISTINE: Yes.

MISS JULIE: [*Wearily*] I don't know. I don't believe in anything any longer. [*She falls on to the bench and puts her head on the table between her hands*] Nothing. Nothing at all.

CHRISTINE: [*Turns right to where* JEAN *is standing*] So! You were thinking of running away!

JEAN: [*Crestfallen, puts his razor down on the table*] Running away? Oh now, that's exaggerating. You heard Miss Julie's plan, and although she's tired now after being up all night I think it's a very practical proposition.

CHRISTINE: Listen to him! Did you expect me to act as cook to that——?

JEAN: [*Sharply*] Kindly express yourself respectfully when you refer to your mistress. Understand?

CHRISTINE: Mistress!

JEAN: Yes.

CHRISTINE: Listen to him, listen to him!

JEAN: Yes, listen to me, and talk a little less. Miss Julie is your mistress, and what you despise in her you should despise in yourself, too.

CHRISTINE: I've always had sufficient respect for myself——

JEAN: To be able to turn up your nose at others.

CHRISTINE: To stop me from demeaning myself. You tell me when you've seen his lordship's cook mucking around with the groom or the pigman! Just you tell me!

JEAN: Yes, you managed to get hold of a gentleman for yourself. You were lucky.

CHRISTINE: Yes, a gentleman who sells his lordship's oats, which he steals from the stables——

JEAN: You should talk! You get a percentage on all the groceries, and a rake-off from the butcher——

CHRISTINE: What!

JEAN: And you say you can't respect your employers! You, you, you!

CHRISTINE: Are you coming with me to church, now? You need a good sermon after what you've done.

JEAN: No, I'm not going to church today. You can go by yourself, and confess what you've been up to.

CHRISTINE: Yes, I will, and I'll come home with my sins forgiven, and yours too. The blessed Saviour suffered and died on the cross for all our sins, and if we turn to Him with a loyal and humble heart He'll take all our sins upon Him.

JEAN: Including the groceries?

MISS JULIE: Do you believe that, Christine?

CHRISTINE: With all my heart, as surely as I stand here. I learned it as a child, Miss Julie, and I've believed it ever since. And where the sin is exceeding great, His mercy shall overflow.

MISS JULIE: Oh, if only I had your faith! Oh, if——!

CHRISTINE: Ah, but you can't have that except by God's special grace, and that isn't granted to everyone——

MISS JULIE: Who has it, then?

CHRISTINE: That's God's great secret, Miss Julie. And the Lord's no respecter of persons. There shall the last be first——

MISS JULIE: Then He has respect for the last?

CHRISTINE: [*Continues*] And it is easier for a camel to pass through the eye of a needle than for a rich man to enter the Kingdom of Heaven. That's how it is, Miss Julie. Well, I'll be going—and as I pass the stable I'll tell the groom not to let any of the horses be taken out before his lordship comes home, just in case. Goodbye. [*Goes*]

JEAN: Damned bitch! And all this for a greenfinch!

MISS JULIE: [Dully] Never mind the greenfinch. Can you see any way out of this, any end to it?

JEAN: [*Thinks*] No.

MISS JULIE: What would you do in my place?

JEAN: In your place? Wait, now. If I were a lady—of noble birth—who'd fallen——? I don't know. Yes. I know.

MISS JULIE: [*Picks up the razor and makes a gesture*] This?

JEAN: Yes. But *I* wouldn't do it, mind. There's a difference between us.

MISS JULIE: Because you're a man and I am a woman? What difference does that make?

JEAN: The difference—between a man and a woman.

MISS JULIE: [*Holding the razor*] I want to do it—but I can't. My father couldn't do it, either, the time he should have.

JEAN: No, he was right. He had to be revenged first.

MISS JULIE: And now my mother will be revenged again, through me.

JEAN: Have you never loved your father, Miss Julie?

MISS JULIE: Yes—enormously—but I've hated him, too. I must have done so without realising it. But it was he who brought me up to despise my own sex, made me half woman and half man. Who is to blame for what has happened—my father, my mother, myself? Myself? I haven't any self. I haven't a thought I didn't get from my father, not an emotion I didn't get from my mother—and this last idea—that all people are equal—I got that from him, my fiancé whom I called a wretched little fool because of it. How can the blame be mine, then? Put it all on to Jesus, as Christine did—

no, I'm too proud to do that, and too clever—thanks to my father's teaching. And that about a rich person not being able to get into heaven, that's a lie, and Christine has money in the savings bank so she won't get there either. Whose fault is it all? What does it matter to us whose fault it is? I shall have to bear the blame, carry the consequences——

JEAN: Yes, but—

[*There are two sharp rings on the bell.* MISS JULIE *jumps up.* JEAN *changes his coat*]

JEAN: His lordship's home! Good God, do you suppose Christine ——? [*Goes to the speaking tube, knocks on it, and listens*]

MISS JULIE: Has he been to his desk?

JEAN: It's Jean, milord. [*Listens. The audience cannot hear what is said to him*] Yes, milord. [*Listens*] Yes, milord. At once. [*Listens*] Yes, milord. In half an hour.

MISS JULIE: [*Desperately frightened*] What does he say? For God's sake, what does he say?

JEAN: He wants his boots and his coffee in half an hour.

MISS JULIE: In half an hour, then——! Oh, I'm so tired! I can't feel anything, I can't repent, can't run away, can't stay, can't live—can't die. Help me! Order me, and I'll obey you like a dog. Do me this last service, save my honour, save his name! You know what I ought to will myself to do, but I can't. Will me to, Jean, order me!

JEAN: I don't know—now I can't either—I don't understand—it's just as though this coat made me—I *can't* order you—and now, since his lordship spoke to me—I can't explain it properly, but—oh, it's this damned lackey that sits on my back—I think if his lordship came down now and ordered me to cut my throat, I'd do it on the spot.

MISS JULIE: Then pretend that you are he, and I am you. You acted so well just now, when you went down on your knees—then you were an aristocrat—or—haven't you ever been to the theatre and seen a hypnotist? [JEAN *nods*] He says to his subject: "Take the broom!", and he takes it. He says: "Sweep!", and he sweeps——

JEAN: But the subject has to be asleep.

MISS JULIE: [*In an ecstasy*] I am already asleep—the whole room is like smoke around me—and you look like an iron stove—which resembles a man dressed in black, with a tall hat—and your eyes shine like coals, when the fire is dying—and your face is a white smear, like ash——[*The sun's rays have now reached the floor and are shining on* JEAN] It's so warm and good——! [*She rubs her hands as though warming them before a fire*] And so bright—and so peaceful——!

JEAN: [*Takes the razor and places it in her hand*] Here's the broom. Go now—while it's bright—out to the barn—and——[*Whispers in her ear*]

MISS JULIE: [*Awake*] Thank you. Now I am going to rest. But just tell me this—those who are first—they too can receive grace? Say it to me—even if you don't believe it.

JEAN: Those who are first? No, I can't! But, wait——Miss Julie— now I see it! You are no longer among the first. You are—among the last!

MISS JULIE: That's true. I am among the last of all. I am the last. Oh! But now I can't go! Tell me once more—say I must go!

JEAN: No, now I can't either. I can't!

MISS JULIE: And the first shall be last.

JEAN: Don't think, don't think! You take all my strength from me, you make me a coward. What? I thought the bell moved! No. Shall we stuff paper in it? To be so afraid of a bell! Yes, but it isn't only a bell—there's someone sitting behind it—a hand sets it in motion—and something else sets the hand in motion—you've only got to close your ears, close your ears! Yes, but now he's ringing louder! He'll ring till someone answers—and then it'll be too late. The police will come—and then——!

[*Two loud rings on the bell*]

JEAN: [*Cringes, then straightens himself up*] It's horrible. But there can be no other ending. Go!

[MISS JULIE *walks firmly out through the door*]

Stanley Richards

Since the publication of his first collection in 1968, Stanley Richards has become one of our leading editors and play anthologists, earning rare encomiums from the nation's press (the *Writers Guild of America News* described him as "Easily the Best Anthologist of Plays in America") and the admiration of a multitude of devoted readers.

Mr. Richards has edited the following anthologies and series: *America on Stage: Ten Great Plays of American History; Best Plays of the Sixties; Great Musicals of the American Theatre: Volume One; Great Musicals of the American Theatre: Volume Two; Best Mystery and Suspense Plays of the Modern Theatre; 10 Classic Mystery and Suspense Plays of the Modern Theatre* (the latter six, The Fireside Theatre-Literary Guild selections); *The Tony Winners; Best Short Plays of the World Theatre: 1968–1973; Best Short Plays of the World Theatre: 1958–1967; Modern Short Comedies from Broadway and London; Canada on Stage;* and, since 1968, *The Best Short Plays* annuals.

An established playwright as well, he has written twenty-five plays, twelve of which (including *Through a Glass, Darkly; Tunnel of Love; August Heat; Sun Deck; O Distant Land;* and *District of Columbia*) were originally published in earlier volumes of *The Best One-Act Plays* and *The Best Short Plays*.

Journey to Bahia, which he adapted from a prize-winning Brazilian play and film, *O Pagador de Promessas,* premièred at the Berkshire Playhouse, Massachusetts, and later was produced in Washington, D.C., under the auspices of the Brazilian Ambassador and the Brazilian American Cultural Institute. The play also had a successful engagement Off-Broadway and subsequently was performed in a Spanish translation at Lincoln Center. During the summer of 1975, the play was presented at the Edinburgh International Festival in Scotland, after a tour of several British cities.

Mr. Richards' plays have been translated for production and publication abroad into Portuguese, Afrikaans, Dutch, Tagalog, French, German, Korean, Italian, and Spanish.

He also has been the New York theatre critic for *Players Magazine* and a frequent contributor to *Playbill, Theatre Arts, The Theatre,* and *Actors' Equity Magazine,* among other periodicals.

As an American Theatre Specialist, Mr. Richards was awarded three successive grants by the U. S. Department of State's International Cultural Exchange Program to teach playwriting and directing in Chile and Brazil. He taught playwriting in Canada for over ten years and in 1966 was appointed Visiting Professor of Drama at the University of Guelph, Ontario. He has produced and directed plays and has lectured extensively on theatre at universities in the United States, Canada, and South America.

Mr. Richards, a New York City resident, is now at work on several new play anthologies.